J. E. (Joseph Epiphane) Darras, Charles I. (Charles Ignatius) White

A General History of the Catholic Church

From the Commencement of the Christian Era until the Present Time

J. E. (Joseph Epiphane) Darras, Charles I. (Charles Ignatius) White

A General History of the Catholic Church
From the Commencement of the Christian Era until the Present Time

ISBN/EAN: 9783742852601

Manufactured in Europe, USA, Canada, Australia, Japa

Cover: Foto ©Lupo / pixelio.de

Manufactured and distributed by brebook publishing software (www.brebook.com)

J. E. (Joseph Epiphane) Darras, Charles I. (Charles Ignatius) White

A General History of the Catholic Church

New-York.

A

GENERAL HISTORY

OF THE

CATHOLIC CHURCH:

FROM THE COMMENCEMENT OF THE CHRISTIAN ERA
UNTIL THE PRESENT TIME.

M. L'ABBÉ J. E. DARRAS.

FIRST AMERICAN FROM THE LAST FRENCH EDITION.

WITH AN

INTRODUCTION AND NOTES

BY THE MOST REV. M. J. SPALDING, D. D.,
ARCHBISHOP OF BALTIMORE.

VOL. I.

NEW YORK:
P. O'SHEA, PUBLISHER,
27 BARCLAY STREET.
1868.

RECOMMENDATIONS

OF

The General History of the Church

LETTER FROM

HIS HOLINESS POPE PIUS IX.

TO THE

AUTHOR OF "THE GENERAL HISTORY OF THE CHURCH."

Dilecto filio presbytero J. E. Darras, Lutetiam Parisiorum.

To our beloved Son, J. E. Darras, Priest at Paris.

PIUS P. P. IX.

Dilecte Fili, Salutem et Apostolicam Benedictionem:

Litteræ Tuæ XIII. Kalendas Aprilis proximi ad nos datæ, quibus exemplar offerre nobis voluisti operis de historiâ Ecclesiæ generali, fuerunt nobis ipsis quam gratissimæ. Significas enim id Tibi fuisse consilii, quod virum certe decet

PIUS P. P. IX.

Beloved Son, health and the Apostolic Benediction:

Your letter of the twentieth of March, accompanied by a copy of your General History of the Church, was most grateful to us. The plan of your work testifies your zeal for sound doctrine and your singular and praiseworthy devo-

germanæ doctrinæ studio ac singularis erga Nos ipsos sedemque Apostolicam devotionis et observantiæ laude præstantem. Si, ut confidimus, consilio ipsi opus quod adhuc legere Nos non potuimus, exacte respondeat, magno illud usui erit istic futurum addetque omnibus stimulos ad gravissimam eam ecclesiasticorum studiorum partem pœnitius internoscendam. Meritas pro oblato ipso operis munere cum Tibi, Dilecte Fili, persolvimus gratias, omnipotentem Dominum suppliciter exoramus, ut sua in te munera multiplicet ac tueatur. Et tanti hujus boni auspicem adjungimus Apostolicam Benedictionem, quam intimo paterni cordis affectu, ipsi Tibi, Dilecte fili, amanter impertimur.

Datum Romæ apud S. Petrum, die 8 augusti, anni 1855, Pontificatus Nostri anno X.

Pius P. P. IX.

tion towards us and the Apostolic See. If, as we trust, the work (which we ourselves have not as yet been able to read) fulfils the design proposed, it will be of the greatest use, and will tend to stimulate a more profound study of this most important branch of Ecclesiastical Science. We give you, therefore, beloved son, merited thanks for your offering to us, and we earnestly pray Almighty God that He will multiply and preserve His gifts in you. And as a pledge of this great favor, we add the Apostolic Benediction, which, with the sincere affection of our paternal heart, we lovingly impart to you.

Given at St. Peter's, Rome, the 8th of August, in the year of our Lord 1855, and the tenth of our Pontificate.

Pius P. P. IX.

RECOMMENDATIONS.

FROM THE
MOST REV. JOHN McCLOSKY, D. D.,
ARCHBISHOP OF NEW YORK.

DEAR SIR:—I am very glad to learn that you are about publishing an English version of the excellent Ecclesiastical History of the Abbé Darras. The auspices under which the translation is made, will, I am confident, secure for it both elegance and fidelity. I trust that your laudable enterprise will meet all due encouragement from the Catholic public.

Very truly, your friend and servant in Christ,
✠ JOHN, *Archbishop of New York.*

P. O'SHEA, Esq.

NEW YORK, *Dec.* 12, 1864.

FROM THE
MOST REV. M. J. SPALDING, D. D.,
ARCHBISHOP OF BALTIMORE.

Mr. P. O'SHEA:

THE conviction grows upon me, that the History of Darras, so warmly commended by many learned men in France, will meet a want which has been so long felt in this country—that of a good Church History, neither too lengthy nor too compendious, and at the same time replete with interesting and edifying details.

The four volumes which you are publishing contain a rich array of facts, well stated and well put together, which will be

RECOMMENDATIONS.

most agreeable and instructive to our Catholic people, all of whom will of course seek to obtain the work for family use. This Church History will also be found very opportune and useful in our numerous Seminaries, Colleges, and Academies. I wish you every success in your praiseworthy undertaking, and hope you will receive sufficient patronage to defray all expenses.

✠ M. J. SPALDING, *Archbishop of Baltimore.*

BALTIMORE, *Dec.* 7, 1864.

FROM THE
MOST REV. J. B. PURCELL, D. D.,
ARCHBISHOP OF CINCINNATI.

CINCINNATI, *Nov.* 15, 1864.

Mr. P. O'SHEA:

DEAR SIR:—Permit me to take this occasion, in answering your Circular, to signify my concurrence in the judgment pronounced on the Ecclesiastical History of the Abbé Darras. Please send me five copies in volumes, cloth binding.

Respectfully yours,

✠ J. B. PURCELL, *Archbishop of Cincinnati.*

INTRODUCTION.

If History be "Philosophy teaching by example," that kind is certainly the most excellent, whose lessons are the most elevated in their character and important in their bearing. According to this principle, *Church History* is immeasurably superior to that which is secular or profane; for while the latter is a record of human events, together with the motives which impel the merely human actors, and the influence of their actions on society and the world, the former treats of the establishment and varied fortunes of a divine institution, founded in this world, but not of this world—of a Church which, but a pilgrim and a stranger upon the earth, is ever looking with straining eyes towards Heaven. The interests bound up with secular history are limited to time; those associated with Church History extend to and embrace eternity. The teachings of the former may tend to promote man's well-being in this world; those of the latter enlighten him as to the means necessary for securing his eternal happiness in the next. As heaven, then, is lifted above earth, as eternity is elevated above time, as God is exalted above man, so is the history of God's Church raised above that which treats merely of human events.

According to Cicero, all history is, or should be, "the witness of ages, the torch of truth, the life of memory, the oracle of life, the interpreter of the past." This is a beautiful theory;

alas! that it should be so often marred in the practice! Instead of being "the torch of truth," history has but too frequently become the lurid beacon of error; instead of being "the witness of ages," and "the interpreter of the past," it has too often been but the time-serving witness of men's present theories or prejudices, and the interpreter of men's present opinions. Passion obscures, and prejudice distorts the facts of the past, until, instead of standing forth in the stately dignity of their own native truth, they are made to pass before us, as phantoms dimly revealed through the hazy atmosphere of the present.

What is called the Philosophy of History, is not unfrequently but a weaving together of the crude and unsound theories of the day, more plausibly than solidly confirmed by the distorted records of ages past. The theory is first adopted, as a foregone conclusion; and then the facts of history are bent and moulded to the theory. The philosopher of history plumes himself on his triumphant success, in making out his thesis by stubborn and incontrovertible facts; whereas, all the time, he is but deluding himself and others by a sophistry as mischievous as it is specious. His method should really be called the highly-wrought romance, or the fascinating poetry, rather than the true development or the genuine Philosophy of History. The historical structure thus reared may please the eye and flatter the fancy; it crumbles into dust or vanishes in thin air before the slightest touch of sound critical inquiry.

If this be true of secular, it is still more strikingly so of Church History. Here, the interests embraced being of a much higher order, and the consequent duties involving more abnegation and self-sacrifice, the temptation to conceal or distort facts becomes much greater. The way to heaven, pointed out in the Church of God, is narrow, rugged, and strewn with thorns; human frailty and human wickedness are but too prone to widen it, to soften its asperities, and to pluck away its thorns, leaving only the roses to delight the senses with their brilliancy and fragrance. Whatsoever is hard to flesh and blood; whatsoever wars with the passions, or involves the necessity of self-restraint; whatsoever is opposed to the free range and unrestricted indulgence of the three great concupiscences, which make up the life of the world, is carefully concealed or skilfully kept in the background, with an instinctive dread of the practical consequences likely to result from too candid an admission. On the other hand, those aspects of the facts, which are of a more genial character, and which soothe without irritating the sensual man, are as carefully brought forward, and are made to occupy a prominent place in the History. Under the hands of this class of writers, Church History becomes, not a reliable record of facts, as they really occurred, with their surroundings, in the past, but an elaborate adaptation of these facts to what they regard as the exigencies of modern progress and civilization. Men write out their own theories and prejudices, and call the production the Philosophy of History!

Such being the case, can we wonder at the assertion by a distinguished modern writer,* to the effect, that for the last three centuries, History, and especially Church History, has been a grand conspiracy against the truth? We firmly believe that this statement is scarcely an exaggeration. Those who have taken the trouble to look over the more usually read text-books of Church History at the present day, written by men opposed to the Catholic Church, though frequently blessed with no particular religious convictions themselves, will, we

---

* The late Count de Maistre.

think, agree with us in this opinion, provided they approach the subject with calm and unbiassed minds. We may mention, without intending to slight others of perhaps higher pretentions, two of those works, which are of such dimensions as bring them within the reach of the ordinary reader, and which now happen to occur to our minds: we refer to Milner's History of the Church, and Gieseler's Text-Book of Ecclesiastical History; the former English, the latter German, translated into English. In both of these, especially in the latter, much learning is expended to very little purpose that is commendable. While they may both be cited as pretty fair examples of the kind of historians we have been describing, they agree in one remarkable particular—in which most other productions emanating from men of a kindred spirit fully agree with them— they both present rather the shadows than the lights of Church History. Had their fixed purpose been to blacken the good and to brighten the bad, they would scarcely have written differently. Almost every vile schismatic and heretic is deified; almost every champion of orthodoxy and holiness is crucified, with his divine Lord and Master! Every one of those scandals, which our Blessed Master foretold should come, and which therefore should not surprise His true disciples, is carefully brought out and greatly magnified; while most of the counterbalancing evidences of holiness of life, are either concealed, or sneered at as superstitious, by these modern *Christian* philosophers of History!*

---

* Mosheim is probably more fair and plausible; but even Mosheim is amenable to much of the censure conveyed in the text. His learning is undoubted, though he often distorts his facts and authorities; while his seeming moderation is not unfrequently a cloak for the most determined partisanship. His Ecclesiastical History (in 4 vols. 8vo) is much prized by those outside the Church. It has been translated, and it appears to be much used as a text-book, or referred to as an authority. The author was a prejudiced Lutheran, who seems to have occupied a high position among his co-religionists. His zeal for his sect, however, often gets the better of his judgment. Whatever may be his fairness in statements, regarding controversies

CATHOLIC CHURCH HISTORIES.

The Catholic Church is exceedingly rich in works on Ecclesiastical History. From the great annalist and father of Church History, Baronius, down to the learned, eloquent, and voluminious Rohrbacher,* we have them of all sizes and in

among the several discordant sects, whether of ancient or modern times, his authority is more than questionable in matters connected with the distinctive doctrines and practices of the Catholic Church. In this respect, he is sometimes even less fair than the sworn and envenomed enemies of all Christian truth, Voltaire and Gibbon. These sometimes catch a glimpse of the sun through the opening in the clouds of prejudice; a privilege which their more partisan or less candid Lutheran brother in *protesting* does not often seem to enjoy. Thus Mosheim, while he surely had learning and penetration enough to know that the story of the Popess Joan was a clumsy fiction and a stupid imposture, has not the candor openly so to denounce it, but prudently leaves the matter in doubt; whereas Gibbon not only declares it to be a groundless fiction in the text, but proves it to be such in a note remarkable for its condensation and learning.

* The Annals of Baronius embrace thirteen large folio volumes, furnishing the History of the Church for thirteen centuries, down to 1299, a volume for a century. The work has had many continuators, abridgers, and commentators. Among the first, we may mention Raynaldus and Laderchius, who bring the Annals down to 1565; also Bzovius, a learned Pole, who reaches the same date in seven folio volumes. The learned oratorian Theiner has undertaken the further continuation of Raynaldus and Laderchius, and for this purpose has had full access to even the most secret archives of the Vatican. We have seen but three volumes folio of his continuation, which bring the Annals down to the year 1585—embracing only twenty years! At this rate, the Continuation may make a library in itself, should the laborious author live long enough to carry out his gigantic plan. Among the abridgers of Baronius, Spondanus stands pre-eminent for learning and accuracy. The learned critic Pagi has written a very erudite commentary on the Annals, which is much esteemed for its great moderation and critical acumen. In fine, the vast work of Baronius, with those which it has originated, forms a complete repertory of Church History, and constitutes almost a library in itself.

Among the more celebrated Catholic Historians of the Church, we may also name Natalis Alexander, a learned Dominican, whose work fills ten folio volumes, in Latin, but is more remarkable for its learned essays on difficult points than for its narrative of events, and is rather Gallican in its spirit; Graveson, who wrote, in Latin, a condensed and methodical Church History, in four volumes quarto, which is much esteemed; Fleury's extensive History of the Church, in French, with its continuation by a very inferior writer—the former more remarkable for its beauty of style, and interest of narrative, than for its Catholic spirit and accuracy of statement, the latter possessing few redeeming traits for its numerous errors of omission and commission; Cardinal Orsi, who wrote, in Italian, an extended, learned, and most excellent Ecclesiastical History of the first six centuries, in forty-two volumes, 12mo, with his continuator Becchetti, who followed out very ably the plan of his illustrious predecessor; Palma, lately professor of Church History in the Roman Seminary and in the Propaganda, who has published, in Latin, several volumes of learned and able essays on difficult and interesting portions of Ecclesiastical History, finally Berault Bercastel, whose voluminous and well-written Church History, in French, was very popular some years ago, until it was in a measure superseded by the equally extensive and much more learned and reliable work of Rohrbacher, which now occupies the foreground among those who prefer to read French.

various languages. But hitherto those among us who read only their native English have deeply felt the want of a comprehensive, reliable, and sufficiently extended history of the Church, in our own tongue; those of Gahan, Reeve, and Pise being either mere abridgments, or in other ways very deficient.* This want is now happily supplied by the publication, in an English translation, of the Church History by the Abbé Darras, written in French, in four volumes octavo. Though not altogether perfect, we regard it, upon the whole, as the best compendious digest of the facts which has yet appeared. It may not, perhaps, be so learned or methodical as Alzog, Palma, Wouters, Döllinger, or even Alber, but as a book for the people, it is believed to be preferable to them all.† The author narrates the principal events in a flowing and popular style, devoid of formal divisions and technicalities; while, by ranging all the facts under the successive Roman pontificates, he preserves the

---

This brief reference to some of the principal Catholic works on Ecclesiastical History shows, that what is stated in the text about the great richness of our literature in this department is not at all exaggerated. We have not referred to works of the kind written in Spanish or German, with which we are not so well acquainted. Nor have we alluded to the partial Church Histories, or cognate works, of Muratori, Tiraboschi, Tillemont, Mabillon, Hurter, Voigt, and many others of the kind, to say nothing of the truly colossal Acta Sanctorum, by the Bollandists. Compared with the labors of Catholic publicists in this field, those of Protestants—including the once popular, but now almost forgotten, Centuriators of Magdeburg—sink into insignificance.

* Döllinger's History of the Church appeared in London in A. D. 1840, in an English translation by the Rev. Edmund Cox, D. D., in four thin volumes octavo. It comes down only to the Reformation, the author having written a separate and more elaborate work on this great religious revolution. The translation has not been republished in this country, and but few copies are to be found. While it displays very considerable learning, and is in the main accurate in its statements, it is perhaps a little too stiff and scientifically methodical for the ordinary reader. Besides, the learned writer is occasionally too sharp on the Popes, and he permits his German prejudices to have too much influence on his opinions. He scarcely does justice to Boniface VIII., nor even to the least defensible of all the Popes—Alexander VI.

† In Theological, Philosophical, and Scientific works, method is important, if not essential. It is not so, at least to the same extent, in History, which deals with human actions. Men do not usually act scientifically or even methodically, and the historian who faithfully records their acts, may well frame his narrative accordingly, without being fairly open to the charge of not having adapted it to the subject-matter.

chronological order, and directs attention to the successors of St. Peter, as the main-springs of all the principal events, and the centres around which they revolve or cluster. Thus he preserves, or rather returns to what is substantially the method of the great Annalist—without being hampered by his division of years—combining with his plan of didactic narrative much of the graceful style and flowing narrative of Fleury and Berault Bercastel. In the main accurate, the work, without being critical, is sufficiently learned for the popular reader; while those acquainted with the languages, and desirous of fuller historical investigation, may easily turn to works of greater volume and more varied erudition. According to our humble judgment, it is the very work which, all things considered, supplies best our present want, and which will do most good to our people; we accordingly augur for it a wide circulation in America, as it has already had in France.

To those who may be inclined to cavil, and to allege that the Abbé Darras is an Ultra-Montane, who is too favorable to the Popes, and cannot therefore be regarded as an impartial historian, we would beg to say, that, in this sense, there are few historians who have not well-defined views of their own, as to the drift and interpretation of the facts which they relate. For ourselves, we candidly avow, that we greatly prefer to trust a writer who has conscientious opinions and lively faith, rather than one who is either an infidel in religion, or has on the subject but crude and ill-digested theories of his own—the mere echo of the passions and prejudices of the hour. One who has faith is generally impressed with the principle of accountability to God, who will judge the living and the dead, and who will certainly punish all falsifiers and prevaricators. We are not of those who believe that a sneering scepticism, such as one witnesses in Voltaire, Paine, and Gieseler, is indispensable for historical impartiality. On the contrary, we are strongly predisposed to distrust all such writers. They evidently wish to make out a case, and to bend all the facts to their own cherished theory, which is, moreover, rather satanical than Christian, because animated more by hatred than by love. It is sad enough to reflect, that most of our English historians belong to this class; those particularly who are most popular and most generally read.

Take, for example, the history of England, by the sceptical Hume, and the brilliant History of the Decline and Fall of the Roman Empire, by the infidel Gibbon. Few works in the English language have been so popular as these, and few have done more mischief to the cause of historical truth and of true religion. Our incautious youth read them on account of their faultless style and splendid narrative, heedless of the subtle poison which is instilled with the well-rounded periods. Gibbon's work, in particular, is marked by an amount of erudition, and a general accuracy of facts that are unconnected or but remotely connected with faith, which render it all the more seductive to those who look only to the good which appears on the surface, and are not sufficiently guarded against the evil which lurks beneath. Originally a convert to the Catholic faith in his early youth, this brilliant historian imbibed infidelity in the school of Geneva, to which his parents had compelled him to go, in order to eradicate Catholicity from his mind and heart. They succeeded but too well! He ceased to be a Catholic, but he was far too logical to halt half way by becoming a Protestant. He accordingly plunged into the gulf of infidelity, and by his seductive writings he has drawn thousands of others into the same fearful abyss. And yet take it all in all, and make proper allowance for the coloring of prejudice, his is, perhaps, the best history of the early and mediæval Church, which was ever written by a non-Catholic.* An infidel the best Protestant Church Historian! This may startle those who do not reflect that the best, if not the only great Protestant epic poem, is entitled *Paradise Lost!* *Paradise Regained*, by the same author, was an utter and irretrievable failure.†

But think or say what you will of particular statements made by Darras, quibble as you may about this or that detail, there are two great, all-pervading FACTS of Ecclesiastical History, which you will not—cannot deny. No sophistry can weaken, no special pleading can obscure, no scepticism can doubt them. We refer to the Perpetuity of the Catholic Church, and the Immortality of the Papacy. These two facts, as indubitable as they are significant, unfold the net results of all Church History. They stand forth amidst the ruins of the past, more solid and immovable than do the pyramids from the sands of the desert. They are as luminous as the sun, which, spite of darkness and storms,

---

* This is, we believe, also the opinion of Dr. Newman, expressed, if we remember aright, in his work on Development.

† We have lately seen, in the library of Emmittsburg, what we suppose to be the original edition of Gibbon's Decline and Fall. It is in fourteen volumes octavo, and it was published at Bâle (or, as it is printed in the edition, Basil) in Switzerland, in A. D. 1788, the very date of the preface written by the author in London. This edition is enriched with learned and racy notes on the margin by the late learned Bishop Bruté, who often disputes the quotations of the infidel historian, laughs at his reasoning, and exposes his sneers to just ridicule. This is perhaps the best way, after all, to answer such philosophic writers. In A. D. 1838, Chryety published at Oxford, Ohio, an edition of Gibbon in two volumes octavo, with a preface and notes by Guizot. In looking over it, we were much disappointed. Guizot's notes do not realize the promises of Guizot's preface, nor are they at all worthy the reputation of the learned publicist. Turning to the famous chapters xv. and xvi., in which Gibbon so insidiously assails Christianity, and perusing the notes of Guizot thereon, we found them exceedingly weak and unsatisfactory. He gives us but few rebutting facts, and these so diluted as to excite our wonder. Professor Palma of Rome, and Spedalieri of Naples, could have given the celebrated author of works on Modern Civilization many useful hints, and furnished him with many important facts on the subject of the early Martyrs, which would have enlightened him, and enabled him effectually to refute the false statements of Gibbon. In some of his other notes, we find the Christian Guizot less exact than the infidel author of the Decline and Fall; as, for instance, in his statement in regard to the constitution of the early Church.

still maintains his undeviating course. Your prejudices and your passions can no more blot them out from the record of the past, than can the mists and the clouds blot out the sun from the heavens. There they are firmly fixed in the firmament of history, and you can neither deny them nor even ignore their existence. In spite of yourself, you cannot fail to be deeply impressed with their significance in settling the practical and vital question : Which is the one true Church of Christ?

To unfold the logic of these two prominent facts, we will offer a few remarks on each of them in succession. They cover the whole ground of Church History, giving a coloring to all its parts, and knitting its facts together into one harmonious and solid whole.

I. Perpetuity of the Church.

Is the Catholic Church human, or is she divine ? This is the important inquiry, the correct answer to which involves our happiness, both in this life and in eternity. If she be human, we would naturally expect to find in her history the evidences of change, decline, and dissolution, which we find in all merely human institutions. Like all these, she would have her beginning, her culminating point, her decline, and her fall. If she be divine, we would not be surprised to find her rudely buffeted indeed by the storms which threaten, and ultimately destroy all human institutions, but we would yet expect to see her come out of all these tempests, not only with the principle of life still strong in her, but even with re-awakened energies and renewed vitality. The principle announced by the wise Gamaliel, when it was question in the Sanhedrim of crushing the Church in her very infancy, will be here appropriate:

"And now, therefore," said the sage, " I say to you, refrain from these men, and let them alone ; for if this design or work be of men, it will fall to nothing; BUT IF IT BE OF GOD, YOU ARE NOT ABLE TO DESTROY IT, LEST PERHAPS YOU BE FOUND TO OPPOSE GOD. (Acts v. 38, 39.)

We are willing to rest the issue upon the application of this test, and we are, moreover, content that even the most bitter adversaries of the Church shall make the application. They dare not deny the great facts to which we shall refer, nor can they logically resist the force of their application to the matter in hand.

Considering the terrible struggles through which the Church has passed during her weary pilgrimage of eighteen hundred years on earth, her permanency, with her ever-increasing extension and vitality, is certainly the most remarkable fact in all history. Were she a merely human institution, according to all the lights of the past, this perpetuity would be utterly incredible—impossible. It would be a greater and more stupendous miracle even, than that of her continued preservation by special divine interposition, which we assert. In this latter hypothesis, the fact would be at least consistent and intelligible; in any other, it would be utterly incomprehensible, and would border on the impossible or absurd. Glance for a moment at the vicissitudes of the strongest human institutions which the hand of man has ever founded. Take, for instance, the Roman Empire, whose framework was of iron, and which for centuries lorded it over the conquered nations of the earth. This huge colossus, bestriding the earth, was most strongly established upon its solid and world-wide base at the birth of Christianity. It had reached its culminating point of prosperity and power at the precise moment, when the Founder of the Church was born in a stable in an obscure village of one of its most remote conquered provinces. The golden age of Augustus had dawned upon the world, and the temple of Janus was closed in token of universal peace and prosperity. Here were then two claimants for universal empire: Augustus the Great, wielding the destinies of the most mighty empire which the world had ever seen; and JESUS OF NAZARETH, the Infant Founder of a new empire, an apparently helpless babe, born in poverty and covered with swaddling clothes, weeping in His manger, and having court paid to Him only by his poor but Immaculate Mother, His devoted foster-father, and a few peasant shepherds. Which of these two, according to all human calculation, was more likely to gain and retain the mastery of the world? Which has actually obtained the ascendency; which has survived, and which has ceased to exist?

Church History solves the problem. The issue was fairly made up between the two empires, and the Church founded by Christ gained the final victory over the splendid empire founded by Augustus. During two hundred and fifty years the contest fiercely raged, the Roman Empire, meanwhile, wielding all its immense and terrible power to crush the infant Church ere she could have time to gain a sure foot-hold on the earth. All the odds were clearly against her in the fearful and bloody struggle. Power, wealth, the passions, the sword, were all arrayed against her, while she could oppose to such fearful weapons nothing but poverty, weakness, and unalterable meekness and patience. The blood of her children flowed in torrents, while under her merciful guidance they repaid evil by good, and shed not a drop of blood in return. Time and again, she was driven from the surface of the earth and the light of day into dark caverns under ground—into the now hallowed Catacombs—where in darkness and sorrow she offered up with trembling hands her pure prayers and holy sacrifice. Still, after so many trials, protracted through so long a period, the triumph over all her powerful enemies remained with her; and the victory, once achieved, was as immortal as herself. The Roman Empire.

drunk with the blood of the saints, toppled over and fell to rise no more; while she calmly built up her temples amidst its ruins, and erected the Rome of the Popes from the *débris* of the Rome of the Cæsars. The former became, in many respects, even more splendid, it was certainly more permanent than the latter. The Cross, which appeared surrounded with a halo of light to the admiring eyes of Constantine, vanquished the Roman eagles which had been borne in all-conquering triumph to the remotest corners of the earth. Who will not say that the finger of God was surely here?

But this was not all; it was but the first part of the Church's triumph, her *début* on the troubled theatre of the world. The Roman Empire fell under the stout and continued blows of the Northmen, who for two centuries poured their almost countless hosts of barbarous invaders into the very heart of its immense territory, where they swept every thing before them, and then came thundering at the gates of the imperial city itself. The Northmen conquered Imperial Rome; did they conquer the Church? No! But the Church conquered them! They came as ravenous wolves to devour; the Church, through the divine power which was in her, converted them into the gentle lambs of her own fold! Under her maternal training these ruthless conquerors of Pagan Rome became the chief of her own disciples, and the founders of new kingdoms and dynasties, to which all the modern governments of Europe trace back their origin. God was surely in her and with her, to enable her to achieve so glorious and so bloodless a revolution, which is the beginning, the fountain-head of all modern civilization. What, in fact, would have become of society had the Church succumbed with the Roman Empire? All would have been anarchy and chaos, and order and civilization would have been simply impossible. If all was not irretrievably lost, we owe it to the Catholic Church, as the hand-maid of God.

After having survived the Roman Empire, and conquered by civilizing barbarism, the imperishable Church was now destined to win unfading laurels in another field, upon which the fate of her own existence as well as that of human liberty and civilization was to be decided; and here, as everywhere else, she came out of the contest, with her garments indeed dripping blood, but bearing the palm-branch of victory in her hands. We refer to the thousand years' contest between the Crescent and the Cross; the most fierce, protracted, and momentous struggle, perhaps, recorded in all history. Our scope does not require us to enter into details, which are, moreover, well known to every reader of history. We are called on merely to chronicle the result. This may be briefly stated, by saying, that the Crescent trailed in the dust, and that the banner of the Cross waved triumphant over the field; and that the Cross, all radiant with light, became a beacon of hope for the civilized world, which thus escaped, as by a miracle, from the horrible thraldom, the debased morals, the brutish darkness, that still prevailed wherever the Crescent continued in the ascendant. Nearly half the world was permitted to share this gloomy destiny; if the other half was rescued from a similar fate, we owe the result to the noble exertions of the Popes, and to the agency of the Church, divinely protected and guaranteed from destruction by the solemn promise of her divine Founder, "that the gates of hell should not prevail against her."

Sneer at the Crusades as much as you will; speak disparagingly of the Popes who planned and animated them; inveigh against "the fanaticism" which kept up this struggle for centuries, in spite of the more *enlightened* principles of modern "Political Economy;" join unblushingly with such heartless infidels as Voltaire and Gibbon, in this fierce, fashionable, and satanic declamation; forget that you are Christians, freemen, and civilized men, in spite of those very declaimers, and in consequence of that very fanaticism:—you move us not. We are not even disappointed at your course; for we have been too long accustomed to hear men of your stamp—the organs of the world which crucified Jesus—railing in this strain. Go on with your denunciations: they hurt us not; they only injure yourselves. The Church will continue to flourish in undiminished splendor for centuries after you are dead, laid in the tomb, and forgotten! Go on: the world will praise you and raise tombs to your memory; and you will thus "have received your reward!" God grant that what the great St. Augustine says of men like you may not be verified in your case! *Laudantur ubi non sunt; cruciantur ubi sunt!* *

But pause one moment, and tell me, whether you question the final and permanent result of the great struggle as above recited? Dare you deny it, or its momentous consequences for civilization and society? Dare you say, or even hint, that scoffers of your class had any thing whatsoever to do with the glorious triumphs achieved by such heroes of chivalry as Godfrey de Bouillon, Tancred, Richard Cœur de Lion, and St. Louis of France, and by such far-seeing and saintly Pontiffs as Gregory VII. and Urban II.? Had those immortal men been imbued with the selfish and sneering spirit of Voltaire and Gibbon, instead of being impelled by that of chivalry, what would, in all human probability, be *your* fate now? Would you be Christians or Mussulmans; would you be free or slaves; would you be civilized or barbarians?

When you will have answered these questions to your own

---

* "They are praised where they are not; they are tormented where they are!"

satisfaction, will you please take the trouble to resolve other of equal significance in relation to the matter in hand—the divinely guarantied perpetuity of the Church? What has become of all those loud-mouthed adversaries of the Church, of that vast and motley host of schismatics and heretics, of infidels and traitors, from Judas Iscariot and Simon Magus in the first century, down to Miller and Joe Smith, and the founder of Spiritism in the nineteenth, who have successively lifted their hands against the imperishable Church of all ages and of all nations? What has been the net and final result of all their fierce declamations, and of their premature shouts of victory? Did they succeed in their contemplated work of destruction, or did they ingloriously fail? Did they ruin the Church by rending her inborn unity, or were they themselves dashed to pieces against the rock upon which she had been divinely built? What was the ultimate fate of the thousand and one heresies and sects, which ambitious or wicked men originated against the unity and divine character of the Church during the first fifteen centuries? They have all vanished from the face of the earth; they are dead and buried, and long since forgotten, except by those who from time to time fitfully and passionately revive their memory, in order to renew their fruitless assaults against the Church. They have nowhere else "a local habitation or a name;" the world knows them not, and heeds not the doom which has overtaken them; God has judged their founders!

And what has become of most of the numerous sects which have sprung up since the sixteenth century? The answer is clear and patent to every reflecting man who has read history, and who is in the habit of studying events in their antecedents and consequents. Their fate was already foreshadowed in that of their predecessors; it was declared in advance by our blessed

Lord himself, when he laid down this great principle: "Every plant which my heavenly Father hath not planted, shall be rooted up. Let them alone: they are blind and leaders of the blind; and if the blind lead the blind, both fall into the ditch." (St. Matthew xv. 13, 14.) Most of these human religions have already "fallen into the ditch;" the others are well-nigh its brink. Some yesterday, some to-day, others to-morrow— all are hastening to the same fearful doom. Germany, the fatherland of these modern sects, has already, to a very great extent, lapsed into infidelity, or into rationalism and pantheism, which are only other names for infidelity. The Bible, which was so much vaunted by the founders of Protestantism, has now become a book of myths and fables; miracles, grace, and every thing that is supernatural have been discarded, and very often only those truths which belong to the natural order, and which even a decent pagan would have maintained, are taught from the chairs of the universities; while from the very pulpit from which Calvin launched his invectives against the Church, the divinity of Christ, and every thing supernatural in His religion, are covertly or openly impugned.

In France, the children of the sturdy Huguenots have, in a great measure, adopted the same tenets of quasi-infidelity; in spite of Guizot and some others, who try to stem the rushing torrent of unbelief, little but the mere lifeless shell of Christianity remains, its vital kernel having long since disappeared. In England, indeed, a semblance of faith is still preserved by the aid of an immense and wealthy Church Establishment, the rich funds of which were *borrowed* from the Catholic Church; but even in England, with all the influence of the Establishment and the prestige of the government, the tendency of belief is downward, rather than upward; Low-Church principles have gained the day over those of the High-Church; and the infidel Bishop Colenso cannot or will not be authoritatively silenced or condemned, while the almost undisguised infidelity of the leading Churchmen who lately published the notorious Essays and Reviews has not been officially rebuked.

A similar development of infidel tendencies is witnessed in our own country; where, beginning with Boston, Unitarianism, Universalism, Spiritism, and a hundred other sects, either directly infidel or bordering on positive unbelief in Christianity as a supernatural religion, are spreading like a canker over the land. Alas! that it should be so; but the truth is even more fearful than what would be conveyed by the picture which we have here hastily drawn of waning Protestantism. The sects, which still love to be called Evangelical, are manifestly on the decline; they are threatened with being ingulfed by the infidel or semi-infidel masses which are ominously l ving beneath them. The day must come, and it is not far distant, when the dissenting sects of this country will go the way of the dissenting sects in Europe. Having left the summit-level of Catholicity, they are all fast hastening down the declivity of unbelief; and it is only a question of time, when they will all plunge headlong together, like their numerous predecessors, into the frightful abyss!

Perhaps the most striking, as it is certainly the saddest evidence of this downward tendency, as existing in England and America, was lately exhibited in the general howl of indignation which went forth from the pulpit and the press of both countries against the sainted and heroic Pius IX., for having, in his Encyclical, with apostolic freedom and firmness, dared hurl his censures against the mischievous and wicked errors of modern revolutionists and unbelievers. In fierce denunciation of the Pontiff, the sects of England and America, penly and without a blush, have joined hands with European

Rationalists, Naturalists, Pantheists, and Infidels; and if there has been any distinction or pre-eminence in the amount of fury thus displayed, it would seem to have been won by the sects calling themselves *Evangelical!*

Amidst all this Babel-like confusion of dissent, and this rapid tendency to dissolution among the sects, what of the Catholic Church! Is she waning in her fortunes, diminishing in her numbers, or losing her influence? Is her dissolution threatened? Is her vitality even imperilled? The answer rises instinctively to the lips of every candid man: she was never stronger, never more thoroughly alive, than she is at this very day. Her terrible conflicts of eighteen centuries—conflicts which may continue for eighteen centuries more, should the world last so long—have left her more vigorous than ever. Her bishops are never before so numerous or devoted; her priests never more active or influential; her spirits never more buoyant; her face never more radiant. She sends her missionaries to the most remote confines of the earth and to the farthest off islands of the sea, with the same exuberant and hopeful zeal which marked the apostolic age; and her modern apostles still pant for, win, and wear the crown of martyrdom, with the same burning charity and the same abounding joy, as did their predecessors in the race of spiritual conquest in the halcyon days of her early history. In the often quoted language of Lord Macaulay:—

"Nor do we see any sign which indicates that the term of her long duration is approaching. She saw the commencement of all the governments, and of all the ecclesiastical establishments that now exist in the world; and we feel no assurance that she is not destined to see the end of them all. She was great and respected before the Saxon set foot on Britain—before the Frank had crossed the Rhine—when Grecian eloquence still flourished at Antioch—when idols were still worshipped in the Temple of Mecca. * * * When we reflect on the tremendous assaults which she has survived, we find it difficult to conceive in what way she is to perish." *

Yes; it is more than difficult, it is simply impossible that she should perish. He who said, "Heaven and earth may pass away, but My word shall not pass away," built her securely upon a Rock, and He pledged His solemn word that "the gates of hell should not prevail against her." History shows the faithful fulfilment of this divine prophecy and promise. Its verdict was already foreshadowed in other prophetic words of the inspired Record: "And the rain fell, and the floods came, and they beat upon that House; AND IT FELL NOT, FOR IT WAS FOUNDED ON A ROCK." (See Matt. vii. 25.) This is the clue to the difficulty, the key of the position; with it all is clear, without it history were an inextricable labyrinth.

"Strong as the rock of the ocean, which stems
A thousand wild waves on the shore,"

she will stand unshaken amidst all the storms of the future, as she has nobly withstood all the storms of the past.

During eighteen centuries the Church has thus triumphantly stood the test of Gamaliel. Empires have arisen, flourished for a time, and then crumbled into ruins, along her pathway in history. Dynasties have changed and been extinguished; thrones have tottered and fallen; sceptres have been broken; crowns have mouldered to dust: but she has survived all; and she still stands up erect and vigorous in the world; not an antique, but a living and breathing existence, having a vitality not sickly, not waning, but superabundant; not only living herself, but bountifully bestowing of her exuberant

* Review of Ranke's History of the Popes.

life upon the nations of the earth, and giving without losing any of it herself; even as the sun giveth forth his light and heat, without impairing his own exhaustless store. She lives, and she will live, "all days even to the consummation of the world." She lives, the only divine and immortal institution of earth. Christ is her Head, and Christ is God, and He stands pledged that she shall share in His own immortality. Christ is her Bridegroom, and she is His chosen Bride, "without spot, without wrinkle," all glorious and undefiled; a divine and blooming Bride, who knows no old age and feels no decay—"doomed to death, but fated not to die." She has walked the world, patiently and lovingly, bearing her crown of thorns, like her heavenly Bridegroom; she has been often scourged through it as He was; but like Him, she bears a charmed life, and cannot be conquered by death. Immortality is written upon her brow, and she will wear the wreath for ever more, in spite of the world, the devil, and the flesh! A pilgrim of faith and of love, with her home in the heavens, she asks only a free passage through this world; and her omnipotent Bridegroom will see that she obtain it, whether men will it or not.

We pass now to the second great FACT of Church History, which, after what we have said, need not detain us long:—

II. THE IMMORTALITY OF THE PAPACY.

Even from a human point of view, there is, perhaps, no more remarkable or magnificent spectacle in history than that presented by the long line of Roman Pontiffs. The golden chain of the succession stretches across the broad historic field, from St. Peter in the first century, to Pius IX. in the nineteenth; and not a link of it has been broken by the changes of time and the rude shocks of events, during more than eighteen centuries! Compared with this venerable line of bishops, the oldest ancestral and royal houses of Europe are but of yesterday. These have all undergone the changes incident to human things; that has proved itself superior to all vicissitudes, and has come triumphant out of every fiery ordeal. Through sunshine and tempest, through whirlwinds and revolutions, through the wreck of empires and the changes of dynasties, through ruins cumbering its pathway during long ages, the Papacy has survived, and it still lives, with undiminished vigor and ever-renewed vitality.

The imperial line of the Roman Cæsars began the race with the Papacy; it was strong and the Papacy was weak; but the line of the Cæsars, which was inaugurated under auspices so promising and so splendid by Augustus, after a period of less than five centuries, terminated disastrously and ingloriously in Augustulus (or the little Augustus); while the Papacy was still young, and had hardly yet gained a firm foot-hold on the earth. The line of the Eastern Cæsars began with Constantine in the fourth century, and closed with Constantine Paleologus in the fifteenth; still the Papacy remained, more firmly seated than ever on the Chair of Peter. The old French monarchy began in the fifth century, and after having undergone manifold vicissitudes, and passed through the various dynasties of the Merovingian, the Carlovingian, and the Capetian houses, it was extinguished for a time at the close of the last century, in the blood of Louis XVI., and though subsequently revived for a brief period, it seems that its sun has now set forever; still the Papacy exhibits no signs of decay. The English monarchy has undergone similar changes, and has passed through the successive dynasties of the British, Saxon, Danish, Norman, Plantagenet, Tudor, Stuart, and Brunswick houses; but the Papacy, which was already four centuries old when Hengist, the Saxon, first set foot on British soil, has outlived the past, and it bids fair to survive the present and future royal lines.* The same may be said of the imperial line of Germany, and of the royal line of Spain—not to speak of the smaller principalities of Europe, or the comparatively modern line of the Russian Czars. They are all of the earth, earthly; they have all in turn bowed to the decree of instability, and to the doom of dissolution, inscribed on all merely human institutions; while the Papacy has plainly risen above this law of change, has exhibited no signs of decay which would indicate approaching dissolution, and, after having bravely battled with events for eighteen centuries, has immortality still engraved on its triple crown.

This wonderful tenacity of life becomes still more astonishing when we reflect upon the terrible conflicts through which the Papacy, like the Church, has passed during its long pilgrimage on earth. For three centuries the sword of persecution, wielded by the mightiest empire which the world ever saw, was seldom returned to the scabbard, and to be a Roman Pontiff was to be a candidate for martyrdom. More than thirty of the early Pontiffs were made to pass from an earthly to a heavenly crown, under the axe of the pagan executioner. At each successive decapitation, the cruel instruments of imperial

* The following tabular view of the Royal Houses of France and England will exhibit, at a glance, the changing fortunes of those famous dynasties:—

FRANCE.		ENGLAND.	
Merovingian line began	A. D. 448	Anglo-Saxon from fifth century to	A. D. 1017
Carlovingian	" 750	Danish, to	" 1042
Capetian	" 987	Saxon again, to	" 1066
House of Valois, Second Capetian Branch	" 1328	Norman, to	" 1138
		Plantagenet, to	" 1399
Valois—Orleans—Third Capetian Branch	" 1498	House of Lancaster, to	" 1461
		House of York, to	" 1485
Bourbon—Fourth Capetian Branch	" 1589	Tudor, to	" 1603
Last of Bourbons—Louis Philippe —expelled from the throne in	" 1848	Stuart, to	" 1649
		Commonwealth, to	" 1660
		Stuart again, to	" 1714
		Hanover and Brunswick, to	" 1865

despotism no doubt boasted that the line was extinct, and that no priest would be found bold enough to step into the dangerous post stained with the blood of the previous incumbent. No doubt the certain downfall of popery was then a hundred times predicted, with at least as much earnestness, and with more seeming probability, than it has been foretold on less plausible grounds by many in modern times, who so loudly vaunt their zeal for Christianity. But as the pagan prophecies were falsified by the event, so may we reasonably hope and confidently expect that those of their *Christian* imitators will not be realized. If history convey any certain lesson, we may safely derive this steadfast conclusion from its faithful and constant verdict of eighteen centuries.

After having survived pagan persecution, the Papacy had to contend successively with the barbarism which had overwhelmed the Roman Empire; with heresy, which in almost every century threatened to rend the bosom of the Church; and with schism, which more immediately assailed its unity, and threatened its integrity and its very life. The Popes triumphed over barbarism, by first converting, and then humanizing and civilizing the barbarians. The greatest obstacles which they had to encounter, in carrying out this benevolent mission, were presented by the untamed passions and the rude violence of the semi-barbarous emperors, kings, and feudal chieftains of the Middle Ages. They quailed not, however, before a long-continued opposition excited by the mighty ones of the earth. In the discharge of their duties, as Fathers of Christendom and civilizers of the newly-converted European nations, they trembled not in the presence of mail-clad warriors or crowned robbers of the Church. St. Gregory VII. confronted the imperial tyrant and debauchee, Henry IV, with as much spirit as that with which his sainted predecessor, St. Leo

the Great, had confronted the ruthless Attila. If persuasion
and expostulation failed, measures of severity were adopted;
and in the protracted and varied contest, the final result was
never doubtful. The Popes always triumphed in the end over
their mighty adversaries, however appalling and seemingly insurmountable were the difficulties against which they had to
contend.

Similar weapons were used against heresy in all its Protean
forms, and with similar results. The stricken monster, after
writhing for a time, and shifting its ground or changing its
form, never failed eventually to yield up its feverish life
under the stout blows of the Papacy. Cast out from the
Church, which is the garden of life, its vitality waned, and it
was doomed to go the way of all flesh; while the life of faith
within the Church was endued with a new vigor, after every
triumphant contest with rebellion against its authority.

But the fiercest trial, perhaps, through which the Papacy had
to pass, was that of schism raising up rival claimants to the
Tiara. Yet through even this dangerous ordeal has the Papacy
passed unscathed. Most of these schisms were of short
duration. The different antipopes, whom the violence of unprincipled emperors or kings set up at various times previous to
the fourteenth century, continued in their unhallowed rebellion
for a very brief period; they were soon deserted by their followers, and after a short career of mischief, the world knew
them no more. It was not so with the great Schism of the
West, which lasted for nearly forty years, at the close of
the fourteenth and the beginning of the fifteenth century. It
would seem as if God wished to test the vitality of the Papacy,
and to show to the world that it was plainly indestructible.
During forty years, Christendom was divided in its allegiance
between two, for a brief space among three claimants of the

papal crown. Christ, the great Head of the Church, seemed to be slumbering, while the Bark of Peter was rudely buffeted by the waves, which threatened it with shipwreck; but, after sufficiently trying the faith of His disciples, He arose from His slumber, and, with the calm majesty of Divinity, rebuked the winds and the waves, and suddenly there came a great calm! The storm-tossed vessel had now escaped its greatest danger, and it was henceforth to pursue its even course on comparatively untroubled waters. If ever the Papacy could have been destroyed, it must have succumbed under the effects of the Great Schism. But, instead of being destroyed, it came out of it stronger even than it went in. It was invested with a new vigor, and was established on a more solid basis than ever, when Martin V., elected by the Council of Constance, in A. D. 1417, was received with universal acclamation by a united Christendom. It was to know division no more; and from that day to this, no schism, worthy the name, has troubled the peaceful career of the Papacy.

To say that the Great Schism, or any previous one of shorter duration, interrupted the line of the papal succession, would betray a very slight and imperfect knowledge of the subject, or a blind partisanship which is proof against calm and logical argument. The succession certainly continued in one or the other of the lines; and for the purpose of establishing its unbroken character, it really matters not much in which. Failing the line of Avignon, we may fall back upon that of Rome—which, we have no doubt, is the true one;— and failing both, during the last eight years, we may still fall back on that created by the Council of Pisa, which elected Alexander V., after having attempted to depose the two other claimants. In any hypothesis, the succession is unbroken. In the whole contest there was no issue as to faith or principles, but only a question as to the matter of fact—which was the rightful claimant? The entire scandal is fairly ascribable, not so much to the Popes, as to the selfish ambition of earthly monarchs, who wished to make the Papacy subservient to State policy; and particularly to that of the most unprincipled, perhaps, among all those who wore the crown at that stormy period—Philip the Fair, of France.

As to the other objections usually alleged against the line of the succession, they are comparatively trivial and unimportant. They are mere straws floating on the current, not impeding its flow, but rather pointing out its course. An interruption of a few months, or even of a few years, induced by the calamities of the times, cannot be fairly objected as a serious break in a line of Pontiffs which extends over eighteen centuries. The succession is moral rather than physical, and a space of time comparatively small is reputed as nothing, according to the canon of sound jurisprudence fairly applicable to such cases. If this rule be very properly brought into requisition in regard to the line of succession in royal houses, why may we not be permitted to extend it to the much longer one of the Roman Pontiffs? The sun is not blotted out from the heavens by the transient cloud which for a day or a week may hide his face; and when the cloud passes away his rays shoot forth with renewed brilliancy. So it has been with the Papacy. It has been so in the matter of temporary interruption or obscuration; it has been so also when its fair face, like that of the sun, has been occasionally and partially obscured by the dark spots of scandal.

And the impartial reader of Church History will not fail to come to the conclusion, that in almost every instance in which troubles and scandals threw a dark shadow for a time over the Papacy, the princes of the earth were mainly the authors of the evils which afflicted Christendom. Thus, for example, the unworthy men, who sat on the papal chair at the close of the ninth and the beginning of the tenth century, were thrust into it by the intrigues and violence of wicked men and women, who happened at that period to hold political power in the Roman territory. Intruded by violence, they became legitimate Pontiffs only by the acquiescence and recognition of the Church; and whatever may have been the private or even public vices of a few of them during these disastrous years, it is not even claimed that they attempted any thing against the faith, or introduced any innovation even into general discipline. The succession was preserved in the unworthy incumbent—unworthy because, owing to the unhappy dissensions of the times, the usual mode of election became impracticable. Is it fair to charge on the Papacy, in its normal state, the evils and scandals which were plainly caused by a departure from the wise rules regulating the order of promotion to the papal chair, which were set aside by the hand of violence? We think not.

If one of the twelve Apostles, who were trained under the immediate eye of our blessed Lord Himself, was permitted to fall away and to turn traitor, to the fearful extent of selling his Master for thirty pieces of silver, and if this sad defection did not break the integrity of the apostolic college, or even destroy its prestige, is it equitable or just to charge that a very few Popes of doubtful morality, in a line numbering more than two hundred and fifty, have ruined the Papacy, or disgraced it in the eyes of fair-minded men? If even one-twelfth of the Popes had led scandalous lives, the proportion would not be greater than that which we would have been led to expect from the precedent set in the first body of Christ's ministers, selected by Himself for the high and holy office of evangelizing the world. But it is scarcely pretended, even by the worst enemies of the Papacy, that the proportion has been so great as this. Besides the few disedifying Pontiffs intruded into the Holy See by wicked leaders of faction, to whom we have already referred, there are, we believe, not more than three or four to whose moral conduct reasonable exception has been taken; and some of these may be plausibly defended without straining the evidence.

The least defensible of all, perhaps, is Alexander VI., who occupied the papal chair at the end of the fifteenth and the beginning of the sixteenth century; but immoral as he certainly was before he was promoted to the Tiara, there seems to be no sufficient evidence to show that his immoralities were continued after he became Pope. His great fault consisted in the favors which he extended to the unworthy children who had been born to him many years before his promotion; and their wickedness was made, fairly or unfairly, to reflect back upon the character of their parent. Much of the obloquy, with which contemporary writers have visited the name of Alexander, is fairly traceable to the scandalous conduct of Giovanni and Cæsar Borgia,* whose justly indignant enemies blamed the father for their excesses and tyranny. Thus, Heli, the high-priest, was censured, and justly, for the permitted or unpunished crimes of his two sons; but it is not pretended, for all this, that Heli was himself a wicked or immoral man. It is not the first, nor the hundredth time, in the history of the world, that parental indulgence and fondness have darkened the mind and blinded the eye to the faults of a wicked offspring. On the other hand, it is not, we believe, even hinted on any side, that Alexander VI., whatever may have been his short-comings as a man, ever attempted, as Pontiff, to adulterate the faith,

---

* For character of Lucretia Borgia, see Note, p. xlv.

or to change any of the time-honored general usages and discipline of the Church. His wickedness, whatever it was, was hurtful chiefly to himself. In his public administration he was a far-seeing statesman, and not an unwise or imprudent Pontiff. His timely interposition, and his wise arbitrament which was accepted by the parties most deeply interested, settled the fierce dispute which had arisen between the Spanish and Portuguese discoverers in the New World, and thereby probably prevented a protracted war and untold bloodshed and confusion of rights and claims among the early American settlers. Whatever opinion men may choose to entertain of his moral character, these things should be fairly taken into the account.

If there are thus lights, as well as shadows, in the character of one so generally censured as Alexander VI., what may we not anticipate as to that of a few other Pontiffs less open to accusation? Time was, and that not long ago, when such Popes as Gregory VII. and Innocent III. were painted with the darkest colors, as marked by all that was odious in rapacity and despotism; but two learned Protestant historians— Voigt and Hurter*—lately stepped forth to the rescue, analyzed and published the original records of their lives; and the resulting verdict of all impartial men has been, that no two Popes in the entire line were surrounded by a greater halo of light and glory.

Take them all in all, the two hundred and fifty Popes and more,† who have successively occupied the Chair of Peter,

---

* Hurter since became a Catholic, probably in consequence of his researches into the records of the Church during the glorious but much maligned pontificate of Innocent III. He found the truth to be so utterly different from the current and accredited representations, that a total reaction took place in his candid and well-balanced mind. While a little learning is a dangerous thing, much is invaluable to an honest man, who sincerely seeks the truth, and is prepared fearlessly to follow its teachings, no matter whither these may lead.

† Without at all breaking, or interfering with the line of the succession, different Catho-

constitute the most respectable and venerable body of men whose deeds are recorded on the pages of history. Nearly all of them were highly respectable men, learned, enlightened, and pious, far beyond their age; very many of them were venerable for their personal sanctity. Seventy-nine of them—nearly a third of the entire number—were so remarkable for their holiness of character as to merit being inscribed on the Calendar of Saints; and this number includes thirty-three who willingly laid down their lives for Christ and His Church. A very large proportion of the others were men of blameless life, and of indefatigable zeal for the propagation of the faith, while not a few of them were possessed of great learning and capacity. Such, for instance, were Innocent III., Innocent

he writers assign different numbers of incumbents, in their catalogues of the Popes. The late learned and holy Archbishop Kenrick reckons the number at two hundred and fifty-one, rigidly excluding all who were in any way doubtful. Other lists, not so critically composed, swell the number to two hundred and sixty-two, or even a few more. The difference is more apparent than real; and close examination will show that it does not in the least clash with the substance of the succession. The following, among other items of difference, will sufficiently establish this statement:—

1. Some historians maintain that Cletus and Anacletus, in the first century, were two men, while others, more probably, believe these to be but two names of the same incumbent. 2. Some admit Stephen VII. (A. D. 896-7) among the genuine Popes, while others, with Graveson, regard him as an intruder, which he certainly was at the beginning of his career. 3. Some lists, even among those published at Rome, admit the names of Alexander V., and of his successor, John XXIII., chosen by the Council of Pisa, while the more judicious catalogues exclude them both. They lived during the later years of the Great Schism, while there were already two other claimants of the Tiara sitting respectively at Rome and Avignon. 4. Other Pontiffs lived for so short a time after their election, as to have been omitted in some of the catalogues. Thus Stephen II., elected A. D. 752, survived only three days; John XV., elected about the year 985, lived also but a few days, and was not consecrated, &c. 5. Some authors, again, with the Count De Maistre, reject several Popes, who were intruded into the Chair of Peter, at the close of the ninth and the beginning of the tenth century; while others, much more reasonably and soundly, still reckon those intruders among the lawful Popes, on account of the subsequent recognition of, or acquiescence in, their authority by the Church.

It is thus manifest that the substance of the succession is not at all affected by the slight differences in the various lists or catalogues of the Popes, drawn up by different authors. These diverging views only exhibit the latitude wisely allowed to criticism in the Catholic Church. Whatever may be the theories broached or maintained by these learned critics, the integrity of the succession remains evidently untouched.

IV., Boniface VIII., and Benedict XIV.—not to name a host of others in the earlier ages of the Church.

In this connection, it is a remarkable fact, and one which shows how effectually Christ has watched over His Church, in the person of His Vicars on earth, that during the last three centuries—since the so-called Reformation—not a single unworthy or immoral Pope has occupied the venerable Chair of Peter. While wickedness has abounded, and the very foundations of the faith have been boldly undermined by wicked men "lying in wait to deceive," God has taken care of His own, and has spared scandals in the high places of His Church. The Reformation has, perhaps, been instrumental in involuntarily and indirectly rendering this signal service to the cause of the Church, which it so unblushingly maligned. By removing from the pale of Catholic Christendom the most turbulent and unrestrained of its members, it has contributed to purify the atmosphere breathed by the great body of Christians, who remained faithful; while by its bitter opposition, it has quickened their zeal and nourished their vigilance. Thus God's providence hath drawn good out of evil.

Compare the Popes with the sovereigns who have contemporaneously filled the various thrones of Europe and the world; and mark the difference, or rather the contrast. While among the latter it is very difficult to discover even one just man, in a long line of incumbents; in the former, it is almost as difficult to find one who is wicked. Among the latter, personal morality, self-restraint, and purity are the exception; among the former, they are the rule. Among the latter, a ruler now and then appears clad with the virtues which mark the saint, as if to show that sanctity is compatible with every condition in life; among the former so many blameless and saintly men appear, that we cease to wonder, and yield to no surprise on discovering a new Pope who is true to the traditions of his order. When we find a solitary flower in the bleak and dreary desert, we are startled into unbounded admiration; when we behold whole clusters of them in a flower-garden, we look with calm pleasure on the beautiful spectacle, but take it as a matter of course, and are not at all astonished.

With the long and brilliant line of the Popes thus staring them in the face, let superficial men of the present day talk of the downfall of the Papacy. So shallow men often prated and predicted, during the centuries which have passed; but the event never failed to falsify their prophecies, begotten by their prejudice and hatred. The Papacy still endures, in spite of their malignity. Let Pius IX. be again driven from his throne, and be even dragged into captivity; many of his predecessors, including the last two who bore his honored name, shared the same fate, and yet the Papacy survived the disaster. The enemies of the Popes were themselves laid low, but in the long run the Papacy itself never failed to triumph. This is the sure conclusion reached by the logic of all history. No one ever attempted to remove or destroy the Papacy, who was not, in his own person, or at least in that of his early descendants or successors, dashed to pieces against that rock upon which the Church was divinely built by the Architect who has guaranteed her safety. This is the true secret of the wonderful permanency, of the divine vitality of the Papacy. Victor Emmanuel and Napoleon III. are protected by no such divine promise, they are clad in no such invulnerable panoply, as that which shields their weak and apparently defenceless victim. Let them beware! Let them learn a lesson from the teachings of the past! They and their dynasties may fall or pass away; the Papacy will surely remain, so surely as God liveth and is true to His word!

At no previous period of its history was the Papacy stronger in its hold upon the confidence and affections of Christendom, than it is at the present day. Eighteen centuries of triumphant conflict with the princes of the earth and the powers of darkness have succeeded in convincing the Christian world of its invincibility, and of the utter futility of opposition to its decisions. Gallicanism has waned, and has now well-nigh disappeared, under the influence of this growing conviction. One of the most gratifying spectacles which modern history presents to the eye of the Christian is the unanimity and enthusiasm with which the Catholic episcopate of the entire world, numbering about nine hundred, and with them all Christendom, have responded to the bold and independent declarations of the late Encyclical. This general and harmonious concert of assent has been marred by no discordant, much less dissenting, voice. In France and in Italy, the bishops have nobly contemned the prohibition and braved the despotic mandates and threats of Napoleon, and of his humble instrument, Victor Emmanuel.

Such being, then, the clear teachings of history in regard to the Papacy, was it not fitting that, in a History of the Church, the Popes should occupy a prominent place? They are the chief executives of the Church, the centres around which cluster all the facts connected with her history; aye, the very pivot on which they turn. This was the happy conception of the Abbé Darras in composing his History, the first volume of which is now presented to the public, for the first time in an English dress. The idea itself, together with the fact that it has become popular, is a hopeful sign of the times. Coming from France, which was erewhile the seat of the time-serving and factious Gallicanism that Napoleon III. is seeking to resuscitate and introduce, it is particularly consoling, as indicating the general predominance, even in that empire, of sounder and more conservative principles of Church polity.

We conclude this Introduction by brief quotations from two African Fathers; one belonging to the second, the other to the fifth century of the Church. Speaking of the heretics of his day, Tertullian says: "Let them exhibit the origin of their churches; let them evolve (unfold) the order of their bishops, so running by succession from the beginning, that the first bishop had for his author or predecessor one of the Apostles, or one of the apostolic men who persevered in communion with the Apostles. For in this way the apostolic churches exhibit their origin, as the Church of Smyrna relates that Polycarp was placed there by John; as the Church of Rome likewise relates that Clement was ordained by Peter; and in like manner the other churches show those who were constituted bishops by the Apostles, and made conservators of the apostolic seed. LET HERETICS PRODUCE (FEIGN) ANY THING LIKE THIS! FINGANT QUID TALE HÆRETICI.*

The great St. Augustine invites dissenters back to the bosom of unity in the following affectionate language:—

"Come to us, brethren, if you wish to be ingrafted in the vine. We are afflicted at beholding you lying cut off from its trunk. Count over the bishops in the very See of Peter, and behold in that list of fathers how one succeeded the other. This is the rock against which the proud gates of hell do not prevail."†

* De Præscriptionibus.   † Contra partem Donati.

NOTE ON LUCRETIA BORGIA.—Most modern writers, following the unscrupulous Victor Hugo, have sought to blacken the character of Lucretia Borgia, whom they represent as a modern Jezabel. Roscoe, in his Leo X., defends her with much plausibility and learning, and the facts which he alleges in her vindication go far towards palliating the conduct of her father. The charges made against both father and daughter seem to have originated with the most violent personal or partisan enemies of the family. See the Special Dissertation on the subject by Roscoe, beginning of second volume, American Edition, 1865.

CONTENTS.

INTRODUCTION...Page xi.

CHAPTER I.

1. Connection of Christianity with the past.—2. The fulness of time. Religious and moral state of the world at the Advent of our Lord Jesus Christ.—3. His life during thirty years.—4. Public life of our Lord.—5. Teaching of the Saviour. Institution of the Sacraments.—6. Foundation of the Church.—7. Passion and death of our Lord Jesus Christ on the cross.—8. His Ascension..Page 13.

CHAPTER II.

§ I. PONTIFICATE OF ST. PETER (A. D. 33, June 29—A. D. 67). 1. Pentecost.—2. Life of the primitive Christians.—3. Election of the seven deacons.—4. Conversion of St. Paul.—5. Calling of the Gentiles.—6. Persecution by Herod Agrippa. Dispersion of the Apostles.—7. First mission of St. Paul.—8. Council of Jerusalem.—9. Second mission of St. Paul.—10. Third mission of St. Paul.—11. Fourth mission of St. Paul.—12. First general persecution under Nero. Martyrdom of St. Peter and St. Paul. § II. PONTIFICATE OF ST. LINUS (A. D. 67-78). 13. Destruction of Jerusalem by Titus.—14. Death of St. Linus. § III. PONTIFICATE OF ST. CLETUS, OR ANACLETUS (A. D. 78-91). 15. Identity of St. Cletus, or Anacletus.—16. Extension of Christianity into Gaul and Germany. § IV. PONTIFICATE OF ST. CLEMENT I. (A. D. 91-100). 17. Letters of St. Clement to the Corinthians.—18. Heresies of the first century.—19. Second general persecution under Domitian.................................Page 28.

CHAPTER III.

1. Importance of studying the first century.—2. Teaching of the Church. Its authority.—3. Its simplicity.—4. Miracles. Confirmation of the doctrine relating to them.—5. Tradition.—6. Holy Scriptures. New Testament.—7. The Gospels.—8. The emblems of the four Evangelists.—9. The Acts of the Apostles.—10. Epistles of St. Paul.—11. Epistles of St. James, St. Peter, St.

CONTENTS.

John, and St. Jude.—12. The Apocalypse.—13. Principal points of doctrine contained in the New Testament.—14. Government of the Church. Authority of the Apostolic See.—15. Episcopacy.—16. Priesthood, Deaconship, Religious Orders, Celibacy of the Clergy, Deaconesses.—17. Discipline.—18. Worship. —19. Conclusion..Page 60.

CHAPTER IV.

§ I. Pontificate of St. Evaristus (A. D. 100-109). 1. Character of the third general persecution under Trajan.—2. Letter of Pliny the Younger to Trajan. —3. Reply of Trajan.—4. Arrius Antoninus.—5. Martyrdom of St. Simeon, bishop of Jerusalem.—6. Sect of Thebutis.—7. Unity of Government a guarantee of purity of faith.—8. Journey of St. Ignatius to Rome.—9. His martyrdom.—10. Martyrdom of St. Evaristus. § II. Pontificate of St. Alexander I. (A. D. 109-119). 11. Regulations of St. Alexander I.—12. Martyrdom of St. Onesimus, bishop of Ephesus—of St. Timothy—of St. Titus, &c.—13. Epistle of St. Polycarp to the Philippians.—14. St. Papias, bishop of Hierapolis. —15. Works of St. Dionysius the Areopagite.—16. Therapentes.—17. Revolt of the Jews.—18. Death of the Emperor Trajan.—19. Character of the Emperor Adrian.—20. Martyrdom of Pope Alexander I. § III. Pontificate of St. Sixtus I. (A. D. 119-128). 21. Gnostics.—22. Martyrdom of St. Symphorosa, and her sons.—23. Martyrdom of SS. Sabina, Serapia, Zoe, &c.—24. Martyrdom of Pope St. Sixtus I................................Page 84.

CHAPTER V.

§ I. Pontificate of St. Telesphorus (A. D. 128-138). 1. St. Telesphorus, Pope.— 2. Apology of St. Quadratus, and of Aristides.—3. Letter of Serenius Granianus, proconsul of Asia, to the Emperor Adrian.—4. Reply of Adrian.—5. Revolt of the Jews.—6. The Talmud.—7. Version of Aquila.—8. Death of Adrian.—9. Martyrdom of Pope St. Telesphorus. § II. Pontificate of St. Hyginus (A. D. 138-142). 10. Heresy of Cerdon and Marcion.—11. Death of St. Hyginus. § III. Pontificate of St. Pius I. (A. D. 142-150). 12. Persecution continued under the reign of Antoninus.—13. St. Justin the Apologist. His conversion.—14. Exhortation to the Greeks, the first work of St. Justin. —15. First Apology of St. Justin, addressed to the Emperor Antoninus.—16. Decree of the Emperor Antoninus Pius in favor of the Christians.—17. Death of Pope St. Pius I...Page 103.

CHAPTER VI.

§ I. Pontificate of St. Anicetus (A. D. 150-161). 1. Different sects of Gnostics. Cainites, Secundians, Ptolemaitans, Ophites, Sethians, Marcosians, Colorbasians, Archontiques, Antitactes, Adamites or Prodicians.—2. Question about Easter.—3. Voyage of St. Polycarp to Rome.—4. Foundation of the churches of Lyons, Vienne, Valence, and Besançon.—5. St. Hegesippus.—6. Dialogue between St. Justin and Tryphon.—7. Death of Pope St. Anicetus and the

Emperor Antoninus. § II. PONTIFICATE OF ST. SOTER (A. D. 162-174). 8. Fourth general persecution under the Emperor Marcus Aurelius.—9. Martyrdom of St. Felicitas and her seven sons at Rome.—10. Letter from the Church of Smyrna to the churches of Asia.—11. Martyrdom of St. Polycarp, bishop of Smyrna.—12. Celsus, the philosopher.—13. Controversy between Crescentius the Cynic and St. Justin.—14. Second apology of St. Justin, addressed to the Emperor Marcus Aurelius.—15. Martyrdom of St. Justin and his companions.—16. Miracle of the thundering legion.—17. Illustrious bishops and doctors under the pontificate of St. Soter.—18. St. Dionysius, bishop of Corinth: his letter to the Church of Rome.—19. Heretics. Tatien, chief of the Encratites.—20. Bardesanus.—21. Apelles, disciple of Marcion.—22. Montanus, Priscilla, and Maximilla.—23. Death of Pope St. Soter ....Page 120.

CHAPTER VII.

§ I. PONTIFICATE OF ST. ELEUTHERIUS (A. D. 174-186). 1. The persecution renewed, A. D. 177. Martyrs of Lyons: Sanctus, Maturus, Attalus, and Blandina.—2. Journey of St. Irenæus to Rome.—3. Martyrdom of SS. Epipodius and Alexander at Lyons.—4. Of St. Symphorian at Autun.—5. Apology of Athenagoras. His treatise on the resurrection of the dead.—6. Apologies of St. Melito, bishop of Sardis; of Claudius Apollinaris, bishop of Hierapolis; and of Miltiades.—7. Hermias. St. Theophilus, bishop of Antioch. Heresy of Hermogenes.—8. Conversion of King Lucius of Great Britain to Christianity.—9. Death of Marcus Aurelius. Commodus succeeds him.—10. Apology and martyrdom of the Senator Apollonius.—11. Version of the Holy Scriptures by Theodotion. Work of St. Irenæus against Heresies.—12. Death of St. Eleutherius, A. D. 186 ....Page 143.

CHAPTER VIII.

§ I. PONTIFICATE OF ST. VICTOR I. (A. D. 186-200). 1. Question of Easter.—2. Letter from Polycrates, bishop of Ephesus, to Pope St. Victor I.—3. Letter from St. Irenæus to Pope St. Victor I.—4. Letter from the bishops of Palestine to Pope St. Victor I.—5. Heresy of the Theodotians.—6. The Priest Gaius refutes the Theodotians.—7. Other apologists of the Christian faith.—8. Christian schools.—9. Christian school of Alexandria, of St. Pantænus.—10. Clement of Alexandria, his works.—11. Death of Pope St. Victor I ....Page 159.

CHAPTER IX.

§ I. PONTIFICATE OF ST. ZEPHYRINUS (A. D. 200-217). 1. Fifth general persecution, under Septimus Severus.—2. Scyllitan martyrs at Carthage.—3. Martyrdom of St. Perpetua, St. Felicitas, and their companions, at Carthage.—4. Martyrdom of St. Leonides, father of Origen, at Alexandria (202).—5. Martyrdom of St. Irenæus, bishop of Lyons.—6. Martyrdom of the disciples of Origen at Alexandria (204).—7. Martyrdom of Potamiana, of St. Marcella, her mother, of the soldier Basilides, at Alexandria (204).—8. Tertullian.—9. Conference between Gaius and Proclus, at Rome.—10. Voyage of Origen to Rome. The Octapla, Hexapla, Tetrapla. Bible of Origen.—11. St. Narcissus, bishop of Jerusalem.—12. St. Alexander, coadjutor of St. Narcissus, and bishop of Jerusalem.—13. Minucius Felix, Octavius, and their friend Cecilius.—Caracalla, emperor.—15. Massacres at Alexandria. Flight of Origen to Cæsarea.—16. Condemnation of the heretic Noetus.—17. St. Hippolytus, bishop of Porto. His works.—18. Fall and penitence of Natalis, confessor of the faith. Death of Pope St. Zephyrinus..Page 171.

CHAPTER X.

§ I. PONTIFICATE OF ST. CALLISTUS I. (A. D. 217–222). 1. Heliogabalus, emperor.—2. Interview between Origen and Alexander Severus.—3. Labors of Origen.—4. Journey of Origen into Greece. His ordination.—5. Julius Africanus.—6. Death of St. Callistus I. Decrees of this Pope. § II. PONTIFICATE OF ST. URBAN I. (A. D. 222–231). 7. Alexander Severus emperor.—8. Church of St. Mary beyond the Tiber.—9. Excommunication of Origen.—10. Persecution at Rome.—11. Martyrdom of SS. Valerianus, Tiburtius, and Maximus.—12. Martyrdom of St. Cecilia.—13. Martyrdom of St. Urban I. § III. PONTIFICATE OF ST. PONTIANUS (A. D. 231–235). 14. Exile of Pope St. Pontianus.—15. Death of Demetrius, patriarch of Alexandria.—16. Sixth general persecution by Maximus the Thracian. Martyrdom of St. Pontianus. § IV. PONTIFICATE OF ST. ANTHERUS (December, A. D. 235–January, A. D. 236). 17. Conversion of Ambrose, friend of Origen, and of Protoctites, priest of Cæsarea.—18. Martyrdom of Pope St. Antherus..Page 193.

CHAPTER XI.

§ I. PONTIFICATE OF ST. FABIAN (A. D. 236–250). 1. Election of Pope St. Fabian (A. D. 236–250).—2. St. Gregory of Neocæsarea. Plan of Christian education of Origen.—3. Election of St. Gregory Thaumaturgus to the bishopric of Neocæsarea.—4. His miracles.—5. Election of St. Alexander the collier to the bishopric of Comana.—6. Relaxation in the morals of the faithful.—7. The Emperor Philip checked by the Bishop St. Babylas at the gate of the church at Antioch.—8. Heresy of Beryllus, bishop of Bozra (A. D. 242). Heresy touching the resurrection.—9. Elcesaites.—10. Conversion of St. Cyprian.—11. Treatise on the vanity of idols. The Book of Testimonies of St. Cyprian.—12. Promotion of St. Cyprian to the bishopric of Carthage.—13. Massacre of the Christians at Alexandria.—14. Seventh general persecution, under the Emperor Decius. Death of St. Fabian. Works of his pontificate.....Page 217.

CHAPTER XII.

§ I. VACANCY IN THE SEE OF ROME (January 20, A. D. 250—June 2, 251). 1. Character of the seventh general persecution, under Decius (250).—2. Martyrs of Rome, Jerusalem, Antioch, Alexandria, &c.—3. Martyrs of Asia.—4. Interrogatory of St. Acacius, bishop of Antioch, in Pisidia.—5. Defections at Car thage.—6. *Thurificati, Sacrificati, Libellatici, Lapsi.* Billets of recommendation from the martyrs.—7. Letter of Lucian, confessor of Carthage, to St. Cyprian, on the question of apostasies.—8. Reply of the clergy of Rome to St. Cyprian on the question of apostasies.—9. Schism of Felicissimus and Novatus at Carthage. § II. St. Cornelius Pope (June 2, A. D. 251—September 14, 252). 10. Election of Pope St. Cornelius, June 2, 251.—11. Novatian, first antipope. —12. Death of Decius (251). End of the seventh general persecution. St. Paul, first hermit.—13. Council of Carthage (252). Treatises of St. Cyprian: *De Lapsis, De unitate Ecclesia.*—14. Council of Rome.—15. Second Council of Carthage under St. Cyprian (252). Schism of Fortunatus at Carthage.—16. Confession, exile, and death of St. Cornelius (September 14, 252). § III. St. Lucius I., Pope (October 1., A. D. 252—March 14, 253). 17. Election, pontificate, and death of Pope St. Lucius I.—18. Death of Origen. Doubts of his orthodoxy. § IV. St. Stephen I., Pope (A. D. 253-257). 19. Election of Pope Stephen I.—20. Universal plague (253-260).—21. Charity of the Christians.— 22. Letters and decisions of St. Cyprian on various ecclesiastical affairs of his time.—23. Question of the baptism of heretics.—24. Council of eighty-five bishops at Carthage (September 1, 256).—25. Eighth general persecution, under Valerian. Martyrdom of Pope St. Stephen I. (257). § V. St. Sixtus II., Pope (August 24, A. D. 257—August 6, 258). 26. Election of Pope St. Sixtus II. End of the affair of the rebaptizers.—27. Martyrdom of St. Cyprian, at Carthage. Principal martyrs of the eighth general persecution, in the various provinces of the empire.—28. Martyrdom of St. Cyril, a child of Cæsarea, in Cappadocia.—29. Martyrdom of Pope St. Sixtus II. (August, 258). —30. Martyrdom of St. Lawrence.—31. End of the eighth general persecution...Page 282.

CHAPTER XIII.

§ I. Pontificate of St. Dionysius (July 22, A. D. 259—December 26, 269). 1. Election of St. Dionysius. Charity of the Christians. Progress of Christianity. —2. Decay of the empire under Gallienus.—3. Heresy of Sabellius.—4. Paul of Samosata.—5. Death of St. Dionysius of Alexandria, and of St. Gregory Thaumaturgus.—6. Death of Pope St. Dionysius. § II. Pontificate of St. Felix I. (December 27, A. D. 269—December 22, 274). 7. Election of Pope St. Felix I.—8. Manes.—9. Letter of Manes to Marcellus.—10. Fundamental principles of the error of Manes.—11. Conference between St. Archelaus, Bishop of Carrhes, and Manes. Another conference between the Priest Diodorus and Manes.—12. Ninth general persecution, under Aurelian.—13. Martyrdom of Pope St. Felix I. § III. Pontificate of St. Eutychian (January 4, A. D. 275—December 7, 283). 14. Election of St. Eutychian. End of the ninth general persecution.—15. Dorotheus, priest of Antioch. Achillas, of Alexandria.—16. St. Felix, of Nola.—17. Progress of Manicheism in Egypt and Syria.—18. Death of St. Eutychian. § IV. Pontificate of St. Caius (December 10, A. D. 283—April 22, 296). 19. Election of St. Caius.—20. Martyrdom of St. Sebastian.—21. Martyrdom of the Theban legion.—22. Martyrdom of St. Victor, of Marseilles.—23. Cruelties of Riccius Varus.—24.

Sect of the Hieracithæ in Egypt.—25. Conversion of Arnobius. His seven books against the Gentiles.—26. Election of Constantius Chlorus and Galerius to the empire.—27. Instructions of St. Thomas, bishop of Alexandria, to the Christian officers of the court of Dioclesian.—28. Death of Pope St. Caius.
Page 268.

CHAPTER XIV.

§ I. St. Marcellinus, Pope (June 30, A. D. 296—October 24, 304). 1. Election of Pope Marcellinus.—2. Galerius begins the persecution.—3. Schism of the Meletians. Council of Elvira.—4. Tenth general persecution, under Dioclesian (A. D. 303).—5. General sketch of the tenth general persecution.—6. Martyrs in the house of the emperor. The Sophists. Hierocles.—7. Martyrs in the East.—8. Martyrs in the West.—9. Martyrdom of Pope St. Marcellinus (October 24, A. D. 304). § II. Vacancy of the See of Rome (October 24, A. D. 304—May 19, 308). 10. Continuation and end of the persecution of Dioclesian in the West.—11. Martyrdom of St. Genesius.—12. Abdication of Dioclesian.—13. Maximin Daia.—14. Continuation of the persecution in the East.—15. Conventicle of traditor bishops at Cirtha. Canons of St. Peter, patriarch of Alexandria. § III. St. Marcellus, Pope (May 19, A. D. 308—January 16, 310). 16. Election of Pope St. Marcellus.—17. Constantine proclaimed emperor by the legions of Great Britain.—18. St. Methodius, bishop of Tyre.—19. St. Anthony.—20. Death of St. Marcellus, pope. § IV. St. Eusebius Pope (April 2, A. D. 310—September 20, 310). 21. Election, exile, and death of Pope St. Eusebius. § V. Vacancy of the See of Rome (September 25, A. D. 310—July 2, 311). 22. Last crimes and punishment of Maximian-Hercules.—23. Edict of Galerius favorable to Christians. Death of Galerius.—24. Deliverance of the Christian prisoners in the East. § VI. St. Melchiades, Pope (July 2, A. D. 311—January 10, 314). 25. Election of Pope St. Melchiades.—26. Schism of the Donatists at Carthage.—27. Maximin Daia attempts, in spite of the edicts of Galerius, to renew the persecution.—28. War between Maxentius and Constantine. Labarum. Victory of Constantine.—29. Edict of Constantine proclaiming the Christian religion the religion of the empire.—30. Council held at Rome, at the Lateran Palace, against the Donatists.—31. Death of St. Melchiades.—32. End of the first epoch of ecclesiastical history. . . . . Page 292.

CHAPTER XV.

§ I. Review of the First Period of the Church (A. D. 1-312). 1. Rapid extension of Christianity in Italy.—2. Throughout the West.—3. In the East.—4. Obstacles to the development of Christianity.—5. Causes favorable to this development.—6. Pagan writers and philosophers hostile to Christianity: Lucian, Celsus, Porphyry, Jamblicus, Philostratus's Life of Apollonius of Thyanea, Hierocles.—7. First apologists.—8. Heresies. Schisms.—9. Government, discipline, and worship.—10. Conclusion . . . . Page 323.

SECOND PERIOD.

CHAPTER I.

§ I. PONTIFICATE OF ST. SYLVESTER I. (January 31, A. D. 314—December 31, 335). 1. Second period of ecclesiastical history.—2. Election of Pope St. Sylvester.—3. Lactantius. His works.—4. Eusebius of Cæsarea. His works.—5. Solitaries. St. Anthony, St. Ammon, St. Pacomius, St. Hilarion, Fathers of the Desert.—6. Council of Arles against the Donatists.—7. Councils of Ancyra, in Galatia; of Neocæsarea, in Pontus; and of Gangres, in Bithynia.—8. Christian legislation of Constantine.—9. Cruelties of Constantine.—10. Reaction against Christianity. Persecution of Licinius. Martyrs.—11. War between Constantine and Licinius. Defeat and death of Licinius.—12. Antecedents of Arius.—13. Heresy of Arius.—14. Council of Alexandria against Arius.—15. St. Athanasius, deacon of Alexandria.—16. League of Arius and Eusebius of Nicomedia. Composition of the Thalia.—17. Letters of the Patriarch St. Alexander against Arianism.—18. Intervention of Constantine in the affairs of Arianism.—19. First œcumenical council at Nice, in Bithynia (A. D. 325).—20. Opening of the council.—21. Public sitting of the Council of Nice.—22. Profession of faith known as the Nicene Creed.—23. Quartodecimans. Question of Easter judged by the Council of Nice.—24. Affair of the Meletians treated by this council.—25. Canons of discipline of the Council of Nice, or *Apostolic Canons*.—26. Hierarchic authority of the patriarchs regulated by the Council of Nice.—27. Election and ordination of bishops and priests.—28. Celibacy of the clergy.—29. Rules for the reconciliation of heretics, schismatics, and *lapsi*.—30. Ecclesiastical discipline relative to marriage regulated by the apostolic canons.—31. Close of the Council of Nice.—32. Deposition of Eusebius of Nicomedia, and Theogni of Nice, by the Council of Alexandria.—33. Foundation of churches and pious donations of Constantine.—34. Discovery of the true cross by St. Helena, mother of Constantine.—35. Progress of the faith beyond the limits of the Roman Empire.—36. Foundation of Constantinople.—37. St. Athanasius, patriarch of Alexandria. Intrigues of the Eusebians against Eustathius, patriarch of Antioch.—38. Arius is prevented by the resistance of St. Athanasius from entering Alexandria. St. Anthony at Alexandria.—39. Arian Council of Tyre against St. Athanasius.—40. Exile of St. Athanasius to Treves by the Emperor Constantine.—41. Dedication of the church of Jerusalem (September 13, A. D. 335).—42. Death of Pope St. Sylvester (December 31, A. D. 335)..Page 353

CONTENTS.

CHAPTER II.

§ I. PONTIFICATE OF ST. MARK (January 18, A. D. 336—October 7, 336). 1. Election of St. Mark to the Sovereign Pontificate.—2. Arian Council of Constantinople. Deposition of Marcellus, bishop of Ancyra. Restoration of Arius. His tragic death.—3. Death of Pope St. Mark (October 7, A. D. 336). § II. PONTIFICATE OF POPE ST. JULIUS I. (February 6, A. D. 337—April 12, 352). 4. Election of Pope Julius I.—5. Letter of St. Anthony to the Emperor Constantine. Exile of St. Paul, patriarch of Constantinople. Death of Constantine the Great.—6. Recall of St. Athanasius to Alexandria, and of St. Paul to Constantinople. Second exile of Paul. Eusebius of Nicomedia takes possession of the Patriarchal See of Constantinople.—7. First Arian Council of Antioch. —8. St. Athanasius is a second time driven from Alexandria. Gregory of Cappadocia takes possession of his See. Council of Rome, convoked by Pope St. Julius I.—9. Recall of the Patriarch St. Paul to Constantinople. His third exile.—10. Second Arian Council of Antioch.—11. Catholic councils of Milan and Sardica.—12. Return of St. Athanasius to Alexandria after his second exile. Return of St. Paul, patriarch of Constantinople.—13. Death of St. Paul, the first hermit.—14. Circumcellians. Council of Carthage in regard to them.—15. Persecution of the Christians by Sapor II., King of Persia.—16. Raising of the first siege of Nisibis by Sapor II. Continuation of the persecution in Persia.—17. Raising of the second siege of Nisibis by Sapor II. St. Ephrem, disciple of St. James of Nisibis.—18. Murder of Constans, Emperor of the West. Triple usurpation of the empire.—19. Council of Sirmium. Fourth and last exile of St. Paul, patriarch of Constantinople. His martyrdom.—20. Apparition of a miraculous cross at Jerusalem.—21. Death of Pope St. Julius I .... Page 413.

CHAPTER III.

§ 1. PONTIFICATE OF LIBERIUS (May 22, A. D. 352—September 24, 366). 1. Election of Pope Liberius.—2. The Arians bring new charges against St. Athanasius. Fall of Vincent of Capua.—3. Pope Liberius disavows the conduct of Vincent of Capua, his legate.—4. Council of Milan (A. D. 355).—5. St. Athanasius banished by Constantius (A. D. 355).—6. Letter of Pope Liberius to the exiled prelates.—7. Banishment of Pope Liberius to Berea, in Thrace.—8. Fall of Osius of Cordova. Second Arian Council of Sirmium.—9. The controverted fall of Liberius. State of the question—10. Semi-Arians. Anomœans. Ætians. Eunomians. Eupsychians.—11. Arian Councils of Cæsarea, Antioch, Ancyra, and third of Sirmium.—12. Council of Rimini (A. D. 359).—13. Council of Seleucia (A. D. 359).—14. Council of Constantinople (A. D. 360). First Council of Paris.—15. Council of Antioch (A. D. 361).—16. Death of the Emperor Constantius.—17. First studies and intimacy of St. Gregory Nazianzen and St. Basil of Cæsarea.—18. St. Cyril of Jerusalem. His catechetical instructions.—19. St. Nerses, patriarch of Armenia.—20. Doctors of the West. St. Hilary of Poitiers. St. Martin of Tours. St. Eusebius of Vercelli. St. Paulinus of Treves. Lucifer of Cagliari. Birth of St. Ambrose. Jerome and Augustine.—21. Julian the Apostate, emperor.—22. Nature and causes of the persecution of Julian the Apostate.—23. Edict to recall the banished, and to deprive the clergy of their immunities, and the churches of their possessions.—24. Return of St. Athanasius to Alexandria (A. D. 362).—25. Council of Alexandria.—26. Edict of Julian the Apostate, forbidding the study of Belles-Lettres to the Christians.—27. Julian's attempt to rebuild the Temple of Jerusalem. Death of Julian.—28. Macedonius. His heresy.—29. Death of Pope Liberius..Page 446.

CHAPTER IV.

§ I. PONTIFICATE OF ST. DAMASUS (September 24, A. D. 366—December 11, 384). 1. Ursinus Antipope.—2. Arianism in the East, under the Emperor Valens.—3. Basil of Cæsarea and the Prefect Modestus. Death of St. Athanasius at Alexandria.—4. St. Martin, bishop of Tours. Election of St. Ambrose to the Episcopacy.—5. St. Optatus, bishop of Milevum. St. Jerome.—6. Gratian calls Theodosius the Great to the Government of the East. Death of St. Basil the Great.—7. St. Gregory Nazianzen is appointed to the See of Constantinople. Schism of Maximus at Constantinople.—8. Council of Constantinople. Death of St. Meletius. Troubles arising from it. Retirement of St. Gregory Nazianzen. Rights of the various Patriarchates.—9. Priscillian. His heresy condemned in the Council of Saragossa. Death of St. Damasus. § II. PONTIFICATE OF ST. SIRICIUS (January 1, A. D. 385—November 25, 398). 10. Decretal of St. Siricius to Himerius, bishop of Tarragona.—11. St. Ambrose persecuted at Milan, by the Empress Justina. Mission of St. Ambrose to the Usurper Maximus.—12. Revolt of Antioch. St. Flavian. St. John Chrysostom. Clemency of Theodosius.—13. Massacre at Thessalonica. Penance of Theodosius. Massalians. Death of Theodosius the Great. Death of St. Ambrose.—14. Conversion of St. Augustine.—15. St. Jerome retires to Bethlehem. St. Martin of Tours. St. Paulinus of Nola. St. Delphin and St. Amandus of Bordeaux. St. Victrix at Rouen. St. Sulpitius Severus.—16. St. John Chrysostom elected to the See of Constantinople. Synesius. Death of St. Siricius. § III. PONTIFICATE OF ST. ANASTASIUS I. (November 26, A. D. 398—April 27, 402). 17. Dismissory Letters. First Council of Toledo.—18. Disgrace of Eutropius. Discussion between St. Jerome and the Priest Rufinus.—19. Death of St. Martin, bishop of Tours. Death of St. Anastasius I.
Page 502.

CHAPTER V.

§ I. PONTIFICATE OF ST. INNOCENT I. (April, A. D. 402—March, 417). 1. Letters of St. Innocent I. to various bishops of France, Spain, and Africa.—2. First exile of St. John Chrysostom.—3. Second exile and death of St. John Chrysostom.—4. Invasion of Rome by Alaric.—5. *City of God*, by St. Augustine. Pelagianism.—6. Death of St. Innocent I. § II. PONTIFICATE OF ST. ZOSIMUS (August, A. D. 417—December, 418). 7. Labors and death of St. Zosimus. § III. PONTIFICATE OF ST. BONIFACE I. (December 30, A. D. 418—October 25, 422). 8. Election of St. Boniface I. Antipope Eulalius. Question of the right of appeal to the Holy See agitated by the Bishops of Africa.—9. Pretensions of Atticus, Bishop of Constantinople, to jurisdiction over all the Asiatic churches.—10. Death of St. Jerome and of St. Boniface I. § IV. PONTIFICATE OF ST. CELESTIN I. (November 3, A. D. 422—April 6, 432). 11. Semi-Pelagianism.—12. Cassian. St. Simeon Stylites. Invasion of Africa by Genseric. Death of St. Augustine.—13. The Franks in Gaul. St. Lupus, of Troyes; St. Eucherius, of Lyons; St. Germanus, of Auxerre, &c.—14. Nestorius. Third general council at Ephesus. Death of St. Celestin I. § V. PONTIFICATE OF ST. SIXTUS III. (April 26, A. D. 432—March 28, 439). 15. Election of St. Sixtus III.—16. Prudentius. Sedulius. Predestinarianism. St. Prosper.—17. Theodosian Code. Barbarian invasion of the different provinces of the Empire. Death of St. Sixtus III................................Page 545.

CHAPTER VI.

§ I. PONTIFICATE OF ST. LEO I., THE GREAT (September 1, A. D. 439—April 11, 461). 1. Works of St. Leo the Great against different Heresies.—2. Eutyches. *Latrocinale of Ephesus.*—3. Marcian, Emperor of the East.—4. Council of Chalcedon, the Fourth of the General Councils.—5. Attila. He invades Gaul and Italy. Retires before the Majesty of St. Leo the Great.—6. New troubles raised in the East by Eutychianism.—7. Invasion of Rome by Genseric.—8. Timothy Ælurus at Alexandria. Death of St. Leo the Great. § II. PONTIFICATE OF ST. HILARY (November 12, A. D. 461—September 10, 467). 9. Election of St. Hilary.—10. Efforts of St. Hilary to uphold the Laws of the Ecclesiastical Hierarchy.—11. Councils of Arles, of Tours, and of Vaunes, in Gaul.—12. Earthquake at Antioch. Burning of Constantinople. Death of St. Simeon Stylites. § III. PONTIFICATE OF ST. SIMPLICIUS (September 27, A. D. 467, to the fall of the Western Empire, August 23, A. D. 476). 13. Election of St. Simplicius.—14. St. Epiphanius of Pavia. St. Patiens of Lyons. St. Sidonius Apollinaris.—15. Odoacer, King of the Heruli, overthrows the Western Empire...Page 581.

CHAPTER VII.

§ REVIEW OF THE SECOND PERIOD OF THE HISTORY OF THE CHURCH (A. D. 312—476). 1. Advance of the Gospel in the East.—2. Advance of the Church in the West.—3. Pagan Polemics. Apologists of the Second Period.—4. Heresies, Doctors, and Councils.—5. Growth of Monastic Institutions.—6. Government, Discipline, and Worship......................................Page 615.

NOTES...Page 622.

DIVISIONS

OF THE

GENERAL HISTORY OF THE CHURCH.

The History of the Church is divided into eight periods.

The first includes from the birth of Jesus Christ to the conversion of Constantine the Great, A. D. 1 to A. D. 312.

The second includes from the conversion of Constantine to the fall of the Western Empire, A. D. 312 to A. D. 476.

(The history of these two periods forms the first volume.)

The third includes from the fall of the Western Empire to its re-establishment under Charlemagne, A. D. 477 to A. D. 800.

The fourth includes from Charlemagne to Pope Sylvester II., A. D. 800 to A. D. 999.

(The history of these two periods forms the second volume.)

The fifth includes from Pope Sylvester II. to Pope Boniface VIII., A. D. 999 to A. D. 1303.

The sixth includes from Pope Boniface VIII. to Luther, A. D. 1303 to A. D. 1517.

(The history of these two periods forms the third volume.)

The seventh includes from Luther to the treaty of Westphalia, A. D. 1517 to A. D. 1648.

The eighth includes from the treaty of Westphalia to the accession of Pope Pius IX. to the sovereign pontificate, A. D. 1648 to A. D. 1846.

(The history of these two periods forms the fourth and last volume.)

A REMARK

UPON THE

CHRONOLOGY OF THE CHURCH.

The chronology adopted in this work is that of the "Abrégé Chronologique de l'Histoire Ecclésiastique," 3 volumes, 12mo, published in 1757, on the model of the great work on the history of France by the President Hainault. It is no part of our plan to enter into the discussions that have arisen on the numerous difficulties of chronology. We have adopted a system already completed, not that it may, perhaps, be the most exact in all its details, but because it is the one most generally followed. We leave to the learned professors of that branch of science the care of pointing out, if they judge it best, the chronological systems which present divergences more or less important from the system we follow.

GENERAL HISTORY OF THE CHURCH.

CHAPTER I.

1. Connection of Christianity with the past.—2. The fulness of time. Religious and moral state of the world at the Advent of our Lord Jesus Christ.—3. His life during thirty years.—4. Public life of our Lord.—5. Teaching of the Saviour. Institution of the Sacraments.—6. Foundation of the Church.—7. Passion and death of our Lord Jesus Christ on the cross.—8. His Ascension.

1. THE establishment of Christianity, which divides the history of the world into two distinct periods, was not an isolated fact, unconnected with past ages;—the forty preceding centuries served as a vast avenue leading towards it. "The fall of the earthly Adam," says St. Augustine, "called forth the heavenly Adam, the Redeemer of the first." The promise of a Saviour, made in the garden of Eden, was borne with them in their exile by our first parents, and the remembrance of it was perpetuated in the hearts of succeeding generations. God renewed it to the patriarchs; Abraham, Isaac, and Jacob transmitted it, with the privilege of seeing the expected Messiah born of their race. By means of a phenomenon unique in history, a people was chosen whose sole mission was to guard the deposit of tradition, the Testament of the covenant made between God and man; and this people, confined within the narrow limits of Judea, obscure, destitute of national renown or military glory, alone survives amid all the vicissitudes of empires. Egyptians,

Assyrians, Medes and Persians, Greeks and Romans, succeed each other, then fall and vanish. Sesostris, Nabuchodonosor, Cyrus, Alexander, Cæsar, made the world resound with the noise of their victories. The Jewish people, sometimes protected, sometimes enslaved by all these conquerors, resisted their oppression or submitted to their yoke without any radical change in their own constitution, or mingling their blood with that of the stranger races; and did not disappear like other conquered nations. Errors the most heterogeneous, modes of worship without end, creeds the most absurd and the most opposite, successively swayed the earth under the banners of the great conquerors of the world. Their religions shared the fate of their empires—Anubis is dethroned by Mithra, who is the Zeus of the Greeks, the Jupiter of the Romans. The Jewish people, alone, offer no example of variation in their faith. They carry with them everywhere a book dictated to Moses many ages earlier than the epoch assigned by the Greeks to the invention of writing. This book contains a legislation, a ceremonial, and religious, civil, and military codes. Their laws, rites, creeds, subsisted in the same forms, from the epoch of Sinai to that of Cæsar. One hope, one image, one aspiration pervades their history : it is the hope of the Redeemer; the image of the Messiah, represented by the patriarchs and the just of the Old Testament; the aspiration for the promised Christ, son of David and of Abraham, the Pontiff King, whose reign shall have no end. Under whatever point of view we judge this great fact, of a people the most obscure, the least powerful of all, who maintain, in the midst of the overthrow of other nations, their own perpetual duration, we are obliged to recognize in it a miraculous history, without precedent and without imitation. Poets, such as Homer or Hesiod; men of genius, such as Socrates, Plato, Aristotle, charmed the rest of mankind by their theogonies or philosophic systems. The Jewish people paid no homage to their schools, whose renown extended throughout the earth. They had no part in the altars raised, or sacrifices of

victims made, to any idol, for the Jew disdained the wisdom
of the sages of Greece. His sacrifices are for Jehovah; his
masters, his doctors, are the prophets, from Moses to Malachias,
through David, Elias, Eliseus, Isaias, Jeremias, Ezechiel,
Daniel, and others; who all portray, in some form, the expected Messiah, and add new traits to His anticipated history, or reveal with greater clearness the date of His advent. The all-absorbing expectation of this people is the
coming of a Saviour, whom they are charged to announce to
mankind. It is wonderful to observe how this necessity of a
Saviour dominates, in spite of them, the pagan religions of
antiquity. Among them all, in fact, we find human sacrifices,
as if mankind had felt that they must be redeemed, but that
they were themselves insufficient for their ransom. Where
human blood did not flow, that of bulls and heifers inundated
the temples. A perpetual libation of blood was established,
which had its source in a confused idea of expiation, or of
religious redemption. Ancient civilization was established
upon two principles, which were derived from the same idea,
viz.: the inferiority of woman, and the common right to hold
slaves. To explain the debased condition of the first is
impossible, without recurring to the fall of man, as it is
related by Moses. Slavery, subsisting without question during
forty centuries, implies the principle of universal consent,
which flowed from the idea of religious expiation. The Jewish people alone possessed the key to these enigmas, which
troubled the entire existence of pagan nations. They alone
had the secret of those vague hopes, of those aspirations for
an unknown liberator, for the new golden age, sung by Virgil,
and mysteriously agitating the East and the West.

2. Christ was to come, said St. Paul, in the fulness of time—
Ubi venit plenitudo temporis. The epoch of Augustus seemed to
realize the fulness of time of the ancient civilization. The
Roman empire, at its summit of power, had for its limits—on
the north, the Rhine and the Danube; on the east, the Euphrates; on the south, Upper Egypt, the deserts of Africa, and

Mount Atlas; on the west, the seas of Spain and Gaul—nearly three-fourths of the habitable globe. The power of Alexander had, in some measure, approached this immense extent; but the Macedonian conqueror, from his dying-bed at Babylon, might have caught a glimpse of the dismemberment of his empire. Nationalities, for a moment merged under his victorious hand, were reconstituted as soon as his sword was broken The Romans, on the contrary, had not so suddenly reached universal domination; but, when they had attained this object, the entire world was modelled under their yoke; their pioneers opened roads, which began at the eternal city, to end at the extremities of the earth; their language was adopted, as a mark of servitude, by the conquered nations; and the world, for ages, was Roman. Under the influence of a political condition at once so brilliant and durable, the intellectual powers had acquired the perfection of the age of Pericles, and its

alone regenerate the world. It was for this peaceful Conqueror that the Roman slaves opened vast highways among the nations; it was to hear the glad tidings of His Gospel that all people forgot their foreign idioms and spoke the language of Rome, which was destined to become, at a later period, the language of the Church.

3. Under the twelfth consulate of Augustus, in the 750th year of the founding of Rome, the angel Gabriel was sent to Nazareth, a little city of Judea, to a virgin whose name was Mary, of the tribe of Judah, and of the line of David. He announced to her that by the operation of the Holy Spirit, and apart from the ordinary laws of nature, she would give birth to the Son of David—to the Christ—to the Son of God—to the Messiah, whose reign would be without end. Nine months later, an edict of Cæsar Augustus was published, commanding a census to be made of the inhabitants throughout the world; and Mary went, with Joseph her spouse, a saintly old man, to be registered at Bethlehem, the city of David. "And it came to pass, that, when they were there, her days were accomplished that she should be delivered. And she brought forth her first-born son, and wrapped him up in swaddling-clothes, and laid him in a manger: because there was no room for them in the inn." The first who came to adore Jesus Christ, the Sovereign of the world, whose birth was so strange, were shepherds. The Magi from the East, warned by a miraculous star, came in their turn, and laid at the feet of the infant the tributes proper to be offered to a king, to man, and to God—gold, myrrh, and incense. The legal ceremonies were performed around His crib. Jesus Christ submitted to the expiatory rite of circumcision. Mary, virgin before, during, and after the birth, accomplished the rites of her purification in the manner of other Jewish women. God, the Redeemer, presented in the temple which He was to replace by the temple of His everlasting Church, was redeemed from the hands of the High-Priest at the price of two doves. Meanwhile, the Son of God could not descend upon earth without bringing disquietude to the

powers of the world. Herod, king of Judea, tributary to Rome, considered his throne endangered by the advent of the King of Heaven. He ordered a general massacre of the children of Bethlehem and its environs, "from two years old and under." Mary and Joseph had conveyed the infant to Egypt, from whence God recalled Him, after the death of Herod. The Gospel is silent upon the earliest years of Jesus. At the age of twelve He appeared at Jerusalem, in the temple, in the midst of the doctors, who were astonished at His wisdom. He then returned into obscurity, "growing in age, in grace, and in wisdom," and, according to tradition, aiding His adopted father in his trade of carpenter.

In the fifteenth year of the reign of Tiberius, the banks of the Jordan witnessed the appearance from the desert of a man clothed in camel's hair, who neither ate nor drank with other men, whose life was austere and mortified, who preached penance, and who called himself the voice of the Lord, to announce the coming of the Lamb of God. It was John, son of Elizabeth and Zachary, whose birth had been foretold by an angel, and who had leaped in his mother's womb on the visit of the Virgin Mary. The people, in multitudes, followed John, asking of him the baptism of penance. But he showed them that his ministry was of a transitory character, and sent the Jews "to Him, the latchets of whose shoes he was not worthy to loose." And he practised what he avowed, with a sublime humility. Jesus came to demand of His precursor baptism in the waters of the Jordan. A voice was heard from heaven, saying, "This is my beloved Son, in whom I am well pleased." The Holy Spirit descending upon Him in the form of a dove, completed the manifestation of the Trinity, by the voice of the Father, the corporeal presence of the Son of God made man, and the mysterious figure of the Dove, symbol of the Holy Spirit. Henceforth, said John, of Jesus, "He must increase, but I must decrease." The precursor made himself as nothing before his Master. He won the glory of martyrdom, and died a victim to the revenge of an immodest woman, for having reproached the tetrarch Herod, because of his impure life.

4. Here begins the public life of Jesus Christ, and His mission in the world, which, to a certain extent, the baptism of John had inaugurated. Like Moses on Mount Sinai, Jesus withdrew during forty days into the desert, and there maintained a victorious combat with the prince of darkness, that, being in all things like His brethren, the apostle could say, "He had passed through all our temptations." To establish distinctly the difference between His spiritual royalty and the sovereignty of this world, Jesus Christ in the first place manifested His power by miracles: the wedding of Cana, which He honored by His presence, as if to sanctify humanity in marriage, which is its source, beheld the change of water into wine. From this moment, His steps were marked by prodigies. All infirmities, all disorders, every class of suffering, yielded to His word. The daughter of Jairus was restored to life at the voice of God, who is the author of life; sight was restored to the blind; the possessed were delivered from the power of the demon. A paralytic of thirty years was publicly cured on the Sabbath day. Jesus healed also a leper, the servant of a centurion. On a highway He met the widow of Naim, who followed the funeral of her son. He approached the bier, recalled the dead to life, and restored him to his mother. The elements obeyed Him; the winds and tempests became still on His command. He walks on the water, and enables Peter also to walk upon it at His side, a living image of the Catholic Church, of which St. Peter was to be the first pontiff, and which the waves were never to submerge. A simple touching of the clothes of the Saviour cured a woman of an issue of blood. A secret and divine virtue went forth from Him and wrought wonders. The faith of the Canaanite was recompensed by the cure of her daughter. The deaf and dumb, by His power, were restored to hearing and speech. The multitudes who followed Him into the desert having forgotten to provide food for the

journey, Jesus Christ multiplied seven loaves and five fishes, until they were sufficient to satiate more than five thousand persons. In the presence of Peter, James, and John, His disciples, He was transfigured, and appeared in all His glory on Mount Tabor. Descending again among the Jews, He went about doing good, and working miracles. A man born blind opens his eyes to the light; a woman who had been ill eighteen years, recovers her health by His word; one sick of dropsy is cured in the same manner. Finally, He closes this series of marvellous works, which were public and well attested, which, in fact, during three years, all Judea had witnessed, by the resurrection of Lazarus, after he had lain three days enclosed in his tomb, and his body had already become a prey to the corruption of death.

5. We have begun by enumerating, in a summary way, the principal miracles of Jesus Christ, because, in the eyes of the multitude, they were the most substantial proofs of His divinity. His doctrine was not less marvellous, and it was to produce in the religious and moral world the same transformation which the power of the Son of God wrought upon the material world. His mode of teaching resembled in nothing the methods of the philosophers and sages. He made no showy display of words, no oratorical pretensions. He was simple and familiar in His discourse, presenting His sublime ideas under the forms of parables or images. It was on the heart He wished to engrave His law of charity, and it was to the heart that He addressed himself. Especially He sought to teach the *unity of God*, the Father of all men. He established this fundamental principle, not by arguments nor disputations, but with the simple, natural, candid tone of a son who speaks of his father. The idea which predominated in the ancient world was that of a God angry and terrible, whom none could look upon and live, and who must be appeased by the blood of victims and of hecatombs. In the doctrine of the Saviour, God appeared only as the father of the prodigal son; as the fountain of living waters for the thirsty soul, such as he was to the Samaritan

at Jacob's well; or like the good shepherd who bears on his shoulders the wandering sheep which he leads back to the fold: finally, as the God of mercy and forgiveness. This is the true and attractive characteristic of the New Testament, which, for this reason, is called the law of mercy. The grace of God thus descending upon earth, Jesus Christ established the channels through which it was to be communicated to men. These are the sacraments, the visible signs of the mysterious and invisible operation of grace upon the soul, viz.: Baptism, Confirmation, the Eucharist, Penance, Extreme Unction, Holy Orders, and Matrimony.

It must be distinctly remembered that nothing in the past bore any resemblance to such institutions, or doctrines, or works, as these. "How the teachings of Jesus Christ stand out in bold relief, detached by their divine character from all the errors which surround them, in the midst of hypocritical doctors, of captious scribes, of proud Pharisees! How the Man-God detects their cunning by His own wisdom! How He, anathematizes all the vices by His sanctity! How He exhausts all the passions by His patience! By His meekness, He imparts strength to every weakness! And how ready is He to help in every affliction."*

6. To perpetuate the benefits of the redemption which He brought to mankind, and to insure to them the purity of His doctrine and the integrity of the sacraments which He instituted, it was incumbent on Jesus Christ to found, and, in fact, He did found, a visible society, always teaching, always one, which He made the depository of His doctrines. This is the Catholic Church, whose history we now study, and whose divine institution, such as it was given by the Saviour, we now proceed to examine in detail. Two objects are here worthy of especial attention: (1.) the instruments chosen; (2.) the form given.

(1.) "Jesus, walking along the shore of the sea of Galilee,

---

* AUGUSTE NICOLAS, Études sur le Christian. t. iv. p. 15

and seeing the fishermen, said to them, Come with me, and I will make you fishers of men." These fishermen, whose whole fortune was in their nets, who had no knowledge but that of their trade, were the chosen instruments, the first founders of the Church; that institution which was destined to bear throughout the earth the light of truth—to confound the wisdom of the philosophers, to seat itself in the Capitol, and to reign, without limits and without end, over the world. The names of these elect of God to conduct this grand enterprise were utterly unknown to the world of philosophers and the powerful of their time: Simon, who was called Peter, John and James, sons of Zebedee, Andrew, Peter's brother, Philip, Thomas, Bartholomew, Matthew, James, son of Alpheus, Simon of Cana, Jude, brother of James, and Judas Iscariot, who betrayed his master. The weakness, the obscurity, the ignorance of these twelve Jews were well calculated to throw into strong relief the divinity of the doctrines which they were commanded to teach to mankind. Jesus Christ purposely selected the weak things of the earth to confound the strong. He instructed them, as a characteristic of the success of their mission to remain *weak*, humanly speaking, and not to rely upon any earthly help, or artifice, or defence. "Do not possess gold nor silver, nor money in your purses. . . . . And when they will not receive you nor hear your words, going forth out of that house or city, shake off the dust from your feet. . . . . Behold I send you as lambs in the midst of wolves."

It is evident that Jesus Christ designed to reject, in the composition of His Church, all that a man of the commonest prudence would have sought for, and to incorporate with it all that the same man would infallibly have rejected. It is this which St. Paul terms the folly of the cross, and which the most unexampled, the most brilliant, and the most enduring successes have never ceased to proclaim, everywhere, to be the wisdom of God.

(2.) The apostles of His Church being thus selected,

Jesus Christ organized them in unity, and with authority—two correlative principles, without which no institution can subsist. The twelve apostles were as yet like separate blocks awaiting the foundation-stone, in order to form with it, and by means of it, one edifice. Simon was chosen for a special calling; henceforth he was to be called Peter; *et imposuit Simoni nomen Petrus*, a prophetic name, for he was to become the rock on which the Church should be built. His mission was explained to him a few days after, in a more explicit manner. "I say unto thee, that thou art Peter, and on this rock I will build my Church, and the gates of hell shall not prevail against it, and I will give thee the keys of the kingdom of heaven. Whatsoever thou shalt bind on earth, shall be bound in heaven, and whatsoever thou shalt loose on earth, shall be loosed in heaven." Here, then, is already a supremacy constituted in the hierarchy of the Church; a chief placed above the other chiefs; a foundation-stone selected among the other stones of the edifice. The authority of this sovereign chief is more distinctly proclaimed by these words: "Feed my sheep; feed my lambs." To complete our citations on this subject, let us add a passage which is too often neglected, yet which, from its connection with others, places in still greater prominence the prerogatives and functions of the *Prince* of the apostles. "Simon, Simon, Satan hath desired to sift you as wheat, but I have prayed for thee, that thy faith fail not, and when thou shalt be converted, confirm thy brethren." Certainly Jesus Christ could not more plainly manifest His will to establish His Church on the unity of Peter, and to constitute it under the authority of this supreme pastor, who is to feed the sheep and the lambs,—that is to say, following the interpretation of the Fathers and doctors, the bishops and the faithful,—who holds in his hands the keys of the kingdom of heaven, and who is charged to strengthen his brethren in the faith. Peter and his successors were then invested with the authority, the primacy of the apostleship. They are the centre of the Church, and from them must radiate her history, based on the unity of one headship and one faith, with the assurance of that divine saying, "I have prayed that thy faith fail not." This promise of infallibility is afterwards renewed by another solemn declaration: "Behold I am with you all days even to the end of the world." And to seal the unity of this divinely constituted hierarchy, Jesus Christ thus addresses his Father: "Holy Father, keep them in Thy name whom Thou hast given me, that they may be *one* as we are. . . . . And not for them only do I pray, but for them also, who through their word shall believe in me" (Christians in every place and in all time, at that moment present to the thought of the Saviour), "that they may all be one, as Thou, Father, in me and I in Thee, that they may also be one in us." Thus this nascent Church, destined ever to increase more and more, will remain united to Jesus, its founder, by the uninterrupted tradition of Peter and his successors; and whoever would seek for salvation, must adhere to this unity, to this authority of Peter and his successors: for Jesus Christ has promised to be with them even to the consummation of ages.

7. The public mission of the Saviour, the preaching of His doctrine supported by miracles, the institution of the Church, and of the sacraments which she was to dispense, occupied only three years. The Jewish people had been witnesses of this extraordinary life, they had seen the miracles which Jesus had strewed about His path, yet in this Messiah, true son of David, whose every trait had been so clearly defined by the prophets, they failed to recognize "*the Desired of all nations, the Expectation of the world, the Desire of the everlasting hills.*" But this blindness had been predicted, and is the more easily understood, because Christ, in the ideas of a gross and carnal people, was to be a conqueror, a hero, surrounded with glory and magnificence. Jesus Christ, on the contrary, declared that His kingdom was not of this world; He preached a doctrine totally opposed to the maxims of the world; He taught men to detach themselves from earthly inclinations, desires, and hopes, and

to conquer, by mortification and sacrifices, the kingdom of heaven, which suffers violence. The Pharisees, whom He compared to whitened sepulchres, and whose hypocrisy He unmasked; the great, whom He alarmed by accepting the title of king, the spiritual and pacific king of souls; the doctors of the law, the priests, and scribes, whom He accused of "imposing on their brethren burdens which they would not touch with the point of their finger," united their common hatred, and resolved upon the death of one whom they regarded as only a man. Jesus Christ was acquainted with their conspiracy; without fearing, but without provoking them, He came to Jerusalem. It was a short time after the resurrection of Lazarus; the people gave Him a triumphal entry, waving palm branches around Him, and spreading their vestments for the passage of the humble animal which bore the new king of Sion; one only cry escaped from every lip: "Hosanna! Glory to the Son of David!" Five days later, these acclamations of triumph were changed into tumultuous vociferations: "Crucify Him! Crucify Him! Let His blood be upon us and our children!" What had occurred during this interval? Nothing that can explain such a change. But the hour was come when the Son of Man was to be delivered into the hands of His enemies. Jesus Christ had celebrated the Passover with His disciples, and had instituted at the last supper the Holy Eucharist, the permanent miracle of the love of a God who dwells in the midst of men, to become their food and drink. The same night, Judas Iscariot, his lips still tinged with the Eucharistic blood, had sold his Master to the chief priests for thirty pieces of silver, and betrayed the Son of Man by a kiss. The crime was no sooner committed than despair entered the traitor's soul: he hastened to cast the money into the midst of the temple, and hung himself. The Pharisees, the council of the priests, and the people who had plotted the death of Jesus, followed Him with shouts, crying, "He is a blasphemer." They accused Him also before the governor, Pontius Pilate, as the enemy of Cæsar. Led before him, and questioned, if He were the Christ—if He were a king—"I am," he replied, for, from this moment, He spoke openly, and without parable. He was then given over to the insults of the populace, spit upon, beaten, stripped of His garments, fastened, naked, to a column; and Pilate, showing Him to the people, exclaimed "Ecce Homo!" Yes, behold the man who pays the ransom of all men, by suffering Himself in their place. His disciples abandoned Him; John and the holy women alone remained faithful. A heavy cross was laid on His shoulders; He falls under its weight, but is forced on to Golgotha. His holy Mother meets Him on this path of dolors. The daughters of Jerusalem weep for Him, and He predicts to them, that soon they will weep for the fate of their country and their children. At the foot of Calvary the soldiers cast lots for his clothing; they nail Him to the cross between two malefactors, one of whom is converted, and becomes the first saint, under the new law, who enters heaven, which is now opened to man by the passion of the Son of God. At length He cries, "It is finished!" and He dies. All nature was moved—the rocks were rent—the dead arose. The curtain of the holy of holies was rent from the top to the bottom, and darkness covered the earth. Witnesses of this divine death exclaimed, "This, truly, was the Son of God!" Joseph of Arimathea solicited and obtained from Pilate permission to bury the body of Jesus. They laid it in a sepulchre cut in the rock, placing at the entrance an enormous stone. The Jews fixed their seal upon it, and set a guard there (A. D. 33).* The *consummatum est*—It is consummated—of Calvary announced to the world the accomplishment of all the prophecies. At the precise moment when Jesus Christ expired, the seventy weeks of years predicted by the prophet Daniel were ended. The fall of Adam was repaired by the sacrifice of a God. The mediation of the Redeemer, the reconciliation of man with God, was now an accomplished fact.

* We adopt here the most simple chronology, without pretending to impose a preference. We know the opinion which places the death of our Lord Jesus Christ under the consulate of the Geminii, the 23d year of our era. It is supported by respectable authorities, and has been adopted by some learned critics.

8. Three days after His death, Jesus Christ rises victorious from the tomb—the guards are overturned, the stone of the sepulchre is moved, the disciples once more behold their Master, now become glorious, immortal. St. Thomas, still incredulous, touches the scars of His wounds, and places his hand in the wound in His side. During forty days, Jesus remains in the midst of them, renewing His instructions for the completion of His work, and performing a multitude of miracles. This fact of the resurrection, perfectly established by the four Evangelists, superabundantly demonstrated by even the incredulity of St. Thomas, "who refused, obstinately, to believe," said St. Leo the Great, "in order that the world might be more fully assured of the fact," is the basis of our faith, and the confirmation of the divinity of the Church. "If Jesus Christ be not risen again," said St. Paul, "then is our preaching vain, and your faith is also vain." It was during the forty days our Saviour remained on earth after His resurrection that His disciples, having seen Him, touched Him, spoken with Him, and received His instructions, derived from Him their undaunted courage to announce the Gospel. Finally, Jesus united them around Him for the last time at Bethania; and on a mountain near this city, He addressed to them these words: "All power has been given to me in heaven and on earth. Go preach the Gospel to every creature, baptizing them in the name of the Father, and of the Son, and of the Holy Ghost." He then extended His hands over them and blessed them. At the same moment He was raised up towards heaven, and a cloud received Him out of their sight.

CHAPTER II.

§ I. Pontificate of St. Peter (a.d. 33, June 29, a.d. 67). 1. Pentecost.—2. Life of the primitive Christians.—3. Election of the seven deacons.—4. Conversion of St. Paul.—5. Calling of the Gentiles.—6. Persecution by Herod Agrippa. Dispersion of the Apostles.—7. First mission of St. Paul.—8. Council of Jerusalem.—9. Second mission of St. Paul—10. Third mission of St. Paul.—11. Fourth mission of St. Paul.—12. First general persecution under Nero. Martyrdom of St. Peter and St. Paul. § II. Pontificate of St. Linus (a.d. 67-78). 13. Destruction of Jerusalem by Titus.—14. Death of St. Linus. § III. Pontificate of St. Cletus, or Anacletus (a.d. 78-91). 15. Identity of St. Cletus, or Anacletus.—16. Extension of Christianity into Gaul and Germany. § IV. Pontificate of St. Clement I. (a.d. 91-100). 17. Letters of St. Clement to the Corinthians.—18. Heresies of the first century.—19. Second general persecution under Domitian.

§ I. Pontificate of St. Peter (a.d. 33, June 29, a.d. 67).

1. In ascending to heaven, the Son of God left to His disciples the charge to continue His mission, and to preach the Gospel to all people. To fulfil their sublime calling, they had need of great strength and high intelligence; of nothing less than the fulness of the Holy Ghost, which, according to the promise of the Saviour, *would instruct them in all things.* Until their apostleship was confirmed by the coming of the Holy Spirit—the same which had descended upon Jesus, in the form of a dove, at the commencement of His public life—the apostles remained in the cœnaculum,* or upper supper-room, "with Mary, mother of Jesus, and the holy women, persevering in prayer." During these days of expectation, Peter, for the

---

* Used frequently by the primitive Christians as an oratory and place of public worship.—A. B.

first time assuming the authority with which he had been invested, "to feed the sheep and the lambs," in virtue of his primacy, spoke, and explained the necessity of preserving the original number of the Apostolic College, and of filling the place of the traitor Judas by the election of a new apostle. The choice fell upon Matthias. Thus were filled the twelve thrones on which were to be seated the judges of the twelve tribes of Israel. Several days after, on the festival which commemorated the promulgation of the law on Mount Sinai, the Holy Spirit, in the form of tongues of fire, descended upon the assembled apostles and disciples, and communicated to them the intelligence and ardent zeal which were destined to renew the face of the earth. Since that moment this vivifying Spirit remains indissolubly united to the Church, His mystical spouse, and preserves within her the unity of love and of faith. Every period of ecclesiastical history presents to us the trace of His fecundating inspirations. His gifts were soon made manifest in the Apostles. These men, hitherto so slow to believe, so narrow in their views, so vacillating and timid, from this marvellous hour display an energy, a zeal, a courage, which faltered not until death. But it was the gift of languages which at first made the strongest impression upon the Jews and proselytes, who were assembled from all quarters of the globe to celebrate, at Jerusalem, the feast of Pentecost. Parthians and Medes, inhabitants of Asia Minor and Mesopotamia, Jews from Egypt and Rome, from Lybia, Crete, and Arabia, were amazed to hear, each in his own language, the words of the disciples. The voice of the Prince of the Apostles converted on this day to the faith three thousand men. Some days later, Peter—for from him emanated all the earliest acts of the rising Church—Peter, with a word, cured a man lame from his birth, on the steps of the temple. The people assembled in wondering crowds to see the prodigy. The Chief of the Apostles preached to the multitude the name of Jesus Christ, and five thousand of them were converted. The leaders of the Jews began to be alarmed at such a manifestation of power in works and in words. The priests and Sadducees commanded Peter and John to be seized and cast into prison; and the following day they were summoned before the Sanhedrim. In the presence of these judges Peter preached the divinity of Jesus Christ, and His resurrection from the dead. They commanded him never to pronounce this divine name before the people. "Judge for yourselves," he replied, "if it be right to obey you rather than God. For we cannot but speak the things which we have seen and heard." They were liberated. Every day augmented the number of believers who were converted to Jesus Christ by the preaching, not less than the miracles of the Apostles. The sick were placed in the streets, that, while Peter was passing, his shadow might fall upon them; and the people of the adjacent towns brought to Jerusalem the possessed and the sick of every description, and they returned healed. The rigorous measures of the synagogue were powerless to arrest the rapid progress of the Church. Peter was thrown into prison, but in the night he was delivered by an angel; the Apostles were beaten, but they rejoiced to *bear this opprobrium for the name of Jesus Christ.* Already the question of putting them to death had been agitated in the Sanhedrim, but one of its members, Gamaliel, prevented this crime.

2. The multitude of the believers were of one heart and one mind, and formed but one family, who held every thing in common. There were no poor among them, because they who had lands or houses sold them, and brought the price to the Apostles for distribution among the needy.* They continued the religious exercises in common use with the Jews, frequenting the temple at the hours of prayer and sacrifice, where they were accustomed to assemble under Solomon's porch. They also assembled in the cœnacles or oratories of the most commodious or spacious houses of the Christians, under the direction of the Apostles or of priests appointed by them. There they

---

* Hæc erat angelica respublica nihil ducere proprium, hoc protulit primum germen nascens Ecclesia.—Chrysost., *In Act. Apost.*, 7.

were instructed in the mysteries of faith and the maxims of Jesus Christ, persevering with fervor in prayer and in the communion of the breaking of bread; that is to say, in the reception of the sacrament of the Holy Eucharist. After it they took, in common, their ordinary nourishment. These were the repasts afterwards called *agapæ* (charity and affection). The community of goods did not lead to an entire relinquishment of the right and possession of property—it was never imposed on any one as a duty, nor was it ever introduced into the other Churches. It is, therefore, a gross historic error to pretend that the spirit of the Gospel in the primitive Church was destructive of the rights of property. When Ananias and Sapphira sought to deceive the Apostles, in reserving for themselves a part of the sum which they had received for their goods, Peter said to them, "Why have you lied unto God? Were you not free to keep all for yourselves, and to enjoy it?" The sudden death with which they were smitten at the feet of the Prince of the Apostles demonstrated to the faithful that they could not, with impunity, deceive the ministers of the Lord. In exterior things, the Christians lived like the Jews, with whom certain pagan contemporary authors have confounded them. They still observed the ceremonies of the law, although, after their fulfilment in the person of Jesus Christ, they had, in their figurative character, ceased to be obligatory. This was an epoch of transition, which was not to close until after the ruin of Jerusalem, announced by the prophetic words of the Saviour, who had warned His own generation that they would witness the catastrophe.

3. The complaints of certain Hellenistic Jews, that is, of Greek origin, who represented that their widows were forgotten in the distribution of alms daily dispensed by the Apostles, gave occasion, about this time, to the election of seven deacons (A. D. 33). They were chosen by the faithful, and presented to the Apostles, who imposed hands on them. Stephen, Philip, Prochorus, Nicanor, Timon, Parmenas, and Nicolas, a proselyte of Antioch (Acts vi.), were charged with this ministry,

which consisted in providing food for the poor and the distribution of the alms. They also served at the administration of the Eucharist and preached the Gospel, as is proved by the example of St. Stephen, the most prominent among them. The numerous conversions which God wrought through his word, marked him as a subject for the fury of the priests. Accused by them of blasphemy, Stephen was dragged without the walls of Jerusalem and stoned. He died praying for his murderers, and was the first among those martyrs of the Church whose blood has not ceased to flow for the cause of God, and in vindication of the truth, during eighteen centuries. The immediate effect of the persecution which followed, and extended to all the Christian inhabitants of Jerusalem, was to disperse the faithful over the adjacent cities, and through them to found new churches in Palestine, Samaria, and even in Phœnicia, Syria, and Cyprus. The preaching and the miraculous cures of the Deacon Philip gained over to the Gospel a great number of Samaritans, who afterwards received the sacrament of Confirmation and the gifts of the Holy Spirit from the hands of Peter and John. A providential meeting of Philip with an Ethiopian eunuch—of great authority under the Queen Candace—who was returning from Jerusalem, led to his conversion and baptism. On his return to his country, he there propagated Christianity. About this time, Simon the Magician, proposing to purchase from the Apostles, for money, their power of communicating the gifts of the Holy Spirit, was repulsed with horror by St. Peter. Such was the first attempt to commit the abominable crime of simony, which has preserved the name of its author, and which consists in the sacrilegious desire to purchase spiritual gifts with material offerings. Simon, far from repenting his error, employed his imperfect knowledge of the truths of the Gospel to broach a heresy, the first which appeared in the Church. He claimed, as a principle, that as no actions are good in their nature, therefore works are of no avail for salvation; and that grace alone is sufficient to save men, without co-operation with it on their part. This was the germ of the heresy of Predestinarianism.

His doctrine consisted in a sort of fusion of the elements of Christianity with the fables of pagan mythology. This was the germ of Gnosticism.

4. Among the persecutors of the faithful, who made himself most remarkable by his indefatigable activity, his passionate and almost ferocious zeal, was Saul, still young, born at Tarsus, in Cilicia, of Jewish parents, of the tribe of Benjamin, but Roman citizens. During the martyrdom of St. Stephen, Saul had charge of the garments of those who stoned the holy deacon. Since then he had not ceased to pursue the Christians; but the time was come when the wolf was to be changed into a lamb, the persecutor into an apostle. This young Cilician, of unprepossessing exterior,* was destined to preach the Gospel before kings and peoples. The classic culture which he had acquired in the flourishing schools of Tarsus, his native city, and his eloquence, which the celebrated Longinus has placed by the side of that of Demosthenes, Æschines, and Isocrates, served to prepare him to preach the name of Jesus Christ to the Gentiles. The knowledge of the Hebrew Scriptures and traditions, which he gained at the feet of Gamaliel, eminently enabled him to expound the doctrines of Christianity to the Jews. By the sublimity of his talents, the energy of his will, the ardor of his character, he was called to propagate afar the Church of Christ, and to make known all the depth and the riches of the evangelic doctrine, by expounding it with marvellous clearness in face of the prejudices of Judaism and the errors of paganism. To stay the progress of the Gospel, Saul, in the years 35, 36, obtained letters from the grand council, or Sanhedrim, of the Jews, addressed to the chiefs of the synagogues in Palestine and Syria, which granted him full powers to bring in chains, to Jerusalem, all Christians on whom he could lay hands. He was on his way to Damascus, when, suddenly, on the road, he was enveloped by a supernatural light. Stricken and dazzled, he fell to the

* Bossuet, Panégyrique de St. Paul.

ground, and heard a voice, saying, "Saul, why persecutest thou me?" On his asking, "Who art thou, Lord?" he received the answer, "I am Jesus, whom thou persecutest." At the same moment he was ordered to proceed to Damascus, where he should learn what he must do. During his sojourn in that city, the disciple Ananias, warned by a heavenly vision, came to visit him; and, laying his hands upon him, restored his sight, which he had lost on the road to Damascus, and baptized him. Saul, entirely changed, began immediately to preach the name of Christ, of whom he had been the most ardent persecutor. He travelled over Arabia Petræa, either to preach to the Jews whom he found there, or to prepare himself, in retreat, for his apostolic mission. After three years, returning to Damascus, he was obliged to fly in the night, to escape the snares of the Jews, who would have killed him. He then made his first visit to Jerusalem, to see Peter, " to observe, to study him," says St. Chrysostom, "as one greater, as well as older, than himself." "To see him," according to Bossuet, "in order to establish forever the principle, that however learned, however holy one may be, he must see Peter." Saul, the persecutor, afterwards changed his name into that of Paul the Apostle, to express, in a way to be understood, the interior transformation which grace had wrought in him. He courageously preached the Gospel in the synagogues, but the murderous attempts of the angry Hellenists against him having soon obliged him to leave Jerusalem, he returned to Tarsus.

5. About this time (A. D. 35) the Apostle St. James was chosen by St. Peter, and raised to the dignity of Bishop of Jerusalem. His merit had obtained for him the surname of the Just. He was called the brother of the Lord, according to the genius of the Hebrew tongue, because, being the son of Alpheus and Mary, sister of the Blessed Virgin, he was related to Jesus Christ. Leaving the disciples of Jerusalem under the direction of this holy pastor, Peter began to travel over the towns of Judea, to visit the saints, for so the first Christians

were often called, and confirm them in the faith. Miracles, then necessary to the propagation of the Gospel, accompanied his word. At Lydda, otherwise called Diospolis, he restored a paralytic to health, and all the inhabitants of this town and of the country of Sharon were converted to the Lord. At Joppa he recalled to life the widow Tabitha, and restored her to the saints, for whom she was a model; to the poor, of whom she was a benefactress. Meanwhile, the hour was come when the gates of the Church, hitherto open only to the Jews, were to be equally free for the entrance of pagans. Peter, who went about Palestine, employing the time which the persecution allowed in forming and enlarging the new churches, was prepared for this great event by a warning received in a vision, that he should no longer consider as unclean that which God had pronounced clean. At the same time, another vision directed a man who feared God, the centurion Cornelius, of Cæsarea, to send for the Chief of the Apostles at Joppa, where he had just recalled to life Tabitha, the widow. Peter obeyed the summons, and announced the Gospel to the centurion and his friends who shared his sentiments. While he explained the divine doctrine, his auditory, composed chiefly of pagans, received, all at once, the Holy Spirit; and the faithful, who came with Peter, heard them speak in languages which they had never learned. Peter, therefore, had no hesitation in baptizing men so evidently called of God. Thus the Church received these first-fruits of the Gentiles into her bosom. It should be remarked, that to Peter alone, among the Apostles, God at first revealed the mystery of the union of the Jews and Gentiles in the same fold—a mystery the most difficult for the early disciples to believe, educated as they had been in the maxims of Judaism, and in a legal and absolute separation from other nations. The fact of the calling of the Gentiles was soon solemnly consecrated by the foundation of the apostolic see of Antioch, of which St. Peter was the first Bishop, and where the faithful were for the first time called Christians (*Christiani*). The Latin termination of this word gives reason to conclude that it was originally employed by Romans living at Antioch.

6. A second persecution, but at this time especially directed against the chiefs of the rising Church, was instigated by Herod Agrippa, grandson of Herod the Great, on whom the Emperor Claudius had conferred, at the same time, the royal dignity and that of governor of Judea. To prove himself a zealous Jew, and desirous to please the people, Herod Agrippa ordered the decapitation of St. James, son of Zebedee, and the imprisonment of Peter under a rigorous guard. The head of the Church, for whose deliverance the faithful continued in fervent prayer, was set at liberty during the night by an angel. He left Jerusalem immediately, and the sudden death of Agrippa, after which Judea became a Roman province, put an end to the persecution. In the interval, the Apostles separated, to go and preach the Gospel to all nations. Before their departure they composed a substantial abridgment of Christian doctrine, commonly called the Apostles' Creed, the object of which was to secure unity of faith, as the primacy of St. Peter would maintain unity in government. The history of most of the Apostles, after their dispersion, is involved in nearly impenetrable obscurity. St. Luke, from this period, treats only of the acts of St. Paul, St. John, and St. James, of whom we have more precise information than of the others. Brief notices, which are often uncertain, are all that remain to us. St. Matthias went to preach the Gospel in Colchis; St. Jude, in Mesopotamia; St. Simon, in Lybia; St. Matthew, after having written his Gospel, at the request of the faithful in Judea, went into Ethiopia; St. Bartholomew, into the Greater Armenia; St. Thomas, to the Parthians, and even to India; St. Philip, after having evangelized Upper Asia, died at Hierapolis, in Phrygia; St. Andrew was sent to the Scythians, whence he passed into Greece and Epirus; James, son of Alpheus, remained at Jerusalem, of which he had been appointed Bishop; St. John preached in Asia Minor. According to the most probable opinions, the Blessed Virgin

accompanied him in his apostolic journeys. An ancient and generally received tradition attests that she died at Jerusalem; and the belief of the Church is, that, after her death, she was, by a glorious assumption, taken up body and soul into heaven."* She died, so far as is known, at Jerusalem, about the year 45 or 47. St. Peter had, in the first place, fixed his see at Antioch, of which he was the first Bishop. After remaining there nearly seven years, he quitted it, to establish at Rome the future residence of the vicars of Christ. These two episcopates of St. Peter have been considered of such importance by the faithful, that, since the first ages of the Church, two solemn festivals have been established as memorials of them. In the interval between the foundation of these two sees, the holy Apostle preached the Gospel in Pontus, Galatia, Bithynia, Cappadocia, and Asia Minor, followed by Mark, Pancratius, Marcian, Rufus, and Apollinaris, future Bishops of Alexandria, Syracuse, and Capua. Mark, his disciple, was, however, sent by St. Peter to found the Church of Alexandria. The capital of Egypt thus received the faith, by this intermediary, from St. Peter, as Rome, the capital of the West, and Antioch, the capital of the East, were founded, also, by the great Apostle. Before leaving his master, St. Mark wrote his Gospel, at the request of the faithful at Rome, who desired to preserve the remembrance of the preaching of the head of the Apostles.

7. About the same time, St. Paul received at Antioch his consecration to the apostleship. To this consecration he appeals (Gal. i. 1) when he says that it is not by man, but by the grace of Jesus Christ, that he has been made an Apostle. Taking with him Barnabas and John Mark, they set out together on their first mission. They preached the Gospel at Salamina, capital of the Isle of Cyprus, first addressing them-

---

* The Assumption of the Blessed Virgin has never been defined an article of faith. It is with it, as it was with the Immaculate Conception before the dogmatic decree of December 8, 1854, which filled the Catholic world with joy. Nevertheless, the belief of the Assumption of the Blessed Virgin, consecrated by tradition and by the feast celebrated in her honor, in both the Latin and Greek Churches, is, of right, dear to all the faithful.

selves to the synagogues, to which their Jewish origin gave them free entrance. Called to Paphos by the proconsul, Sergius Paulus, Paul struck the impostor Elymas (Bar-jesu), who was in the city, with blindness, and gained the proconsul to the faith.* From Paphos these messengers of good tidings returned to the Asiatic continent, and from Perge, in Pamphylia, where Mark left them, they went to Antioch of Pisidia. There, and at Iconium, in Lycaonia, their word converted to the Gospel a multitude of Jews and pagans. Among the new disciples at Iconium was a young maiden, St. Thecla, whose memory antiquity has celebrated, and placed her name by the side of that of St. Stephen, because she was the first martyr of her sex who had the glory of suffering for the name of Jesus. Dragged before the pagan judges, who would have forced her to deny her faith, she courageously resisted the torture, and, by their order, was exposed to the beasts in the amphitheatre. But the lions came crouching to her feet, not daring to harm the body of the saintly virgin. The people, touched by this spectacle, demanded the release of St. Thecla, who ended her days in peace. She received, nevertheless, the title of martyr, in accordance with the usage of the early ages of the Church, when this name was given to all who had suffered for the Gospel from torments fatal in their nature, even though they had miraculously survived. At Lystra, where a word from St. Paul publicly restored to a lame man the use of his limbs, the two Apostles were supposed to be gods, and the people proposed to offer sacrifices to them, as to Jupiter and Mercury; but the same people suddenly changing their minds, under the influence of the Jews, pursued Paul with stones, and dragged him out of the city. They thought him dead, but the will of God preserved him for other combats and other triumphs. The Apostles departed the next day for Derbe, which also they evangelized. In another visit to the believers of

---

* It is supposed by many that the Apostle changed his name from Saul to Paul in honor of this distinguished convert. This opinion is confirmed by the fact that he is constantly called Paul from this period.—A. B.

Lystra, Antioch of Pisidia, and Iconium, they appointed pastors to these rising churches; and returning to Antioch, in Syria, closed their first mission.

8. Called to the apostleship in an extraordinary manner, St. Paul had received directly from God the understanding necessary for his work. But, in order to give to his instruction and discipline the exterior sanction of the truth, and a perfect accordance with the doctrine and conduct of the other Apostles, and urged, too, by a superior inspiration, he went to Jerusalem, the second time since his conversion, accompanied by Barnabas, and by Titus, whom he had brought from the darkness of paganism to the light of the Gospel. There he met St. Peter, who had just arrived, and SS. James and John. From this time the question of the positive obligation of the Mosaic law was agitated among them; and it was one of decided importance to the progress of the Christian society. No question, indeed, presented greater difficulties to the Jews—particularly to those who lived at Jerusalem, in view of the temple, and in the midst of the still subsisting sacrifices—than that of divesting themselves of the prejudices through which they regarded the exact observance of the law as the only means of justification and salvation. It was only with extreme difficulty they could conceive that faith in Jesus Christ was sufficient for the justification of the pagan converts, without submitting to circumcision and other legal prescriptions; and they refused to communicate with them so long as they failed to bear those marks of the law of servitude. St. Paul opposed these requirements with all his energy. The three Apostles, Peter, James, and John, held the same doctrine, recognizing him and Barnabas as their true colleagues, and decided that the two latter should be specially sent to preach to the pagans, while the former continued to evangelize the Jews. Soon after the return of Paul and Barnabas to Antioch, Peter joined them, and made no scruple to eat with the uncircumcised believers, until the arrival of some Christian Jews, sent by St. James. Fearing to scandalize these austere zealots for the law, who regarded

the uncircumcised and their repasts as unclean, St. Peter withdrew himself from the table of the pagan converts. The agitation which this incident occasioned in the Church at Antioch showed the necessity of an authoritative decision on the part of the Apostles united at Jerusalem. Paul and Barnabas were sent thither as deputies. The five Apostles, Peter, James, John, Paul, and Barnabas, with the priests and faithful, constituted the first council, known as the Council of Jerusalem. St. Peter, in his quality of head of the Church, opened the assembly. He declared that in calling them to the faith, God had made no difference between the Jews and Gentiles. The Church of Jesus Christ was the prophetic mountain of Isaiah, where all nations of the earth were to meet in the unity of faith. St. Paul and St. James spoke in the same sense, and the final decision of the council reduced the obligations of the pagan converts to the following: 1st. To abstain from meats offered in sacrifice; 2d, from the flesh of strangled animals, and from blood; 3d, from fornication. The prohibition to participate in the meats of sacrifices was necessary to preserve the new Christians from relapsing into paganism. As to fornication, the moral sense of the pagans was so extinct that they looked upon it as an action of no consequence; and it was important that purity of manners should become a distinctive mark of the new law. The prohibition of strangulated flesh was sustained by the Church out of regard to the health of her children; that against blood had a higher origin. Blood, in the sacrifices, was the principal offering reserved for the Lord. So long as sacrifices continued to be offered in the temple of Jerusalem, it may readily be conceived that the Christians respectfully observed this prescription. To the Jewish mind abstinence from blood was a divine precept, obligatory on all men; it was therefore necessary, in order to lessen their repugnance to any kind of communication with the Gentiles, to impose, for the time, the same prohibition on all Christians. The decision of the council, preceded by these solemn words—"It has seemed good to the Holy Spirit and to us," was sent to the Churches of Syria and Cilicia; and Paul, with Barnabas, returned to Antioch, while Peter took the way to Rome.

9. In a short time St. Paul began a second mission, accompanied by Silas only—Barnabas having separated from them because St. Paul refused to take John Mark with him. Barnabas, therefore, and John Mark embarked for the Isle of Cyprus; Paul and Silas went into Asia Minor, Providence having permitted this separation, that the Gospel might be preached in a greater number of places at the same time. A. D. 53 St. Paul first visited the Churches of Northern Syria, Cilicia, and Lycaonia. At Lystra he was joined by the young Timothy, who was the son of a Greek father and a Jewish mother, now a Christian. Conformably to the desire of St. Paul, Timothy, in order to obtain easier access to the Jews, was circumcised. The three heralds of the faith then travelled over Phrygia, Galatia, and Mysia. At Troas the physician and evangelist, Luke, joined them. A vision which St. Paul had in a dream, induced him to quit Asia and go into Macedonia. At Philippi, a seller of purple, named Lydia, was converted, with all her household. In this same city, on account of the cure of a slave who was possessed by an evil spirit, Paul and Silas, by order of the governor, after having been beaten with rods, were cast into prison, as seducers of the people, and as preachers of a new and not authorized religion. The joyful constancy of the Apostles, and the miracle which opened their dungeon in the night, so troubled the jailer, that, having been instructed by St. Paul, he believed in Jesus Christ, and received baptism, with all his family. The authorities of the city, alarmed at the precipitation with which they had maltreated a Roman citizen, for St. Paul enjoyed this title by birth, restored the prisoners to liberty with much respect, praying them, nevertheless, to depart. But the foundations of the Church were already laid in Philippi. The Apostles made a longer stay in the populous city of Thessalonica, where there was a synagogue, and formed among the Jews a church, which soon became flourishing. Meanwhile, the unbelieving

Jews having sought, by calumnious charges, to extort from the pagan authorities the condemnation of the holy missionaries, they departed in the night for the neighboring city of Berea, where, among the Jewish inhabitants, they found greater sympathy. Pursued, even in this city, by the Jews of Thessalonica, Paul left Silas and Timothy, and, alone, sailed for Athens. This city, the centre of civilization, arts, and letters, now despoiled of her political importance, and reduced to be the mere slave of Rome, still governed her masters by her science and genius. The future consuls and Cæsars came to learn, in her schools, to think justly and to speak well. The eye encountered, everywhere, statues and temples raised in honor of the gods with pagan pomps and bloody sacrifices. One nameless altar in this capital of polytheism, dedicated to the Unknown God, furnished the Apostle a favorable subject for the commencement of his work. Led by Stoics and Epicureans before the Areopagus, the supreme tribunal in religious matters, St. Paul announced, in the presence of an astonished auditory, the one God Almighty, "in whom we live, and move, and have our being," and who will judge the world by Him whom He has raised from among the dead. Some replied to him in mockery; others, that "they would hear him another time." A few believed in Jesus Christ, among whom were Dionysius, member of the Areopagus, and an humble woman named Damaris. From Athens St. Paul went to the capital of Achaia, the voluptuous Corinth, where he dwelt with a converted Jew named Aquila, laboring with his own hands for his support as a tent-maker, and preaching in the synagogue. But here also the greater number of the Jews received his doctrine with such hostility, that at length he turned, with more success, towards the Greeks. He formed, in a short time, a community of believers, of whom Crispus, chief of the synagogue, was a member, which, during the year and a half it was under the direction of the Apostle, became one among the most flourishing and numerous. A second time the Jews carried their complaints before the proconsul Gallio, brother of the famous philosopher, Seneca; but he dismissed them, declaring that he would not interfere in a Jewish religious quarrel. During these proceedings, Silas and Timothy, returning from Macedonia, brought to St. Paul consoling accounts of the state of the Churches in that country. This was the occasion of the First, and, soon after, of the Second Epistle of St. Paul to the Thessalonians. The Apostle returned to Syria, and, after a brief sojourn at Jerusalem, proceeded to Antioch, having accomplished this second mission A. D. 56.

10. A third soon followed, which he began in Asia Minor. He paused three years at Ephesus, preaching the Gospel to the inhabitants and the numerous strangers attracted to this opulent city, by commercial relations and the magnificence of the Temple of Diana, which was reckoned among the wonders of the world. There, was awakened the first suspicion that the reign of Christ menaced the worship, until then all-powerful, of the idols; and that the great Diana of the Ephesians might fall into dust before the Crucified. A tumult, excited by the goldsmith Demetrius, whose models of the temple of the great goddess might fall into discredit, endangered the life of the Apostle; but one of the magistrates of the city found means to tranquillize the people. During this sojourn at Ephesus, St. Paul wrote to the Christians of Galatia, to guard them against the false judaizing doctors, who taught the positive obligation of the Mosaic law. It was during this same interval that he sent Titus with his First Epistle to the Church at Corinth, then threatened with intestine dissensions. Feeling an ardent desire to see once more the faithful of Philippi, Thessalonica, and Berea, he went, in the year 59, by Troas into Macedonia, where he wrote his Second Epistle to the Corinthians. From this it appears that for the accomplishment of his mission he had suffered, chiefly from the Jews, the most barbarous treatment, and incurred dangers of which St. Luke makes no mention. It is probably at the same epoch that he sent to his disciple Timothy, left by him at the head of the church in Ephesus, a First Epistle, containing instructions on

his duty as Bishop. Having afterwards turned his apostolic zeal towards the churches of Greece, he sent by the deaconess Phœbe, who was going to Rome, his admirable Epistle to the faithful of that city, who were beginning to form a church. In the year 60, he hastened his return to Syria, with many others from the churches of Achaia and Macedonia, to be present at Jerusalem on the feast of Pentecost. At Miletus, having assembled the bishops and priests of Ephesus and the neighboring churches, he conjured them, in a touching discourse, to guard the flocks confided to their keeping; he warned them against the false doctors who would soon appear; and after praying with them, he departed, with a presentiment of the perils that awaited him. At Cæsarea, he saw the deacon Philip and his four daughters, who were endowed with the gift of prophecy. At Jerusalem he found none of the Apostles except St. James, Bishop of the city. The numerous members of the Church at Jerusalem, all composed of converted Jews, still held strongly to the observances of the Mosaic law. Many of them were hostile to St. Paul, and accused him, falsely, of having urged the Jews of the Diaspora to set aside the law and circumcision.* St. James advised him to remove this suspicion by undertaking a Jewish ceremony for four of the faithful, who now accomplished, in the temple, the vow of the Nazarite. St. Paul consented, but having been recognized by certain Jews of Asia Minor, they pointed him out to the fanatical fury of the people as a contemner of the law and profaner of the temple; and he would have been massacred, but for the intervention of the Roman tribune, Lysias. Conducted by Lysias himself before the Sanhedrim, at the head of which was seated the high-priest Ananias, a bitter enemy of the new faith, the sentence of death was prepared, when Paul reminded the Pharisees present in the assembly, that he had become an object of hatred to the Sadducees for having maintained the doctrine of the resurrec-

* The Jews who were dispersed in the Roman provinces were called of the Diaspora, from two Greek words, διά and σπείρω.

tion. The spirit of party, kindling at once the whole nature of the Pharisees, rendered them, for the moment, oblivious of their former animosity against him who had deserted their sect, and they declared that they found nothing in him worthy of chastisement. Lysias profited by this declaration to withdraw St. Paul from the rage of the Sadducees; but knowing that forty Zelotes (fanatical Jews) had sworn his death, he had him conveyed to Cæsarea, before Felix the governor, with a certificate of innocence. His enemies, and the high-priest with them, pursued him to that city. Felix, not daring to attack a Roman citizen, and hoping, also, that St. Paul would purchase his liberty, remanded him to a not strict confinement, where he passed two years. The implacable persecutors of the Apostle accused him before Portius Festus, the successor of Felix, and neglected nothing to procure his condemnation. St. Paul appealed from him to the emperor, and Portius accepted the appeal. Soon after these proceedings the young King Agrippa,* with Berenice his sister, wife, first of Herod, King of Chalcis, and later of Palemon, King of Pontus, having come to visit the new governor, Festus, and desirous to know the celebrated prisoner who was spoken of by all Judea, St. Paul was brought before them. The Apostle seized this occasion to preach the Gospel before the powerful of the earth. King Agrippa was a Jew. "Believest thou the prophets?" demanded St. Paul of the king. "I know that thou believest." And Agrippa said to Paul: "Almost thou persuadest me to be a Christian." "Would to God," replied St. Paul, "that not only thou, but also all that hear me this day should become such as I am, except these bonds!" And the king rose up, and the governor, and Berenice, and they that sat with them, saying: "This man has done nothing that merits either death or the prison. He might have been set at liberty, if he had not appealed to Cæsar." In the year 62, St. Paul

---

* This Agrippa was a son of Herod Agrippa, deceased in A. D. 43 or 44. He was present with Titus at the siege of Jerusalem, and was the last king of the Jews. His fate after the dispersion, is not known. He probably died during the reign of Domitian.

set out, as a prisoner, for Rome, accompanied by St. Luke and Aristarchus. In consequence of a shipwreck on the coast of Malta, he was delayed three months on that island. On his arrival at Puteoli (Pozzuoli), he received a fraternal welcome from the Church which was already formed there; and finally, in the year 63, the eighth of the reign of Nero, he made his entry into the capital of the empire, in the midst of the Christian brethren who had hastened to meet him. Two years he lived at Rome, under a slight restraint, enjoying the permission to occupy a private lodging with the soldier who had charge of him, and to receive those who came to visit him; consequently he was free to preach the Gospel. Here ceases the narrative of the Acts of the Apostles by St. Luke. This monument of the primitive Church is the most precious of its history. The first conquests of the Gospel in the pagan world do not present a triumph, the import of which is limited to the times when they occurred. The position of the Church remains the same in all ages. She has always had fierce enemies to combat—Jews or Gentiles, heretics or unbelievers, philosophers or executioners. St. Paul, that sublime missionary, who, in passing, wins cities and kingdoms, is the model above every other for all the teachers, all the ministers of Jesus Christ. For them, as for him, their strength is in their own weakness; they triumph when they are vanquished.

11. During his captivity of two years at Rome, besides the short letter sent to Philemon by Onesimus, a fugitive and converted slave, whom he sent back to his master, St. Paul wrote the Epistle to the Ephesians, which is a true evangelical letter, addressed to the faithful in Asia Minor; the Epistle to the Colossians, and that to the Philippians, in which he sets forth, touching the resurrection of our Saviour, the principles of faith, the redemption of fallen man, and the calling of the Gentiles. At the same time, probably, he wrote the Epistle to the Hebrews, addressed to the Jews in Judea and Jerusalem. In this epistle, St. Paul explains how Christianity came forth from the Jewish religion, and how immeasurably superior the new

law is to the ancient. The apostolic zeal of St. Peter and St. Paul, united in the same city, occasioned a rapid progress of the church at Rome. The teachings of Christianity had found their way even into the imperial court, so that St. Paul could write to the Philippians: "All the faithful salute you, especially those of Cæsar's household." At this epoch is placed the apocryphal interview of St. Paul with Seneca. The almost Christian maxims spread over the works of this philosopher, leave no doubt that he had at least known the morals of the Gospel. It was, apparently, to the good offices of influential friends and disciples that the Apostle owed his deliverance from imprisonment, in the beginning of the year 65. He availed himself of his liberty to undertake immediately new missions, of which, unfortunately, we have no precise information. There is, nevertheless, reason to believe that he executed the project of a visit to Spain, which he mentions in his Epistle to the Romans. This opinion is confirmed by the testimony of a contemporary author, Clement of Rome, who informs us, "that Paul was the herald of the Christian faith to the whole world, and penetrated even to the limits of the West." The Apostle went also into the Island of Crete, accompanied by his disciple Titus, whom he left there as overseer of the newly-founded churches, with power to institute bishops and priests. He sent to him afterwards, from Nicopolis (Epirus), an instruction on the manner of directing the flock confided to his care. This is the Epistle to Titus, in the canonical Scriptures. From Nicopolis Paul went to Corinth, visited once more the churches of Troas and Miletus, and returned to Rome towards the end of the year 66.

12. The first general persecution of the Church had just begun, by order of Nero. The pretext was worthy of the tyrant. Disgusted with the simplicity of the ancient edifices of Rome; or, rather, by a barbarous caprice, being disposed to give a spectacle which might rival the taking of Troy, Nero commanded the city to be set on fire. Of the fourteen divisions which then composed it, four only escaped the flames.

The emperor, to exculpate himself from the infamy of his own act, endeavored to fix it upon the Christians. He had them arrested and condemned to the most horrible torments. Some, covered with skins of wild beasts, were hunted, torn, and devoured by dogs, in imitation of a barbarous chase; others were crucified. Some were enveloped in resinous and other combustible matters, and fastened to posts along the streets, or in the alleys of the imperial gardens. In the evening they were set on fire, like torches destined to illumine the night. Nero, meanwhile, walked about his gardens, or drove himself in a car, by the light of these homicidal illuminations. St. Paul was arrested and brought before the tribunal of this crowned monster; but he spoke with such eloquence and courage, "that he escaped," as he says himself, "from the fury of the lion." Nero was satisfied with sending him to prison. At this time St. Peter was still free, in the midst of Rome, to yield to the ardor of his zeal, to fortify the Church, or extend the empire of faith, and, in the presence of Nero himself, to confound the sacrilegious audacity of Simon Magus. He celebrated the divine mysteries in the house of a Christian named Pudens. Tradition has regarded this house as the first church in Rome consecrated to divine worship by the Prince of the Apostles. Paul, meanwhile, detained in strict captivity, and in the near expectation of martyrdom, addressed a farewell epistle to his well-beloved disciple, Timothy (A. D. 67). He warned him to be on his guard against heretics, and, under this name, he seems to designate more especially the followers of Simon Magus and the Nicolaites. These last, availing themselves of an equivocal expression of the holy deacon Nicolas, pretended, upon this authority, to support a debauched sect, who admitted promiscuous intercourse and the most revolting excesses. We know not on what pretext they mingled the name of Nicolas with such scandals. Whatever it may be, St. Irenæus informs us that these heretics taught the same errors as the Cerinthians, of whom we shall treat hereafter. St. John has refuted both, in the beginning of his Gospel. At length the conversion of one of the concubines of Nero by St. Peter, brought upon him the wrath of the tyrant. He was arrested and committed to the Mamertine prison, where he converted to the faith his two guards, Processus and Martinianus. Finally, St. Peter and St. Paul were summoned before the governor of Rome. They, together, confessed the faith to which they had consecrated their lives, and both were condemned to capital punishment. According to a tradition of the highest antiquity in the Church, the two Apostles prophesied, before their death, the approaching ruin of Jerusalem. St. Peter, after having been beaten with rods, was crucified, his head downwards, on Mount Janiculum, and buried in the Aurelian Way, near the Temple of Apollo, in the same spot which is now covered by the palace of the Vatican and the Church of St. Peter, whose grandeur yields in nothing to the most imposing ruins of the Rome of the Cæsars (June 29, A. D. 67). The same day, St. Paul, as a Roman citizen, was beheaded near the Fulvian waters, in a place now nearly desert, a short distance from the Basilica, entitled, *St. Paul outside of the Walls.** The pontificate of St. Peter lasted thirty-three years, of which twenty-five were passed at Rome. None of his successors have reigned so long in the see of Rome. From this exceptional duration originated the celebrated sentence pronounced at each exaltation of the Roman pontiffs: *Annos Petri non videbis*—a wholesome reminder of the brevity of human things amid the most sublime grandeur here below.†

§ II. Pontificate of St. Linus (a. d. 67–78).

13. St. Linus, born at Volterra, in Tuscany, one of the disciples mentioned in the Second Epistle to Timothy (iv. 21),

---

* The precise spot is marked by the handsome little church of the Three Fountains—delle tre Fontane—so called from a beautiful legend that the head of the Apostle, after being severed from the body, made three leaps, fountains springing up at each point of contact with the earth. Most visitors to the Eternal City have seen this church, and proved the existence of the fountains.—A. B.

† For all that regards the pontificate of St. Peter, see the "Origin of Christianity," by Dr. Dœllinger, from whom we have borrowed much in this chapter.

was the immediate successor of St. Peter. In the lifetime of the Prince of the Apostles, he had been appointed to aid him in the government of the Church. Under his pontificate an event, matured by the divine justice, and predicted forty years before by Jesus Christ, was consummated. Jerusalem had to expiate a deicide, and history furnishes no record of so terrible a chastisement as hers. By a design of Providence, this city was spared so long as she remained the cradle of Christianity; but when faith had extended her conquests; when, far from being useful for the propagation of the Gospel, the existence of Jerusalem was rather an injury to its progress, from the attachment of the Jewish converts to the Mosaic ceremonies which they saw practised in the temple, then the vengeance of God called the Roman legions around the walls of the holy city. The generation who had heard the threatenings of Jesus Christ had not passed away. St. Peter and St. Paul had foretold the near accomplishment of the prophecies, so that the ruin of Jerusalem was at once the punishment of the most horrible of crimes, a clear proof of the divinity of the Saviour and of the religion which He had founded, the final separation between Christianity and the law of Moses, and the seal of reprobation, impressed in characters of blood, upon the Jewish nation. From the year 66, the party of Zelotes, or Zealots, had taken up arms to shake off the Roman power. Some slight successes gained over Cestius Gallus, proconsul of Syria, exalted the hopes of the fanatics. Warned by the predictions of the Saviour, the Christians, on the contrary, retired to Pella, to avoid the disasters of the coming war. In fact, Nero, on hearing of the defeat of Cestius Gallus, appointed Vespasian to conduct the war against the Jews; and he, with his son Titus, seized immediately the fortresses of Palestine, and then slowly approached the territory of Jerusalem, counting on the intestine divisions of the enemy to attain his end. John of Guiscala, from the name of the fortress which he commanded in Galilee, escaped from it, and, followed by a numerous band, threw himself into Jerusalem.

where he took the government into his own hands, and maltreated those who wished for peace. This served to produce internal dissensions in face of the enemy; and, as if to prolong the agony of Jerusalem, Vespasian, on hearing that the legions of Belgic Gaul had revolted against Nero, and proclaimed Galba emperor, resolved to abandon the Jewish war for the present, and, with his army, sailed for the shores of Italy, to hold himself prepared for events. This interruption of the war served only to augment the woes of Jerusalem and of all Judea. The parties of Simon and of John Guiscala fought against each other even within the city. Famine, earthquakes, the sinister lamentations of Jesus, son of Ananus, mysterious voices which issued from the inner temple, were presages of the ruin of this people. Vespasian, become emperor himself after the transient reigns of Galba, Otho, and Vitellius (A. D. 68), gave orders to his son Titus to pursue vigorously the siege of Jerusalem. An immense multitude of Jews were gathered within the city, for the festival of the Passover, when Titus invested it with a wall of circumvallation, which rendered all communication from without impossible. The city was surrounded by a triple girdle of walls, protected by deep valleys. But the Roman soldiers, encouraged by the presence of the son of their emperor, succeeded in scaling the first ramparts. Five days after the commencement of the siege, the second wall crumbled under their powerful machines. A Jewish author, Flavius Josephus, who was with the army of Titus, was sent to the besieged, and he used every means of persuasion which might incline them to surrender, but they drove him back with reproach and outrages. The famine, meanwhile, had become so fearful in this doomed city that the inhabitants had recourse to the most horrible expedients to procure a single morsel of food. They dragged the dead from their graves, in the wild hope of finding aliment. A woman, a mother, murdered her own infant, roasted and ate one-half of its body, and presented the remainder to the famished soldiers, whom the odor of this execrable meal had attracted to the spot.

"It is my son," she said; "be not more tender than a woman, nor more compassionate than a mother." On hearing of it, Titus declared that the ruins of Jerusalem should bury the remembrance of such a crime. Among those who had succeeded in escaping from the city, one was found who had swallowed a number of small pieces of gold. A report of this discovery being bruited about the camp, the soldiers captured not less than two thousand fugitives, who were disembowelled, in order to search for the treasures they were supposed to contain. At length, on the fifth of July, A. D. 70, the third wall was carried by assault; but the besieged, more obstinate than ever, refused to yield, and took refuge in the temple. This magnificent edifice was built like a fortress, and completely defended by a square enclosure of impenetrable walls. Titus had commanded that, at all hazards, this monument should be preserved. But a soldier, lifted up on the shoulders of his comrades, "and instigated," said Josephus, "by a supernatural impulse," threw in a firebrand, thus kindling a conflagration that Titus strove in vain to extinguish. The Jews within the temple were all burned, or they perished by the sword. The conqueror passed a plough over the ruins of Jerusalem, and left only three towers standing—Phasael, Hippicus, and Mariamne. Eleven hundred thousand Jews, according to Josephus, lost their lives during the siege; ninety-seven thousand were sold as slaves; John of Guiscala was condemned to perpetual imprisonment; Simon, led to Rome in chains, served to adorn the triumph of Titus, and was then executed. Such was the end of the Hebrew nation. The temple, the sacrifices, the legal priesthood, the distinction of tribes—all disappeared before the sword of Titus, who proclaimed himself the instrument of divine vengeance, August 20, A. D. 70. The Christians, conducted by their Bishop, St. Simeon, successor of St. James, returned to inhabit the ruins of Jerusalem. Great numbers of Jews, enlightened at last by the terrible accomplishment of the prophecies, opened their hearts to the light of the faith.

14. After a pontificate of twelve years, St. Linus died at Rome. The most ancient monuments give him the title of martyr. We have already remarked that the usage of the primitive ages gave this title to those who had suffered for Jesus Christ, even when their persecutors had not pursued them to death. The Liber Pontificalis—Book of the Popes—attributes to St. Linus an ordinance which prohibits women from entering the assemblies of the faithful without a veil.

§ III. Pontificate of St. Cletus, or Anacletus (a. d. 78-91).

15. The succession of the Popes here presents an historical difficulty which has been fruitful in controversies—Is St. Cletus different from St. Anacletus? Critics are divided on this question. The learned researches of the Rev. Fathers Lazzari and Pappenbrock have at length settled the question by adopting the identity of the two names in the person of the same pontiff. According to their opinion, which is now generally followed, Cletus, elected the successor of St. Linus, a. d. 78, was comprised in an order of exile against the Christians, enacted under Vespasian by the governor of Rome. During the reign of Titus, the pontiff, returning to his episcopal city, took the name of Anacletus, or *iterum Cletus*.[*] Thus is reconciled the authority of the ancient Fathers and catalogues, who name this Pope sometimes Cletus—sometimes Anacletus. In the first year of his pontificate, a violent plague ravaged the city of Rome (a. d. 78). The Christians manifested their charity and devotion by their care of the infected, whom the pagans abandoned in the streets. There was not, at that time, any open persecution against the faithful, but the magistrates could readily find occasions and pretexts for exiling them, or delivering them to the executioner. In this manner St. Apollinaris, first bishop of Ravenna, suffered martyrdom, January 23, a. d. 79. Vespasian had no inclination to attach his name to bloody edicts of proscription. Of a character merciful and clement, he was but slightly moved by the charms of idolatry.

[*] Cletus again.

His last words, on the approach of death, contained a jest upon the doctrine of the apotheosis: "Behold," said he, "I am becoming a god!" (June 24, 79.) Titus, his son, the conqueror of Jerusalem, succeeded him, and, in too short a reign, merited the title of "The delight of the human race."

16. The Gospel was now making itself heard in all countries. Gaul, that land which the arms of Cæsar had opened for the Apostles, received the messengers of good tidings in her principal cities. At Tours flourished St. Gatien; at Arles, St. Trophimus; at Narbonne, St. Paul; at Toulouse, St. Saturninus; at Paris, St. Dionysius; at Clermont, in Auvergne, St. Austremonius; at Limoges, St. Martial, &c. Although the origin of these rising churches may be enveloped in obscurity the traditions of the people, and the formal testimony of St Irenæus and Tertullian, who mention, in their writings, the churches of Gaul existing in their time, which was the second century, do not allow us to refer to the third century the birth of Christianity in Gaul.* At the same time, St. Maternus founded the Church in Strasburg, and perhaps also that of Cologne; St. Clement, that of Metz; St. Eucherius, that of Treves; St. Crescentius, that of Mayence. According to the testimony of Tertullian, Christianity was already flourishing in Spain. Thus the Church, half a century after the ascension of the Saviour, had already won her title of Catholic, and had representatives throughout the world. To Titus succeeded his brother Domitian (September 13, A. D. 81), who made men almost regret the loss of Nero. He had all his cruelty, and united to it paroxysms of rage bordering on madness. His first act was to banish philosophers from all Italy. Under this name the Christians were included, and Pope St. Anacletus suffered martyrdom at Rome, A. D. 91. He had established twenty-five priests to fulfil the pastoral duty in the different quarters of Rome.

* Baronius, Mabillon, Pagi, Nat. Alexander, Mamacchi, and the most learned modern critics, have refuted, on this point, the opinions of the historians of the seventeenth and eighteenth centuries.

§ IV. Pontificate of St. Clement I. (a. d. 91-100).

17. St. Clement, the successor of St. Anacletus, was a Roman, and a disciple of St. Peter. St. Paul eulogizes him in his Epistle to the Philippians (iv. 3): "And I entreat thee also, my sincere companion, help those women that have labored with me in the Gospel, with Clement, and the rest of my fellow-laborers, whose names are in the book of life." The first care of the new pontiff was to appoint at Rome seven notaries, whose duty was to collect the acts of the martyrs, and place them in the registers of the festivals of the Church. Hence arose the institution of the Apostolic Prothonotaries Participants, who were increased to the number of twelve by Sixtus V. The Church of Corinth was at this time troubled by a small number of its members, who, jealous of the reputation of certain virtuous priests, had deposed them. The case was referred to the judgment of St. Clement I., who addressed two letters to the Corinthians, which have been praised by all antiquity, and which, a century later, were still read publicly in assemblies of the faithful. A fragment only of the second epistle is extant. The first, which the erudite believed to be lost, was published almost entire in the last century, at Oxford, by Patricius Junius, a Scotchman, from an ancient manuscript in the Royal Library, that dates from the time of the first Council of Nice. The authenticity of this precious document is generally admitted. St. Clement there speaks with the authority which he held from the chair of St. Peter; he decides the question as supreme judge, and announces to the Corinthians that he sends to them five legates: Claudius, Ephebius, Valerius, Vitonius, and Fortunatus, who are charged to deliver this letter, and to use all means for the re-establishment of peace among them. In proportion as the Church enlarged the circle of her conquests, error, by a parallel movement, seemed to develop itself to hinder the progress of the Gospel. The heresies of this epoch arose, some from expiring Judaism, others from Paganism and

ing to defend itself. After the ruin of Jerusalem, the Christians born Jews, who still held strongly to the forms of the Mosaic religion, were divided into three sects, viz.: the Ebionites, the Nazarenes, and the Cerinthians.

18. The Ebionites, sectaries of the Stoic Jew, Ebion, gave a predominance in their doctrine to Judaism. They regarded all the ceremonies of the law as obligatory, and pretended that Jesus Christ was merely a man, the son of Joseph and Mary. They treated St. Paul as an apostate, because this Apostle, on every page of his writings, demonstrates the divinity of the Saviour. For the same reason they rejected all the Gospels except that of St. Matthew, because there the testimony of the dogma which they denied seemed to them less precise. The Nazarenes, on the contrary, recognized the divinity of Jesus Christ, but they mingled in His history certain errors borrowed from an apocryphal gospel, which, to the exclusion of others, they had adopted. They maintained that the obligations of the Mosaic law were binding only on the Jewish converts. The doctrine of Cerinthus, a Jew of Antioch, partook of the errors of both the Ebionites and the Nazarenes. With the first, he maintained the indispensable obligation of all to submit to the law of Moses; with the second, he agreed that Jesus Christ was God, but only since His baptism by John in the waters of the Jordan. Up to that time He was nothing more than man, born, according to the Ebionites, of Joseph and Mary. At the moment of the Passion, the Christ, the Son of God, returned to His father; the man alone had suffered, died, and risen again. Pagan philosophy also sought to mingle itself with the verities of faith, to deprive them of their character of divine revelation. The Docetes, from the Greek word Δοκέω, *to appear*, destroyed the humanity of Jesus Christ in pretending that He had never had more than the appearance of a body, and that all His life had been a sort of mysterious illusion, deceiving men by the phantom of a body. Menander, also, a disciple of Simon Magus, undertook to ally the doctrine of the Gospel with the Platonic system on the formation of the

world. He taught that God, the supreme intelligence, had given being to a multitude of inferior genii, who had moulded the world and the human race. In his system, Jesus Christ is not God, but merely an envoy of the good genii. This idea was developed at a later period by the Gnostics, in their genealogies of Eons.* By the side of these teachers of impiety, Catholic writers consoled the Church by their zeal and talents. The Pastor, by Hermas, appeared about this time. Under the allegory of the sheep which the shepherd guides to more abundant pastures, the author describes the interior life of grace and holiness of the primitive Christians. St. John, at the age of more than ninety years, wrote his Gospel to refute Ebion and Cerinthus, in their attack upon the divinity of Jesus Christ and the reality of his human nature. His three epistles are equally intended to combat these heretics.

19. The second persecution burst forth suddenly in the midst of these pacific contests. Under the reign of Domitian, virtue had become an unpardonable crime—for this reason the Christians were entitled to the hatred of the tyrant. In the year 95, an imperial edict was sent into all the provinces, commanding the faithful to be treated as declared enemies of the state. The first victim at Rome was Flavius Clemens, first cousin to the emperor, and his colleague in the consulate. He had scarcely time to resign the fasces, the ensigns of his dignity, when, by order of Domitian, he was led to execution. Flavia Domitilla, his wife, was exiled for the same crime as her husband. Another Flavia Domitilla, mother of Flavius Clemens, was banished to the Isle of Pontia. She is honored as a martyr, with Saints Nereus and Achilleus, her eunuchs. St. John was then at Rome. He was plunged, near the Latin gate, into a caldron of boiling oil, from which, by the power of God, he escaped without the least injury. Domitian exiled him to the Island of Patmos, where he wrote the Apocalypse, according to a vision, in which the Saviour revealed the future

* This Greek term means spiritual beings intermediate between man and God—A. B.

to him under mysterious symbols. St. Andrew was martyred in Achaia. He suffered on a cross in the form of X, which, since then, bears the name of St. Andrew. The death of Domitian, A. D. 96, and the accession of Nerva to the throne, restored peace to the Church, and St. John to liberty. The Saint returned to Ephesus, where he continued to preside over the Christians of Asia. We may refer to this epoch the touching history, recounted by Clement of Alexandria, of a young man, who, on his departure for Rome, had been left by St. John in the care of a bishop of Asia, to be brought up and instructed in religion. On his return from Patmos, the Apostle heard that he had abandoned his faith and joined a band of malefactors. St. John, despite his extreme age, was conveyed to the mountain where the robbers had their cave. He pressed the miserable youth to his bosom, kissed his bloody hand, assured him of pardon, if he would only repent; and having brought about his reconciliation with the Church, with God and man, he conducted him back to Ephesus. The holy Apostle, careful to preserve the deposit of faith in its utmost purity, deposed a priest who was convicted of having published an apocryphal work on the Acts of St. Paul. Sentiments of the most tender charity overflowed his soul. "Love one another," he often said to his disciples; "this precept contains all the law." His whole life was an exemplification of this heavenly principle drawn from the heart of his divine Master. He died, in extreme old age, A. D. 100, the only one of the Apostles who did not suffer martyrdom.

St. Peter and St. Paul had poured out their blood for Jesus Christ; St. James the Less, at Jerusalem, had been killed in a popular tumult; St. Bartholomew had been flayed alive in Armenia; St. Thomas had suffered martyrdom in India; St. Matthew, in Persia; St. Andrew, in Achaia; St. Jude, in Mesopotamia; St. Simon, in Lybia; St. Philip, in Phrygia; St. James the Greater was put to death by Herod Agrippa at Jerusalem; St. Matthias was martyred in Colchis. Thus, all the Apostles, save one, only laid the foundation of the Church in their own blood. Pope St. Clement I., spared in the persecution by Domitian, was exiled in the year of the accession of Trajan to the empire (A. D. 100). The Church honors him as a martyr, but history has not preserved the details of his death.

CHAPTER III.

1. Importance of studying the first century.—2. Teaching of the Church. Its authority.—3. Its simplicity.—4. Miracles. Confirmation of the doctrine relating to them.—5. Tradition.—6. Holy Scriptures. New Testament.—7. The Gospels.—8. The emblems of the four Evangelists.—9. The Acts of the Apostles.—10. Epistles of St. Paul.—11. Epistles of St. James, St. Peter, St. John, and St. Jude.—12. The Apocalypse.—13. Principal points of doctrine contained in the New Testament.—14. Government of the Church. Authority of the Apostolic See.—15. Episcopacy.—16. Priesthood, Deaconship, Religious Orders, Celibacy of the Clergy, Deaconesses.—17. Discipline.—18. Worship.—19. Conclusion.

1. THE first century presents a view of institutions in their germ, which, at a later period, were developed in the bosom of the Church. Unlike human society, the Church was not left to be perfected by time. Her constitution, established by God, contained, in its origin, the same elements which the course of history has developed in all their fulness, by exhibiting their influence on mankind. The study of this century is, therefore, of the highest importance; because all the dogmas which heresy has attacked, as well as most of the institutions which, through error, have been calumniated or rejected, find a signal confirmation in the Apostolic teachings and traditions.

For the sake of method, we shall treat this subject under four principal heads: the doctrine of the Church, her government, her discipline, and her worship.

§ I. DOCTRINE OF THE CHURCH.

2. The first point to be observed in the Apostolic teaching is the authority, as witnesses, of the disciples who were in-

structed by the Saviour Himself, and who alone form the link between the Divine Word and the faith of succeeding ages.

3. From this principle of authority arose the simplicity which marked their doctrine. They expounded the faith in the face of Judaism and of pagan philosophy, without the resources of eloquence or any of the artifices of human language, with a force of conviction derived from well-known, recent, and incontestable facts. But this divine simplicity cannot be attributed, solely, to the character of the Apostles, illiterate as they were. It entered into the designs of Providence to proportion the evangelical teaching to the intelligence of the poor and the lowly, by whom Christianity began her conquests in the world: so that it is no slight proof of the divinity of the Church, to find that the simplicity of her Apostles, which, humanly speaking, would have been the first and greatest obstacle to her progress, was, on the contrary, the most influential cause of her triumphs.

4. The teaching of the Apostles derived also a supernatural force from the wonderful miracles which attested its truth We have seen that the shadow of St. Peter healed the sick His alms were—to the infirm, health; to the deaf, hearing; to the blind, sight. The disciples of Jesus Christ wrought more miracles in proof of His teaching than He had wrought Himself. The power of performing miracles, which God imparted to His Church, and which she has always possessed, was exhibited to a remarkable extent in the first century, in confirmation of a doctrine, so marvellous in itself that it has been said, "That the conversion of the world to Christianity, without the aid of miracles, would have been the most wonderful of all miracles."

5. This doctrine was transmitted by the oral teaching of the Apostles to their disciples, for Jesus Christ did not, like Moses, write His law. The new dispensation was to be engraven on the heart by charity, before being set forth in books.

Besides this, the oral teaching of the Apostles was as much divinely revealed as are the Holy Scriptures. To assert the contrary would be to deny the Apostles a prerogative which all succeeding ages have accorded them. And, in fact, the Church could not have lasted, without some guarantee that the teaching of its founders was infallible. It is therefore a fundamental error to neglect the teaching of tradition, and admit no other authority than that of the Scriptures, in deciding all questions of dogma, morals, discipline, and worship. A great many regulations were prescribed to the early Christians concerning the rising institutions, the external ceremonies which should accompany the celebration of the holy mysteries, and the rites to be observed in the administration of the sacraments, which form no part of the Scriptures.

The Apostles, in obedience to the command of their divine Master, went about the world—not composing treatises like the philosophers, nor disputing like sophists or rhetoricians, but teaching with authority. Souls were drawn to them by the supernatural force of grace. The principal points of faith having been explained to these new converts, they were baptized and admitted to the communion of the body and blood of Jesus Christ. The imposition of hands conferred upon them the gifts of the Holy Ghost, and the Apostles then left them, and went in pursuit of other conquests.

6. But, when the Christians increased greatly in numbers, the Apostles, notwithstanding the activity and fruitfulness of their zeal, were unable to convey orally to all their disciples the teachings of divine truth. Moreover, false doctrines threatened to corrupt the deposit of tradition, and it became necessary to refute them. Jews and Gentiles were equally hostile to the Christian faith, and they must be combated. Hence it was of the highest consequence to fix with certainty, and in writing, the doctrine of Jesus Christ. And the New Testament, the Word of God, inspired by the Holy Spirit, came forth from the consecrated hands of the Evangelists and Apostles.

7. Never before was the human tongue employed to teach truths so sublime; never were truths taught with such simplicity. The Gospel is not only the recital of the wondrous

actions of a God descended among men, it is also a code of laws which has regenerated mankind. Without it, there is neither salvation for individuals nor repose for society. It is a clear and precise revelation of the divine law, infinitely surpassing, in every respect, the highest conceptions of the most celebrated philosophers of antiquity; it is a system of moral precepts so perfect, that no higher idea of virtue can be conceived of than is therein set forth; yet, nevertheless, so adapted to all the wants of mankind, that this sublime virtue has become popular among the disciples of the Gospel. To the teachings of this divine book alone can be attributed the heroic sanctity of thousands of virgins, confessors, and martyrs, of every age and condition, at all times, in all countries of the world. We find in it, not the ordinary forms of human reasoning, nor the scientific methods of the moralists and orators,—but each of its words is like an immediate revelation from the Divinity. We feel at every page that the most exalted authority, the most merciful omnipotence condescends to come down to the level of the intellect and heart of man.

8. The early Fathers, followed by all the doctors of the Church, have compared the four Evangelists to the four symbolic creatures, who, in the vision of Ezechiel, formed the car of God. The Man is employed as emblematic of St. Matthew, who begins his Gospel with the recital of the human genealogy of Jesus Christ. The Lion is the emblem of St. Mark, who begins with the "voice of one crying in the desert." The Ox, an animal used for sacrifice, is the emblem of St. Luke, whose Gospel commences with the sacrifice of Zachary. Finally, the Eagle, with his lofty flight, his intrepid mien, is the emblem of St. John, whose vigorous wing elevates him above the things of earth, whose eye penetrates even unto the throne of the Divinity!

9. The Acts of the Apostles were written, at Rome, by Saint Luke, two years after St. Peter had made this capital the centre of Catholicity. They contain the history of the first years of the Church, and a narrative of the voyages and

labors of the Apostles, particularly of St. Paul, of whom St. Luke had been, for some time, the companion. They conclude with the arrival of St. Paul at Rome, where, having appealed to Cæsar, he was to be judged.

10. The fourteen Epistles of St. Paul, addressed to the Romans, Corinthians, Hebrews, &c., follow next after the Acts of the Apostles, in the catalogue of the canonical books as arranged by the Church. This arrangement does not imply any supremacy or claim over St. Peter, whose epistles are placed third in order, but is owing to their number, their excellence, and the importance of the subjects they treat of. Their sublimity surpasses all human eloquence and reasoning. They were addressed to persons who had been recently converted from the darkness of paganism to the light of the Gospel, and were intended as spiritual nourishment for children in the faith, as the milk of the word, to be dispensed to the little ones and the weak; yet this has not hindered men of the loftiest genius, from St. Chrysostom to Bossuet, from finding in the teaching of St. Paul an inexhaustible source of fruitful inspiration and of admirable precepts.

11. We have already mentioned the Epistle of St. James, addressed to the whole Catholic Church. It is placed immediately after the epistles of St. Paul in the canonical books of the New Testament. This monument of the holy bishop of Jerusalem is so much the more precious, because it is the only one of the inspired books which expressly mentions the sacrament of Extreme Unction (chap. v. 14). Catholic tradition shows, that the Church has always interpreted this passage in the same manner that she does at present. Heretics have labored, on their side, to alter this clear and precise text of the Apostle. Some have entirely suppressed it; so that it is not found in the Bibles published by some of their societies established to propagate Protestantism. The two Epistles of St. Peter, the three Epistles of St. John, and the Catholic Epistle of St. Jude, complete the series of letters written by the Apostles to the churches they had evangelized. Received with the respect

due to the word of God, read in the assemblies of the faithful before the celebration of the divine mysteries, commented on by the bishops or priests who presided at these assemblies, communicated to various churches, they have been transmitted, as a sacred deposit, to future ages. The severest penalties were enacted against those who should alter the text or change its sense. The solicitude of the primitive Christians for the preservation of the Scriptures, is, for us, a sure guarantee of their integrity. The vigilance with which they condemned all private interpretations confirms the certitude of tradition, which has preserved for us, through the succession of Fathers and doctors, the true spirit of the Gospel, a living and sound intelligence, within the bosom of the Catholic Church.

12. Finally, the Apocalypse of St. John completes the list of the sacred Scriptures. With that eagle glance which penetrates the future, even to the gates of eternity, he closes the sacred volume in a wonderful manner. In the Old Testament, four thousand years of expectation form, so to speak, an immense avenue which ends in Jesus Christ. In the Apocalypse, the world goes onward from Jesus Christ the Redeemer to Jesus Christ the Supreme Judge—the glory of the elect, the terror of the condemned. Between the first and the last coming of our Lord there can be no new dispensation, because there cannot be a second redemption The design of the Apocalypse is to disclose to us, in a special manner, the great work of God, whose justice inflicts terrible chastisements upon the enemies of His Church, and makes her triumph, not only in heaven, where He crowns the martyrs with eternal glory, but even on earth where He establishes her, with all the lustre which had been foretold by the prophets. There are two ways of interpreting this mysterious book. One is general, the plan of which is traced by Saint Augustin, in his great work, *The City of God*. This method of interpretation is to consider, in history, two empires mingled physically, but morally separate. One is the empire of Babylon, which signifies confusion and trouble. the other is that of Jerusalem, which

signifies peace. The former is the world, the latter is the Church, but the Church in her highest character, that is, in the Saints, in the elect: In that, Satan reigns; in this, Jesus Christ: impiety and pride rule in that; in this is the seat of religion and truth: in that there is the joy which shall be changed into eternal woe; in this, the suffering which shall lead to eternal happiness. Wherever we find the world vanquished, or Jesus Christ victorious, there we shall meet with a wise interpretation of this divine prophecy. We may even feel assured, according to the rule laid down by St. Augustin, that we have divined in some degree the intention of the Holy Spirit, who from all eternity has foreseen every meaning which would be given to His Scriptures, and has always approved those which were good, and were edifying to the children of God.* The second manner of interpreting the Apocalypse, is purely historical. It consists in applying the symbols, described by St. John, to particular events. "This book," says St. Dionysius of Alexandria, "contains a wonderful but deeply hidden knowledge, of what happens every day." With the exception of some of those remarkable portions, of which the early Christian tradition has preserved the meaning, such as the application to pagan Rome of the character attributed by St. John to Babylon, interpretations of every kind have been given to the Apocalypse. The Church has passed sentence only upon such of these interpretations as attacked principles of the faith; so that, after the labors of the most erudite commentators, the opinion of St. Jerome is still sustained in all its force: "The Apocalypse," says this great doctor, "is as full of mysteries as of words."

13. The Holy Scriptures, those venerable monuments of the Apostolic age, were, from their origin, received with the respect due to the word of God. We find them quoted in the Pastor of Hermas, in the letters of St. Clement, and in the letter to Diognetus. Heretics endeavored, either to alter the sacred text, or to introduce apocryphal gospels, under the names of

* Bossuet, *Explication de l'Apocalypse*, passim.

the Apostles, such as the "Gospel of the Infancy," the "Proto-Gospel," attributed to St. James, &c. But their efforts to corrupt the Apostolic teaching at its source, have ended only in demonstrating the importance which the Church attached from the beginning to the preservation of the New Testament pure from all foreign admixtures. The sacred books and the writings of the Apostolic Fathers, which have come down to us, do not form a collection of works in which the Christian doctrines are set forth in a didactic manner, but rather their history and morals. The *Discipline of the Secret*, which was so inviolably observed in the face of paganism, or of Judaism, explains sufficiently this reserve of the ecclesiastical authors. From this reserve, or silence, Protestants have sought to draw conclusions adverse to all points of dogma, or discipline, that are not explicitly mentioned by those early writers. Their arguments rest on a capital historic error. They argue, as if religious initiation had been effected in the first century by written instructions; whereas it is the contrary which is true. Oral instruction, or the setting forth of the truth, without any medium but the living voice, was the striking characteristic of Apostolic teaching. Such is the sacred origin of that tradition, or oral transmission of religious truth, which began with the Saviour, and has pursued its course amid persecutions and heresies, always unchangeable, always respected. Tradition completes the written doctrine, the sacred text confirms tradition; we cannot separate one from the other; we cannot shake either of these two columns of the temple without crumbling the whole edifice. "When we hear the Fathers of the eleventh century proclaim the existence of oral tradition and the secret transmission of doctrine as a fundamental and preliminary article; when we find them laying down as a final rule the authority of tradition, in determining matters of Christian faith; when we see all the succeeding Fathers recognizing the force of tradition, and appealing in the last resort to the tradition and authority of the ancient Fathers in determining the teachings of the

Church, it is scarcely possible to conceive the bad faith which has dared to reject it."* If, also, we examine, in detail, the particular points of doctrine set forth here and there in several passages of Holy Writ, and by the writers of the Apostolic age, we shall find, contained in them, nearly the whole of Catholic theology: 1st. The origin and reason of our existence; the root of Christianity in the history of the Hebrew people, who were only the continued promise, the prophecy and figure of it; the mystery of the Redemption, which was a necessary consequence of the dogma of original sin; the Adam of the new law of love, who was to redeem the first Adam—the Adam of the law of fear. 2d. The precise and marked distinction between the law of Christ and the law of Moses; the extension of the kingdom of God over all people; the diffusion, among all nations, of the truth, which, until then, was confined to one privileged people: The Decalogue, or the moral law of the Jews, become the moral code of the universe, while the ceremonial prescriptions, particular rites, and legal observances of Moses ceased to have any obligatory force. 3d. The divine inspiration of the Scriptures recognized and proclaimed. 4th. The establishment of the ecclesiastical hierarchy in its degrees of order and of rank: St. Peter taking the first place in the council of Jerusalem; bishops appointed by the Apostles, and placed at the head of the new churches; and the orders of priests and deacons. 5th. The three fundamental mysteries of Catholic dogma: the Trinity, the Incarnation, the divinity and humanity of Jesus Christ; the redemption or satisfaction made by Jesus Christ; and His Grace, the fruit of that redemption. 6th. The sacraments, channels of grace, the sources of spiritual life and regeneration. 7th. Morality, of which their notion was the same as that which obtains now. We can borrow from the writers of the Apostolic age their own expressions, to exhort to good works, to penitence, fasting, detachment from the world, and prayer. This doctrine of the early Church is

* M. L'Abbé Blanc, Cours d'Histoire Ecclés., passim.

the same that she will continue to teach during all succeeding ages. The necessity of upholding the truth against heretical attacks will lead to the successive development of each particular point of doctrine; but the Popes and councils, in defining each dogma, will accept only the tradition which comes directly from the Apostles.

§ II. Government of the Church.

14. The integrity of doctrine and the purity of tradition required for their preservation the guaranty of a regularly constituted government. The first century of the Church, the Apostolic age, while the first ministers of the good tidings were dispersed throughout the world to preach the name of Jesus Christ, could present, it will readily be conceived, only the elements of a hierarchy, which, at a later period, when the world should become Christian, would be organized in a definite form. But these elements sufficed to establish then the principles which are still in vigor in the government of the Church. The primacy of St. Peter is evident from the facts themselves: he it was who presided at the election of Matthias; he was the first to preach to the Jews; it was he whom St. Paul came to see and to *study*, as Bossuet expresses it; it was he who presided at the Council of Jerusalem, and promulgated its decision; it was he who proclaimed the mystery of the vocation of the Gentiles, which was a scandal in the minds of the Jews; it was he who founded the Patriarchal See of Antioch, which became the first in the East, because St. Peter had his seat there; it was he who came to plant the cross in Rome, the capital of the world, and, since then, the centre of Catholicity; it was he who sent from Rome his disciple St. Mark to establish the Church of Alexandria, which also became a Patriarchal See in memory of St. Peter, who had founded it through his envoy. These marks of honor, these singular prerogatives would be inexplicable, if we did not presuppose the principle of the primacy of the pon-

tificate, legitimately exercised and unanimously recognized in the person of Peter, by the other Apostles.

No personal advantages could be attributed to St. Peter over any of the other Apostles. Was not St. John the disciple whom Jesus loved, to whom in dying He confided His mother? And yet it was not St. John who presided, who opened councils, who promulgated decisions. Was not St. Paul, by the miracle of his conversion, by the grandeur of his eloquence, by the depth and sublimity of his doctrines, more especially pointed out for the veneration of the faithful? And, nevertheless, it is St. Paul who comes to St. Peter to give an account of his apostleship. Even from the fact of the famous discussion between the Apostles, is it not to be supposed that to St. Peter were referred the questions of dogma and discipline which required an authoritative decision? The words of Jesus Christ, "Thou art Peter, and upon this rock I will build my Church," were interpreted in the first century in the same sense which we now give to them. They constituted supremacy in the pontificate and unity in its authority. The primacy of St. Peter existed and was exercised under a paternal form, as was in accordance with the wants of the infant Church.

15. Bishops constitute the second rank of the hierarchy. The election of St. Matthias to the apostleship long served as a model to the Church in the choice of bishops. When the suffrages were found to be balanced between two persons equally worthy of this honor, they recurred to a choice by lot, thus leaving the decision to God alone. Bishops were also elected by assemblies of the clergy and people, and consecrated by other bishops. It is a fact worthy of remark, that nearly all the bishops of the first centuries were inscribed in the catalogue of the saints. The heritage of virtue seemed as if transmitted with the episcopal dignity. The example came from the See of Rome, where, up to A. D. 500, scarcely three or four Popes can be found who are not acknowledged as saints. In the second century, the Emperor Alexander Severus referred to the example of the Christians, to show what strictness should

be observed in the choice of public officers. "The bishop was elected, in the presence of the people, by the bishops of the province, assembled in the cathedral church of the vacant see, to the number of at least two or three; for in those times it was difficult to hold large councils, except in the intervals between persecutions, and occasionally some of the sees remained a long time vacant. The presence of the people was deemed necessary, so that all being persuaded of the merit of the candidate elected, should obey him the more willingly."*
St. Paul made a law against the elevation of neophytes to the episcopal dignity, in order to prevent the government of the Church from being committed to the domination of proud or ambitious men, or the deposit of tradition to the imperfect knowledge of a new Christian. The bishop was, at once, the father and the judge of the Christians in the primitive ages. His decisions terminated the disputes which arose among the faithful. He was charged with the care of the poor, of the widows, and the orphans, and he presided at the distribution of the alms which the early Christians placed at his disposal. These alms are frequently mentioned in the Epistles of St. Paul, under the name of "collections." It was also the duty of bishops to preach; the ministry of the word was, for a long time, almost their exclusive privilege. Early in the fifth century, we see that Valerius, the aged bishop of Hippo, made a glorious exception to this usage, in confiding to St. Augustin, then only a priest, the honor of taking his own place in the pulpit. The election of bishops was, therefore, an event of extreme importance in the various churches. It was always preceded by public fasting and prayers. Usually the election was made during Saturday night or Sunday morning; the consecration followed, of which the principal ceremony has always been the imposition of hands; and this was immediately preceded by the holy Sacrifice of the Mass. We find, in ancient authors, that while performing sacred rites the bishops wore some exterior mark of their dignity. Polycrates, bishop of Ephesus, at the

* Fleury, *Mœurs des Chrétiens.*

close of the second century, writes that the Apostle St. John wore on his head a plate of gold. St. Epiphanius relates the same thing of St. James, the first bishop of Jerusalem. Others make a like observation relative to St. Mark, first bishop of Alexandria. "For the rest, the government of the bishops was a government of charity. The clerics and, above all, the priests formed a sort of permanent council for the bishop. They assisted him in all public functions, as disciples who followed their master; for they were attached to him as the Apostles were to Jesus Christ."* The bishops never failed to preside at the public offices and prayers, to explain the Holy Scriptures, and to offer the Sacrifice of the Mass on Sundays and Holydays.

In the canons of the first centuries, we find a prohibition against the celebration of the holy mysteries by a priest in the church of a bishop, unless the latter be hindered by sickness from fulfilling this august function. The dignity of the bishop was held by the faithful in the highest honor; and St. Polycarp remarks, that they vied with each other in trying to be first to take off his shoes. These testimonials of veneration, of which we find traces in the remotest ages of the Church, are a sufficient reply to the calumnies of that party spirit which presumes to accuse the episcopacy of having usurped, in later times, distinctions and honors unknown to the Apostolic age.

16. Next to the bishops ranked the *presbyteri, seniores*, or priests chosen, as their name indicates, either from among the elders, or the clerics most esteemed for the purity of their morals and their holiness of life. The bishop often selected them in accordance with the requests of the people, or at least with their participation, and always with the counsel of his clergy, and after a careful examination. They were often obliged, in the Apostolic and earlier times of the Church, to constrain those who were to be ordained to accept an honor which their humility induced them sometimes positively to refuse. The priests of each church were almost always chosen

---

* L'Abbé Fleury, *Mœurs des Chrétiens.*

from among those who had been baptized and who had exercised
the duties of clerics during several years. After ordination it
became their duty to reside in their diocese, unless their own
bishop yielded them to another. They received an appointed
stipend, on account of their ministry, and lived by the altar,
fulfilling the counsel of the Apostle. The Church furnished
from her treasury all that was needful for the subsistence of
her clergy, and each of them received, by the week or month,
a portion, in kind or in money. The distribution of these
salaries was usually confided to a deacon, who, we find, as far
back as the second century, was called archdeacon in the
annals of the Roman Church. We have already seen that
deacons were instituted by the Apostles, to aid them in dispensing the alms of the Church. To this function they united
others of a more elevated character, viz., to administer, in default of priests, the Sacrament of the Eucharist to the faithful,
and even to preach the Gospel, as may be observed in the example of St. Stephen, the first of the deacons and martyrs.
The priesthood and the diaconate were, up to the twelfth century, the only orders termed *major* or *holy*. This fact is made
known by a canon of the Council of Benevento, A. D. 1091,
under the presidency of Urban II. "We term," said he, "the
diaconate and the priesthood holy orders." The elevation of
the sub-diaconate to the rank of holy orders is attributed to
Innocent III., at the end of the twelfth century. However
this may be, "it is known," and these are the words of the
Council of Trent, "that from the foundation of the Church the
name and particular functions of the orders of subdeacon, of
acolyth, of exorcist, of reader, and porter, were in use." From
the first century, ecclesiastical celibacy was rigorously exacted
from the two holy orders, the diaconate and priesthood. St.
Epiphanius and St. Jerome, who attest this tradition, leave no
doubt in regard to it. They affirm that the usage of the three
great patriarchates of Rome, Alexandria, and Antioch was, to
ordain none but virgin or continent clerics; and that if they
had been married before their ordination, they ceased from

that moment to live in common with their wives. In the first century we find also the germ of religious orders, who were destined to become afterwards the soul of the Church. There were from that time Christians called to a higher perfection, who voluntarily practised all the exercises of penance, training themselves in piety, after the model of St. Paul, "by chastising their body, and reducing it to servitude." They were called ascetics, that is to say, *exercitants*. They lived in retreat and in continence, and they joined to Christian frugality extraordinary abstinence and fasting. They practised *zerophagy*—eating only dry food—sleeping on the bare earth, and dividing their time between prayer, the study of the Scriptures, and manual labor. "We have seen," says St. Paul, "these men, of whom the world is not worthy, wandering in deserts, in mountains, covered with skins, living in dens, and in caves of the earth." From the first century we find also virginity, that other glory of the Church, practised in the midst of the disorders and immorality of the pagan world. If, in the transformation wrought at once by the Gospel in pagan society, all were not equally exemplary, we must still regard it as an extraordinary miracle of heroism to behold generations of youthful maidens arise, offering to God the sacrifice of all the joys of the world, to bury their lives in retirement, in fasting, watching, and mortification. Such examples had no parallel either in Judaism, where virginity was regarded as an opprobrium, or in paganism, where the most infamous passions had their gods, their priests, and their altars. The Christian virgins of the primitive age led an ascetic life in the bosom of their families, renouncing even the most innocent indulgence in dress or amusements. Silence, retirement, poverty, labor, abstinence, and continual prayer were the objects of their preference; and thus the rising Church was edified by the spectacle of their virtues, and by their meritorious prayers and good works. Another institution, which lasted only during the first ages, had its origin from the Apostles. It is that of *deaconesses*. Widows, the most sensible and experienced, were selected for this honor.

The age for admission was first fixed at sixty years, but afterwards at forty. The deaconesses exercised towards women a part of the functions of deacons. Their charge was to visit all persons of their sex whom poverty, sickness, or other misfortunes rendered fit subjects for the care of the Church. They instructed the catechumens, under the direction of the priests, presented them for baptism, and moulded the newly baptized in the Christian life. In the assemblies they guarded the doors of the women's side, taking care that each was placed according to her rank, and observed silence and modesty. The deaconesses gave an account of all their functions to the bishop, and, by his order, to the priests and deacons. The institution of deaconesses went out of use by degrees. Such is the form under which the first century presents the Catholic hierarchy and the government of the Church.

§ III. Discipline.

17. The regeneration of the moral nature of man, effected by the coming of the Redeemer, was to exhibit itself in the bosom of Christianity by a new life, and by manners unknown to the corruption of ancient society. The picture of the rising Church forms a striking contrast between the virtues inspired by the doctrines of the Gospel and the vices of the pagan world. The first church at Jerusalem was composed of three thousand converts; these converts heard the instructions of the Apostles, prayed together, and in private houses broke bread together. They placed their goods in common, and sold their inheritances to distribute the price among their brethren. Their mode of life, which conformed to the counsels of evangelic perfection, has been depicted by the apologists of the first centuries. "Among us," says Athenagoras, "will be found the ignorant, the poor, laborers, and old women, who cannot perhaps prove, by reasoning, the truth of our doctrine; they do not enter into discussions, but they do good works. Loving our neighbor as ourselves, we

have learned not to strike those who strike us; not to go to law against those who have robbed us; if any one gives us a blow on one cheek, we present the other; if they ask of us our coat, we offer them also our cloak. Allowing for the difference of years, we regard some as our children, others as our brethren and sisters. The most aged we honor as our fathers and mothers. The hope of another life makes us despise the present, even in the midst of lawful pleasures. Marriage with us is a holy vocation, which imparts the grace necessary to bring up our children in the fear of the Lord. We have renounced your bloody spectacles, being persuaded that there is very little difference between looking on murder and committing it. The pagans expose their children to get rid of them; we consider this action as homicide." "We are accused of being factious.* The factiousness of Christians is to be united in the same religion, in the same morals, in the same hope. We conspire to pray to God in common, and to read the Holy Scriptures. If any one of us has sinned, he is deprived of communion, and of taking part in our assemblies of prayer, until he has done penance. Old men, whose wisdom merits this honor, preside in these assemblies. Every one contributes a monthly sum, according to his means and inclination. This treasure serves to feed and bury the poor, to support orphans, shipwrecked sufferers, exiles, and those condemned, for the cause of God, to the mines or to prisons. Every thing is in common among us, except women. Our repasts in common are explained by their name of *agape*, which signifies *charity*." Certainly there must have been a strange blindness in the pagan world not to have been seized with admiration at the view of such noble sentiments and generous actions, in the midst of the general enervation of manners and debasement of character. There was found also a pretext for the disdain which the pagans at first affected for the religion of Jesus Christ, in the choice of the persons from whom it seemed that recruits were taken by preference. According to them, the

* Tertullian, *Apologeticus*.

Christians were nothing more than coarse, ignorant, fanatical sectaries, who would neither give nor discuss the reasons for their worship, and were accustomed to reply, "Do not inquire about it; the wisdom of this life is an evil, and its folly is good."* In the first century, the pagans confounded the religion of Jesus Christ with Judaism, and treated it with equal contempt. But the rapid propagation of the Gospel called the general attention to a doctrine which controlled the most exalted intellects as well as the humblest, and which at the same time invaded every country on the globe. The ruin of Jerusalem, by separating Judaism in so decided a manner from Christianity, no longer permitted them to be confounded with each other. The pagan world, alarmed at the view of its deserted temples, its gods despised, its sacrifices fallen into neglect, its morals, superstitions, and fables so boldly combated, essayed to resuscitate its dying institutions by the sword, and to drown Christianity in a sea of blood. The popular hatred, skilfully directed by the emperors, magistrates, and priests of the false gods, subserved their projects of vengeance, and history presents the unheard of spectacle of three centuries of massacres, of murders, and of judicial tortures, publicly perpetrated against thousands of victims of every age, and rank, and sex, in all parts of the world, without the elevation of a single voice among the spectators to utter, in the face of their murderers, even one cry of indignation!

In the quotations from Athenagoras and Tertullian which we have made, we find the principal features of the discipline practised in the primitive age. We propose to examine them a little more in detail. Baptism was usually administered by immersion. The subject was three times plunged in the water, and each time the minister named one of the Divine persons of the Trinity; but baptism by aspersion was judged sufficient in cases of necessity—as, for example, for sick persons. The people gave the name of *Clinics* to those who had been baptized in this way in their beds. To baptism was united the anoint-

* Origen, Cont. Cels., lib. 1.

ing with oil blessed at the altar. The newly baptized were presented to the bishop, and, by the imposition of hands, they received the Holy Ghost, or the Sacrament of Confirmation. They were given honey to eat, to mark their entrance into the true land of promise, and their spiritual infancy. During the first week, the neophytes wore a white robe which they had received on rising from the holy laver of water, as a type of the innocence which they ought to preserve. Adults did not always change their names—as we find in the 1st century many saints whose names were derived from false gods, as Dionysius, Demetrius, &c. The custom of changing the name, to take that of a martyr or confessor, was not introduced until after the Council of Nice. Solemn baptism was conferred only on Easter eve, in order that the neophytes should rise with Jesus Christ, or on the eve of Pentecost, that they might receive the Holy Ghost with the Apostles. The sacrament of the Eucharist was immediately administered to them. None were admitted to baptism but after long and serious trial. Gladiators, comedians, circus-riders, women of bad lives, and diviners, could be baptized only after having renounced their former modes of living, and given marks of a true and sincere conversion. The Christians had for their rallying sign, or as an abridged creed, the sign of the cross, which preceded each of their actions. All their works—their labor, the seed-time, the harvest, and the gathering of fruits—began and ended with prayer. A house newly constructed, or newly inhabited, received a special benediction, and each meal always began with prayer. The study and meditation of the Holy Scriptures was the constant occupation of every Christian family. Many saints of the primitive ages have been found buried with the book of the Gospels on their breast. The austerity of their lives fostered the spirit of prayer in the early Christians. They at first counted as fasting days of obligation only those which preceded Easter, now called Lent. The Church observed them in memory of the passion of Jesus Christ. The fast of Wednesday and Friday was not obligatory, being left to the devotion of the faithful. All these fasts were in different degrees, according to their duration and their rigor. Those of Wednesday and Friday lasted until None—three hours after midday. Those of Lent, much more rigorous, extended to vespers, that is, to sunset, nearly six o'clock in the evening. The reason of fasting until None, was to honor the death of Jesus Christ; to vespers, to honor His burial. The degrees of abstinence were also different: some observed *homophagy*—abstinence from all cooked food; others *zerophagy*, which consisted in partaking only of dry fruits, such as nuts, almonds, and things of that kind; others contented themselves with bread and water. The *agape*, or repast of Christians in common, had been instituted in memory of the supper, when Jesus Christ gave His body and blood as food and drink to His Apostles. Each contributed his part towards furnishing it. St. Paul specifies certain abuses which were introduced into these assemblies. In their origin, the *agape* were preceded by the breaking of bread, or the reception of the Eucharist; but as early as the end of the first century, from respect to this august mystery, the custom had already prevailed in many churches, to administer it only in the morning, and to those who were fasting. The frequent persecutions had given rise to a peculiar custom. Each Christian conveyed occasionally to his dwelling the eucharistic species, to communicate himself, in case of necessity.

Much has been said in these latter times of the community of goods, which seems to be indicated by the passage in the Acts of the Apostles: "*The Christians sold their property, and brought the price, and laid it at the feet of the Apostles.*" Recent systems, which, under the modern name of Socialism, seek to renew in the public mind the Utopias of the ancient spoliators, have striven to place themselves under the patronage of the primitive Church, and to have it believed that their principles were the principles of the Gospel. There is in this a double error of fact and of right, which needs only to be noted. In fact, the placing of the goods of the faithful in a common fund, never was, even in the first century, a general measure. The widow Tabitha, whose liberality is praised in the Acts of the Apostles, had reserved to herself the administration of her fortune. St. Paul said to the rich, who complained of the simplicity of the *agape*, that they were at liberty to provide better things in their own houses As to the point of law, the community of goods was not obligatory upon the early Christians; it only afforded to some an occasion to practise in a special manner evangelic perfection. Thus, when Ananias and Sapphira brought to the Chief of the Apostles only a part of their possessions, St. Peter said to them: You were free to keep all your fortune in your own hands; but because you have intended to deceive the Lord, behold, His hand will fall heavily on you. To extend to all Christians of the present day the community of goods, would be the same error as to declare as obligatory and universal the vows of poverty, obedience, and chastity, which members of religious communities impose on themselves. From the first century public penance for great faults was introduced into the Church. The various degrees of this penance were successively regulated by the canons.

§ IV. Worship.

18. Public prayers occupied much time in the life of the early Christians. Each congregation assembled on Sunday,* which the pagans named the *day of the sun*, and which, immediately after the resurrection of our Lord and Saviour, was substituted by the Apostles for the Saturday of the Jews. The place of meeting was at first one of those dining-halls which the Latins called cœnacles, and which were in the upper part of the house. Such was the hall from which the young Eutychius fell, whom St. Paul restored to life. Later, the persecutions obliged them to retreat into the crypts, or subterranean caverns formed by quarries out of the city. Such were the catacombs, which still exist in Rome, and which are so well

* Called *Dies Dominica*, or the Lord's day.—A. B.

described in the magnificent works on the Catacombs. The great object of these assemblies was the celebration of the sacrifice, to which the different names were given, of the *Lord's Supper*, the *Breaking of Bread*, the *Oblation*, the *Collect* (collecta—assembly), *Eucharist* (act of thanksgiving), the *Liturgy* (public office). There was but one daily sacrifice in each church; it was offered by the bishop, assisted by his priests. The celebration could be made by priests only in the absence or illness of the bishop. The order of the Liturgy has changed, according to times and places; certain ceremonies have been added or retrenched; but the essentials have always remained intact. From the earliest times, as we learn from their writers, after the prayers they read certain passages, first from the Old Testament, afterwards from the New. The reading of the Gospel was followed by a discourse upon it from the bishop, who added exhortations suited to the wants of his flock. This first part of the sacrifice was the only one at which the catechumens, who were being instructed in the faith, but were not yet baptized, had a right to be present. After they had withdrawn, the gifts were offered, viz., bread and wine mixed with water, which were to become the elements of the sacrifice. The people then gave to each other the kiss of peace—the men to men, the women to women—as a sign of perfect union. The action of the sacrifice now commenced; the words of consecration were pronounced over the sacred species; the Lord's Prayer was recited; the celebrant received the Holy Communion, and caused it to be distributed by the deacons to all present.* Regularly, all who came within the Church communicated: even children received the sacrament of the altar. The Communion was distributed under both species. The agape, which followed the celebration of the holy mysteries, was an ordinary repast, composed of offerings from each of the Christians. All the ministers of the altar had a right to a special portion of it.

---

* The celebrant distributed only the Eucharistic wine through the deacons.—Note of the Commission for the Examination of Books, appointed by the Archbishop of Avignon to give an account of this History of the Church.

This fact explains the origin of the distributions in kind, of which the custom was maintained, even in France, until the Revolution of 1793. Several chapters still retain traces of it. Besides the celebration of the holy mysteries, the Christians assembled for public prayers at different hours, both morning and evening. The recitation or chanting of the Psalms occupied the greatest part in these offices. Matins seem to have succeeded to the morning sacrifice of the ancient law. Vespers took the place of the evening sacrifice, and they were instituted to sanctify the beginning of the night. They were sometimes called *lucernarium*—the prayer of lamps—because it was the hour when they were lighted. The prayers of tierce, sext, and none, passed also into the use of the Christians, who adopted them from the Jews. We find traces of them in the Acts of the Apostles, and in authors of the first centuries. The use of varied chants, kneeling and prostration during prayer, lighted lamps, incense, holy water, all belong to the Apostolic age, in which we also find all the elements of public worship as it is regulated at the present day. Whatever regarded the Liturgy was then carefully veiled in mystery; and it is important to establish this fact, since it explains the silence of the writers of those ages on a multitude of questions and details. The fear of exposing the evangelical doctrine and the sacraments to the profanation and railleries of the infidels, caused them to be enveloped in inviolable secrecy. Not only did the priests never celebrate the mysteries in the presence of a pagan, even of a catechumen, but they regarded it a crime to mention to them what passed there, or even to pronounce the solemn words in their presence, or speak of the nature of the sacrament. In their writings or public discourses, if the mysteries were alluded to, only obscure or enigmatic expressions were employed. Thus, in the New Testament, to *break bread* signifies to consecrate and distribute the Eucharist; but the pagans could not understand it. This law of silence gave occasion for the most absurd calumnies against the Christians. The apologists then spoke, and the necessity of defending the Church from the accusations of her enemies overcame the less important rule of secrecy.*

19. It has been shown, that the first age of the Church presents to the view of the observer a doctrine, a hierarchy, a discipline, and a worship, regularly constituted and solemnly recognized. At the moment when the Church, founded by Jesus Christ, took her place in pagan society, and announced publicly her intention to overcome the world, she united all the elements of strength and unity which could secure her duration. Scarcely come forth from the hand of the Man-God, she bore within her, in her constitution and laws, the character of her divinity. We shall behold her in the coming ages, with an unbounded expansion, extend her power throughout the world, speak the language of every people, and bend all to her yoke; her discipline will be modified according to the wants of her new children; her worship will display the most solemn and majestic pomp; her government will enlarge its resources and multiply its means in proportion to the increase of her empire; her doctrine, attacked by heresy, will be vindicated, and all questions will be successively defined, by her Sovereign Pontiffs and her councils; but this development, in time or space, will lead to no new dogma, no rule, no measure, no law, which does not find its warrant in the time of the Apostles, from whom it is derived through a legitimate and uninterrupted tradition. Men pass away; empires, forms of government, institutions, human laws fall, one after the other, each paying their tribute to the decay which awaits every work of man: the Church alone remains to-day as she was yesterday, and such as she will be at the consummation of ages, having sustained from time, the great spoiler of all human institutions, neither radical change nor tarnish, because she has within herself the truth, which naught can modify nor change—*Justificata in semetipsa.*

---

* This important point of discipline, which throws so much light on many things connected with the usages of the early Church, was called the Disciplina Arcani.—A. B.

CHAPTER IV.

§ I. PONTIFICATE OF ST. EVARISTUS (A. D. 100-109). 1. Character of the third general persecution under Trajan.—2. Letter of Pliny the Younger to Trajan.—3. Reply of Trajan.—4. Arrius Antoninus.—5. Martyrdom of St. Simeon, bishop of Jerusalem.—6. Sect of Thebutis.—7. Unity of government a guarantee of purity of faith.—8. Journey of St. Ignatius to Rome. —9. His martyrdom.—10. Martyrdom of St. Evaristus. § II. PONTIFICATE OF ST. ALEXANDER I. (A. D. 109-119). 11. Regulations of St. Alexander I. 12. Martyrdom of St. Onesimus, bishop of Ephesus—of St. Timothy— of St. Titus, &c.—13. Epistle of Polycarp to the Philippians.—14. Papias, bishop of Hierapolis.—15. Works of St. Dionysius the Areopagite.— 16. Therapeutæ.—17. Revolt of the Jews.—18. Death of the Emperor Trajan.—19. Character of the Emperor Adrian.—20. Martyrdom of Pope Alexander I. § III. PONTIFICATE OF ST. SIXTUS I. (A. D. 119-128). 21. Gnostics.—22. Martyrdom of St. Symphorosa, and her sons.—23. Martyrdom of SS. Sabina, Serapia, Zoe, &c.—24. Martyrdom of Pope St. Sixtus I.

§ I. PONTIFICATE OF ST. EVARISTUS (A. D. 100-109).

1. THE second century opens with the third general persecution under Trajan. The persecution of the Christians by this prince presents several points which distinguish it from the cruelties of Nero and of Domitian. The rapid propagation of the Gospel had already made the Church powerful, as well by the number as by the union and devotedness of its members. Roman policy began to be alarmed at the progress of a religion which threatened to leave neither purchasers for the victims, nor adorers for their false gods. The emperors had accustomed the people to an idolatrous worship, the ceremonies of which excited the ridicule of their own ministers. The Cæsars thought in sustaining polytheism to support their authority—to strengthen their power—to save

the empire. There was no want of legal enactments to repress a new religion which they deemed seditious. One of the most ancient ordinances of Roman legislation prohibited the recognition of any god, without the approbation of the senate; and Trajan, although he was resolved to oppose the progress of the Church, published no sanguinary edict, but interdicted associations and nocturnal assemblies in the provinces. The persecution was merely a political affair; the Christians were accused of no crime; their innocence was not denied; still less did the judges institute rigorous inquests respecting the character, the doctrines, or the aims of the religion of Jesus Christ. It sufficed that this religion was new, that it opposed the established worship, that the senate had not sanctioned it, to make it the duty of the magistrates to sentence its disciples to death; and they were applauded "for preserving the multitude from a superstition, whose confessors obliged themselves by an oath to avoid any crime."

2. Pliny the Younger, governor of Bithynia, the friend of Trajan, wrote to him: "I have examined the conduct of the Christians for myself. They are accustomed to assemble on a certain day before sunrise, and to sing together hymns in honor of Christ, whom they revere as a God. They oblige themselves by an oath to avoid all crimes—to commit neither fraud, nor adultery, nor robbery; never to break their word nor violate a trust. They then retire, and reassemble to partake together of *an ordinary and innocent repast.*"* These last words evidently refute the popular prejudice which accused the Christians of immolating, in their assemblies, an infant, which they divided among themselves and devoured; an absurd interpretation of the dogma of the Eucharist.

"By this proscription of the Christians," adds Pliny, "a multitude of persons of every age, sex, and condition, are placed in peril, for this superstitious contagion has gained not only the cities, but the towns and rural districts. The temples of the gods are abandoned, the solemn sacrifices have long

* Plin., Lib. x. Epist. 97.

been interrupted, and none purchase the victims. I have hesitated not a little, to decide whether there ought not to be some difference allowed in cases like these, with respect to age or rank ; whether tender infants ought not to be otherwise dealt with than adults; whether the penitent should not be pardoned; or whether it be not sufficient that they renounce Christianity, if they have once professed it; finally, whether they are to be punished for the name only, without any other crime, or for other crimes attached to the name."

3. The emperor replied by an unheard of rule—"not to search for the Christians, but to punish them if they persevered in their profession of faith when they had been denounced and convicted. *Conquirendi non sunt: si deferantur et arguantur puniendi sunt.*" "It was," said Tertullian, "a strange decree, which, in forbidding the Christians to be searched for, implicitly recognizes their innocence, and which nevertheless ordains their punishment as criminals, upon a simple denunciation." Such, in regard to the Christians, was the Roman policy, caring little for virtue or truth, but fully alive to providing for the interest of the moment.

4. The proconsuls, sent into the different provinces of the empire, met everywhere Christians who, it was made to appear, were enemies of the law. While Pliny governed Pontus and Bithynia, Arrius Antoninus persecuted the faith in proconsular Asia. In his passage through a city of his government, all the Christians presented themselves at once before his tribunal. Alarmed at their multitude, he sent only a limited number to execution, and said to the others : "Wretches that you are, if you are so determined to die, can you not find precipices or cords ?"

5. About the same time, Atticus, governor of Syria, ordered the arrest of the holy Simeon, bishop of Jerusalem, first cousin of our Lord, and then a hundred and twenty years old. He was tortured during several days, and he endured his sufferings with such constancy as to astonish even the proconsul, who did not expect so much strength in a man of his age. Finally, he was

fastened to a cross, and thus closed his glorious career—having governed for forty years the Church of Jerusalem, which he had the happiness to preserve from any invasion of heresies or sects, during his whole pontificate. But when all the disciples who had seen the Lord with their own eyes had passed from earth, error began its work in the Church with more success.

6. The death of Simeon having left the See of Jerusalem vacant, a schism arose, where hitherto all had been peace. Thebutis, a converted Jew, aspired to the honor of succeeding the holy bishop. The Christians made choice of Justus, whose doctrines and morals inspired greater confidence; and Thebutis, in revenge, set himself at the head of a new heresy. He taught, with the other sectaries educated in Judaism, the necessity of the works of the Mosaic law for salvation, and that baptism and the other sacraments were insufficient for spiritual regeneration.

7. The principle of unity in government established in the Church by Jesus Christ Himself, as a safeguard of her doctrine, had been misunderstood by certain Christians of Philadelphia. The illustrious bishop of Antioch, St. Ignatius, surnamed Theophorus, happened to pass by this place. While he was in the midst of the faithful, who had assembled to hear this heir of the apostolic traditions, who was the most celebrated bishop of the East, he suddenly exclaimed, inspired by the Spirit of God, who revealed to him the secrets of men's hearts: "Stand fast by your bishop, your priests, and deacons; be immovable in unity and subordination." At these unexpected words, the culprits supposed that he had been informed of their tendencies by the bishop of Philadelphia; but he called God to witness that no human voice had mentioned them to him, but the Holy Spirit had inspired him to say: "Do nothing without the bishop, love unity, and fly dissensions." His exhortations re-established calm among the Christians of Philadelphia. This was, in some sort, the testament of the holy bishop to the churches of Asia.

8. A short time afterwards, Trajan came to Antioch, on his

return from an expedition against the Parthians. St. Ignatius was summoned before his tribunal. "Who art thou, malignant devil?" demanded the emperor. "No one has ever so named Theophorus,"* he replied. "And who is Theophorus?" "He who bears Christ in his heart." "Dost thou not believe that we also bear in our hearts the gods who have aided us to vanquish our enemies?" "There is but one God, who created the world; there is but one Jesus Christ, His only Son," returned St. Ignatius. "What!" said the emperor, "that Jesus Christ whom Pontius Pilate nailed to the cross?"

After this interrogatory, Trajan pronounced his sentence. "We ordain that Ignatius, who boasts that he carries the Crucified in his heart, shall be chained and taken to Rome, to be exposed to the beasts of the amphitheatre during the public festivals."

9. Was it the intention of the emperor, by transporting the holy bishop to meet his death at Rome, to remove from the Christian population in Asia the contagious spectacle of his constancy, so that the blood he was about to shed might not become the fruitful seed of new martyrs? Did he hope, in exposing Christian bishops to the outrages of the people in the capital of the world, by showing them mixed up with the vilest criminals and barbarian captives, to extinguish their religion by public contempt? Or did he perhaps rely on the long and wearisome voyage, the weight of his chains, the privations and fatigues of captivity, to triumph over the strength and patience of an infirm old man? However this may be, the event falsified all his calculations. Never had the sanctity of Ignatius attracted such homage as in his fetters—never was his eloquence so far-reaching, so brilliant. His voyage was a continued triumph. Arrived at Smyrna, St. Polycarp, the bishop, came to kiss his chains. He received three deputations from the churches of Ephesus, Magnesia, and Tralles, and sent to each of them epistles which breathe the true charity of the Apostles. Above all, he feared that the faithful, through their prayers, might obtain from God the

* Theophorus, from two Greek words, means literally God-bearing.—A. B.

delay of his martyrdom, or that, by human means, they might obtain his pardon of the emperor. He addressed to the Church, "which *presides* at Rome in charity," touching supplications on this point. From Smyrna he was taken to Troas, and embarked for Macedonia, which he traversed, and, taking ship at Epidamnus (Durazzo), passed down the Adriatic gulf, and by the straits of Sicily entered the sea of Tuscany. He hastened to reach Rome before the close of the festivals, that he might soon consummate his martyrdom. The soldiers who guarded him, revering his sanctity, were grieved at their approaching separation from the holy man. Finally they landed. The faithful came to meet him with mingled joy and sadness; happy to embrace the saintly bishop, afflicted at his approaching death. Some flattered themselves with the hope of gaining the people to his cause, and perhaps of procuring his pardon. St. Ignatius, enlightened by the Holy Spirit, was aware of their thoughts, and besought them to love him with a true love, and not to hinder his happiness by delaying his martyrdom. He then knelt on the shore, and prayed with the whole assembly, imploring the Son of God to have mercy on His Church, to put an end to the persecution, and to preserve among Christians the spirit of charity. At length, conducted to the amphitheatre, he was, by the emperor's orders, exposed to the wild beasts. Torn in pieces by two lions, he had the happiness which he had so much desired, to be ground, as he expressed himself, like pure wheat, in order to be admitted to the feast of the Lamb. His martyrdom occurred December 20th, A. D. 107. His acts were recorded by eye-witnesses, and sent to the churches of Asia, so that the remembrance of his death might continue to confirm the faithful whom his eloquence and example had edified during his life. The deacon Philo of Cilicia, and Reus Agathopodus, who had accompanied the holy martyr on this last voyage, piously conveyed to Antioch his larger bones, which the teeth of the lions had spared, as most precious relics.

10. Nearly at the same time, St. Evaristus gave his life

for Jesus Christ, whose representative he had been on earth. During this century, the chair of St. Peter was but a throne for martyrs. Pope Evaristus gave titles to the churches of Rome, and appointed priests for their spiritual government. He ordained that seven deacons should accompany the bishop when he preached, either to sustain the dignity of his ministry or to serve as witnesses of the truth, *propter stylum veritatis.* In the course of his pontificate, from A. D. 96 to 109, he instituted and ordained fifteen bishops.

§ II. PONTIFICATE OF ST. ALEXANDER I. (A. D. 109–119).

11. St. Alexander, by birth a Roman, succeeded Evaristus. In the midst of the persecutions by which the rising Church passed through a baptism of blood, he ordained that the priests should recall the remembrance of the passion of the Saviour before the consecration; a remembrance expressed in the words: "*Qui pridie quam pateretur,*"* &c. He also ordained the mingling of water with wine in the chalice. To repel the attacks of the devil, the most fearful enemy of Christians, he recommended that the dwellings of the faithful should be purified by water mixed with salt, which had received the blessing of a priest. In this solicitude of St. Alexander for the spiritual wants of the Church, we recognize his vigilance to preserve and fix by decrees the Apostolic traditions. These three institutions came, in fact, from the Apostles. The last had particular advantages for the recently converted people. It sanctified a pagan custom, and replaced the lustral waters by a Christian symbol of tears of penitence; and it was a reminder of the waters of baptism, to which the blood of Jesus Christ, as a divine salt, had imparted a regenerative virtue. There have been, from that time, special prayers for the blessing of water. Some of these which the Church has preserved for this ceremony, and which breathe a perfume of holy and ancient simplicity, are, perhaps, the same of which St. Alexander regulated the use in the second century. *Thus,* according to the remark of Baronius,

* Who, the day before he suffered, &c.—A. B.

the pious traditions that came from the Apostles were confirmed, and received a regular sanction from their immediate successors.

12. While Antioch sent her saintly bishop to Rome to receive the crown of martyrdom, the church of Ephesus had the same glory. St. Onesimus, a disciple of St. Paul, was taken, enchained for Jesus Christ, to the capital of the empire, where he was stoned. It seemed that the greatest examples of constancy and of noble sacrifices were to be given in the very centre of paganism; that the prodigious fecundity of Christian blood, on so vast a theatre, might be made still more glorious.

A little earlier, St. Timothy, also the disciple of St. Paul, to whom St. Onesimus had succeeded in the episcopal See of Ephesus, had likewise sealed his faith with his blood. Titus, bishop of Crete, had preceded him in the same glorious end. He was martyred at the age of ninety-four.* St. Antistius, bishop of Dyrrachium, in Macedonia, died, like his divine Master, on the cross. St. Phocas, bishop of Synope, in Pontus, gave also his life for Jesus Christ. The persecution extended to the extremities of the earth, in order to strike everywhere, at once, a religion which, though yet in its infancy, already embraced the whole world. In proportion as the sword of the executioner removed the bishops from their churches, the election from among the clergy and the faithful in union with the See of Rome gave successors to the martyred prelates. Heron succeeded St. Ignatius in the See of Antioch; Zaccheus succeeded the bishop Justus, in the See of Jerusalem; Primus succeeded the bishop Cerdon,† in the See of Alexandria. The other churches, also, had their episcopal succession; and the tyrants, in sending her bishops each day to die, made still more resplendent the immortality of the Church, and the divinity of an institution which had from that time such an abundance of life, that she developed it only the more in proportion as she was persecuted.

13. St. Polycarp, bishop of Smyrna, a disciple of St. John

---

* There is no evidence of his martyrdom. His office in the Roman Breviary is that of Bishop-Confessor.—A. B.

† Cerdon, bishop of Alexandria, was not Cerdon the heretic, who lived in the reign of Antoninus Pius.

the Evangelist, inherited the influence which St. Ignatius had exercised over the churches of Asia. On the occasion of the martyrdom of the bishop of Antioch, his friend, he wrote to the Philippians a celebrated epistle, which, in the times of St. Jerome, was still read in the solemn assemblies of the faithful of Asia. Although it is rather a moral exhortation than a dogmatic treatise, it contains precious evidence on the dogmas of the incarnation, of the atonement of Jesus Christ, of the reality of His human nature and His passion, and on the ecclesiastical hierarchy. In the rules of conduct which he addresses to all conditions of life—to young men, to virgins, to the faithful engaged in marriage, to widows, to deaconesses, to ministers of the altar themselves, and to deacons and priests— he insists particularly on the necessity of prayer, fasting, and other mortifications; and on the fear of the last judgment, on chastity, on subordination, on condescension, and mutual charity. His words, often borrowed from the Holy Scriptures, especially from the New Testament, the Evangelists, the Acts of the Apostles, the Epistles of St. Paul, St. Peter, St. John, superabundantly prove the respect in which at that time the Church held those Apostolic monuments.

14. Nearly at the same time, Papias, the bishop of Hierapolis, in Phrygia, the friend of St. Polycarp, and perhaps, like him, a disciple of St. John, made a collection in writing of the oral traditions concerning the Saviour and His Apostles. He composed five books, entitled *Exposition of the Discourses of the Lord*, of which Eusebius has preserved some fragments. Antiquity has praised the eloquence, zeal, and piety of this holy bishop. He fell, nevertheless, into the error of the Millenarians, attributed before him to Cerinthus. Misled by a false interpretation of this passage of the Apocalypse, *The just shall rise, and shall reign a thousand years with Christ*, he concluded that after the resurrection there would be a reign of the just on earth. Yet he did not people this new Eden with material enjoyments or carnal delights, as Cerinthus had done, who was imbued with the gross ideas of Judaism upon the

reign of the Messiah. Papias, in maintaining this second advent of Jesus Christ, admitted nothing but a spiritual happiness, more worthy of Christian hope. The austerity of his doctrines and his known virtue caused several Fathers to adopt, somewhat later, the error of millenarianism, often called chiliasm, from the Greek word χιλον.

15. Among the contemporary writers of these holy personages, the name of St. Dionysius the Areopagite must not be omitted. Certain critics of the sixteenth and seventeenth centuries have very unwisely endeavored to contest the authenticity of the works which bear his name. This error has been learnedly refuted by the Reverend Fathers Honoré de St. Marie and Natalis Alexander. The books of this doctor which have come down to us are the *Treatise on the Divine Names*, *The Books of the Celestial Hierarchy, of the Ecclesiastical Hierarchy*, a book on *Mystical Theology*, and Letters. Embracing in a sublime trilogy the entire world of the intelligences, "his eagle flight," said St. Thomas Aquinas, "has borne him successively to the heaven of the most Holy Trinity, to the heaven of angelic nature, and to the heaven of human nature." The magnificence of his style is worthy the grandeur of his subjects, yet sometimes there is found an obscurity, which the critics attribute to three causes: 1st, the difficulty of expressing with perfect clearness so abstruse a doctrine; 2d, the peculiar style of St. Dionysius the Areopagite, who wrote in the manner of the Platonists, of whom the moderns have preserved no clear knowledge; 3d, the Discipline of the Secret, which interdicted precise developments or explications, from the fear of exposing the mysteries of our religion to the contempt of the pagans.

16. In the book of the *Ecclesiastical Hierarchy*, he speaks of the faithful who in his time gave themselves up to contemplative life in separation from the world. This passage should be placed beside that of Philo the Jew, a contemporary writer, on the subject of the Therapeutes, or monks of the church of Alexandria. "They construct," said this author, quoted by Eusebius in his ecclesiastical history, "small oratories in re

tired places in the country, to which they give the name *monasterium*. There they pass their life, far from other mortals, in the exercises of piety, and celebrate the august mysteries. The law of God, the oracles of the prophets, and other Scriptures, are the continual subjects of their meditations. The whole day, from dawn till sunset, is consecrated to pious exercises, to singing Psalms and holy canticles. They reproach themselves if they lose, in the care of their bodies, any part of the day, which they reserve entirely for the contemplation of heavenly things. Only after sunset they permit themselves to partake of a frugal and scanty meal. To animate their solitude, they have the writings of the ancients who founded their religion, and from these they take their rule of conduct, and the models whom they ought to imitate." The writings which Philo mentions, adds Eusebius, are nothing else than the Gospels, the Epistles of the Apostles, and some commentaries composed by the doctors of the Apostolic age.

These witnesses of Christian antiquity, which place monastic institutions in the very earliest days of the Church, are not without historic interest. What a spectacle the Christians, newly withdrawn from the errors and corruption of paganism, offered to the world! Whilst the maddest cruelty and the most degrading passions sat in turn on the throne of the Cæsars, and so pervaded the morals of society that they scarcely excited a movement of indignation, the disciples of Jesus, recalling the exiled virtues to the earth, gave the degenerate Romans examples of disinterestedness, of mortification, of contempt of earthly interests, of abstinence, and of virtue, unknown to the best days of the republic; or rather they proved, in the midst of the amphitheatres, in the jaws of the lions, in the flames of the pyre, under the sword of the executioner, that a divine virtue flowed from the very name of Jesus into their hearts.

17. The Jews, after the ruin of Jerusalem, were dispersed abroad, and carried with them everywhere in their exile a hatred of the Roman name. Towards the end of the reign of

Trajan, A. D. 114-117, they revolted at Alexandria, in Egypt, and in Cyrenaica, where they were very numerous. It would be difficult to conceive how this unhappy nation dared to match itself against the forces of the empire, and at the very moment when the victory of Trajan over the Parthians had given new power to the Roman arms, if we did not remember that, always seduced by false prophets, they believed themselves at length called to inaugurate the reign of the Messiah, whom they still expected, and to enter into the realization of these chimerical hopes. This insurrection was marked by unparalleled cruelties. Not satisfied with the murder of the Greeks and Romans among whom they lived, their infuriate rage led them to eat their flesh, to drink their blood, to make girdles of their intestines, and to cover themselves with their skins. Great numbers were cut through the middle of the body, some were exposed to beasts, or forced to kill each other like the vilest gladiators. It was computed that two hundred thousand victims were sacrificed to their fury in Libyan Cyrenaica. Two hundred and forty thousand were massacred in the isle of Cyprus. Trajan sent Martius Turbo against them in Egypt and Libya, who destroyed an immense multitude of the insurgents by the sword. Lucius Quietus made an equal carnage in Mesopotamia. This first sedition was thus stifled in the blood of its authors.

18. Trajan was not destined to see the end of these troubles. Insatiable of triumphs, after having conquered the Parthians, subjugated Armenia and Babylonia, and ravaged a part of Arabia, he laid siege to Afra, a city of the Agarenian Arabs. A check obliged him to retreat, and he went to die at Selinonte, in Cilicia, A. D. 117, at the moment when his recent conquests were escaping from his authority, and throwing off the yoke which he had imposed on them. A wise administrator in peace, a skilful general in war, Trajan merited the love and admiration of the Romans; but he tarnished his glory by the indulgence of shameful passions, and by his cruelties towards the Christians. The persecution which he ordered against the Church placed

him in personal relations with some of the most heroic among her martyrs, most venerable among her bishops and confessors. He did not comprehend that the vitality of the empire was weakened by the loss of those Christians whom he commanded, on a single denunciation, to be thrown to the lions. He was not capable of a sentiment of admiration for the constancy and generous intrepidity of St. Ignatius and the other pontiffs, whom he sent to die for the entertainment of the Roman populace.

19. He bequeathed the purple to Adrian, his adopted son, whom the Empress Plotina charged herself to make acceptable to the senate. The new Cæsar had all the vices opposed to his good qualities. He loved the arts, yet sometimes sentenced artists to death from jealousy; he was eager in the pursuit of knowledge, but descended to the ridiculous superstitions of judicial astrology and magic; he affected a profound respect for the senate, to whom he owed the throne, yet had no scruple in condemning the most virtuous senators to death to gratify a caprice. With these inconsistencies in his character, the diversities of opinion respecting Adrian are readily explained. He changed nothing in the last decisions of Trajan respecting the Christians, who saw themselves still exposed to the hate of the pagans.

20. Pope St. Alexander experienced about this time its effects. He had converted to the faith many of the principal citizens of Rome, among whom was Hermas, prefect of the city. The priests of the idols and the pagan magistrates, irritated by his zeal, condemned him to death, with his two priests, Eventius and Theodulus. They were beheaded May 3d, A. D. 119. In the course of his pontificate he consecrated five bishops. Besides the decrees relative to the Passion of the Saviour, on mingling wine and water in the chalice, and on holy water, he is regarded as the first who, from respect to the Divine Victim, ordered unleavened bread to be used in the holy sacrifice. Of the flourishing condition of the Roman Church at this time, we are enabled to judge from the high eulogium

pronounced by St. Ignatius, in his epistle from Smyrna. He calls it "the well-beloved Church, filled with light, worthy of God, abounding in sanctity, justly blessed, meriting all praise, perfectly governed, presiding in charity, having the deposit of the law of Christ, bearing the name of the Father, united according to the flesh and the spirit, full of the grace of God, without division or any impure alloy."

§ III. PONTIFICATE OF ST. SIXTUS I. (A. D. 119-128).

21. Twenty-five days after the death of St. Alexander I., St. Sixtus I., succeeded him. Under his pontificate the Gnostics developed their erroneous doctrines, and led many of the faithful into their errors. If we would have a true idea of Gnosticism, we must abstract ourselves from the intellectual centre in which we live, and return to the system of pagan theogony which Basilides, Carpocrates, Epiphanius, and Valentinus, who were the principal heads of the Gnostics, strove to adapt to the Christian dogma. This fusion was effected under the influence of the Alexandrian school, which, since the Ptolemies, had become the centre of the philosophic movement during this epoch. Oriental science met in this common arena with the systems of Pythagoras and Plato. Idolatry was purified, and elevated to the eminence of a scientific combination. They left gross forms and fabulous mythology to the superstition of the vulgar, reserving to themselves more exalted knowledge and higher science, which they concealed under this deceptive appearance. This sublime doctrine was decorated with the ostentatious name of *Gnosis*, knowledge *par excellence*. In commencing the study of all philosophy the human mind finds two problems, on the solution of which depend the results of its investigations: viz., the existence of matter, and the existence of evil. Following the materialists, matter is eternal; according to the dualists, the principle of evil has maintained its existence parallel with that of good from all eternity. The pantheists insist that matter is God, and that evil

is only the prejudice of an intelligence too narrow to embrace at once the entire proportions of being; therefore, it does not exist. Gnosticism tries another system, that of *emanation*. Matter was not the immediate work of the Eternal Intelligence: it owes its existence to an inferior demiurge, descended by a series of successive generations from the first principle of all being to the extreme confines of the divinity. The first Gnostics, Saturninus, of Antioch, a disciple of Menander, Basilides, of Alexandria, Carpocrates, and his son Epiphanius, also of Alexandria, dogmatized, in the first thirty years of the reign of Adrian, and gave circulation to the principles of Gnosticism. But it was reserved to Valentinus to give their latest form to these yet fluctuating doctrines. He appeared, only twenty years later, under the pontificates of SS. Pius and Anicetus; but not to intercept the historic narrative, we will here give a succinct analysis of his system. According to Valentinus, the First Cause of Being inhabited an invisible and unexplored abyss, which he designated under the name of Βύθος, *depth*. This eternal principle of life had remained many ages unknown, in silence and repose, accompanied in this mysterious solitude by Ἔννοια, *thought*. They engendered Νοῦς, intelligence, with Ἀλήθεια, truth. The four *Eons* (the name which Valentinus gave to these spiritual principles) formed the sacred Titrada, an imitation of the mysterious Quaternas of Pythagoras. *Intelligence* and *truth* produced λογός, the word, and Ζωή, the life, who in their turn engendered *man*, Ἄνθρωπος, and Ἐκκλησία, the *church*. From these eight superior Eons proceeded, always by Syzygies, twenty-two other generations, completing the whole of the superior world, which he named Pleroma, πλήρωμα, *plenitude*. The last Eons of Pleroma produced, by successive generations, three essences: the *pneumatic*, or spiritual, immutable, and indestructible; the *psychic*, or animal, capable of good and evil; the *hylic*, or material, subject to destruction and death. To these three constitutive elements of the human race corresponded three different classes of men. The first was that of pneumatics, or spirituals; in them all was life, worth, and light: the Gnostics ranged themselves in this category. The second, the psychites, mixed natures, who led an animal life, yet preserved a ray of intelligence. The third, hyliques, or materials, an effete race, who led an earthly and abject life of the senses. The pneumatics only can reascend to the eternal principle in the joy of the Pleroma, as a subtile vapor traverses all the lower strata to resume its place in the higher regions of the air. The psychites, to be lifted up from their lower state, must be redeemed by the Eon Jesus, who was incarnate in the womb of Mary, and who withdrew at the moment of the Passion, so that only the animal Christ suffered. The redemption was not extended to the hyliques, who are devoted to eternal death, through the imperfection of their own substance. This presumptuous classification established the Gnostics in impeccability. Formed of a purer element than other men, their souls, in their own esteem, could never be soiled by corruption. The disorders of the senses, the movements of concupiscence changed not the tranquil peace they enjoyed in a region superior to passions or desires. Such doctrines justified every excess and legitimated every crime. All actions, even the most culpable, became indifferent. All virtues, the grace of the Incarnation, the Redemption, faith, good works, mortifications, even martyrdom, were only so many superstitions, as ridiculous as they were useless. It is not difficult to conceive the attraction which perverse human nature found in these doctrines, and consequently the Gnostics multiplied rapidly in the first two ages of the Church, and strangely compromised the true faithful, who were supposed to hold the same opinions. The accusations of nocturnal and infamous assemblies, of homicidal festivities, of execrable orgies, fell upon Catholics, whom the pagans took neither time nor pains to distinguish from the sectaries; and when the persecution was kindled, the culpable went with incense in their hands to seek their safety at the feet of idols, while the innocent and faithful Christians hastened to martyrdom.

22. These calumnies had excited the popular hatred against the Christians to the highest degree in the first year of the reign of Adrian, A. D. 117. Although this prince had issued no edict against the faithful, the persecution, which towards the end of Trajan's reign had relaxed, now assumed a new degree of fury, and everywhere resounded the tumultuous cry, *Death to the Christians!* which made many martyrs. Among those who then sealed the Catholic faith with their blood, the Church particularly honors St. Symphorosa and her seven sons. This admirable widow lived with her family on the hill of Tibur (Tivoli), near which the Emperor Adrian had just constructed a magnificent palace, which he wished to open by solemn sacrifices in honor of the gods of the empire. Following his superstitious custom, in the midst of the ceremony he interrogated the oracles. Their response, suggested perhaps by the hatred of the priests against the Christians, was that the widow Symphorosa, who lived on the neighboring heights, made them mute by invoking her God, and that she should first be constrained to offer incense to the idols. Led before the prince, the heroic widow thus replied to his demands: "Getulius, my husband, and Amantius, his brother, were tribunes in your armies: they preferred death to apostasy; and if their punishment was disgraceful in the eyes of men, in heaven it has covered them with immortal glory." "Either sacrifice to the all-powerful gods, with thy sons, or I will make thee offer thyself in sacrifice with them." "And whence comes to me the happiness to merit, with my children, to be offered as a holocaust to my God?" "It is not to thy God that I shall sacrifice thee, but to mine." "Your gods cannot receive me in sacrifice. If you order me to be burned for Christ, the fire which consumes me will torment your demons far more than me." "Make your choice; either sacrifice to my gods or die in torments." "It is vain to think of moving my resolution by your threats. My most ardent desire is to rest with my husband, whom you sent to die for the name of Christ." The emperor commanded that she should be conducted to the

temple of Hercules, that her face should be bruised with blows, and that afterwards she should be suspended by her hair. As she continued unshaken in her holy resolution, she was cast into the river, with a heavy stone fastened about her neck. The following day he caused seven stakes to be planted around the temple of Hercules, on which were extended by pullies the seven brothers, who were put to death by various modes of punishment. Crescentius, the eldest, was pierced in the throat by a sword; the second, Julian, was transfixed by many points of iron buried in his breast; Nemesius received a lance in his heart; Primitivus, in the stomach; Justin had his back broken; Stracteus was disembowelled; and Eugene, the youngest, had his body riven from head to foot.

23. About the same time St. Sabina, widow, and St. Serapia, virgin, received the crown of martyrdom in Umbria; and St. Zoe, with her children, in Pamphylia. At Rome, St. Eustachius also, with his wife and children, suffered death for their Lord. He was an illustrious captain of the imperial army; but he preferred to give his life for the King of Heaven rather than, by betraying his conscience and the truth, to pass it in glory and honor. Another soldier, probably a tribune, suffered martyrdom. His memory is preserved in the following inscription, graven on the stone of his sepulchre in the catacombs: "In the time of the Emperor Adrian, Marius, officer of the soldiers, and still young, has lived long enough, for he has given his blood with his life for Jesus Christ. He rests in peace."

24. The Pope St. Sixtus was one of the last victims of the persecution under the reign of Adrian. He died towards the year 128, after governing the Church ten years. According to the *Liber Pontificalis*,* St. Sixtus made a decree which reserved to the ministers alone the power of touching holy things. He added to the Liturgy of the Mass the chant of the *Sanctus*. Finally, he ordained that the bishops who had been called to Rome on business should not be again re-

* Book of the Popes.

ceived in their respective places of jurisdiction without letters from the Holy See, addressed in the form of greeting to their people. These letters were called *formalæ*. In the same manner clerics could travel only with letters of communion from their bishops; the bishops themselves were to bear letters of communion from the Holy See. By these, the hierarchy was constituted in unity of government, under the immutable authority of the pontiffs, successors of St. Peter.

CHAPTER V.

§ I. Pontificate of St. Telesphorus (a. d. 128-138). 1. St. Telesphorus, Pope.—2. Apology of St. Quadratus, and of Aristides.—3. Letter of Serenius Granianus, proconsul of Asia, to the Emperor Adrian.—4. Reply of Adrian.—5. Revolt of the Jews.—6. The Talmud.—7. Version of Aquila.—8. Death of Adrian.—9. Martyrdom of Pope St. Telesphorus. **§ II. Pontificate of St. Hyginus (a. d. 139-142).** 10. Heresy of Cerdon and Marcion.—11. Death of St. Hyginus. **§ III. Pontificate of St. Pius I. (a. d. 142-150).** 12. Persecution continued under the reign of Antoninus.—13. St. Justin the Apologist. His conversion.—14. Exhortation to the Greeks, the first work of St. Justin.—15. First Apology of St. Justin, addressed to the Emperor Antoninus.—16. Decree of the Emperor Antoninus Pius in favor of the Christians.—17. Death of Pope St. Pius I.

§ I. Pontificate of St. Telesphorus (a. d. 128-138).

1. St. Telesphorus succeeded St. Sixtus I. Before his elevation he had led the life of the anchorites, as we learn from the *Liber Pontificalis, ex Anachoreta.* To preside over the Christian assemblies in the catacombs; to ordain priests* and consecrate bishops, to take the place of those who had suffered from the sword of persecution; to confirm in faith and patience the churches shaken by the fury of tyrants; to regulate the order of the sacred ceremonies, and the forms of prayers or hymns that accompanied them; to place the ecclesiastical hierarchy on solid foundations; to watch over the maintenance of the holy doctrines and traditions; finally, to close a life of privations and pious toil by the torments of martyrdom;—such were the glorious privileges of the earliest Roman Pontiffs. 1st. The Apostolic institution of Lent was maintained and confirmed

---

* These ordinations were usually held about Christmas, *mense decembri.* The Church, from the earliest period, observed the practice of reserving fixed epochs for these important ceremonies, which perpetuate the priesthood in the world.

by St. Telesphorus, who ordained a fast of seven weeks before Easter. 2d. The custom of celebrating Mass only at the hour of tierce—nine o'clock in the morning—was also maintained by this pope, who allowed no exception but on the feast of the Nativity, when it was celebrated in the night. 3d. He was the first who introduced into the liturgy the *Gloria in Excelsis*.

2. While Adrian visited the various provinces of his empire, he left behind him, together with shameful monuments of his passions, useful ameliorations, and durable reforms. Athens was especially the object of his care; he did much for its embellishment, and gave it his name—the *City of Adrian*. During one of his visits there, St. Quadratus, whom Eusebius represents as a disciple of the Apostles, a man of brilliant genius and of apostolic zeal, availed himself of the occasion to address to him an apology, or defence, on behalf of the Christians, A. D. 126. This work, the first of its kind, was still extant in the time of St. Jerome, who mentions it with high eulogium. Only a fragment remains to us, on the reality of the miracles of Jesus Christ, as distinguished from the enchantments and transient impressions of magic. "The miracles of the Saviour," said the holy apologist, "were always visible, because they were always true. Those whom He cured, those whom He recalled from death to life, were seen, not only at the moment of their cure, or of their resurrection, but long afterwards; not only during the lifetime of the Saviour, but many years after He had ascended to heaven; some of them, indeed, are still living."

Aristides, a Christian philosopher of Athens, about the same time, presented another apology to Adrian, in which he relies on the testimony of the ancient philosophers to prove the sublimity of the Catholic faith. This work is also lost to us. The emperor, touched by these just representations, seems to have adopted sentiments more favorable to the Christian religion.

3. But that which chiefly contributed to put an end to the persecution was the letter which, nearly at the same time,

Serenius Granianus, proconsul of Asia, addressed to Adrian on the subject of the cruelties practised by the multitude upon the Christians. It was a custom at the public festivals, that the people of Rome, or of the provinces present, should have liberty to ask of the prince or proconsuls any thing which their passions, excited by the bloody spectacle, could suggest. "*The Christians to the lions*" was the cry in every amphitheatre, and without interrogatory, or process of law, or any valid judgment, Christians, by thousands, were cast to the wild beasts. Serenius, in his letter to the emperor, did not hesitate to pronounce upon these proceedings as monstrous iniquities. To sacrifice to the clamor of the populace a multitude of victims of every age and rank, of both sexes, when they were not even accused of any judicial crime, seemed to him a barbarism unworthy of Rome and of Adrian.

4. The reply of the emperor was not addressed to Serenius Granianus, who, in the interval, had probably relinquished the government of Asia, but to his successor, Minucius Fundanus. It is thus recorded by Eusebius: "I have received the letter addressed to me by the illustrious Serenius Granianus, your predecessor. The affair appears to merit serious attention, in order to protect these men (the Christians) from similar vexations, and that pretences may be withdrawn from informers for future calumnies. If the inhabitants of any district have charges to make against the Christians, which they are able in person to sustain before your tribunal, let them have recourse to this judicial mode; but they must not be permitted to pursue them with foolish or tumultuous clamor. Reason demands that if there be any ground of accusation, you should have cognizance of it. If they are convicted of actions contrary to the laws, decide the case according to the gravity of the crime. If, on the contrary, the accusation proves to be calumnious, let the informer suffer merited punishment."

This rescript was sent to other governors of provinces, and the fury of persecution was relaxed, though not entirely extinguished; for, on the one hand, the passions of the populace, and, on the other, the hatred of the proconsuls for the very name of Christian, together with the progressive decline of respect and obedience towards the central authority, continued still to leave multitudes of Christians a prey to the blind passions of the populace, or to judges misguided by their prejudices.

5. The Jews, always conquered, and always rebellious, availed themselves of the absence of the emperor in distant provinces to attempt a new insurrection. They were embittered against the sovereignty of Adrian by a double motive. This prince, who had undertaken to raise all the cities of his vast empire from their ruins, had sent a pagan colony to rebuild and inhabit Jerusalem. He also changed the name of the ancient City of David to that of Ælia Capitolina. The Jews could not endure without indignation the presence of these idolaters, who raised altars to false gods in the very places where the God of Abraham had been so long invoked by their fathers. Another measure, too, had outraged their devoted attachment to the law of Moses. Adrian had prohibited, under pain of death, the circumcision of their infants. This was to take away the seal of their covenant with God—the sacred sign which distinguished them from the pagans. A sullen discontent soon became apparent among them. They assembled in the vast subterranean cavities near their cities, and secretly organized a revolt. A cunning impostor contrived to turn these hostile inclinations to the profit of his own ambition. He was *Barchocebas*, or *the Son of the Star*. He announced himself as the envoy of God, to deliver the Jewish people from the oppression of their enemies. The star of Jacob, predicted by Balaam, was the sign of his advent; he was the Messiah promised by the prophets, and expected by the patriarchs. The rabbi Akiba placed the resources of his science and influence at the service of the false prophet, and Barchocebas was hailed as the Saviour of Jerusalem. He soon found himself at the head of a multitude of partisans, and the first use he made of his power was to persecute with the greatest cruelty the Christians who refused to abjure their faith in Jesus Christ,

and to enter into the league which he formed against the Roman domination. The tortures to which he condemned these victims surpassed in barbarity and cruelty all that pagan rage had hitherto invented. Meanwhile he extended his intrigues throughout the East among the Jews, and sought for the enemies of the empire in all directions. In the neighboring tribes he found a multitude greedy for pillage, ready to swell the number of his troops. The Romans, at first, despised this insurrectionary movement in a nation which they had so often conquered, and its importance was only discovered when the extent of its ramifications became apparent. The governor of Judea, Tinnius Rufus, began by sending to execution a crowd of persons, without distinction of age or sex. This act of cruel severity served only to excite the insurgents to greater fury. Their revolt at once, in every point in Syria, alarmed the governor, who called on the emperor for re-enforcements. Adrian summoned from Great Britain Julius Severus, reputed to be the greatest general of his time, and dispatched him to the aid of Tinnius Rufus. Seeing the numbers of his enemies, Severus avoided a general attack, preferring a slower mode of warfare to the dangers of an uncertain combat. He therefore attacked them separately, to force them into narrower limits, and to cut off their supplies. His skilful manœuvres were completely successful. Within two years he captured, in succession, every fortified place in Judea, and destroyed more than six hundred thousand Jews, without including those who perished by famine, fire, or want. An immense multitude were sold in the markets of Terebinth and Gaza. Such as were not sold in those cities were transported into Egypt. This frightful disaster surpassed those which Nabuchodonosor and Titus had inflicted upon Judea. Barchocebas lost his life at the siege of Bether, where the rebels had fixed the centre of their operations. Jerusalem no longer preserved any traces of her past glories. The stones which had served in the erection of the temple, were now employed to build a theatre. Over one of the gates was placed a marble hog, to the Jews the most impure of animals. A statue of Jupiter was set upon the Holy Sepulchre; and one of Venus was raised upon Calvary. A sacred wood for pagan sacrifices was planted at Bethlehem The consecration to Adonis of the grotto where Jesus was born, profaned this holy place. The dispersed Israelites were prohibited from entering Jerusalem—neither were they allowed to approach it—however strong might be their love of Sion. They were obliged to purchase at a great price the permission, on one day of the year, to bathe with their tears the places upon which, in other times, their religion had shed such splendor. St. Jerome, who, in his time, was a witness of this lugubrious ceremony, says: "After having purchased the blood of the Saviour, they purchase their own tears; they pay a ransom for the privilege of weeping. What a dismal spectacle, on the anniversary of the day when Jerusalem was taken and destroyed by the Romans, to see the approach, in mournful attire, of a multitude of people—of women and men, bending under the weight of years, and covered with rags, whose bearing attests the anger of the Lord, in the exhaustion of their bodies, and in their torn garments!"

This catastrophe was advantageous, however, to the Christian Church in Jerusalem, which hitherto had been governed by bishops converted from Judaism, and was consequently attached to the observances of the Mosaic law. A residence in this city being now permitted only to the Gentiles, the Church was recruited chiefly by her conquests among them. Besides, in the utter dispersion of a people condemned by God, this last tempest gave a new force to the proofs of Christianity, which, according to the prophets, was to succeed Judaism, and rise on its ruins, A. D. 134.

6. Far from confessing their offences in the presence of these terrible judgments of Heaven, the Jewish doctors sought more diligently than ever to blind themselves, and to lead their unhappy compatriots into the same errors. From hatred to Christianity, and in order to weaken the proofs of the divinity of Jesus Christ, which is made so evident in the prophecies,

they began the composition of the *Talmud*, or *doctrine*, an enormous compilation of their oral traditions. This work is divided into two parts; the *Mischna*, or *law*, which is the text, and the *Ghemur*, or *complement*, which is a commentary on the other. The entire collection forms twelve volumes in folio. Among its fables and puerile inventions there is a hatred of the name of Christian, which is not even dissembled. This book is perhaps the greatest obstacle to the conversion of the Jews.

7. At this epoch, a work of another class, but with the same object, was undertaken by an apostate Christian. Aquila, a native of Sinope, in Pontus, was first a pagan. The miracles which he saw performed among the Christians converted him, and he was baptized; but his attachment to astrology, which, in spite of the counsels of the bishops, he refused to abandon, caused his excommunication, and he was excluded from the Church. To avenge this injury, he was circumcised, and openly embraced Judaism. Carrying his hatred still further, he applied himself to the study of the Hebrew tongue; and after acquiring a thorough knowledge of it, he commenced a new Greek version of the Scriptures, to correct that of the Septuagint. He endeavored especially to make it literal, and succeeded so well that even St. Jerome pronounces his translation very exact. But the same Father reproaches him for having designedly weakened the passages which serve to establish the divinity of Jesus Christ.

8. All these desperate efforts to hinder the progressive advancement of the Catholic Church ended by imparting to it new strength. The dispersed Jews carried everywhere the testimony of the victory of Christianity, and the heretics, in yielding to the disorders of an infamous life, condemned themselves; in fine, the emperors achieved the ruin of their own authority by the excesses of every description to which they abandoned themselves. Adrian expired A. D. 138. Towards the close of his life, this prince became melancholy and cruel. He condemned to death his brother-in-law Servienus, and Fuercus, his grand-nephew. He was suspected of poisoning

his wife Sabina, whom he afterwards placed among the divinities of the empire. He complained that he, who at his will had sent so many to execution, could not die himself. Finally he expired, suffocated by an excess in eating, cursing the physicians, and jesting upon his soul. Antoninus Pius, his adopted son, a prince worthy of the surname which his virtues and his gratitude towards his benefactor had gained for him, succeeded to the throne. His fine qualities endeared him to the Romans and made him venerable to strangers, even to the barbarian sovereigns, who chose him more than once for arbiter in their disputes.

9. The same year Pope St. Telesphorus ended his Apostolic career by a glorious martyrdom. He had governed the Church ten years. St. Hyginus, converted from philosophism—*ex philosopho*—was his successor.

§ II. PONTIFICATE OF ST. HYGINUS (A. D. 138–142).

10. At this time Cerdon, a Syrian Gnostic, came to Rome, where Valentinus was preaching his heresy, and Marcion followed soon after. Cerdon had borrowed his fundamental errors from the Gnostics, but he had given them a new form. Though condemned and excommunicated by St. Hyginus, he continued, nevertheless, to spread the poison of his doctrines among the faithful, and openly taught the principles of dualism. According to his system, there are two gods; one who is good and beneficent, the other just and severe; one invisible and unknown, the other visible and apparent; the first, the father of Jesus Christ, the second, creator of the universe; the former, author of grace, the latter, of the law.

Marcion, originally from Sinope, in Pontus, was at first his disciple. The son of a holy man, who in the end was made a bishop, he had received a Christian education, and in his early youth made a profession of ascetic life. But having had the misfortune to yield to an impure passion, his father, who suffered from the disgrace of his ignominy, excommunicated him and drove him from the Church. In spite of his entreaties to be readmitted to the communion of the faithful, the bishop continued inflexible, and Marcion went to Rome. Being of an active and enterprising disposition, he undertook to propagate the doctrines of Cerdon, which he had adopted, and he brought so much ardor and success to his work that he outshone his master. He denied that the Son of God was really incarnate, and that our bodies would rise again; because, he said, it was repugnant to the Son of God to be clothed with the corruption and impiety of matter, and to the soul to have for its companion in glory a body evil in its nature. But his system was particularly remarkable in its moral part. Adopting seriously the warfare which the Gnostics declared against the body, Marcion and his disciples fasted to mortify the flesh; they preached virginity, and had among them austere virgins; they received for baptism only those who lived in continence. From the same principles they exalted martyrdom, and pretended to seek for it. In thus avoiding the impurities of the other Gnostics, Marcion rendered his doctrine more dangerous for weak minds, who had enough of natural probity to avoid those degraded sects. This circumstance explains the rapid progress of the Marcionites in the East and West—a progress attested by St. Justin during the lifetime of this sectary.

11. Again the See of St. Peter was left vacant. St. Hyginus occupied it only four years. It is not known by what kind of torments he obtained the title of martyr. It is believed, from an expression in the *Liber Pontificalis*, that he made a decree relative to the various orders and functions of clerics. In this decree, it has been thought, is discovered the origin of cardinals. If it be meant that St. Hyginus was the first to fix the titles of the suburbicary bishops,[*] which were afterwards given exclusively to cardinals, this remark may have some foundation. The name and dignity of the cardinalate we believe to be of a far more recent date.

St. Pius I. succeeded St. Hyginus.

---

[*] The Bishops occupying Sees in the neighborhood of Rome.

§ III. Pontificate of St. Pius I. (a. d. 142–150).

12. Although mildness and clemency were characteristic of the Emperor Antoninus, the faithful during his reign were not the less a prey to the most cruel persecution. The following inscription in the cemetery of St. Calixtus, to the martyr St. Alexander, furnishes us with a proof of it: "Alexander has ceased to live on earth, only to begin an immortal life in heaven. He closed his career under the Emperor Antoninus, who, beholden to the Christians for great services, returns to them evil for good. For whoever bends the knee to offer homage to the true God is conducted to punishment. Oh, wretched times! when we can avoid the executioner neither in caverns nor even in the midst of sacrifices and prayers! What is more miserable than life? At the same time, what is more miserable than death, when parents and friends are not permitted to render sepulchral honors to the objects of their tenderness?" These touching complaints, mingled with Christian resignation and holy hope, doubtless afforded consolation to the sorrows of the faithful who lost their brethren in the faith in the midst of torments; but they could not reach the throne of the Cæsars. An eloquent voice about this time brought them before it.

13. St. Justin was born at Neapolis,[*] a city of Palestine, of a family of pagan colonists, established there by the Emperor Vespasian. It had pleased God, whose grace brought him to a knowledge of the truth, to endow him with an ardent temperament, eager in the pursuit of science, and with a natural preference for philosophic researches. He yielded to them from his youth with a passionate attachment. Having exhausted the doctrines of the Stoics, the Peripatetics, the Pythagoreans, without allaying the thirst after truth which consumed his soul, he had embraced the Platonic philosophy, the spiritualism of which accorded best with his elevated intellect. One day, while walking alone on the border of the sea which

---
[*] The ancient Sichem.

bathes the shores of his country, in order to abandon himself more quietly to his accustomed meditations, he met with an unknown man, of venerable exterior, who entered into conversation on wisdom, on God and His perfections, and on the destiny of man; and he intimated how much philosophy, even that of the divine Plato, is powerless to enlighten the human mind on these fundamental points. "What guides, then, have we to follow," asked Justin, "if these have been unable to arrive at truth?" "At a remote period," replied the old man, "long before those who are called sages, there were just men, friends of God, who, speaking under the inspiration of the divine Spirit, foretold the events which are now passing in the world. They were termed prophets. They only have known the truth; they only have brought it to mankind. When we read their works with faith, they reveal to the mind the only doctrines worthy of true philosophy. In their discourses they do not confine themselves to syllogistic forms or subtle reasonings; the testimony which they give to truth is superior to all demonstration. Their oracles, which are now fulfilled before our eyes, command our belief in their truth. Add to these the miracles which they performed in the name of the one God, Creator and Father of all things, and in predicting the advent of His Son Jesus Christ. Pray, then, that the gates of light may be opened to your mind, for no one can either see or understand the truth unless God and His Christ prepare his soul for it."

The fruitless study of the vain systems and contradictions of pagan philosophy had left the heart of Justin in agitation and disquietude; these words inspired him with a strong desire to draw from a source hitherto neglected. "I was soon convinced," he adds, in finishing this relation, "that there alone was to be found a philosophy well grounded and useful to men; and it is for this reason that I am now a Christian." This important conquest of the Gospel over the wisdom of paganism was made during the last years of the reign of Adrian, A. D. 132 to 138.

14. Justin retained in his new sphere of life the *pallium*, or mantle of the philosophers. It is believed that he became a member of the Roman clergy. Hitherto the education of youth had remained in the hands of pagan philosophers. St. Justin was the first to open a Catholic school, where he moulded the minds of his pupils in the faith. The celebrated Tatian was one of his disciples. His ardent and efficacious faith manifested itself in eminent works. His first publication, entitled *Exhortation to the Greeks*, was written to dissipate the prejudices of the pagans against Christianity. He proves, with an erudition which is never at fault, that the books of Moses are anterior to all the writings of the pagan philosophers and poets, and that the Mosaic traditions, disfigured by a multitude of accidental and local errors, are to be found in their principal data in the pagan theogonies; and he refers, as an example, to the dogma of the unity of God, the basis of Jewish revelation, which is preserved in the works of the most esteemed pagan authors. From this the enemies of Catholicity, from Julian the Apostate down to the Protestant sects, have taken occasion to accuse St. Justin, and the Fathers of the earliest ages, of Platonism. This charge cannot be sustained. The philosophy of Plato is mingled with so many obscurities, contradictions, and errors, that to extract Catholic truth from it is impossible. Besides, Aristobulus, Josephus, St. Justin, Origen, and Eusebius of Cæsarea, have proved that Plato had knowledge of the Hebrew books, and that he had drawn this part of his doctrine, so little resembling that which belonged to himself, from them. And even if it were possible that a man possessed of a genius which antiquity had denominated divine, had, by help of the scattered traditions surviving in the bosom of humanity, arrived at the attainment of some few of the sublime verities which Christianity has established, far from making it a subject of reproach to the doctors of the Church who avail themselves of the use of testimony so precious, why cannot it be seen that their object was to bring forward the evidence of a new and admirable argument for the faith, since it is

proved that it is conformable to the natural religion of the highest intellects?*

15. This work was only a prelude to the publication by St. Justin of his first Apology, which the persecutions, now more active against the Christians, rendered highly opportune. He addressed it in these terms to the princes who then governed the Roman world : "To the Emperor Titus Ælius Adrianus Antoninus Pius, Cæsar Augustus; to Verissimus, his son, a friend of truth; to Lucius, equally a friend of truth, son of Cæsar, and adopted son of Pius; to the Sacred Senate; and to all the Roman people, on behalf of the men of every condition, who, as Christians, are unjustly hated and persecuted, I, Justin, son of Priscus, grandson of Bacchius, of the colony of Flavia Neapolis, in Syrian Palestine, as one of them, have presented this address."

"Reason," he continues, "makes it a duty in those who are truly pious and philosophic to love truth, and to love it so much as to sacrifice to it the prejudices which they have inherited from their ancestors, and even life itself. Princes, you are denominated pious and philosophic, the guardians of justice and the friends of truth : we shall see if you merit these titles. For although we address to you this appeal, do not imagine that it is intended to flatter you or to ask favors. Our only desire is, that you will order a severe inquest to be made, and if we are found guilty, let us be punished with all the rigor of the law. And be not deceived : if in judging us you listen only with the intention of gratifying superstitious men blinded with passion, or believing idle rumors, your sentence will injure only yourselves. For us, although you cannot convict us of any crime, you may immolate us, but you cannot hurt us."†

This firmness and elevated mode of reasoning are sustained

---

* See, on this subject, the *Études Historiques* of M. de Châteaubriand, Étude deuxième, seconde partie.

† We have taken this elegant analysis from the exordium to the Apology by the skilful pen of M. L'Abbé Blanc. Cours d'Histoire Ecclésiastique, seconde partie, 181, première édition.

throughout the Apology. He is indignant that the simple avowal of being a Christian is sufficient to lead to condemnation, while those who apostatize before the tribunals are absolved with the honors due to innocence and virtue; as if justice did not rigorously demand, first of all, an examination of the conduct of the accused, in order to condemn or absolve him according to his works. "It seems," he adds, with a rare energy of expression, "that you fear lest all the world should become virtuous, and that you will no longer find subjects for punishment: a thought more worthy of executioners than of just and generous princes." He passes on to a simple, clear, and precise exposition of the Christian doctrines. Without pretension, as without timidity, he gives a portrait of their manners. "We have," said he, "among us men who formerly were violent and passionate—but now humble and patient, converted by the exemplary lives of the Christians, or by their integrity in business." In reply to the reproach of rebellion against the princes and the laws of the empire by which the generous constancy of the Christians was dishonored: "We adore one only God, but in all else we obey you with joy, acknowledging you as the emperors and masters of men, and we pray that, with sovereign power, you may also be just." Finally he approaches the most delicate part of his work, that of the accusations which were heaped upon Christians. He was unable to refute them victoriously without violating the *Discipline of the Secret*,* which, as we have stated, was rigorously observed from the first century. Yet it was impossible to recede before a public opinion which the infamies of the Gnostics contributed every day still further to mislead. "It is reasonable," said an historian, "to believe that in this part of his address St. Justin had an understanding with Pope St. Pius I., and that it was by his consent he treated of certain dogmas so explicitly, especially of the Eucharist." He explains the Catholic doctrine on this sacrament, and that of

---

* For a full account of this Discipline of the Secret, a most important feature in early Church History, see Bishop Trevern's excellent Amicable Discussion.—A. B.

Baptism, avoiding, however, the sacramental forms. "We do not," said he, "receive the Eucharist as common bread, nor as an ordinary beverage. But as, by the word of God, Jesus Christ was incarnate and took upon Himself flesh and blood for our salvation, thus the bread and wine, sanctified by the prayer of His Word, becomes the flesh and blood of the same Jesus Christ incarnate, to become our flesh and our blood by its transformation into our food." Here follow details of other circumstances which accompany the principal action of the sacrifice, of which he might speak without impropriety; such as the prayers, exhortations, readings of the lives of the Saints, the kiss of peace, and the collections for the poor.

Having completed this faithful portrait of the usages of Christians, and of their conduct in the religious assemblies, he concludes with the same independence of language and thought which attended his exordium: "Such is our doctrine: if you find it reasonable, respect it—if you see in it only frivolities, despise it; but condemn not, on this account, thousands of innocent persons. We might demand justice of you, in virtue of the letter of the great and illustrious Cæsar, Adrian, your father; but we prefer to rely on the merits of our cause and the justice of this appeal. If you persist in sacrificing the truth to popular fury, do what is in your power. When princes prefer to flatter public opinion rather than to respect the interests of right and justice, they act no better than the brigands in the forests."

16. Did this work, which breathes the dignity and moderation of virtue herself, touch the heart of Antoninus? From the imperial rescript, of which Eusebius has preserved the text, we are permitted to conjecture that it did. The faithful of Asia and Greece, persecuted like those of Rome, also addressed complaints to the emperor upon the vexations of every kind which they suffered from their countrymen. The pagans cast upon the Christians the odium of every public calamity, which they considered as divine vengeance for the outrages perpetrated on the gods by this impious sect. About this

period, A. D. 148–150, many terrible calamities broke out, all at once—a cruel famine, the inundation of the Tiber, and an earthquake, which overwhelmed many cities in Asia and in the isle of Rhodes. The sanguinary cries of the populace against the Christians then resounded with greater fury than ever; and to check the effects of this blind rage, Antoninus found himself obliged to send to the Asiatic cities the following decree in favor of the disciples of Christ :*

"The Emperor Titus Ælius Adrianus Antoninus Augustus Pius, sovereign pontiff, in the fifteenth year of his tribunitial authority, consul for the third time, father of his country, to the people of Asia, health:

"I doubt not that the gods themselves take care to detect the Christians, whatever efforts they may make to conceal themselves. In fact, they have both more interest and more power than you, to punish those who refuse to adore them. But you, who never cease to torment those people, to accuse their doctrines of atheism, and to impute to them crimes for which you can furnish no proofs, beware, lest instead of bringing them to better ways of thinking, you do but render them the more obstinate; for they desire less to live, than to die for their God. As they are always ready to yield up their lives rather than submit to your will, they seem to remain victors in their combats with you. As for the earthquakes, past or present, be advised, and compare your conduct with that of the Christians. When these misfortunes occur, you become entirely discouraged, while the Christians, on the contrary, feel their confidence in their God redoubled. In the midst of public calamities, you seem to have no confidence in the gods, you neglect the sacred worship, you forget the Divinity, and, unable to endure that others should honor him, you become envious, and persecute them to death. Many governors of provinces wrote to my divine father on this sub-

* Tillemont, Pagi, and Orsi, have sufficiently proved that this Edict should be attributed to the Emperor Antoninus, and not to Marcus Aurelius, his successor, as some historians have supposed, after Fleury.

ject, and he replied that the Christians should not be disturbed, unless they were convicted of violating the laws of the empire. A great number of letters have been addressed to ourselves, all demanding instructions relative to the same subject, and our responses have been made conformable to the intentions of our divine father. When hereafter any action is brought against a Christian on account of his religion, let the accused be released, and see that the accuser is punished according to the rigor of the laws."

This ordinance of Antoninus was solemnly promulgated at Ephesus, the seat of the general assemblies of Asia.* Copies were sent to the governors of other cities: Larissa, Thessalonica, Athens, &c., and peace for a short time was granted to the Church.

17. During this interval, Pope St. Pius I. died, A. D. 150. Some martyrologies bestow on him the title of martyr, without informing us of the manner of his death. From the *Liber Pontificalis* we learn that he commanded those who returned to the faith, after renouncing the heresy of the Jews, to be rebaptized.† By this heresy of the Jews is meant the error of the Jewish converts who remained attached to the legal observances, believing them to be obligatory and indispensable for salvation. This decree of St. Pius I. intimates, according to a remark of Baronius, that there existed sects separated from Catholic unity, in which baptism was preserved, so that it was unnecessary to renew it, in the case of a conversion to the Catholic faith; and others, wherein it had been corrupted, especially among the heresies born of Judaism. Such was probably that of the Corinthians. St. Anicetus succeeded St. Pius I. in the government of the Church, A. D. 150.

---

* We find from this epoch a sort of national representation for the various provinces of the Roman empire. The deputies of each town assembled in a city, called *communs*, to deliberate on public affairs.

† Constituit hæreticum venientem ex Judæorum hæresi suscipi et baptizari.

CHAPTER VI.

§ I. Pontificate of St. Anicetus (A. D. 150-161). 1. Different sects of Gnostics: Cainites, Secundians, Ptolemaitans, Ophites, Sethians, Marcosians, Colorbasians, Archontiques, Antitactes, Adamites or Prodicians.—2. Question about Easter.—3. Voyage of St. Polycarp to Rome.—4. Foundation of the churches of Lyons, Vienne, Valence, and Besançon.—5. St. Hegesippus.—6. Dialogue between St. Justin and Tryphon.—7. Death of Pope St. Anicetus and the Emperor Antoninus. § II. Pontificate of St. Soter (A. D. 162-174). 8. Fourth general persecution under the Emperor Marcus Aurelius.—9. Martyrdom of St. Felicitas and her seven sons at Rome.—10. Letter from the Church of Smyrna to the churches of Asia.—11. Martyrdom of St. Polycarp, bishop of Smyrna.—12. Celsus, the philosopher.—13. Controversy between Crescentius the Cynic and St. Justin.—14. Second apology of St. Justin, addressed to the Emperor Marcus Aurelius.—15. Martyrdom of St. Justin and his companions.—16. Miracle of the thundering legion.—17. Illustrious bishops and doctors under the pontificate of St. Soter.—18. St. Dionysius, bishop of Corinth: his letter to the Church of Rome.—19. Heretics. Tatian, chief of the Encratites.—20. Bardesanus.—21. Apelles, disciple of Marcion.—22. Montanus, Priscilla, and Maximilla.—23. Death of Pope St. Soter.

§ I. Pontificate of St. Anicetus (A. D. 150-161).

1. It is the nature of error to be always variable, and to multiply itself under divers forms, but never to re-establish the unity from which it separated, when it departed from the truth. During the pontificate of St. Anicetus, numerous sects, the impure vegetation of Gnosticism, raised their heads, having nothing in common but their hatred and contempt for Catholic dogmas, and for Christians who continued faithful to the doctrines of Jesus Christ and Apostolic instruction. It will be sufficient to give only the names of these absurd systems, the offspring of the Gnosis of Valentinus, and so low in rank that

most of them have not even secured to their authors the pitiable notoriety of heresiarchs.

First, the *Archontiques* (from ἀρχων, prince), who attributed the creation of the world to different rival powers. They rejected the sacraments, and gave themselves up to shameful disorders. The *Adamites*, disciples of an impostor named Grodicus, who would have the world to return to the nakedness of Adam. The *Cainites*, who, by a strange inversion of ideas, had a devotion towards all whom the Scriptures signalized for impiety and crimes.

The *Antitactes*, or *Contraries*, followed the same system. They regarded the Divinity as the evil principle, and maintained, consequently, that virtue is worthy of all chastisements, and vice, of every recompense. The *Ophites* were distinguished by their veneration for the serpent, which they respected as the author of all wisdom, in memory of the serpent that beguiled the first woman in the earthly Paradise.

2. While these absurd fancies divided Gnosticism into as many parties as there were doctors in its circle, the Church continued to organize herself more completely in unity and discipline. The question of the day on which Easter should be celebrated, began to be agitated between the Eastern and Western Churches. In the time of the Apostles, Sunday had been substituted for Saturday for the assemblies of the faithful, yet by complaisance towards the newly converted Jews, there had been a certain toleration for their observance of Saturday. The Apostolic institution naturally led to the transfer of the celebration of Easter from the fourteenth day of the month of Nisan (March—April) to the Sunday which followed it. St. Peter established this usage in the Church of Rome, which ought to be the model of all the other churches, as she is their mistress and mother. But this disciplinary measure was not made general at that time. The memory and the traditions of St. John still lived in the person of his disciple St. Polycarp; the churches of Asia preserved the usages which the beloved Apostle had there introduced: Rome, in her prudence, toler-

ated a divergence which had so respectable a beginning, but prepared in the end to adopt such measures as circumstances might dictate.

3. It was probably with a view of conferring on this subject with Pope St. Anicetus, that the illustrious bishop of Smyrna came to Rome. He was received there with all the demonstrations of esteem and respect due to the merit and eminent sanctity of this illustrious disciple of the Apostles. St. Anicetus and St. Polycarp held a friendly discussion upon the question on which the two churches were divided. The Pope considered it of the highest importance to persuade St. Polycarp to abandon his ancient custom, knowing the powerful effect of his example upon the Asiatic bishops. His predecessors had labored with prudent zeal to remove, by degrees, the Judaic observances introduced into the Church by Jewish converts, and their efforts had been crowned with success. This one point alone remained to be cleared up. But the authority of St. John, and the inviolable attachment which St. Polycarp cherished for his venerated master, overshadowed in his mind all the arguments of this sovereign pontiff. St. Anicetus then regarded it as a duty to leave the matter on its ancient footing, and to tolerate, even in Rome, their accustomed observance by Asiatic visitors to that city. This diversity of opinion in no way weakened the ties of concord. To pay more honor to his guest, St. Anicetus invited him to celebrate the holy mysteries in his presence, in the city of Rome. The Easter controversy was not again renewed, until the pontificate of St. Victor, towards the close of this century. The sojourn of St. Polycarp at Rome was marked by the conversion of a large number of heretics, who were restored to the unity of the faith as much by the power of his example as by the authority of his age, his zeal, and his wisdom. He had conversed familiarly, in his youth, with the Apostles and disciples of the Lord. Imbued with the doctrines of such excellent masters, and full of their spirit, whenever he heard the blasphemies of some innovator he was accustomed to exclaim, with indignation: "For

what times, Lord, hast Thou then reserved me?" In conferring with the Marcionites and Valentinians, whose errors were then the most widely diffused, he protested, in a loud voice, that the doctrine of the Catholic Church was the only one he had learned from the lips of the Apostles. His testimony made a favorable impression upon many of them. Having one day met the heretic Marcion, the latter had the boldness to ask if he recognized him. "Yes," replied St. Polycarp, "I know thee for the first-born of Satan." At length he bade farewell to the sovereign pontiff, and the two saints separated with tender embraces, having given reciprocally the kiss of peace. They were to unite again only in heaven, which both were destined to reach by the path of martyrdom.

4. It is generally believed that the foundation of the church at Lyons may be dated from this epoch. St. Pothinus, disciple of St. Polycarp, went thither to preach the faith, and he established the episcopal see. St. Irenæus succeeded him. SS. Ferreolus, Ferrutius, Felix, Fortunatus, and Achilles, their disciples, evangelized the cities of Besançon, Vienne, and Valence.

5. St. Hegesippus, by origin a Jew, had passed from the profession of Judaism to that of Christianity, and he came to Rome under the pontificate of St. Anicetus. Following the example of the ancient sages of Greece, who travelled into the distant regions of Italy, Egypt, and the most remote provinces of the East, to enjoy the conversation of the celebrated men of those countries, Hegesippus had undertaken a voyage to the Christian cities to confer with their holy bishops and the most illustrious doctors. He could himself claim a place among them, for Eusebius of Cæsarea places him in the number of the defenders of the truth, who vindicated it against the attacks of heresy in works full of erudition and eloquence. But the limit of his learned pilgrimage was Rome, the seat of religion from which proceeded all the churches of the universe, like rays from a common centre. It was there he composed an ecclesiastical history, in which he points

out the succession of the popes from St. Peter to St. Anicetus. This precious work, the loss of which we cannot too much deplore, was, it appears, the object and the fruit of his travels. He wrote it in a simple and familiar manner, to imitate the style of the saints whose virtues he recorded.' He died about the year 180, in the reign of Commodus; and the Church has inscribed his name among the holy priests whose memory she celebrates.

6. About the time of the visits of St. Hegesippus and St. Polycarp to Rome, St. Justin made a voyage to Asia. The philosopher's mantle, which he had never laid aside, attracted to him, at Ephesus, the Jew Tryphon, who, driven from Jerusalem by the events of the last war under Adrian, had retired into Greece, where he occupied himself in constant application to the study of philosophy. Always consumed by zeal for the salvation of souls, St. Justin strove to lead him to the knowledge of the truth, to faith in Jesus Christ. In a discussion, which lasted two days, he endeavored to prove to him, in the first place, that the law of Moses had been abolished; secondly, to demonstrate the divinity of Jesus Christ, of whom he relates the incarnation, the life, the doctrines, the death, and resurrection; thirdly, to explain the vocation of the Gentiles to the light of the Gospel and the divine institution of the Church. The strength of his reasoning, his profound doctrine and eloquence, reduced Tryphon to silence, but they failed to convert him. God reserves the understanding of the truths of the Gospel to humble and docile hearts; He refuses it to the proud, puffed up by false philosophy. On his return to Rome, St. Justin wrote a report of his conferences with the Hellenist Jew, according to the promise which he had made to him, as a guarantee of the sincerity of his arguments. It would appear that the Hebrews could never abandon the hope of seeing Jerusalem one day flourishing as in the times of David and Solomon. This sentiment obtained credence even among faithful Catholics, on the authority of Papias and other millenarians. The Church had not yet condemned

this opinion, therefore it remained open. St. Justin appears to have favored it; for, in closing his discussion with Tryphon, he says to him that Jerusalem would be rebuilt, and that the saints would reign there with Christ in His glory. The Jew refused to believe that he really thought so, imagining that he held this language only to flatter his secret hopes, and more surely to attract him to the doctrines of the Gospel. Offended by such a suspicion, St. Justin replied: "I am not so vile as to hold language opposed to my thought. I am not alone in this opinion. Many Christians as well as myself regard it as indubitable. I will not, however, conceal from you that many others are of a different opinion. But to convince you that I have no intention to deceive, I will write, in a special treatise, all the conferences which we have had together, and I will profess publicly this article, as I have done to you." In fact, the zealous doctor seeks to support this error by many texts from the Holy Scriptures, among which he quotes particularly from the Apocalypse. Certain innovators have made use of this fact as a point from which to attack the authority of tradition. But the sincerity with which St. Justin admits that this doctrine was far from being universal in the Church, is sufficient to prove that it was merely the private opinion of individuals, and not one of the dogmas transmitted in Catholicity through the channels of Apostolic tradition.*

7. The Emperor Antoninus having died, after a reign of twenty-two years, A. D. 161, Marcus Aurelius, the philosopher, his adopted son, hastened to place him among the gods, and to possess the inheritance which he had left on earth. To his great regret, he found himself obliged to share it with Lucius Verus, his adopted brother, who was designated by the will of the deceased emperor as his colleague in the empire. But a few years later he disembarrassed himself of him by poison. The

* The error of the Millenarians, advocated by Papias, Bishop of Hierapolis, and a few others of the early Christian writers, was entirely different from that broached by Cerinthus and his detestable followers. The latter maintained a thousand years' reign of impure orgies and carnal delights. This horrible system, akin to that afterwards adopted by Mohammed, was always repudiated by orthodox Christians.—A. R

universe was disposed to bless this crime; for, during his brief reign, Lucius Verus proved himself, by his cruelties and debaucheries, the equal of Tiberius or Nero. In the same year another prince, whose power continued to grow beside the palace of the Cæsars, died, covered with the glorious purple of martyrdom. The Pope, St. Anicetus, marked by his death the transition from the pacific reign of Antoninus to the fourth general persecution under Marcus Aurelius. The *Liber Pontificalis* informs us that, according to the precept of the Apostle, Anicetus forbade the clerics to wear long hair. We understand this ordinance doubtlessly to refer to the clerical tonsure, which dates from the Apostolic age. After a vacancy of several months, St. Soter was called to succeed him in the chair of St. Peter, and to guide the helm of the Church during the tempest just rising against her (A. D. 162).

II. PONTIFICATE OF ST. SOTER (A. D. 162–174).

8. Marcus Aurelius, in ascending the imperial throne, brought to it virtues which history has eulogized. But his love of philosophy made him unjust towards the Christians. Of the Stoic school, he liked not the disciples of the Cross. "We should always be ready to die," said he, in one of his maxims, "in virtue of a judgment of our own, and not from pure obstinacy, like the Christians." In spite of the firmness of soul which he displayed in his sentences, he proved himself the most superstitious of idolaters. On the point of departure for an expedition into Germany, he celebrated, during seven days, a solemn festival to the gods, to render them propitious. Sumptuous tables were spread in the temples, on which the most exquisite viands were served for the idols of wood, stone, or metal, which were placed around on rich cushions. He immolated for this ridiculous ceremony so many white beeves, that a pithy epigram on the subject was circulated. "The white bullocks to the Emperor Marcus Aurelius: If thou shouldst return victorious, we are all lost."

In the first years of his reign he addressed the following decree to the governors of the empire, which was the signal for the fourth general persecution against the Church: "The Emperor Marcus Aurelius, to all his administrators and officers: We hear that those who in these times call themselves Christians, violate with impunity the laws of the empire, and the ordinances of our predecessors. Arrest them, and if they refuse to sacrifice to our gods, punish them with divers torments. Be careful that justice be always allied with severity, and that punishment cease with the crime."

9. The popular fury, long restrained by the benevolence of Antoninus, burst forth with new violence so soon as this sanguinary edict was promulgated in the different provinces. While St. Glyceria died for the faith at Heraclea, in Thrace, St. Felicitas and her seven sons were the first victims stricken at Rome by the persecution. The pagan pontiffs denounced to Marcus Aurelius the attachment of this noble family to the law of Christ. The prefect of Rome, Publius, received orders to compel Felicitas and her sons to sacrifice to the gods. Led privately before him, the holy widow heroically protested that neither promises nor menaces could shake her resolution. "Wretched woman," said Publius, "if death has so many charms for you, do not at least hinder your children from preserving their lives!" "My children will live," replied Felicitas, "if, like me, they refuse to sacrifice to your idols; but if they should have the misfortune to commit such a crime, their death will be eternal."

The next day Felicitas and her sons were brought before the tribunal of Publius, which was prepared in the field of Mars. "Have pity on your children," said the judge. "Destroy not, in the flower of their age, young people of such high promise." "Your compassion," she replied, "is an impiety, and your soft words cruel. My sons, raise your thoughts and desires to heaven. There Jesus Christ awaits you with His saints. Combat for your souls, and prove yourselves worthy of His love." At these words, Publius commanded her to be struck in the face. "Dost thou dare," he cried, "in my presence, to excite them to despise the orders of my master?" He then called up the seven children in succession. They all confessed the faith of Jesus Christ with equal firmness. With the worthy sons of Felicitas the persuasions of Publius failed, as well as his threats of the most cruel tortures. Januarius, the eldest, merited, by the holy boldness of his answers, to be scourged with rods. Felix, the second, showed the same constancy. "They to whom you wish me to sacrifice are neither gods nor have they any power at all. Whoever sacrifices to these mute idols plunges himself into eternal misery." "We know," replied Sylvanus, "what recompense is reserved for the just, and that chastisements without end await sinners; therefore we disobey the edicts of men, that we may follow the eternal laws of God." "I am the servant of Jesus Christ," exclaimed Alexander; "I confess Him with my lips; I believe in Him with my heart; I adore Him without ceasing. This God gives to youth the wisdom of age. As to your divinities, they, with their adorers, will be cast into eternal punishment." Vital and Martial also continued immovable. A report of this case having been laid before the Emperor, the seven Christian heroes were sent to different judges to be put to death by various modes of torture. The first expired under whips armed with lead. The second and the third were beaten to death with sticks. The fourth was thrown headlong from a height. The three others were beheaded. St. Felicitas, already seven times martyred, ended her life by decapitation.

10. The persecution raged with equal violence in Asia. A celebrated letter addressed by the Church of Smyrna to that of Philadelphia, and to all the churches in the world, has preserved details of the combats which the Christians had to support against the enemies of their faith: "The martyrs' flesh was so torn by the whips that their bones were laid bare, and their veins and arteries might be counted. Touched by compassion, the spectators could not refrain from expressions of pity; but e martyrs uttered not a sigh, nor a groan, as if they were

strangers to themselves, or Jesus Christ himself was there to console them by His presence. They who were condemned to the beasts, were subjected to various tortures in the prisons. The tyrants hoped by these measures to make them deny their faith, but their hellish efforts proved useless. The young and courageous Germanicus signalized his constancy above all the others. When the moment for his combat approached, the proconsul exhorted him to have compassion upon himself. Without replying, the intrepid Christian champion, with a single bound, threw himself before the beasts, who quickly tore asunder his bleeding limbs! Surprised and irritated at this heroic courage, the populace shouted as if with one voice: 'Death to the atheists'" (this name was given to the Christians because they refused to sacrifice to the gods); "'let Polycarp be brought!'"

11. The saintly bishop, on the approach of the storm which burst upon his flock, had at first refused to leave Smyrna, where he had been pastor during seventy years. He long resisted the entreaties of his people, but at last consented to be removed to a country house, near the gates of the city. Three days before his arrest, he had a divine revelation, after which he said to his disciples: "I shall be burned alive." A domestic betrayed his retreat, and towards evening guided the soldiers to the apartment in which he reposed. On seeing the bishop so full of majesty, so affable, so gentle and dignified, they were seized with a respectful fear, and, astonished at the exasperation of the magistrates, many of them regretted that they had come to arrest this admirable old man. The disciple of St. John, in obedience to the orders of the proconsul, made his entry into his episcopal city on an ass, as Christ had done in Jerusalem. The people cried out, "Here is the doctor of Asia! the father of the Christians, the enemy of our gods. Let loose a lion on Polycarp!" This could not now be done, because the combats with the beasts were ended. Then the populace renewed their shouts: "Let Polycarp be burned alive!" In vain the proconsul ex-

horted him to spare his white hairs, and blaspheme Christ. Polycarp replied: "I have served Him these eighty and six years, and never has He done me evil. How can I blaspheme my Saviour and my King?"—"If you do not change your sentiments, I shall order you to be consumed by fire." "You speak to me of a fire which burns for an hour, and is then extinguished, because you know nothing of the judgment to come, and the eternal torments that are reserved for the impious." During this time the people ran in crowds to bring wood from houses, and from the public baths. The wood and other combustibles were heaped all round him. The executioners would have nailed him to the stake, but he said to them: "Suffer me to be as I am. He who gives me grace to undergo this fire will enable me to stand firm in the midst of the flames." He was then left unbound on the pyre, "like a sheep chosen from the flock," records the letter from Smyrna—"like an agreeable holocaust, and accepted of God." Looking up to heaven, he prayed: "O Almighty Lord God, Father of thy beloved and blessed Son Jesus Christ, by whom we have received the knowledge of Thee, God of angels, powers, and every creature, I bless Thee for having been pleased, in Thy goodness, to bring me to this hour, that I may partake of the chalice of thy Christ for the resurrection to eternal life in the incorruptibleness of the Holy Spirit, and receive a portion in the number of Thy martyrs, amongst whom grant me to be received this day as a pleasing sacrifice. Wherefore for all things I bless and glorify Thee, through the eternal High Priest Jesus Christ, Thy beloved Son, with whom, to Thee and the Holy Ghost, be glory, now and forever!"

He had scarcely finished, when fire was set to the pyre. The flames, by a wonderful prodigy, ranged themselves around the martyr's head like the sails of a ship swelled by the winds. His acts relate that his body resembled silver or gold tried in the crucible, and exhaled an odor of incense, as of precious perfumes. The pagans seeing that it could not be consumed by the flames, commanded a spearman, one of those who in the amphitheatre gave the last stroke to the wild beasts, to plunge a sword into his bosom. The man, obeying this barbarous order, pierced Polycarp, when his blood poured forth in such streams that it extinguished the fire. The Christians were glad of this phenomenon, as it nurtured in them the pious hope of being able to obtain at least some holy relics of their bishop, but the pagans kept a careful guard around the pyre. The officer who presided at the execution, according to the Gentile custom, burned the body of the holy martyr. "For ourselves," continues the letter from the faithful of Smyrna, "we took up the bones, more precious than jewels or gold, and deposited them honorably in a place at which may God grant us to assemble with joy to celebrate each year the birthday of the martyr, that it may remind us of those who have fought, and renew the courage of generations to come, by the noble examples of their forefathers in the faith." Such is the narrative of the death of St. Polycarp, which, according to the most probable calculations, occurred February 23d, A. D. 166. All the churches of Asia Minor, and throughout the world, desired to read the account of this glorious combat; and the example of the saintly bishop of Smyrna, who in his lifetime converted so many infidels, had, after his death, the privilege of confirming the Christians in their faith.

12. While the generous blood of the martyrs flowed at the stake, under the fangs of wild beasts, or the sword of the executioner, the pagan philosophers sharpened the weapons of their irony and sarcasm against the Christians, and gathered courage to insult men who knew how to die for their faith. Celsus, the Epicurean, made himself notorious in this kind of warfare, which was both cowardly and cruel. His book entitled *Discourse upon Truth*, was nothing more than a bitter satire upon the Jews and Christians, whom the philosopher seems to confound in equal contempt. He repeats all the calumnies which had been vulgarly accredited among the Romans of this epoch against Moses and his legislation. He then engages a Christian and a Jew in a discussion, and fin-

ishes by turning both into derision. Although he maintains the most insulting tone in this diatribe, admissions escape from him which are sufficient alone to establish against him the truth of Christianity. He grants that this religion, whose limits, even in his time, had no bounds short of the known world, had been founded by a crucified Jew, who had for his associates in this great work a dozen unknown and illiterate fisher men. He reproaches the Christians for no other crimes than those of holding secret assemblies which were prohibited by the magistrates, of detesting idols and their altars, and of blaspheming the gods. He does not deny that Jesus Christ and His disciples, even those who were then living, wrought miracles; but instead of receiving them as proofs of divine power, he attributes them to enchantment and the artifices of magic. His work is the first which had for its object a direct attack upon Christianity. The Fathers of the Church, especially Origen, have victoriously refuted all the sophistries of Celsus.

13. Another philosopher of the Cynic school, also wrote against the Christians, about this time. It was Crescentius, known for his baseness, and his sordid avarice, which did not, however, hinder him from being a pensioner of Marcus Aurelius, and being publicly honored by imperial favor. St. Justin provoked him to a public controversy. In the presence of a crowd of witnesses, he clearly convicted him of being either entirely ignorant of the Christian doctrines, or of being the most flagitious of men; supremely ignorant, if he really believed the absurdities which he circulated against the religion of Jesus Christ; and wicked, above all, if, knowing the doctrine and mysteries taught by the Church, he dared to defame the faithful and to induce princes, magistrates, and people, to believe them to be men without religion, piety, or faith in God. Their conferences were frequent, and ended each time to the greater glory of Christianity and to the confusion of philosophy. Crescentius, a dishonest adversary, in revenge for his defeat, denounced Justin to the judges appointed to pursue the Christians. The

intrepid defender of the truth showed no hesitation in sustaining it, even at the peril of his life.

14. St. Justin published a second apology about this time, which he addressed to the Emperor Marcus Aurelius. He recapitulated the ideas which he had developed more at length in his address to Antoninus. The superiority of the doctrines of Jesus Christ is established by quotations even from the poets and sages of Greece. "The Christians," he says, "possess the truth entire, the perfect Word in Christ; whilst each philosopher, in so far as he has taught any thing good, possessed it only in parts, or fragments of truth." He yields to the just indignation which the blind cruelty of the magistrates towards the faithful naturally excited in every generous soul. "The Christian Ptolemy," said he, "is conducted before the governor, who asks him, 'Are you a Christian?' Strong in the purity of his conscience and the holiness of his faith, he bravely confesses that he has studied in that school of virtue. On the order of the judge, Ptolemy is conducted to execution. Another Christian, Lucius, who was present at these strange proceedings, could not refrain from speaking to the governor. 'By what law do you condemn a man to death who has been convicted of neither adultery nor fornication, nor homicide, nor theft, nor, in fact, of any crime, a man who is guilty only of being a Christian? The sentence you have just pronounced in the name of Cæsar and of the august senate of Rome dishonors the religious emperor, the son of Cæsar, who is proud of being called the friend of wisdom.' The only reply was, to send Lucius to die, as an adherent of the Christians. In submitting himself to the executioners, he thanked the unworthy magistrate for delivering him from the service of such barbarous masters, and sending him by a speedy death to the Father and Lord of heaven. You accuse us," continues St. Justin, "of committing horrible crimes in secret. But these abominations, with which, by the most atrocious calumnies, you charge us, and which we detest, you fear not to commit yourselves, in public. Might we not, taking advantage of your example, boldly assert that these actions

are virtuous? May we not reply that in murdering children, as you falsely accuse us, we celebrate the mysteries of Saturn, in which the hands of the most illustrious personages of the empire are stained with human blood? And as to our pretended incests, may we not assert that we follow the example of your Jupiter and other gods,—that we practise the morals of Epicurus,—of your philosophers, and your poets? And yet it is because we teach that these maxims must be scrupulously condemned, and that we must practise the virtues opposed to these monstrous vices, that you persecute us without relaxation, and send us to death." The genius of St. Justin had not been enfeebled by years. We recognize, in these manly accents, the vigorous independence, the lofty and proud eloquence of the newly converted Christian. "Whatever may be the judgment you form of us," he adds, in conclusion, "our doctrine is worth more than all the writings of the Epicureans, or the infamous verses and the immodest books that are represented on the stage, and read with entire liberty."

15. The lips of this eloquent apologist were soon closed by martyrdom. Shortly after the publication of his address to Marcus Aurelius, St. Justin and several of his disciples were arrested, through the denunciation of the Cynic Crescentius. "What philosophy dost thou teach?" demanded Rusticus, the prefect of Rome. "I have tried all sorts of doctrine," replied Justin, "and finally I have adopted that of the Christians, although it is calumniated by those who know nothing of it." The disciples of the holy doctor, Chariton, Hierax, Pion, Evelpistus, and Liberienus, also generously confessed their faith. Then addressing himself anew to Justin, "Listen," said the prefect; "thou, who passest for eloquent, and who believest that thou hast found the true wisdom, when thou shalt be torn with whips from head to foot, dost thou imagine that thou canst mount to heaven?" "I imagine nothing," replied St. Justin; "I know it. I am so assured of it, that not a doubt remains. Jesus Christ has promised this recompense to all who shall have obeyed His law." Rusticus, finding the

holy confessors immovable in their resolution, pronounced their sentence in these terms: "Let those who have refused to sacrifice to the gods, and to conform to the edict of the emperor, be publicly whipped, and then led to death, as prescribed by law." They were conducted to the place of punishment, and, after suffering flagellation, were beheaded. Their bodies, secretly brought away by some of the faithful, were buried with the honors due to martyrs.

16. But a miraculous event obliged Marcus Aurelius, and the people of his empire, to show themselves less hostile towards the Christians. This prince, surprised in the country of the Quadi, was shut in, with his legions, among the mountains of Bohemia, by the barbarians (A. D. 174). Superior in numbers, the enemy seized all the passages, and deprived the Romans of every means of getting water, hoping, by the intensity of their thirst, to overcome a force which they were unable to conquer by arms. There were in the imperial army many Christian soldiers, chiefly from Melitene, in Armenia, and its neighborhood. In this extremity these threw themselves on their knees, and offered fervent supplications to God for relief. Suddenly, thick clouds accumulated in the air above them, and soon a beneficent rain fell over the camp. So terribly pressed were the Romans by thirst, that they first raised their heads and received the water in their mouths; then gathering it in their bucklers and casques, they drank abundantly, and watered their horses. Profiting by this disorder, the enemy fell upon them, so that the Romans were obliged to drink and fight at the same time, for they were so parched by thirst that there were wounded men who drank their own blood, mixed with the water which had fallen from their casques. The rain was soon attended with thunder and lightning, which, falling on the barbarians, without touching the Roman army, they were repulsed, and forced to sue for the emperor's clemency.

After a miracle so unquestionable, granted to the solicitations of the disciples of Jesus Christ, the evidence of which the emperor could not deny, he commanded a cessation of the persecutions which he had ordered against them. The brief peace now allowed to the Christians, is the strongest proof that the general opinion attributed to them the victory over the barbarians, and the safety of the imperial army.

17. The decimation of her children by the executioners served to display the wonderful fecundity of the Church.

There flourished under the pontificate of St. Soter a great number of illustrious persons and holy doctors, whose noble example and learned works made them the edification of the faithful and the glory of their age. Besides Hegesippus and St. Justin, of whom we have spoken, Philip, bishop of Gortyna, in the Isle of Candia, employed his talents and learning to refute the errors of Marcion. Modistus and Musanus combated the heretics of their time, with equal success. St. Apollinaris, bishop of Hierapolis, St. Meliton, bishop of Sardis, Athenagoras, a Christian philosopher of Athens, opened the way by their pious studies and labors to the apologies for Christianity which were to be published at a later period. Finally, Irenæus in Gaul, first a simple priest in the church of Lyons, of which he was destined to be the most illustrious bishop, prepared his magnificent work against Heresies—one of the most precious monuments of the primitive Church.

18. St. Dionysius, successor of Primus in the episcopal see of Corinth, was one of the most distinguished prelates of this epoch. His zeal and charity were not limited to the instruction of his own flock; he extended them to other churches, and, after the manner of the Apostles, maintained an epistolary correspondence with the bishops of the different provinces. Eusebius of Cæsarea has preserved fragments of his epistles to the churches of Lacedæmon, Athens, Nicomedia, Gortyna, and Gnosse in Crete (Candia). The most remarkable of them is unquestionably that addressed to the church of Rome. He justifies himself, with Pope St. Soter, in regard to certain errors which it was supposed were contained in his letters to different churches. "The apostles of falsehood," said he, "have altered my epistles, adding or retrenching at their pleasure, so as to

favor their heresies. Need we be astonished that they have attempted to corrupt even the Holy Gospels, when they suppose it to be to their interest to alter the writings of so inferior an authority?" Another passage recalls the ancient and touching charity of the Roman pontiffs, who, in their paternal solicitude, ministered to the wants of all the churches in the world, and to the indigence or necessities of the faithful exiled for the faith, or condemned by the persecutors to the quarries and mines.. "Your blessed bishop, Soter," he adds, "not only preserves this usage, but does still more, in distributing more abundant alms than his predecessors to the indigent in the provinces, and in receiving, with affectionate charity, the brethren who visit Rome; lavishing upon them the consolations of faith, with the tenderness of a father who receives his children into his arms."

19. By the side of these illustrious doctors, whose genius shone in the bosom of Catholic unity with all the splendor of truth, the Church was grieved by sad defections. Tatian, a native of Assyria, one of the most celebrated disciples of St. Justin, had at first edified his brethren in the faith by the example of his virtues, as much as by the wisdom of his writings. He had composed a polemical treatise after the manner of his master, entitled an *Oration against the Greeks*. Eusebius and St. Jerome extol it highly. It is remarkable that in this discourse he branded, in advance, the errors of the Gnostics, which unhappily he afterwards adopted. Inflated with his success and the brilliancy of his reputation, he disdained the simplicity of faith, and despised its rule, to follow his own reason: he wished to have a system of his own; to found a school; and he became merely a sectary. He threw himself into Gnosticism, and adopted the Marcionist theory, with the sons of Valentinus. Admitting the two principles of Marcion, to explain the origin of evil, he distinguished himself by pressing more vigorously this error to its consequences, and reducing these to practice. He condemned marriage, as an adultery and a fornication; he forbade, as Theodoret reports, to

eat the flesh of animals and to drink wine. This abstinence from all sensual pleasures gave to his disciples the name of *Encratites*, or *Continents*. This new heresy soon split up into several sects. The Severians, from the name of their chief, Severus, admitted the Law and the Prophets, but they interpreted them in accordance with their own views. Later, the Apotactitae, or Renouncers, added to the errors of Tatian an absolute renunciation of all earthly goods, condemning the holding of property as an injustice, and pretending to conform, in this manner of life, to the precepts and example of the Apostles. Tatian, whose misfortune it was to serve as the chief of these innovators, composed, after his separation from the Church, a great number of works, which are all now lost He wrote, among others, a *Concordance of the Four Gospels*— the first attempt of this kind. The title alone of this work is sufficient to establish the fact that the Church was in tranquil possession of the four Gospels as early as the middle of the second century.

20. During the same period, a learned Syrian afflicted the faithful by the scandal of his revolt from the Church. Bardesanus had a cultivated mind, was a fervent Christian in the first years that followed his conversion, and, like Tatian, an intrepid defender of the truth. Eloquent in his native tongue, the Syriac, full of fire and vivacity in controversy, he wrote various polemical treatises, and an infinity of lesser works against Marcion and the other heresiarchs. These productions, translated into Greek by his disciples, preserved, even in a foreign idiom, an elegance and force which St. Jerome admired. The most celebrated is the *Dialogue on Destiny*, against judicial astrology, which seems to have been addressed to the emperor Marcus Aurelius, who was known for his superstitious faith in impostors and diviners. The reputation of Bardesanus was so distinguished, that the Pagans, considering him as an important conquest, sent to him Apollonius, the favorite of Marcus Aurelius, to persuade him by the most seductive promises to quit the Christian religion. He replied to their advances, with as

much courage as wisdom: "I do not fear death, neither can I avoid it, even if I were to yield to the desires of the emperor." His firmness on this occasion placed him, in the opinion of the faithful, almost in the rank of the confessors of the faith. But the more his attachment to the truth had elevated him in the Church, the deeper was his fall. He embraced the errors of Valentinus, which he taught a long time to the disciples whom his talents had seduced. Having at length recognized the absurdity of Gnosticism, and returned to more Christian sentiments, he combated the system which had misled him. But he still preserved some remains of his errors, which formed a sort of middle system of semi-Gnosticism, to which he gave his name. Marinus, one of his sectaries, informs us that Bardesanus admitted two principles, the one good, the other evil; this was the dominant idea of the Syrian school and of Marcion. According to him, the body of Christ came down from heaven, and not from the womb of Mary, and there was no resurrection of the dead.

21. The heresy of Marcion, which then infected the Church, had taken a new growth from the false preaching of Apelles, the most famous disciple of this sectary. Chased from the company of his master, on account of a great scandal which he had given, he took refuge at Alexandria, where he propagated his own errors. He said that the Creator had wished to form the visible universe in imitation of a superior world, but had been unable to attain to its perfection. For this reason, He had repented of His imperfect work. He said that Jesus Christ had not had even the appearance of a body, as Marcion pretended, nor true flesh, as the Gospel teaches, but, in descending from heaven, He had made for Himself an aerial body, formed of the most subtile parts of each of the regions He traversed; and that, after His resurrection, He had restored each part to its original element, so that the spirit alone returned to heaven. This system induced him to deny the resurrection of the body, with the other Marcionites. To seduce the simple-minded more easily, he pretended to possess

secrets of the future, and published, under the name of *Phanerosis, or Revelations*, the hallucinations of a girl named Philumena, whom he gave out as a prophetess. Apelles lived to an advanced age. As an old man, he affected austere morals, and a grave and severe exterior. Rodon, a Catholic doctor, in a public conference with him, having found him contradicting himself several times, constrained him finally to assert that a man's religion ought not to be so scrupulously examined; that each should remain firm in the belief which he has once embraced; and that they who place their hope in Jesus Christ, to whatsoever sect they may belong, will be saved, provided they be found full of good works. Thus it is that, by an inexorable logic, all heresies, all errors, necessarily force themselves into a universal indifferentism.

22. Montanus, an epileptic, or rather demoniac, as the fathers style him, or, perhaps, simply an impostor, born in Mysia, a province which then, formed part of Phrygia, gave birth to a new sect, about the middle of the second century, of which illuminism seems to have been the most salient characteristic. Subject to convulsions of an extraordinary nature, he pretended that during these attacks he received divine inspirations, to give a new degree of perfection to the Christian religion and morals. Two opulent women, Priscilla and Maximilla, carried away by some gross illusion, or by their passions, deserted their families to follow this fanatic. After his example, they also had ecstasies, prophesied, and shared with Montanus the honor of figuring at the head of their party. They claimed to have succeeded the Catholic prophets Agab, Judas, Silas, the daughters of St. Philip, Quadratus, and the prophetess Ammia, of Philadelphia, affirming that God had given them a mission to perpetuate the gift of prophecy, which was never to be lost in the Church. Montanus boasted of having in himself alone the plenitude of the Holy Ghost, which the Apostles had received only in part on the day of Pentecost. Consequently, he named himself the Paraclete, and claimed the office of reforming the Church. St. Paul had per-

mitted second marriages; Montanus interdicted them as infamous. The Church taught the indissolubility of marriage, supported by the text of the Gospel; Montanus pretended that it is permitted at any time to sunder its bonds. The Apostles had instituted one Lent only; Montanus ordered three in the year. His sectaries fasted with so much rigor that they sometimes passed the whole day without food. There were other fast-days in which they ate only towards evening. He forbade his disciples to fly in times of persecution, and recommended them to offer themselves voluntarily for martyrdom. Inexorable towards sinners, he rarely admitted any to penance. He did not deny the power of the Church to remit sins, but he granted it only to spiritual persons—to an apostle, or a prophet. His partisans affected to establish among themselves a regular hierarchy, at the head of which they placed a patriarch, as the supreme chief of the sect. Next came those whom they named *Cenomes*, then the bishops, who occupied only the third rank. They had fixed the seat of their heresy in Pepuza, a little town of Phrygia, which, among themselves, they agreed to name Jerusalem. There it was that, under the appearance of an inflexible austerity, they indulged themselves in all the disorders of a licentious life, according to the testimony of Apollonius, an ecclesiastical writer of that time, who utters vehement reproaches against them. Under the denomination of Phrygians, or Cataphrygians, the Montanists spread themselves over a great part of Asia, and infested even Africa, where, at the commencement of the second century, they already had several churches. Meanwhile, the bishops began to move against these scandalous innovations. Serapion, bishop of Antioch, Apollinaris, of Hierapolis, Aelius Publius, of Thrace, meeting together in solemn council, formally condemned the new heresy and its supporters. They had already been denounced by Pope St. Soter, who now confirmed the sentence of this council, and anathematized Montanus and his disciples, and this judgment was afterwards renewed by St. Eleutherius. Montanus, blinded by his pride and the madness to which he had surrendered himself, refused submission to the sentence pronounced against him. He continued to play the part of an illuminee; and it is believed that in one of his transports, in concert with Maximilla, his prophetess, he committed suicide—probably with a view the sooner to enter into possession of the eternal beatitude.

23. In the midst of these struggles against heretics within and persecutions without, Pope St. Soter received the recompense of his toils. He died in the year 174. The Roman Martyrology gives him the title of martyr, without any details as to the mode of his execution. He suffered for the faith, apparently before the miracle of the Thundering Legion, which took place the same year, and, for a season, arrested the persecution against the Christians. The *Liber Pontificalis* attributes to him a decree, which prohibits religious women (nuns) to touch the sacred pall, or offer incense in the church. He was distinguished for his charity in aiding poor churches and suffering Christians, according to the testimony of St. Dionysius of Corinth, to whom he had written a letter, which is lost. St. Eleutherius, who had been a deacon under Pope Anicetus, was his successor.

CHAPTER VII.

§ I. PONTIFICATE OF ST. ELEUTHERIUS (A. D. 174–186). 1. The Persecution renewed, A. D. 177.—Martyrs of Lyons—Sanctus, Maturus, Attalus, and Blandina.—2. Journey of St. Irenæus to Rome.—3. Martyrdom of SS. Epipodius and Alexander at Lyons.—4. Of St. Symphorian at Autun.—5. Apology of Athenagoras. His treatise on the resurrection of the dead.—6. Apologies of St. Melito, bishop of Sardis, of Claudius Apollinaris, bishop of Hierapolis, and of Miltiades.—7. Hermias—St. Theophilus, bishop of Antioch—Heresy of Hermogenes.—8. Conversion of King Lucius of Great Britain to Christianity.—9. Death of Marcus Aurelius. Commodus succeeds him.—10. Apology and martyrdom of the Senator Apollonius.—11. Version of the Holy Scriptures by Theodotion. Work of St. Irenæus against Heresies.—12. Death of St. Eleutherius, A. D. 186.

§ I. PONTIFICATE OF ST. ELEUTHERIUS (A. D. 174–186).

1. THE calm which the Church enjoyed after the miracle of the Thundering Legion lasted scarcely three years. The persecution was rekindled with greater violence than before, yet it is probable that Marcus Aurelius was not the author of this sanguinary reaction. Some historians even assure us that, about this time, he issued an edict favorable to the Christians. But the popular hatred, restrained during a brief period, broke out with the greater violence, because the Gnostic sects, which were increasing every day, furnished by their disorders occasions for multiplied calumnies against a religion which they profaned, while bearing its name. The monuments of this epoch all attest that the pagans accused the Christians of renewing the horrors of the Feast of Thyestes and the Marriage of Œdipus in their nocturnal assemblies.* These

---

* Letters from the Church of Lyons to the Churches of Asia and Phrygia.—EUSEBIUS of Cæsarea, *Hist. Eccles.*

reproaches would seem inexplicable, if the conduct of the Gnostics had not given rise to them. The Discipline of Secret regarding the Sacrament of the Eucharist, though it was inviolably respected during the first century, had not prevented St. Justin from exculpating the faithful from the accusation of infanticide; and no Christian usage could serve as a pretext for the accusation of incestuous unions, which was reiterated against them. It was heresy, then, which supplied arms to the pagans, and delivered the Christians to their fury. The new storm was most severe in Gaul, which then gave to the Church its first fruits of martyrdom. Following the touching custom which had been established, of sending to the other churches narrations of the combats sustained for the faith, the confessors of Lyons and Vienne, who were the principal sufferers from the cruelty of the persecutors, addressed a letter to their brethren in Asia, in which they recounted the glorious conflicts of their martyrs. Eusebius has preserved this monument of faith and charity, which is as remarkable for the purity and charm of its style as it is interesting in its matter. "The animosity of the pagans against us was such," they say, "that they drove us out of private houses, as well as from the baths and other public places; our presence, in whatever place we might be, was sufficient to bring upon us the outrages of the populace. The confessors endured, with the most generous constancy, all that could be suffered from the cruel insults of the insolent mob. Their goods were pillaged, they were stoned, and exposed to every excess which a furious people could invent against those whom they regarded as their enemies. Dragged to the forum and questioned by the magistrates, they bravely confessed their faith, and were cast into prison until the arrival of the governor. As soon as he was informed of the affair, he ordered the arrest of the most distinguished Christians and firmest supporters of the two churches of Vienne and Lyons. The fury of the multitude, of the governor, and of the soldiers, was fiercest against Sanctus, deacon of Vienne; Maturus, a neophyte, full of zeal and courage; Attalus, originally of Pergamus, one of the most intrepid defenders of the faith; and Blandina, a young slave, delicate and fragile, but who had fortitude enough to weary the executioners employed to torture her, by turns, from morning until evening. After having subjected her to every kind of pain, they confessed themselves vanquished, and wholly unable to comprehend how she could still breathe after enduring such a succession of torments, any one of which seemed enough to put an end to her life. The deacon, Sanctus, proved himself not less firm in his faith. To all the interrogations of the governor as to his name, his origin, his country, his only response was, 'I am a Christian.' Plates of red-hot copper were applied to the most tender parts of his body. The holy martyr saw his flesh thus roasted without changing his posture, because Jesus Christ, the source of life, shed upon him a heavenly dew which refreshed and strengthened him. Some days after his persecutors subjected him to new torments, when the inflammation of his former wounds had rendered them so painful that he could hardly bear the slightest touch. His body, exhausted by pain, far from sinking under this new trial, recovered its former suppleness, so that, by the grace of Jesus Christ, the last wounds became a remedy to the first. At length, they condemned these heroic confessors to be exposed to the wild beasts. Maturus and Sanctus were the first taken to the amphitheatre. They were beaten with rods, and then made to sit upon a red-hot iron chair, their burning flesh diffusing an insupportable odor. Yet the spectators were impatient in demanding other torments, to overcome their inexhaustible patience. They were afterwards exposed to the wild beasts, and in this manner furnished, during a whole day, the cruel amusement to the people, which is usually given by the combats of gladiators. As, notwithstanding all these tortures, they still breathed, the executioners were obliged to slaughter them under the amphitheatre. Attalus was known to the people as an intrepid champion of the faith. The spectators, with loud cries, demanded that he should be brought on the arena. To satisfy their rage, the holy martyr was led there. They forced him to walk around the amphitheatre, bearing a placard with these words in Latin written upon it: '*This is Attalus, the Christian.*' Before being exposed to the beasts he was placed on the heated chair. While his flesh broiled, and the odor of this human holocaust was spread around, he said, in reply to the accusations of homicide which these people made against the Christians: 'You yourselves roast human flesh as if it were to be eaten; but for us, we never eat men, and our religion forbids all crimes.' Blandina, the last of this heroic society of martyrs, entered the lists with as much joy as if she had been conducted to a nuptial feast. After she had suffered the whips, the lacerations of the beasts, and the heated chair, she was fastened in a net and laid before a bull, who threw her up many times into the air. But the saint, filled with the hope which her faith imparted to her soul, thought only of Jesus Christ, and was insensible to her torments. Finally they pierced the throat of this innocent victim, and the pagans confessed that they had never seen a woman suffer such horrible tortures with so great courage.

2. "The disciple of St. Polycarp, the venerable St. Pothinus, first bishop of Lyons, bore witness, by his death, to the faith which he had brought to this city. More than ninety years old, he was so very sick and feeble that it was necessary to carry him to the tribunal. It seemed that his soul still remained attached to his body, only to serve for the greater triumph in it of Jesus Christ. As the soldiers bore him along, he was followed by a crowd, who vociferated the vilest insults; but these outrages neither disturbed the holy man nor hindered him from boldly confessing his faith. 'Who is the God of the Christians?' the governor asked him. 'You will learn it, if you become worthy of the knowledge,' replied the intrepid bishop. Immediately, and without regard to his age, he was most outrageously treated by the furious populace; those nearest struck him with their fists and feet; those

farther removed hurled at him any projectile they found at hand. They would have reproached it themselves as a crime not to have insulted the holy old man, only thinking of avenging on his person the honor of their gods. After enduring this horrible treatment without a complaint, St. Pothinus was thrown into prison, where, two days afterwards, he died of his wounds."—St. Irenæus succeeded him in the episcopal chair of Lyons. He went to Rome to receive the episcopal consecration from the hands of Pope St. Eleutherius. Another object made the journey necessary. The errors of Montanus and the false prophecies of Priscilla and Maximilla threatened to spread into Gaul. Some Christians, even among the confessors of the faith, had given examples of abstinence which seemed, by their scrupulous austerity, to approach the erroneous rigorism of the heretics. It was to inform the sovereign Pontiff of this state of things, and to receive his advice, that St. Irenæus undertook the journey to Rome, charged with letters to the Pope from the clergy and faithful of Lyons.

3. The persecution continued with the same violence against this people thus left for a time without a pastor. No retreat could secure the victims from the researches of their enemies. Two young men—Alexander, a Greek, and Epipodius, a native of Lyons, both in the flower of their age—were closely united by the ties of Christian friendship. Both belonged to illustrious families; they stimulated each other to piety, and prepared for martyrdom by the purity of their lives, their innocence of heart, and by works of charity and mercy. At the commencement of the persecution they retired into the village of Pierre Encise, near Lyons, and lived together in solitude with a Christian widow who had offered them an asylum. Discovered by the satellites of the governor, they were cast into prison; and three days afterwards, with their hands tied behind their backs, like the vilest criminals, they were led before the tribunal. On the demand of the magistrate, they replied, "We are Christians." "Of what use

has it been to torture so many of these Christians to death, if they still dare to speak of Christ?" cried the angry judge. Separating the two friends, to prevent their mutual exhortations to remain faithful to their God, he first called up Epipodius. "The crucified, whom you adore," said he to his prisoner, "forbids the joys and pleasures that form the charm of life; our gods, on the contrary, receive our joyous homage in the midst of festivals and flowers: change, then, this austerity so intolerable, for the agreeable pleasures of youth." "With the Christians," replied the generous martyr, "the soul commands, the body obeys. The atrocities by which you suppose you honor your idols, can only procure for you eternal death." The judge, on this, ordered him to be struck on the face with the fist. His mouth all bloody, Epipodius cried out, "Jesus Christ is my God, one only God, with the Father and the Holy Ghost." They then extended him on the instrument of torture, and the men approached to tear his sides with iron claws. But the people, fearing to see the victim expire in the hands of strangers, vociferously insisted that he should be given to them, that they might rend him in pieces. The tumult increasing, there was danger of a riot. To prevent it, the governor hastened to order Epipodius to be beheaded; and the martyr's soul departed, to receive in heaven the reward of his constancy. The next day the governor summoned Alexander. "Sacrifice to the gods," said he; "take warning by the example of the others, for we have so pursued the Christians that you alone remain of all that impious race." "You are mistaken," Alexander replied; "the name of Christian cannot perish. The life of men perpetuates it, and their death propagates it." The holy martyr was then extended, his legs separated, and in this state three men by turn relieved one another in beating him. He endured this slow and cruel torture without uttering a complaint. At last the governor, finding him immovable, condemned him to die on the cross. The sentence was executed. The Christians were fortunate in eluding the vigilance of the soldiers while they gained possession of the bodies of these saintly martyrs, and the same tomb reunited the heroic friends. To the names of these noble confessors of the faith, should be united those of SS. Marcellus and Valerian, who, having escaped from Lyons, suffered martyrdom in two neighboring cities; the first at Châlons sur Saône, the second at Trenorchium, now Tournus.

4. The city of Autun was a witness, at the same time, of the devotion and courage of St. Symphorian. Descended from one of the best families of the city, and distinguished by his brilliant education, this young and intrepid Christian met one day a solemn procession, made in honor of Cybele, the mother of the gods. He was unable to refrain from public expressions of his contempt for idols, and boldly ridiculed this superstitious worship. The offended pagans dragged him before the proconsul Heraclius, as a seditious man, who refused to adore the divinities of the empire. "Why dost thou refuse to pay homage to the mother of the gods?" demanded the judge. "I adore the true God," replied Symphorian. "As for this idol of your demons, if you will allow me, I will break it with a hammer before your eyes." "Is it not enough to be sacrilegious? wilt thou also be chastised as a rebel?" Heraclius then ordered him to be beaten with rods, and taken to prison. Some days after, he was subjected to an interrogatory, and the most seductive promises were made to him. Wealth, gratifications, military honors, imperial favors, every thing was offered that could minister to his enjoyment, if he would but consent to sacrifice to the immortal gods. "I go," said Heraclius, "to decorate with flowers the altars of Apollo, Cybele, and Diana, and you will unite with me in a solemn sacrifice." The saint rejected these insidious propositions of the judge with horror. He portrayed, in all their extravagance and absurdity, the insensate dances of the Corybantes, in honor of Cybele, the impostures of the priests who gave out the oracles of Apollo, and the superstitious games in honor of Diana. Heraclius condemned him to be beheaded. As they led the martyr to the

place of execution, without the walls of the city, his mother, venerable for her piety and her age, hastened, not to unman him by her tears, but to fortify and animate him by her exhortations. From the height of the ramparts, she cried out: "Symphorian, my son, my dear son, lift up your thoughts to the living God; prove your courage and your faith. Death is not to be feared when it surely leads to life. That you may not regret the earth, raise your eyes towards heaven, and despise the torments which last but for a little while; if you are constant, they will be changed into everlasting happiness." Sustained by the voice of his tender mother, and by the strength of divine grace, the young Christian generously submitted to martyrdom. His precious relics, gathered by the piety of the faithful, were deposited in a narrow cell, over which a majestic church and a celebrated monastery were in after-times erected.

5. From the violence of the persecution in Gaul may be conjectured the ravages which it made in the other provinces of the empire. So many atrocities committed against the Christians inspired eloquent writers to embrace with ardor the defence of faith and virtue, so shamefully misunderstood. In the name of all the faithful of Greece, Athenagoras, a Christian philosopher of Athens, addressed to the Emperor Marcus Aurelius and his son Commodus, recently associated with him in the empire, an apology, entitled *Legation*, because it was an embassy from the oppressed to their persecutors. In this work, which has a style full of dignity and force, and a clear and precise logic, he exposes and victoriously refutes the accusations of the pagans against Christianity. "You permit," said he, "all nations, all cities, all citizens, to live according to their laws, to profess their religion, to preserve their ceremonies, to honor the gods of their fathers, even where they are so ridiculous as the cat-gods and crocodile-deities of the Egyptians; to us, alone, you have interdicted the privilege of bearing the name of Christian, and of living according to our laws; and yet this name is innocent, and our laws are just and

good. The pretext for the violence practised against us is the vulgar accusation of atheism, incest, and inhuman repasts. If the Christians were convicted of such crimes, it would be just to exterminate their sect; to wash out in their blood so much wickedness, without sparing age, or sex, or rank. But the emperors themselves are the irrefragable witnesses of the injustice of these and similar calumnies, since by many edicts they have forbidden pursuits against the Christians; whereas, such researches could never be too exact or severe, if the abominations of which we are accused had the least foundation." Athenagoras then examines in detail the grounds of each accusation, and demonstrates its frivolity and injustice. He concludes by expressions full of fire and eloquence, when replying to the impostures circulated among the people, of the pretended homicidal festivals of the Christians: " We are accused of this frightful crime, we who have renounced your spectacles of gladiators and wild beasts, because we find but small difference between applauding murder and committing it! We believe that it is a crime to expose an infant, as is done every day at the gates of your palace, in the streets, and in public places; yet you accuse us of murdering them for a barbarous feast! Our religion commands us to believe in the resurrection of the dead; if this belief appears to you devoid of reason, ridicule, if you choose, our simplicity, but never accuse us of making ourselves a living tomb of those who are one day to be resuscitated from the dead!"

It seems that the dogma of the resurrection was a frequent object of attack by the pagans. The saintly apologist, who only slightly touches this point of Catholic faith at the close of his *Legation*, wrote a treatise especially *On the Resurrection of the Dead*, in which he proves its possibility, against the objections drawn from the transformation of the body, and shows its reality by reasons drawn from the divine order of things, from propriety and justice.

We remark, in general, in these two works of Athenagoras, the only ones of his which are extant, the ideas and reasonings of St. Justin, presented in a more cautious style. He insists less on the Scriptures, and more on reason. Yet he does not confine himself to the part of the accused who merely defends himself. The apologist makes himself, little by little, the accuser, and attempts chiefly to show how much of absurdity and impurity there is in paganism, which he places in contrast with the doctrine and manners of the Christians.

6. About the same time (178), St. Melito, bishop of Sardis, also presented an apology to the two emperors. The earthquake which had recently overthrown the city of Smyrna, had directed the popular fury against the Christians of Asia, who were held responsible for every public calamity. "In virtue of the new decrees published in our provinces," said the bishop, "the Christians are exposed to a persecution such as they have never before suffered. Their greedy calumniators take advantage of these ordinances, to rob openly their unhappy victims. For this reason, we supplicate you to take cognizance of those who are accused, and to judge whether they merit such treatment. If, among your predecessors, Nero and Domitian gloried in their cruel persecutions of the Christians, Adrian, your grandfather, and Antoninus, your father, have signalized towards us their justice and clemency. In addressing our supplications and our hopes to the foot of your throne, we doubt not, that we shall find the same benevolence, the same humanity." This fragment, cited by Eusebius, is all that remains of the work of St. Melito. Claudius Apollinaris, bishop of Hierapolis, in Phrygia, also proved his zeal for religion, by an apology addressed to the Emperor Marcus Aurelius. Christian antiquity has praised the elegance of his style and his erudition in sacred and profane letters, but his works have not reached us. The same must be said of Miltiades, whom Tertullian numbers among the eminent men who had refuted the errors of Valentinus. He also composed, for the defence of Christian philosophy, which he professed, a remarkable apology, addressed to the *Heads of this Age*, that is to say, to

the governors of provinces and cities, where their duties brought them into contact with the Christians.

7. At the same epoch lived Hermias, a writer celebrated for the new method which he employed to confound paganism. Until this time, the Christian authors had confined themselves to proofs of the superiority of the evangelic dogmas over idolatry, by placing in a strong light the doctrines of Jesus Christ, in order to vindicate them from the calumnies with which they were loaded; but Hermias adopted the opposite method. He attacked the pagan worship with the arms of ridicule and bitter irony. He was surnamed the Christian Lucian. His work, entitled *The Philosophers Rallied*, is the most adroit ridicule which has been brought to bear against paganism. A masterpiece of its kind, it is as remarkable for clearness and precision as for its vivacity, wit, and grace. He passes the philosophers in review. Each of them sets forth his system on the gods, the soul of man, and the beginning of things; and the succeeding one always overturns what his predecessor had attempted to construct.

All the cultivated and superior minds then living within the Church employed their talents in eloquent works, to establish the divinity of religion. St. Theophilus, sixth bishop of Antioch after St. Peter, published three discourses against the detractors of the Christian faith. He addressed them to Autolycus, a learned pagan, whom, in his pastoral solicitude, he sought to enlighten in the Christian faith. The principal subjects treated by the illustrious bishop are, the nature of God, His providence, the order of the world, the absurdity of idolatry, the ignorance of the philosophers, and the vain chimeras of the pagan poets on the origin of being, as opposed to the purity of Christian doctrine and morals. In another work, he undertakes to refute Hermogenes, a heretic of his time, who taught, with the Platonists and Stoics, that matter is eternal. His disciples, of whom Hermias and Seleucus were the most celebrated, received from Tertullian the name of *Materiarii*, and they were the precursors of the modern Materialists.

8. Notwithstanding the efforts of these able apologists, the fire of persecution was not extinguished. But if the Church, decimated by the executioners, lost her children by martyrdom in the different provinces of the Roman empire, she expanded her bosom to receive distant nations, who felt themselves mysteriously attracted by the light of divine truth. Lucius, king of one of the small states of Great Britain, sent a solemn embassy to the Pope, to ask for missionaries to instruct his people, and procure for them the knowledge of the Gospel. St. Eleutherius received the envoys with joy. He gave them priests, whose preaching was so successful, that in the time of Tertullian, the cross had already been planted in the most northern regions of Great Britain, which hitherto had proved inaccessible to the Roman eagles. Lucius is honored with a public devotion, December 3d.

9. The Emperor Marcus Aurelius, after having entered (A. D. 180) Pannonia, to engage in a war with the Marcomanni, expired, leaving the purple to his son Commodus, who was suspected, and not without foundation, of having abridged the days of his father. The cruelties and debauchery of the new reign surpassed all that was remembered of Nero or Domitian. Commodus had all the beggars and cripples of the city disguised as giants or monsters, only that he might massacre them with his club, and give himself the name of the Roman Hercules. Meeting one day a man of extraordinary height, he cut him in two, to exhibit his strength, and to enjoy the pleasure of seeing the entrails of his victim fall out. He ordered that Rome should change her name, and be called the *Colony of Commodus*. Incest, and the most abominable crimes, defiled the palace of this crowned fool, who was seated on the throne of the world. By a secret design of His providence, God suffered to be thus loosened the reins of the most shameful passions of humanity, that, at last, frightened at her own excesses, she might throw herself into the arms of a religion which alone preserves the secret of virtue. The persecution continued during the first two years which followed the

death of Marcus Aurelius. It ceased afterwards, perhaps through the influence of Marcia, to whom Commodus had just granted the honor of empress, and who was favorably disposed towards the Christians.

10. The calm of this unexpected peace, after tempests of such long duration, produced numerous conversions. At Rome many personages of the highest distinction embraced the faith with their families. Apollonius, a senator, illustrious in letters and philosophy, was of this number. One of his slaves denounced him as a Christian before Perennis, the prætorian prefect. The ordinances which forbade the accusation of Christians, under pain of incurring the chastisement due to calumniators, had just been restored. Perennis, consequently, ordered the slave to be crucified and his legs broken. By a strange contradiction, he afterwards ordered Apollonius to justify himself before the Senate, and give an account of his conduct. Apollonius composed a solid and eloquent apology, in which he candidly confessed the Christian religion, and defended it from the accusations brought against it. He read this discourse before the assembled Senate, but he soon sealed with his blood his courageous profession of faith; for, according to the edict of Trajan, still in force, a Christian, once brought to justice, could not be released unless he apostatized. A decree of the senators, his colleagues, condemned Apollonius to be beheaded. The sentence was executed A. D. 189.

11. We know of no other martyrs who suffered under Commodus. But if the faithful had peace with the idolaters, the Church had still to suffer from the heretics. Theodotion, of Ephesus, first a disciple of Tatian, afterwards a Marcionite, and finally a Jew, undertook a translation of the Holy Scriptures into Hebrew Greek. His intention was, to weaken the force of those passages of the prophets which teach the divinity of the Messiah. In spite of his hostile purpose, he did not succeed to any extent in altering these sacred sources, and his version became a new arm in favor of evangelic truth in the

hands of the fathers of the Church. St. Irenæus notices it in his great *Treatise against Heresies.* The holy bishop of Lyons, on his return to his flock, where the persecution had made such terrible ravages, found the churches of Celtic Gaul infested with the errors of the Marcosians, whose sacrilegious impostures and pretensions had seduced the weak. They allowed their adepts the most monstrous excesses, under the pretence of impeccability common to all the Gnostic sects. Irenæus combated the heresies of these false doctors, and was led, with this view, to compose a complete refutation of the whole Valentinian system. To succeed in such a work, it was necessary to unite to a profound knowledge of the Scriptures, and a rare penetration of spirit, the study of the Greek and Oriental systems of philosophy. St. Irenæus, formed by St. Polycarp, had drawn from his lessons the Apostolic doctrines and traditions in all their purity. While still young, he was familiar with the works of the profane poets and philosophers, as is proved by the frequent quotations he makes from their maxims; and he had studied with care all the writings of Valentinus and his disciples. Prepared by these labors for the work which he meditated, he at length finished his immortal production, "Against Heresies." He wrote in Greek, his mother tongue, but we have only a few fragments of the original text, preserved by Eusebius. That which we have is a Latin translation, made, probably, in the lifetime of St. Irenæus, for the use of his people in the churches of Gaul. It is divided into five books. The first is devoted to the exposition of the Gnostic heresies, all included in Valentinianism. Considering this system as the latest development of Gnosticism, he makes it the centre of all his arguments. In the second he combats all these errors with the arms of good sense and sound logic, showing their absurdities and incoherencies, and opposing them with arguments drawn from reason. In the third book he refutes them by tradition, by the Holy Scriptures, and the text of the four Evangelists. He continues the same mode of reasoning in the fourth and fifth books, where he cites the

Epistles of the Apostles, which he had particularly reserved for the close. The chief source from which St. Irenæus draws his proofs is tradition, of which he shows the existence, the character, and sacred authority, in the Church. Not being able to follow up the succession of the bishops in each see, he contents himself with appealing to the tradition of the Roman church, the greatest and most venerable of all. "It is necessary,"* said he, "for the faithful of every country, to conform to the teachings of the See of Rome, because of its eminent primacy, in which has always been preserved the tradition of the Apostles." The heretics, on the contrary, being new men, have no root in the past. They each date from a chief, whose name they take in borrowing his doctrines. With them there is no succession of authority, doctrine, or apostleship; the caprice of an arrogant spirit is their only law, their sole origin. The argument of tradition, which all the fathers have unceasingly employed in their controversies, had a peculiar force under the pen of a writer who counted, between the Apostles and himself, no other intermediary than the illustrious martyr, St. Polycarp, bishop of Smyrna. Nothing is more touching than the manner in which St. Irenæus speaks of his ancient master, in a letter to the priest Florinus, who had the misfortune to fall into the snares of the heretics. "While yet a child," says the illustrious bishop, "I saw you in Asia Minor, in the house of Polycarp, where you, who were living in the court of the emperor, came to see the holy bishop, and strove to obtain his esteem. The memory of childhood grows with the understanding and mingles with it, so that I could point out the place where the blessed Polycarp was seated when he spoke, his bearing, his mode of life, and the discourses he made to the people. He told us how he had lived with John and the

---

* Ad hanc enim Ecclesiam, propter potiorem principalitatem, necesse est omnem convenire Ecclesiam, hoc est, eos qui sunt undique fideles, in qua semper ab his qui sunt undique conservata est ea quæ est ab Apostolis traditio.—*Advers Hæres*, lib. iii., cap. 3, No. 2.

others who had seen Jesus Christ. He related to us their instructions, and many things which he had heard them say concerning the Lord, His miracles, and His doctrines. God gave me the grace to listen to these discourses with the greatest attention, and to engrave them on my heart." It was thus in the century succeeding the Apostles, that St. Irenæus, relying on the tradition and doctrine which he had received from them, combated the false novelties of his time.

12. The illustrious bishop of Lyons did not finish his great work during the pontificate of St. Eleutherius. This Pope died A. D. 186. He is honored with the title of martyr, which is given him in the Roman Martyrology. He renewed, says the *Liber Pontificalis*, the prohibition to regard as impure any ordinary aliment proper for the food of man.* This ordinance was provoked by the immoderate and superstitious abstinences of the Encratites and Montanists. St. Victor, an African by birth, was elected to the sovereign pontificate, A. D. 186.

---

* Et hoc iterum firmavit, ut nulla esca usualis a Christianis repudiaretur, maxime fidelibus, quam Deus creavit, quæ tamen rationalis et humana esset.

CHAPTER VIII.

§ I. Pontificate of St. Victor I. (a. d. 186-200).—1. Question of Easter.—2. Letter from Polycrates, bishop of Ephesus, to Pope St. Victor I.—3. Letter from St. Irenæus to Pope St. Victor I.—4. Letter from the bishops of Palestine to Pope St. Victor I.—5. Heresy of the Theodotians.—6. The priest Gaius refutes the Theodotians.—7. Other apologists of the Christian Faith.—8. Christian Schools.—9. Christian school of Alexandria, St. Pantænus.—10. Clement of Alexandria, his works.—11. Death of Pope St. Victor I.

§ 1. Pontificate of St. Victor I.

1. The question respecting the time of celebrating the festival of Easter, raised a quarter of a century before, by St. Polycarp, in his interview with Pope Anicetus, had not been decided by the predecessors of St. Victor I. The Asiatics had, therefore, continued their old usage of celebrating it on the same day with the Jews. As time passed on, this erroneous custom seemed to have acquired also the right of prescription. It maintained, besides, between the Asiatic and Latin Churches, a troublesome divergence in regard to festivals, to fasts, and to whatever was regulated by the day of the Easter celebration. Since the final destruction of Jerusalem by Adrian, the motive of complaisance to the Jews newly converted, who still cherished a very strong attachment to the Mosaic rites, had ceased to exist. On the other hand, the obstinacy of the Asiatics had been increased by the sort of tacit consent of Pope Anicetus, and by the authority of St. Polycarp. Even at Rome, the priests Blastus and Florinus from Asia, had endeavored to persuade the faithful that they could not, in conscience, follow the usage of the Latin Church for the celebration of Easter. Matters went so far that,

fearing a schism, the Pontiffs SS. Soter and Eleutherius found themselves obliged to withdraw from the Asiatics resident at Rome the permission to conform to the custom of their country; so that by the exaggerated ideas of the Asiatics a point of discipline had become a doctrinal question. St. Victor would no longer tolerate this error; he therefore resolved to labor efficaciously to establish a perfect uniformity in all the churches. With this design, he convoked at Rome a council of all the bishops of Italy. It was there solemnly decided that Easter should be celebrated on Sunday, a day consecrated from the time of the Apostles to the memory of the glorious resurrection of Christ; and the fathers interdicted the observance for the future of the Jewish usage in the celebration of this solemnity. Victor sent the synodical letter to the bishops of all the provinces of the Catholic world By his order, Theophilus of Cæsarea assembled the bishops of Palestine; St. Irenæus of Lyons, those of the Gauls; Bacchylus of Corinth, those of Achaia; Demetrius of Alexandria, those of Egypt; and Palma d'Amastris, those of Pontus. These assemblies unanimously adopted the views of the Pontiff, and the letters which they addressed to him are all agreed on the necessity of conforming to the custom of the Latin Church for the celebration of Easter.

2. But Polycrates, bishop of Ephesus, had been appointed by St. Victor to preside in the council of proconsular Asia. As might have been easily foreseen, the bishops of this country were not disposed to abandon an ancient custom in their province, supported, too, by a venerable tradition. "It is among ourselves," wrote Polycrates to St. Victor, in returning to him an account of the operations of the assembly, "it is in Asia that these great lights of the Church sleep in the Lord. Philip, one of the twelve, at Hierapolis; John, who reposed on the bosom of the Lord, the holy pontiff who wore the frontlet of gold, martyr and doctor, came to die at Ephesus; Polycarp, the illustrious bishop of Smyrna; Thraseas, bishop and martyr of Eumenia; the blessed Melito, bishop of Sardis, who

in all his thoughts and actions was inspired and directed by the Holy Ghost. These great personages have celebrated Easter on the fourteenth day of the lunar month, following the text of the Gospel, and observing the rule of faith. And I, Polycrates, the humblest of the bishops, having lived sixty-five years in the service of the Lord, observe the tradition of my masters and my fathers. I will not suffer myself to be alarmed by threats, knowing the word of the Apostles, 'It is better to obey God than man."' In proportion as the letters of the other councils had brought consolation to the Pope, that of Polycrates grieved him. The bishop of Ephesus intrenched himself behind a tradition, respectable doubtless, and for which the Roman pontiffs had shown much consideration, by tolerating it during a century and a half; but he did not enter into the motives which had actuated the Pope. Far from this, he insinuated that the usage of the Asiatics only was founded on the rule of faith. This was to favor the schismatics, whom the Pontiffs had to combat in the bosom of Rome herself. One fact worthy of remark in this discussion is, that the supremacy of the Pope is not questioned by the Asiatic bishops. They make no complaint of his interference, by an abuse of power, in the conduct of remote and independent churches. On the contrary, Polycrates, in closing his letter, implicitly recognizes that the authority of the Pope, which he believes himself in conscience obliged to resist, has no equal among men, nor can be controlled, except by the authority of God. However this might be, Victor felt that the period of compromise was past. He prepared a sentence of excommunication against the Asiatics, and in his letters declared them henceforth separated from the unity of the Church.*

3. This determination of the Pope re-echoed throughout the Catholic world. Ephesus, Smyrna, and so many other sees, illustrated by the Apostles or their disciples, under the weight of sentence of excommunication, offered an afflicting spectacle to the bishops of other provinces, most of whom were

---

* Ab unitate Ecclesiæ prorsus alienos esse pronuntiat.—EUSEBIUS, lib. v, cap. 23.

in relations of friendship or gratitude with the Churches of Asia. Besides, the bond of charity united them more closely at this epoch, when they were threatened with the same menaces and persecutions. The greater number of the bishops wrote to the Pope, some with force and vehemence, others with wise reserve and praiseworthy moderation. St. Irenæus was of the latter number. He began his letter by stating the conformity of his belief with that of the Roman Church, and the necessity of celebrating Easter on Sunday; but he did not see, in the attachment of the Asiatic Churches to their ancient usage, a sufficient reason for separating them from Catholic communion. "The pontiffs," said he to St. Victor, "who before Soter governed the Roman Church, viz., Anicetus, Pius, Hyginus, Telesphorus, Sixtus, preserved peace with the Churches whose observance was not conformable to theirs. This divergence of opinion did not hinder them from sending official letters to the bishops of Asia, and thus maintaining communion with them." He cited, as a proof of this tolerance, the interview between St. Polycarp and St. Anicetus, on this same question. "Be cautious," added the holy bishop of Lyons, "in cutting off from catholic unity entire Churches, for a custom which they have received from their fathers in the faith." St. Irenæus wrote, in the same spirit, to a large number of bishops, to interest them on behalf of the Asiatics. From the quotations we have made, it is evident that St. Irenæus considered the controversy between the Pope and the dissidents as purely a point of discipline.

4. The bishops of Palestine, nearer to the centre of this dissension, and consequently better situated to appreciate its true character, judged otherwise. Narcissus of Jerusalem, Cassius of Tyre, Clarus of Ptolemais, and other prelates of the provinces, came together in council, under the presidency of Theophilus of Cæsarea, to whom Pope St. Victor had delegated his authority,[*] wrote to the Pope a synodical letter, in which

---

[*] Papa Victor direxit auctoritatem ad Theophilum, Cæsariensis Palestinæ antistitem.—Labbe, tome I., (col. 596.)

they declare their attachment to the tradition of the Latin Church in the celebration of Easter. They establish its authority on irrefragable proofs, and end by praying the Pope to give to their letter the greatest possible publicity, " in order," they say, " that the Catholic world may not suspect us of being accomplices with those who separate themselves from the way of truth." St. Victor, meanwhile, touched by the solicitude of so many illustrious and saintly bishops, softened the rigor of his first sentence. It satisfied him to know that the improper custom of the Asiatics met with general disapprobation. The tolerance of it was interrupted, and the error could no longer claim prescription. Its extinction had become only a question of time. It was important, henceforward, to guard against wounding susceptibilities, to leave minds leisure to comprehend and digest the truth, in proportion as the question disengaged itself from the personal animosities with which it had been environed. The sequel showed the prudence and wisdom of the pontiff. In the following century, the Asiatics returned to the universal practice; and this question was again agitated at Nice, only because certain bishops of Syria and Mesopotamia still thought it a duty to resume, for their particular usage, the Asiatic custom, unanimously abandoned by the Catholic world.

5. St. Victor, at the same time, excommunicated the heresiarch Theodotus and his adherents. Theodotus of Byzantium was a currier, but his reputation for learning and virtue raised him above his profession. Arrested as a Christian, during the persecution under Marcus Aurelius, he apostatized, to escape its torments. The reproaches which his cowardice brought upon him induced him to quit Byzantium, and to take refuge in Rome, where he hoped to remain unknown. But the indelible brand of apostasy seemed marked upon his brow, and he did not find at Rome the repose which his own country had refused him. Weary of conflict, he thought to justify his crime by becoming a heresiarch. " It is not God that I have denied," said he, " it is only a man ;" and henceforth he taught

publicly that the Word was not God, thus renewing the heresies of Cerinthus and Ebion. The universal tradition of the Church was totally opposed to this new system. Theodotus essayed to prove that tradition had been corrupted by the later Popes. The Holy Scriptures, whose precise and formal texts could not be distorted to sustain the erroneous interpretations of the apostate, were altered in the editions which he placed in the hands of his disciples. Artemas, one among them, contributed to bring some reputation to the sect, by his talents and eloquence. Soon afterwards, another Theodotus, called the *Banker, Argentarius*, also a disciple of the currier, added a new error to those of his master. He pretended that Jesus Christ, a pure man, conceived of the Holy Spirit and the Virgin Mary, was inferior to Melchisedec, because it was written of him, *Thou art a priest forever, according to the order of Melchisedech*. It appears that the text where St. Paul represents Melchisedech "without father, without mother, without genealogy, having neither beginning of days, nor end of life, but likened to the Son of God, continueth a priest forever,"* served the *Melchisedechians* as a pretext to make of him a superhuman being, incomprehensible, and almost divine, and as a consequence to elevate him above Jesus Christ, whose divinity they denied.

6. The priest Caius, who lived at Rome at the end of the second century, refuted these innovators. "The Theodotians," said he, "are confounded first by the testimony of the Holy Scriptures, afterwards by the writings of Justin, Miltiades, Tatian, and others, who have defended the true doctrine against the heretics, who were their contemporaries; and they all attest the divinity of Jesus Christ. From the first age of the Church, hymns and sacred songs have celebrated Jesus Christ, the Word of God, and attributed divinity to Him."†

7. The truth did not fail of eloquent defenders. Men of the finest genius, unsurpassed by any whom the Church had,

* Hebrews, vii, 8.
† Psalmi quoque et cantica fratrum jampridem a fidelibus conscripta, Christum Verbum Dei concelebrant, divinitatem ei tribuendo.

until that time, numbered within her bosom, adorned the closing years of the second century. While Irenæus shed lustre upon Gaul, Pantenus and Clement, in Egypt, set forth the brilliant treasures of their knowledge and eloquence in the Christian school of Alexandria, which they, alone, would have been sufficient to immortalize. Origen, yet a child, gave astonishing proofs of early intelligence. Tertullian, in Africa, the first among the Latins, entered the lists with his crushing logic and his powerful eloquence. To these celebrated names, Eusebius adds those of other writers whose works, unhappily for us, are lost. The philosopher Maximus, who had composed several important treatises on the questions so much debated by the heretics—viz., the origin of evil and the existence of matter—Candidus and Appion, who wrote commentaries on the work of the six days—Sextus, author of a book on the resurrection—and Heraclytus, who left analytical treatises on the epistles of St. Paul. But above all these glories of the Church, the attention of the Catholic world was particularly attracted to the school of Alexandria, which then shone with the greatest splendor.

8. The Apostles had laid the foundations of those institutions, which, under the name of Christian schools, perpetuated in the bosom of the Church the tradition of teaching. It entered into their mission to provide for all that was necessary to prepare subjects able at a later day to preach, and govern the churches. St. Paul having formed his disciple Timothy by his own example and instruction, recommended him, in his turn, to choose able men, and to exercise them in the evangelic ministry of the word. Tradition has preserved the memory of the numerous disciples of St. John, at Ephesus, where this Apostle passed the last years of his life. The bishops, successors of the Apostles, and stationed in each see, did not fail to give a more stable form to these establishments, and to form them into regular schools.

9. Alexandria contained an establishment of this kind, which St. Jerome informs us was the creation of St. Mark the

Evangelist. A city, peopled by philosophers, the centre of the prevailing opinions; an intellectual focus, where all the sciences then known were cultivated, had need of a system of Christian instruction more developed, more complete. It was time to exhibit Catholic science in its own brilliant lights —to oppose it to the vain systems of human philosophy—to demonstrate its superiority: to produce its evidences—to unfold it as a whole—and to present a just appreciation of its consequences upon the happiness of mankind. To found a seminary for the truth, in the midst of the seats of error, was the intention of the bishops of Alexandria. To place before the most learned auditory in the world apostles of pre-eminent sanctity and eloquence, was their constant aim, and they succeeded. In the year 179, the illustrious Pantenus occupied this eminent post. A Sicilian by birth, he had been educated at first in the principles of the Stoic philosophy—had discovered the truth, and was converted to the Christian faith. He brought to the service of this sacred cause an indefatigable zeal, useful and varied knowledge, and an eloquence the reputation of which had overleaped the bounds of the Roman empire, and passed into India. An embassy had been sent to him from that country, praying him to announce the Gospel to them. Clement of Alexandria, his disciple, said of him: "This bee of Sicily, from the juice of the flowers which he has gathered in the celestial meadows of the Apostles and Prophets, produces in the minds of his auditors a treasure of immortal learning and virtue." He tore himself away, nevertheless, from the applauses of the Alexandrian youth, and from the successes of an apostleship which he had made illustrious, to undertake the toils of the distant mission that was opened to him. Appointed by Demetrius, patriarch of Alexandria, apostle and bishop of the oriental nations, he penetrated the Indies, whither he was called. It was not until long years after, when age had broken his strength, that he returned to Alexandria. The see was then held by Origen, disciple and successor of Clement of Alexandria. Pantenus felt his youth, in some sort, revive in this young man, whose glory was then without an equal. He took pleasure in praising his doctrines and eloquence, and in conciliating for him the veneration, friendship, and esteem, with which the greatest men of the age honored himself. St. Pantenus died about the year 216.

10. His most glorious conquest had been the conversion of Clement of Alexandria, who succeeded him as director of the Christian school. Titus Flavius Clement, a native, according to some authorities, of Alexandria, according to others, of Athens, had been educated in paganism. An insatiable desire of knowledge had enabled him, in his laborious youth, to exhaust the treasures of human learning and the principal systems of philosophy. Wearied by the doubts and contradictions which he encountered at each step, he applied himself to the examination of the modes of worship and religious doctrines of Greece, Rome, and of the different nations of the world. With this object, he travelled in the East, in Greece, and in Italy, and finally terminated his wanderings in the pursuit of truth in Egypt, at the feet of St. Pantenus, whose persuasive and touching eloquence put an end to all his irresolution, and attached him forever to the Christian religion. At first, a fervent neophyte; later, a zealous priest; he became an indefatigable apostle. After the departure of St. Pantenus for the Indies, Clement of Alexandria continued his work. He brought to his task an immense erudition, language full of unction and charm, and a sanctity of life which imparted to his instructions the irresistible authority of example. Not content with instructing his auditory by his voice alone, he wrote many treatises, for the benefit of such as were unable to follow the course of his lessons. "The ancient priests," he said, "did not write, because they could not lay aside teaching. Perhaps, also, they thought that the same talents could not successfully be applied to both; but written works serve to protect doctrines, in transmitting to posterity the primitive traditions." In fact, the Fathers had not written

until this time, except to meet the urgent necessities of controversy with paganism or heresy. The Church, essentially dogmatic, especially in her first age, as we have already said,* had not yet found, amid the tempests which agitated her, the leisure to develop, in learned works, the sublime philosophy she taught in the world. Clement of Alexandria took the first step in the new path which was opened to Christian genius. In the three books of the *Pedagogue*, and in the eight *Stromata*, the two most important of his works still extant, he constantly places religion at the summit of science, by proving the excellence of its dogmas, and their harmony with sound reason. The *Pedagogue*, composed for the Catechumens, whose spiritual infancy was directed by Clement, is an abridgment of the whole of Christian morals. Jesus Christ himself, the Word of God, and wisdom incarnate, is presented as a model and master. He teaches the true wisdom. He bestows on simple and pure hearts solid grandeur, durable happiness, and the supreme good. This work of initiation into the faith, ends with a description of the holy practices, the austere morals, and the inexhaustible charity of the Christians. The author afterwards rendered it complete, by his great composition, which he called the *Stromata*, or Miscellanies, which he himself says were to contain "the Catholic truth, mingled with the instructions of philosophy; or, rather, they would present it covered and hidden, like the nut in its shell." These expressions indicate the state of mind of Clement of Alexandria, in commencing this work, which he terms, in another place, *The son of his soul*.† On the one hand, he was restrained by the prejudice which had grown up among Christians, of the inutility of writings on religion purely philosophical; and, by the Discipline of Secret, which imposed entire reserve on the subject of the mysteries, dogmas, and sacraments. On the other hand, he felt himself invincibly attracted to engage in a controversy with Pagan philosophy,

---

* Chap. I.—State of the Church in the first century.
† Animæ liberi sunt scripta.—Stromat, lib. 1, § 1, p. 316.

which should result in the triumph of the evangelic doctrines over all merely human conceptions, and which should also serve for the instruction of the faithful, in giving them sound ideas of a superior order, on the practice of Christian perfection, and preserve them from the seductions of false mystics, which at that epoch Gnosticism had multiplied. Divided between these two considerations, he endeavored to conciliate them in his work. He informs us "that he has sowed the Christian dogmas in his book in such a way that the uninitiated in the knowledge of the mysteries cannot easily discover our holy traditions."* The obscurity of the terms which he employs in treating of the sacraments, is transparent to the faithful, and is equivocal and ambiguous only to the Pagans, to whom it was important that the secret of the Church should not be revealed. The affected disorder of the matter was also a part of his general design. He compares the *Stromata*, "not to those beautiful gardens, where all is disposed with art and elegance, but to a mountain, covered by nature with forests and plants of every kind, growing all together, as if thrown there by chance."† In spite of his precautions, his plan is perceptible, at least in its fundamental ideas. He treats first of philosophy in general, and presents it under its various aspects. He then speaks of faith, the foundation of Christian life; of the virtues which purify and ornament the soul, in delivering it from the unregulated movements of the passions. He combats briefly the errors of the Encratites, on the subjects of continence, marriage, and martyrdom. He then comes to the picture of the true sage, the philosopher, the *Gnostic par excellence*, that is to say, of the Christian, elevated by the practice of all the virtues, to the contemplation of God, and of His sublime beauty; living, henceforth, a life almost superhuman, and exhibiting on earth the perfections of evangelic virtue. To reach this eminent

---

* Ut a quolibet eorum qui mysteriis non sunt initiati non facile inveniri possint sanctæ traditiones.—Strom., lib. iv., § 1, p. 565.

† Strom., lib. vii., § 18, p. 901.

degree of Christian sanctity, to triumph over the miseries, the imperfections, the weaknesses of fallen humanity, is not this the supreme end which Religion points out to all her children? Is it not in this way that she advances them, each according to his vocation, and his co-operation with the graces which are imparted to him by the Holy Spirit? This, also, is the end which Clement of Alexandria proposed to himself in this work.

We have also from the same author an *Exhortation to the Gentiles*, in which he magnificently sets forth the excellence and purity of the Christian religion, by comparing it with the idolatrous worship, whose infamous mysteries he unveils without mercy, and a short treatise which has for its title and subject, *Who of the rich can be saved?* He composed, besides, eight books of *Hypotyposes*, or *Instructions*: a grand commentary on the whole Scriptures, on which Eusebius and St. Jerome bestow the highest encomiums—unhappily only some incomplete fragments remain to us—a controversial treatise on the question of Easter, in which he opposes the usage of the Asiatics; and various controversial works against the Encratites and Montanists.

11. While Clement wrote his *Stromata* at Alexandria, St. Victor closed his pontificate, in the year 200. The *Liber Pontificalis*, and the *Roman Martyrology*, both give him the title of martyr, without mentioning the particulars of his death. Eusebius informs us that the holy pontiff composed several writings, now lost, and St. Jerome places him first among the Fathers of the Latin Church. Besides his decree relative to the celebration of Easter, he declared, by an ordinance, that the common water of a fountain, pond, river, or sea, could be used in case of necessity, in the administration of baptism. This leads to the supposition that, until then, it had been the rule to use holy water in administering this sacrament. St. Zephyrinus, a Roman by birth, succeeded him.

CHAPTER IX.

§ 1. Pontificate of St. Zephyrinus (a. d. 200–217). 1. Fifth general persecution, under Septimius Severus.— 2. Scyllitan martyrs at Carthage.— 3. Martyrdom of St. Perpetua, St. Felicitas, and their companions, at Carthage.—4. Martyrdom of St. Leonides, father of Origen, at Alexandria (202).—5. Martyrdom of St. Irenæus, bishop of Lyons.—6. Martyrdom of the disciples of Origen at Alexandria (204).—7. Martyrdom of Potamiana, of St. Marcella, her mother, of the soldier Basilides, at Alexandria (204). 8. Tertullian.—9. Conference between Gaius and Proclus, at Rome.—10. Voyage of Origen to Rome. The Octapla, Hexapla, Tetrapla. Bible of Origen.—11. St. Narcissus, bishop of Jerusalem.—12. St. Alexander, coadjutor of St. Narcissus, and bishop of Jerusalem.—13. Minucius Felix, Octavius, and their friend Cecilius.—Caracalla, emperor.—15. Massacres at Alexandria. Flight of Origen to Cæsarea.—16. Condemnation of the heretic Noetus.—17. St. Hippolytus, bishop of Porto. His works.—18. Fall and penitence of Natalis, confessor of the faith. Death of Pope St. Zephyrinus.

§ I. Pontificate of Pope St. Zephyrinus (a. d. 200–217).

1. Commodus, having been strangled by his principal concubine, aided by two prefects of the Prætorium, ended his life on the eve of the day on which he had ordered the assassination of the two consuls of Rome by a troop of gladiators. Pertinax, an old general, who had risen by his genius, having been the son of a slave who sold charcoal in Liguria, reigned ninety-seven days. Fearing that he intended to establish the ancient discipline, the pretorian soldiers cut off his head, and bore it in triumph round their camp, on the end of a pike. From the ramparts of Rome, the empire was offered to the highest bidder. Didius Julianus purchased it at the price of twelve hundred drachms for each soldier, nearly six hundred dollars, payable immediately to him; the empire was thus

disposed of by the legions, and the senate ratified the bargain. But the purchaser was unable to pay the price agreed upon. Sixty-six days after, he was deposed by the senate, and conducted to execution. Three generals were then each proclaimed Emperor by their troops, and assumed the purple at the same time: Pescennius Niger in the East, Blodius Albinus in Great Britain (England), and Septimius Severus in Illyria. The last, three times victorious over Niger, in Asia, was equally fortunate against Albinus at the battle of Lyons. The crown remained his own. Severus was born at Leptis, on the coast of Africa. He had both the Punic faith and cruelty. His first act of authority was to force the senators to place Commodus in the rank of the gods. "It becomes them, indeed," said he, "to be scrupulous! Are they any better than that tyrant?" Nevertheless, he was at first favorable to the Christians, and confided the education of his son to one of them, named Proculus, and he protected those members of the senate who had been converted to Christianity. But afterwards he changed these happy dispositions, and in the year 202, he forbade, under the heaviest penalties, the profession of the religion of Jesus Christ. He enforced this decree with the obstinacy natural to his character; and, as the multitude had not even awaited this signal to gratify their fury against the Christians, the persecution soon became general.

2. At Carthage, the proconsul Saturninus summoned before his tribunal Speratus, Narzalis, Citlinus, Veturius, Felix, Aquilinus, Lotantius, Januaria, Acyllina, Generosa, Vestina, Donata, and Secunda. When the proconsul ordered them to sacrifice to the false gods, Speratus replied: "We have never violated the laws. No one can accuse us of any crime. Our religion commands us even to pray for those who unjustly persecute us." "We also," rejoined the proconsul, "have a religion full of good and pious teaching. Swear, then, with us, by the genius of the emperors, our masters." "I know not the genius of the emperors, but I can loyally maintain faith, hope, and charity. We adore only one Lord and one God, King of kings, Empe-

ror of all nations." Each of the confessors replied with the same courage, and Saturninus sent them all to prison. The trial was resumed the next day. On this occasion, Saturninus addressed the women: "Obey the emperors, our masters, and sacrifice to the gods." Donata replied: "We desire to pay to the emperors all the homage and respect due to them, but we can adore Jesus Christ only, who is the true God." Vestina followed: "That which I must always meditate in my heart, and pronounce with my lips, is that I am a Christian." Secunda added: "And I also am a Christian. I will persevere in this faith of my companions, and my own. Never will we adore your gods." Speratus was then interrogated anew. Full of holy enthusiasm, he exclaimed, addressing the crowd who filled the pretorium: "If you wish to know the thoughts of my heart, listen: I am a Christian." All the other confessors with one voice repeated the same profession of faith. "I give you a respite of three days," then said Saturninus, "to reflect on the part you may wish to take, and to retract the errors of this impious sect." "No delay will change our belief," replied Speratus; "we will die with joy for the religion of Jesus Christ. Rather take time yourself to deliberate—abandon the shameful worship of idols, and become a disciple of the Gospel. Have courage to do so, or hesitate no longer to pronounce sentence against us." Saturninus then commanded these generous Christians to be decapitated. "We give thanks to God," they said, while they were being conducted to the place of execution, "that He does us the honor this day to receive us into heaven, for the confession of His name"—and the noble victims were immolated. Their martyrdom took place on the seventeenth of July, A. D. 200.

3. Soon after this, Vivia Perpetua, of Carthage, twenty-two years of age, and of illustrious birth, was arrested. Her father and mother were still living. She was married, and nursed an infant. They seized with her Felicitas, a Christian slave, married, and pregnant. Revocatus, Saturninus, Secundulus, and Saturus, were joined with them as companions in captivity. The

father of Perpetua, a zealous pagan, besought his daughter to sacrifice. "Some days having elapsed since I last saw my father" (it is Perpetua herself who writes this narrative of the commencement of her martyrdom), "I gave thanks to God for this, and his absence strengthened me. It was in this interval that we were baptized"—(she and also Revocatus were only catechumens when they were arrested). "I prayed for naught else, on coming out of the water, but patience in my bodily sufferings. A few days afterwards they threw us into a dungeon. I was frightened, for I had never seen such darkness. It was a bitter day! The heat was stifling because of the crowd; the soldiers pushed against us; and I was dying of anxiety on account of my infant. Then the blessed deacons, Tertius and Pomponius, who assisted us, obtained, by means of money, permission for us to go out, and pass some hours in a more commodious place than the prison. We profited by this advantage. I suckled my infant, and commended him to my mother's care; I encouraged my brother, but I was parched with grief to see how much sorrow I caused them. Several days I passed in this anguish. There was a rumor that we were to be interrogated. My father came from the city to the prison, overwhelmed with distress. He said to me: 'My child, have pity on my white hairs; have pity on me! If I am worthy of being called thy father, if I have brought thee up to this age, if I have preferred thee to thy brothers, make me not a reproach among men. Think of thy mother: see thy son, who cannot live when thou art gone. Lay aside this obstinacy, lest we all be ruined!' My father expressed his tenderness for me by kissing my hands, throwing himself at my feet, weeping, not calling me his daughter, but his *lady*. I grieved for him, seeing that of all my family he would be the only one who would not rejoice at our martyrdom.* I said, to console him, 'Whatever happens on the scaffold will be that which is most pleasing to God; for be assured that we are not in our own power, but in His.' He went away sorrowful.

* All the other members of her family were Christians.

"The next day, while at dinner, they came to take us to be interrogated. The report of it had reached the neighboring districts, and a crowd of people assembled near the tribunal. The others underwent the interrogation, and generously confessed Jesus Christ. When my turn came, my father approached me, holding my son in his arms, and said: 'Have pity on your child!' The procurator Hilarian added, 'Spare the age of your father; spare the infancy of your son. Sacrifice to the gods, for the prosperity of the emperor.' 'I cannot,' said I. 'Are you a Christian?' 'I am a Christian.' As my father endeavored to withdraw me from the tribunal, Hilarian commanded that he should be driven away, and he received a blow from the rod of a lictor. I felt it as if I had been stricken myself—so much did I suffer to see the white hairs of my father insulted, because of me. Hilarian then pronounced our sentence, condemning us all to be exposed to the beasts. We returned joyfully to the prison."*

"Secundulus died there. Felicitas was in the eighth month of her pregnancy: seeing the day of the spectacles so near, she was greatly afflicted, fearing that her martyrdom would be deferred, because it was not permitted to put pregnant women to death. The prayers of the confessors obtained for her a prompt and happy delivery. She gave birth to a girl, whom a Christian woman brought up as her own child. On the eve of their combat they were given, according to custom, their last supper, which was termed the free repast, and which was made in public. The Christians obtained permission on this occasion to remain within the prison, the keeper of which was already converted. The martyrs changed

---

* We have scrupulously reproduced the recital of St. Perpetua. "Human literature," says M. Rohrbacher, "has nothing approaching it. A young woman, a mother, of distinguished birth, cherished by all her friends, beholds herself separated from her father, mother, brothers, husband, and her infant, to be devoured by wild beasts, before all the people: she sees her aged father, whom she loves, and who loves her most tenderly, kiss her hands, throw himself on his knees, to prevail with her to pronounce one word which will save her from danger: she compassionates the sorrow of her father, she consoles him but she will not pronounce that word, because it would be an apostasy: and she writes al this on the eve of her torments, with a candor and a calm above human nature."

their dying feast into an agape. To the people around them they said: 'Observe our faces well, that you may know us on the day of judgment.'"

"The next morning they left the prison for the amphitheatre, as if on their way to heaven. Their faces shone with ineffable joy. At the door they were required, according to custom, to put on the ornaments worn by those who appeared at this spectacle. These were, for men, a red mantle, the habit of the priests of Saturn; for women, a fillet around the head, the symbol of the priestesses of Ceres. The martyrs refused these liveries of idolatry. 'We are here only to maintain our freedom,' they said; 'we have sacrificed our lives rather than do any thing of this kind; we have already told you so.' Saturninus and Revocatus were first abandoned to the fury of a leopard and a bear, who dragged them about some minutes, without inflicting serious injury. Saturus was exposed to a wild boar, who, respecting the martyr, attacked the hunter, and inflicted upon him a mortal wound. Perpetua and Felicitas were stripped and put into nets, to be exposed to a furious cow; but the people revolted at this refinement of cruelty. These generous women were then clothed in flowing garments. Perpetua, the first exposed, was thrown into the air, and fell on her back; she sat up, gathering her loosened hair, to avoid the appearance of mourning, and seeing Felicitas all bruised by her fall, she extended her hand to aid her in rising. Both then stood, prepared for a new combat; but the people, whose cruelty was softened, would not have them exposed a second time, and they were reconducted to the Sanavivaria gate, where Rusticus, the deacon, was unbounded in his cares for them. Saturus was now presented to a leopard, who, seizing him in his jaws, at once threw him on the ground, bathed in blood. 'There is a baptism that will save him,' shouted the people; an ironical allusion to the sacrament of the Christians. But the martyr, turning towards the soldier Pudens, whose conversion he had undertaken, 'Adieu,' he said; 'remember my faith; let my death confirm you in fidelity to Jesus Christ.' He then asked for the ring which Pudens wore, bathed it in his wound, and restored it, as a pledge of their friendship, and a memento of his blood. Finally, he expired in the place where they were accustomed to put an end to those whom the beasts had left still breathing. The people demanded that the other martyrs should be brought again to the centre of the amphitheatre, to have the pleasure of seeing them receive their death-blows, and accustom themselves to the view of homicide. They rose and came of themselves, to consummate their martyrdom, after giving to each other the holy kiss of peace. Saturninus and Revocatus received the last stroke immovable and in silence; Felicitas fell into the hands of an inexpert executioner, who forced from her a cry of pain (for these murders were a sort of apprenticeship for unpractised gladiators); Perpetua herself guided the trembling hand of the man to her throat."*

4. The persecution was not less furious in Egypt. Alexandria was especially marked for vengeance by the Pagans, because of her eminence in Catholic science. Septimius Severus visited the city soon after his edict of persecution was proclaimed, and ordered the Christians to be pursued with the utmost rigor. They were arrested in the Thebaid, and in every province in Egypt, wherever they could be seized, and brought to the city for execution, so that it became the capital of proscriptions. Clement of Alexandria, obliged to fly from the murderers, wrote, from his place of concealment: "Every day we see fountains of Christian blood flowing; every day we see our martyrs consumed in the flames of the pyre, interrogated in the midst of tortures, decapitated by the sword. Their fidelity to Jesus Christ leads them to these glorious combats, and teaches them to testify their piety by the effusion of their blood."† Leonides was arrested with an innumerable crowd of Christians. Origen, his son, whom he had brought up with the greatest care, had just reached his seventeenth year. "But," said St. Jerome, "from his childhood he was a great

* Act Sincer, p. 80 et seq. † *Stromata*, lib. L, p. 414.

man." Besides the liberal arts and belles-lettres, St. Leonides had given him a knowledge of the Scriptures, some sentences of which he made him every day commit to memory, and recite before beginning his profane studies. Origen devoted himself with an application which was not content with merely the literal sense, but sought for the more hidden meaning. St. Leonides discouraged this excessive ardor for knowledge, yet from the depths of his heart he blessed God for giving him such a son. Often, while Origen slept, he approached the bed where his child lay, and opening his bosom, kissed it with respect, as a sanctuary where dwelt the Spirit of God. So holy an education produced its fruits. When Origen heard of his father's imprisonment for the faith, neither the tears nor the supplications of his mother could retain him. She was obliged to have recourse to a maternal stratagem, and conceal his clothing, to prevent him from going to offer himself a captive for Jesus Christ. He was consoled by writing to St. Leonides a letter, full of eloquence and force, in which he encouraged him to martyrdom. "Have confidence," he wrote; "give yourself no trouble about us" (he had six brothers younger than himself). "Leave all for Jesus Christ; He will be your recompense." St. Leonides was beheaded, and his property confiscated for the benefit of the public treasury, A. D. 202.

5. St. Irenæus, at the same time, had the happiness of shedding his blood for the faith which he had so gloriously defended in his works. Septimius Severus, on hearing that the numbers of the faithful were multiplying in Lyons, through the zeal of this pious prelate, adopted measures worthy of his cruelty. He sent orders to his soldiers to surround the city, and put to the sword all who confessed themselves Christians. The massacre was almost general, and the blood of the martyrs flowed in streams through the public places. St. Irenæus was led before the tyrant, who commanded him to be put to death, applauding himself for having thus silenced both the pastor and his flock. An ancient inscription, still to be seen in

Lyons, at the door of the principal church, says the holy victims of the faith numbered nineteen thousand men, without including women and children. Among the martyrs of Gaul, at this epoch, was St. Andeolus, subdeacon, sent by St. Polycarp to preach the Gospel, who was put to death at Viviers.

6. After the departure of Clement of Alexandria, who had retired into Cappadocia, to the house of bishop Alexander. the Christian school had been for some time dispersed by the violence of the persecution. Origen had the courage to revive it, even under the sword of the persecutors, A. D. 203. He sold his books of grammar and profane science, on the condition that he should be furnished with four oboli* a day for his sustenance. Thus freed from the care of his daily wants, he commenced his work with incredible ardor. He passed the whole night in study and watching, to prepare the eloquent instructions which he addressed on the morrow to his disciples. When nature, overcome by sleep, yielded to the necessity of repose, he rested some moments on the bare ground, and quickly resumed his work. In a few years he had committed to memory all of the Holy Scriptures, and, with the knowledge of the text which his memory furnished, applied himself to the immense labor which he bestowed on the Bible. The austerity of his life corresponded to his indefatigable ardor for learning. He never drank wine. His frequent fasts and his habitual abstinence had nearly cost him his life. Even in winter he went barefoot, allowed himself only a single habit, and refused all that his friends wished to give him. Such sanctity, united to his prodigious talents, attracted a crowd of disciples, even from among the most distinguished learned men and philosophers. Heraclas, who afterwards became bishop of Alexandria; Plutarch, his brother; the two Sereni, Heraclides, Heron, and many other young men, eagerly placed themselves under his direction By this, they exposed themselves to the vengeance of the persecutors, who did not spare them. They were sent to prison

* About eight cents of our money.—*Am. trans.*

Heraclas alone escaped their search; Providence had other views for him. Origen made incredible efforts to bear to his spiritual children the consolations and encouragements of religion. He visited the martyrs in their prison, accompanied them to the interrogatory, exhorted them even in their place of torments, and gave them, in the presence of the pagans and the soldiers, at the last moment, the kiss of peace. It was miraculous that he escaped the rage of the Gentiles, who were several times on the point of stoning him. They even posted soldiers at the door of his residence to murder him, and the furious people often dragged him along the streets of the city. Several times he was tortured, but God would not permit him to be removed from the Church of which he was one of the glories. One day the infidels seized him, and, having shaved his head, in imitation of the priests of the idols, they clothed him in robes worn by those who sacrificed; thus attired, they placed him in the highest step of the temple of Serapis, and gave him palms to be distributed, according to custom, to those who ascended. Origen received them, and, lifting them up, "Come," he cried, "come and receive these palms; not as those of your idols, but as the palms of Jesus Christ, my God." His disciples were sent to be executed. Plutarch, Heraclides, Heron, and one of the Sereni, were beheaded; the other was burned alive. They also sent to the flames the young catechumen, Herais, who was preparing to receive baptism, and attended the instructions of Origen.

7. At the same time, Alexandria witnessed the death of a young Christian, a martyr to chastity. Potamiana was a slave. Her master, inflamed by her rare beauty, could not obtain her consent to his infamous desires. He delivered her to the governor of Alexandria, Aquila, in the hope that the view of torments and threats of death would subdue her virtuous constancy. Aquila, having found her immovable, applied the torture. The executioners exhausted their strength in vain against this noble victim. At length, the governor ordered an immense caldron filled with pitch to be placed over a fire, and

when it was boiling, "Obey thy master," he said to Potamiana, "or I will plunge thee, living, into this heated caldron." "God forbid," replied the saint, "that any judge should be so wicked as to condemn me to do a criminal action." Other threats of Aquila having had no more effect than this, he commanded that she should be stripped and cast into the caldron. The chaste martyr had the right of repelling the outrage offered to her modesty, and she was plunged with her garments on into the heated caldron. The governor appointed one of his guards, Basilides, to preside at the execution. On approaching the martyr, the soldier felt his heart moved by a supernatural grace. He drove away the people who crowded on the passage of Potamiana, to insult her virtue. When on the point of being thrown into the caldron, she promised to intercede for him with the Lord, assuring him that he would speedily feel the effects of her gratitude. When she had ceased to speak, they lowered her gradually into the boiling pitch, until her head was submerged. At the same time her mother, St. Marcella, was burned alive.

Some days after, the soldiers, companions of Basilides, having endeavored to force him to swear, with them, by the gods of the empire, Basilides refused, declaring that he was a Christian. The soldiers at first supposed he was merely in jest; but, becoming convinced of the sincerity of his declaration, they conducted him to the governor, who threw him into prison. The Christians, astonished at so sudden a conversion, came to visit the new brother whom the Lord had given them. "Potamiana appeared to me," he said, "three days after her martyrdom. She placed a crown on my head, saying that she had obtained for me grace from the Lord, and that soon He would call me to His glory." He was baptized, and the next day the lictor's axe opened for him the gates of eternal life.

8. "A secret power of conversion arose from the blood of the martyrs, which thus became the seed of Christianity." This is an expression of Tertullian, who had himself yielded to the marvellous attraction. Quintus Septimius Florens Tertullianus,

the son of a centurion of pro-consular troops, was born at Carthage, A. D. 160. He studied all the sciences, and succeeded in each of them. His style, lively, concise, energetic, brilliant in metaphors and novel thoughts, and in expressions of an always happy audacity, recalled the thunders of Demosthenes, in the language of Tacitus. It would seem that if Logic wanted to choose a style of eloquence, she would select that of Tertullian. In his writings, each word is a sentence, each argument a victory. The African Bossuet, nothing would be wanting to his glory if he had always made humility the safeguard of his genius.

Although a pagan by the prejudices of birth and education, he was unable to resist the profound impression made on his soul by the invincible constancy of the martyrs. He embraced the faith of Jesus Christ, became a priest, and soon after addressed to the magistrates of the Roman empire the most eloquent apology which had yet been written.

"It is not a favor which the Christian religion demands of you," said he, "for she is not herself surprised at her reception. A stranger in this world, she knows that among strangers, enemies are easily found. Her origin, her home, her hopes, her credit, and her glory, are in heaven. She only asks that she shall not be condemned without being known.

"The proof that she is unknown is, that ceasing to be ignorant of her, men cease, at the same time, to hate her. It is the knowledge of our faith that gives us Christians by thousands. Behold, and see why it is that we fill your cities, your islands, your villages, and your fields, with a multitude which alarms you, and yet you never suspect that there may be, in this strength of attraction, some good that you do not comprehend. A criminal trembles when he is detected—denies when he is interrogated, or confesses only with tears. No Christian blushes before your tribunals; his only regret is that he has not always been a child of the faith. It is a strange sort of crime, which has no vicious character, no fear, no confusion, no evasions, no repentance, no regrets!

"You proceed against us by a singular subversion of all justice. You torture criminals to force them to confess their crime: you apply it to Christians to constrain them to deny it. When a man cries out, 'I am a Christian,' he tells you what he is; you torture him to make him say what he is not. Appointed to search for the truth, you would force us into falsehood. Such a contradiction ought to make you fear, lest there be some secret and unknown power which inclines you thus to violate all the forms of equity and law. You believe that a Christian is guilty of all crimes, that he is the enemy of the gods, the emperors, the laws, morals, and of all nature—yet you force him to deny it, to be absolved!

"It is said that we have the barbarism to murder, in our assemblies, an infant, whose flesh we eat, and that to this feast of Thyestes, succeed the most infamous orgies. It is said, and notwithstanding the long time during which it has been repeated, you have never yet taken the pains to verify the facts. Either prove these accusations, if you believe them to have any foundation, or cease to credit them, when you have not verified them. Every day we are hunted—we are surprised in the midst of our assemblies—has any one ever met with any thing on which to ground these accusations?

"People thirsting for Christian blood, upright judges, magistrates, so rigorous towards us, what will be your reply when I reproach you with being yourselves the murderers of your own children? You expose them by thousands, in the streets and public-places, to the dogs which devour them; you rid yourselves of them by drowning, or you leave them to perish of hunger—to die by the sword would be a death too gentle for these tender victims. Among Christians, homicide is unknown. In our eyes, it is murder even to prevent a birth—while you sow everywhere the fruit of your debauches. If you had taken notice of the disorders which are committed among yourselves, you must have perceived that they have no existence among Christians. There are two kinds of blindness, which often go together; that of not seeing what is, and of imagining that which is not."

We regret that we cannot reproduce the whole of this most eloquent pleading. What a spectacle was offered to the world in this champion, who stood alone to defend the truth, and whose voice rose above the clamors of the amphitheatre, the threats of the persecutors, and the clank of chains! Never was the struggle of the two powers which divide the world,— the struggle of material power against truth,—better delineated. The logic of Tertullian did not arrest the persecution, and yet, in the last analysis, this logic remained victorious. It was sufficient for the moment, that, on the ground of the discussion where the Christian doctor was placed, he had obliged paganism and philosophy to serve as footstools to the throne of Christ. This new character of religious controversy is revealed in other writings published by Tertullian, nearly at the same time as the *Apologeticus*. The treatises, *Ad nationes libri duo: De Testimonio Animæ: Adversus Judæos: Adversus Hermogenem, Valentinianos, Marcionem: Adversus Praxeam: De carne Christi: De resurrectione carnis*,[*] succeeded each other without interruption, in less than five years. Pressed by the numerous adversaries whom he attacked all at once, and equally pressed for time which seemed always insufficient for his indefatigable zeal, Tertullian purposed to group together all the enemies of the Church, all the heresies of his time and of the ages to come, in order to oppose to their pretensions a general argument proving their inadmissibility. He realizes this idea in the capital dissertation, *De Præscriptionibus*, the most important of his works, without excepting even his immortal *Apologeticus* (208). The arguments which he uses had already been employed by St. Irenæus in his work, *Adversus Hæreses*, but Tertullian gives them a wider application. He says to the chiefs of sects: "You are innovators; you teach doctrines con-

---

[*] In English: *To the Nations* (Gentiles)—*The Testimony of the Soul*—*Against Jews*—*Against Hermogenes, the Valentinians, Marcion, Praxeas*—*The Flesh of Christ*—*The Resurrection of the Flesh*.

trary to those that we hold from the Apostles. Where are your titles against our possession?" *Olim possideo, prior possideo.* Tertullian's works on morals are neither less important nor less numerous. They amount to twelve, published between the years 198 and 204. In the last, entitled *De Patientiâ*, there is a passage which the sad defection of this great genius renders almost prophetic: "It is bold, I confess, in me, to venture to write on patience—I, who am utterly incapable of giving an example of it. It is, nevertheless, a sort of consolation to occupy myself with a virtue which it is not granted to me to enjoy, like the sick, who never cease to speak in praise of the health which they have not. The virtue of patience bears such a preponderance in the things of God, that we can neither fulfil any precept, nor do any acceptable work, without it." In these words there is a kind of presentiment of the extremities into which the violence of his character might hurry him. During fifteen years, Tertullian deserved well of the Church by his labors as a writer, while he edified her as a priest by his sacerdotal virtues. He had reached the age of forty-five years. His talents had been ripened by controversy. His style, bold and picturesque, had received a higher lustre from the uninterrupted series of his triumphs. What promise for an old age so crowned with glory! Wounded pride, the burning ardor of a character which years had not served to render more flexible, crushed forever this brilliant destiny. Certain affronts received from inferior or jealous clergymen, personal injuries, of which St. Jerome, who reports the fact, does not mention the nature, but which Tertullian should have despised, in the high position in which his works had placed him, were the first causes of this lamentable separation. A decree of St. Zephyrinus, admitting penitent adulterers to penance, appeared to Tertullian to indicate a relaxation of doctrine. He made it an occasion to consummate his schism. Disregarding all propriety, he directed his attacks against this immutable rock of the Church, which is destined to witness innumerable, yet always impotent revolts. Alas! Tertullian, the author of the *Apologetica* and of the Book *de Præscriptionibus*, was a Montanist! Priscilla and Maximilla became in his eyes inspired prophetesses, whose sanctity he feared not to celebrate, whose miracles he published. But it was chiefly against the authority of the sovereign Pontiff, that he was excited beyond measure. "I hear," said he, "that a solemn decree has been published. The Bishop of bishops says, 'I remit the sins of adultery and fornication to those who will accomplish their penance.' Such a doctrine ought to be read, not in the churches, but in the dens of crime." The question of second marriages is treated by Tertullian with the same disdain of tradition and authority. The constant teaching of the Church regarded them as legitimate. Although the first Christians, from the desire of a more perfect life, abstained, for the greater part, none thought of blaming them as being contrary to the law of God. Tertullian assumed that as Jesus Christ had repealed the *libellum repudii* granted to the Jews by Moses, *ad duritiam cordis*, so the Holy Spirit, by the mouth of Montanus and his two prophetesses, had forbidden second marriages. Montanus and two poor visionaries were legislators of the same authority as Jesus Christ! This fallen genius did not stop with these absurdities. He continued to follow the path of the inexorable rigorism in which he had engaged. We seek in vain, through the pages on which he pours out the full bitterness of his soul against the authority of the Church and her Head, some indication of a return, some trace of repentance. His old age passed on in this afflicting obstinacy, which was a perpetual insult to the glory of his youth. Antiquity, it is true, informs us that he separated from the Montanists, but it was only to form another sect, who were named *Tertullianists*, the last remains of whom St. Augustine restored to Catholic unity. The death of Tertullian is placed about the year 245.

9. The heresy of Montanus, supported by the name of Tertullian, caused, even at Rome, and under the eyes of the holy Pontiff St. Zephyrinus, some deplorable perversions. The Pope pronounced a sentence of excommunication against

the sectaries of the new prophets (for this was the name given to the Montanists). Under his direction, orthodox doctors labored to refute the heresy. A celebrated conference was held about the year 212, between the Catholic Gaius and the Montanist Proclus. The conversion of the latter was the fruit of the learning and eloquence of Gaius, who wrote a report of the controversy. His work has not reached us.

10. While the West resounded with the din of Tertullian's fall, the East lent an ear to the instructions of Origen. This young doctor had won the admiration of the Roman world. Even the polytheists paid homage to his learning and talents. The pagan philosophers consulted him, dedicated to him their works, or cited his authority in their writings. One day he entered the school of Plotinus, at the moment when the latter was giving a lesson. The philosopher blushed, interrupted his discourse, and only resumed it at the solicitation of his illustrious auditor, on whom he pronounced a pompous eulogy in continuing his instruction. The zeal of Origen, and the simplicity and ardor of his faith, equalled his genius. The excess into which he was led by his timorous conscience, and the interpretation, in too absolute a sense, of an allegorical expression in the Gospel, are known. This action excited, in the sequel, persecutions of which we must speak hereafter. At the moment, Demetrius, patriarch of Alexandria, his bishop, regarded it as nothing more than the exaggerated fervor of a young man. He made him sensible of his fault. Origen acknowledged it with humility, and afterwards disavowed it publicly, in his homilies on the Gospels. Meanwhile, the desire to see Rome, the principal Church,* induced him to undertake the voyage thither (212).

We may readily imagine the reception which St. Zephyrinus would give to a man whose reputation, since the defection of Tertullian, was unequalled in the Church. At this epoch, Origen was engaged in a gigantic work on the Holy Scriptures. His voyage to Rome, like those which he undertook at a later

---

* In Matth., Tract., 7 sub fin.—ORIGEN, *Opera.*

period to the different countries of the known world, was perhaps connected with the project he had conceived. Struck by the variety of readings presented by the different editions of the Sacred Writings, he purposed to embrace them all in a single edition, which should thus become a universal Bible. On returning to Alexandria, he commenced the work, which occupied him during twenty years. To gain time for this and his lessons on theology, the Holy Scriptures, and philosophy, which he gave to the multitude of his disciples, he divided the care of instructing the catechumens with Heraclas, a distinguished scholar and philosopher, whom he appointed to train the neophytes in elementary knowledge. Having completed this arrangement, Origen set himself to the study of Hebrew, with his accustomed energy. When he had overcome the difficulties of this idiom, so foreign to the genius of the Greek tongue, he published his great edition of the Scriptures in eight columns, which took the name of *Octapla*. The first column contained the Hebrew text in Hebrew letters; the second, the same text in Greek letters (for the convenience of those who understood Hebrew, without being able to read it); the third, contained the version of Aquila; the fourth, that of Symmachus; the fifth, the Septuagint; the sixth, that of Theodotion; the seventh and eighth, two Greek versions of unknown authors, which Origen had found, one at Jericho, the other at Nicopolis, in Epirus. The *Hexapla* did not include the two last versions, and had, consequently, only six columns. Desirous to place this work within the reach of a greater number of readers, he put forth another edition, which contained only the four most important versions—that of Aquila, of Symmachus, of the Septuagint, and Theodotion. This edition was called *Tetrapla*. It is to be remarked that Origen was always careful to place the Septuagint in the midst of the other interpretations, to serve as a standard of comparison among them. The principal object of Origen was, in fact, to complete the version of the Septuagint, while retaining it for the basis of his work; for it was at that time the authorized version of the Catholic Church, which regarded it as the canonical version, in spite of the opposition of the Samaritans and Jews. Origen notes scrupulously all the additions which he believes ought to be made to it. To this effect, he uses the following signs: 1. That which is wanting in the Septuagint, is marked by an asterisk. These gaps are filled, by preference, from the version of Theodotion; in his default, from that of Aquila; and finally, in default of both, from that of Symmachus. 2. Another sign, called *obelos*, marks the words or phrases of the Septuagint which are wanting in the original Hebrew. Hence, there are two kinds of copies of the Septuagint: those which contain the primitive text, and those of the text collated by Origen. The first is called *Editio* κοινη, or *Vulgaris*; the other, *Editio Hexaplaris*. During more than fifty years the original copy of the *Octapla* remained hidden in a corner of the city of Tyre, where Origen expired, probably because the expenses of copying a work in forty or fifty volumes exceeded the resources of a private individual. This precious work would perhaps have perished, had not Eusebius brought it to light, and placed it in the library of Pamphilus, the martyr, at Cæsarea.

11. While the illustrious Origen adorned the Church of Alexandria by his labors, St. Narcissus, bishop of Jerusalem, edified his episcopal city by the example of his virtues. This venerable man had received from God the gift of miracles. Eusebius of Cæsarea relates, that in the night on the eve of Easter, the oil failed, and the deacons were unable to light the lamps of the church. St. Narcissus directed them to draw water from a well near by, and bring it to him. Having blessed this water, he had it poured into the lamps, when it was found changed into oil. But his sanctity could not protect him from calumny; or rather, his zeal and apostolic vigor made him a mark for the shafts of the wicked. Certain Christians, unworthy of the name, unwilling to bear the severity with which the pious bishop reproved their disorders, conspired against him, and accused him of an atrocious crime.

They attested their deposition by perjury, accompanied by imprecations. "If I do not speak the truth, let me die in flames," said one. "I consent," said another, "to be a prey to the most horrible diseases." "And I am willing to lose my sight," said a third. Narcissus, unwilling to continue a ministry which suspicion had compromised, tore himself away from the tears and supplications of the faithful. He had long desired the happiness of solitude; he withdrew into a desert, and during many years nothing was heard of the saintly bishop of Jerusalem. Meantime, his calumniators received the due chastisement of their crimes. The house of the first took fire, and he perished in it, with all his family; an unknown malady consumed the second; his body was but one infected wound, and he expired in frightful torments; the third, seized with fright at this manifestation of divine vengeance, publicly confessed his fault, and was so deeply penetrated with remorse, that by continual weeping he lost his sight. Three bishops, Dius, Germamon, and Gordius, had succeeded each other in the Pontifical See of Jerusalem, when Narcissus, then nearly a hundred and ten years old, reappeared in his episcopal city. They besought him to resume the government of his flock, and he consented with reluctance, because of his great age.

12. It pleased God soon to send him an assistant worthy of discharging his eminent functions. In a vision the Lord commanded him to choose for his successor the traveller whom he should meet the next morning at the gate of the city. Several of his people, who had had the same revelation, went out with him at the dawn of the day. A venerable stranger presented himself, who came on a pilgrimage to visit the places consecrated by the life, miracles, and passion of the Saviour. It was Alexander, bishop of Cappadocia. A disciple of St. Pantenus and of Clement of Alexandria, he had passed his youth in the study of theology. His merit had elevated him to the episcopate, and in it he had given an example of every virtue. The persecution of Septimius Severus presented him with an occasion of generously confessing his faith. Seized by

the persecutors, he was thrown into prison, where he remained seven years, encouraging the faithful by his letters, to persevere in the practice of religion. After his long and hard captivity, he undertook this voyage to Jerusalem. The clergy of the city, with Narcissus at their head, saluted the holy confessor, and in spite of his humble resistance, retained him as their bishop. This is the first instance of a bishop being transferred from one see to another, and given for a coadjutor to a bishop still living.

13. Never had the Church been more fruitful in saints and great men, than at this epoch. She extended her conquests everywhere; philosophy bowed before her. The time when the rhetoricians and sophists, proud of a vain learning, regarded her as the asylum of all material and moral poverty, and fit only for slaves, was already far away. Clement of Alexandria, Tertullian, Origen, had, in the estimation of the pagans, reconciled her with genius. The persecutions only made her power more manifest. A supernatural strength was necessary to train so many thousand men for martyrdom. There must be a vigorous sap in that religion, to transform into heroes so many disciples, recruited from all classes of Roman society, in the midst of a degenerate people. We have seen soldiers embracing the Christian religion, converted by the constancy of the martyrs whom they tortured; and now we find judges themselves, who, on quitting the tribunal where they had just condemned the witnesses of Jesus Christ, could not resist the evidence, and demanded baptism. Minucius Felix, and his friend Octavius, Roman magistrates, were remarkable for the violent hatred they bore to the Christian name. The most cruel torments, the most frightful tortures were employed by them against the disciples of the Gospel. Some months later, they made a public profession of belonging to that sect which they had hitherto persecuted, and abjured Paganism. One who was a friend of both, Cecilius of Ostia, had not yet opened his heart to the light of faith. They went to visit him at his country

house, and undertook that conversion of which Minucius has left a history in the dialogue which bears his name. One morning the three interlocutors were walking together on the sea-shore : at first, they watched the children, who amused themselves in skimming flattened pebbles along the surface of the water; after a little time, Minucius seated himself between his two friends. Cecilius, who had saluted an idol of Serapis, inquired "why the Christians hide themselves; why they have neither temples, nor altars, nor images? Who is their God? Whence does he come? Where is this only, solitary, abandoned God, whom no free nation knows? a God of so little power that he, with his adorers, is a captive of the Romans? The Romans, without this God, reign and enjoy the empire of the world. You Christians make no use of perfumes; you do not crown yourselves with flowers; you are pale and trembling; you will never rise again, as you imagine; and you do not really live now, while awaiting this chimerical resurrection." Octavius replied that the world is the temple of God; that a pure life and good works are the true sacrifice. He refutes the objection drawn from Roman grandeur, and turns to their advantage the reproach of poverty addressed to the disciples of the Gospel. He overthrows the calumnies which the pagans disseminate against the faithful; the nocturnal orgies, the infanticide repasts, the incestuous unions. Finally, he unfolds to his friend the Christian philosophy, free from the clouds that prejudice, error, and popular passions, accumulated around it. Few of the dialogues of Plato offer a finer scenic effect, or a more noble discourse. Cecilius was converted, returned to Cyrtha, in Africa, his country; became a priest, and had, as it is believed, the happiness to convert St. Cyprian to the faith, at a later period.

14. Meantime, Septimius Severus, who had allied his name with the seventh general persecution, died at York, in Great Britain (A. D. 211), while pronouncing these words, since become celebrated, "*Omnia fui, et nihil expedit*," "I have been every thing, and it amounts to nothing." The year before, just as he

had gained a great victory over the Caledonians, with whom he was at war, on returning from the field of battle, he saw Caracalla, the eldest of his sons, with a naked sword in his hands, prepared to strike him from behind. The wretched father entered his tent, placed himself in his bed with a sword beside him, and ordered his son to be called. "If thou wishest to kill me," he said to him, "take this sword, or command Papinian, here present, to pierce my throat; he will obey thee, for I make thee emperor." Caracalla, in fact, succeeded Septimus Severus. The first use he made of his authority, was to put to death his brother Geta, who had been associated with him in the empire. Twenty thousand Romans, who were suspected of having lamented the young prince, were murdered. Notwithstanding his cruelty, the new emperor did not revive the edicts of persecution; he left the magistrates and people free to continue or to cease to persecute the Christians.

15. Having heard that the inhabitants of Alexandria had indulged themselves in certain pleasantries concerning his sacred person, he took occasion to visit that city. Disguising his ulterior projects under the mask of gentleness and clemency, he entered the city, and received all imaginable honors. Suddenly, by order of the tyrant, the soldiers of his army spread themselves in every quarter, and massacred, during several days and nights, all whom they found, without distinction of age, sex, or condition. Caracalla amused himself with viewing these scenes of horror from the top of the temple of Serapis. Origen had recently returned from a journey in Arabia, having been invited by the governor—who had heard of his great reputation—to confer with him on scientific subjects. He was obliged again to leave his country, to escape the fate reserved for his unhappy townsmen. He therefore went to Cæsarea, in Palestine, and began a course of public instruction. The bishops of this province invited him—although not a priest—to expound the Scriptures in their presence to the assemblies of the faithful. Demetrius, patriarch of Alexandria, made objection to it; but St. Alex-

ander, bishop of Jerusalem, and Theoctistus of Cæsarea, replied to him in these terms: "You say it is contrary to all tradition that laymen should speak before bishops and expound the Scriptures: this opinion seems to us erroneous. In fact, when bishops find laymen capable of aiding their brethren in the interpretation of the holy books, they request them to instruct the people. For example: at Laranda, Bishop Neo caused Evelpius to speak; at Iconium, Bishop Celsus employed Paulinus; at Synnada, Bishop Atticus availed himself of the services of Theodosius. This discussion proves two things: 1st. That the usage of the primitive Church had been, sometimes to permit laymen of eminent learning and sanctity to speak in the assemblies of the faithful in order to explain the Holy Scriptures; 2d. That this usage in the third century was falling into disuse. However, Demetrius does not seem to have relished the reasons alleged by his colleagues in the episcopate, or probably happy to find a pretext for recalling to Alexandria a man who was the glory of his church, he sent two deacons to Origen, who determined him to return to Egypt.

16. About this time, by a singular coincidence, there was at Ephesus a heretic, who, reasoning on the same principles as Praxeas, with whom he had never had any connection, had arrived at the same errors, which he taught in Asia, while Praxeas disseminated them in the West. Noetus, originally of Smyrna, vain to an extravagant degree, fancied himself called to restore the Catholic dogma to its ancient purity, which, according to him, it had lost. He declared seriously that the authority of Moses and Aaron had been bestowed upon him. He taught that God the Father united Himself to the man Jesus Christ, was born, had suffered, and died with him, whence it followed that the same divine person was called sometimes the Father, sometimes the Son, indifferently. This gave to his partisans the name of *Patripassians*, because they believed that God the Father had suffered. The priests of the Church of Smyrna, under the presidency of the bishop,

summoned the heretic before them. He obstinately persisted in his false doctrines, and was, with his disciples, cut off from the Church.

17. Precisely as Praxeas had encountered a doctor who victoriously maintained the defence of catholic truth, Noetus found in St. Hippolytus, then a priest of the Roman Church, afterwards bishop of Porto, and martyr of the faith, a vigorous antagonist. St. Hippolytus, like St. Alexander, of Jerusalem, and Origen, had been a disciple of Clement of Alexandria.* The taste for study and the love of science which he had acquired at this school, grew in him with his age. Many works were the fruits of his erudition and vigils. Few of them have reached us. There remain only fragments of his work against Noetus and some extracts, gathered in 869 by Anastasius, the Librarian, of a refutation of the heretic Beron, who dogmatized at the same time as Noetus and Praxeas, under the Pontificate of St. Zephyrinus. This new sectary, first engaged in the Gnostic systems of Valentinus, had abandoned them, to fall speedily into other errors. Confounding the two natures united in Jesus Christ, but distinct, one from the other, he pretended that the body of the Saviour wrought the same things as the divinity, and that, by reciprocity, the divinity was subject to the same accidents as the flesh. St. Hippolytus combats with great precision this false doctrine which Nestorius, Eutyches, and the Monothelites, renewed, in the fourth, fifth, and sixth centuries. To mark more clearly the distinction of the two natures, he uses an

---

* In 1551, as some excavations were being made near the Church of St. Lawrence, without the walls of Rome, on the road to Tivoli, there was found in the ruins of an ancient church of St. Hippolytus, a marble statue, representing a man seated in a pulpit, on the two sides of which were graven, in Greek characters, two cycles, each of sixteen years, and which, repeated seven times, determine for a hundred and twelve years, the one the fourteenth day of the moons of March, the other the Easter Sundays. In this statue, now deposited in the Vatican, all the learned agree in recognizing St. Hippolytus, who, the ancients inform us, really composed a pascal cycle of sixteen years. The saint gives notice that his cycle begins in the first year of the reign of Alexander Severus, and that this year the pascal term fell upon April 13th, on Saturday, and that Easter was celebrated the 21st—which marks the year 222.

ingenious and very just comparison. "When I speak with the tongue, or write with the hand, I express outwardly by both of them only one and the same thought of my mind; but it does not follow that this thought is the natural product of the tongue or the hand. In the same manner, the most blessed flesh of Jesus Christ in being the instrument of the Divine operations, did not, for that reason, become of itself a creating power."

We have, besides, from this writer, two dissertations entitled, the one, *Oratio de Consummatione Mundi;* the other, *De Antichristo et Secundo Adventu Domini nostri Jesu Christi.*[*] When St. Hippolytus was occupied in the composition of these various works, he was only a priest. About the year 251 he was named the first bishop of Porto, near Rome, by Pope St. Cornelius.

18. Thus Catholic truth found faithful defenders, who consoled her under the rigor of the persecutions, and the ravages of heresy. About the same time, St. Zephyrinus had the happiness of receiving into the bosom of the Church an unhappy victim of error. Under his pontificate, a Christian named Natalis, after having generously confessed the name of Jesus Christ, before the tribunals, had allowed himself to be seduced by the disciples of Theodotus, the currier. He had even consented to be ordained bishop of this sect, on the promise of a monthly pension of a hundred and fifty Roman denarii (about twenty-five dollars of American money). "But," says a contemporary author, "our God and Lord Jesus Christ, full of mercy and not willing that a confessor who had had a part in His sufferings should be left to perish out of the Church, gave him the grace to acknowledge his crime. One morning, clothed in sackcloth, covered with ashes, and shedding torrents of tears, he came to throw himself at the feet of St. Zephyrinus. He confessed his fault, in presence of the faithful, who were touched by his humility and repentance—

---

[*] In English · *Discourse on the End of the World—Antichrist, and the second coming of our Lord.*

the sovereign Pontiff reconciled him with the Church, and admitted him to her communion.

19. Soon after, St. Zephyrinus went to receive in heaven the recompense of his labors. Some martyrologies give him the title of martyr; other historians observe, on the contrary, that he was the first Roman pontiff who had not died in torments. He expired in 217, the same year that saw Caracalla perish near Carrhas, in Mesopotamia, under the blows of Macrinus, prefect of the prætorium. The *Liber Pontificalis* attributes several decrees to St. Zephyrinus: 1st. That the deacons and priests shall be ordained in the presence of all the clergy and people. 2d. That henceforth, for the consecration of the precious blood of Jesus Christ, cups of glass or crystal shall be used, and not vases of wood, as had been hitherto the practice. 3d. That all the priests should assist at the church when the bishop celebrated the holy mysteries. St. Callistus I., by birth a Roman, succeeded him.

CHAPTER X.

§ I. Pontificate of St. Callistus I. (a. d. 217-222).

1. Heliogabalus emperor.—2. Interview between Origen and Alexander Severus.—3. Labors of Origen.—4. Journey of Origen into Greece. His ordination.—5. Julius Africanus.—6. Death of St. Callistus I.—Decrees of this Pope.

§ II. Pontificate of St. Urban I. (a. d. 222-231).

7. Alexander Severus emperor. 8.—Church of St. Mary beyond the Tiber.—9. Excommunication of Origen.—10. Persecution at Rome.—11. Martyrdom of SS. Valerianus, Tiburtius, and Maximus.—12. Martyrdom of St. Cecilia.—13. Martyrdom of St. Urban I.

§ III. Pontificate of St. Pontianus (a. d. 231-235).

14. Exile of Pope St. Pontianus.—15. Death of Demetrius, patriarch of Alexandria.—16. Sixth general persecution by Maximinus the Thracian. Martyrdom of St. Pontianus.

§ IV. Pontificate of St. Anterus (December, a. d. 235—January, a. d. 236).

17. Conversion of Ambrose, friend of Origen, and of Protoctites, priest of Cæsarea.—18. Martyrdom of Pope St. Anterus.

§ I. Pontificate of St. Callistus I. (a. d. 217-222).

1. Frivolous and inconsistent in his character, Macrinus had coveted the empire. A crime had placed him on the throne, from which he was soon driven. His genius was not equal to his ambition. After a reign of fourteen months, the army removed the usurper from power as easily as it had permitted him to assume it. Macrinus was murdered by the soldiers of the legion of Emessa, in Syria, who brought in triumph to Rome the young Heliogabalus, grand nephew of Septimius Severus. "It was necessary," says a celebrated

writer, "that all the vices should be seated on the throne, before men would consent to place there a religion which condemned all vices and all passions."* The city of Romulus, of Scipio, and of Cæsar, beheld the arrival of a young Syrian, a priest of the sun, having a painted circlet around his eyes, cheeks colored with vermilion, and wearing a tiára, a collar, bracelets, a tunic of cloth of gold, a silk robe of the Phœnician pattern, and sandals ornamented with carved stones; this young Syrian, surrounded by eunuchs, buffoons, chanters, and dwarfs, danced and marched backwards before a triangular stone, the image of the god whose priest he was. This was Heliogabalus, the new emperor. He surpassed Nero in cruelty, Caracalla in prodigality: but the vice which chiefly governed the world under his reign was impurity. He converted the imperial palace into a sink of debauchery. His prefect of the prætorium was a buffoon; coachmen and strollers became senators and consuls. He created a senate of women, to decide upon questions of fashion.

2. While this crowned fool dishonored the throne, Alexander Severus, his cousin, acquired, under the direction of his mother, Mammæa, the great art of ruling. Mammæa loved and admired Christianity; it appears that she even professed it. In the year 218, four years before the elevation of her son to the empire, having heard at Antioch, which at that time was her place of residence, of the great reputation of Origen, she sent an escort of honor to accompany the great doctor to her palace. Origen remained some time near Mammæa and the future emperor; he discoursed with them on the Christian religion, the divinity of its origin, the sublimity of its dogmas, and the purity of its morals. The young prince was pleased with these lessons; and if in the sequel he exhibited no taste for the dissolute habits of his cousin Heliogabalus, if he appeared in the whole course of his life a lover of justice and humanity, his contemporaries, as well as posterity, have attrib-

---

* Etudes Historiques, par M. de Chateaubriand.

uted these high qualities to the Christian influence of his early education. Origen left Antioch loaded by his illustrious host with honors, and returned to Alexandria to devote himself to the studies which he loved.

3. He had recently converted to the Catholic faith Ambrose, a rich man of Alexandria, who had been attached to the sect of the Valentinians. This new disciple, charmed with the eloquence and erudition of his master, stimulated still further the natural ardor of Origen for labor. He requested of him a general commentary on all the books of the Holy Scriptures: the doctor set himself to work, and composed his Εξηγητρια (*commentaries*)—*Treatise against Celsus—Defence of the Christian Religion against Celsus the Philosopher*, one of his best productions. Ambrose furnished all that was necessary to meet the expenses of these works. He induced his master to lodge in his house, that he might be in a better position to promote his studies—and he placed at his disposal seven secretaries, *notarii*, to write at his dictation. Other scribes, *librarii*, made neat copies of the first proofs of the *notarii*. Finally, others again multiplied copies of the same works. Stenographers reproduced the oral instructions, which the learned doctor gave every day to his auditory. Origen revised the manuscripts, in the presence of his friend, during the hours of repasts, that not a moment of his precious time should be lost. Origen yielded to the well-intentioned exactions of Ambrose, whom he sometimes laughingly called his *overseer*. The multiplicity of his labors, and the diversity of his occupations, excited his imagination instead of exhausting it. He labored night and day with incredible ardor. His constitution, though frail and delicate, nevertheless sustained this lengthened toil. In this way he composed nearly six thousand works, if we include in the number his homilies and letters. This indefatigable application gave him among his contemporaries the name of *Adamantinus* (constitution of diamond).

4. Meanwhile, the churches of Greece were lamenting the

ravages made among them by the heresies of the Valentinians, of the Montanists, and of Noëtus. They called for Origen, that prodigy of eloquence, in whom was revived the learning of the holy Fathers, to combat these new sectaries. He forced himself away from his studious retreat and his laborious exercises, to yield to this call of charity. Ambrose would not be separated from his illustrious friend, and accompanied him in his journey. Origen travelled by land, and entering Palestine, went to salute St. Alexander, bishop of Jerusalem, and Theoctistus, of Cæsarea, his ancient hosts. Demetrius, patriarch of Alexandria, had given him, on his departure, letters of communion, in which he referred in the highest terms to the knowledge and virtue of his catechist. The bishops of Palestine, from their admiration of this great man, desired to attach him in a special manner to the Church, which, as a simple layman, he had served with so much glory. They therefore imposed hands on him, and ordained him priest. He was then forty years of age. Origen continued his journey. At Nicopolis (the ancient Emmaus), he saw the learned Julius Africanus; and, passing on to Ephesus, reduced the heretics to a humiliating silence. In every city he held conferences with the sectaries, whom he confounded by the clearness of his arguments, leaving them no other resource to cover their defeat than that of changing the published reports of the controversies, and of attributing to the Catholic doctor, in these intentional falsifications, opinions and reasonings which he had never pronounced—a species of calumny which they used without scruple.

Demetrius, having heard at Alexandria of the ordination of Origen, wrote to the bishops of Palestine to complain of this irregular proceeding. Whether it was jealousy, as is intimated by Eusebius and St. Jerome, or simply zeal for the preservation of ecclesiastical discipline, which actuated Demetrius under these circumstances, is a question which probably may never be determined. However it may have been, the patriarch of Alexandria made bitter recriminations. He informed the bishops of Asia, in circular letters, that Origen, by an action until now unknown, had infringed the laws of the Church, and had incurred canonical irregularity. Alexander replied that he had conferred the priesthood on Origen on the strength of the letters of recommendation given by Demetrius; and that he was ignorant of the facts mentioned in the subsequent letters of the patriarch. After rather long negotiations, this difference was settled, and Origen returned to Alexandria. But the peace which he enjoyed was not of long duration.

5. Julius Africanus, whom Origen met in Palestine, was one of the most learned men of this epoch. He was from Emmaus, a small country town, which Vespasian changed into a city, under the name of Nicopolis. It had been recently burned by Quintilius Varus, governor of Syria. Julius Africanus, sent as a deputy by his compatriots to the Emperor Heliogabalus, had obtained its restoration. The chronological labors of Julius Africanus have made him celebrated. To prove the antiquity of religion, and the novelty of the pagan histories, he wrote in Greek, his mother-tongue, a universal history, from the creation of the world to the fourth year of the reign of Heliogabalus, A. D. 221. This important work, which still existed in the time of Photius, is now lost. He wrote another book, which he named *Kestos;*[*] or, *The Embroidered Girdle*, in imitation of the *Stromata*, or *Tapestry*, of Clement of Alexandria. Natural history, agriculture, geography, history, geometry, and medicine, furnished the materials for this work, which has reached our days. An Epistle to Aristides, in which Julius Africanus seeks to reconcile the two genealogies of Jesus Christ according to St. Matthew and St. Luke, has also escaped the wreck of time. "It is," said the author, "a common tradition in Palestine, that Jacob and Heli were uterine brothers; Heli dying without children, Jacob espoused his widow, and was the father of Joseph according to nature, while Heli was

---

[*] Histoire de la littérature Grecque profane, t. v. p. 269: Paris, librairie Gide, 1832.

his father according to law." The interview between Origen and Julius Africanus gave rise to a bibliographic controversy between these two learned men. Origen employed, in presence of Julius Africanus, a quotation from the History of Susanna. Africanus declared it to be apocryphal. In a letter which he wrote to Origen on this subject, which is still extant, he defends his thesis, relying for the principal foundation of his argument on the absence of the History of Susanna in the copies of the Jews. Origen replied from Nicomedia, that the catholic tradition, until then unanimous, was a sufficient guarantee of its authenticity. He added, that it was not safe to remove the bounds fixed by the Fathers; and besides, in the present question, the tradition of the Jewish doctors was itself in conformity with the opinion of the Church. The Alexandrian doctor at the same time engaged St. Hippolytus to write a commentary on the History of Susanna. This is all that is known of the labors and history of Julius Africanus.

6. St. Callistus did not live to witness the last persecutions of Origen. Although the Christians generally were less disturbed, and the edicts of Septimus Severus had fallen into desuetude, the emperors lost no occasion to wound, in the persons of popes, bishops, and priests, a religion which they always hoped to destroy.* In the latter years of the pontificate of St. Callistus, the saintly priest Callipodius was beheaded. His body, ignominiously dragged through the streets of Rome, and cast into the Tiber, was buried with the highest honors by the holy pope. A similar fate awaited the latter. Some time afterwards he was imprisoned, and left to suffer all the horrors of famine. His persecutors allowed him only food enough to preserve his strength sufficiently to endure the torment of the rods with which he was beaten every day. The good old man was finally precipitated from the

---

* Such were, in fact, according to St. Cyprian, a few years later, the dispositions of the Emperor Decius: "Cum tyrannus infestus sacerdotibus Dei fanda et nefanda comminaretur cum multo patientius et tolerabilius audiret levari adversus se æmulum principem quam constitui Romæ Dei sacerdotem."—ST. CYPRIAN: *Epistola ad Antonianum*.

window of his prison to the bottom of a well, where he expired, October 14th, A. D. 222. The reign of Heliogabalus ended the same year. He had prepared himself for all emergencies, when it might become necessary to die by his own hand; cords of silk, a golden poniard, poisons enclosed in vases of crystal and porphyry—an interior court, paved with precious stones, upon which he intended to throw himself from a lofty tower. But all these resources failed him. He had lived in dens of infamy—he was killed in a sewer; and his body was thrown into the Tiber, where he had cast the good priest Callipodius. The *Liber Pontificalis* attributes to St. Callistus a decree which, according to apostolic tradition, regulated the Ember-Days. This Pontiff ordained that three times in the year, a fast on bread, wine and oil, should be observed on Saturday, according to the words of the Prophet. Baronius believes that it should read *four times*, because the prophecy of Zacharias, to which it alludes,* says positively that the thanksgiving fast for the blessings of Providence should be celebrated four times in the year. St. Callistus gave his name to the celebrated cemetery of the Appian Way—in which were deposited the glorious remains of forty-six popes and many martyrs.† Among the bishops ordained by this pontiff may be named Hippolytus, of Porto, whom we have already mentioned. St. Urban I., by birth a Roman, was elected to succeed St. Callistus.

§ II. PONTIFICATE OF ST. URBAN I. (A. D. 222–231).‡

7. The death of Heliogabalus left the throne to the son of Mammæa, the young disciple of Origen. Alexander Severus had conceived for Christianity and its divine founder a respect

---

* Thus saith the Lord of hosts: The fast of the fourth month, and the fast of the fifth, and the fast of the seventh, and the fast of the tenth, shall be to the house of Judah, joy, and gladness, and great solemnities: only love ye truth and peace.—ZACH. PIAS viii, 19.

† The number is estimated at 174,000.

‡ See, for this period of ecclesiastical history, *L'Histoire de Sainn Jean*, par le R. P. dom P. GUÉRANGER.

which he ever preserved. The *Lararium* (oratory) of his palace included not only the statues of the gods, and the emperors who had merited most of the human race; Alexander had also placed there the statue of Jesus Christ, to whom he rendered divine honors. His admiration for the Son of Mary was so unfeigned, that he even laid a proposition before the senate to admit to a rank among the gods the founder of a religion whose morals were so pure. The senate desired to consult the oracles upon this imperial proposition, and Lampridius, a contemporary author, reports their response to have been, that if this new apotheosis were to be celebrated, the temples would be soon abandoned, and all the world would become Christian. The maxim, *Do unto others only that which you would wish them to do to you*, was constantly on the lips of Alexander, and he freely acknowledged that he had borrowed it from the Christians. He had it engraved in his palaces and on the public edifices. By his order, a herald proclaimed it publicly in the punishment of criminals. A fact related by Lampridius, and which throws great light on the situation of the Church in Rome, will serve to make known the impartiality of Alexander in cases affecting the Christians.

8. In the region beyond the Tiber, at the foot of the Mount Janiculum, was situated the famous *Taberna meritoria*, from which it was said that in the year of Rome 718, a fountain of oil had burst forth and flowed a whole day, like a mysterious river.* Under the pontificate of St. Callistus I., this celebrated place had passed into the possession of the Christians. The pontiff erected a church on the spot, and dedicated it to the Mother of the Saviour. The new sanctuary bore the name of "St. Mary beyond the Tiber." But the *Popinarii* (tavern-keepers) laid complaints before Alexander, because a place hitherto open for the advantage of the public, had been taken from them to be consecrated to a worship which was not recognized by the

---

* This fact is reported in the chronicles of Eusebius, and in those of St. Prosper, Idacius, and Orosius. Dion Cassius mentions it in his History of Rome, lib. xliii. p. 385, edit. of 1606.

laws of the empire. The good dispositions of the prince towards the Christians appear in his decision of this case. "I prefer," he said, "that God should be honored in this place in any manner whatever, rather than to restore it again to the venders of wine."

9. Meanwhile the East, warmly interested in the glory and reputation of Origen, engaged passionately in the discussion which had arisen at Alexandria regarding him. A council of bishops of the province, with the patriarch Demetrius at their head, had begun by examining the affair of his ordination. It was decided that Origen should not be deposed from the priesthood, but that he should withdraw from Alexandria, and that he should no longer have the privilege of continuing his lessons. The celebrated catechist had not awaited the result of the deliberations of the assembly, but had retired, in advance, to Palestine, leaving the direction of the catechumens to Heraclas, his disciple. The affair could not stop here. In the prodigious number of the works that had issued from the pen of the Alexandrian doctor, numerous errors were believed to exist. Were they the work of heretics, who had interpolated them without his knowledge? or, were they simple hypotheses which his rich imagination had taken pleasure in creating on points not yet defined? or, were they a consequence of the human weakness to which the loftiest minds must pay their tribute whenever they depart from the rule traced by the Church? To whatever cause they may be due, when examined in a second council, assembled by the care, and under the presidency of Demetrius, they were judged to be of sufficient gravity to lead to the deposition and even the excommunication of Origen. St. Jerome, while warmly defending the learned Alexandrian, informs us that Rome and the bishops of the Universal Church adhered to the acts of the council of Alexandria. But the Bishops of Palestine, Arabia, and Phœnicia, refused to believe in the culpability of Origen. This illustrious doctor, on learning his condemnation, addressed to the churches of Egypt a letter, in

which he explains himself in an orthodox manner on all the contested points, and demands that they shall not render him responsible for interpolations made in his writings. These spontaneous testimonies of attachment to catholic truth were sufficient to establish the innocence of Origen with his friends. Yet some erroneous doctrines are still imputed to him, for the most part extracted from his book *Peri archon; or, Of the First Causes*. He says there, 1st. That matter was created from all eternity; that, after this world, there will be many others, as before it many others had an existence; God being never unoccupied, creation is for him a necessity. 2d. That all souls were created before the world in a perfect equality, and with subtile bodies which are inseparable from them; that, having fallen into various faults, they were exiled in the angelic nature, in human forms, and even to the sun and stars, according to the degree of their culpability; that the soul which continued intimately united by charity to its Creator, merited, by its perseverance, to be joined, by an indissoluble tie, to the person of Christ. 3d. That, delivered from their bondage, souls go to heaven to receive the prize of their merits, or to hell, to endure the pain of their sins; but that neither recompense nor punishment is eternal, because the damned and the blessed, preserving their free will, the latter can be expelled from heaven by a new fault, and the former, by their repentance, may participate in the benefits of the universal redemption, from which the Divine Goodness does not even exclude the devil. 4th. That the fire of hell is nothing more than remorse of conscience. Origen has also been accused of favoring Pelagianism; of supposing man capable of elevating himself to a perfection which could free him from all sin, or even from all temptation; of not having a firm belief in the transmission of original sin; and of treating as irremissible, sins committed after the reception of the Holy Spirit. If we are permitted to think that Origen himself was a stranger to these errors, it cannot be denied that heretics have given them as from him It is a misfortune of great men that their authority often serves to accredit opinions which were not theirs, but the germ of which may be detected in their writings. All the East was troubled by innovators, who, under the shadow of Origen's name, denied the divinity of Jesus Christ, and the eternity of punishment; and maintained the pre-existence of souls, and the reality of an anterior life, in which they had been capable of merit or demerit. At a later period, A. D. 553, we shall see Origenism condemned by the second council of Constantinople, the fifth ecumenical council.

10. In spite of the good-will of Alexander towards Christianity, and the thirty years of peace which had followed the fifth general persecution under Septimus Severus, the Roman legislation had not been changed in its hostile disposition against the disciples of Jesus Christ. The legists of the imperial palace, Domitius Ulpian and Julius Paulus, whose names are as imposing in the origin of jurisprudence as they are odious in the annals of Christianity, had taken pleasure in bringing together, in their compilations, the ordinances which devoted the faithful to death. The Roman superstition and the hatred of the people against the Christians, watched together over the maintenance of those sanguinary edicts, and the tolerance of the prince, which could provisionally suspend the execution of them, went not so far as to efface them from the code of the empire. A caprice of the populace, or the ill-will of some subaltern magistrate, sufficed to renew the ancient persecutions against the Church. In this way the virgins Martina and Tatiana gave their lives for Jesus Christ. The Pope St. Urban I., twice summoned to the pretorium, generously confessed his faith. It had been impossible for him to live within the city, and his ordinary retreat was in the catacombs of the Appian way, in the cemetery which his predecessor, St. Callistus, had recently enlarged. In the spring of the year 230, the Emperor Alexander quitted Rome to direct an expedition against the Persians. He left, in the quality of prefect, Turcius Almachius, a personage known for his hatred against the Christians.

The occasion appeared to him favorable to indulge in violence towards them, and he exercised it at first on those belonging to the lower orders. Not content with mangling their bodies by tortures of all kinds, Almachius resolved that they should be deprived of sepulture. It was with gold that devoted Christians had to purchase from the executioners the precious remains of the martyrs. They lovingly reunited the limbs, separated by the sword, and gathered their blood with sponges, which they afterwards pressed into vials or ampullæ; and to preserve for Christian posterity the full testimonials of their victory, they sought diligently even for the instruments of torture.

11. Illustrious victims, also, were reserved for the fury of Almachius and the palm of martyrdom. Cecilia, a Roman virgin, descended from the ancient and noble race of the Cecilii, in the midst of a pagan family had received the faith in her earliest infancy, and devoted to God her virginity. Her parents had married her, against her wishes, to a young pagan, named Valerian. Marriages between Christians and pagans still occurred at this epoch, and if they sometimes led into difficult situations, they were often the instruments employed by God to gain the infidel party to the true faith. The Church, conformably to the Apostolic doctrine, strongly disapproved them, and necessity alone could excuse the faithful who contracted them. However it might have been in this instance, Cecilia said to Valerian, "I am under the care of an angel whom God has appointed protector of my virginity. Be cautious, therefore, to do nothing which can excite against you the anger of the Lord." Astonished at this language, the young pagan respected his spouse, and said that he would believe in Jesus Christ, if he could see the angel who guarded Cecilia. The pious virgin availed herself of the occasion to instruct him in the truths of the Gospel, and soon Valerian declared himself ready to receive baptism. He went into the catacombs of the Appian way, to throw himself at the feet of St. Urban, who conferred on him the sacrament of regen-

eration. Tiburtius, his brother, had, soon after, the same happiness. These two neophytes distinguished themselves among all the Christians of Rome, by their zeal in gathering the bodies of the martyrs immolated by the orders of Almachius. Soon they were denounced to this magistrate, who commanded them to appear before his tribunal. They courageously confessed their faith, and refused to offer libations to the gods. "To what god do you pay homage?" inquired Almachius. "Is there any other," replied the martyrs, "that you should ask us such a question in regard to God? Is there more than one?" "But at least tell me the name of this one God, of whom you speak?" "The name of God neither you nor any mortal can discover. It is incommunicable." "But Jupiter, is not that the name of a god?" "You are under a mistake," said Valerian, "Jupiter is the name of a corrupter, a libertine. Your own authors represent him as a homicide, a man guilty of all the vices; and you dare to call him a god! I am astonished at your hardihood; for the name of God can only belong to a being who has nothing in common with sin, and who possesses all the virtues." "And so," replied Almachius, "the entire universe is in error; you and your brother only know the true God." "Do not deceive yourself," said Valerian; "the Christians, those who have embraced this holy doctrine, are already innumerable in the empire. It is you who form the minority; you are the planks which float on the sea after a shipwreck, and have no other destination than to be burned." The generous boldness of Valerian had its immediate recompense. Almachius ordered him to be scourged with rods. During his punishment, the young patrician addressed the crowd: "Citizens of Rome," he cried, "let not the view of these torments hinder you from confessing the truth: believe in the Lord, who alone is holy. Destroy the gods of wood and stone to which Almachius burns his incense: crush them into dust, and know that they who adore them will be eternally tormented." At length Almachius condemned the two brothers to be decapitated, and sent them to Maximus, his registrar, with orders to execute the sentence the following day, at a spot four miles from Rome. During the night, the holy confessors, and Cecilia, who came to visit them, converted Maximus, his family, and the soldiers who guarded their prison; and, at the appointed hour, they finished, together, their glorious martyrdom. Almachius, informed of the conversion of Maximus, caused him to be beaten to death with whips loaded with lead, which was the punishment of persons of inferior rank. St. Cecilia deposited the bodies of the three martyrs in the cemetery of St. Callistus, and, foreseeing that the persecution would soon fall upon herself, she prevented the confiscation of her goods by distributing them to the poor, and employed the last hours which she had still to live, in the conversion of a multitude of pagans whom her example and instructions led to the faith. Pope St. Urban had the joy to receive in his arms these new children of the Church.

12. As she had anticipated, Almachius gave the order for her appearance before him. The virgin answered the questions of the prefect with a holy assurance. "Whence comes it that you have this boldness before me?" said he to her.—"From a pure conscience, and a simple faith."—"Art thou ignorant that thou art in my power?"—"And you—do you know who is my spouse and my defender?"—"Who is he?"—"The Lord Jesus Christ."—"Knowest thou not that our masters, the invincible emperors, have ordered that those who will not deny they are Christians shall be punished, and they who will consent to deny shall be acquitted?"—"Your emperors are in error. The law on which you rely proves only one thing—it is, that you are cruel, and we are innocent. In fact, if the name of Christian were a crime, it would be our part to deny it, and yours to force us by torments to confess it."—"Unhappy creature, knowest thou not that the power of life and death is placed in my hands by the emperor?"—"How can you say that the prince has conferred on you the power of life and death? You well know

that you have only the power of death. You can take away life from those who enjoy it, but you cannot restore it to the dead. Say, then, that the emperor has made of you a minister of death, and nothing more."—"Cease this audacity, and sacrifice to the gods."—"You call these mute stones gods? They are incapable of protecting themselves from the flames, or of drawing you out. Christ only can save from death, and deliver the guilty man from the fire." These were the last words of Cecilia before the judge. Almachius gave orders that she should be taken home, and inclosed in the bath-room of her palace, called by the Romans the *Caldarium*, which should be heated to the degree of suffocation, and continued until the virgin, left without air under its burning vault, should die without the necessity of an executioner. But the saint, after remaining three days in this heated atmosphere, was still living. Almachius then sent a lictor into the bath-room to take off her head. The soldier struck her three times with his axe, and, his work unfinished, withdrew (the law forbade its further continuance), leaving the saint bathed in blood. St. Cecilia lived three days afterwards, and finally yielded to God her glorious soul, November 22d, A. D. 230.

13. Some time after this event, Pope St. Urban was brought before Almachius. "Is this," said he, "that seducer whom the Christians have made their pope?" "Yes," replied the venerable man, "it is I, who have seduced men to abandon the ways of iniquity, to lead them into the ways of justice." St. Urban was cast into prison with two priests who had been arrested with him. A second interrogatory was equally unfavorable to the views of Almachius. The two priests, having generously confessed their faith, were scourged with loaded whips. During this torture, Almachius said to the pontiff, "Thou art old, and for this reason thou regardest death as rest; thou art jealous of these young men; thou persuadest them to sacrifice their lives, because thy own is nearly at an end." One of the priests, indignant at this outrage, interrupted the prefect: "Your words are evident false-

hoods," he said. "Our father, from his youth, has always regarded Jesus Christ as his life, and death as a gain. More than once he has confessed Christ, and exposed his life for the flock confided to him." Led back to prison, Urban converted to the faith the jailor, Anolinus, who soon paid with his life for the honor of being enrolled among the followers of the Lord. Finally, by the order of Almachius, the confessors were led out on the Nomentana road to be decapitated. On the way, Urban thus exhorted his companions: "It is the Lord who calls us; He who has said: 'Come to me, all ye that labor and are burdened, and I will refresh you.' Until now we have known the Lord only as in a glass, and as an enigma; behold the moment when we go to see Him, face to face!" The persecutors beheaded them, and the bodies of the martyrs were taken by Christians to the cemetery of Pretextatus, May 25th, A. D. 231. St. Urban provided for the dignity of the service in the churches of Rome. He replaced the vases of the altar with silver ones, and caused to be made, among other things, twenty-five silver patens for various churches of the city. These patens were of large dimensions, for they were destined to receive the breads which each one of the faithful, who was to communicate, brought as an offering. The *Liber Pontificalis* makes no mention of the decrees attributed, afterwards, to St. Urban, on the doubtful authority of Mercator. Pontianus, a Roman, was elevated to the see of St. Peter in the following month of June.

§ III. PONTIFICATE OF ST. PONTIANUS (A. D. 231–235).

11. The return of Alexander Severus restored, for some time, tranquillity to the Church of Rome—at least, the violence of Almachius does not seem to have been prolonged beyond this epoch. The impressions of the emperor, when he was made acquainted with the acts of the prefect, are not known. It is to be supposed that this prince, who detested cruelty, must have blamed the excesses of the prefect, but it does not

appear that he expressed in any way his displeasure at the judicial murder of so many Christians. However this may have been, the system followed under the reign of Alexander in regard to the sovereign pontiffs, was not slow in being applied to Pontianus. This saintly pope had to suffer persecution for his ministry: he was not condemned to death, but an order emanating from the imperial court exiled him, with the priest Hippolytus (not the bishop of Porto), to the isle of Buccina, one of the wildest on the southern coast of Sardinia. Separated from his see, Pontianus abdicated.

15. As yet, the affair of the excommunication of Origen was not concluded. This doctor always complained that the bishops called together by Demetrius, the patriarch of Alexandria, had judged of his doctrine from interpolated books which the heretics circulated in his name. Palestine continued to offer him the hospitality which Egypt, his native land, refused. His habitual residence was at Cæsarea. Theoctistus, and St. Alexander of Jerusalem, had confided to him the charge of interpreter of the Scriptures, and found so much utility and pleasure in his learned discourses, that they were rarely separated from him. Firmilianus, bishop of Cæsarea, in Cappadocia, shared in their admiration for this great man. Sometimes he sent for Origen, for the benefit of the churches which he directed; sometimes he went to visit him in Judea, to confer on divine things. Demetrius died A. D. 231, having occupied the see of Alexandria forty-three years. The affection which he manifested for Origen during the first period of his episcopate, the severity which he used against him afterwards, the cause of the Alexandrian doctor sustained by holy bishops, his contemporaries, and embraced with warmth by St. Jerome—present a problem that has never been solved, and leaves posterity in doubt of the true sentiments of Origen. But the death of the patriarch, and the election of Heraclas, the disciple and friend of Origen, who was elevated to the see of Alexandria, put an end to the strife. The chair of catechist, left vacant by the promotion of

Heraclas to the episcopate, was confided to another disciple of Origen, St. Dionysius of Alexandria, who was also destined to fill the patriarchal see.

16. Alexander had undertaken an expedition against the Germans. The legions, dissatisfied with his severity in the re-establishment of military discipline, and instigated by Maximinus, of Thrace, assassinated him near Mayence, in the twenty-eighth year of his age (A. D. 235). Maximinus hastened to reap the fruits of the crime. The new emperor, formerly a shepherd in the mountains of Thrace, was a giant of eight feet and a half in height, coarse and ignorant, speaking the Latin very imperfectly, despising men, and of a character arrogant, hard, and ferocious. His first act was to publish edicts of death against the Christians, whom he detested for the sole reason that Alexander had loved them. This was the sixth general persecution of the Church. The decrees of Maximinus were specially directed against those who taught in the Church, or governed it. The material impossibility of extending them to all the faithful without depopulating the empire, not less than the hope of extinguishing religion in the blood of its chiefs and pastors, had dictated this policy. An order was immediately expedited to the isle to which Alexander had banished him, for the execution of Pope St. Puntianus (November, A. D. 235). His body was afterwards transported to Rome, and deposited, under the pontificate of St. Fabian, in the cemetery of St. Callistus. Eleven days afterwards, St. Anterus, a Greek by birth, succeeded him, December 3d, A. D. 235.

§ IV. PONTIFICATE OF ST. ANTERUS (DEC. A. D. 235–JAN. A. D. 236).

17. The reputation of Origen, in the East, pointed him out to the persecutors as the most indefatigable of the doctors of the Church, and he was sought for with particular care. But having retired into Cappadocia, near the Bishop Firmilianus, his friend, he lay concealed two years in the house of

a rich and pious woman, named Juliana. His friend Ambrose, then a deacon, and Protoctites, a priest of Cæsarea, in Palestine, were seized and conveyed into Germany, where Maximinus then was. Origen wrote to his friend an exhortation to martyrdom. The two confessors gave, in the presence of the tyrant, a solemn homage to the Christian faith; nevertheless, they were not put to death; and the end of the reign of Maximinus, which happened at the close of the same year (236), restored them to liberty. The martyrdom of St. Ursula and her companions at Cologne, is placed at this epoch.* These were, with the Pope St. Anterus, the only known victims of the sixth persecution by Maximinus.

18. St. Anterus signalized his pontificate, which lasted only a month, by the care he took to put together the acts of the martyrs, collected by notaries appointed for the purpose since the time of St. Clement I. These glorious archives were to teach Christians, in ages to come, the worth of a victory purchased with so much blood. Anterus was denounced before Maximinus, as one affecting to honor the memory of the enemies of the empire and of the gods. He was beheaded January 3d, A. D. 236.

* The common tradition of the eleven thousand virgins reposes evidently on the false manner of reading the expressions: *Ursula et XI. M. V.* Some authors pretend that the name of *Undecimilla*, companion of St. Ursula, has given rise to this error.*

* The martyrdom of St. Ursula and her numerous companions has been established very conclusively by the learned investigations of the Rev. Victor de Buck, published in 1858, in the ninth volume of the Bollandists for October. They were martyred by the Huns who retreated through Cologne after the defeat of Attila at Chalons Sur-Marne, A. D. 451. Father de Buck's investigations verify in a remarkable manner the pious traditions of the faithful regarding St. Ursula and her companions. S

CHAPTER XI.

§ I. Pontificate of St. Fabian (A. D. 236–250).

1. Election of Pope St. Fabian (A. D. 236-250).—2. St. Gregory of Neocæsarea. Plan of Christian education of Origen. 3. Election of St. Gregory Thaumaturgus to the bishopric of Neocæsarea. 4. His miracles. 5. Election of St. Alexander the collier to the bishopric of Comana. 6. Relaxation in the morals of the faithful. 7. The Emperor Philip checked by the Bishop St. Babylas at the gate of the church at Antioch. 8. Heresy of Beryllus, bishop of Bozra (A. D. 242). Heresy touching the resurrection. 9. Elcesaïtæ. 10. Conversion of St. Cyprian. 11. Treatise on the vanity of idols. The book of Testimonies of St. Cyprian. 12. Promotion of St. Cyprian to the bishopric of Carthage. 13. Massacre of the Christians at Alexandria. 14. Seventh general persecution, under the Emperor Decius. Death of St. Fabian. Works of his pontificate.

§ I. Pontificate of St. Fabian (A. D. 236–250).

1. The usurpation of Maximinus had been the signal for the most complete anarchy in the empire. The legions created at will new Cæsars, who appeared a moment on the throne, and fell under the poniard of a rival, abandoned by their soldiers almost as soon as they were elected. From the year 235, in which Maximinus died, to the year 244, the Gordians, father and son, Puppianus, Balbinus, and Gordian III., in turn assumed the purple, which soon served as their winding-sheet. "But, by the side of these elections by the sword, the peaceable elections of those other sovereigns, who reigned by the staff, continued."* Eusebius relates the marvellous circumstance which attended the promotion of St. Fabian to the sovereign pontificate. As the brethren were assembled for the election, several persons of distinction were proposed. No

* M. de Chateaubriand: *Études Historiques*. Discours, Ire partie.

one thought of Fabian, when a dove, flying above the assembly, came to rest on his head. He was unanimously proclaimed, January 10th, A. D. 236.

2. By a privilege common to all great men, the name of Origen is found mingled in all that was most holy and illustrious in his time. He was still at Cæsarea when Providence led there a young man destined in the designs of God to become the instrument of great things. Gregory, of Neocæsarea, in Pontus, of noble and worthy but pagan parentage, accompanied his sister, who was married to a jurist whom the governor of Palestine had brought with him, as recorder, to aid in the administration of the provinces. He had just closed his course of study of the Roman law, with high distinction, and had already appeared at the bar with success, when, by the grace of God, he met with Origen. The sort of charm which the eloquent Alexandrian exercised over others acted with the more power upon Gregory, as the young man was better prepared for it by chaste morals and a life exempt from the corruption so frequent in the Pagan world. Having come to Cæsarea only to escort his sister, and to return forthwith to his home, the young orator soon formed such an attachment for Origen that they were compared to Jonathan and David. From that time, forgetting affairs, country, parents, ambitious projects, or profane studies, he thought of nothing but to profit by the lessons of a master who led him into a heavenly country, until now unknown. He afterwards wrote the method used by the Christian philosopher to bend his soul, by slow degrees, under the yoke of faith. This plan of Christian education in the third century presents, in its vast extent, the best reply to those who pretend that in its origin the faith was disseminated through the world by the fanaticism of narrow and ignorant minds. It may, at the same time, give an idea of the universality of Origen's knowledge. "Like a skilful agriculturist," said St. Gregory, "who examines in all its aspects the land which he intends to prepare for cultivation, Origen sounded and penetrated the sentiments of his disciples, making

inquiries, and reflecting upon their replies. When he had prepared them to receive the seed of truth, he instructed them in various branches of philosophy : in logic, to form their judgment, by teaching them to discriminate between solid reasonings and the specious sophisms of error; in physics, to make them admire the wisdom of God by an analytic knowledge of His works; in geometry, to habituate their minds to rectitude by the rigor of mathematical propositions; in astronomy, to elevate and extend their thoughts, by giving them immensity for a horizon; finally, in morals—not those of the philosophers whose definitions and sterile divisions give birth to no virtue, but practical morals, making them study in themselves the movements of the passions, so that the soul, seeing itself as in a mirror, may extirpate every vice, even to the roots. He then approached theology, or the knowledge of God. He made them read on Providence, which has created the world and governs it, all that has been written by the ancients, philosophers or poets, Greeks or barbarians, without otherwise minding their systems, their sects, or their particular opinions. In this labyrinth of pagan philosophy he served as their guide to discern whatever might be really true and useful, without allowing them to be fascinated by the pomp and ornaments of language.* He laid it down as a principle, that in whatever regards God, we must trust only God, and the prophets inspired by him. And then he commenced the interpretation of the Scriptures, which he knew thoroughly, and which, by the grace of God, he had penetrated in all their most secret depths."

3. After five years employed in these studies, Gregory received baptism, and prepared to leave the master who had revealed to his youth a new path and another life. In presence of a numerous assemblage, he addressed to him, with a trembling voice, his last adieu. "Pray the Lord," he said,

---

* "It is permitted," wrote Origen to Gregory, "in coming out of Egypt to enter the land of promise, to bring away the riches of the Egyptians, and to use them for the construction of the tabernacle, although experience has taught me that this is useful to few."

at the close, "to console us in this separation; pray Him to send His good angel for our guide; but pray Him, above all, to bring us back near to you; more than all the rest, this would console us." Such were, in those happy days of the rising Church, the ties of gratitude and attachment that united the Christian disciples to their learned masters. On his return to Neocæsarea, Gregory, in whom his countrymen expected to find an eloquent orator and an eminent jurist, showed himself to his astonished fellow-citizens only as the most fervent of neophytes. He abandoned all that he possessed in the world, and retired into a solitary country-house, to be there alone with God. Such conduct, in a city which counted only seventeen Christians, seemed folly; but it was the folly of the Cross which converted the world. Phedimus, archbishop of Amasea, elected Gregory to the episcopate of Neocæsarea. It was difficult to overcome the resistance of the saint, who fled from solitude to solitude, to escape the burden of the episcopate. Here is revealed, in all its plenitude, the power of miracles which Jesus Christ imparted to His disciples, when He said that they should do still more wonderful things than Himself. Each step of the new bishop was accompanied by prodigies.

4. "Command this rock to go to such a place," said a pagan priest to him, "and I will believe in Jesus." Gregory, animated by that faith which removes mountains, spoke to the rock, which displaced itself and went to the designated spot. Each morning the house of Busonius, which had given hospitality to the man of God, was invaded by a crowd of sick persons, whom Gregory healed, in passing. He soon became the spiritual king of this city, though, when he entered it, he had not a roof under which to rest his head. "Of what consequence is it," he said, to his murmuring disciples, "are we not protected under the wing of God? Do you find the vault of heaven too narrow for you? Think of building the house of your soul, and do not afflict yourselves that you do not find edifices prepared for you." Quickly he laid the plan of a

church, and all hastened to contribute money or labor for its construction. He reconciled disputes; the tribunals were deserted. He controlled the elements as he regulated consciences; the overflowing waves of the Lycus obeyed his voice. The name of Wonder-Worker (Thaumaturgus) was given him, and history has preserved it. The prodigies he wrought have been attested by all contemporary writers: St. Gregory of Nyssa, St. Basil, Rufinus, St. Jerome, the historian Socrates, Sozomen, and Theodoret; so that on this point history can defy the most malevolent criticism. Their authenticity, besides, can be immediately established by this fact, that in dying, the saintly bishop, who had found but seventeen Christians in taking possession of the see of Neocæsarea, left there scarcely as many infidels. So rapid, so complete a conversion, would be an inexplicable miracle, without the numerous miracles which effected it.

5. The divine power, which shone in the person of St Gregory Thaumaturgus, multiplied the number of Christians in all that country. The city of Comana requested him to come and organize a church, by giving her a bishop. On the day fixed for the assembly, the chiefs and magistrates of the city sought one among the most noble, the most eloquent, the most distinguished for the qualities which they saw shining in St. Gregory, to be presented to him. "You ought not," said the illustrious bishop, "to exclude from your choice the humblest and poorest. The Spirit breatheth where He willeth."—"If you wish to choose from among the citizens," laughingly replied one of the magistrates, "take Alexander the collier."—"Well! who is this Alexander?" responded Gregory. They led before him a man half naked, clothed only in rags, his face and hands blackened by charcoal. All the assembly began to laugh at his appearance; the collier alone remained calm, seeming contented with his position, and by his grave and modest exterior giving evidence of his interior recollection and peace. Gregory took him aside. After a serious conference with him, the Thaumaturgus returned alone to the assembly, and pronounced

a discourse on the fearful responsibilities of the episcopate. He was closing his remarks, when a man, vested with the pontifical ornaments, was introduced. Every eye was turned towards him; it was Alexander the collier, who, by the order of Gregory, had been thus transformed. "Do not be surprised," said the Thaumaturgus, "if you were mistaken in judging according to the senses. The demon wished to have rendered this vessel of election useless, by keeping him concealed." After the consecration, which took place immediately, the new bishop delivered a discourse to the people. His speech was solid, strong, and full of good sense, though with few ornaments; his air and demeanor were noble and majestic. Under the exterior of a collier, Gregory had discovered true merit and solid virtue. St. Alexander worthily governed the church of Comana, and suffered martyrdom by fire in the persecution of Decius.

6. These generations of illustrious saints, produced by the power of the Gospel, labored together to propagate and maintain the sacred fire which Jesus Christ came to bring upon earth. It would, however, be a mistake to suppose that no disorder then existed in the Church, no irregularity to be deplored. Certain writers have drawn a picture as much the more brilliant of the Christian perfection of the third century, as they were preparing themselves to be more severe on the ages following. The truth is, that Jesus Christ remains with His Church at all times, but at no time is absolute perfection to be found on earth. In all ages, we recognize, in the bosom of the Church, man and God; the miseries of the one, and the mercies of the other. Origen complains "that many come to the assemblies of the faithful only on the holydays, and come much less to be edified and instructed than to follow custom, or place themselves more at their ease." "Some," he says, again, "remain to chat about things indifferent, or even profane. Even the women disturb the silence and recollection of the holy mysteries."* He reproaches the

* Exod., Hom. 12 et 13.—ORIGEN.

Christians with attending exclusively to their temporal affairs, to their fields, their commerce, their litigations. "Instead of applying themselves to the meditation of the divine word, they are passionately addicted to the spectacles of the circus, horse-races, and the combats of wrestlers."* Some there are, who have faith, who come to church, bow to the priests, show themselves devoted and affectionate towards the servants of God, give voluntarily for the decoration and support of the altar; but they take no care to correct their morals, nor quit their former life, but remain in their vices and iniquities. The evil was not confined to the laity. Origen laments that already in his time there were found ambitious men who intrigued for the honors of the priesthood, or the episcopate, in spite of their personal unworthiness, and who sought in their holy functions only the profit and pomp of the highest ranks. "Let prelates learn," he says, "from Moses, not to appoint their successors by testament among their relatives or connections, as if the government of the Church were an inheritance." Elsewhere, speaking of the display made by bishops: "We would almost," he said, "have guards like kings; we make ourselves terrible and difficult of access, chiefly to the poor; we treat them who speak with us and ask for some favor, in a manner which the most cruel tyrants and governors would not assume towards suppliants." These passages, and others of a similar character, which we may remark in the writings of the Fathers of the third century, prove that at that epoch, as in every other in the history of the Church, the tares were found mingled with the good grain. The work of God, nevertheless, was going on, in spite of these stains, propagating itself and gradually bringing the world under the yoke of the faith.

7. A fact which proved all the power of ecclesiastical discipline at this epoch, occurred A. D. 244. The Emperor Philip had assassinated Gordian III., to usurp his power. This prince, if his conduct was not that of a Christian, had at least

* Levit. Hom. 9.—Origen.

the faith of one. The testimony of contemporary authors leaves no doubt of it. But political prudence forbade the public profession of a faith proscribed by the laws and usages of the empire. Nevertheless, in cities where Christians were in the majority, he did not hesitate to show himself at their ceremonies. Being at Antioch in A. D. 244, on the 14th of April, the day on which the Easter festival was celebrated, he presented himself to the assembly of the faithful. But St. Babylas, bishop of that city, stopped him at the door, and reproached him for the murder of Gordian, and the ambition which had tempted him to commit this crime, declaring that he was unworthy to participate in the holy mysteries, until he had expiated his sin by penance. Philip submitted, and was afterwards reconciled to the Church. Origen, at a later date, wrote to him and to the Empress Severa two letters, which were still extant in the time of St. Jerome. In them was remarked a certain tone of authority, which denotes a Christian doctor writing to Christians.

8. Origen had been called, two years before, to the council of Philadelphia, in Arabia, to defend the doctrine of the Church against Beryllus, bishop of Bozra. This prelate, who, with this exception, has left the reputation of a pious and learned doctor, had fallen into a heresy which was a renewal of that of the Theodotians. He pretended that Jesus Christ had not existed before the incarnation, and had only begun to be God on being born of the Virgin. He added that He had been God only because the Father dwelt in Him, as in the prophets. He thus denied the divinity of the Word. These grave errors were exposed by the bishops of Arabia, who endeavored to recall Beryllus to the orthodox faith; but by an obstinacy fearful in a prelate, whom, in spite of the heresy into which he had fallen, St. Jerome places among the most illustrious and learned writers of the Church, he refused to yield. Origen then was called to the Council of Philadelphia, convoked for this object; its acts were still preserved in the time of Eusebius. Private conferences not

having had, at first, the success which had been anticipated, Origen, in a public discussion, proved, with so much clearness and strength, the true Catholic dogma, that Beryllus, convinced by his arguments, finally acknowledged the truth. He was grateful to Origen, and expressed his thanks in several touching letters. It seemed that wherever error showed itself, Origen was called to resist its progress, and that this great man was, in some sort, tradition personified. Several years later we find him again in Arabia, crushing a sect of heretics, who taught that the soul died with the body, to resume a new life at the resurrection. Origen explained Catholic truth in a manner so intelligible, that they who had embraced this heresy abandoned it entirely.

9. The study of the Holy Scriptures, which formed the ordinary occupation of the new converts, gave rise at this time to a sect of heretics, of whom Elcesai seems to have been the head. They rejected certain parts of the sacred books, and selected, at their pleasure, such passages as were agreeable to them in the Old or the New Testament, and proscribed all the remainder. They rejected altogether the Epistles of St. Paul, and extolled a book, the work, doubtless, of one of their chiefs, whose words they regarded as inspired by the Holy Spirit. Faith in this work remitted sins. They maintained that it is allowable to yield to persecution, to dissemble the faith, and to adore idols, provided the heart has no part in it. Origen wrote several treatises against them, and combated their heresies with the victorious eloquence of genius, resting on tradition and Catholic belief.

10. Another light arose at this time on the soil of Africa, so prolific in men of sanctity and faith. St. Cyprian was one of the most brilliant conquests of the Gospel over pagan philosophy. Of an illustrious family, who had long been habituated to proconsular honors, he had enriched the heritage of his ancestry by the lustre of his talents and eloquence, and the pagans considered him as the rampart of expiring idolatry. The truth had long pressed upon his heart, and it was not

until after ripe deliberations that he yielded to the voice of the holy priest Cecilius, whose name he afterwards united to that which he rendered so celebrated. But finally, Thascius Cæcilius Cyprianus received baptism, and made a public profession of Christianity. Here is the account which he gave to a friend, of the great victory he had just gained over his doubts and hesitation: "It seemed to me," he wrote, "very hard to be born again, to lead a new life, and to become another man in the same body. Is it possible, said I, at once to lay aside the deeply rooted, the inveterate habits which seem born with us, and which long use has strengthened, even to old age? How can he learn frugality who has been accustomed to an abundant and delicately served table? And he who has always been clothed in rich fabrics, in shining purple and gold, how can he bring himself down to a simple and common habit? Accustomed to the splendors of the *fasces*, to honors, to a numerous retinue of friends and clients, how can a man resolve to sink into private life, into the obscurity of a solitude which is looked upon with disdain? Thus I thought within myself, and in despair of finding any thing better, I loved the evil which had become natural to me. But when this life-giving water had washed away the stains from my past life, when my purified heart had received the light and the heavenly spirit from on high, my doubts, to my infinite astonishment, had vanished; all was open, all was luminous; what before seemed impossible, was now easy. I perceived that that which was born according to the flesh, and lived under the law of sin, came from the earth, and that what is animated by the grace of the Holy Ghost, comes from God. You know it, assuredly, my dear friend, and you acknowledge the blessing that has delivered us from the death of sin, to restore us to the life of virtue."

In these accents we recognize the wondrous transformation which the grace of baptism had wrought in the soul of the neophyte, and the superabundance of joy of a renewed heart. The pagans, from whom he had separated, returned to him in sarcasms all the discredit which such a conversion cast upon their doctrines. They ironically named him *Coprianus*, by a poor comparison of his name to a Greek word which means a *dunghill*. But the humiliations of the Gospel were glorious to the disciple of the Cross. He embraced holy austerities with fervor. His wealth, the inheritance of a long line of ancestors, augmented by the places he had occupied and the services he had rendered, was distributed to the poor. He made vows of perfect continence, wore the humble mantle of the Christian philosophers, like St. Justin and Tertullian, and commenced the study of Scripture, less to satisfy a vain desire of knowledge, than to seek for rules of conduct. Among ecclesiastical authors, he loved most his compatriot Tertullian, with whom his genius had the greatest affinities. He did not allow a day to pass without reading some passages from this author; and when he asked for his works, he was in the habit of saying, "Give me the master."

11. As a response to the reproaches of the pagans, who demanded an account of his conversion, he first wrote his *Treatise on the Vanity of Idols*, where he proves the absurdity of idolatrous worship, and demonstrates the unity of God and the divinity of Jesus Christ. His work *Of the Testimonies* appeared soon afterwards. A general view of religion is there presented, with the method which was afterwards followed and developed more largely in the scholastic theology. The first part is a treatise on the true religion against the Jews. He proves that the law of the Jews had a character essentially temporary, and transitory; that it was to be destroyed; that in it Christ was announced, to establish a new temple, a new sacrifice, a new priesthood, and a new church; that the nations were called to obtain, by His merits, the remission of their sins. The second part is a dogmatic treatise on the divinity and the incarnation of Jesus Christ. He proves that Jesus Christ is the Word of God; that He is God and man; that the prophets had predicted His passion, His crucifixion, His resurrection, His ascension, and His eternal reign by the power of the Cross. The third part is a moral theology, treat-

ing of the practical consequences of the Christian dogmas, and of the rules of conduct for the direction of souls.

12. So much knowledge and piety authorized a departure from the prescription of St. Paul which prohibits the ordination of a neophyte, and which had been hitherto observed in all the churches. St. Cyprian was, therefore, elevated to the dignity of the priesthood, and a year after (A. D. 248), the death of Donatus having left the episcopal see of Carthage vacant, the faithful unanimously demanded him for their bishop. He alone believed himself unworthy of the honor, which he preferred, he said, to leave to his elders in the faith. But the people besieged his dwelling, and closed all the avenues leading to it. The modest prisoner was finally led, against his will, to the episcopal chair, where his election was confirmed by the judgment of the bishops of the province and the acclamations of the multitude. Five restless and ambitious priests protested against his election. The saint pardoned them with a kindness which was admired by every one, and treated them as his best friends. But this condescension did not succeed in touching these envious and obstinate spirits; their jealousy became the germ of long and envenomed discords, the echoes of which resounded through all the Church at a later period. The distrust that was entertained by some persons, owing to his sudden promotion to the episcopate, joined to his profound humility, determined St. Cyprian to do nothing without the counsel of his clergy and the participation of the people; not that he believed it an obligation, for he wrote afterwards to the Bishop Rogatian, who consulted him on the subject, that by the authority of his chair he had all the power necessary to govern his church, and chastise the rebellious members of his clergy and people. It would be, then, a mistake to conclude, from the single example of St. Cyprian, that all the bishops of his time did the same, and that the bishops of all times ought to imitate him. Providence, in placing St. Cyprian in the episcopal see of Carthage, prepared for this church a powerful defence against

the persecution which a year later was to fall upon the Christians.

13. From the last year of the Emperor Philip (A. D. 249), and while all the rest of the Church was in peace under the government of this prince, a storm, the precursor of more violent tempests, broke out in Alexandria. This tumultuous city, the emporium of all the commerce of the East, and the home of every sect, was inhabited by a numerous and hardy population, whose manners verged on ferocity and whose hands were often bloody. The popular passions were easily excited, and the massacres which followed their civil discords more than once caused the Roman governors to tremble. A pagan poet attempted to revive the idolatrous superstitions of which the progress of Christianity threatened every day the approaching ruin, and soon after the election of Heraclas to the patriarchate, profiting by the attention which this event had turned towards the faithful, he excited the populace against the adorers of Christ. His burning words, the inspired tone in which he gave utterance to them, reanimated all the ancient fury. The cry, *Away with the Christians!* became the universal cry, and the extermination of the faithful began with a saintly old man named Metras, whom the seditious attempted to force to apostatize. On his refusal, they seized him, beat him down with sticks, tore out his eyes, and transpierced his face with sharpened reeds. Having dragged him in this state through the streets of the city, they took him into a suburb and finished his martyrdom by stoning him. This innocent blood only whetted their fury. A devout woman, called Quinta, became their next victim. They led her, in a crowd, to a temple of idols, and commanded her to adore their gods. She repelled, with horror, the incense they offered her. Instantly her feet were bound, and she was dragged, her head downwards, over the pavements of the city, where she left fragments of her bleeding flesh, and finally was stoned in the suburb. These first violences still further stimulating the rage of the populace, they invaded the houses of the faithful, pillaged them of their

furniture and precious vases, then, throwing the rest through the windows, they made bonfires of it in the streets. It seemed as if one half of the city were taking the other by assault. In the midst of these excesses, the conduct of the Christians was admirable. Scarcely a single example of apostasy could be found. The children, the women, the virgins, generously confessed their faith, and lost, with joy, their worldly goods, to acquire rights in the heavenly kingdom. The seditious had seized a virgin named Apollonia. They broke all her teeth with clubs, and, leading her without the walls of Alexandria, kindled a large fire, ready to cast her into it if she refused to adore the gods. She begged for a little time, as if it were for reflection, but when they had left her to herself, urged, doubtless, by an inspiration, she darted into the fire and was consumed. A fervent Christian, Serapion, was taken in his own house. They broke all his limbs at the joints, and as he still lived after this horrible torture, they cast him out of a window on the pavement, where he expired. Tracked like wild beasts, massacred by those who passed by, the Christians could not leave their houses, and the number of victims was immense. The vengeance of the pagans only relaxed when the civil war turned their arms against each other, and left the faithful to a repose which was not of long duration.

14. Great events had just changed the face of the empire. Decius, sent by the Emperor Philip as his lieutenant into Pannonia, corrupted the legions, and returned at their head to attack their master, who was vanquished and murdered by his own soldiers at Verona (A. D. 249). The throne was once more the recompense of crime. Decius bore a savage hatred against the Christians, and inaugurated his reign by a bloody edict against the faithful, addressed to all the governors of the provinces. It was the signal for the seventh general persecution. The first victim was the saintly Pope Fabian, who was beheaded January 20th, A. D. 250. He illustrated a pontificate of fourteen years by his piety and labors. As soon as promoted, he had caused to be transported from Sardinia to Rome the body

of St. Pontianus, the predecessor of St. Anterus, who had died in that island, and whom he buried in the cemetery of St. Callistus. He raised many altars over the tombs of martyrs, and recommended to notice carefully the day of their death, in order to celebrate their anniversary. With the same object he established a commission of seven sub-deacons to edit the acts of the martyrs. Baronius attributes to him the conversion and baptism of the Emperor Philip and his son. Attentive in watching over the deposit of faith which was confided to him, he wrote many letters to repress the heresy of Privatus, bishop of Lambesa, a Roman colony in Numidia. History does not relate the nature of this heresy. St. Cyprian informs us only that Privatus was condemned and deposed for his crimes, in a council of ninety bishops, held at Lambesa and confirmed by the letters and authority of St. Fabian. We shall soon find again the name of Privatus, in the schism of Novatus, against St. Cyprian, at Carthage. St. Fabian regularly divided the resources which the charity of the faithful placed in his hands for the poor. He confided their distribution to the seven deacons of the Roman Church; giving each the care of two of the fourteen districts of the city. Such are the details furnished by the *Liber Pontificalis* concerning the pious labors of St. Fabian.

CHAPTER XII.

§ I. Vacancy in the See of Rome (Jan. 20, A. D. 250—June 2, 251).

1. Character of the seventh general persecution under Decius (250).—2. Martyrs of Rome, Jerusalem, Antioch, Alexandria, etc.—3. Martyrs of Asia.—4. Interrogatory of St. Acacius, bishop of Antioch, in Pisidia.—5. Defections at Carthage.—6. *Thurificati, Sacrificati, Libellatici, Lapsi.* Billets of recommendation from the martyrs.—7. Letter of Lucian, confessor of Carthage, to St. Cyprian, on the question of apostasies.—8. Reply of the clergy of Rome to St. Cyprian on the question of apostasies.—9. Schism of Felicissimus and Novatus at Carthage.

§ II. St. Cornelius Pope (June 2, A. D. 251—Sept. 14, 252).

10. Election of Pope St. Cornelius, June 2, 251.—11. Novatian, first antipope.—12. Death of Decius (251). End of the seventh general persecution. St. Paul, first hermit.—13. Council of Carthage (252). Treatises of St. Cyprian, *De Lapsis, De unitate Ecclesiæ.*—14. Council of Rome.—15. Second council of Carthage under St. Cyprian (252). Schism of Fortunatus at Carthage.—16. Confession, exile, and death of St. Cornelius (Sept. 14, 252).

§ III. St. Lucius I., Pope (Oct. 18, A. D. 252—March 14, 253).

17. Election, pontificate, and death of Pope St. Lucius I.—18. Death of Origen. Doubts of his orthodoxy.

§ IV. St. Stephen I., Pope (A. D. 253–257).

19. Election of Pope St. Stephen I.—20. Universal plague (253–260).—21. Charity of the Christians.—22. Letters and decisions of St. Cyprian on various ecclesiastical affairs of his time.—23. Question of the Baptism of heretics.—24. Council of eighty-five bishops at Carthage (Sept. 1, 256).—25. Eighth general persecution, under Valerian. Martyrdom of Pope St. Stephen I. (257).

§ V. St. Sixtus II., Pope (Aug. 24, A. D. 257—Aug. 6, 258).

26. Election of Pope St. Sixtus II.—End of the affair of the rebaptizers.—27. Martyrdom of St. Cyprian, at Carthage. Principal martyrs of the eighth general persecution, in the various provinces of the empire.—28. Martyrdom of St. Cyril, a child of Cæsarea, in Cappadocia.—29. Martyrdom of Pope St. Sixtus II. (August, 258).—30. Martyrdom of St. Lawrence.—31. End of the eighth general persecution.

§ I. Vacancy in the See of Rome (a. d. 250-251).

1. The seventh general persecution opened with such violence, that it was not possible for the Church of Rome to assemble for the election of a successor to the late Pontiff St. Fabian. A copy of the edict of proscription was sent to all the governors of provinces at the same time that the elevation of Decius to the empire was announced to them. The new prince declared "that, resolved to treat all his subjects with clemency, he was hindered by the sect of Christians, who, by their impiety, called down the anger of the gods, and all other calamities upon the empire. He commanded, therefore, that every Christian, without distinction of quality or rank, of sex or age, should be compelled to sacrifice in the temples; that such as refused should be confined in the public prisons, and subjected at first to the lesser punishments, to overcome, by degrees, their constancy; and, finally, if they continued obstinate, they should be cast into the sea, or thrown alive into the midst of flames, or exposed to beasts, or suspended upon trees to become the food of birds of prey, or torn to pieces in many ways, by the most cruel torments." The new edict, read publicly in the prætorian camp, was affixed on the capitol, and successively in all the cities and towns in the empire. A peculiar character, noted by St. Augustine, marks this proscription. "The persecutors," said this father, "had observed that, in proportion as the Christians were put to death, their numbers increased from their martyrs' blood. They feared to depopulate the empire if they destroyed so many thousands of the faithful. The edicts no longer bore the ancient form, 'Whoever confesses himself a Christian *shall be put to death;*' but only, '*shall be tormented until he renounces his faith.*' Under this apparent mildness, the demon of the south concealed a fire far more dangerous. How many, in fact, who would have courageously suffered a speedy death, became disheartened at the view of long and varied torments!" Never was a more formidable tempest raised against the Church of Jesus Christ.

Princes, governors, people, and senate, all that was most distinguished among the Romans, joined together to efface from the earth the name of Christian. Decius was convinced that, in its essence, Christianity was incompatible with the constitution and spirit of the empire. "The magistrates suspended all cases, private or public, to apply themselves to the great, the important affair—the arrest and punishment of the faithful. The heated iron chairs, the steel claws, the pyre, the sword, the beasts, all the instruments invented by the cruelty of man, lacerated, by night and by day, the bodies of martyrs; and each tormentor seemed to fear that he might not be so barbarous as his fellows. Neighbors, relatives, friends, heartlessly betrayed each other, and denounced Christians before the magistrates. The provinces were in consternation; families were decimated; cities became deserts; and the deserts were peopled. Soon the prisons were insufficient for the multitudes arrested for their faith, and most of the public edifices were converted into prisons."* St. Gregory, of Nyssa, who gives us this picture of the Christians, has exaggerated nothing. All the pagan authors agree that Decius had imposed two tasks upon himself: to put a stop forever, in the whole extent of the Roman empire, to the propagation of the Christian religion, and to the invasion of the barbarians. He succeeded in neither. Faith emerged triumphantly from this rude trial, and the Goths, under their King Cuiva, captured Nicopolis and Martianopolis, took Philippopolis by assault, massacred a hundred thousand inhabitants, and carried away a crowd of illustrious prisoners, under the eyes of the powerless emperor.

2. These reverses served only to redouble the wrath of Decius, who attributed them to the impiety of the Christians. At Rome, Moses and Maximus, priests, Nicostratus, a deacon, and an immense multitude of the faithful, filled all the state-prisons. SS. Abden and Sennen, Persians, SS. Victoria and Anatolia, Romans, shed their blood for Jesus Christ. The venerable St. Alexander, bishop of Jerusalem, was dragged to

* St. Gregory, of Nyssa, p. 518.—*Vita Thaumat.*

the tribunal of the governor of Palestine, at Cæsarea, and put in irons, where he died from bad treatment. At Antioch, the bishop, St. Babylas, was sent to prison, and desired to be buried in the chains in which he died. Origen, whose reputation marked him as one of the noblest victims, was thrown into a dungeon, with an iron collar about his neck, and shackles on his feet, so fastened as to separate his legs as far as possible. They did not let him die, in the hope that his fall might draw many Christians after him. He remained immovable, and found means, from his prison, to write letters of encouragement to his brethren, sufferers like himself for the faith. At Comana, the bishop, St. Alexander, whose election we have mentioned, was burned alive. In Alexandria, where the Christians had, in the preceding year, been so cruelly persecuted, the most sanguinary scenes were renewed. The sight of the torments intimidated many of the faithful, especially among the higher classes, and, unhappily, many defections took place. Some allowed themselves to be conducted, pale and trembling, to the altars of the false gods; others hastened there of themselves, crying out that they had never been Christians, and proving it but too truly by their conduct. There were those who allowed themselves to be dragged to prison, yet scarcely waited a day to sacrifice to the idols; or, if they had the courage to endure the first tortures, yielded to the second. The faith, nevertheless, counted glorious martyrs. The aged Julian, broken by infirmities, and Eunus, resisted all menaces: they were placed on camels, and whipped while they were driven through the city. At length they were cast into the flames, around which the populace danced and insulted their victims. St. Macarius, an Egyptian, met the same fate. SS. Epimachus and Alexander, after suffering the whips, the iron claws, and many other tortures, were also burned alive. Four women, Mercuria, Dionysia, and two of the name of Ammonaria, were beheaded. Heron, Ater, Isidore, and Nemesian, Egyptians, and four soldiers, Ammon, Zeno, Ptolemy, and Ingenuus, were burned alive. A child named Dioscorus was brought before the judge, who, having in vain tried to vanquish him by flatteries and torments, astonished at his courage and the wisdom of his answers, ended by setting him at liberty, "because of his age, which," he said, "made him not responsible for his conduct." A Christian called Ischyrion was the steward of a magistrate, who commanded him to sacrifice to the gods; on his refusal, this barbarous master seized a stake, with which he transpierced his bowels and laid him dead at his feet. St. Dionysius, bishop of Alexdria, escaped, as by a miracle, from the hands of his persecutors, and took refuge in a deserted place, whence he consoled and governed his church through devoted priests and deacons, who found means to preserve secret relations with him. Thus the general persecution succeeding the temporary violence of intestine riots, at Alexandria, perfected more and more the virtue of the servants of God. During the sedition, there was only one apostate; after the edict of Decius, on the contrary, few truly faithful were found. It is certainly less difficult to resist a popular tumult, of which we hope soon to see the end, than a sovereign power, against which there is no resource but in an humble and generous faith, ready to expect all from God and to suffer all for His name.

St. Gregory Thaumaturgus, at Neocæsarea, in Pontus, was successful in preserving all the faithful of his jurisdiction in the faith and courage of the true servants of Jesus Christ. He advised the Christians to avoid the dangers of persecution by flight, and he himself retired to a deserted valley, where he eluded the vigilance of the soldiers sent in pursuit of him. The executioners revenged themselves by carrying off a crowd of Christians who had taken refuge in the neighboring country. All generously confessed their faith, and several of the number had the glory of giving their lives for it. Troad, a young man of a noble race, was of this number; after frightful tortures, he received the crown of martyrdom.

3. All the churches of Asia counted multitudes of courageous Christians, whom torments could not move. St. Maxi-

mus, St. Peter of Lampsacus, inscribed their names, in the outset, on the list of martyrs. The last, young and of remarkable beauty, received an order to sacrifice to Venus. "I am astonished," he replied, "that a magistrate would wish to force me to adore an infamous prostitute, all the actions of whom were crimes which it is your duty to punish in others with severity." On this refusal, the proconsul ordered him to be extended on a wheel, between pieces of wood fastened to his body with iron chains, so arranged that the wheel, in turning, crushed, gradually, all his bones. The courage of the Christian hero failed not for an instant during this cruel torture, and the proconsul ended by ordering his head to be struck off. As this magistrate, named Optimus, was departing for the city of Troad, three other Christians were brought before him—Andrew, Paul, and Nicomacus. The latter, full of an impatient presumption, cried out, in a loud voice, that he was a Christian. His two companions, more modest, awaited their trial, and humbly replied that they, too, adored Jesus Christ. The proconsul commanded Nicomacus to be laid on the rack, but he was unable to bear the torments, and cried out in the midst of them, "I have never been a Christian! I sacrifice to the gods!" The proconsul ordered him to be instantly released, but the unhappy apostate failed to enjoy the life he had so unworthily purchased, and soon expired. Among the crowd of spectators, a young virgin named Dionysia, about sixteen years of age, called out, "Miserable man! to gain a momentary ease, must you precipitate yourself into eternal punishment!" For these courageous words she was taken before the proconsul, who endeavored to intimidate her by frightful threats. "My God is greater than you," she said; "He can give me strength to suffer all your torments." The proconsul ordered her to be removed to an infamous house, and Andrew and Paul were returned to prison. By a miracle of divine power, Dyonisia escaped from the den of corruption without stain, and was beheaded on the day following. Andrew and Paul were delivered to the people, who were not less cruel than the beasts of the amphitheatre. They were publicly whipped in the streets of the city, then bound by the feet, and dragged, their heads downward, into a suburb, and stoned by the populace.

When we insist on the narration of those horrors, which were renewed with the same courage on one side and the same barbarity on the other, throughout the empire, it is to add more strength to the argument for the divinity of the Church, which is drawn from the violence of the persecutions. The philosophy of the last century has sought to question the atrocities charged upon the pagan emperors, and has taken the side of the persecutors against their victims. It is our part to state the facts in all their bloody reality. To this long martyrology we might add a hundred other illustrious names: at Smyrna, the saintly priest Pionius; at Cæsarea, in Cappadocia, St. Mercurius; at Melitene, in Armenia, St. Polyeuctes—the two latter, distinguished officers of the army; at Pergamus, St. Carpus, bishop of Thyatira, and his companions; in Syria, St. Christopher and St. Themistocles. This last pastured his sheep on a mountain where a Christian was concealed, and he suffered death rather than to betray the retreat of the proscribed victim. In Ionia, the seven sleepers, that is to say, the seven brothers, who, to escape the persecution, left Ephesus, and entered a cavern, where they were shut in, and thus slept in the Lord. In Pamphylia, St. Nestor, bishop of Side, with St. Conon, a gardener, and many others. In Crete, St. Cyril, bishop of Gortynas, and ten other martyrs. At Nicea, in Bithynia, the saints Tryphon and Respicius; at Nicomedia, in the same province, the saints Marcian and Lucian. And, finally, in Sicily, the illustrious virgin and martyr, St. Agatha. She was as distinguished by her birth as by the virtues with which her soul was adorned. The governor, captivated by her beauty, caused her to be arrested as a Christian, and had her placed in the hands of a woman of evil life, to be corrupted. His infamous calculation was baffled. In a trial, where he referred to her noble birth, "The most illustrious nobility," she replied, "consists in being the servant of Jesus Christ." When he commanded her to adore the gods, she asked: "Would you like your wife to be a Venus, and would it please her to have you imitate Jupiter?" The governor made no reply, but ordered her to be smitten on the face and returned to prison. The next day she suffered the torture with such courage that the angry judge added torments still more horrible, and had her breasts torn away. God willed to manifest the glory of His servant; during the following night she was miraculously healed. But, four days afterwards she expired, in the midst of tortures, while making this prayer: "Lord, my God! Thou hast protected me from my cradle; Thou hast uprooted from my heart the love of the world, and hast given me patience to suffer. Lord, receive now my spirit."

4. We should not omit a trait which contrasts with the general cruelties; it relates to St. Acacius, bishop of Antioch, in Pisidia. He was brought before the proconsul Marcion, with Piso, bishop of Troas, and the priest Menander. "You ought to love our princes well," said the proconsul, "you who live under the Roman laws." "And who loves the emperor more than the Christians?" replied Acacius. "We pray continually for him, that he may live long—that he may govern the people with justice, and that his reign may be peaceable; we pray, also, for the soldiers, and for all the world." The holy bishop continued to reply with so much wisdom and good sense, that the proconsul considered it his duty to send a report of his examination to the emperor. Decius admired it so much that he released the bishop, and gave as a recompense to Marcion the government of Pamphylia. A profound lesson may be learned from this fact; it shows us, in practice, the real policy of Christians, who have only prayers, even for the governments that oppress them. The words of St. Paul are: *obedite præpositis vestris.** If, in the sequel of history, certain events appear at the first glance contrary to this general rule, it will not be difficult to discover that they

---

* Obey those placed over you.

occurred in a society greatly modified, the bases of which had become Christian. The faithful were not then, on one side subjects, and on the other, Christians. These two duties were blended together. They were subjects of Jesus Christ, of whom the sovereigns proclaimed themselves the ministers; and this was admirably expressed by the word, then in use, the Christian republic. At a later period we shall see the application of this doctrine.

5. While these noble examples of courage produced so many martyrs and confessors in all parts of the world, the Church had to mourn many terrible defections. The bishop of Smyrna, Eudemon, the unworthy successor of the great saints who had illustrated that see, fell into apostasy, and by his fall led away many of the faithful. Repostus, bishop of Suturna, in Africa, Jovinius and Maximus, whose sees are unknown, of the same province, Fortunatian, of Assur, also of Africa, all sacrificed to the idols. In Spain, Basilides, bishop of Leon, and Martial, bishop of Merida, declared, by a public edict, that they renounced the faith. But no city, after Alexandria, saw more lamentable apostasies than that of Carthage. The fury of the pagans at first was turned entirely against the Bishop St. Cyprian. The circus and amphitheatre resounded with incessant shouts of *Cyprian to the lions!* The holy man hoped by his withdrawal to appease the violence of the sedition. He was proscribed—a price was set upon his head, and his property confiscated. From his retreat he assisted his flock by his exhortations, encouragements, and prayers; but he had the grief to perceive that his efforts were too often useless. He thus expresses himself. "On the first threatenings of the enemy, the greater number of our brethren betrayed the faith; they were not prostrated by the violence of the persecution, but cast themselves down by a voluntary fall." Before they had even been taken, or questioned, clergy and people ran, of their own accord, to the public place, as if they had only awaited the occasion to apostatize. They came in such crowds, to renounce Christianity, that the

magistrates proposed to postpone it until the next day, because of the lateness of the hour; but they besought them not to defer it. Many, not content with ruining themselves, persecuted others, and led them off to the altars of the idols. Some brought their children to the pagan priests, to destroy in them the grace of baptism. The rich, especially, showed the greatest weakness, and their wealth became the cause of their ruin. Many, however, suffered death courageously for Jesus Christ. Mappalicus, Paul, Fortunion, Bassus, all expired in torments, and a large number of confessors died in prison.

6. There were several degrees of apostasy: these timid Christians were classed in three different categories, which were termed the *thurificati, sacrificati, libellatici*. The *thurificati* had only offered incense to the idols. The *sacrificati* had sacrificed to the false gods, or eaten immolated viands. The *libellatici* had gone to the magistrates, declaring that, as Christians, they were not permitted to offer sacrifice, but they offered money in order to procure an exemption from this ceremony. Through avarice or humanity, the proconsuls and governors gave them then a billet (*libellum*), purporting that they had renounced Jesus Christ, and sacrificed to the gods of the empire, though they had done no such thing. These billets were read publicly, and their bearers were left in peace. All who belonged to these three categories were, without distinction, named *lapsi* (fallen), and for each of them canonical penances were appointed. In proportion as the persecution abated from exhaustion, or because the governors awaited the issue of the war in which the Emperor Decius was engaged against the Goths, many fallen Christians, among both the clergy and the people, wished to re-enter the Church to participate in the holy Eucharist, or resume their functions, without a preparatory penance. To accomplish this, they abused a very holy practice. The martyrs or confessors gave to those who had had the misfortune to apostatize, letters of recommendation to the bishops. The Church had much respect for these missives, and when the suppliants were otherwise well

disposed, she abridged for them the period of satisfactory penance. But they did not confine themselves to this. Several confessors, and particularly one among them named Lucian, of Carthage, undertook to give, without distinction, either in their own name or in that of martyrs from whom they said they had received the order, letters of recommendation, expressed in general terms: "Let N., and they who are with him, be admitted to the communion;" so that a single person could present twenty or thirty others, as members of his family, or of his household. Men were even found who made a traffic of these billets of indulgence; and some priests, without consulting the bishop, arrogated to themselves the right to reconcile to the Church, and admit to the sacraments, all who presented themselves furnished with one of the recommendations just referred to.

7. St. Cyprian protested in the strongest terms against these unworthy abuses. From the place of his concealment he gave the most precise instructions, and sent to the clergy of Rome all the details of this affair. At the same time he explained the cause of his retreat, which had been misinterpreted at Rome. Lucian, on his side, urged by certain undisciplined priests and deacons, pressed the reconciliation of the apostates, on the strength of the billets from the martyrs. He dared even to address to St. Cyprian, in the name of all the confessors, this letter: "All the confessors to the Pope* Cyprian, greeting: Be it known to you, that we have given the peace to all of whom you have taken information on the subject of their conduct since their fall, and we request that you apprise of it the other bishops. We wish that you may have peace with the holy martyrs. Written by Lucian, in presence of an exorcist and a reader." In consequence of this strange letter, the people in various places rose against their prelates, and exacted from them, on the instant, the communion which they believed had been granted to all by the martyrs and confessors. St.

---

* The name of Pope, or Father, was given at that time to all the bishops in general, and sometimes to simple priests.

Cyprian, in this difficult situation, again wrote to the church of Rome, and transmitted to it the billet of Lucian, and all the other documents relative to this affair.

8. The priests who administered the church of Rome during the vacancy in the Holy See, responded by an admirable letter in which they entirely approved the conduct of the holy bishop, blamed the arrogance of the apostates, and still more the indiscretion of those who instigated them. "Nothing is more advisable in time of peace," they say, "nothing more necessary during the war of persecution, than to cling inviolably to the discipline of the Church: to abandon it, is to abandon the rudder in the midst of a tempest. This is not a maxim of recent growth among us: this severity, this faith, this discipline, prevailed from the earliest times. The Apostle could not have said that our faith was spoken of in all the world, if at that time it had not taken deep roots; and it would be a great crime to degenerate from such glory.

"May God forbid that the Roman Church should lose her vigor by a profane indulgence; or that she should relax the bands of severity by overturning the majesty of the faith. In presence of the defections which are each day more numerous, to grant to those who have fallen the remedy of a reconciliation which can be of no service, is, by a false compassion, to add new wounds to that of apostasy, by taking from these unfortunate people the resource of a healing penance: it is not to cure—it is to give a death-blow. Since the martyrdom of Fabian, of glorious memory, we have been unable, from the difficulties of the times, to elect a bishop who may regulate all these affairs, and examine with authority and prudence those who have fallen. But we think, with you, that we must await the close of the persecution to consider the question of apostasies, and consult with the bishops, the confessors, and laymen, who have remained firm. For it seems to us that it would give too much ground for offence if one only gave sentence on a crime so universal.

"Behold, in fact, the entire world full of the ruins of

those who have fallen. An evil of such extent demands great prudence and efficacious remedies; and those who would repair it ought to act with circumspection, lest that which might be done against the rules should be judged null by all. Let us pray for each other. Let us pray for the fallen, that they may rise and recognize the magnitude of their crime, that they may become penitent and patient; that by their restlessness they may not trouble the yet insecure state of the Church, nor kindle within it an intestine persecution; that they may knock at the doors, but not break them open.

"Assembled with some bishops of the adjacent cities, and with those whom persecution has driven here from other distant provinces, we have thought we would innovate in nothing before the election of a bishop of Rome. Until that time, let all be held in suspense who can wait. In regard to those who are in imminent danger of death, when they give signs of a true repentance, let them be admitted. But let us take care that the froward have no occasion to praise our extreme leniency, and that the truly penitent do not accuse us of excessive severity."

This decree, especially addressed to St. Cyprian, was sent to all the churches in Christendom, because it responded to a general demand. Such was then the Roman Church. Deprived of her chief by martyrdom, exposed to the rudest blows from persecutors, not only she remained unshaken, but communicated her firmness to the other churches over which she ceased not to watch. Attentive to all the designs of error, she knew how to resist its snares and to forewarn the faithful. An instance of this occurred in the case of Privatus, the heretical bishop of Lambesa, who, taking advantage of the persecution and the vacancy of the Holy See, had sent to Rome for letters of communion. St. Cyprian had warned the Roman clergy to guard against his artifices. "You have followed your custom," replied the priests of Rome to the bishop of Carthage, "in giving us notice of what concerns you, for we ought all to watch over the body of the Church, whose members are distributed throughout the provinces. But before the receipt of your letters, the underhand dealings of that heretic had not escaped us. Futurus, an agent of Privatus, came to obtain from us letters of communion; his attempts have been fruitless." History records facts of this nature with care; they prove, on the one hand, the anxiety of the heretics of that time to obtain the support of the see of Rome, as the centre of doctrine and authority; and on the other, the vigilance with which the see of Rome guarded the deposit of faith.

9. The question of the apostates did not cease, in spite of this decision, to agitate the church of Carthage. St. Cyprian sent two priests to examine the age, the condition, and the merits of those who were to be promoted on his return to ecclesiastical functions, and to give an account of those who had fallen. This mission excited the displeasure of some malcontents. An artful man, named Felicissimus, sustained by the five priests who had been opposed to the election of St. Cyprian, declared himself openly in revolt againt his bishop. Among these was Novatus, an unworthy priest, whose crimes were equally atrocious and notorious. By his own authority, he appointed Felicissimus a deacon, and, leaving him at Carthage, he went to Rome with the intention, doubtless, to present these facts in colors which would be advantageous to himself.

§ II. St. Cornelius, Pope (June 2, a. d. 251—Sept. 14, 252).

10. The widowhood of the church of Rome had ceased. Many bishops, whom the persecution had brought to Rome, united with the clergy and the faithful, and elected, as pope, St. Cornelius. "It was necessary," said St. Cyprian, "to constrain the new pontiff to accept this dignity. Nothing was seen in him but the tranquillity and modesty belonging to those whom God chooses for bishops. It was thus that he reached the highest degree of the priesthood, after having passed through all the grades of the hierarchy; having shown himself, in each, an instrument of divine grace."

11. An election so conformable to ecclesiastical discipline

was, nevertheless, contested. Novatus had brought to Rome his turbulent and factious spirit. He allied himself to an ambitious priest named Novatian, who intrigued for the sovereign pontificate. Novatian protested against the election of St. Cornelius, calumniously accusing him of being a *libellatic*, which means, as we have already explained, that he had purchased his life for money, during the persecution. At length, yielding to the counsels of Novatus, he, with four Roman priests, separated entirely from St. Cornelius, and got himself ordained by three bishops from remote parts of Italy, whose good faith he grossly imposed on, by plunging them into a state bordering on ebriety, and thus became definitively the first antipope whose pride afflicted the Church. To schism he joined heresy. According to him, the Church had no power to grant peace to the fallen in the persecution, whatever penance they might accomplish, and never was it permissible to communicate with them. He also positively condemned second marriages. His disciples named themselves, on account of this affectation of severity, *Cathari*, or *Puritans*. To retain them in schism, he made them swear, on the holy Eucharist, to remain faithful to him. "Swear to me," he said, when giving them communion, "swear to me, by the body and blood of our Lord Jesus Christ, never to leave me to return to Cornelius." The misguided people whom he addressed never received the Eucharist without having made this oath, and a malediction against the venerable pontiff took the place of the word *Amen*, which they were accustomed to say when communicating. That which rendered this schism most dangerous, was the reputation of eloquence and authority which Novatian enjoyed. He spared nothing to attract the faithful into his perverse way. St. Jerome has preserved a list of his numerous writings. He sent deputies to various churches, with letters to inform them of his election. He spoke seriously of the constraint which had forced him to accept the pontificate. The names of the confessors whom he had seduced contributed to mislead the simple-minded, and to trouble the consciences of many.

12. Thus, to the horrors of the seventh general persecution succeeded the disorder of schism. After the death of the emperor, who was defeated and killed by the Goths (251), near Philippopolis, the instruments of torment ceased to lacerate the Christians. The violence of Decius was transient, like his power. He had been the scourge which God had used to punish the relaxation of the faithful. From his short but terrible persecution may be dated the movement which, at a later epoch, peopled the desert with the faithful, and gave birth to the wonders of monastic institutions. A young man of the lower Thebaid (A. D. 251), named Paul, flying from the persecutors, found a grotto, shaded by a palm-tree, near which rippled a fountain. Paul took possession of this grotto, lived alone in it, under the eye of God, ninety years, and acquired from this solitude the glory of being the first Christian hermit.

13. The schism and heresy of Novatian found able adversaries in that Christian society which, always invincible, came forth from the persecution of Decius. St. Dionysius, bishop of Alexandria, replied in these terms to the letters of notification from the antipope: "If you have been ordained against your wish, give proof of it by abdicating, of your own free-will, for you ought to suffer every thing rather than to divide the Church of God. The martyrdom which you will have endured to avoid a schism, will not be less glorious than the other." A council of seventy bishops, assembled at Carthage by the care of St. Cyprian, pronounced the same decision, and St. Cornelius was acknowledged as the lawful pope. Felicissimus and the five priests who had caused so much trouble in the Church were anathematized. The question of the apostates, seriously examined, was solved by framing penitential canons, which are thus summed up: 1st. The *libellatici*, who had undertaken penances immediately after their fall, were to be from that time admitted to communion. 2d. The *sacrificati* were treated with more severity, without, however, taking from them the hope of pardon, lest an excessive rigor might throw them into schism or heresy. The duration of their

canonical penitence should be proportioned to the degree of their culpability and to their present dispositions. They who had yielded to the violence of torture, would be admitted after three years of penitence. All the details for the examination which the *lapsi* should undergo were regulated, and also the various penances to be imposed on them. These regulations, with the acts of the council, were sent to Pope St. Cornelius. As a commentary on these disciplinary ordinances, St. Cyprian composed and published his treatise, *De Lapsis*, where are found all the eloquence of a Father of the Church and all the love of a good pastor. A short time after he wrote his book, *De Unitate Ecclesiæ*, to forewarn the faithful against the schism of Novatian.

14. St. Cornelius also had called at Rome a council of sixty bishops. They anathematized Novatian and his errors. The pope gave notice of the fact to all the churches, and the schismatics were overwhelmed by the powerful unanimity opposed to them. Maximus, Urban, Sidonius, and Macarius, Roman priests, who had followed the antipope, submitted, with the faithful whom they had led into rebellion. St. Cornelius received them with benignity to the communion of the Church, and restored their dignities. He had also the joy to receive the abjuration of one of the bishops who had consecrated Novatian, but he admitted him only to lay communion, and named another bishop in his place. These happy tidings imparted joy to all Christendom. St. Cyprian wrote to assure the pope of his own satisfaction at these events.

15. He held, at this moment, a second council at Carthage, composed of forty-two bishops. The penitential canons relative to the apostates were rendered more mild. They ruled that the *lapsi* might be admitted to communion, even when they were not in danger of death, and without insisting on the precise duration heretofore fixed for doing penance. The Church, at that time, attentive as ever to the spiritual good of her children, knew how to apply, to modify, to temper, her regulations according to circumstances; and, immovable in her

faith, she proportioned her discipline to the various wants of the times. Privatus, the heretic bishop of Lambesa, in Numidia, whose seditious proceedings we have already noted, presented himself at the second council of Carthage, to justify himself respecting the crimes for which he had been deposed. This new attempt failed, like its predecessors. In revenge, he assembled a conventicle, in which, after having anathematized St. Cyprian, he ordained, as bishop of Carthage, Fortunatus, one of the five seditious priests who fostered the troubles of this Church. The schismatics dispatched Felicissimus to Rome, and, what was very remarkable, directed him, not to Novatian, so much was the influence of the antipope lessened even among his partisans, but to St. Cornelius. The pontiff rejected his advances with apostolic vigor, and wrote of it to St. Cyprian, reproaching him, in terms full of kindness, that he had not received advices from him on this subject. The illustrious bishop of Carthage replied in these words:[*] "The schismatics have, then, dared to cross the seas, and present their letters before the chair of St. Peter—to the Church of the churches, whence emanates sacerdotal unity, without reflecting that they to whom they address themselves are those Romans whose faith the apostle so highly praised, and to whom infidelity can find no access. Condemned by our council, these desperate men doubtless regard the authority of the African bishops insufficient. Their cause has been examined, their sentence is pronounced." Certain writers, unfavorable to the primacy of the see of Rome, have affected to find in this letter of St. Cyprian a protestation against appeals in general to the sovereign pontiff. But Cecilian, successor of St. Cyprian, who appealed to Rome against the Donatists; St. Athanasius, who appealed to Rome against the Arians; St. John Chrysostom, who appealed to Rome against his private enemies; St. Cyprian himself, who had previously appealed to Rome against Novatus and Felicissimus, suffice to establish, by striking examples, the doctrine of the Church on this point

[*] The whole of this passage may be found, Opera S. Cypr. Epist. 55.

In point of fact, the schismatics in question did not appeal: knowing, as all the world knew, that the chair of St. Peter was, as it is still, the source of unity and sacerdotal legitimacy, they demanded letters of communion merely to gain authority for their false bishop.

16. The glorious pontificate of St. Cornelius was drawing to its close. The Emperor Gallus, on succeeding Decius, had preserved his hostility to Christianity. He ordered St. Cornelius to prison. "The empire," in the magnificent language of St. Cyprian, "was again vanquished by the priesthood." The pope nobly confessed the name of Jesus Christ, and was exiled to Civita Vecchia, where his glorious death* occurred, September 14, A. D. 252. "He merited," said St. Cyprian, "the palm of confessors, for he had defied the fury of tyrants, by daring to accept a title which then was a sentence of death." A virginal purity, with the greatest prudence and firmness, characterized St. Cornelius. A decree is attributed to him which forbade any Christian to take an oath, or to pronounce vows, until he had reached fourteen years of age.

§ III. St. Lucius I., Pope (Oct. 18, A. D. 252—Mar. 4, 253)

17. St. Lucius I., one of the priests who had been banished with Pope St. Cornelius, was appointed his successor, amid the applauses of the universal Church. But his promotion only made him a mark for the proscription of Gallus, whose policy in regard to the Christians seems to have been to strike chiefly the pastors, the better to destroy the flock. St. Lucius, like his predecessor, was banished; and received, in his place of banishment, letters from St. Cyprian, who felicitated him on his generous confession. Some months afterwards, the holy pope was restored to the affection of the faithful at Rome, who received him with transports of joy. The persecution, nevertheless, continued. The emperor had given orders to his governors to spare all the schismatics of the party of the anti-

---

* Pontificate of Bucherius.

pope Novatian, hoping, probably, that intestine dissensions would have better success against the Church than the violence of arms. "The Lord," said St. Cyprian, on this subject, in a second letter to Lucius, "wishes, by this, to confound the heretics, and to show which is the true Church; who is the one bishop legitimately elected; who are those whom the enemy attacks, and those, on the contrary, whom the demon spares, as belonging to himself." St. Lucius survived these testimonials of the fidelity and devotion of Christian Africa only a few months. He died March 4, A. D. 253. In the short period of his pontificate, he sanctioned, by a decree, the doctrine of the Church touching the *lapsi;* admitting them to communion after a sufficient penance. He renewed the ordinances of his predecessors relative to the serious examination of the capacity and morals of the candidates for holy orders, and prohibited the clergy from having in their houses, or in their service, other women than their near relatives.

18. In the beginning of this same year (253), a man died, exhausted by gigantic labors, leaving a great name, on which history is divided. Origen expired at Tyre, bequeathing to posterity as many disputes, after his death, as during life. To say of him only what is incontestible, we will merely recapitulate the principal facts of his stormy life. His virtue, his love of poverty, his humility, the courage with which he confessed the faith, his immense labors, can never be doubted by any one. He had the glory to count among his disciples, martyrs, doctors, and illustrious bishops: St. Heraclas and St. Dionysius, both bishops of Alexandria, St. Gregory Thaumaturgus, and his brother St. Athenodorus, also bishop in Pontus, St. Firmilian, Beryllus, bishop of Bozra, whom he reclaimed from heresy, St. Alexander, bishop of Jerusalem, &c. But, as if every thing that relates to the reputation of Origen should offer a contrast, he had on the one hand a crowd of illustrious disciples, while on the other, most detestable heretics called themselves *Origenians.* This sect, which still existed in the time of St. Epiphanius, renewed all the abomi-

nations of the Gnostics, and pretended to justify them by the doctrine of Origen. The prodigious number of the writings of this great man contributed, perhaps, to bring them into disfavor. He had composed not less than six thousand. In the rapidity of composition which so enormous a production demanded, in the necessity of dictating to two or three at the same time, and of leaving to the care of the stenographers themselves afterwards to collect and publish his discourses, it is not possible to suppose that many involuntary errors have not escaped attention. When we add, that the doctrine of the Church was not, at this epoch, as it was afterwards, fixed and defined by the councils in proportion as heresy, calling attention to each dogma in particular, provoked an infallible decision, we shall, perhaps, find the errors of Origen, of which we have already recapitulated the chief, more excusable. However it may be, these fearful words have been pronounced of this great genius: *No one has surpassed him, either in good or in evil. Ubi bene, nemo melius; ubi male, nemo pejus.* His eternal salvation remains among the secrets of God. "But, if we must fear for him," said Le Nain de Tillemont, "let us fear still more for ourselves, lest we fall into faults which make us tremble for an Origen."

§ IV. St. Stephen I., Pope (May 13, a. d. 253—Aug. 2, 257).

19. St. Stephen was elected sovereign pontiff, May 13, a. d. 253. He was designated, in advance, to the suffrages of the clergy and faithful of Rome, by the confidence placed in him by his two predecessors. St. Cornelius had confided to him the administration of the Church property. St. Lucius I., at his death, had confided to him the care and guidance of the Church.

20. The two first years of his pontificate were marked by one of the most horrible plagues of which history has preserved the remembrance. From Ethiopia, where it first appeared, it spread over every part of the empire, leaving victims by myriads in its track. At Rome, five thousand were carried off

in a single day. St. Stephen proved himself the worthy pastor of his suffering flock. He sent supplies to Syria, to Arabia, and wherever the plague broke out. St. Dionysius, of Alexandria, wrote to thank him for his attentive charity. The deportment of the Christians, in these distressing circumstances, commanded the admiration even of their enemies. The pagans had so great a horror of the contagion, that, forgetting all the laws of nature, they threw their diseased relatives out of the windows, as if they could banish death at the same time with the infected. St. Cyprian, who gives us many frightful details, relates, that the streets of Carthage were full of the dying, and of unburied corpses. Houses, made empty by the pestilence, became a prey to infamous thieves, who profited by the calamity to enrich themselves with the spoils of the dead. At the call of their bishop, the Christians assembled, and took charge of the different quarters of the city, aiding, without distinction, the pagans and the faithful. The rich contributed from their wealth, the poor their labor, and order was soon restored. The pagans, touched by this sublime devotion, were converted in great numbers to the religion that inspired it. St. Cyprian exerted himself in every way to provide for so many wants; he encouraged the weak, directed the ardor of the most zealous, and consoled all in their sufferings. In the midst of the ruins created by the plague, he wrote his *Treatise on Mortality*, where he mingled all the tenderness of his feelings with the elevated conceptions of faith. At Neocæsarea, St. Gregory Thaumaturgus gave the same example to his people. St. Dionysius at Alexandria, St. Maximus at Nola, in short, all the Catholic bishops, offered this eloquent spectacle to the pagan world; and these Christians, who, by order of the emperor, were hunted in every place to be thrown to the lions, rushed with intrepidity amidst the dangers of pestilence and the terrors of death, to the relief of those self-same men who so often had been their persecutors.

21. Christian charity increased with the misfortunes of the empire. The Scythians, the Goths, the Persians, precur-

sors of the formidable army of barbarians who were surrounding more and more closely the Roman provinces, devastated the frontiers in turn, ruined the cities, and led away captive those whom the plague had spared. Eight bishops of Numidia had the grief to see their flocks thus dragged into slavery. They wrote of this disaster to St. Cyprian, who, with many tears, read these letters to his people, from whom he collected alms, to the amount of a hundred thousand sesterces, which he sent to the bishops. "If," he wrote, " to try our charity, God sends you another such calamity, fear not to let us hear of it. We pray constantly that this misfortune may not be renewed; but be assured, if the case should happen, we will gladly give all that is in our power." To encourage still more the charitable inclinations of his people, the eloquent bishop wrote his book, *On Good Works and Alms-deeds*, an admirable exhortation to Christian charity.

22. The reputation of St. Cyprian for virtue and learning, caused him to be consulted as the oracle of the universal Church. He succeeded to the brilliant heritage of Origen, and his voluminous correspondence attests his zeal for the maintenance of faith and ecclesiastical discipline. He wrote to a bishop of a strange abuse which had been introduced in the holy sacrifice of the Mass, during the persecution. As it was celebrated at the dawn of day, and as the custom of the primitive Church was to distribute the communion under the species of wine, as well as of bread, it was feared that the odor of wine might betray the faithful, and some ignorant ministers put water, only, in the chalice. St. Cyprian restored the apostolic tradition on this point, and taught that the mingling of water with the wine signified the union of the Church with Jesus Christ, from whom she could not be separated. Fortunatian, bishop of Assur, having apostatized during the persecution, had been deposed, and replaced by Epictetus. When peace was restored to the Church, Fortunatian wanted to resume the possession of his see. St. Cyprian wrote to Epictetus and to the faithful at Assur, that it must

not be permitted. Encratius, a bishop, consulted St. Cyprian concerning a comedian, who, after having left the theatre, was converted, but still continued to prepare young men for the stage. "It is my opinion," replied the bishop of Carthage, "that it is not becoming, either to the majesty of God or to the discipline of the Gospel, to sully the purity of the Church by such a scandal. If the comedian is poor, let him be assisted with the other brethren who are poor like himself." A priest of the Church of Furnes, in Africa, called Geminius Faustinus, had accepted the administration of a wardship. St. Cyprian recalled the discipline then in force, and especially a decree of one of the preceding councils of Carthage, which forbade the nomination by testament of a clergyman as tutor or guardian, that he might not be drawn away from prayer and the ministry of the altar. "If any one, in spite of this prohibition, dare to disobey it, the holy sacrifice shall not be offered for him." Marcion, bishop of Arles, in Gaul, left the Catholic Church, to attach himself to the anti-pope Novatian. Faustinus, bishop of Lyons, and the other bishops of the province, wrote of it to St. Cyprian, who referred the subject to the pope, and prayed him to interpose his authority in this affair. "Send," he wrote to St. Stephen, "to the clergy and people of Arles letters by which Marcion may be excommunicated, and another bishop appointed to gather the flock of Christ, which is still scattered." St. Cyprian acted with the same respect for the decisions of the Holy See in another affair belonging to the Church in Spain. Basilides, bishop of Leon, and Martial, bishop of Astorga, had fallen, during the persecution, into the cowardice of the *libellatici*. After the peace, they deceived the confidence of the Holy See by false representations, and, by means of the letters which they had fraudulently obtained, they pretended to retain their sees. St. Cyprian, who at this time was presiding over a council of thirty-eight bishops, wrote a letter, in the name of his colleagues, to the priest Felix, to the people of Leon and Astorga, and to the deacon Lelius. "Let them observe," said he, "what has been ordained by Pope St.

Cornelius. The *libellatici* can be admitted to penance, but they must be excluded from the honor of the priesthood, and from all clerical functions."

23. A question of still more serious importance had arisen in the Church. St. Cyprian took an active part in it. Unhappily his zeal was not always confined within the limits of true wisdom; and when we see this illustrious doctor openly resist St. Stephen, we are reminded that a saint is always a man. The question to be decided was, whether the baptism conferred by heretics is valid or not; and whether those among them who were restored to the bosom of the Church should be rebaptized. In our times, such a question would be decided as soon as proposed. Baptism is a sacrament which can be validly conferred even by a pagan, provided the prescriptions of the Church are observed. To make the effects of the sacraments dependent on the dispositions of those who are their ministers, is an error notorious, defined, condemned; which would lead, in practice, to the most disastrous consequences. Heretics and schismatics cannot lawfully administer the sacraments, but they do it validly. This distinction, evident to us, was not so clear before the decision of the Church. St. Cyprian took the opposite view, and maintained, openly, that the baptism performed by heretics and schismatics was null, and that those who were converted should be baptized: *baptized*, he said, for he would not use the word *rebaptized*, the better to show that they had not been baptized up to that point. He held the erroneous doctrine of Agrippinus, one of his predecessors in the see of Carthage. The schism of the antipope, Novatian, had given much actuality to this question, by the great number of sectaries who demanded re-entrance into the Catholic communion. The particular councils of Synnada, and of Iconium in Phrygia, had just decided that the baptism of heretics was null, by the mere fact that it was conferred out of the Church. Pope St. Stephen I. immediately wrote to the bishops of the neighboring provinces not to communicate with those who rebaptize heretics. The bishops of Numidia,

consulted St. Cyprian on this question. In the name of thirty-two bishops, assembled in council at Carthage, he replied that, following the doctrine of his predecessors, none could be baptized out of the Church. "To confer the grace of a sacrament," he says, "he who administers it must first possess it: since no one can give that which he has not." He admits that the custom had generally prevailed, not to rebaptize heretics; "but," he adds, "it is not custom, but reason, which ought to prescribe the rule." A bishop of his party, at a later period, expressed this thought in another form: "Jesus Christ said, 'I am the truth,' but not, 'I am the usage.'" Such is the thesis which St. Cyprian supported with all the vigor of his eloquence, in a multitude of private letters and treatises, in which he does not always spare St. Stephen. The year following (256), he held another council of seventy-one bishops, at Carthage, when he decided according to his own views the question of the baptism of heretics. He sent the acts of this council to the pope. "It is especially to you," he said in his letter, "that we should send all that more closely concerns the sacerdotal authority, or the unity and dignity of the Catholic Church. We have judged that they who have been defiled by the profane water of the heretics, ought to be baptized when they return to the Church, and that the laying on of hands is not sufficient to give them the Holy Spirit." This was the state of the question when it reached the tribunal of the Roman pontiff. Two councils of Phrygia, two councils of Africa, and a considerable number of bishops of all the provinces, had openly embraced the error. The most illustrious doctor in Christendom, the eloquent bishop of Carthage, whose decisions all the Church had been habituated to regard as oracles, supported them by the mighty power of his reasoning, of his authority, and reputation. The Church has rarely found herself in such peril. It was not sufficient for the Holy See to proclaim the truth; circumspection was required, which could control the situation, and, by indulgence, reclaim those whom an intemperate rigor might drive into a hopeless heresy

St. Stephen comprehended his position, and acted with merciful firmness. Without undertaking discussions with minds prepossessed, he was content to declare, with simplicity, the apostolic doctrine, leaving to the truth the time to germinate in their souls. Unfortunately, we have only fragments of his letter to the African bishops, but these are sufficient to manifest the spirit in which it was composed. He speaks of the chair of St. Peter, the foundation of the Church, on which he is seated, after an uninterrupted succession. He lays down the traditional doctrine, which is opposed to the council of Carthage. He defines the rule by this precept, which has passed into a theological axiom, *Nihil innovetur nisi quod traditum est* (Let there be no innovation unless by the sanction of tradition). He declares, at the close, that if they persevere obstinately in their error, he shall be forced to break with the bishops of Africa.

24. Rome had spoken: there lay the truth: there was the right. Yet we must confess, in sorrow for the weakness of human nature, St. Cyprian yielded not. "What presumption does it not indicate," he wrote to the Bishop Pompey, when sending him the pope's reply, "to prefer a human tradition to the order of God!" He convoked at Carthage a council of the three provinces of Africa, Numidia, and Mauritania: eighty-five bishops answered his call, and assembled September 1, A. D. 256. In his opening discourse, he complains of the tyranny which the *Bishop of bishops* pretends to exercise in the Church. When the votes were taken, all were unanimous in supporting the opinion contrary to the papal decision; one saying, "*that it was in the Scriptures;*" another, "*that no one can give that which he has not;*" another, "Jesus Christ said, '*I am the truth,*' not, *I am the usage;*" finally, another, "*that no one prefers usage to reason and truth, for reason and truth always exclude usage.*" From these forms of expression may be seen how much the discussion had tended to embitter their minds. St. Cyprian would not, in spite of this unhappy dissension, break with Pope St. Stephen. He sent a deputation to convey

to him the acts of the council. His envoys were badly received, and the new incident only complicated the question, and still more envenomed it. St. Stephen having proclaimed the law, judged it best not to execute the threatenings he had expressed, but left events to time and reflection. St. Cyprian, on his side, in the height of the controversy, published two tracts, which could not fail in the sequel to react most favorably upon himself: the first, *De Utilitate Patientiæ;* the second, *De Invidia.* And St. Augustine writes, that "he cannot doubt of the return of this great man to the truth, although the authentic proofs of it were suppressed, probably by those who, possessed by the same error, were unwilling to be deprived of such patronage."

25. The eighth general persecution cut short this question in blood, and sent the defenders of both sides to martyrdom. If we were tempted to judge great and holy bishops with severity for a transient aberration, who would not pause, filled with respect and admiration, before these glorious champions of the faith? They had a right to sustain with some warmth, in a pacific discussion, what they believed to be the truth, when they had the courage to profess the truth under the sword of their executioners. Their fault was nobly effaced, before God and men, in their own blood. During the five years since the Emperor Valerian ascended the throne, he had constantly favored the Christians; and doubtless by the permission of Providence, success had crowned his enterprises. Suddenly he changed his conduct, and at the same time the fortune of his arms failed him, and, three years later, he was captured by the Persians, and reduced to serve as a footstool to their king when he mounted his horse. In A. D. 257, yielding to the solicitations of Macrinus, his favorite, he signed the edict of the eighth general persecution. Paganism, after so many sanguinary and useless attempts, still hoped to extinguish the religion of Jesus Christ by persecution. A Christian named Hippolytus; Adrias and Paulina, with their two young children, Neo and Mary; the deacon Marcellus, the tribune

Nemesius, and his daughter Lucilla; Sempronius, Olympius and Exuperia, with their son Theodulus, were the first victims at Rome, where the persecution commenced. Pope St. Stephen was particularly sought for by the persecutors. He was taken, with the clergy who had not left him, and Valerian admitted him alone to his presence. The two sovereignties of the faith and of the sword were face to face: the one could give sentence of death, but the other knew how to die; the future was the heritage of the latter. "Is it thou," said Valerian, "who seekest to overthrow the republic, and who persuadest the people to abandon the worship of the gods?" "I seek not to overthrow the republic," replied Stephen; "but I exhort the people to abandon the worship of demons, which they adore in the idols, and to know the true God, and Him whom He has sent, our Lord and Saviour Jesus Christ." Valerian ordered the saintly pope to be taken to the temple of Mars, to hear his sentence, and he was beheaded August 2, A. D. 257. His body was deposited in the cemetery of St. Callistus; but it was removed, August 17, A. D. 762, under St. Paul I., to the church of SS. Stephen and Sylvester, built by this pope, which is now called St. Sylvester *in capite*, because the head of St. John Baptist is preserved there.

§ V. St. Sixtus II., Pope (Aug. 24, A D. 257—Aug. 6, 258).

26. Notwithstanding the violence of the persecution, the clergy and faithful assembled to give a successor to St. Stephen, in the person of Sixtus II. The new pontiff had long been archdeacon of the Roman Church—an office of considerable dignity, to which belonged the administration of ecclesiastical property, and which now passed into the hands of St. Lawrence. The sovereign pontificate, under existing circumstances, was only a shorter road to martyrdom. St. Sixtus II. proved himself worthy of this sublime vocation. Under the shadow of the persecution that threatened him, he found enough of calm and tranquillity of soul to terminate, in concert

with St. Dionysius, of Alexandria, the question of rebaptism. St. Dionysius, driven from his see by Emilianus, prefect of Egypt, had been exiled to Lybia, in the little town of Cefro. The inhabitants, all pagans, were converted by him, and he soon formed, in this remote country, a church as fervent as that from which he had been separated by violence. He wrote several times to St. Sixtus, to inform him of the efforts he had made to lead back the dissidents to the decision of Pope St. Stephen I. He had the consolation to witness the return to unity of all whom a transient error had separated.

27. St Cyprian, on the first intimation of the approaching persecution, had written, in a style of great fervor, an *Exhortation to Martyrdom*, which he addressed to all the faithful of his church. He was the first seized, and conducted before Paternus, the proconsul of Africa, who merely sent him in exile to Curuba, a seaport, twenty leagues distant from Carthage. But Galerius Maximus, successor of Paternus, came to Carthage with more hostile designs. He ordered the bishop to be led to the pretorium. An immense crowd gathered to hear the trial of the illustrious doctor. "Are you Thasius Cyprianus?" demanded the proconsul. "I am," replied the saint. "Are you the bishop of these sacrilegious Christians?" "I am." "The august emperors command you to sacrifice to the gods." "I shall do nothing of the kind." "Think of what you are doing." "In a cause so just, there is no time for deliberation. Execute your orders." The sentence was prepared, and the proconsul read the decree: "Thascius Cyprianus shall die by the sword." "*Deo gratias*," responded the noble bishop. The Christians in the crowd cried out, "Let us die with him." A tumultuous scene then followed the judgment, and the proconsul ordered the removal of St. Cyprian from the city, to prevent the sedition that he feared. The bishop of Carthage bandaged his own eyes; a priest and deacon who accompanied him to the place of execution, bound his hands; he gave twenty-five pieces of gold to the swords man, and presented his head, which was struck off with

single blow The Christians collected the blood of the martyr, in cloths of linen and silk, September 14, A. D. 258. Eight of his disciples—most of them clerics of the Church of Carthage—Lucius, Montanus, Flavianus, Julian, Victoric, Primulus, Renus, and Donatian, imitated their sainted bishop in his courage and in his death. The city of Cyrtha, in Numidia, counted its martyrs by thousands. They were led into a valley bordering on the river, between two ranges of hills, elevated on both sides, as if to favor the spectacle. They were then ranged in line, their eyes bandaged, and the executioner passed on from one to another, striking off their heads. This atrocious butchery lasted a great part of the day. In Spain, St. Fructuosus, bishop of Tarragona, with his two deacons, was led before the imperial governor, Emilianus. "Have you heard the order of the emperors?" demanded the proconsul. "I know not what they have ordered," replied the bishop; "as for myself, I am a Christian." "They have ordered that the gods shall be adored." "I adore one only God, who has made heaven and earth, and sea, and all that they contain." "Know you not that there are gods?" "No." "Well, we will instruct you." The governor, turning to Augurus, one of the deacons, counselled him not to be hindered by what Fructuosus had just said. Augurus declared that he also adored the one Almighty God. "And you," said Emilianus to Eulogius, the other deacon, "do you, too, adore your bishop, Fructuosus?" "I adore, not Fructuosus, but the God whom he adores." "Are you, then, a bishop?" The saint replied, "I am." "Say, rather, that you have been." And he condemned all three to be burned alive. At Antioch, the governor ordered the priest Sapricius to be put to death. A Christian, Nicephorus, who, for some years, had entertained a bitter enmity against this priest, followed him in the crowd, and, while on the way, entreated his pardon before he ascended to heaven. But Sapricius was inexorable. Arrived at the place of execution, this unhappy priest, so hard towards his brother, had not the courage to face death, and cried out that he was ready to sacrifice to the gods. He was released. "What have you done?" said Nicephorus. "Martyr of Jesus Christ, lose not the crown that you have already merited by so many torments." His exhortations were in vain; and this immortal crown, of which Sapricius had made himself doubly unworthy, was transferred to Nicephorus; for the tormentors merely changed their victims, and, by order of the governor, they beheaded him. At Toulouse, in Gaul, St. Saturninus was dragged by a furious bull, and died for the faith.

28. At Cæsarea, in Palestine, three friends sealed their friendship by martyrdom. They presented themselves together to the governor, who condemned them to the beasts. These three heroes of Christian friendship were Priscus, Malchus, and Alexander. An instance, still more remarkable, was that of a child, named Cyril, which excited the admiration of Cæsarea, in Cappadocia. The father of this boy was an idolater, and, in his hatred of the name of Christian, had driven his son from his house, and abandoned him entirely to public charity. Cyril was brought, by soldiers, into the presence of the governor. "My child," said the judge, with gentleness, "I can easily pardon your fault, in consideration of your age. You need nothing but to be restored to your father's favor. Do right, and renounce your superstition." The holy child replied: "I am glad to suffer reproaches for my conduct. I rejoice to be driven from my father's house; God will receive me in one much more grand and beautiful. I willingly renounce the goods of this world, that I may be rich in heaven. I am not afraid of death, because it is followed by a better life." Then the judge, assuming a tone calculated to intimidate a child, threatened him with cruel torments; had him bound, as if to be taken to the place of execution; ordered a pyre to be prepared and set in flames. The courage of Cyril seemed to be only the more assured. He allowed himself to be led about, without shedding a single tear. They approached the fire, as if to cast him into it, but his constancy was unmoved. The judge had secretly ordered them to go no further. When it was evident

that the view of torments had made no impression upon him, he was brought back to the judge, who said to him, "You have seen the fire, you have looked at the sword; now will you be good, and, by submission to my will, and that of your father, will you not deserve to regain his affection, so that you can return home again?" The young Cyril replied: "You have done me a great wrong to recall me; I fear neither the fire nor the sword; I am anxious to go to a home far more desirable, and I sigh for riches more solid than the possessions of my father. Do not delay, but let me die, that I may the sooner be with God." The assistants wept to hear him speak thus; but he said: "You ought to rejoice, instead of weeping. Far from desiring to soften me by your tears, you ought to encourage me to suffer every thing. You know not what glory awaits me; nor what is my hope; nor the heavenly city to which I am going. Let me end this earthly life!" With these sentiments, he received the crown of martyrdom. While reading this page of Church history, we know not which should most excite our astonishment, the faith that, at so tender an age, inspires such noble and heroic sentiments, or the blindness of the pagans, who could hope to triumph over such faith by the sword or the pyre.

29. St. Sixtus II. had preceded, on his way to heaven, this pleind of glorious martyrs whom the edicts of Valerian multiplied in all parts of the empire. History has not preserved more than a few brief records of their heroic acts. On the 6th of August, A. D. 258, while the holy pontiff celebrated the holy mysteries in the cemetery of Callistus, the soldiers laid hands on his person, and bore him off to execution. "Where are you going, my father, without your son?" cried Lawrence, archdeacon of the Roman Church; "Whither do you go, holy pontiff, without your deacon?" St. Sixtus replied: "It is not I, my son, who abandon thee. But a more fearful combat awaits thee: in three days thou wilt follow me." As he spoke these words, a soldier smote off his head. He had occupied the Holy See eleven months and six days. He

had sent to Gaul St. Peregrinus, first bishop of Auxerre, and had transferred the bodies of SS. Peter and Paul to the catacombs, in order to place the precious deposit in greater security. Among the praises which antiquity bestowed on St. Sixtus II., we remark especially that of being a mild and pacific pontiff. It was to his meekness that was reserved the consolatory mission of terminating the question concerning rebaptism, which had filled the pontificate of his predecessor with bitterness.

30. The prefect of Rome, possessed with the belief that the Christians had great treasures in concealment, which he coveted, ordered Lawrence, who had the care of them, to be brought before him. "You complain," he said, "that you are treated with cruelty. There is now no question of punishments; I require only what depends on yourself. It is reported that in your ceremonies the pontiffs offer libations in golden vases; that the blood of the victims is received in chalices of silver; and that, to illuminate your nocturnal sacrifices, you have wax lights fitted upon golden chandeliers. It is said, too, that, to furnish these offerings, the brethren sell their inheritances, and often reduce their children to poverty. Bring to the light these hidden treasures. The emperor has need of them to pay the soldiers, and to re-establish the finances of the state. I understand, that, according to your doctrine, we must render to every one that which belongs to him. The emperor claims, as his own, the money which bears the stamp of his image: render, then, as you say, to Cæsar that which belongs to Cæsar. If I mistake not, your God does not coin money; he has not brought silver into the world, he brought only words. Give us, then, the money, and keep the words." "I confess," returned Lawrence, "that our Church is rich: the emperor himself has not such great treasures. You shall see all that she has most precious, but give me time to put all in order, and make an inventory and valuation." The prefect gave him three days of delay. In this interval, Lawrence went about the city, seeking, in every street, the poor, to whose wants he

administered. He brought them all—lepers, blind, lame, paralytic, sick, many covered with ulcers—and ranged them in the court of the church. "Come," said he to the prefect, "you will find a great court full of precious vases, and ingots of gold heaped under the galleries." Then, opening the door, he exhibited to the prefect an assemblage of all human infirmities. "These," said he, "are the treasures I promised you. I add to them pearls and precious stones; you see the virgins and widows—they are the crown of the Church. Make the best of this wealth for Rome, the emperor, and yourself." The only reply of the prefect was to order an immense gridiron, under which burning coals were placed. The holy deacon was extended upon it, and had the strength, in the midst of the tortures of this holocaust, to say to the tyrant, "Turn me on the other side, I am sufficiently roasted on this. It is cooked enough; you can eat it." And thus he gave up his soul to God, a martyr to faith and charity.

31. After the death of the victim comes the punishment of the persecutor. Rarely has divine justice marked this truth in a more striking way. The plague recommenced its ravages with a fury hitherto unknown. Even the elements seemed to lend themselves to avenge the blood of the just which had inundated the earth. During many days, Italy was enveloped in thick darkness. Rome, Libya, and Asia, were covered with ruins by frightful earthquakes, and the barbarians began to take possession of the Roman world. The Germans invaded Gaul to the Pyrenees, crossed these mountains, ravaged a part of Spain, and showed themselves on the shores of Mauritania to a people astonished to behold this new race of men. The Alemanni, another German tribe, advanced upon Italy, to the number of three hundred thousand, even to the vicinity of Rome. The Goths, Sarmatians, and Quadi, devastated Illyria. Scythia poured forth her populations on Asia Minor and Greece. These warriors, half naked, embarked on the Black Sea in a kind of floating cabins, trusting themselves to a stormy sea and to timid mariners. They surprised Trebi-

zonde, ravaged Pontus, and, chaining the Roman captives to the oars of their vessels, returned triumphant to their deserts. Other Goths or Scythians, encouraged by this example, compelled their prisoners to construct a fleet, left the borders of the Tanais, passed the Bosphorus, entered Asia, pillaged Chalcedon, and retired by the light of the flames which consumed Nicea and Nicomedia. In fine, to complete the picture of all these disasters, Valerian, who had deluged the world with Christian blood, became a prisoner of Sapor, king of Persia, and served as a footstool to his conqueror when he mounted his horse; and, as if vengeance is ever destined to survive crime, after the death of the Roman emperor, his skin, stuffed, tanned, and painted red, remained suspended, during several centuries, under the vaulted roof of the great temple of the Persians. The son of Valerian, Gallienus himself, regarding his father's misfortune as an abdication, said no more, on receiving this frightful intelligence, than, "I knew my father was mortal." This series of disasters put an end to the eighth general persecution.

CHAPTER XIII.

§ I. PONTIFICATE OF ST. DIONYSIUS (July 22, A. D. 259—Dec. 26, 269).

1. Election of St. Dionysius. Charity of the Christians. Progress of Christianity.—2. Decay of the Empire under Gallienus.—3. Heresy of Sabellius.—4. Paul of Samosata.—5. Death of St. Dionysius of Alexandria, and of St. Gregory Thaumaturgus.—6. Death of Pope St. Dionysius.

§ II. PONTIFICATE OF ST. FELIX I. (Dec. 27, A. D. 269—Dec. 22. 274).

7. Election of Pope St. Felix I.—8. Manes.—9. Letter of Manes to Marcellus.—10. Fundamental principles of the error of Manes.—11. Conference between St. Archelaus, Bishop of Carrhœ, and Manes. Another conference between the priest Diodorus and Manes.—12. Ninth general persecution under Aurelian.—13. Martyrdom of Pope St. Felix I.

§ III. PONTIFICATE OF ST. EUTYCHIAN (Jan. 4, A. D. 275—Dec. 7, 283).

14. Election of St. Eutychian. End of the ninth general persecution.—15. Dorotheus, priest of Antioch. Achillas of Alexandria.—16. St. Felix, of Nola.—17. Progress of Manicheism in Egypt and Syria.—18. Death of St. Eutychian.

§ IV. PONTIFICATE OF ST. CAIUS (Dec. 10, A. D. 283—April 22, 296).

19. Election of St. Caius.—20. Martyrdom of St. Sebastian.—21. Martyrdom of the Theban legion.—22. Martyrdom of St. Victor of Marseilles.—23. Cruelties of Riccius Varus.—24. Sect of the Hieracitæ in Egypt.—25. Conversion of Arnobius. His seven books against the Gentiles.—26. Election of Constantius Chlorus and Galerius to the empire.—27. Instructions of St. Thomas, bishop of Alexandria, to the Christian officers of the court of Diocletian.—28. Death of Pope St. Caius.

§ I. PONTIFICATE OF ST. DIONYSIUS (July 22, A. D. 259—Dec. 26, 269).

1. ST. DIONYSIUS was elected pope July 22, A. D. 259, and consecrated by Maximus, bishop of Ostia. The ancient usage, then in vigor, which St. Augustine remarked in his time, gave to the bishops of Ostia the privilege of consecrating the

Roman pontiffs. The calamities which desolated the empire offered, from the first, a vast field to the zeal and charity of St. Dionysius. He sent considerable sums of money to Cæsarea, in Cappadocia, to redeem the captives who had fallen into the hands of the barbarians. It might be said that the Christians were wholly occupied in paying, by benefits, for the torments which they had suffered from their persecutors. The other St. Dionysius, the illustrious bishop of Alexandria, on returning from exile, found his episcopal city in all the horrors of civil war. Each edifice of this immense city became a fortress, each street a field of battle. Many of its population had perished, and the Bruchion was empty. It was not permitted to pass from one quarter to another, and it was less difficult to write or to receive an answer from the East to the West, than from Alexandria to Alexandria. To the civil war, succeeded famine and pestilence. The bishops and the Christians multiplied themselves, as it were, to supply every want, to calm all animosities, to console the unfortunate. It was a glorious spectacle to see Christianity bear sway amid all these ruins that human passions had accumulated around themselves, and to increase by means of all that seemed destined to annihilate it. The barbarians began to yield to its influence. Among their captives, they had taken many holy bishops and priests, who healed the sick, expelled demons, in the name of Jesus Christ, and taught virtue by their discourses and example. The barbarians admired them, and became persuaded that, by imitating their virtues, they would render God propitious. Many made themselves the disciples of their slaves, received baptism, and founded new churches. Such was the commencement of Christianity among the Goths, Sarmatians, and Germans.

2. While a life-giving virtue thus flowed from the name of Jesus Christ over the Roman and barbarian world, paganism exhausted itself in pleasures or in idle dreams. On each new disaster, Gallienus laughed, and inquired what would be the amusements, or the plays, for the next day. Porphyry wrote treatises against the Christians whom the emperors condemned

to death; and Plotinus, his master of philosophy, obtained of Gallienus the gift of a ruined city of Campania, to which he gave the name of Platonopolis, where he proposed to establish the famous republic of Plato. These fine projects failed, in spite of imperial favor and gold. They were all that expiring paganism found to oppose the invasions of the barbarians and the conquests of Christianity, which profited by every blow directed against it. At the death of Gallienus, thirty generals took the purple at the same time, which served them oftener as a winding-sheet than a mantle. The moral world already belonged to the Christians; the empire was soon to become the possession of barbarians.

3. Intestine dissensions, meanwhile, were not wanting to this religion, so often tried by violent persecutions. In A. D. 257, Sabellius had renewed, in Libyan Cyrenaica, the heresy of Noetus and Praxeas. With them, he denied the Trinity, and the real distinction of the three divine persons. Many Egyptian bishops adopted these errors, and heresy was propagated to such a degree that one hardly dared to call Jesus Christ the Son of God. St. Dionysius, bishop of Alexandria, multiplied, in this peril of the faith, his exhortations, his letters, his efforts, to second the triumph of sound doctrine. He insisted, with great force, in his discourses and treatises, on the distinction of the three persons in the holy Trinity. "Jesus Christ, in His Gospel, says of himself: 'I am the vine, my Father is the Husbandman.' Now the vine and the husbandman, the work and the workman, are not the same thing." Certain of the faithful, well instructed in doctrine, on reading these words of the bishop of Alexandria, imagined that he taught that the Son was a creature, and that he did not regard Him as ὁμοούσιος, or consubstantial with the Father. This term consubstantial, which, at a later epoch, was to raise so much opposition, is remarkable in the mouth of simple Christians, sixty years before the council of Nice. From this, they took occasion to accuse St. Dionysius of Alexandria, before the Pope St. Dionysius. The sovereign pontiff convoked, at Rome

(A. D. 261), a council, which at once condemned the two opposite but equally impious errors, of those who held the doctrine of Sabellius, and of those who said that the Word had been created, made, or formed, and that He was not *consubstantial* with the Father. The pope afterwards wrote to St. Dionysius of Alexandria, desiring him to explain his doctrine, and to justify himself from the errors imputed to him. The patriarch of Alexandria replied by protesting his faith in the word *consubstantial*. In his letter to the pope, and in a special treatise, he gives the reasons which had induced him to insist more particularly on the proofs of the distinction of the persons in the holy Trinity, in his reply to Sabellius. His justification was complete, because his attachment to the true doctrines had never varied. At a later period St. Athanasius used his name and his works to confound the Arians.

4. A heresiarch, more formidable than Sabellius, dogmatized in Syria—Paul, of Samosata, bishop of Antioch (A. D. 263). Of morals more than suspected, his character was arrogant; loving splendor and show, he had sought, in the high dignity he had attained, only the means of gratifying his passions. He affected the luxury of the Roman magistrates and proconsuls. His episcopal chair resembled the tribune of a provincial governor, and he required applauses to enhance the eloquence of his discourses. The favor of Zenobia, queen of Palmyra, which he enjoyed, contributed much to nourish his pride. This princess, in religion a Jewess, desired to be instructed in the Christian doctrine, and addressed herself for this purpose to Paul of Samosata. This unworthy bishop pretended to explain the Incarnation by admitting in Jesus Christ two persons, or, following the Greek, *hypostases*, the one, Son of God, by nature, and existing before time began; the other, son of David, born in time, and who had only received the name of the Son of God after His union with the Word, as a city receives the name of its sovereign, a house that of its founder. This error, which was afterwards developed by Nestorius, and to which he gave his name, was vigorously refuted

by St. Dionysius of Alexandria, who is everywhere found in the breach when the true faith needs a defender. "The Word made Himself flesh," said the holy patriarch, "without division or separation. Two persons do not exist in Him, as if the Word dwelt in man, but was not united to him. How dare you, then, speak of Jesus Christ as a man distinguished for his genius—He, the true God, adored by all creatures, with the Father and the Holy Spirit, incarnate of the Holy Virgin Mary, Mother of God?" The name of the Mother of God, given to the blessed Virgin by St. Dionysius of Alexandria, and afterwards confirmed by the general council of Ephesus, was not new in the Church. St. Methodius, of Patara, had already employed it. Origen had used it, in his commentary on the Gospel of St. Luke; and in his treatise on the epistle to the Romans, he develops, at large, the reasons why he has given this name to the blessed Virgin. Two councils assembled in succession, at Antioch (A. D. 264–268), condemned the errors of Paul of Samosata; but their author, by the use of subterfuges, and by protesting his submission, had succeeded in avoiding a personal anathema. Finally, a third council (A. D. 269), held in the same city, solemnly deposed him, and elected another bishop in his place.

5. St. Dionysius, of Alexandria, did not live to close this affair. He expired A. D. 264, during the first council of Antioch, which had been convoked, in great part, through his influence. He filled the patriarchal see of Alexandria seventeen years, and his name is gloriously identified with all the conflicts of that stormy period. His works, his courage under persecution, his virtues, and his genius, have won for him the title of Great. Nearly at the same time, another disciple of Origen died, the not less illustrious St. Gregory Thaumaturgus, bishop of Neocæsarea, whom even the enemies of the Church called a second Moses, on account of his miracles. "I give thanks to God," said he, before his death, "that, having found, on coming to this city, only seventeen Christians, I leave to my successor only seventeen infidels." He forbade that a place

should be purchased for his sepulchre, "so that posterity shall know that Gregory had no possession on this earth, not even a tomb." That was a happy age in the Church, where sanctity was left as a heritage, and where she always found a disciple to receive the mantle of Elias!

6. The Pope St. Dionysius died December 26, A. D. 269, after a pontificate of ten years. St. Basil calls him a pope illustrious for the purity of his faith and virtues. The two heresies of Sabellius, and Paul of Samosata, had found in him a formidable adversary. He apportioned the churches of Rome, and the cemeteries, among the priests, and completed the boundaries of the dioceses and parishes. He ordained St. Zamas, first bishop of Bologna, and took great pains to restore their primitive vigor to the various canons and usages of discipline, which had been disturbed by the persecution of Valerian. This excellent Pontiff had a profound knowledge of the doctrines of the Church, which he proved at the time of the discussion on the baptism of heretics; when, being only a priest, he warmly sustained the decision of St. Stephen I.; and at a later period, by uniting with his namesake, St. Dionysius of Alexandria, when the latter sought to moderate the severity of the sentence, and to counsel pacific measures.

§ II. St. Felix I., Pope (Dec. 27, A. D. 269—Dec. 22, 274).

7. On the day following the decease of Pope St. Dionysius, St. Felix, the first of the name, was elected to succeed him. Shortly after, he received a letter, addressed to his predecessor, in which the bishops of the council of Antioch informed the holy see of the condemnation of Paul of Samosata. The new pope confirmed it by his authority, and wrote, on this subject, to Maximus, bishop of Alexandria, who had succeeded St. Dionysius in the government of that Church: "We believe," said he, "in Jesus Christ, our Lord, born of the Virgin Mary. We believe that He is the eternal Word, the only Son of God. No: He was not a man, in whom God only sojourned.

Son of God, He was perfect God, and perfect man, after His Incarnation, and no distinction of two persons could be found in Him."

8. From the remote bounds of Persia, another heresiarch, whose name and aberrations were destined to a longer duration, prepared new troubles for the Church. He announced himself as the envoy of God, to recall the world to the truth, and Christians to purity of faith. His costume was as strange as his doctrines, and its singularity struck the imagination of the multitude. He wore sandals, with soles of great thickness, to add to the height of his stature, and a flowing mantle of many colors, which gave something aerial to his movements. He had a large staff of ebony, on which he leaned as he walked. Under his arm he carried a book, written in Babylonish characters. One of his legs was covered with red cloth, the other with green. In this guise, resembling that of a Persian satrap, the slave Cubricus exhibited himself as Manes, the heresiarch, the father of Manicheism. He claimed to possess the gift of miracles, and pretended to cure all diseases by the virtue of his prayers. Cast into prison for impostures, he killed his jailor; he succeeded in escaping from his prison and from Persia, his native country, and presented himself at Carrhes, in Mesopotamia, the ancient Haran of the Scriptures, preceded by the reputation which, with the aid of his dupes or accomplices, he gained, and by the following strange letter, which he addressed to Marcellus, disciple of St. Archelaus, bishop of that city:

9. "Manes, apostle of Jesus Christ, and all the saints and virgins who are with me: to Marcellus, my well-beloved son: grace, mercy, and peace, from God the Father and our Lord Jesus Christ. May the hand of light preserve thee from the evils of this present world, from its dangers, and from the snares of the principle of evil. Amen.

"I have heard, with joy, that thy charity is great, but it grieves me to see that thy faith is not conformable to the true doctrine. Sent from God to restore the human race, which has gone astray, I have considered it needful to write to thee for the salvation of thy soul, and for the spiritual good of those who surround thee. Learn, then, my son, to discern the errors which the common doctors teach. They declare that good and evil, light and darkness, the flesh and the spirit, arise from the same principle, and they continually confound one with the other. How dare they to say that God is the author and the creator of Satan and his works of wickedness? They go still farther, and are not ashamed to affirm that the Word, the only Son of the Father, is the son of a woman named Mary, and formed of flesh and blood, the principles of corruption and of death. I do not, at this time, note other errors, reserving them until I shall be near thee. I doubt not the eagerness with which thou wilt embrace the true doctrine, as soon as thou shalt know it. For the rest, it is not by constraint, like the other doctors, it is by persuasion that I shall diffuse the faith."

10. The system of duality, which Manes brought to the West, was not new. The ancient belief of the Persians in the genius of good, and the genius of evil, had given it birth. In ascending to the origin of this doctrine, we find it stated in the system of Pythagoras, and later personified in Ormuzd and Zerdast, the Persian gods. The work of Manes was, however, from these pagan elements to compose a theogony, which, to a certain point, adapted itself to the Christian dogma. He taught the existence of two eternal gods, born of themselves, but opposed to each other: one, the principle of good, which he named Light; the other, the principle of evil, which he named Darkness. The human soul was a spark from the light; the body, a portion taken from darkness. Then followed the emanations and generations of principles, which Manes borrowed from Gnosticism.

11. The presence of Manes at Carrhes had attracted to the conferences which he opened with the saintly Bishop Archelaus an immense auditory. Despite the *prestige* of his renown, and his wonderful art in speaking, to which he owed his name—for Manes, in the Persian tongue, signifies the son of eloquence—

the heresiarch was vanquished by the simple logic and the ardent faith of the bishop. This triumph, which all the assembly acknowledged by applauses, was such, that Turbon, a favorite disciple of Manes, abandoned his master, to place himself on the side of Archelaus.

The new Paraclete—for Manes assumed this title also—had, if possible, still less success in another conference with Diodorus, a holy priest in a neighboring town. The multitude, assembled to hear this controversy, took so warmly the part of the true doctrine, that they drove away the heresiarch, threatening to send him before the king of Persia. Manes contrived to escape, and sought refuge in a fortress on the frontier. He was soon seized by soldiers of the king of Persia, who flayed him alive, to avenge the death of the jailor. His body was abandoned to the dogs and birds of prey; and his skin, stuffed, was exposed over the gate of the city, A. D. 284, where it was still to be seen in the time of SS. Cyril and Epiphanius.

We have anticipated events to bring into connection all that history has preserved of importance in the life and actions of Manes. His doctrines died not with him; and we shall frequently have occasion to meet them in conflict with the faith of the Church.

12. Aurelian, become emperor in A. D. 270, was at first favorable to the Christians. Soon afterwards, the idea of attaching to his name the destruction of a religion which he saw extending with such rapidity in all parts of the empire, made him a persecutor. At the moment when he was about to sign his first edict of proscription, a thunderbolt fell near him, and forced the pen from his hand. This warning was insufficient to change his sanguinary purpose; and, some months after, A. D. 274, he instituted the ninth general persecution. As if God had chosen to measure the years of his reign by his protection of the Christians, scarcely eight months had passed, when, on his way to the East, in prosecuting the war against the Persians, he was killed by the officers of his army, between Heraclea and Byzantium. His edicts

had not even had time for publication in the distant provinces; but it was sufficient that his hostile intentions against the Christians were known, to make many martyrs. In the provinces of Gaul, where he had signed the edict of general persecution, they were most numerous. St. Columba at Sens, St. Patroclus and St. Savinian at Troyes, St. Reverianus at Autun, St. Priscus at Auxerre, were the most celebrated. Italy had also her victims: St. Agapitus of Palestrina, St. Restituta of Sora, in Latium, SS. Felix and Irenæus, and St. Mustiola of Sutri, gave their lives for the faith. In the East, history has preserved the names of the holy martyrs Conon and Mamas.

13. The dignity of Pope St. Felix I. had attracted towards him the attacks of the persecutors. He expired in torments, December 22, A. D. 274. The *Pontificalis* attributes to him the renewal of the already ancient ordinance to celebrate the holy sacrifice of the Mass on the tombs of martyrs. He also instituted the consecration of altars, by placing in them relics of martyrs. St. Felix governed the Church nearly five years. He was deposited in the cemetery in the Aurelian Way, on the spot where a church was afterwards consecrated by Felix II., two miles distant from Rome.

§ III. St. Eutychian, Pope (Jan. 4, A. D. 275—Dec. 7, 283).

14. Eutychian succeeded St. Felix Jan. 4th, A. D. 275. The ninth general persecution had just ceased with the life of Aurelian, whose last victim had been Pope St. Felix I. It was a passing storm, the precursor of another, the most terrible of all that had yet raged around the bark of the Church. Under the government of Eutychian, the faithful breathed in peace, while the imperial purple passed, by turns, to the shoulders of Tacitus, Probus, Carus, Carinus, and Numerianus, whom a caprice of the prætorians placed on the throne and on the scaffold. Barbarians, under the various names of Gepidæ, Jutes, Vandals, Blemmyes, Alani, Goths, Franks, Burgundians, availed

themselves of this rapid succession of emperors, to invade different portions of the empire. Sometimes conquered in gigantic combats, where four hundred thousand were left on the field of battle, their innumerable hordes sent forth their incessantly renewed myriads into Syria, Asia Minor, Thrace, and on the shores of the Bosphorus. In the West, they assailed Great Britain, Germany, Gaul, Spain, and the frontiers of Italy. Christianity gained in power by all the losses of the empire. The barbarians found in the Roman world but one principle possessing vitality and strength—the Christian faith—and gradually they yielded to its mysterious influence.

15. Saintly bishops succeeded each other in the sees of the great cities. At Antioch, St. Cyril effaced the last traces of the heresy of Paul of Samosata, and reconciled with the Church St. Lucian, the priest, who, for a brief period misled by error, was, in the end, one of the martyrs of Dioclesian's persecution (A. D. 279). At the same time, a patriarch of Christian virtues and learning, Dorotheus, a priest of Antioch, left, at the age of one hundred and five years, the example of a long life passed in the study and practice of a religion which was his happiness and glory. Profoundly versed in human learning, he had applied his knowledge to the interpretation of the Scriptures, which he read in the original text. He died full of years and merits, leaving the reputation of one of the most learned doctors of his time. Alexandria, under the government of her bishop, Theonas, sustained her ancient renown. Achillas occupied the chair of Clement and Origen. He was a profound philosopher and a fervent Christian. Another priest, Pierius, also gave lessons there. Rich in the treasures of science which he had amassed, he lived in poverty. A powerful dialectician, he applied to theology the method which he acquired from the ancient philosophy, and merited, at the same time, by his eloquence, the surname of the new Origen. In Pontus, the excellent Bishop Meletius was called the *Attic honey*, from the sweetness and florid eloquence of his speech.

16. At this time, a holy confessor edified the city of Nola,

in Campania, by his virtues, and the tranquil death that crowned them. Felix, a priest, had been imprisoned in the persecution of Decius; while his bishop, St. Maximus, had, through his precautions, reached an asylum in the desert. Miraculously delivered, Felix returned to his astonished fellow-citizens. The persecution of Valerian obliged him to seek concealment in a dry cistern, where a poor woman every day brought him a little bread. Solitude developed the faculty of meditation in the soul of Felix to a high degree. On returning to his country, after the death of Valerian, he refused the episcopate, which the faithful offered him, that he might occupy himself entirely in the contemplation of divine things. His speech was full of gravity and solemn instruction. The ministry of preaching alone brought him among men. The remainder of his time he lived in an isolated garden, which he cultivated with his own hands, dividing its products with the poor. Poor himself, he had only a single garment, which he often exchanged with some mendicant; and when he was urged to accept the presents of the rich, he replied that he wished only to abound in the grace of Jesus Christ, and in eternal goods. He thus finished his pilgrimage in a happy old age, and was buried in his beloved solitude, to which he would be faithful, even after his death.

17. Yet, side by side with these illustrious confessors, error still found ardent sectaries. Hermias in Egypt, Addas or Adimantus in Palestine and Syria, Thomas in Persia, and even in India, all disciples of Manes, propagated the doctrines of their master. The obstacles they encountered in this work of darkness only stimulated them to stronger efforts; and these tares, which the enemy by their hands cast into the field of the husbandman, fructified under the cover of night. Their seeming austerities, and the hypocrisy with which they dissimulated the impiety of their belief, attracted proselytes. They slept on mats of rushes or reeds, laid on the ground; had particular days for fasting and abstinence; and affected, before simple people, to honor the Blessed Virgin and the relics of saints,

while they considered such devotion as profane and superstitious. By these means, they had such success in propagating their heresy, that, in the time of St. Augustine, it was spread throughout the world; and this great genius, before his conversion, was long held in its chains.

18. Pope St. Eutychian died December 7, A. D. 283, having governed the Church nearly nine years. With the exception of some cruelties perpetrated in their own name, by certain governors, in their provinces, the faithful were in peace during his entire pontificate. The Saints Trophimus, Sabbas, and Dorymedon, at Antioch in Pisidia, are the only martyrs of this epoch whose names have been preserved. The hour of the great persecution was not yet come. St. Eutychian prescribed, under certain circumstances, the benediction of branches of trees and fruits. He instituted, according to Bury, the offertory of the Mass. Full of solicitude for the preservation of the relics of the martyrs, he commanded that their bodies should always be buried in a *colobio* or dalmatic of a red color; formerly, they were wrapped in white linen tinged with their blood. St. Eutychian was deposited in the cemetery of Callistus, and afterwards transported to the city of Luni, his native place. After the ruin of this city by the barbarians, he was deposited at Savona, to which the episcopal see of Luni was transferred.

§ IV. St. Caius, Pope (Dec. 16, A. D. 283—April 22, A. D. 296).

19. St. Caius was elected to succeed St. Eutychian in the chair of St. Peter (Dec. 16, A. D. 283). A circumstance of some note has been preserved respecting Caius. His family, originally of Dalmatia, was united by close ties of relationship with that of the future Emperor Dioclesian, who, at first, a slave of the Roman senator Anullinus, amused himself by killing all the wild boars in the forest of his master, because a Druidess had promised him the purple *de sanguine Apri*. He had not yet met the prefect of the prætorium, Aper, whom he pierced with

his sword, crying, "I have killed the fated boar." Providence destined to two members of the same family two sovereignties widely different: one purchased, by murder, a crown which he was to stain with the blood of thousands of Christians; the other, by his virtues, obtained a spiritual royalty which so many of his predecessors had purchased with their blood. These two events succeeded each other, at the interval of a year, and the name of Dioclesian was inscribed in the calendars of the empire, A. D. 284. Perhaps to this relationship of the pope with the emperor are due the fourteen years of peace that elapsed between the coronation of Dioclesian and the tenth general persecution which he afterwards ordered. Not that this interval was passed in tranquillity by the faithful—for the last edicts of Aurelian had never been revoked, and Christians were always regarded as a sect inimical to the empire, whom the governors gloried in opposing. Besides, Dioclesian had associated with him the son of a poor laborer of Pannonia, who, under the name of Maximian-Hercules, saw himself, in one day, created Cæsar, sovereign pontiff, and god. Dioclesian appropriated the East to himself, and left the West to the new Cæsar. This latter professed the most violent hatred for the Christians, and lost no occasion to persecute them. There were not wanting martyrs to satisfy his cruelty.

20. The Church of Rome then counted among the most fervent of the faithful a distinguished officer of the imperial army. Sebastian, captain of a company of prætorian guards, was a native of Narbonne, in Gaul. He visited Christians who were imprisoned for the faith, assisted them with his credit and the influence of his rank, encouraged the weak, and exhorted the pagans, whom he converted in great numbers to the religion of Jesus Christ, by his example and conversation. Even the prefect of Rome, Chromatius, with all his family, his clients, and his slaves, to the number of fourteen hundred persons, received baptism through his zeal. The house of Chromatius became like a temple, where Pope St. Caius celebrated the divine mysteries, and distributed to these neo-

phytes the body of Jesus Christ and the bread of the evangelic word. Meanwhile, the progress of Christianity gave umbrage to Maximian-Hercules. To avoid an open persecution, Chromatius, whose quality of senator detained him at Rome, solicited and obtained from the emperor, under the pretext of restoring his feeble health, permission to retire to his estates in Campania. The day of separation came, and Caius went yet once more to offer the holy sacrifice in this house of benediction. Addressing them at the close, he said: "Our Lord Jesus Christ, knowing our human frailty, has formed two classes among those who believe in Him—confessors and martyrs—in order that they who do not think themselves strong enough to endure the weight of persecution may withdraw, leaving the chief glory to the soldiers of Christ, whom they can, at least, assist in their combats. Let those, then, who desire it, follow Chromatius and his son Tiburtius in their retreat; and let those who have the courage, stay with me in the city. Distance cannot separate hearts united by the grace of Jesus Christ; and if, with our mortal eyes, we see you no more, you will ever be present with us in the interior of our souls." He was like Gideon, selecting only the bravest soldiers for the combat. Tiburtius, hearing his counsels, cried out, "I conjure you, O father, and Bishop of bishops, command me not to fly the persecution. All my desire is to give my life for my God. Would that I had a thousand to offer Him!" St. Caius yielded, though with tears, to the supplications of this noble youth, and the assembly separated: some followed Chromatius to Campania; others remained with the pope. St. Sebastian was one of the latter. Castulus, another officer, steward of the baths, received them in the imperial palace itself, where Caius was in greater safety than elsewhere. Maximian had now begun to persecute the Christians. St. Zoe, a devout lady, going to pray at the tomb of SS. Peter and Paul, on the day of their festival, was dragged before a magistrate, who, unable to compel her to sacrifice to the gods, ordered her to be suspended, by the hair, to a tree, and a fire of dung to be lighted at her feet, which suffocated her. They then fastened a large stone to her neck, and threw her into the Tiber, "fearing," the pagans said, "that the Christians might make her a goddess." Nicostratus, first secretary of the prefecture of Rome, husband of St. Zoe, Tranquillinus, Claudius, Castor, Victorinus, and Symphorian, were also arrested as Christians; the Roman prefect ordered all to be cast into the sea. Tiburtius, the generous son of Chromatius, was taken, through the perfidy of a false brother bribed by the imperial police to act as a spy in the Christian assemblies. "What!" said Tiburtius to the magistrates, "because I refuse to adore a harlot, in the person of Venus, the incestuous Jupiter, a cheat like Mercury, and Saturn the murderer of his children, I dishonor my race, I am infamous?" This Christian hero was beheaded. Castulus, the harborer of the Christians, a victim of the same treason as Tiburtius, suffered torture, and was finally cast, living, into a pit, which was then filled with sand. St. Sebastian, in his uniform as captain of the prætorian guards, had never ceased to visit the martyrs, to encourage them in their tortures, and to gather their remains after death. Maximian-Hercules, who had commanded all these punishments, had gone into Gaul to repress a formidable insurrection of the Bagaudes—Belgian peasants—who commenced a revolt somewhat similar to those which broke out in France during the middle ages. It is asserted, but without proof, that their chiefs, Elianus and Amandus, were Christians. The exactions of the Roman governors had aroused these rustic legions against their pitiless masters. In the absence of Maximian-Hercules, St. Sebastian was denounced to Dioclesian as encouraging the impiety of the Christians. The captain of the guards appeared before the emperor, who reproached him with ingratitude in thus repaying his obligations to him, and of using against his government the authority with which he had himself invested him. Sebastian replied, that "he had not ceased to be faithful to his duties, and to offer prayers for the health of the prince and the empire; but having long since discovered the folly of adoring gods of stone, he had addressed his prayers to the true God, who is in heaven, and to His Son Jesus Christ." Dioclesian was irritated by this language, and calling for a company of Mauritanian archers, who served among his guards, Sebastian was stripped of his clothing, the archers pierced him with their arrows, and left him for dead on the spot. Irene, widow of Castulus, came at night to take away the martyred body. As he still breathed, she conveyed him to her abode within the imperial palace, and, some days afterwards, Dioclesian was astonished to find in the midst of his courtiers, ranged along his passage on the main staircase of the palace, Sebastian, the captain of his guards. The emperor was furious, and ordered him to be taken instantly to the hippodrome of the palace, where the holy martyr was beaten to death with clubs: his body was cast into a sewer, from which it was drawn by the Christians (A. D. 288).

21. Christianity had invaded every place, even the imperial army. Maximian-Hercules resolved at all hazards to prevent its propagation among his soldiers, especially at the moment when he marched against the Bagaudes, who, it was said, with or without truth, had Christian leaders. He had paused, while crossing the Alps, at the village of Octodurus, now Martinach, in Valais, to give some repose to his troops. At this place he was joined by the Theban legion, which Dioclesian had ordered from the East, and which he now sent to increase Maximian's forces. This legion, composed entirely of Christians, had its cantonments at Agauna, at the foot of what is now the Great St. Bernard. Maximian-Hercules intended to employ them, like the others, in searching for the Christians of the country, whom he put to death. The Theban legion formally refused to obey his orders. Maximian replied to this first act of disobedience by ordering them to be decimated. All the soldiers who composed it were ranged at random in several lines. The executioners passed, counting the soldiers, and every tenth man was beheaded. Those who remained, after this butchery, refused again to obey the order of Maxi-

mian. A second decimation had no other result. The angry Cæsar preferred to endanger the success of his arms, rather than to yield to what he chose to term the obstinacy of these mutineers. Without awaiting the answer to an address which the Theban legion had sent to Dioclesian, he brought them all together into a valley, which he surrounded with his troops, and ordered to be massacred before his eyes this band of heroes, who suffered themselves to be murdered for the name of Christ, whose soldiers they had been before they had enlisted in the service of the empire.

22. The march of Maximian-Hercules across Gaul was tantamount to a general execution of the Christians. On his way through Marseilles, Victor, a Christian officer, having refused, before the Cæsar himself, to sacrifice to the gods, was dragged through all the streets of the city, his feet and hands bound, exposed to the outrages of a vile population. Afterward tortured on the rack, then cast into a subterranean dungeon, Victor converted the soldiers who guarded him, and at night procured them baptism. The day following, these new Christians were decapitated in his presence, by order of Maximian. Victor was suspended upon a beam and scourged, until, weary of their toil, the executioners threw him, dying, into his dungeon. Maximian-Hercules essayed to overcome the patience of the martyr by the duration and diversity of his torments. Three days afterwards, he ordered him into his presence, and, directing him towards a tripod on a portable altar, commanded him to lay incense upon it, in honor of Jupiter. Victor approached, as if to obey, and with his foot overturned both the altar and tripod. The enraged emperor ordered his foot to be cut off on the spot. He was then placed under the stone of a hand-mill, which his tormentors turned slowly, to break his bones by degrees. During this terrible operation, the machine broke. To finish him, Maximian ordered his head to be removed from his bruised and mutilated body, which was thrown into the sea; but the waves brought it back to the shore, and these precious remains were gathered by Christians, and buried in a grotto cut in the rock.

23. Arles had also her celebrated martyr in the person of St. Genesius, recorder of the proconsular tribunal, who, not able to endure the work of transcribing the unjust sentences dictated against the Christians, threw at his feet the wax tablets on which he wrote, fled, and crossed the Rhone by swimming. Arrested on the opposite bank, he declared himself a Christian, and atoned, by the loss of his head, for this act of courageous indignation. Every step of Maximian was marked by new victims. St. Foi, a virgin, near Agde; St Capiais, bishop of Agen; Tiberius, Modestes, and Florentius, at Vienne; Ferreol, a military tribune, and one of his soldiers named Julian, at Brioude; Vincent, Orontius, and Victor, at Embrun; at Nantes, SS. Donatian and Rogatian, two brothers, illustrious by their birth, were beheaded after suffering every species of torture. Belgium was the chosen theatre for the cruelties of Maximian-Hercules, seconded in his sanguinary projects by Riccius Varus, governor of Belgic Gaul, which comprehended a part of what is now northern France. The most distinguished martyrs were—at Amiens, the bishop St. Firmin, Victorius, Lucian, and Gentian, their host; at Augusta, capital of Vermandois, since destroyed, St. Quentin; at Soissons, SS. Crispin and Crispinian; at Tournay, St. Piat, a priest; at Fismes, near Rheims, the virgin St. Mæcra; at Louvre, near Lutetia, St. Just or Justin; besides a great number at Trèves, the ordinary residence of Riccius Varus. The East, though more tranquil, had also proconsuls who distinguished themselves by their cruelties to the Christians. Lysias, governor of Asia Minor, exhibited there the inhumanity of Riccius Varus in the West, and these two names have a cruel celebrity in the martyrologies of this epoch. Claudius, Asterius, and Neo, Domnina and Theonilla, and the two illustrious brothers SS. Cosmas and Damian, physicians of the town of Egea, in Lycia, suffered martyrdom by his orders.

24. About A. D. 290, a new sect arose in Egypt. Hierax, of Leontopolis, its author, was a man of austere life, of rigid morals, eating nothing which had had life, and abstaining from

wine. He seems to have belonged to that class of minds, of overstrained views, who would impose on all Christians a life holy in itself, but to which all are not called. The rigorism of his principles carried him so far as to see in the body only an emanation of the genius of evil; and, on this point, he agrees with the Manichees, among whom Baronius ranks him. From this foundation he proceeds to deny the resurrection of the flesh, insisting that the most precise texts of Scripture on this subject refer only to the spiritual resurrection of the soul. He condemned marriage, and admitted to his communion only virgins, excluding all others from the kingdom of heaven. He rejected, also, the doctrine of the Church concerning baptized infants who die before the age of reason, and held that they could not enter heaven, nor be crowned, because they had never combated. Other errors are found in his writings on the Holy Trinity, the mystery of which, according to the usual process of heretics, he proposed to elucidate by images and ideas entirely human. For example: he compared the three divine persons to three wicks lighted in the same lamp, by the same oil; which seems to indicate a distinct substance in the three persons. The regularity of his morals, and the erudition displayed in his works, led many Christians into his false doctrines; and when he died, pen in hand, at the age of more than ninety years, the sect of the Hieracites was one of the most considerable in Egypt. We do not perceive that the Church condemned them until the council of Nice, which answered them victoriously, and, in particular, the errors on the Trinity, by the magnificent and most just expression of "*Light of light*," applied to the generation of the Son of God.

25. While Maximian-Hercules multiplied martyrs, to extinguish in their blood the religion of Jesus Christ, a famous rhetorician of Suia, in proconsular Africa, studied in silence this so much persecuted faith. The truth shone into his soul, hitherto sincerely attached to the pagan worship. He avows frankly that he was honestly a practical idolater. "When I saw," said he, "the richly colored bands in the hollow of a tree,

or the stones bedewed with oil, I adored them; I offered petitions, as if they had possessed some secret virtue, and addressed my vows to an insensible trunk." At length, grace was victorious, and Arnobius asked for baptism. As a pledge of his conversion, he did not hesitate to burn publicly that which he had adored. He wrote, in a vigorous and energetic style, seven books against idolatry, in which he answers all the objections of the pagans against the Church. The scandal of the Cross especially astonished the Gentiles: "Your God," said they to the Christians, "died on a gibbet."—"Well, what of that?" replies Arnobius. "Pythagoras was burned alive; Socrates was condemned to drink hemlock; Regulus perished by a most cruel death: are they dishonored? It is not the sentence, it is the crime which constitutes the infamy. You have made a god of Bacchus, because he taught men the use of wine; a goddess of Ceres, because she taught them to make bread. What honors, then, are not due to Jesus Christ, even though He had been only a man, to have brought us the knowledge most necessary to the human race, and to have taught us to know God, the world, and ourselves! But Christ is not a man; Christ is God; God above all things; God by the nature of His being. Yet, once again, in spite of your sneers, in spite of your abuse, once more, though your ears split in hearing it, Christ is God—God appearing to us in the form of a man! You have the most striking proofs of it before you: the most incontestable proofs. Do you not see in how short a time His religion has spread over the whole earth? Is there a nation so barbarous that it has not softened and civilized? Observe this crowd of men of genius, of orators, grammarians, jurists, philosophers, who solicit its instructions, and for it abjure the belief of their whole life. The more you multiply threats and tortures against this religion, the more this religion is augmented. You employ tormentors and racks to destroy the faith; and these racks and these tormentors are a new attraction to believe in Christ, and to prefer His doctrines to all earthly goods. Is not the finger of God in this? You scoff at our credulity—our inclination to accept the faith. But all in this world begins by faith. You yourselves, in the intellectual order, have faith in some certain philosopher. We have faith in Christ, because He has proved by miracles the truth of His doctrines. Your philosophers, your chosen ones, what miracles have they wrought? Where is he among them whose word has ever been capable of calming the tempest, of restoring sight to the blind, of raising the dead?" The whole work of Arnobius is full of passages similar to these. He wrote in the first fervor of his conversion, when he was only a catechumen, and little instructed in the truths of faith. This circumstance explains why we find in his works a certain inexactness, and even some errors, which ancient Christianity did not reprove, because of the peculiar situation of the author. The greatest glory of Arnobius, after this, is to have had for his disciple Lactantius, who has been surnamed the Christian Cicero.

26. Dioclesian did not consider himself strong enough to support, with the aid of Maximian-Hercules only, the weight of an empire which the barbarians disputed with him on every side. He therefore resolved to create two new Cæsars, and to give them the guardianship of the Rhine and the Danube. The new masters of the world, whom the will of a crowned slave called to the throne, were Constantius Chlorus and Galerius. The first repudiated the Princess Helena, by whom he had a son who was afterwards Constantine the Great, to espouse Theodora, daughter-in-law of Maximian-Hercules. Already, among the names of these persecutors, we see the dawning destinies to which were attached the victory of the Church. Galerius espoused Valeria, daughter of Dioclesian. He was a Cæsar more barbarian than Roman. His mother, a slave from beyond the Danube, had given him the full type of the savage nations of Dacia. His height was colossal: his look, voice, gestures—all were terrible. The four new sovereigns went to fix themselves, Dioclesian at Nicomedia, Maximian at Rome, Constantius Chlorus in Great Britain, and Galerius at Trèves.

27. To console himself in the division of the empire, Dioclesian modelled his court after the magnificence of Olympian royalty. He gave himself the surname of Jupiter. Instead of the laurel crown, he assumed the diadem, and to the purple mantle he added a robe of silk and cloth of gold. Whoever was introduced into the presence of the emperor, prostrated himself and adored him. He obliged them to address him as *Your Eternity*, a title which his successors, who passed like shadows, took great care to preserve. Meanwhile, he allowed Christians very freely to approach his presence. Many filled important functions around him. Such were Dorotheus, Gorgonius, St. Peter, and Lucian, invested with the dignity of major-domo, or grand chamberlain of the palace. We still have the instructions that St. Theonas, bishop of Alexandria, addressed to the latter, which are not the least interesting pages of the ecclesiastical history of that epoch. It is curious to note how the Church, through her bishops, commanded her children to practise obedience, respect, devotion, affection, towards princes, in whose name religion was so often persecuted. St. Theonas exhorts the grand chamberlain and all the Christian officers to make themselves agreeable to their master, by the regularity, the promptitude of their service, and, at the same time, by the gayety and amiability of their character—"in order," he said, "that the sovereign, fatigued with the affairs of state, may find his joy and repose in the gentleness, the patience, the open countenance, and exact obedience of his servants. His orders, when they are not in opposition to God, should be regarded as the orders of God himself." He instructs them that no influence of money or of interest should ever induce them to give bad advice to the prince, to sell their credit, or to strengthen injustice. He recommends them to avoid all rivalries—hatred, disputes, intrigues; never to allow their names to be mixed up with parties who contend for influence at court, and lose in questions of personal vanity the spirit and time which ought to be employed only for the public good. He exhorts them to be affable, ready to serve others—

to aid men of merit; in fine, to use their power for the good of all. Christianity had made such progress at the court of Dioclesian, that the Empress Prisca and her daughter Valeria received baptism; and Constantine, brought up in the interior of the palace, learned to love the Christian piety which he afterwards professed.

28. Pope St. Caius expired April 22d, A. D. 296, having governed the Church twelve years. He confirmed, by decrees, the usage which required clerics to pass, in the seven inferior orders of the Church, a suitable time, before they could be eligible to the episcopal office. Worthy of executing the apostolic ministry in so stormy an epoch and in the midst of the dangers of a persecution incessantly renewed, St. Caius merited the eulogiums which antiquity has pronounced upon him. He was, say the historians, a pontiff of rare prudence and of courageous virtue. The body of the blessed pope was deposited in the cemetery of St. Callistus.

CHAPTER XIV.

§ I. St. Marcellinus, Pope (June 30, a. d. 296—October 24, 304).

1. Election of Pope Marcellinus.—2. Galerius begins the persecution.—3. Schism of the Meletians. Council of Elvira.—4. Tenth general persecution under Dioclesian (a. d. 303).—5. General sketch of the tenth general persecution.—6. Martyrs in the house of the emperor. The sophists. Hierocles.—7. Martyrs in the East.—8. Martyrs in the West.—9. Martyrdom of Pope St. Marcellinus, October 24, a. d. 304.

§ II. Vacancy of the See of Rome (October 24, a. d. 304—May 19, 308).

10. Continuation and end of the persecution of Dioclesian in the West.—11. Martyrdom of St. Genesius.—12. Abdication of Dioclesian.—13. Maximin Daia.—14. Continuation of the persecution in the East.—15. Conventicle of traditor bishops at Cirtha. Canons of St. Peter, patriarch of Alexandria.

§ III. St. Marcellus, Pope (May 19, a. d. 308—Jan. 16, 310).

16. Election of Pope St. Marcellus.—17. Constantine proclaimed emperor by the legions of Great Britain.—18. St. Methodius, bishop of Tyre.—19. St. Anthony.—20. Death of St. Marcellus, pope.

§ IV. St. Eusebius, Pope (April 2, a. d. 310—Sept. 20, 310).

21. Election, exile, and death of Pope St. Eusebius.

§ V. Vacancy of the See of Rome (Sept. 25, a. d. 310—July 2. 311).

22. Last crimes and punishment of Maximian-Hercules.—23. Edict of Galerius favorable to Christians. Death of Galerius.—24. Deliverance of the Christian prisoners in the East.

§ VI. St. Melchiades, Pope (July 2, a. d. 311—Jan. 10, 314).

25. Election of Pope St. Melchiades.—26. Schism of the Donatists at Cartha.—27. Maximin Daia attempts, in spite of the edicts of Galerius, to renew the persecution.—28. War between Maxentius and Constantine. Labarum. Victory of Constantine.—29. Edict of Constantine proclaiming the Christian

religion the religion of the empire.—30. Council held at Rome, at the Lateran palace, against the Donatists.—31. Death of St. Melchiades.—32. End of the first epoch of ecclesiastical history.

§ I. St. Marcellinus, Pope (June 30, a. d. 296—Oct. 24, 304).

1. Marcellinus, a Roman priest, was elected successor to St. Caius. Theodoret pronounces an appropriate eulogium on this pope, by declaring that he proved himself as strong as the persecution that came in his time. God reserved for him, indeed, the glory of being one of the first victims of this last terrific storm, which, according to all human probability, should have annihilated the Church at the commencement of the fourth century. The Donatists, nevertheless, dared to attack his illustrious memory. In the conference at Carthage, a. d. 311, they produced the pretended acts of a false council of Sinuessa, which accused St. Marcellinus of having delivered to the persecutors consecrated vessels and the books of the Scriptures;* but Catholic antiquity has sufficiently avenged this calumny. The pontiff, who offered his head to the executioner, and who died for his faith, is so far above such attacks that there is no need of refuting them.

* Bossuet, in his *Defence of the Declaration of the Gallican Clergy* (lib. ix. cap. 32), expresses himself on the subject of St. Marcellinus and the council of Sinuessa as follows: "What shall I say of Marcellinus, who, as many once believed, burnt incense to the idols; or what of that council of Sinuessa, which, it was said, was convoked against him? Whether false or true, is of no importance to us. Most canonists for three hundred years, believed it true, and held it so for the reason that on certain occasions a synod might be convened, not, indeed, to judge the supreme pontiff, but to persuade or remonstrate, in order that he should be induced, from modesty, at least to abdicate." But in a note we read further: "No controversy now exists concerning the council of Sinuessa among the learned, for that it was suppositious, the barbarous style and absurd opinions clearly prove. As to the incense-burning of Marcellinus, of which none of the ancient writers speak, it is fabulous. And it is the more so, because Theodoret (lib. II., cap. 3) says that Marcellinus flourished in a time of persecution, which he would not say of a pontiff who had offered incense to idols. And although the Donatists brought this charge of idolatry against Marcellinus, it was false, and unsustained by a single witness, as they were accustomed to accuse many others—among them the most saintly pontiffs Melchiades, Marcellus, and Sylvester. But the synod of three hundred bishops was never mentioned by them, nor by St. Augustine in his books against Petilianum. Neither was it very practicable, in a time of persecution, to assemble three hundred bishops; for, in a time of general peace, Constantine was barely able to bring together an equal number at the council of Nice. These remarks are sufficient for a bungling fable."

2. Galerius, the crowned Dacian, had inherited from his idolatrous mother a violent hatred of Christianity. His first experience in arms was unsuccessful; sent by Dioclesian against Narses, king of Persia, A. D. 294, he was thrice beaten. On his return, clothed as he was with the purple, he was suffered to walk unnoticed the length of a mile, by his stern master's chariot. Galerius felt the lesson. The following year, after a second expedition, he presented to Dioclesian, in chains, the most illustrious Persian warriors; all the family of Narses, as captives; all the equipages and all the riches of the army which he had completely vanquished. From this day he became formidable to Dioclesian himself, and claimed the right to avenge his past humiliations upon the Christians. He began, therefore, on his own account, and without giving himself the trouble to ascertain the sentiments of the three other princes, to put in action the most rigorous measures against the faithful (A. D. 298). His vengeance fell first upon the officers of his household, and the soldiers and most notable Christians of his army. He deprived them of their employments, drove them from his presence with insults, and sentenced to the last degrees of punishment those whom he judged to be the most obstinate. History has preserved the names of some of the soldiers who suffered under these circumstances: Maximilian, who was beheaded at Tebesta, in Numidia; Marcellus, a centurion of Trajan's legion, at Tangier, in Mauritania, who, on the day of the emperor's festival, refusing to offer sacrifice for the life of *His Eternity*, threw away the symbol of his office, the vine-branch, with which the centurions chastised the soldiers, removed his baldrick and military girdle, and avowed himself a Christian. He was beheaded. While Agricola, prefect of the pretorium, dictated the sentence, Cassian, the recorder, declared that he never would consent to write so unjust an act, and trod under foot both the stylet and tablets. Martyrdom was the price of his generous indignation. It is reported that at the same epoch forty Christian soldiers were martyred for the faith, in the province of Lauriac, a

city now ruined, which was situated near the mouth of the Ems.

3. These cruelties of Galerius were in some some sort personal, although his colleagues did nothing to hinder them. The greater part of the Church continued in peace, and enjoyed even a kind of favor in the opinion of Dioclesian, who had just issued an edict against the Manichees, condemning them to the punishment of fire. The schism of Meletius alone troubled the harmony of the Church, whose dogma was being more explicity defined and better comprised under the influence of frequent minor councils. Meletius, bishop of Lycopolis, in the Thebais, had been convicted of many crimes, and, among others, of having sacrificed to idols. He was deposed in a council held at Alexandria by St. Peter, successor of St. Theonas. Far from submitting to this condemnation, and to the canonical penance, he separated from the communion of the bishop of Alexandria and his other colleagues, thus commencing the schism of the Meletians, which afterwards increased, and was not ended until A. D. 325, at the Council of Nice. A council held at Elvira, in Spain (A. D. 301), is celebrated for its disciplinary canons, the most ancient that have been perfectly preserved. Valerius, bishop of Saragossa, and Osius of Cordova, took part in it. Severity prevails in these eighty-one canons, where, in twelve cases, the bishops refuse, even to the end of life, not penance, it is true, but communion, to the culpable. They decree this punishment against the Christian who has voluntarily apostatized; to him who, after baptism, accepts the charge of flamen, or priest of the idols, and offers sacrifices; to the informer, who, by his perfidy, has caused the death of any one; to homicides; to women who have left their husbands to marry again; to virgins consecrated to God, who have betrayed their vows to live in disorder, etc. There is a remarkable decree which forbids having pictures in the churches, "fearing," say the Fathers, "lest the object of our worship and adoration be exposed on the walls." They feared, doubtless, lest these paintings, in times of perse-

cution, should be profaned by the infidels, or serve as a pretext for their outrages and calumnies. Christian antiquity has always given this interpretation to this canon, which has nothing in common with the iconoclastic fury.

4. Towards the close of the year 302, frequent and mysterious interviews were remarked between Dioclesian and the Cæsar Galerius, at the palace of Nicomedia. It was a question with them to resume the design of Nero, and to take such skilful measures, that they might, at length, by a terrible but decisive blow, exterminate Christianity forever. The old emperor — history renders him this justice — long resisted the proposal. "It was dangerous," he said, "again to trouble the peace of the world, and to shed torrents of blood. Besides, punishments led to nothing; for the Christians asked for nothing better than to die." In fine, urged by Galerius, Dioclesian consented to submit the question to a council of magistrates and officers of the army. The counsellors trembled before the Cæsar on the banks of the Danube; all voices agreed upon the necessity of pursuing the enemies of public worship. Dioclesian, still hesitating, sent to consult the oracle of Apollo of Miletus. Apollo replied, "*That the just, spread over the earth, hindered him from speaking the truth.*" The Pythoness complained that she was mute; the diviners declared that the *just*, to whom Apollo referred, were the Christians. The persecution was resolved upon, and the time fixed for commencing it was the feast of the Terminales (February 23, A. D. 303), the last day of the Roman year, which was expected also by the persecutors to decide the fate of the Christian religion. The decree of extermination was, in substance : "The churches shall be destroyed and the sacred books burned; the Christians shall be deprived of all honors, all dignities, and condemned to punishment without distinction of order or rank; they may be cited before the tribunals, but will not be permitted themselves to cite any one, even in cases where they have to complain of robbery, injury, or even adultery. Christian freedmen shall again be reduced to slavery." A special edict

was directed against the bishops, which commanded that they should be put in irons and forced to abjure. The attack commenced with the church of Nicomedia, in the presence of the two emperors. At break of day, the prefect of the city, followed by generals, officers, and a detachment of soldiers, arrive at the church, situated on a hill, and surrounded by noble edifices. They break the doors, and seek everywhere some figure of the God whom the Christians adore. The writings which they find are delivered to the flames, and all the rest to pillage. Dioclesian and Galerius stood at a window of the palace, presiding at this first execution, and encouraging their emissaries by voice and gestures. Galerius wished the church to be fired; but Dioclesian, fearing lest the flames should be communicated to the rest of the city, sent the pretorians, armed with axes and hammers, and in a few hours the building was razed to the ground. Couriers were dispatched to the Emperor Maximian-Hercules and to the Cæsar Constantius Chlorus, to convey the new decree, and the orders for its execution. The aged Maximian received them with joy—for they had long been the object of his desires. Constantius, when made acquainted with them, summoned all the Christian officers of his palace, and proposed to their choice either to retain their offices, if they would sacrifice to the idols, or, if they refused, to be banished from his presence, with the loss of his favor. Some, preferring their worldly interests to their religion, declared themselves ready to offer sacrifice. The others remained immovable in their faith. But what was their surprise, on hearing Constantius declare that he held the apostates as cowards; and that, since he could not hope they would be more faithful to their prince than to their God, he dismissed them forever from his service. The others, on the contrary, he retained near his person, made them his body-guard, and considered them as the most devoted of his servants. Gaul, which was under his jurisdiction, escaped the general persecution through his benevolent protection, as if God had been satisfied with the martyrs that Maximian-Hercules had strewed along his passage sixteen years before (A. D. 287), while the Church, elsewhere, was in peace. Constantius, however, to avoid irritating the emperors by openly making light of their decrees, permitted the church buildings to be destroyed, "considering," said Lactantius, "that after the storm they could be rebuilt."

5. Meanwhile, the persecution had at once extended from the Tiber to the extremities of the empire, Gaul only excepted. Everywhere churches fell in ruins under the blows of the soldiers. The magistrates fixed their tribunals in the temples or near the statues of the false gods, and compelled the multitude to sacrifice; whoever refused to adore the gods was condemned and delivered to the executioner. The prisons were overcrowded with victims; the roads were covered with troops of mutilated men, who were sent out to die, either in the depths of the mines or in the public places. Whips, racks, iron hooks, the cross, or ferocious beasts, mangled the flesh of tender infants and their mothers; here, naked women were hung upon posts by the feet, and left to die by this immodest and cruel torture; there, the limbs of martyrs were fastened to trees forcibly drawn together, which, when loosened, tore them in fragments. Each province had its peculiar torments: in Mesopotamia it was a slow fire; in Pontus, the wheel; the axe in Arabia; melted lead in Cappadocia. Frequently, when the sufferer was expiring from excess of torture, the executioners relieved the thirst of the confessor, or threw water on his face, lest his burning fever should hasten his death. Sometimes, weary of consuming their victims separately, the pagans threw many at once into the flames; the bones of the victims, reduced to ashes, were scattered to the winds.*

6. The household of the emperor was the first exposed to the tyrant's cruelty. Valeria, daughter of Dioclesian, and his wife, Prisca, had not strength to resist the torture, and offered sacrifice. Dorotheus, chief of the eunuchs, Gorgonius, Peter, Judas, Mygdonius, and Mardonius, suffered death at Nicomedia. The tormentors poured salt and vinegar on the wounds

* M. DE CHAUTEAUBRIAND: *Etudes Historiques.*

of Peter. He was stretched on a gridiron, and his flesh roasted like the meats for a feast. Women, children, and old men were cast indiscriminately into fires prepared for the purpose, while other victims, crowded into barks, were precipitated into the sea. St. Anthimus, bishop of Nicomedia, and all the priests, deacons, and clerks of that church were seized, and on their confession alone, without any other examination, they were led to execution. To enforce the decree which prohibited Christians from prosecuting any cause before the tribunals, there were placed in each hall of justice, even in the cabinets of the judges, portable altars, on which parties were made to offer sacrifice before pleading their cause. At Nicomedia, the governor of the province of Bithynia appeared as much transported with joy as if he had conquered a barbarous nation, because a Christian who had resisted him during two years at last yielded to the violence of his torture. Two pagan sophists of Nicomedia, while surrounded by victims accumulated in all the prisons of the city, while bleeding and mutilated bodies encumbered the streets, had the ferocious courage to write books against these Christians, whom they might at least have left to die in peace. One of them, a professor of philosophy, whose work is analyzed by Lactantius, without caring to preserve his name, had filled his treatise with so much abuse of the victims, and such base adulation of the tyrants, that he gained only contempt even from the pagans. The other, not less violent, but more artful, was a judge at Nicomedia, named Hierocles. He entitled his book *Philalethes, The Friend of Truth*, as Celsus had called his *Discourse of Truth*. He addressed it to the Christians, and "touched," as he said, "by their deplorable situation, he would not attack them, but merely offer them some salutary counsels." Thus he skilfully takes the double part, dear to his malevolent soul, of tormentor and philanthropist; he made himself the counsellor of those whom, as judge, he sent to execution. In other respects his book was only a tissue of objections against the truth of Christianity, chiefly drawn from the works of Celsus. His success surpassed, if it were possible, the hopes even of the author, for in recompense of his abusive libel Hierocles was appointed, by Galerius, governor of Bithynia, and, soon after, of the important province of Egypt. He exhibited such animosity against the Christians that he is ranked among the most sanguinary enemies of a religion which, during the space of three centuries, had almost as many persecutors as the empire had counted sovereigns.

7. It would be impossible to enumerate the names of all who belonged to that heroic army of martyrs, sent to heaven from all parts of the earth, in execution of the imperial decrees. Pontus, Cappadocia, Phrygia, Armenia, Mauritania, Thrace, witnessed the renewal, at the same moment, within their borders, of all the horrors which had ensanguined the whole of Nicomedia and Bithynia. St. Theodotus, an innkeeper of Ancyra, in Galatia, merited admiration for his courage and his faith. He suffered martyrdom with a crowd of Christians whom he strengthened by his exhortations and example. Seven virgins, companions of St. Thecusa, exposed by the infamous magistrates in places of debauchery, miraculously preserved their honor, to present it pure, with their blood, on the altar of the Lamb. Antioch had her legion of confessors, among whom was St. Romanus, who was strangled, after Dioclesian had ordered his tongue to be cut out and subjected him to intolerable tortures. During his interrogatory, the judge having attempted to prove the superiority of the pagan over the Christian religion, Romanus requested permission to address some questions to a little child, that the pure truth might be heard from his lips. Barallah, a boy seven years old, was brought. Romanus asked: "Is it more reasonable to adore one God, than to adore thousands who fight against each other?" Barallah replied: "There is only one God; we ought not to adore many." The judge ordered him to be whipped so cruelly that his blood flowed profusely. The spectators were melted to tears. The judge—if we can associate the name of justice with such misdeeds—condemned this

heroic child to be beheaded. The mother of Barallah carried him in her arms to the place of execution. She kissed him tenderly, recommended herself to his prayers, placed him in the hands of the murderer, spread her mantle in a position to gather the blood of the young martyr, and gained leave to take away his precious remains. At Tyre, the tormentors, weary of torturing their victims, having exhausted all known means of punishment, sent them to the beasts of the amphitheatre to finish their work. Lions, leopards, bears, or wild boars, were loosed upon them. But these animals, by divine permission, or perhaps disdaining these bloody remnants of human cruelty, refused to touch the martyrs, and furiously attacked the pagans, who provoked them with boar-spears and spikes. In fine, they were obliged to behead these generous confessors of the faith. At Cæsarea, in Palestine, Procopius, exorcist of the church in Jerusalem, who had just arrived in the city, was led before the governor, who offered him incense and commanded him to burn it to the divinity of the four emperors. Procopius replied by this saying of Homer, $εἷς κοίρανος ἐστώ$—*One master is enough*—when he was immediately beheaded. All the bishops of Palestine were transported to Cæsarea to be subjected to the most hideous tortures. The judges held it of the highest importance to make the people believe that the bishops had sacrificed, hoping, by the pretence of their example, to influence their flocks. They bound the hands of a bishop to an altar of the idols, while they burnt incense upon it; then sent him away, declaring that he had sacrificed. Another was released, half dead, from the rack; he was carried off, while they published that he had finally denied his faith. If any one had yet strength enough to protest against this imposture, he was struck in the face, many hands stopped his mouth, and he was sent elsewhere, and declared to have a place among the apostates. Egypt witnessed frightful scenes of cruelty. In the Thebais, martyrs were fastened to stakes, exposed to the burning sun, and left to die of hunger. Instead of iron claws, fragments of broken glass and pottery were used to lacerate their bodies; their nails were torn up with iron points, and boiling oil poured on the wounds; women were suspended naked by one of their feet, the head downwards; some were burned on a gridiron, or crucified, generally the head down; others were cut in pieces, or fastened to the tails of wild horses. These horrors were renewed during two entire years, and sometimes a hundred executions were counted in a single day in the same city. Among this array of martyrs were Philoroma, a military tribune of Alexandria, and Phileas, bishop of Thmouis, whose constancy and heroism drew tears even from their murderers. These execrable cruelties, scarcely to be believed—if, from examples too recent we did not know to what degree of barbarity a people can descend when they yield to their bloodthirsty instincts—were sometimes extended over entire cities. In Phrygia there was a town of eight to ten thousand inhabitants, whose governor, treasurer, all the officers, and all the people, declared themselves Christians. The matter was referred to the emperor; but Dioclesian, who had beheaded the principal citizens of Antioch because a pretender to the empire had, during two days, occupied that city, and had been driven from it by the inhabitants on the third, felt no embarrassment on account of a miserable little town of Phrygia. He sent soldiers who set fire to every part of it, burned the place and all its population, without even sparing children at the breast, and returned only after they had converted it into a heap of ashes. Carthage and Numidia were equally the scene of bloody persecutions. In this province they sought especially the inspired books. Mensurius, then bishop of Carthage, to save them from the soldiers, had them carried away from the basilica, and left there only heretical writings. The emissaries of the proconsul, in making their perquisition, took off and burned all the books without examination; but Paul, bishop of Cirtha, now Constantine, in Algeria, and twelve other bishops of this province, delivered up the Scriptures and the consecrated vessels, to avoid torture The name of *traditors* was given to all who betrayed the same.

weakness. At a later period we shall see how disastrous were the consequences of their cowardice.

8. The West was not less fruitful in confessors of the faith. Spain, that land in which Christianity had already cast such deep roots, counted her martyrs by thousands. The proconsul Dacian was charged with the execution of the edicts against them, and he spared no exertions to persecute to the utmost a multitude of the faithful, who looked upon death as a great blessing. At Saragossa eighteen gave their lives for Jesus Christ. The most celebrated of these was St. Vincent, who had the glory of being praised by St. Augustine and by the poet Prudentius. He was archdeacon of Valerius, the bishop of Saragossa. This prelate, too aged to dispense the word in person to his people, imposed this duty on Vincent. The young deacon, full of zeal and erudition, and fortified by the meditation of the Holy Scriptures, applied himself efficiently to the holy ministry. On the coming of Dacian, his reputation for sanctity and eloquence marked him at once for persecution. He was arrested, with his bishop Valerius, whom the proconsul, on account of his advanced age, merely sent into exile. Vincent was put to the rack. At each torture, when the rack dislocated his bones, or the iron claws mangled his limbs, the martyr turned laughingly towards Dacian, saying, "No one has ever been more friendly to me than yourself;" or he would reproach the tormentors, who were covered with sweat, for their want of strength and courage. Twice these ministers of a superhuman cruelty interrupted the torture to regain their strength, and to leave the wounds of the martyr to cool, in order to redouble his sufferings when renewed. Dacian burned with rage. He ordered this mutilated body, of which the intestines were already exposed, to be taken from the rack and laid on an iron bed, over a heated brazier. Those parts of the body which were not turned towards the fire were burned with blades of red-hot iron. On the bleeding wounds they threw salt, the sting of which, aided by the fire, penetrated the flesh. This punish-

ment, the atrocity of which revolts the imagination, made no change in the constancy of the Christian hero, and the proconsul ordered him to be thrown into a dungeon which had been strewed with fragments of broken pottery. The guards, half opening the door of the dungeon, were amazed to see the martyr walking, and singing the praises of God. This spectacle of an invincible faith converted them to the Christian religion. Dacian, by a refinement of cruelty, and resolved to deny Vincent the glory of dying in torments, had him placed on a soft bed, where he intended to have his wounds dressed, that he might be prepared for new tortures; but scarcely had the martyr been laid there, when he expired. His body was thrown into a field, to be devoured by wild beasts and birds of prey. There it remained, untouched and incorrupt, for fifteen days. The governor then ordered it to be sewed in a sack, and thrown into the sea. The waves brought it ashore, and the Christians gave it sepulture in a neighboring church. A child twelve years old, named Eulalia, at Merida, gave evidence, at that tender age, of courage equal to St. Vincent. Dacian, at whose tribunal she, of her own accord, presented herself to confess her faith, at first attempted to gain her by caresses. He then commanded the instruments of torture to be placed before her, and, at the same time, incense, to be offered to the gods. Eulalia spit in his face, overturned the idols, and threw the offerings far from her. On the instant, the tormentors tore her delicate limbs with iron hooks. As she counted the strokes, she said: "This is a writing which engraves on my body the victory of Jesus Christ." Lighted torches were applied to her bleeding wounds; her hair, with which she covered her bosom, caught fire and smothered her. At Complutum, two youthful brothers, Justus, thirteen, and Pastor, seven years old, rivalled the heroism of Saint Eulalia. On learning the arrival of Dacian, they left school and went to declare to the proconsul that they were Christians. After having them whipped until they bled, Dacian sent them to be decapitated. Sicily, and all Italy, counted thousands of martyrs. At Catania, the deacon Euplius was arrested while he was reading the Gospel to the people, and taken at once to execution. At Syracuse, the illustrious virgin St. Lucy, whose name is inserted in the canon of the Mass, died to preserve the honor of her virginity, which the protection of her God guaranteed in the infamous den to which the magistrate had consigned her. In Tuscany, Sabinus, bishop of Assisi, suffered martyrdom with Marcellus and Exuperantius, deacons, and many clerks. Venustianus, governor of Tuscany, whom St. Sabinus had cured of an inveterate ophthalmia, embraced the faith of his victim. He was beheaded, with his wife and children, who were converted by his example.

9. Every thing leads to the belief, according to Tillemont, that St. Marcellinus at this time (October 24, A. D. 304) received the crown of martyrdom. He was deposited in the cemetery of St. Priscilla, in the *Via Salaria*, near the bridge of Salaro. We have mentioned that the Donatists, some years later, dared to calumniate the memory of this holy pontiff. They pretend that St. Marcellinus, unable to endure the torture, had denied his faith. This falsehood was ornamented by all the circumstances which could give it the appearance of truth. It purported that the pontiff, acknowledging his fault, had presented himself as a suppliant before a council of three hundred bishops, assembled at Sinuessa. There he had confessed it, and requested, with tears, that a penance should be imposed on him proportionate to the guilt he had incurred. The council was said to have replied: "Pronounce your sentence yourself; the chief See ought not to be judged except by itself." But in this odious fabrication all is false; the accusation is now recognized as calumnious, and, consequently, the innocence of the pontiff is admitted. St. Augustine, speaking of Petilius, the author of this fable, says: "He accuses Marcellinus of being a traditor, a wicked and sacrilegious man; I declare him innocent. It is not necessary to weary myself to prove his innocence, for Petilius does not venture to prove his accusation." This falsehood has been repeated in our

day,* but the learned labors of Schelstrate, Roccaherti, Peter de Marca, Peter Constant, Papebrock, Nat. Alexander, Pagi, Aguirre, Sangallo, Xavier de Marca, have fully vindicated the innocence of St. Marcellinus, and cleared him from all calumnies.

§ 11. Vacancy in the See of Rome (Oct. 20, a. d. 304—May 19, 308).

10. The violence of the persecution, which fell chiefly on the ministers of the Church, prevented the Roman clergy, for nearly four years, from holding an election for a successor to St. Marcellinus. The number of Martyrs, meantime, was continually increasing. St. Agnes, a Roman virgin, is one of the most celebrated. She had scarcely reached the age of fifteen; her rare beauty had captivated a son of the Roman prefect, who wished to make her his wife. But the young Christian had chosen Jesus Christ for her spouse. Forced by the prefect into a place of prostitution, her virginity was miraculously preserved. The flames of a pyre, prepared to consume her, separated around her body without touching it. Finally, her head was stricken off by the sword of a soldier, and she was united forever to her God. The name of Agnes was placed in the canon of the Mass. Nearly at the same time, St. Soteris, virgin, the exorcist Peter, Arthemius, jailer of the prison, converted by the captive Christians, his wife Candida, his daughter Paulina, and the priest Marcellinus, all suffered martyrdom at Rome. Other parts of Italy were not spared. At Bologna, Agricola was taken, with Vitalis, his slave, who was

* The Roman breviary (26th April, Lectio V.) admits the fall of St. Marcellinus. Baronius warns us, on this point, that the Roman Church has no intention to impose on us, as proved facts, the historic facts reported in the legends of the saints. There are some which criticism can and ought to contest, when it is supported by grave authority and peremptory proofs. Lambertini, afterwards pope under the name of Benedict XIV. (*De Servorum Dei Beatificatione*, lib. iv., p. 2, c. 13, No. 8), pronounces in the same sense in connection with the question which occupies us. He assures us that the fact cited by the Roman breviary, respecting the fall of St. Marcellinus, is false: 1st. Because of the silence on this point of all the ancient writers on the lives of the pontiffs. 2d. Because of the impostures of the Donatists, who could never prove the truth of their assertions: and he recalls the words of St. Augustine which we have already quoted.

fastened to a cross and executed first, to intimidate his master. Both were interred in the Jewish cemetery; St. Ambrose afterwards removed them. At Milan, SS. Nazarius and Celsus, Nabor and Felix, Gervase and Protase, whose relics were also discovered by St. Ambrose. At Aquila, SS. Cantius and Cantianus, with their sister, Cantianella, of the consular family of Anicius. At Augusta, in Rhetia (Augsburg), a courtesan named Afra, converted to the faith, gave an example of heroic courage; she was burned alive on an island of the Lech, by order of the proconsul Gaius. In Pannonia, St. Ireneus, bishop of Sirmium, and Victorinus, bishop of Petaw, gave their lives for Jesus Christ. In Thrace, Philip, bishop of Heraclea, Severus, priest, and Hermes, deacon, were burned alive.

11. These were the last victims of the persecution in the West. A great event, which was destined to change the face of the world, placed the whole of western Europe in the hands of Constantius Chlorus. This prince, equitable, virtuous, benevolent to Christians, extinguished the fires which, during two years, had not ceased to devour them by thousands. Diocleisan had come to Rome at the commencement of the year 304, to celebrate his triumph over the Persians, Egyptians, and the tribes of Libya. The medals struck in his honor, the arches ranged along his passage, named him, among his other titles of glory, *the emperor victorious over the Christian impiety*. In the theatre the mysteries of that religion were parodied, which Dioclesian boasted to have effaced from the world. In presence of the emperor and all the court, and the populace, drunk with joy, the comedian Genesius, clothed in the white dress of a neophyte, simulated with sacrilegious railleries all the ceremonies of the Christian baptism. Each gesture of the actor was saluted by frenzied applauses from the crowd. Meantime, the water fell upon the body of Genesius, while the consecrating words were pronounced. The actor rose a Christian. He advanced to the front of the stage. "Hear me," he exclaimed, "august emperor, officers, philosophers, and people of Rome! Whenever the name of Christian has reached my

ears, it has penetrated me with horror. I have informed myself with exactitude of the mysteries of this detested religion, only to amuse you; but when the baptismal water touched me, I saw a hand which came from heaven, and shining angels above me. They read in a book all the sins I had committed since my infancy, and washed them in the water in which I had been baptized, and presented me with the book, which was whiter than snow." It was at first supposed that these words belonged to the part, and the applauses were redoubled; but the new Christian insisted on his sincerity, and finally triumphed over the incredulity with which he had been received. Dioclesian, incensed, ordered him to be beaten with clubs; after this, he was laid on the rack; his body was torn with iron hooks, and lighted torches were applied to his wounds. Finally, he was beheaded for that God who had been so late revealed to him, but whom he had so faithfully confessed from the instant that he had known Him.

12. The martyrdom of St. Genesius was the last ordered by Dioclesian. Some days after, he departed from Rome, where his Oriental luxury had awakened the raillery of the *Quirites*. The Cæsars had begun to find the morals of the degenerate Romans too austere, and royalty fled from the ancient capital. A fearful malady attacked this emperor, who had presumed to measure his power with that of the true God. On his return to Nicomedia, where his mind was weakened by suffering, he met Galerius, who assumed the tone of a master, and spoke of having him massacred by the troops if he persisted in holding the empire. Upon this, the aged tyrant, in a plain, crowded with multitudes of the great, the people, and the soldiery, mounted upon an elevated tribune, from which he declared, that having need of repose, he ceded his power to Galerius. At the same time he nominated a new Cæsar: it was Daia, or Daza Maximin, formerly a keeper of flocks, and son of the sister of Galerius. The emperor threw his purple mantle over the shoulders of the late shepherd, and

Dioclesian, now Diocles, pursued the way to Salona, his native land (A. D. 305). Maximian-Hercules also laid down the sovereign authority at Milan, in favor of Constantius Chlorus, and nominated as Cæsar, Valerius Severus, an obscure favorite of Galerius, on the same day on which Dioclesian accomplished his sacrifice at Nicomedia. Maximian having in the sequel again seized the purple, invited Dioclesian to follow his example. The latter replied: "If you could see the fine cabbages I have planted at Salona, you would not speak to me of empire." These stoical words were falsified by bitter regrets. The hand of God was heavy on these two persecutors and on their race; Lactantius has recorded their end in his magnificent work, *De Morte Persecutorum*. Maximian was murdered, with his son of eight and his daughter of seven years of age. His wife was thrown, living, into the Orontes, where he had ordered so many Christian women to be drowned. Dioclesian, an emperor without empire, tormented by regret, and doubtless also by remorse, could not sleep, could not eat in his solitude of Salona; he resolved to die of hunger, and St. Jerome informs us that before he expired he vomited out his tongue, all eaten by worms. Prisca, his wife, and Valeria, his daughter, as fugitives, disguised under wretched clothing, were recognized, arrested, beheaded at Thessalonica, and cast into the sea. Why had they not the courage to die for the God whom they had so deplorably denied!

13. As yet the Christians had gained nothing by these changes of the Cæsars. In the East, Maximin Daia, to whom was assigned the government of that part of the world, or rather the power of treading it under foot, understood nothing of either war or civil affairs; he brought into the service of the empire nothing but an insatiable ferocity; it was through this quality that he had gained Galerius. This last, a crowned monster, gave to the world examples of cruelty which, even after Nero, Tiberius, or Caligula, might still seem new. He kept a number of bears to whom he gave his own name, and every day several Christians were thrown to them in his

presence, while he laughed with hideous enjoyment as he saw the brutes grind their yet palpitating limbs. It was especially at his banquets that he indulged himself in this ferocious pleasure. Another mode of torture, of his own invention, pleased him still more, because it prolonged his horrid diversions. Martyrs were fastened to a stake, and a slow fire was kept burning under the soles of their feet, until the flesh, completely charred, fell from the bones. Then, with torches which burned without flames, each of the members was roasted in succession, until no part of the body remained untouched. Meantime, the head was sprinkled with fresh water, and the lips and mouth were moistened, to prevent the victim from dying too soon. Some are known to have lived several days in these tortures, to the great delight of Galerius, who gloated over their sufferings.

14. The blood of martyrs, therefore, continued to flow in the East. At Aquileia, St. Anastasia, widow of a Roman ambassador in Persia, was beheaded on the same day as the priest St. Chrysogonus, who had instructed her in the faith and sustained her in her captivity. Both names were placed by the Church in the prayers of the Canon. At Thessalonica, St. Agape, St. Chionia, and St. Irene, were burned alive. Irene, before her torture, had been exposed several days in a house of debauchery, where she was divinely preserved stainless. At Tarsus, in Cilicia, Taracus, Probus, and Andronicus, dragged successively from Tarsus to Mopsuesta and Anazarba, cities of Cilicia, to be interrogated by the proconsul Maximus, exhausted, in turn, all manner of tortures—the rack, the hooks, and the red-hot spits on which they were impaled. No part of their bodies was left without a wound. The eyes were put out, the teeth broken, the tongue cut off; in fine, more resembling mutilated corpses than living men, they were thrown to the beasts in the amphitheatre of Tarsus, in presence of the whole population. A she-bear and a furious lioness came one after the other to lick their bleeding wounds, and caressingly crouched at their feet. Maximus, more cruel than these ani-

mals, commanded the gladiators to behead the martyrs, who were thus released to receive the recompense of their courage and unshaken constancy. In this same province of Cilicia lived St. Julitta, who was arrested by order of the governor, with her son, St. Cyr, four years of age. This child, seeing the tortures of his mother, cried out that he was a Christian like her. Alexander, the governor, took him by the foot and dashed his head against the steps of his tribune. His brains were scattered near the courageous mother, who uttered only these words: " I thank Thee, my God, for having crowned the son before the mother." The judge ordered her feet to be plunged in boiling pitch, while her flesh was torn by the iron hooks. Julitta ceased not to confess her faith. Finally, this judge, or rather this torturer, gagged her, and ordered her to be decapitated. Another martyrdom occurred at Tarsus, in Cilicia, under extraordinary circumstances. Boniface, a pagan, steward of Aglae, a Roman lady, had long maintained a criminal intercourse with his mistress. Touched at length by grace, and resolved to change her life, Aglae sent her steward into the East to bring her some relics of the martyrs. Boniface, on quitting her, said in pleasantry, "that he prayed her to receive his own relics, if ever they should be brought to her under the name of a martyr." On his arrival at Tarsus, he found the public place filled with Christians, who were suffering the most horrible tortures. Deeply moved by the spectacle, he approached the martyrs, and was so touched by their constancy, that he exclaimed, " I, also, am a Christian." The governor ordered him to be seized and joined to the band of holy confessors. His body, redeemed by the domestics he had brought with him, was conveyed to Aglae, who placed these precious remains in a magnificent oratory which she erected fifty stadia from Rome. At Cæsarea, in Palestine, Appian and Edesius, brothers by birth and faith, were cast into the sea. Agapius was devoured by beasts in the amphitheatre. Theodosia, a virgin eighteen years of age, was torn by the iron hooks, and drowned in the Mediterranean. The priest Pamphilus, Valens, a deacon, and a great number of other Christians, were beheaded at the same time. St. Pamphilus had written an apology for Origen. Eusebius, of Cæsarea, had conceived so high an esteem for him, that he bore the surname of Pamphilus, from respect to the memory of this saint. In Syria, St. Domnina and her daughters Prodosca and Berenice, to avoid the torments and outrages to which the persons of their sex were exposed, drowned themselves in a river.* At Amasea, the soldier Theodorus confessed Jesus Christ before the judges, who granted him time to deliberate. He profited by it to set fire to the temple of Cybele. Retaken, and long tortured on the rack, he was burned alive. In Egypt, more than two hundred and fifty confessors were sent to the mines, after having each their right eye destroyed, and the tendon of the left foot burned, so as to make their lives only a long martyrdom. At Antioch, St. Pelagia, a virgin, seeing her house surrounded by persecutors, threw herself from the roof. Her mother and sisters having learned that they, too, were sought for, threw themselves into a river, and clasping each other by the hand, they were drowned. In Palestine, thirty-nine confessors were beheaded at a single execution. Four others, among whom were Peles and Nilus, Egyptian bishops, were consumed by fire.

15. This long martyrology, of which every detail is a trait of heroism and of faith, was filled within the years 304, 305, 306, 307—during the vacancy of the see of Rome. An instant of relaxation gave the opportunity (A. D. 305) to eleven or twelve bishops of Numidia to assemble at Cyrtha, now Constantine, in Algeria. This conventicle, formed of traditor bishops, who at first reproached each other for their crimes, and who finished by a compact of alliance, elected for bishop of Cyrtha another traditor, named Sylvanus. By a contradiction, which might appear strange if experience had not taught that men the most indulgent toward themselves are usually most severe to others, these same bishops, six years later, deposed Cecilian, bishop of Carthage, as having been ordained

---

* Such cases as these, independently of an extraordinary impulse of the Holy Ghost, would be contrary to the dictates of Christian morality.

by traditors. While ministers, unworthy the God of peace, and charity, gave this scandal to the world, St. Peter, patriarch of Alexandria, gave to his Church canons or rules of conduct for the feeble Christians who had been unable to resist the violence of the persecution. This monument of the ancient discipline of the Church breathes the gentleness and compassionate discretion of the good pastor. The longest of the penalties prescribed by St. Peter of Alexandria is three years. It includes masters who had sent their Christian slaves in their place to the tribunals, to suffer for them. They who had yielded only from weakness or pusillanimity, even without having given battle, could be received into communion after a year of penance. Such is the virtue of the saints, full of that merciful condescension of *the Son of man, who came to seek, not the just, but sinners.*

§ III. St Marcellus, Pope (May 19, a. d. 308—Jan. 16, 310).

16. Long after the bloody persecution had ceased at Rome, the clergy were sought after and imprisoned. It was not until May 19, a. d. 308, that they could assemble and put an end to the vacancy of the Holy See and the widowhood of the Church. They elected Pope St. Marcellus, one of the priests whom St. Marcellinus had had almost constantly with him. Christian antiquity praises his firmness in maintaining the vigor of discipline. After the ravages of persecution, large numbers of Christians, who had not had the courage to confess their faith in presence of the tormentors, tumultuously demanded to be restored to the Church without passing through the salutary tests of canonical penance. To receive them at once would have been merciful, but weak. St. Marcellus comprehended this, and resisted their attempts, even at the expense of his personal repose and tranquillity. This is the eulogy which Pope Damasus made of him, without adding other details on the circumstances of the conflict which he was obliged to sustain.

17. And now the name, so dear to the Church, of Constan-

tine the Great began to dawn upon the world. Providence that watched over his destiny, disengaged him by degrees from the trammels which it seemed must bind down his rising glory. Son of Constantius Chlorus and of Helena, the daughter of a Roman inn-keeper—left, through the repudiation of his mother, without favor or protection—he was induced to attach himself to the court of Dioclesian, and bore arms in Egypt and Persia. His valor and affability soon won him popularity in the camp. The abdication of Dioclesian threw him into the power of Galerius, who, jealous of his credit with the soldiers, wished to get rid of him by engaging him in combat—first with a Sarmatian, afterwards with a lion. Constantine, happily escaping in both these trials, withdrew by flight from the snares of Galerius. To prevent pursuit, from post to post he hamstrung the horses he had used, and rejoined his father at Boulogne at the moment when, having vanquished Carausius, he was embarking for Great Britain. Constantius died at York, some months afterwards (A. D. 306). The legions, by a last essay of their power, and without awaiting the election of the palace, proclaimed Constantine emperor. Galerius, despite his ill will, was constrained to have this detested rival in power. Other discomfitures awaited him. His tyranny had revolted the Romans, who threw off the yoke, and offered the purple to Maxentius, son of Maximian-Hercules. The father left his retreat, joined his son, gained by presents the army which Galerius sent against them under the command of Severus, his colleague in the empire, and forced the general to bleed himself to death (A. D. 307). Galerius hastened in person with his legions to the gates of Rome. He found it fortified, and defended by Maximian and Maxentius, who had foreseen his attack. Two legions abandoned him, and he shamefully fled with the rest, ravaging all the country on his passage, to prevent the possibility of being pursued by the two emperors (A. D. 308).

18. While the Church, agitated by the storm of persecution, was calumniated by the philosophers, she found among

her children able and ardent defenders. Christian antiquity has preserved the memory of the learned and numerous works of St. Methodius, at first bishop of Olympia, a maritime city of Lycia, afterwards bishop of Tyre. St. Jerome calls him *the copious orator;* St. Epiphanius, *a glorious champion of the truth;* St. Gregory of Nyssa, *a well of erudition;* Andrew of Cæsarea, *the great Methodius.* He wrote during the persecution of Dioclesian, and was one of its illustrious victims. His greatest work was a refutation of the fifteen books of impious calumnies which the philosopher Porphyry had compiled against Christianity. Nothing now remains of this admirable production of St. Methodius but the fragments cited by St. John Damascene. It needed courage to defend the cause of Christians under the ban of the world, when they met only tormentors and death. The errors of Origen, or rather those which were accredited under this name in the East, also attracted the attention of Methodius. He wrote, to controvert them, several special treatises, *On the Resurrection,* on *The Episode of the Witch of Endor,* who made Samuel appear to King Saul, on *Free-will,* and on *Creatures.* Commentaries on the greater part of the Scriptural books completed the cycle of this useful and laborious life. All these works, written in Greek, are lost to us.

19. The persecution which closed the world to Christians, had opened their way to solitude. At this epoch, the desert, according to the prophetic expression, was seen covered with flowers. We have already mentioned St. Paul, the first hermit, who, A. D. 250, in the persecution of Decius, entered on this way, where generations of recluses were to follow him. Another patriarch of anchoritic life illustrated the desert at this time. It was St. Anthony, born in Egypt, of noble and worthy parentage. At twenty years of age he one day heard in church those words of the Gospel, "If thou wilt be perfect, go sell what thou hast, and give to the poor, and come, follow me, and you shall have treasures in heaven." He received the evangelic counsel to the letter. The next day, possessing

nothing of all the opulence he had inherited, he left his family and country, and placed himself under the care of a holy old man who had lived many years in solitude. The product of the rush mats which he made with his own hands sufficed for the support of this youth, reared in luxury and ease. He strove to stifle in his heart all remembrance of the world, and occupied himself constantly in meditations on the Scriptures, which he suceeded in committing entirely to memory. The demon struggled energetically to crush in this heroic soul the germs of the virtues which were to be developed at a later period with so much splendor, for the honor and spiritual advantage of the Church. Impure phantoms, worldly reminiscences, his nobility of birth, the desire of glory, the pleasures of life, incessantly revisited the thoughts of the young anchorite, who, to overcome them, plunged into still deeper solitude and redoubled his prayers, his vigils, fasts, and austerities. These interior conflicts, so well known under the name of *Temptations of St. Anthony*, ended by a brilliant victory over the spirit of darkness. As he exclaimed, one day, in the bitterness of his heart, "Where art Thou, Lord, and why hast Thou abandoned me?" a voice replied, "I have been ever at thy side; I wished to be a spectator of thy courage. Because thou hast resisted, my help shall never fail thee." Anthony returned thanks to his Deliverer, and the following day settled himself in a retired mountain of the Thebais, in the midst of abandoned ruins, to live far from the sight of men, only supported by the favors of God. There he passed twenty years, unknown to the world. The reputation of his sanctity then brought to him a crowd of disciples. At length (A. D. 307) he came forth from his mysterious abode, healing the sick on his way, consoling the afflicted, quieting dissensions, reconciling inveterate enemies, and visiting the monasteries which had been peopled under his direction, some east, some west of the Nile, near the city of Arsinoë. The solitaries listened to his words as oracles. "The mountains of the Thebais were full of Christians, who passed the day and night in chanting psalms, in study, fasts, prayers, labor, and alms-giving; preserving among themselves the spirit of peace, union, and charity. At the view of these pious solitaries, whose whole conversation was in heaven, we can hardly avoid crying, with the prophet, 'How magnificent are thy tabernacles, O Jacob! how beautiful thy tents, O Israel! As woody valleys, as watered gardens near the rivers, as tabernacles which the Lord hath pitched, as cedars by the water-side.'"* These expressions, full of holy enthusiasm, which such a spectacle drew forth some years later, are from the eloquent St. Athanasius, bishop of Alexandria. God thus prepared, in the labor of a fruitful solitude, soldiers for the truth, ready to come down into the lists, as did St. Anthony afterwards, to be her courageous defenders. The time had not yet come.

20. St. Marcellus gave his blood for that faith which nearly all his predecessors had confessed, like him, in torments. He was to be the last pope of the early ages to suffer martyrdom. Imprisoned by command of Maxentius, who ordered him to renounce the title of bishop and sacrifice to the idols, he was condemned to serve among the slaves employed in the imperial stables. After nine months of this odious punishment, the holy pope was delivered at night by his clergy, and received into the hospitable dwelling of Lucina, a Roman lady, who concealed him with the greatest care. The house of this noble widow was from that time consecrated into a church, to which the faithful came in secret to receive instructions from the courageous pontiff. But this retreat was discovered by the police of the tyrant. Maxentius ordered St. Marcellus to be seized and condemned to death. Constantine was to avenge on the tyrant the effusion of this innocent blood. The body of the blessed martyr was piously interred by Lucina, who was faithful to him in death, as she had been in life. He was afterwards removed into the Church of St. Marcellus, which he had founded. The firmness of this pontiff in main-

---

* St. Athanasius.—*Vita S. Anton.*

taining the rules of canonical penance, caused him to be unjustly accused of excessive rigor by certain writers.* This conduct was conformable to the rules of the Church, and to the duty of a pope charged to make them respected by all catholics.

§ IV. St. Eusebius, Pope (April 2, a. d. 310—Sept. 26, 310).

21. St. Eusebius, by birth a Greek, who in the world had practised the profession of medicine, succeeded St. Marcellus. During the brief term of his pontificate, St. Eusebius signalized his zeal and vigilance for the maintenance of the faith in all its purity. Some heretics troubled the peace of the Church of Rome; so far as we can judge from an ancient inscription of this epoch, their errors were chiefly on questions of discipline. St. Eusebius exhibited the same firmness as his predecessor to secure the integrity of canonical penances in regard to the *lapsi*. Maxentius, whose power, in spite of Galerius, was consolidated at Rome, did not persecute the Christians; but he pretended, by an abuse which we shall often find renewed in the course of history, to intermeddle with their internal government. Two months after the election of St. Eusebius, Maxentius exiled him into Sicily, as a punishment for his apostolic vigor in maintaining the laws of discipline, of which he, Maxentius, could not understand the necessity. The saintly pope died there, September 26, of the same year, 310, having governed the Church nearly five months.

§ V. Vacancy in the See of Rome (Sept. 26, a. d. 310—July 2, 311).

22. The commencement of the year 310 witnessed the punishment of one of the persecutors of the Church. Maximian-Hercules had soon become embroiled with Maxentius, his son, who reigned at Rome. He passed into Gaul, and

---

* Fleury.—*Histoire Ecclésiastique*, tome 11, p. 573.

received from Constantine, the husband of his daughter Fausta, a noble and generous hospitality, which he repaid only by crimes.* When Constantine (A. D. 308), occupied with some of his legions in repressing, on the shores of the Rhine, the incursions of the Franks, had left his father-in-law with the rest of the army in Provence, Maximian seduced the principal officers and the governors of the city, and seized the reins of power. On this intelligence, Constantine hastened, by forced marches, to Arles, which opened her gates to him. He pursued and captured the usurper under the walls of Marseilles, and took no other vengeance than to despoil him of the purple, and to keep him in his palace, near his person. Impunity emboldened this veteran in crime. He obliged Fausta to promise to leave open the door of Constantine's sleeping-chamber; and one night, escaping the vigilance of the guards, he approached the imperial bed, and pierced the slumberer with his poniard: it was a eunuch, whom Constantine, informed of the plot by the faithful Fausta, had placed in his bed. Maximian, taken in the act, with the bloody poniard in his hand, and exulting in the assassination of his son-in-law, was permitted to choose the manner of his own death, and strangled himself with his own hands—thus avenging the blood of so many martyrs which he had taken a cruel pleasure in shedding (A. D. 310).

23. During eight years the persecution commenced by Dioclesian weighed upon the East. Of all who had taken part in it, and who glorified themselves for having annihilated the Christian name,* none were now living except Galerius. His hour was approaching. He prepared by new cruelties to celebrate the twentieth anniversary of his reign, when the hand of God was laid upon him. A frightful ulcer extended over the lower part of his body, from which there escaped

* "Dioclesian, Cæsar-Augustus, after having adopted Galerius in the East, abolished the superstitions of Christ, and extended the worship of the gods." And this other inscription, also found in Spain: "Dioclesian Jupiter, Maximian-Hercules, Cæsar-Augustus, after having extended the Roman empire in the East and in the West, and abolished the name of Christians who overturned the state."—(*Inscrip. numism. apud Gruter*, p. 280.)

continually black and corrupted blood, with worms constantly reproduced, and an intolerable odor. The upper portions of his bust were so reduced, that they resembled a skeleton, on the bones of which a livid skin had been drawn; but the legs and feet were so swollen as to have lost all shape. Amid these horrible sufferings, caused by an incurable disease, Galerius changed from an excessive cruelty to an unaccustomed clemency. In the first period of his sickness, he ordered the unsuccessful physicians to be thrown to the beasts in the amphitheatre. As these executions failed to cure him, he began to make salutary reflections on his past life. The remembrance of the Christians whose blood he had shed in torrents troubled his sleepless nights, and, weary of human remedies, he was disposed to appease the wrath of God, whom he had so outraged. The city of Sardica, witness of his sufferings, was also the witness of his tardy repentance. From this city he dated an edict which restored to the Christians the free exercise of their religion. All the titles that he assumes in this monument, which Eusebius has preserved, only prove the more his inability to destroy a religion that forced from him, on his bed of death, a testimony of benevolence.* Galerius

---

* Here is the text of this edict: "The Emperor Cæsar Galerius Valerius Maximian, invincible, august sovereign Pontiff—great in Germany, in Egypt, in Sarmatia, in Thebais, in Persia, in Carpathia, in Armenia, in Media, in Adiabene, the twentieth year of his tribunitial power, the nineteenth of his empire, consul for the eighth time, father of the country, proconsul, to the inhabitants of the provinces, greeting:—

"In the constant care which we take of the public interests, we sought at first to revive the manners of the ancient Romans, and to bring back the Christians to the religion of our ancestors, which they had abandoned. Yielding to a new influence, they had rejected the maxims of their fathers, and organized assemblies for a new worship. In consequence of our ordinances, a great number of them were punished by divers tortures. Nevertheless, since we see that those who remain persevere in their sentiments, and refuse to serve the gods, although they have no liberty to adore the God of the Christians, consulting only our clemency and *that natural goodness which has ever inclined us to the side of indulgence*, we have thought it a duty to extend even to them our paternal mercy. They can, therefore, freely profess their religion, and re-establish the places of their assemblies, in subjecting themselves to the laws of the empire. We shall make known to the magistrates, by another decree, the course they will have to pursue. In virtue of this favor which we grant to them, the Christians are required to pray to their God for our health, and for the welfare of the republic, that the empire may prosper in every part, and that they may themselves live in security and peace."

did not long survive this final act of justice. He died like
Antiochus, after having lived like him. Before his death, he
recommended his wife, Valeria, and Candidianus, his son, to
Licinius, whom, from nothing, he had elevated to the rank of
Cæsar. Licinius hastened to put both of them to death as
soon as Galerius had closed his eyes, by way of discharging
his debt of gratitude. The Divine justice made use of the
fury of these crowned monsters, to inflict on all the race of the
persecutors the chastisements of their fathers' crimes. The
death of Galerius left the empire legitimately divided between
Constantine, Licinius, and Maximinus, who, recognizing each
other as august, but aspiring all three to pre-eminence, reigned,
the first in Gaul, Spain, and Great Britain; the second in Illyria; the third in Asia, the East, and Egypt. The centre of the
empire—that is to say, Italy and Africa—was in the power of
Maxentius, who, never having been regularly proclaimed emperor, either by Dioclesian or Galerius, was regarded as a
usurper, in Latin, *tyrannus*.

24. The news of the edict of Galerius produced throughout the East, on behalf of the Christians, that which the Jews
had experienced at the close of the Babylonian captivity. All
the confessors detained in dungeons were released: those who
labored in chains, at the bottom of the mines, were restored
to light and liberty. In all the cities the Christians again
celebrated their assemblies, made their ordinary collections for
the poor, the widows, and orphans. Charity reappeared in the
world with the religion of Jesus Christ. The pagans, who fancied
they had assisted at the funeral solemnities of Christianity,
were surprised at so unexpected a revolution, and proclaimed
aloud that the Christians' God, who had conquered the Cæsars,
was the only great, the only true God. The confessors, delivered from their chains, returned to their country, and moved
about the cities in the midst of acclamations and songs of
triumph. They were seen in numerous troops on the great
roads and in the public places, chanting psalms and canticles.
The population, even pagans, participated in their joy, and the

reappearance of the Christians was like a public festival for the empire, which, for the space of eight years had labored to exterminate them throughout its extent.

§ VI. St. Melchiades, Pope (July 2, a. d. 311—Jan. 10, 314).

25. After a vacancy of nine months, the reason of which history does not record, the chair of St. Peter was occupied by Melchiades. It was the lot of this pontiff to gather in peace what his predecessors had sowed in storms and blood. His first act was to send the deacons Strattan and Cassian to resume the possession of churches and other properties, which, according to the new edicts, were to be restored to the Christians.

26. The first year of the pontificate of St. Melchiades (a. d. 311) was marked by the consummation of the schism of the Donatists at Carthage. The African bishops, profiting by the peace of the Church, assembled at Carthage to give a successor to Mansurius, bishop of that city, who died during the persecution. The deacon Cecilian was elected by a unanimous vote. Felix, bishop of Aptongus, imposed hands on him, seated him in the episcopal chair, and gave him the inventory of the vases of gold and silver which Mansurius had confided to the care of the elders of the Church. Some unfaithful depositors had hoped to turn certain of these precious objects to their own advantage, and leagued with two intriguing deacons, Botrus and Celeusius, who had carried their pretensions even to the see of Carthage. In concert, they called together the Numidian bishops who had not been convoked for the ordination of Cecilian. These prelates were the same who in 305, as we have seen, assembled to ordain the traditor Sylvanus, bishop of Cirtha. Under the direction of *Donatus*, bishop of Casa Nigra, in Numidia, they formed a false council and deposed Cecilian, on the pretext that Felix of Aptongus, who had imposed hands upon him, was a traditor; that besides this, Cecilian had refused to appear at their assembly; and

finally, that while he was still a deacon, he had hindered the faithful from bearing succors to the martyrs in prison during the persecution of Dioclesian. Considering, for these reasons, the see of Carthage vacant, they elected and ordained as bishop the reader Majorinus, thus raising altar against altar in the same church. Such was the origin of the long schism at Carthage, which took its name from Donatus, of Casæ Nigræ, who was its most ardent and chief instigator. Cecilian was not moved by these troubles and calumnies. He considered himself as sufficiently justified by the sole fact that he remained, said St. Augustine, "united in communion with the Roman Church, where the principality of the apostolic chair has always been in vigor, and where he was ready to plead his cause." We shall see, in the sequel, the Church of Rome pronounce her judgment, and render justice to innocence and truth (A. D. 311).

27. The edict of Galerius which gave freedom to Christians had been executed, as soon as known, in all the provinces of the empire. None of the colleagues of the aged Cæsar would have dared to resist the expression of his will, authentically promulgated. But it was a dear sacrifice to the sanguinary instincts of Maximin Daia to relinquish the daily executions, the cruel diversions of the amphitheatre, which had to cease now for want of victims; and in the year that followed the death of Galerius (October, A. D. 311) he published a decree forbidding Christians to assemble in the cities for the exercise of their worship, on the pretence that they disturbed public order and tranquillity. The governors and proconsuls, divining the intentions of the emperor under the milder forms that still veiled them, comprehended that a new persecution was in view; they consequently recommenced by calumniating their morals, and outraging the memory of their divine Founder. The false acts of Pilate, filled with blasphemies against Jesus Christ, were scattered over all the East which was under the control of Maximinus, as if taken from the imperial archives. Women of vicious life were suborned, who declared, before the

tribunals, that in their assemblies the Christians celebrated infamous mysteries, and that they had themselves taken a part in them. The tormentors were soon again at work. The eyes of confessors were torn out, or their hands, or feet, or ears were cut off. Maximinus had forbidden their punishments to be carried further than mutilation; but this recommendation soon fell into oblivion: the age of martyrs seemed to have returned. St. Peter, bishop of Alexandria, gave his life for the faith, and also SS. Theodore, Hesychius, and Pachomius, bishops of different churches. At Antinous, the monk Apollonius, thrown upon a burning pyre, was miraculously preserved from the flames. This prodigy converted the judge who had condemned him. He was named Arianus; in his turn he became a martyr to this new faith, which had but just subdued his heart, but already was stronger than death. He was thrown into the sea, with many other confessors, by order of the prefect of Alexandria. At Emesa, the bishop Sylvanus was devoured by the beasts of the amphitheatre. At Nicomedia, the priest St. Lucian suffered a new species of punishment. After being left several days without food, when he was tortured by the pangs of hunger, a sumptuous table was placed before him, covered with meats and viands offered to the idols. He resisted this temptation, the most violent, doubtless, to nature; his head was struck off. Maximin Daia carried his hatred to Christianity and his fanaticism for idolatry to insanity. The Armenian nation, and their king, Tiridates, had just been converted to the faith of Jesus Christ by the preaching of St. Gregory, surnamed the Illuminator, the apostle of Armenia. On hearing of this, Maximinus, without regarding the respect due to the title of ally of the Romans, which Armenia merited by her traditional fidelity, instantly declared war, and entered the country at the head of a formidable army. But the Armenians could easily deal with this barbarian, destitute of intelligence and military talent. They beat him in every encounter, and drove him ignominiously from their country. In the cities of Armenia subject to the Romans, there was at this epoch a great number of martyrs. As a nation, these Christians of the first ages defended the true religion, arms in hand; as individuals, they died for it.

28. Meantime, the great event of the fourth century was accomplished at the gates of Rome (A. D. 312). Maxentius had declared war against Constantine to avenge, as he said, the death of Maximian-Hercules, his father; but, in reality, to accomplish a long cherished design to take possession of Gaul. Constantine resolved to anticipate the plans of his enemy. Maxentius had re-established the pretorians; his army was composed of a hundred and seventy thousand infantry and eighteen thousand cavalry. Constantine did not hesitate to attack Maxentius and this formidable force with only his forty thousand veterans. He passed the Cottian Alps on one of those indestructible roads made by the Romans, took Susa by assault, defeated a corps of heavy cavalry near Turin, another at Brescia; Verona capitulated; the captive garrison were bound in chains forged from the swords of the vanquished; and in this triumphal march Constantine arrived at the gates of Rome. Maxentius remained within the walls, because an oracle threatened him with death if he came out of them; but his captains, chiefly men of experience, held the country for him. Constantine was encamped opposite the Milvian bridge, now Ponte Molle. One day, as he advanced at the head of a body of troops, towards mid-day, a brilliant cross of light formed itself in the midst of the sky, in the direction of the sun. On this miraculous cross appeared, in letters of fire, these Latin words: *In hoc signo vinces*. The apparition of this prodigy, which was seen by the whole army, deeply moved Constantine, who, long years afterwards, related it himself to Eusebius, bishop of Cæsarea. All that day he was preoccupied with this marvellous vision. The night following, the same cross appeared to him anew, and Jesus Christ, revealing Himself, ordered him to place this image upon his standards. The next day, at the side of the Roman eagles, a

banner of a form hitherto unknown was remarked. It was a long staff of gilded wood, bearing near the top a transverse beam, forming a cross, from the arms of which floated a banner of cloth of gold and jewels; above it sparkled a crown of gold and precious stones, in the midst of which was the monogram of Christ, formed of the two Greek initials of this name. This monogram and the image of the cross were also placed on the casques of the soldiers. Such was the famous *Labarum*: and in this manner the cross, reserved until then as an infamous gibbet for the vilest criminals, after three centuries of outrages, incredulity, and persecutions, triumphed over the world, took its place among the most sacred things, and became the standard of the Roman legions, which the conquered world regarded only with respect and admiration. "The battle which was about to be fought between Maxentius and Constantine," says M. de Chateaubriand, "is of the small number of those which, as a material expression of the conflict of opinions, became, not a single fact in war, but a veritable revolution. Two religions and two worlds met at the Milvian bridge; two religions were face to face, armed, on the bank of the Tiber, in view of the Capitol. Maxentius interrogated the Sybilline books, sacrificed lions, and opened pregnant women to search the bosom of infants torn from their mother's bowels—for it was supposed that hearts that had never palpitated could not conceal an imposture. Constantine came by a divine impulse and the greatness of his genius. These words are engraven on his triumphal arch: *Instinctu Divinitatis, mentis magnitudine*. The ancient gods of the Janiculum had, ranged around their altars, the legions who in their name had conquered the world: in the face of these soldiers were those of Jesus Christ. The *Labarum* surmounted the eagles, and the earth of Saturn beheld the reign of Him who preached on the mountain; time and the human race had made a step in advance."* This battle of Actium, for Christianity, was fought

* M. DE CHATEAUBRIAND: *Études Historiques*. Ed. Charpentier, p. 213.

October 28, A. D. 312. Maxentius, at length unfaithful to the vow he made not to fight outside of Rome, crossed the Tiber, throwing up behind him a wooden bridge, divided into two movable parts. His plan was to draw Constantine on this bridge, then to separate its parts, and to drown his enemy in the river beneath. He ranged his army in order of battle, the rear being backed by the Tiber—a fault in strategy, and an enormous imprudence, since the soldiers, if obliged in the least to fall back, were instantly precipitated into the river. Constantine, as a skilful general, deployed his army advantageously in the plain, and by masterly combinations supplied his deficiency in numbers. The troops of Maxentius were broken at the first shock. The bravest were killed at their posts, the others, confused, blinded, threw themselves into the Tiber, and the greater part were swallowed up. The flying Maxentius hastened towards the bridge he had constructed. The weight of the multitude who passed upon it at the same moment broke it down, and Maxentius, falling into the water, perished by the means which he had prepared for the destruction of his rival. The God of the Christians had fulfilled His promise to Constantine, and the *Labarum* was victorious. The following day Constantine made his triumphant entry into Rome, where the joy of all classes equalled his own. The terror of the name of Maxentius was so great that the people were reluctant to give credit to the report of his death, fearing his terrible vengeance if the rumor should prove false. But the body of the tyrant, which had sunk in the mud of the river, having been found and recognized, was brought into the city as the proof and pledge of the deliverance of the Romans. Their joy was no longer concealed, and the eager crowd pressed around to gratify themselves with a view of the conqueror's face, all flushed with victory. "Never was there a day," said the orator Nazarius, "since the foundation of Rome, that was happier than this; none of the boasted triumphs of antiquity can enter into comparison with the triumph of Constantine. In it there were not exhibited the chiefs of the enemy in chains, marching before the car of the conqueror, but all of the Roman nobles, delivered from the exactions which the tyrant had imposed on them. Barbarians were not cast into the dungeons, but citizens of consular rank were released, whom the avarice and cruelty of Maxentius detained there. They who formed the procession in this festival were not captive strangers, but Rome herself, set at liberty. She had gained no conquest over an enemy, but she had regained herself; she had not enriched herself with new spoils, but she had herself ceased to be the prey of a tyrant; and her crowning glory is, that in exchange for servitude, she has resumed her right to empire. In place of prisoners of war, which the conqueror disdained to mingle with this pomp, each substituted in his thought another kind of captives: they saw enchained the monsters most terrible to the human race; impiety subjugated; perfidy vanquished; audacity enchained; tyranny, fury, cruelty, pride and arrogance, license and debauch, furious enemies whose excesses we had felt, and who now chafed with rage to perceive that they were powerless to injure us."*

The sword of the victor rested in the scabbard: the fight was ended; the sole act of severity of the Christian hero was an act of rigorous justice, and at the same time of wise policy —he dispersed the pretorian militia, who, during two centuries and a half, had held in check the emperor and the empire, and had set up the purple at auction. Some months afterwards,

---

* Translated from Crevier: *Histoire des Empereurs*, t. xii. We give the text of this eloquent passage: "Nullus post urbem conditam dies Romano illuxit imperio, cujus tam effusa, tamque insignis gratulatio aut fuerit, aut esse debuerit. Nulli tam laeti triumphi, quos annualium vetustas consecratos in litteris habet. Non egebantur quidem ante currum vincti duces, sed incedebat soluta nobilitas. Non conjecti in carcerem Barbari sed deducti e carcere consulares. Non captivi alienigenae introitu millium honestaverunt, sed Roma jam libera. Nihil ex hostili accepit sed seipsam recuperavit, nec praeda auctior facta est, sed esse praeda desivit, et (quo nihil adjici ad gloriae magnitudinem potest) imperium recepit quae servitium sustinebat. Duci sane omnibus videbantur subacta vitiorum agmina, quae orbem graviter obsiderant. Scelus domitum, victa perfidia, diffidens sibi audacia, et importunitas catenata, et cruenta crudelitas inani terrori frendebat. Superbia atque arrogantia debellata, luxuries coercita, et libido constricta noxu ferreo tenebantur."—(NAZAR. PANEG: *Constantin. August.*)

another victory, won by Licinius, near Heraclea, cost Maximinus Daia his power and his life.* With him disappeared the last persecution of the Christian religion.

29. Constantine signalized his accession to the sovereign power in Rome by an edict in favor of Christians. He granted them liberty to build new churches, and to regain possession of those of which the persecution had deprived them. This decree, dated at Milan, was sent to all the consuls and governors of provinces. For the first time during three centuries, an emperor dared openly to proclaim his sympathy for the faith of Jesus Christ, and for the first time this act was received with unanimous consent. Constantine bestowed on the ministers of the Christian religion the privileges enjoyed by pagan priests. Clergy were to be exempted from all imposts, services, and public charges. The pontiffs became men of consideration, having the confidence of the sovereign. Thus was definitively closed a combat of three centuries, between the Church of Jesus Christ and idolatrous Rome. During three centuries, idolatrous Rome persecutes the Church by her emperors and her idols—during three centuries the Church suffers and dies in her martyrs. At the end of these three centuries, idolatrous Rome witnessed the destruction, at once, of idols and persecutors; whilst the Church, overcoming them all, saw a youthful hero display on his banners the sign, hitherto ignominious, of Christ, the cross which, henceforth, will be the glorious standard of regenerated humanity, A. D. 313.

* Maximinus was greatly chagrined at the victory of Constantine and his alliance with Licinius, and, with an army of seventy thousand men, he advanced, by rapid marches, from Syria, to attack them. Licinius, who was his antagonist, had already twenty thousand soldiers. Some days before the battle an angel appeared to him in the night, and warned him to rise quickly, and with all his army to offer prayers to the sovereign God, promising him the victory if he did so. Early the next morning Licinius called his secretary and dictated to him the prayer which the angel had repeated to him, and ordered this writing to be distributed to all his army. On the day of battle, his soldiers having three times recited the prayer, full of confidence, fell upon the troops of Maximinus, so far superior in numbers, and made a great carnage. Maximinus, obliged to fly with his troops, poisoned himself at Tarsus, after having loaded his stomach with wine and meats. He died some days after, in excessive suffering. His death gave liberty to all the churches.—(*Abrégé Chronologique de l'Histoire Ecclésiastique*, t. 1, p. 129.)

30. Scarcely had the successor of the Cæsars entered Rome as victor, when he sought out the representative of a spiritual royalty, whose purple, until now, had been the blood of martyrs. From this time there were two sovereignties recognized and proclaimed in the world, that of the pope, and that of the emperor: one without other force than the Divine promises, without other support than its meekness, without other arms than its faith; the other exterior, ruler by the sword, by legislation, wealth and power, but subject to the authority of the pontiffs in things within the domain of faith. It is the great glory of Constantine that he understood the character and executed perfectly the part of the Christian emperor, who was designated by the name of the *external bishop*. The Donatists, on learning of his accession to the empire, laid before him a request to be supported by his authority. "We have recourse to you, most excellent emperor," they said, "you who came of an equitable race; you whose fathers alone among the emperors never ordered a persecution against Christians; we entreat that it may please you to give us for judges bishops from Gaul, because that country, exempt from the proscription, has not, like us, had the misfortune to know traditors. Let, then, the differences which have occurred in the African Church be judged by the bishops of Gaul. Signed by Lucian, Narsutius, Dignus, Capito, Fidentius, and the other bishops of the party of Majorinus." The response of Constantine to this unworthy supplication ought to be written in letters of gold: "What!" he exclaimed, "you ask judges of me, you, bishops, of me who am in worldly life, and who myself await the judgment of Jesus Christ!" He sent all the memorials and papers of this affair to the pope, St. Melchiades, under whose presidency was opened, October 2 (A. D. 313), at the residence of the Empress Fausta, named the Lateran palace, a council composed of nineteen bishops from Italy and Gaul. Donatus appeared as the accuser of Cecilian, the legitimate bishop of Carthage. Convicted himself of having rebaptized heretics, and ordained traditors as

bishops, he withdrew from the council. The assembled prelates then examined in detail the acts of the conventicle of the bishops of Numidia, who, (A. D. 311) had condemned Cecilian. They were found tainted with irregularities, violence, and party spirit. Each of the heads of accusation alleged against Cecilian was discussed and carefully weighed. None could bear a serious examination. They were only a tissue of false inventions and calumnies. The question thus elucidated, St. Melchiades, with the unanimous concurrence of the bishops in council, proclaimed the innocence of Cecilian and the legitimacy of his ordination. But by that spirit of eminent prudence which distinguishes all measures emanating from the holy see, the pope did not separate from his communion either the bishops who had condemned Cecilian, or those who had been sent to Rome to accuse him. He even offered, adds St. Augustine, to receive in his communion those who had been ordained by Majorinus, the Donatist bishop of Carthage; and it was so ordered, that in all places where there were two bishops, in consequence of the schism, he who had the seniority of ordination should be maintained, and the other should have the first vacant see. Donatus of *Casa Nigra* was alone excepted from these merciful measures. He was condemned as the author of all the trouble. He departed for Carthage more bitter than ever, and ready to foment new discord.

31. Pope St. Melchiades did not live to see the end of this affair. He died three months after the close of the council, January 10 (A. D. 314). His moderation, prudence, and charity were eulogized by St. Augustine, who, referring to this holy pontiff, exclaims: "O excellent man! true son of peace; true father of Christian people!" He was deposited in the cemetery of Callistus, and afterwards removed to the Church of St. Silvester *in capite* by St. Paul I. Constantine, when he gave St. Melchiades the Lateran palace, added to this imperial munificence an annual rent, sufficient to maintain the dignity of the head of the Church; and thus the Roman pontiffs were

placed in a state of independence which allowed them to exercise their ministry with apostolic liberty for the general good of society. The gratitude and confidence of the people gradually invested them with a sovereignty which was consecrated by time and custom. Charlemagne, at a later period, completed this noble thought of Constantine; and the holy see, a spiritual and pacific power, placed in the midst of civil governments, respected by all, and independent of all, became the supreme moderator and arbiter of Christendom.

32. The first period of the history of the Church ends with St Melchiades. The conversion of the Cæsars was about to change the face of the world. "When, after three hundred years of tortures," said the R. P. Lacordaire, "Constantine saw, from the height of Mount Mario, the *Labarum* in the air, it was the blood of Christians which had germinated in the shade, and had risen, like dew, up to heaven, and unfolded itself in the form of the cross triumphant. Our public liberty was the fruit of an unexampled moral liberty. Our entry into the *Forum* of princes, was the fruit of an empire which we had exercised over ourselves even unto death. We might well reign after such an apprenticeship to servitude. We had won the right to clothe our doctrine in a robe of purple after all the blood they had shed upon it. But this reign was not long, if we give this name to the time which passed between Constantine and the barbarians—a time so full of controversies, when the Catholic doctrine never quitted for a single day the pen and the sword."*

* *Conférences de Notre Dame de Paris* (29 Novembre, 1845, par le R. P. H. Lacordaire.)

CHAPTER XV.

§ I. REVIEW OF THE FIRST PERIOD OF THE CHURCH (A. D. 1-312).

1. Rapid extension of Christianity in Italy.—2. Throughout the West.—3. In the East.—4. Obstacles to the development of Christianity.—5. Causes favorable to this development.—6. Pagan Writers and Philosophers hostile to Christianity—Lucian, Celsus, Porphyry, Jamblicus, Philostratus's Life of Apollonius of Thyanea. Hierocles.—7. First apologists.—8. Heresies. Schisms.—9. Government, Discipline, and Worship.—10. Conclusion.*

1. IN concluding the recital of the sanguinary persecutions of three hundred years' duration, it is interesting to note the marvellous extension of Christianity under the sword of the executioner. "At the commencement of the second century," says St. Justin, "there is no people among whom we do not find believers in Jesus Christ." We read also, in St. Irenæus, that "the Church was spread over all the earth, and to the most remote extremities of the world." The expressions of Tertullian are not less remarkable. "We are of yesterday, yet we fill all that belongs to you; we leave to you only your temples. If we would separate ourselves from you, or withdraw into some distant land, the loss of so many citizens would weaken your power; you would shudder over the desolation, the silence of a world in some sort extinct; you would seek in vain for men to command." It would be satisfactory to know what was, at the epoch of the persecution of Diocletian, the relative number of the Christians and of the pagans. In default of precise and positive information on this question,

---

* See, for the first and second periods, the work of Dr. Dœllinger, professor of history in the University of Munich. *Origine du Christianisme*, 2 vols. 8vo., from which we have borrowed the principal ideas of this chapter.

a rapid view taken of the East and West will give us an approximation to the growth of the Church at the close of the third century. Rome had within her walls forty churches under the pontificate of St. Silvester I. (A. D. 314-335). Ancient local traditions attribute the foundation of most of the churches in Italy to the disciples of St. Peter. Lucca regards as her first apostle St. Paulinus, who was sent to Etruria by the prince of the Apostles. Fiesole, St. Romulus; Ravenna, St. Apollinaris; Milan, St. Anathalon; Aquileia, St. Mark; Bologna, St. Zamas, sent by Pope St. Dionysius (A. D. 259); Zeno, first bishop of Verona, suffered martyrdom under the Emperor Gallienus (A. D. 255). Pozzuoli had for its first bishop, Patrobas, mentioned by St. Paul in his Epistle to the Romans. The ancient martyrologies date at an equally remote epoch the apostolic institution of Beneventum, of Priscus at Capua, of St. Asper at Naples, of Philip of Argyrium at Palermo, and St. Marcian, first bishop of Syracuse.

2. The origin of Christianity in proconsular Africa, though rather obscure in the first century, was gloriously developed in the second. The principal see of the Church, from the desert of Barca to the Atlantic, was Carthage, a magnificent and populous city, long since raised from its ruins, and then, through its commerce, connected with the whole world. Towards the end of the second century, Agrippinus, who was bishop of this city, convoked a synod of seventy other bishops. In the time of Tertullian the religion of Jesus Christ had penetrated among the primitive Africans, the Getuli and Moors, who inhabited the interior of the country in the gorges and the valleys of Atlas—chiefly nomadic tribes, speaking an idiom of their own. In the three first centuries the northwest of Africa was divided into three ecclesiastical provinces, viz.: proconsular Africa, Numidia, and Mauritania. In the following century there were six, including those just mentioned, viz.: the Tripolitan, which had only five bishops, the Bysacene, and Mauritania Cæsariensis. The Church of Spain (A. D. 250) appears for the first time in history when two bishops, Basilides of Astorga and

Martial of Leon, having apostatized in the persecution of Decius, were deposed by a synod. The apostolic epoch of the first bishops of that country is not less supported by traditions sufficiently probable. In A. D. 306 the council of Elvira (Eliberis), held by nineteen Spanish bishops, proves that Christianity at that epoch was flourishing in that country. The Gauls, converted as early as the close of the first century by the disciples of the Apostles, who had seen SS. Pothinus and Irenæus at Lyons, St. Trophimus at Arles, St. Benignus at Autun, St. Victor at Marseilles, SS. Donatian and Rogatian at Nantes, could count in the third century almost as many episcopal sees as there were important cities. In the council of Arles, held against the Donatists (A. D. 314), there were present the bishops of Rheims, of Rouen, of Vaison, of Bordeaux, and envoys from the Churches of Mende (Gabales) of Orange, Apt, and Nice. In the countries on the right bank of the Rhine, and divided into upper and lower Germany, the Christian religion was already powerful in the second century. Treves, Cologne, Maestricht, Spires, Mayence, were so many religious centres, whence the doctrine of the Gospel was spread over the more remote countries of Germany. The borders of the Danube, Norica, Vindelicia, and Rhetia (Austria, Bavaria, the Tyrol, and the Grisons), whose principal cities were populated by Roman colonies (Laureacum, Augusta Vindelicorum, Tridentum), Larch, Augsburg, Trent, had early received the seeds of faith, and the persecution of Dioclesian made numerous martyrs there. Great Britain had received, under the reign of Claudius, Roman colonies, who brought with them the doctrines of the Gospel—and almost the entire people were Christians. Gildas, the most ancient writer of this nation, relates that in (A. D. 303) on the promulgation of the sanguinary edict of Dioclesian the churches were demolished, the sacred books burned publicly in the streets, and a multitude of priests and laics were put to death—so that the forests and caverns which served as places of refuge to the Christians seemed to have more inhabitants than the cities.

The first British martyr was St. Alban of Verulam, converted by a fugitive priest to whom he had given hospitality. After the close of the persecution there appeared at the synod of Arles three British bishops, Eborius of York, Restitutus of London, and Adelphius *de civitate coloniæ Londinensium* (perhaps Lincoln). Thrace, Heminontus, Rhodope, Scythia, and lower Mesia had on the shores of the Mediterranean churches as flourishing as those of Great Britain. In Macedonia, Thessalonica, Philippi, Berœa, the apostolic churches had not degenerated in the third century from their primitive fervor. Athens, the capital of ancient Greek civilization, Byzantium, destined to become the queen of a new empire, had long been conquests of the faith.

3. The East presented the same scenes of Christian faith and fecundity. From Jerusalem, the cradle of Christianity, the Gospel had been spread over all the cities of Palestine, Phœnicia, and Syria. The names of Cæsarea, of Palestine, of Tyre, Sidon, Ptolemais, Berytus, Tripoli, Biblos, Seleucia, Apamea, Hieropolis, Samosata, and, above all, Antioch, recall great and illustrious churches. In Roman Arabia, Bozra, in the Osrhoene, Edessa, the capital, had received the Gospel at an early period. In Mesopotamia and Chaldea the churches of Amida, Nisibis, Seleucia, and Ctesiphon were celebrated. Asia Minor, evangelized by St. Paul, had its illustrious sees of Ephesus, Laodicea, Pergamos, Philadelphia, Thyatira, Tarsus, Mopsuesta, Smyrna, Iconium, Myra, Miletus, Antioch of Pisidia, Corinth, Nice, Chalcedon, etc. The isles of Crete, Cyprus, and the Archipelago, were filled with Christians. Armenia, and even Persia, in spite of the frequent persecutions which were directed against Christianity, counted numerous and flourishing churches. Egypt, evangelized by St. Mark, who founded the patriarchate of Alexandria, sent to the Council of Nice the bishops of Naucrates, Phtinontis, Pelusium, Panephysus, Memphis, and Heraclea. The Thebais, which was to be so fruitful in examples of sanctity, had, in the third century, as episcopal churches, Antinoe, Hermopolis, and Lycop-

olis. Ptolemais was the metropolis of the Pentapolis, which numbered many bishoprics.

4. Hence it is evident that the conquests of Christianity in the third century included all the countries of the known world. So rapid an extension has struck historians the most hostile to the Church. They have endeavored to explain the fact by causes purely natural. They have pretended that persecutions directed in the three first centuries against the faithful, were far from having the characters of universality, perseverance and cruelty which we have attributed to them. This last objection, once the watchword of the philosophy of the eighteenth century, will now obtain no credence among enlightened minds. The facts are too palpable, too numerous, too well established by evidence, to be contradicted in so flagrant a manner. To an impartial observer, the propagation of Christianity in the midst of a society where, during three hundred years, the name of Christian was a capital crime, can only be explained by admitting the divinity of its doctrine and mission. Every thing, in fact, was opposed to its diffusion. Polytheism, rooted in the manners, habits, belief, literature, legislation, public and private life, disposed of all power, rallied all sympathies, commanded respect and imposed submission. Despite its moral weakness and the incredulity of the educated classes, it is not the less a fact, that in the early times of the Church the great mass of the people were bound by an old hereditary attachment to the worship of idols. The Gospel had not only to combat the strong impressions of youth, the polytheistic education and prejudices imbibed with the mother's first teachings, but polytheism itself was regarded as the primitive religion, whose origin was concealed in the night of time; under whose protecting influences were formed the families and foundations of empires. In the Roman world, the worship of the gods, and the institutions that belonged to it, were bound by the closest ties to the system of the state, and bore, in the highest degree, a political character. The centre of the empire, the city on the seven hills, was herself the

object of religious worship. The belief in the divinities of the empire was so identified with the sentiment of patriotism, that it seemed impossible to abandon one without violating the other. To attack traditions consolidated by the laws of many ages, confirmed by the victorious majesty and the universal domination of Rome, was high treason—was to shake the very foundations of the state—was to be the declared enemy of the commonwealth. Such was the manner of thinking, deeply rooted and everywhere accepted, against which, as against a wall of brass, it would seem that all the efforts of the evangelic messengers must have been annihilated. To these external obstacles, others were joined arising from the intrinsic severity of Christian morals, the austerity of its dogmas, and the mystery that enveloped its worship. He who sincerely embraced the faith of Jesus Christ at this epoch, virtually banished himself from civil life and from the whole world, such as paganism had made it. He could take no part in the public ceremonies, all being placed under the invocation of the gods; nor in the theatres; nor in the favorite games of the people; nor in the bloody combats of the gladiators. He was excluded from the festivals and joyous solemnities where the emperor distributed the flesh of the victims; he was excluded from the repasts of families or of societies, all preceded by libations to idols. The Christian life, therefore, appeared to the pagans as an unsocial spirit of isolation, indicating a hatred of society. From the little that is known of the kind of frenzy with which the people rushed to the representations of the circus, and to the conflicts of the arena, there is no difficulty in understanding Tertullian, who said: "The idea of being obliged to renounce the pleasures, the sensualities, the passions of the world, deters more from Christianity than the fear of being condemned to death for having embraced it." The dogma of the unity of God, openly professed by the faithful, and falsely interpreted by the pagans, caused them to be held as contemners of all religion, and even atheists. The pagans were the more disposed to entertain this accusation, as the Christians never disguised their contempt for all that, according to idolatrous ideas, was an expression of worship, and nothing analogous was remarked among them. For these reasons, the apparition of Christianity excited the popular hatred as if against an *impious sect* without gods, without temples, and without altars. Imbued with the opinion that Christians were atheists, and that these men, over whom hovered the wrath of heaven, ought to be extirpated, the multitude cried with one voice to the magistrates and governors, Αἶρε τοὺς ἀθέους (exterminate the atheists)! The more the Christians were obliged to hold their assemblies in secret, and in the night, the greater was the facility of the pagans in receiving the calumny, spread abroad at an early period, that they committed in these assemblies horrible crimes against nature. A child, covered with flour, they said, was offered to the neophyte who was to be initiated; he, unconscious of what he did, pierced it with a knife; the blood of the murdered infant was received in a cup; the members partook of it as food; and they were thus united by the ties of a common sacrifice. This horrible feast, they averred, was followed by indescribable scenes of orgies and of incests. The accusation of anthropophagy had its birth, as we have already remarked,* in the disfigured pagan ideas of the Eucharist. The kiss of peace, which the Christians gave each other before the breaking of bread—the name of *agape* (charity), consecrated for the common repast that followed the assemblies—were the innocent origin of the frightful calumnies of incest and unnatural crimes. At a later period, as we have remarked, the striking dissoluteness of the Gnostics seemed to authorize the pagans in extending to the Christian religion, as a whole, the charge of atrocities which were perpetrated only by sects repudiated by all the faithful. In thus bringing together all the motives for the hatred of paganism against the Church, we can easily account for the general explosion of ven-

---

* We may be permitted to remark, on this subject, that these calumnies are an irrefragable proof of the faith of the earliest Christians in the Real Presence, and transubstantiation, now denied by the Protestant sects.

geance, of persecution, of cruelty, which ensanguined the three first centuries. What the emperors proscribed from policy was the object of popular execration. Never did any sentiment of indignation against the torrents of blood, the gratuitous tortures, the unheard of torments inflicted on the Christians, burst forth from the multitude, who, on the contrary, rejoiced to witness the death of the enemies of the gods and of men.

5. To struggle against all the obstacles which the united interests, passions, prejudices, habits, and superstitions of men opposed to her, the Church employed no other arms than the simple power of her doctrines which gained converts even from the midst of her tormentors. The exemplary life of the Christians, the calm of their conscience, their contempt of all that were the chosen objects of life to other men, the ardor with which they hastened to death as to a better and more enduring life, produced deep impressions on minds moulded by paganism to effeminacy, sensuality, and exaggerated enjoyment of luxury. They felt, in spite of themselves, that there was in this doctrine a strength of spiritual regeneration, and, as it were, re-establishment of human dignity. The zeal of the Christians to propagate the faith which they had themselves received, as a supreme good which they were in haste to share with their brethren, contrasted also with the cold indifference of paganism. "Most of these apostolic disciples," said Eusebius, "as soon as they were initiated in the Christian life, wandered over the most distant lands to make known the name of Jesus Christ, and everywhere they spread the Holy Gospel. Thousands of pagans who heard their discourses opened their hearts at once to the adoration of the true God." Immovable in their attachment to their faith, threats, torments, the view of death under the most hideous form only inflamed their courage. "Man is of God only, not of the emperor," they said with Tertullian. Strangers to all human fear, they replied by a tranquil refusal of obedience to each attempt of the State over their life as Christians, and

declared they had no orders to follow in this matter but those of God and His Church. The principal means employed to annihilate the new faith, persecutions and tortures, produced a diametrically opposite effect. "As the fruitful branches of the vine are often cut away," said St. Justin, "to produce stronger and more abundant buds, so the pagans, without intending it, use the same treatment with us; for Christianity is a vine planted by God the Father and Jesus Christ the Saviour." In presence of such a spectacle those of the pagans who were not quite deprived of their senses, nor completely blinded, began to suspect that it was something more than an illusion which raised so many persons of both sexes, and of all ages, above ordinary weakness, and inspired them with invincible constancy. Often, too, this joyous contempt of death and suffering made a powerful impression on some of the spectators, and a spontaneous conversion was the consequence.

6. It was especially by the sword that paganism strove to destroy the religion of Jesus Christ; yet the pagan writers and philosophers undertook, on their part, the task of ruining, in the opinion of men, a doctrine which the emperors and magistrates sought to extinguish in blood. Lucian was conspicuous in this unworthy strife, which he carried on with the weapons of sarcasm and irony that were peculiar to him. This superficial scoffer, a contemporary of the two Emperors Antoninus, was, by his Epicurean opinions, the enemy of all religion, under whatever form it might appear. As a consequence he saw in Christianity only one of the innumerable phases of human folly, on which he poured the gall of his mockery. In his picture of Peregrine Proteus, he introduces this impostor as connected with the Christians, and takes occasion to recount, in a satirical tone, whatever he knows of the disciples of the Gospel. "These poor people," he says, "imagine themselves immortal, soul and body; consequently they hold death in contempt, and many among them offer to meet it voluntarily. Their first legislator has persuaded them that they are all brethren as soon as they deny the Hellenic gods and adore

their crucified sophist. They equally despise every thing else, regarding their property as common, and by this credulity become an easy prey to the first artful impostor, who can soon make his fortune among men of so little sense." Lucian, as it is evident, had lent only a very fugitive attention to the new faith, and suspected nothing of its importance. His friend Celsus, the philosopher, was the first who wrote a work especially directed against Christianity. This volume, entitled *Discourse of Truth*, of which we can only judge by the refutation of it by Origen, includes all the popular calumnies against Christianity and its author. Christians, according to him, were a body of recent growth, who revolted from the Jews. Jesus Christ, born of a vicious mother, educated in Egypt in the occult sciences of the hierophants, gathered around him by magic arts twelve miserable fishermen. The prodigies which occupied his life were mere enchantments and impostures. His doctrine, an absurd mixture of old Jewish traditions, joined to some moral precepts long before professed by Greek philosophers, cannot sustain the examination of enlightened or serious minds. The adepts of this new doctrine find recruits among the vilest and the most ignorant. "There are," he said, "in many private houses coarse and ignorant men, woolen manufacturers, weavers, etc., who say nothing before the elders or fathers of the family. But if they meet in some secluded place a few children or women, they indoctrinate them, telling them that they must not listen to their fathers and teachers, because they have narrow minds, incapable of relishing the truth. They thus induce the children to shake off the yoke of parental authority, engage them to go to some subterranean den, or perhaps to the shop of a fuller or shoemaker, to hear the doctors of the new science and learn what is perfection. To their other follies," he adds, "they unite the absurd pretension of seeing some day their superstition become the faith of all the world. But what man of sense would suppose it possible that all the people in the world, Greek and barbarian, would ever submit themselves to one and the same belief—to one and the same worship?" Yet that which seemed an impossibility to the pagan writer became not the less a prominent and recognised fact, and his testimony brings into a stronger light the triumph of the Gospel over all impossibilities and all obstacles. Porphyry, born at Bactanea, in Syria (A. D. 233), a disciple of Plotinus, and, without contradiction, the first pagan philosopher of his time, followed in the footsteps of Celsus. He wrote, in Sicily, fifteen books against Christianity, which were dignified by the pagans with the surname of divine. The most distinguished of the doctors, Methodius, Apollinaris, Eusebius, refuted him; unfortunately these refutations are all lost, with the work itself, of which, however, we can discover the plan by the passages occasionally quoted by the Fathers. Porphyry directed his attacks particularly against these books of the Old and New Testament, in which he hoped to find contradictions, absurdities, improbabilities, or impossibilities. He applied himself with uncommon zeal to combat the prophecies of Daniel, which he asserts were not written until after the events that they announce. We give place to some of his other objections: "Jesus Christ called himself the son of God; yet he destroyed the sacrifices of the ancient law which had been established by God. God could not thus condemn himself. There is no proportion between the sin committed in time, and eternal chastisement. Therefore, the Christian law which sanctions eternal punishment is a monstrous law. If the Christ is the only way of salvation, as the faithful pretend, why did he come so late?" The miracles wrought at the martyrs' tombs were, in the view of Porphyry, only magical enchantments or demoniac illusions. The question of miracles was that which most embarrassed the philosophers in their hostile arguments. It is remarkable that not one of them attempts to deny them. All their efforts tend to explain them in a manner more or less ingenious, but never to doubt them. Jamblicus, born at Chalcis, in Celosyria, towards the end of the third century, a neoplatonic philosopher of the school of Porphyry, turned all the resources of his mind to discover a satisfactory solution of this difficulty. His *Life of Pythagoras* is still extant, in which he teaches the means of communicating with the divinity or with demons, and pretends to have found the secret of working miracles. In this work Pythagoras is represented as a thaumaturgus as powerful as Jesus Christ, who arrived at this marvellous knowledge by his acquaintance with the theurgic mysteries. But the most audacious attempt of this kind was hazarded by the rhetorician of Lemnos, Philostratus, under the reign of Septimius Severus (A. D. 196–211) in his *Biography* of Apollonius of Thyana. We can conceive that to a certain point, the name of Pythagoras, already surrounded in the shadow of ages with a mythic aureola, could have been brought forward by Jamblicus for the admiration of a distant age, when it was hardly possible to verify the fables which might be attached to his memory. But Apollonius of Thyana died in the year 97 of the Christian era, and the remembrance of his impostures was still recent among an almost contemporary generation. However this may be, the hero of Philostratus appears in this apotheosis as a manifestation of the divinity on earth strewing prodigies along his path, commanding the elements, seeing through distant space, holding converse with spirits, predicting the future, and relating it, not with the conciseness of a prophet, but with the details of an historian. After numerous adventures, and peregrinations worthy of the Odyssey, he is accused, before Domitian, by one of his disciples, the covetous Euphrates. Without being discomposed on account of the danger that awaits him, he goes to Rome, predicts his death, and at the hour of peril is abandoned by his friends. Horribly tortured by order of Domitian, he is left for dead; and afterwards, appearing to one of his friends, he desires him to touch him, to convince himself that he is yet living, and is not a shade come from hell. Such is the gospel of this Messiah of Philostratus. The philosophers of the eighteenth century endeavored, in their turn, to exhume his memory, and to oppose him to the divinity of Jesus Christ. But if Philostratus told the truth, why did not the world adore Apollonius of Thyana? Or, if Philostratus has written only fables, why awaken from the sleep of ages the name of an impostor who had not the ability to find a single disciple to survive him? Hierocles, the governor of Bithynia under Dioclesian, whose furious pursuit of the faithful in the tenth persecution we have already remarked, was careful not to omit Apollonius of Thyana in his hypocritical *Discourse of Truth addressed to the Disciples of Jesus Christ.* "The Christians," he said, "boast always that their Jesus restored sight to several blind persons, and did other similar things; but we possess many distinguished men, to whom, with much more justice, we attribute equal and greater miracles; for, besides Aristeus and Pythagoras, Apollonius of Thyana has accomplished great and wonderful things. Added to this, these doings of Jesus have been reported by Peter and Paul, and other men of their class, jugglers and gross impostors; while the purest motives have actuated men the most enlightened, friends of truth, such as Maximus, Damis, and Philostratus, to signalize the actions of Apollonius." We should regard only the silliness of such expressions, if history did not show us the hand that traced them, covered with the blood of the many noble victims whose faith Hierocles insulted while he held the sword raised above their heads.

7. Contemporaneously with the first pagan edict against the Christians, these began on their side to publish apologies, intended either to inspire the emperors and governors with kinder feelings towards the faithful, or to imbue cultivated minds with more correct notions of a religion so despised and misunderstood, or, in fine, to unveil the vulnerable parts of polytheism, and to justify the disciples of the new faith in their separation from the religion of the state. The first works of this kind presented (A. D. 131) to the emperor Adrian, by Quadratus and Aristides, are lost, as also those of Miltiades, Apollinaris of Hieropolis, and Melito of Sardis. We have mentioned, at their date, the apologies of St. Justin,

Tatian, Tertullian, Clement of Alexandria, and Origen. All the objections of philosophy—all the sophisms and prejudices of polytheism are completely refuted in these works. The truth is vindicated from all calumnies, explained with candor supported by facts, and disengaged from the mists with which passion and ignorance sought to obscure it.

8. It was not from exterior attacks only that the Church was obliged to defend herself. Scarcely organized, adversaries had arisen from her own bosom, so much the more dangerous as they used against her weapons which they might be said to have borrowed from herself. In treating of the heresies, we have remarked the diversity of their characters. Arising at first from the spirit of Judaism, which would have implanted its usages upon the doctrine of the Gospel and survive its defeat by imposing itself on its conqueror, they brought up, at first, only questions of ceremonial. Such are the errors of Cerinthus and Ebion. Paganism, also, essayed an irruption. It brought forth various Gnostic sects, which, from Simon the Magician to Valentinus, multiplied themselves under many forms, of which we have already given a recapitulation so explicit that we need not again return to them. The strength of Gnosticism soon became exhausted, and towards the close of the third century it disappeared. Manicheism, which renewed some of its errors, succeeded it. The dualism of principles, the antagonism between matter and spirit, form the basis of the Manichean doctrine, which finally loses itself in the vast abyss of Pantheism. To accommodate this importation of the religious system of India to the genius of the West, Manes attempted to unite with it a series of emanations, which connected his heresy with Gnosticism. Africa was the first infested by the errors of Manes, which were diffused with great rapidity throughout the empire. In A. D. 296, the Emperor Dioclesian enacted a law of great severity against the Manichees. As they came from Persia, the enemy of Rome, and founded a dangerous sect which gave reason to fear the introduction of the abominable usages and incestuous laws of

the Persians into the empire, the law ordained that their chiefs should be burnt, the others beheaded, and those of a more distinguished rank, after having been despoiled of their goods, should be transported to the mines. Exposed to these terrible edicts, Manicheism, was soon destined to appear, preserving only isolated sectaries, without union or body of doctrine, and without communication among its members. It is given to truth alone to achieve an open triumph in the arena of bloody persecutions. Dioclesian published against the Catholic faith edicts still more cruel than those against the Manichees. Catholicity came forth conqueror from a conflict in which Manicheism sunk irretrievably Besides the greater forms of heresy which have been mentioned, there arose, during the earliest times of the Church, sects which did not attack the whole of her doctrines, but only particular dogmas. Those of the Trinity, the Incarnation, the Redemption, were most frequently called in question by the heresiarchs of the first ages, under various forms and titles. Some, actuated by dispositions radically antichristian, denied the divinity of the Redeemer, and by this, the Redemption itself. Against these, the Church defended the divinity of Jesus Christ, as she had defended His humanity in opposition to the Gnostics. Others taught a union of the divinity with Jesus Christ, rejecting the distinction of persons, and professing to acknowledge, in the names of the Father, Son, and Holy Ghost, the various aspects of only one divine person; they maintained that the *Word* which was united to Christ, was that only God Himself, or the Father. We have in their time signalized the names and tendencies of each of these heretics. Their generation, beginning with Praxeas, and ending, in the fourth century, with Arius, continued, during this interval, to renew their various attacks, which all, in the last analysis, arrived at the same point—the negation of the divinity of Jesus Christ. That no manner of attack on the rising Church should be wanting, and that, by repelling all, she should better prove the measure of divine strength that sustained her, the long and obstinate schisms of

Felicissimus, Novatus, Novatian, etc., raised up new embarrassments and dangers. In these conflicts with their numerous antagonists, the Fathers and doctors appealed unceasingly to tradition as the infallible rule of faith. The Catholic doctrine being a revealed doctrine, it belongs to no human mind to remake it according to the sense of its own inspirations. It is, and it must remain, what it has always been. Any one, at any time, without entering into the details of controversy, can distinguish the true faith from the false and arbitrary systems of heretics, by interrogating this general and infallible rule of Catholic tradition, which condemns in advance all new systems bearing the name of man. All the Fathers appealed to this tradition, the living Gospel completing the written Gospel. They show the necessity of relying on the Church, and her alone, under pain of floating at random, among human opinions, *with every wind of doctrine;* and this demonstration sufficed to guard the faithful from the dangers of dissenting propagators. But they did not confine themselves to this general refutation, and we have seen that each particular error met, in the writings of the Catholic doctors, learned and courageous adversaries.

9. The government of the Church, founded on the principle of unity in the supremacy of the Roman pontiffs, perpetuated by an always living hierarchy, presented an insurmountable obstacle to the invasions of error. We have shown, as early as the close of the first century, the incessant and powerful action of this visible authority—the true rock against which *the gates of hell can never prevail.* To consecrate the succession of the pontiffs by durable monuments, it was an established custom, in the first epoch, to inscribe the names of the bishops of each church on tables, which were called sacred diptychs. The succession of the principal sees was thus known, and they could thus be proved to have descended, by a living and not interrupted chain, from apostolic origin—the source of truth. Discipline, in drawing closer its bonds, aided in the maintenance of faith and the integrity of doctrine. Rules were fixed

for the admission of neophytes into the Church. The catechumens, to whom the most illustrious doctors, such as Clement of Alexandria, Origen, etc., did not disdain to teach the rudiments of Christianity, were admitted to baptism only after a serious and searching examination. Before the period appointed for solemn baptism they were required to pass some days in retreat, fasting, and prayer, and the faithful joined them in their holy exercises. The place of assembly during the season of persecution was, at Rome, in the catacombs, and in other cities, in isolated private houses, or subterranean places, where they met in secret, from fear of the pagans. The singing of hymns and canticles, reading the books of the Apostles and Prophets, or letters addressed to the churches by some holy bishop, and a lively and touching exhortation or homily on some passage of Scripture, usually accompanied the celebration of the holy mysteries. After the consecration of the bread and wine, the deacons distributed them to those present, and carried them to the absent. The custom was also introduced among the faithful to send them common bread which had been served for the agapæ, and had received only an ordinary benediction. This kind of message was named *Eulogy*, and, under the emblem of the bread, in which all participated, signified the union in the same faith and hope in the same life. The custom of blessing bread on Sundays in our churches,* besides reminding all present of the propriety of communicating in the body and blood of our Lord Jesus Christ, belongs also to the primitive traditions of the *Eulogies*. The use of lights in churches, during the divine service, seems to have originated in the necessity for the Christians in the earliest ages to meet often during the night, or in dark places. Most probably, this usage would have been perpetuated, even without necessity, in memory of the Jewish tradition of the golden candlesticks and lamps which burned constantly before the tabernacle. During the intervals of persecution, the Christians

---

* This custom prevails chiefly in France.

profited by the momentary peace to construct churches and basilicas, where they held their assemblies. The persecutions of Maximinus destroyed a multitude of these holy places thus raised by the piety of the faithful. Afterwards, in proportion as paganism abandoned its temples, the Christians purified them and inaugurated there the worship of the true God. The form of these primitive monuments of the rising Church was naturally modelled according to the rules of Roman architecture. The religious archeologists of modern times have carefully studied the modifications which different epochs and the influence of varying climates have produced on the construction of churches. In the three first centuries the principal parts of each basilica were the *atrium*, vestibule, where the catechumens, the penitents, and the neophytes were placed, who had not the right to approach nearer to the celebration of the mysteries, and whom the deacons notified to withdraw from the interior of the temple at the solemn moment; the *baptistery*, with its sacred piscinæ, where baptism was conferred by immersion; ordinarily, there were two piscinæ, one for men, the other for women, for the baptism of whom recourse was had to deaconesses—the *interior* of the basilica separated by a large screen into two distinct parts, for men and for women; finally, the *sacrarium*, sanctuary, so arranged that the seat of the bishop being placed nearest the altar, the other ministers were placed, in their hierarchical order, nearer to the people. Between the *sacrarium* and the interior of the church a sort of *ambo* or tribune placed the preacher in a position to be heard by the men and women at the same time. Most of the basilicas of the third century were disposed in this manner. The holy mysteries were always offered on an altar inclosing the bodies of martyrs. In the catacombs the tombs of the saints served for altars. From this pious practice arose the custom of inserting relics in the consecrated stones on which repose, during the sacrifice of the Mass, the body and blood of our Lord Jesus Christ. The Church, attentive to the preservation of the mortal remains of her children, destined one day to rise in glory, consecrated, from the earliest period, places separate from the pagan depositories to inter her dead. Tertullian mentions these κοιμητήρια,* cemeteries where the bodies of the just repose in the sleep of death, awaiting the hour of resurrection. The tombs of the faithful were often covered with paintings and sculptures illustrative of their faith.† St. Cyprian recommends to the faithful of Carthage to offer prayers for the dead as a holy and charitable office. Thus, in the three first centuries, we find in operation all the Christian institutions which Protestants have rejected as recent innovations.

Public penance was fixed by the canonical rules established by minor councils. This we have had frequent occasion to remark. These rules were not so invariable but that they might be subjected to modifications required by the difference of times and the particular usage of churches. They who were placed under public penance, presented themselves, on the first day of Lent, at the door of the church, in a mourning dress; the prelate put ashes on their heads, and gave them a haircloth to put on; they then prostrated themselves while prayers were offered in their behalf. At the end of the prayers, the prelate made them an exhortation; after which they were led to the door of the church, which was closed upon them. These penitents came, on festivals, to the door of the basilica, and remained there during the offices. After a certain time they were admitted to hear the instructions, but were obliged to go out before the prayers of the consecration. At a later period they were admitted to the prayers, but prostrate. Finally, they were allowed to pray standing, like the others, only with the difference that they were placed on the left side in the church. These four orders of penitents were known by the names of the weepers (*plorantes*), hearers (*auditores*), the prostrate (*prostrati*), and *standers* (*consistentes*.)

---

* From κοιμάν, to sleep.
† See *Rome Souterraine*, and the work of M. Raoul Rochette, Sur les Catacombes.

Such was, in her dogma, hierarchy and discipline, the Church, against which the powers of Roman magistrates and governors were as naught. She had an interior and divine life which neither the sword of the executioner, nor popular hatred, nor the captious arguments of the philosophers, nor the shackles of a hostile legislation could reach. Like Jesus Christ rising from the sealed tomb, the Church was to rise victorious over every obstacle, every enemy, to reign at last over the world.

SECOND PERIOD

OF

THE HISTORY OF THE CHURCH

From A. D. 314 to A. D. 476.

CHAPTER I.

§ I. PONTIFICATE OF ST. SYLVESTER I. (Jan. 31, A. D. 314—Dec. 31, 335).

1. Second period of ecclesiastical history.—2. Election of Pope St. Sylvester.—3. Lactantius. His works.—4. Eusebius of Cæsarea. His works.—5. Solitaries. St. Anthony, St. Ammon, St. Pacomius, St. Hilarion, Fathers of the Desert.—6. Council of Arles against the Donatists.—7. Councils of Ancyra, in Galatia, of Neocæsarea, in Pontus, and of Gangres, in Bithynia.—8. Christian legislation of Constantine.—9. Cruelties of Constantine.—10. Reaction against Christianity. Persecution of Licinius. Martyrs.—11. War between Constantine and Licinius. Defeat and death of Licinius. 12. Antecedents of Arius.—13. Heresy of Arius.—14. Council of Alexandria against Arius.—15. St. Athanasius, deacon of Alexandria.—16. League of Arius and Eusebius of Nicomedia. Composition of the Thalia.—17. Letters of the Patriarch St. Alexander against Arianism.—18. Intervention of Constantine in the affairs of Arianism.—19. First œcumenical council at Nice, in Bithynia (A. D. 325).—20. Opening of the council.—21. Public sitting of the Council of Nice.—22. Profession of faith known as the Nicene Creed.—23. Quartodecimans. Question of Easter judged by the Council of Nice.—24. Affair of the Meletians treated by this council.—25. Canons of discipline of the Council of Nice, or *Apostolic Canons*.—26. Hierarchic authority of the patriarchs regulated by the Council of Nice.—27. Election and ordination of bishops and priests.—28. Celibacy of the clergy.—29. Rules for the reconciliation of heretics, schismatics, and *lapsi*.—30. Ecclesiastical discipline relative to marriage regulated by the apostolic canons.—31. Close of the Council of Nice.—32. Deposition of Eusebius of Nicomedia, and Theogni of Nice, by the Council of Alexandria.—33. Foundation of churches and pious donations of Constantine.—34. Discovery of the true cross by St. Helena, mother of Constantine.—35. Progress of the faith beyond the limits of the Roman empire.—36. Foundation of

Constantinople.—37. St. Athanasius, patriarch of Alexandria. Intrigues of the Eusebians against St. Eustathius, patriarch of Antioch.—38. Arius is prevented by the resistance of St. Athanasius from entering Alexandria. St. Anthony at Alexandria.—39. Arian Council of Tyre against St. Athanasius. —40. Exile of St. Athanasius to Treves by the Emperor Constantine.— 41. Dedication of the church of Jerusalem (Sept. 13, A. D. 335).—42. Death of Pope St. Sylvester (Dec. 31, A. D. 335).

§ 1. St. Sylvester I., Pope (Jan. 31, A. D. 314—Dec. 31, 335).

1. The first period had been as a baptism of blood to the Church. All the strength of a society powerful by its victories —by the splendor of a civilization which reached its highest point in the Augustan age—by the glories of eloquence, poetry, and the arts—all were combined against the religion of Jesus Christ. The struggle, prolonged through three centuries, ended to the advantage of the Church, which, with Constantine, was elevated upon the throne of the Cæsars. It was the commencement of a new era. To the combats with tormentors succeeded combats against errors, false doctrines, heresies. The right of the Church to live was no longer disputed; her possession of the truth will now be contested. Attempts will be made to corrupt the integrity of her dogmas, the purity of her faith, the legitimacy of her divine traditions. Error will rally round herself minds turned astray, but powerful by the seductions of eloquence, and even entire populations, and emperors, and kings. The Church will oppose them by the solemn decisions of her ecumenical councils, the lights and erudition of her doctors.

2. This new era opens with the election of St. Sylvester to the sovereign pontificate, January 31, A. D. 314. He was a Roman priest, the son of Rufinus and St. Justa. God called him to a tranquil pontificate, and the longest since that of St. Peter. The Emperor Constantine enriched the Church which Sylvester governed, with gifts of his imperial munificence. The pontiff addressed to the clergy various regulations appropriate to the new condition of things. Antiquity is

united in praise of their wisdom and importance, without reference to the special subjects of them. St. Sylvester is the first pope who has been represented as crowned with the tiara. This solemn ornament accorded well with the triumph of the Church; she had purchased the right to wear this crown by the blood of her martyrs.

3. The grand spectacle which the victory of the Church over paganism had just given the world, was well calculated to inspire the genius of Christian authors; they were naturally inclined to review the past, to analyze each phase of this heroic conflict, to develop the new principles which the Christian religion introduced into the world, and to record in its history each advance of the Church. Such is the character of the works of two illustrious writers of this epoch, Lactantius, and Eusebius of Cæsarea. Lactantius, who has been named the Christian Cicero, professed rhetoric at Nicomedia, when he was summoned by Constantine to preside over the education of the Cæsar Crispus, his eldest son. The instructions of such a master formed an accomplished prince. On a calumnious accusation of Fausta, his step-mother, Crispus was put to death, and left to Lactantius the sorrow of surviving a pupil worthy of him. The most celebrated work of Lactantius is that *On the Death of the Persecutors*. The tragic end of so many emperors who had shed the blood of Christians, was a subject to tempt the pen of an apologist. The divine justice, whose finger marks each page of his recital, must have made deep impressions on a generation who were contemporaries of these memorable facts. The logical sequence of his subject naturally led Lactantius to compose a second treatise on *The Wrath of God*, where he proves, against the stoic philosophers, that God is not indifferent to good and evil; that He has chastisements and vengeance for the wicked, as He has recompenses for the just. He especially develops the idea of an active and vigilant Providence in his book *Of the Works of God*. The Christian system of Providence is again explained in a work of more importance and extent, entitled, *The Divine*

Institutions, and divided into seven books: 1. Of false religion; 2. Of the origin of error; 3. Of false wisdom; 4. Of true wisdom; 5. Of justice; 6. Of true worship; 7. Of the life of the beatified. This immense work, which included the whole economy of religion, was abridged by the author himself. We have still this double work, that was intended to second the movement which then inclined the minds of men towards the study of Christianity, and responded to the wants of an epoch of transition between pagan errors and the light of the Gospel. The charm of the style of Lactantius, his harmonious and pure Latinity, which brought back the age of Augustus, contributed to disseminate his works and to win souls to the faith.

4. At the same time Eusebius, bishop of Cæsarea, published, in Greek, his great work of *Evangelic Preparation and Demonstration*. In the first part, he prepares the mind to believe the Gospel; in the second, he demonstrates its truth. He takes his reader from the midst of the shadows of paganism to lead him, as if by the hand, to the splendors of the true faith. In the *Preparation*, divided into fifteen books, he begins by refuting the fabulous theogony of the poets, the physico-allegorical theogony of the philosophers, and the political or legal theogony of the cities and provinces. When the moral world left its seat to seek support upon the foundation of evangelical doctrine, it was needful to prove the emptiness of the groundwork on which it had rested for so many ages. Having overthrown the errors of paganism, it remained to be shown how much the Jewish religion had served as an avenue and preparation to that of Jesus Christ. This is the object proposed by the bishop of Cæsarea in a lengthened and profound discussion on the books of Moses and the prophets, which embraced the twenty books of the *Evangelic Demonstration*, of which only the first ten are extant. At this point of view, the religion of Jesus Christ ceases to be a new religion in the world. It begins at the fall of Adam, which leads to the promise of a Saviour; it is perpetuated in the patri-

archs, in the exceptional existence of the Hebrew people, in
the hopes of the just, in the figures of the Old Testament, in
the inspired voice of the prophets, and is finally realized by
the coming of the Messiah, who fulfils all the prophecies,
verifies all the figures, crowns all the hopes, answers the
expectations of the Jews, the desire of the patriarchs, and
the promise of a Restorer of the human race, made by God
Himself in the infancy of the world. The scope of such a
work is evidently no less vast than magnificent, and was
equal to all the exigencies of the then existing polemics.
Eusebius here displays an immense erudition. His style is
simple and pure, clear and precise. The *Ecclesiastical History*
follows closely after the *Evangelic Demonstration*. It is less a
finished work, or history properly so called, than a collection
of historical pieces, of long extracts from ancient authors
whose works have been lost. The conduct of Eusebius of
Cæsarea, in the great question of Arianism, was not exempt
from reproach. Nor is the period of his history which touches
upon the facts of that heresy always as impartial as could be
wished. Apart from this defect, Eusebius rendered an eminent service in preserving to history the precious monuments
of the primitive Church. This work on the Christian religion
in the past may be regarded as the complement of his great
production of the *Preparation* and the *Evangelic Demonstration*.
Eusebius was an indefatigable historian. The better to include
all the great facts regarding the human race, and to connect
them with Christianity, which ascends from the Saviour, by
the prophets, Moses, and the patriarchs, to Adam, *who was of
God:* to unveil the providential designs over earthly empires,
which all meet in the divine and eternal empire of Jesus
Christ, he composed his *Chronicle*, or tables of universal history from the beginning of the world, year by year, to his
own time. It is the plan which, many ages later, Bossuet so
magnificently developed in his immortal masterpiece — the
Discours sur l'Histoire Universelle. Eusebius, in the compilation of his *Chronicle*, availed himself of the analogous labors of

Justin of Palestine, Clement of Alexandria, Tatian of Babylon, Theophilus of Antioch, and Julius Africanus, who had handled this subject before him.

5. While the doctors were employed in thus sustaining the Christian faith by their learning and eloquence, God multiplied in the desert a generation of pious hermits who made it still more respected by their miracles and the example of their virtues. Their inviolable attachment to the maxims and laws of the Church was destined, also, at a later period, to make their monasteries a secure defence against the seductions of heresy and error. Every halt made by St. Anthony in the rocky solitudes was marked by the foundation of a holy retreat, which the ardent piety of those happy ages had speedily filled. The holy patriarch had finally taken up his abode on Mount Colzim, afterwards named St. Anthony, a day's journey from the Red Sea. The animals of the desert respected his labors and the fields he had cultivated. God renewed for him the miracle of the rock of Moses, and caused springs of living water to burst forth under his feet. The sick came in crowds to be healed by his prayers. Pagan philosophers came to ask him questions, and carried away the treasure of true wisdom which they had found in the replies of this man, sublimely ignorant. Other solitudes were peopled by other saints. Ammon, of a noble and rich family, to gratify his parents, had just concluded an illustrious alliance. On the day of his marriage he read to his young bride the praises of St. Paul on the state of virginity, and persuaded her to live, by mutual agreement, in perfect continence. After eighteen years of this angelic life, the death of his parents permitted Ammon to retire to a mountain of Nitria, where, under the direction of St. Anthony, he passed twenty-two years in the practice of all the virtues, founded many monasteries, and closed in peace a career which heaven had blessed. The attraction to solitude exercised its influence in every rank of society. Some young soldiers, enrolled by force during the war between Maxentius and Constantine,

landed one day at Thebes, in Egypt. They were locked up like prisoners, and treated with excessive rigor. Unknown men visited them, embraced them as their children, and procured them all the comfort and consolation within their power. One of the soldiers inquired who these beneficent men were, and learned that they were Christians who lived in retreat, prayer, and the exercise of charity. The young soldier's name was Pacomius. The remembrance lived in his heart, and bore the fruit of salvation. When his military service was ended, he returned to the mountains of the Thebais to knock at the cell-door of the holy hermit Palemon. "Bread and salt are my only food," said the venerable man to him. "I pass half the night in singing psalms, or in meditation upon the Holy Scriptures." Pacomius, though really frightened at such austerities, replied: "I hope in our Lord Jesus Christ, that, sustained by your prayers, I shall persevere until death in this manner of life." He kept his word. After a novitiate of several years he accompanied Palemon to the vast desert of Tabenna, in the diocese of Tentyra or Denderah, and built several monasteries, to which he gave a rule, and which contained, before his death, seven thousand religious. Nearly at the same time Hilarion, of Gaza in Palestine, whose studious youth encouraged the most flattering hopes, having heard of St. Anthony, went to him, and under this great master learned the secrets of ascetic life. He quitted him, to avoid the considerable numbers who were every day attracted by the reputation of the holy patriarch, and, accompanied by several disciples, returned to inaugurate the solitary life in Palestine. His vestments were a sack, a tunic of skins, which St. Anthony had given him, and a peasant's cloak. Some dry figs, which he ate only after the going down of the sun, were his only food during six years. At a later period he increased his austerities. He labored with his hands, cultivating the soil, and weaving rush or wicker baskets, like the solitaries of Egypt. A little cell, constructed by himself, four feet wide, five in height—of course

lower than his own figure, but a little longer, for sleeping—
served for his dwelling, or rather tomb. Even to extreme
old age he rested on the hard ground, and then with extreme
regret consented to make use of a rush mat. The gift of miracles was, even in this world, the recompense of the holy
anchorite; and when the sick Syrians came to ask, at the feet
of St. Anthony, a remedy for their evils, "Why," he would
say, "have you fatigued yourselves to come so far, when you
have near you my son Hilarion?"

6. Meanwhile the council of Lateran, held by the Pope St.
Melchiades, against the Donatists, had not ended the controversy which ambitious bishops, unworthy of their august position, continued still more to embitter. The return of Donatus,
of *Casæ Nigræ*, to Carthage, had been for Cecilian, the Catholic
bishop, the signal to prepare for a persecution more violent and
angry than ever. The schismatics always maintained that the
ordination of Cecilian was null, because Felix of Aptonga, the
consecrating prelate, had been a traditor during the persecution. They pretended that this question had not been sufficiently examined at the council of Lateran, and demanded a
new judgment—refusing to be guided by the first—and again
addressed their complaints to Constantine. "What!" cried the
emperor, on receiving their demands, "they lodge appeals like
the pagans in their suits at law!" To satisfy them, he ordered
juridical information to be obtained by the proconsul of Africa
on the subject of the conduct of Felix of Aptonga during
the persecution. Felix was solemnly recognized as innocent,
and his principal accuser was convicted of having falsified a
public act to give some color to his calumny. This inquest
and the sentence that followed it did not satisfy the animosity
of the schismatics. Their complaints recommenced with the
same obstinacy. Constantine then sent them to a council
which was held at Arles, in Gaul, "not," said St. Augustine,
"that there was need of a new judgment, after that of the
council of Lateran, but to put an end to their importunities, and with the desire to rebuke their impudence." The

emperor assembled, at the expense of the public treasury, the bishops of Italy, Sicily, Africa, Gaul, Spain, and Great Britain. Pope St. Sylvester sent them four legates—two priests and two deacons. The sittings of the council opened August 1, A. D. 314. Cecilian, the accused bishop of Carthage, was there in person. His cause was once more examined. Two charges were laid against him: the first, that, as a simple deacon, during the persecution, he had gone, by order of the Bishop Mensurius, to the door of the prison, with whips and a troop of armed men, to prevent food from being conveyed to the martyrs therein confined; the second, already so often stated, that the prelates who had consecrated him, and particularly Felix of Aptonga, had been traditors. These two points, after full deliberation, were found entirely false. The innocence of Cecilian was proclaimed, his calumniators condemned. The fathers of Arles, having concluded this first and principal question, turned their attention to the framing of canons of discipline, which they sent to the pope, with a synodal letter prepared in the name of all the bishops present. We transcribe here the commencement of this letter, which is a valuable proof of the filial veneration of the ancient Church of Gaul for the Holy See.

"To the well-beloved Pope Sylvester: Marinus, Agrecius, etc., eternal greetings in the Lord. United together in the bonds of charity, in the unity of our holy mother the Catholic Church, assembled in the city of Arles by the desire of the most pious emperor, we salute you, most glorious pope, with the veneration which is your due. We have been called to struggle against turbulent men, who have no respect for the law and traditions of the Church. But by the authority of God, ever present, and by the inviolable rule of the the truth, they have been confounded. There was neither agreement nor solidity in their discourses, their accusations, or proofs. For this reason, in the name of God and the Church, our mother, they have been unanimously condemned And would to God, well-beloved brother, that you had judged it proper to assist at this grand scene: their condemnation would have been more solemn, and our joy more entire. But you cannot quit those places where the Apostles constantly preside, and where their blood continually gives glory to God."

The judgment of the council of Arles did not, more than that of Lateran, impose silence on the Donatists. They dared again to appeal to the emperor. Constantine, with a view of putting an end to this unceasing discussion, brought it before his *consistorium*, or private council. He summoned before him Cecilian and his accusers, heard both parties, listened to all the charges, made himself acquainted with the whole affair, and finally gave a sentence entirely conformable to that of the two councils; he declared Cecilian entirely innocent. The imperial decision had no better results than the decrees of the councils. When men have begun to substitute their views, their judgments, their personal passions, for the voice of authority, it is rare that they pause in this career. The Donatists pretended, this time, that the emperor had allowed himself to be biased by Osius of Cordova, who was favorable to the cause of Cecilian. If they had the right to invalidate his judgment, why had they invoked it? If they invoked it, why did they not yield to it? The logic of error is the same at all times; and the history of the Church will furnish us with many other proofs of the obstinacy of heretics, and their dexterity in creating pretexts to elude all decisions. Constantine, tired of their intrigues, finished by banishing the most seditious. But these rigorous measures against bishops whom he had been inclined to cherish, if they had been worthy of their exalted vocation, were repugnant to his character. He soon recalled them; but clemency towards them was not more successful than justice, and in the sequel we shall find that they filled Africa with murders and violence.

7. In the same year (A. D. 314) were held the councils of Ancyra, in Galatia, and Neocæsarea, in Pontus. The canons of discipline decreed in these councils, together with those of Arles (A. D. 314), Gangres (A. D. 324), and the œcumenical

council of Nice (A. D. 325), form, as a whole, the collection known as the *Apostolic Canons*. We shall analyze them with those of the council of Nice.

8. The influence of Christianity was diffused in the Roman world by means of these assemblies of bishops, where the people gradually habituated themselves to seek for the true principles of justice. Legislation lost its pagan harshness in contact with evangelical charity. Constantine admirably seconded this movement, so advantageous to religion and to civilization. By a law of A. D. 314, he ordained, under the most severe penalties, that any one having knowledge of persons unjustly held in servitude, should give notice thereof to the magistrates, by whom they should be immediately released. And he proclaimed the principle, eminently Christian, that even sixty years of bondage could not debar a man of his right to freedom. The great question of slavery, which then weighed upon half the human race, was worthy of the attention of a Christian emperor. The pagan laws had incumbered emancipation with formalities, which made it rare and difficult. To make it legal, the act had to be performed in the presence of prætors and consuls themselves. Constantine removed all these obstacles, by permitting the manumission of slaves in the Church, in presence of Christian people and the bishops, requiring no other formalities than a simple attestation, signed by the ministers of the Church (A. D. 316). He declared, by a subsequent law, that those who had been manumitted in this way, should enjoy all the rights of Roman citizens. The preceding year (A. D. 315) he had abolished the ancient and barbarous custom of branding on the forehead, with heated iron, those who had been condemned to the amphitheatre or the mines. "We forbid," he said, "that the face of man be thus dishonored, because it bears on it traces of the majesty of heaven." The same year he abolished the punishment of the cross, reserved until then for slaves. Since Jesus Christ had willed to die on it, and the cross had become the standard of the Roman legions, and the ornament

of the imperial crown, its ignominy had become glorious. Constantine published in all the cities of Italy, and caused to be engraved on brass, as if to make it perpetual, a law which withdrew from the father of a family the right to put to death the young infant which he would not or was unable to support. This legalized child-murder, which Rome had borrowed from Sparta, is, without contradiction, the greatest stain on pagan civilization. The emperor ordained that when a father would bring to the officers of finance a child which he could not maintain, they should draw either upon the public treasury or the imperial domain for a sum necessary to feed and clothe the infant, and without delay, because of the feebleness of the child. In A. D. 323, he enacted for Africa a law not less charitable, commanding the proconsuls, governors, and treasurers to give assistance to parents whom indigence obliged to sell their children. In A. D. 325, he interdicted the combats of gladiators. Under the Roman emperors, the standard of public morality was so low, that a shameful calculation had made it necessary to inflict fines and legal punishments upon those who lived in a state of celibacy! Christianity, which condemned licentiousness as a crime, which admits of only two conditions of life, marriage, or perfect continence, and which, at the same time, held virginity in honor, and sanctified the duties of the married, required a modification in the laws created for a state of things which disappeared as evangelical perfection was diffused on a larger scale. Constantine therefore abolished the law of Augustus on celibacy, which had an injurious effect on continence and virginity. To consecrate Christian usages, and to encourage their becoming general, a new law rendered obligatory the observance of Sunday throughout the empire. From the time of the Apostles, this first day of the week, the day of the resurrection of Jesus Christ, and of the descent of the Holy Spirit in the cenacle, had become the *Dies Dominica*, the Lord's Day. It was chiefly on this day that the catechumens received instructions, and that Jews and pagans were admitted to the public instructions of the Church. The decree of Constantine placed the observance of Sunday under the safeguard of the laws. The tribunals were closed, and ordinary labors interrupted. The only exception was in favor of agriculture, where the necessities are sometimes too urgent to admit of delay, and this exception is still consecrated by the discipline of the Church. The faithful interpreter of all Christian sentiments, the emperor did not practise against paganism the violence which paganism had not ceased, during three centuries, to inflict upon the religion of Jesus Christ. He respected in error the sort of right to which immemorial usage had entitled it, and enacted no edicts of proscription; but he prohibited the consecration of new idols. This law was accompanied by another, which ordained the restoration of churches injured during the persecution, and their augmentation or enlargement, or the erection of new buildings, more in proportion to the increase of the faithful. "We hope," he said, "that all our subjects will embrace the faith of the true God." He offered, from his own estates, the necessary expenses for these buildings, and desired that nothing should be spared to make them suitable to the dignity of the great God who was adored in them. All these ordinances were crowned by the law of June 23 (A. D. 318), which permitted parties to decline the jurisdiction of the magistrates, and to submit themselves to the judgment of the bishops. This was to inaugurate the magistracy of the pontiffs, whom we shall see become the judges of their people, as they were their pastors.

9. Such measures, dictated by eminent piety and wisdom, have obtained for Constantine the praises of all historians. Yet, astonishing as it may seem, he was not himself a Christian, though he sought to gain over all his empire to the religion of Jesus Christ. He received baptism only a few days before his death. This delay was to be regretted for his glory. By a strange contrast, but one which is not unique in the annals of mankind, this prince, whose administrative acts

bore so strong an imprint of humanity, whose morals, by the report of all his contemporaries, were chaste and pure, did not always in his conduct observe Christian moderation and gentleness. In his wars against the Franks, he sent his captives, even kings, more than once to be devoured by the beasts in the amphitheatre. This spectacle recalled the sanguinary gods of the Capitol—not the God of the Gospel. We shall see him put to death Licinius, his former colleague in the empire, contrary to his sworn faith; and afterwards, by a still more odious cruelty, sentence to the same fate the young Licinius, his own nephew, a child of eleven years of age. Eusebius of Cæsarea, the exaggerated panegyrist of the emperor, has not considered it his duty to mention these details. But history must be neither a satire nor a eulogy *a priori*; above all, and so far as human judgment will admit, it ought to be and to remain the truth. On the calumnious accusation of Fausta, his second wife, and without taking time for a mature examination of the facts, Constantine condemned to death the eldest of his own children, the worthy pupil of Lactantius, the Cæsar Crispus, at scarcely twenty-five years of age, and when he had just won the brilliant honors of a naval victory. Eusebius himself eulogizes him. He soon after discovered the innocence of the young prince, and that he had been the victim of the artifices of his step-mother. Fausta was then, by his order, suffocated in a vapor bath. Doubtless in these deplorable circumstances Constantine was more unfortunate than culpable. The Roman law which placed the children, the wife, the entire family at the discretion of its head, absolved him according to the laws then in force; but the law of the decemvirs was not the law of Jesus Christ, nor even that of humanity. The titles of eternity, of adoration, introduced into the etiquette of the imperial court by the pride of idolatrous princes, and the impious adulation of courtiers, were not abolished by Constantine. Vanity is the last sentiment that dies in the heart of men, and it requires all the power of the sacraments and the efficacy of grace to combat it with success. These facts, however we may regret them in the life of Constantine, must not make us oblivious of the glory which is due to him, for the wise and Christian institutions which he bestowed on the empire; and the writers who have undertaken to reflect the odium of these particular acts upon his entire reign have yielded too much to a spirit of depreciation, not less unjust and detestable than that of the most ultra panegyrist. In Constantine they especially assail the emperor who had been the first to elevate Christianity upon the throne.

10. The religious movement, favored by Constantine, wounded too many interests and prejudices not to give occasion for a reaction on the part of expiring paganism. Licinius, emperor of the East, put himself at the head of the retrograde movement. After publishing several edicts which attacked, though with a certain reserve, the religion of Jesus Christ, he proceeded to an open persecution, A. D. 319, removed all the Christians from his palace, and sent many into exile. He then commanded all public functionaries to sacrifice to the idols, under pain of removal. His cruelties were especially directed against the bishops, whom he hated, precisely because they were beloved by Constantine. Among his victims was St. Basil, bishop of Amasea, in Pontus, who was put to the torture. The other bishops of this province were not spared. The bodies of some of them were cut in pieces, and cast into the sea, as food for fishes. St. Blaise, bishop of Sebaste, in Armenia, after having had his flesh torn by iron combs, was beheaded, with two young Christian children. Seven women, detected in collecting drops of his blood, were also put to death. In the same city, forty Christian soldiers were exposed at night, naked, on a frozen pond. Near it was prepared a warm bath for those who would have the weakness to apostatize. Only one, renouncing the glory of martyrdom, came to plunge into the warm water, when he immediately expired. Meantime the guard, who watched at the place of execution, saw an angel descend from heaven, bearing forty crowns, but

only thirty-nine were found to receive them. Struck with this heavenly vision, the guard called the commander of the post, declared himself a Christian, laid aside his clothes, and joined the thirty-nine martyrs to obtain the fortieth crown. The following day the bodies were placed on a carriage to be conveyed to the pyre. One of them, the youngest, still breathed. The executioners left him, in the hope that he might change his resolution. But his mother took him in her arms, and laid him herself on the vehicle, saying, "Go, my son, finish with thy companions this happy journey, so that thou shalt not be the last to present thyself to God."

11. This persecution, added to certain political difficulties, brought about a decisive war between Licinius and Constantine. The preparations on both sides were immense. Constantine had a hundred and thirty thousand men, on sea and land; his son Crispus commanded the fleet. The forces of Licinius numbered nearly a hundred and seventy thousand. Constantine placed the *Labarum* at the head of his troops on their march. It was kept in a tent separated from the camp, where the emperor often retired for prayer. Licinius surrounded himself with diviners from Egypt, sacrificers, and soothsayers, who promised him victory in magnificent verses. The battle was fought July 3, A. D. 324, near Adrianople. Licinius, defeated, fled, leaving thirty-four thousand dead on the field. His fleet was destroyed in the waters of the Bosphorus, by Crispus. A second engagement took place under the walls of Chalcedon. The remainder of the army of Licinius was cut to pieces; with difficulty he escaped the sword of the conqueror, with three thousand men, and fled to inclose himself within the walls of Nicomedia, whither Constantine followed to besiege him, and, finally, reduced him to come as a suppliant to implore pardon. Constantine promised to spare his life, but within the same year he put him to death, with his son, the young Licinius, in contempt of his oath and solemn treaties. This event left Constantine sole master of the world,

and through him the Christian religion triumphed in the Roman empire.

12. Scarcely had the last hopes of paganism fallen in the East with Licinius, under the victorious arms of Constantine, when a new enemy, not less dangerous, arose in the bosom of the Church, against the Church herself. An error, which brought back idolatry under another name, and aimed at nothing else than to sap the very foundation of Christianity, spread over the great cities of the East, always eager in the pursuit of novelties, and passionately addicted to discussions and conflicts of ideas. The new heresy bore the name of its author, Arius, and owed its origin, like most of the errors which desolate the Church in all ages, to wounded pride and disappointed ambition. Arius, a priest of Alexandria, was born, like Sabellius, in Cyrenaic Libya. He was tall in stature, of an imposing form, a grave and serious demeanor, of affable manners, and of mild and agreeable conversation. His austere morals, his mortified exterior, an apparent zeal for religion, a rare talent for dialectics, fair acquirements, but superficial in profane and ecclesiastical science, served to conceal a depth of secret restlessness and unbounded ambition. At the time of the Meletian schism, Arius, not yet in orders, was one of the first to throw himself into it. But he soon drew back, was received into the communion of the Church, and ordained priest by the holy Patriarch Achillas, who confided to him the government of one of the principal churches of Alexandria, and even the public teaching of the sacred Scriptures. The vanity of Arius knew no limits; he aspired to the patriarchal seat of Alexandria. When, on the death of Achillas, the election of St. Alexander to the pontificate destroyed his hopes, he threw off all restraint. The morals of the new patriarch were unassailable; he therefore attempted to calumniate his doctrines, and did not hesitate, in the hope of success, to make a public profession of heresy.

13. St. Alexander, following the doctrine of the Gospel and the Apostles, taught that the Son of God is equal to His

Father, and of the same substance. The Greek word ὁμοούσιος, *consubstantial*, which categorically expresses the truth of the Christian dogma, had been employed by the two Saints Dionysius of Rome and Alexandria, and had already become a common expression. Arius pretended that this was the erroneous doctrine of Sabellius, that by it the personality of the Word was annihilated, and confounded with the Father. Under the pretext of a clearer distinction of the Persons, Arius maintained that the Son had been created—that He is not eternal; that He was taken out of nothingness; that of His free will He was capable of vice or virtue, equally with other men. Philosophically, the character of Arianism was the separation of the world from God. He laid down, as a first principle, that God is too great for the creature to bear His immediate action; too great to put Himself in immediate relations with that which is finite. Consequently, when God willed to create the world, He first formed the Word, to create all the rest by Him. In this system, it is evident, the Word is only a creature more distinguished and of a nature more sublime than others. He is not eternal, although He is anterior to the world; He is not even God, though the Arians give Him this name. The worship they pay to Him is merely idolatry under another form. All the heresies, thus pushed to their ultimate consequences, end in absurdity. Arius was careful to hide from his sectaries the logical consequences of his doctrine; the most simple minds would have revolted from them. When three ages had just avowed, by myriads of martyrs, their faith in the divinity of the Son of God, a Christian, a preacher, a priest, who directly opposed this faith, would have been ill received. The heresiarch, therefore, only insinuated that there were degrees in the Trinity, and that the Son, born of the Father, was less great, and less ancient than the Father.

14. At first, these errors were confined to the circle of private conversations. Arius in this way tried his strength in the *role* of heresiarch. He displayed all the resources of his

imagination and eloquence to mislead and seduce his auditors.
Finally, when he felt assured of the dispositions of the greater
number, when he saw himself surrounded, applauded, sustained, he dared the encounter of public discussion, and openly
preached his new doctrine in the pulpits of Alexandria. The
whole city flocked to hear his discourses. Christians learned
from him that the faith of their fathers was a fable, that Jesus
Christ was God only by participation. Arius willingly admitted that the Word had existed before all ages, because the
words of the Scriptures are explicit; but he maintained, at the
same time, that He was not co-eternal with God, and that His
existence had a *beginning*. These errors soon came to the
knowledge of St. Alexander, who, at first, endeavored to win
back the heresiarch by charitable warnings. His measures of
gentleness and conciliation failed before the obstinacy and
vanity of Arius. As his party increased from day to day, St.
Alexander, to arrest the progress of the evil, assembled his
clergy in two solemn conferences. Arius appeared before
them. The controverted points were discussed. The error
was opposed by Catholic tradition, the witness of the Scriptures, and the fathers. Arius refused to yield. Finally, the
patriarch, having exhausted all means of moderation, convoked
at Alexandria a council of nearly a hundred bishops of Egypt
and Libya. Arius having renewed his blasphemies before
them, was, with his principal adherents, excommunicated,
A. D. 320.

15. The Patriarch St. Alexander had with him, to aid in
the struggle with the Arians, a young deacon whose name will
soon become the rampart of the faith and the centre of
ecclesiastical history in the fourth century. This was Athanasius, who thus began, at the side of a holy and pious bishop,
his laborius career of apostle and doctor. Of a faith profound and immovable, a penetration which opened the most
intricate affairs to his vision, a prudence which the snares of
his enemies never found at fault, a logic which dissipated,
like cobwebs, the most astute sophisms, an eloquence which

made the most difficult questions comprehensible to ordinary minds, and a firmness which the entire world could not move, we shall see him in turn pass from triumph into exile—from the patriarchal chair of Alexandria to the deserts of the Thebais and the mountains of Nitria; the model of bishops and the admiration of anchorets, as admirable for his piety as for his knowledge, and always worthy of the hatred and persecutions of the enemies of the faith. The first part of his life was passed in ascetic exercises, under the direction of St. Anthony, to whom he was united by the ties of unalterable friendship. In this austere school he acquired the invincible courage, the persevering energy, which he exhibited against innumerable adversaries, bishops, priests, and emperors, triumphing at the same time, in discussion, by the clearness and precision of his logic, and in the written strife of polemics by the rapidity, the vehemence, the eloquence and vigor of his composition; in persecution, by his unconquerable boldness, and the unalterable tranquillity of his great soul. Such was St. Athanasius, whom we shall see, after half a century of toil, of exile, of constant wanderings, win the glory of uniting his name forever with the triumph of Catholic truth over Arianism.

16. On quitting Alexandria, after his condemnation by the council, Arius complained that he owed this treatment only to the influence of the deacon Athanasius. It was known that the patriarch had the most entire confidence in him, and admitted him to all his counsels. The heresiarch retired into Palestine, where he spared nothing to gain new partisans. He had the address to draw to his party several bishops, the most influential of whom was Eusebius of Nicomedia, his ancient associate. This prelate belonged to that class mentioned in the Gospel, who do not enter the fold by the door, and who, like the hireling, betray the interests of the flock. He was suspected of having apostatized during the persecution. He afterwards became, no one knew how, bishop of Berytus in Phœnicia. An adroit courtier, he had succeeded in

gaining the good graces of the princess Constantia, sister of Constantine, and wife of Licinius. The metropolitan bishopric of Nicomedia becoming vacant, Eusebius, who measured the episcopal dignity by the greatness of its seat, left the little city of Berytus, without any canonical authorization, for the imperial city of Nicomedia. When Licinius, whose residence was in this latter capital, made war at the same time against the Christians and Constantine, Eusebius was the confidential friend of Licinius. But when Constantine was victor, he was among the first to bow for the favor of Constantine. His was one of those servile dispositions which follow every car of triumph, and which all conquerors find in their train—a miserable spoil, which should be cast off as worthless; but such men know how to make themselves necessary by flattering the vanity of the new master, and placing at his command a devotion which, on the first change, will be offered with equal hypocrisy to his successor. Eusebius was thus a worthy patron for an heresiarch. The following letter was addressed to him by Arius, from his retreat in Palestine. We transcribe it, because it clearly explains his heresy.

"To the much esteemed lord—to the man of God, the faithful, orthodox Eusebius, Arius, unjustly persecuted by the Patriarch Alexander, for the victorious truth which you yourself defend, health and benediction in the Lord. My father Ammonius is setting out for Nicomedia, and I have thought it my duty to take this occasion to salute you, and at the same time to inform your charity of the persecution to which we are unjustly subjected by the bishop. He has excited every one against us, and drives us as reprobates from his imperial city. Our only crime is the refusal to adhere to his erroneous doctrine and to say with him, God is eternal; the Son is eternal: the Father and the Son have always coexisted. The Son is from eternity, always begotten. The Father does not precede the Son a moment, not even in thought. God always, the Son always; the Son proceeds from God. Because Eusebius of Cæsarea, your brother, Theodotus, Paulinus, Athanasius, Gregory, Aetius,* according to the faith of all the Orientals, maintain that God is anterior to the Son, they have been anathematized. There have been excepted from this excommunication only Philogonus, Hellanicus, and Macarius, those ignorant heretics who pretend that the Son is, some say, an expiration or breath, the others a projection from the Father. These are so many impieties, which we cannot admit, even if these heretics threatened us with a thousand deaths. For us, that which we profess and believe, we have taught, and we continue to teach. By the will and the counsel of the Father, the Word subsisted before all time and before all ages, in fulness God, only Son unchangeable. But before being begotten or created, He had no existence. We are persecuted for having declared, 'The Son has a beginning, and God has not.' They are violent against us for maintaining that the Word is taken from nothing, which we have said because He is neither a part of God, nor derived from any creature. Behold the cause of our sufferings: you know the rest. I wish you all prosperity in the Lord. Remember us in our afflictions." Eusebius of Nicomedia replied to this letter with the assurance of his entire adhesion to the principles it contained. "Your sentiments are good, and you ought to wish to see them universally adopted. Who can believe that that which has been created could have being before having received it? Must it not first have begun to be?" Not satisfied with giving this encouragement to the heresiarch, he wrote to the bishops his

---

* The bishops whom in this letter Arius mentions as his partisans are Eusebius of Cæsarea in Palestine, the historian, Theodotus of Laodicea in Syria, Paulinus of Tyre, Athanasius of Anazarba in Cilicia, Gregory of Berytus, Aetius of Lydda, or Diospolis; when he adds that they have been anathematized, it is a calumny, since these names were not mentioned in the council of Alexandria. The three bishops, whom he pronounces ignorant, because they were unfavorable to him, are St. Philogonus, bishop of Antioch, whose merit had elevated him to this apostolic see, to succeed Tyrannus, who had occupied it from the year A. D. 299 to 312; Hellanicus, bishop of Tripoli in Phœnicia; and St. Macarius, bishop of Jerusalem, who had succeeded Hermon in A. D. 314. St. Athanasius considered the last as among the greatest bishops of his age.

partisans to rouse their zeal in behalf of the new doctrine. In his letter to Paulinus, the Arian bishop of Tyre, he praises the ardor of Eusebius of Cæsarea in defending their common error. He urges all his adherents to write to the Patriarch Alexander, being persuaded, he says, that he will yield to their reiterated demands. Arius soon went to Nicomedia to join his devoted protector. He was received with the highest honors. The better to diffuse the venom of their heresy, and to popularize it so far as it was in their power, they composed a collection of chants, containing their whole doctrine, which they named *Thalia*. The measure and the airs were the same as those of the obscene songs then in vogue among the populace. They were adapted to travellers, sailors, laborers, and slaves in the tread-mill. We have already seen the same means employed by Valentine, and Harmonius his disciple, to popularize Gnosticism. The instinct of heresy is always the same. It has small regard for the dignity of its dogmas, or for the morality or propriety of its manner of propagating them; success is the only end.

17. Against all these skilfully combined efforts, Catholic truth opposed an old man as her defender—the illustrious patriarch of Alexandria. But this old man, in the ardor of his faith, found the activity of his youth renewed. Besides, he was seconded by the deacon Athanasius. St. Alexander wrote to all the bishops of the East, and to the Pope St. Sylvester, to inform them of the intrigues of Arius, and to brand him with heresy. He sent to them a memorial, or profession of faith, requesting them to subscribe to it, in order to crush the heresy under the weight of their unanimous suffrages. St. Epiphanius knew of seventy of these letters, addressed to different prelates. As the new sect relied especially on the credit which its avowed protector, Eusebius of Nicomedia, enjoyed at court, St. Alexander did not hesitate to attack, publicly, this usurping bishop. He did it in a circular letter addressed to all the churches in the world. "I had at first," said the saintly patri-

arch, "thought it my duty to be silent, to stifle the evil in the persons of the apostates, and not to offend the ears of the pious faithful by the relation of their blasphemies. But since Eusebius assumes the right to dispose of the affairs of the Church, because he left Berytus and usurped the church of Nicomedia without receiving the punishment he deserves, since he places himself at the head of these heretics, and writes on all sides in their favor, I am obliged to raise my voice to make known to all who the apostates are and the nature of their heresy, in order that you may be guarded against their bold attempts." Before dispatching these letters, St. Alexander assembled his clergy, made known their contents, and engaged them to subscribe to what he had written. Eusebius and Arius also convoked an assembly of their partisans at Nicomedia. Their error was solemnly approved, and they wrote to all the churches to communicate with the Arians. Troubles only increased in the midst of this conflict. Not only the bishops and priests entered into the controversy, the whole people were divided, and took part for or against the truth. All minds were in a ferment; the name of Arius occupied every one; the Thalia had done its work.

18. Such was the state of the East when the victories of Adrianople, Byzantium, and Chalcedon, over Licinius, brought Constantine thither. This prince, deceived by the underhand dealing of Eusebius, saw nothing at first in all these debates but an idle war of words. He thought to settle the whole matter by writing to both parties to cease their strife. But matters were no longer at a point where an imperial letter could appease them. It was a question whether Jesus Christ was God. The Catholic bishops could not for an instant leave this question in doubt. On the other hand, the vanity and personal interests of the Arians were engaged in this conflict; they would not recede. Osius of Cordova and St. Alexander advised Constantine to assemble an œcumenical council, $οἰκουμενικῆς$, that is, of the whole world. The emperor saw that it was the only means of ending a controversy which every day became more

bitter. In concert with St. Sylvester, he summoned a general assembly of all the bishops in the world, to meet at Nice, in Bithynia, in the month of June, A. D. 325.

19. The bishops came from every quarter of the globe, to the number of three hundred and eighteen, exclusive of priests, deacons, and acolytes. All the travelling expenses of the bishops and their suites were paid out of the public treasury. Never had a more imposing spectacle been given to the world. The flower of the human race were assembled, not to treat of frivolous or ephemeral questions of politics, divisions of territories, or of the constitutions of empires: immortal interests were at stake, the very principles of faith and religious life. All these venerable relicts, saved from the prisons and torments of the persecutors, these old men, crowned with virtues more than years, who bore the glorious marks of the tortures they had endured for Christ, came to sustain by their testimony the divinity of Him whom they had confessed in the presence of their tormentors. The living echo of Catholic tradition, they brought to this august assembly the doctrines of the past ages; they linked the present to the Apostolic times, and bequeathed to souls yet to come the truth they had drawn almost from its source. Among these great luminaries of the Church, the most remarkable were Osius of Cordova, who was the legate of St. Sylvester, universally celebrated for his learning, piety, and consummate prudence; the holy Bishop Paphnutius, bishop of Upper Thebais, and Potamon, bishop of Heraclea, who had both paid the penalty of their profession of faith by the loss of the right eye; St. Paul, bishop of Neocæsarea on the Euphrates, whose tendons had been burned with red-hot irons during the persecution of Licinius; St. James of Nisibis, in Mesopotamia, and St. Nicholas, bishop of Myra, both illustrious for numerous miracles; St. Amphion, bishop of Epiphania, who had suffered torture for the name of Jesus Christ under Dioclesian; St. Basil, Bishop of Amasea; St. Meletius, of Sebastopolis; St. Hypatius, of Gangres, in Paphlagonia; St. Macarius, patriarch of Jerusalem; St. Eusta-

thius, of Antioch, and that illustrious bishop of Alexandria, St. Alexander, who had been the first to call upon the error of Arius the anathema of the Church. He was accompanied by his deacon Athanasius, who was destined, in his turn, to be the soul of so many councils. At the side of these prelates, these glorious defenders of the faith, the Arians had brought to Nice all their adherents, of whom the principal were Eusebius of Nicomedia, and Eusebius of Cæsarea; Theognis, of Nice; Patrophilus, of Scythopolis; Maris, of Chalcedon, and Narcissus, of Neroniad. Besides Osius of Cordova, papal legate, St. Sylvester had sent, as his representatives, the Roman priests Vito and Vincent, who subscribed their names, before those of the bishops, to the acts of the council.

20. Before the day appointed for the public assembly, the bishops met in a church large enough to contain all of them— these are the very words of Eusebius of Cæsarea; they held there many private conferences, to which Arius was called. He developed the entire series of his errors; he maintained that God had not always been Father; that there was a time when the Son did not exist; that the Word was made from nothing, the creature and work of God, but more perfect than the others. In consequence, Jesus Christ was not God by nature, but only by a sort of participation. He added: "That He was not the substantial Word of the Father, nor His wisdom, by whom all has been made; but that He was Himself created by the eternal wisdom; that He is in all things foreign to the substance of the Father; that He is not the peculiar and natural production of the Father, the natural virtue of God, in the words of the Scriptures, but the effect of His free will. That the Son cannot perfectly know the Father, and that He can possess that knowledge only within the bounds of His finite and limited nature." The fathers stopped their ears in horror at the exposition of these odious blasphemies, and protested, by their indignation, against a doctrine opposed to the belief of the Church. Most of them wished to condemn these impious heretics without further

debate, in order to hold to the faith which they had received by apostolic tradition. But the Arian bishops maintained that an opinion is not to be implicitly followed on the ground of mere antiquity, and they accordingly called for a more thorough investigation of the subject. Each of the propositions of Arius, therefore, became a separate matter of discussion. The orthodox bishops at first urged the Arians to give a clear definition of what they understood by the name of Son, which the sacred text gives to the Word. "For if Christ be not the Son of God by nature, but only by a kind of participation of the divine perfections, what has He above the angels and saints; and why is He called the only son of God?" "He is called the only Son of God," answered the Arians, "because He alone was made by God alone; whereas God made all other creatures through His Son." "Senseless and impious novelty," cried the orthodox fathers, "since it presupposes two absurd and sacrilegious ideas: either that through impotence, God was unable, alone, to create all other creatures, or that through pride He was unwilling to do it, though He possessed the power. The doctrine is, besides, contrary to the very text of Scripture: *God Himself made us. Ipse fecit nos. There is but one God from whom all things are, and one Lord Jesus Christ, through whom are all things.*" The Arians had recourse to another subterfuge: "As other creatures could not bear the immediate action of the Infinite Being, God first created the Son alone, and then, all other creatures through the Son." "The distinction is worthless," replied the Catholics; "for if creatures could not bear the immediate action of God, how could the Son bear this action, since He is also, in your system, but a creature? If creatures needed an intermediate agent between God and themselves, the Son, who is but a creature, needed one also, and this intermediate agent would need another, and so on, *ad infinitum*. But if, to escape this absurd consequence, you admit that the Son, although but a creature, could have been created immediately by the uncreated Being, you must, of necessity, grant that the uncreated Being could have created all other creatures in the same manner, and your necessity of the production of the Word falls to the ground."

21. The 9th of June, A. D. 325, the day appointed for the public session, had arrived. The preliminary discussions, in the preceding conferences, had removed every difficulty. The orthodox bishops were unanimous in heaping anathemas upon the impiety of Arianism. The Emperor Constantine had come to Nice, to add to the solemnity of the sentence the majesty of the imperial presence. All the bishops, priests and deacons, who were to take part in the deliberations of the council, proceeded to the great hall of the palace, which had been prepared for their reception; here, also a throne of gold had been placed for the emperor. When Constantine appeared, clothed in the imperial purple, and wearing a cloak bright with precious gems, the fathers rose, to honor, in his person, the prince who had drawn the Christian religion from the darkness of the catacombs, and brought it into the full splendor of these august solemnities. Constantine received their homage with respectful modesty. On reaching the upper end of the hall, he remained standing, and only the repeated wishes of the bishops could induce him to take his seat upon the throne prepared for him. St. Eustathius of Antioch then rose and addressed the emperor, returning thanks to God for the wonders accomplished during his reign in favor of religion. Constantine replied, in Latin; his discourse was rendered by interpreters into Greek, as most of the Eastern fathers understood that language better, since it was more prevalent in the East. He gave expression to the joy which he felt at the sight of so many prelates assembled from all parts of the world, and to his earnest desire of putting an end by their agreement to such fatal dissensions. He then gave way to those who presided over the council, and left them at full. liberty to enter upon a thorough examination of all doctrinal questions. The discussion with Arius was therefore resumed, before the emperor. His partisans laid before the council a profession of faith drawn up by themselves, and containing all

their errors touching the nature of the Son of God. All the orthodox fathers, who were in overwhelming majority in the council, unanimously rejected it. They then passed to the consideration of the terms to be used in defining the Catholic belief on the generation of the Word, and it was first proposed to use the expression of the Scriptures, *The Son is of God*. But the Arians interpreting it according to their doctrine, made no difficulty about signing the profession, "For it is also written," they said, "in another text, *All things are of God*." This formula, then, did not, in reality, distinguish the Word from creatures. The Catholics then clearly explained that by the words, *The Son is of God*, they meant to express that He is of the very substance of God; which cannot be predicated of any creature. It was next suggested to use the expression that the Son is the *strength of the Father*, His *sole wisdom*, His *eternal image*, which is like to Him in all things. The Arians found means to abuse each of these new terms. The word *strength* is often used in the sacred writings, to designate a created power (Joel ii. 22). The term *image* was not more precise, since it is written that man was made to the image and likeness of God. Seeing this want of honesty in their adversaries, the Catholics were forced, in order to express themselves more categorically, to include the meaning of the Scripture in a single word, and to say that the Son is *consubstantial* with the Father, ὁμοούσιος, an expression which has since gained so much celebrity. "It means that the Son is not only like to the Father, but so united as to be only one with Him, and that the likeness of the Son is not the same as that which is attributed to creatures. Besides, bodies may be alike, and still be separated and distant, as happens among men, in the case of a father and son, however they may resemble each other; but the generation of the Son of God is very different. He is not only like, but inseparable from, the substance of the Father; the Father and the Son are one. The Word is always in the Father, and the Father in the Word,* just as

---

* FLEURY. *History of the Church*, Lib. xi.

brightness is in regard to light." All these ideas were included in the term *consubstantial*, which the Arians refused to receive, alleging that it was not Scriptural, and that it contained a heterodox meaning. "For that which is of the same substance with another," said they, "partakes of it in one of three ways, by division, by emanation, or by production: by production, as a plant from its root; by emanation, as the offspring from the father; by division, as two or three goblets made from a single mass of gold. But no one of these modes of participation can be ascribed to the generation of the Son of God." The Catholic bishops replied that the term *consubstantial*, as attributed to the Word, included no idea of body, and conveyed no meaning of division or lessening of the substance of the Father, which is essentially immaterial and spiritual; that it signifies only the unity of substance in the Father and the Son, coexisting from all eternity, the Father never without the Son, the Son never without the Father. As to the objection that the word *consubstantial* is not found in Scripture, the fathers answered, that the sense is here above the form; and that the idea of *consubstantiality* is embodied in every page of Holy Writ, so that the absence of the word is of no force against the doctrine. Besides, they observed, the term is not new, as both the saints Dionysius use it to explain the nature of the Word, and usage has made it familiar in Christian speech. The alleged passages of the two holy doctors, were referred to, and even Eusebius of Cæsarea was forced to grant the correctness of the quotations. The term *consubstantial* was therefore adopted by all the orthodox fathers, as best calculated to meet all the subtleties and evasions of error, and it has ever been the terror of the Arians.

22. The important question once discussed and settled, it remained to draw up a Catholic profession of faith. Osius of Cordova, the legate of Pope St. Sylvester, composed the formulas, and Hermogenes, afterwards bishop of Cæsarea, in Cappadocia, wrote it at his dictation. This profession, known

as the Nicene Creed, has become the received expression of Catholic faith. It has stood the test of ages, and all generations have used it as a solemn act of faith. Sung in every Catholic Church throughout the world, blended with the prayers of the liturgy on the lips of doctors and faithful, it is the oath of loyalty to Catholic doctrine, pronounced in the consecration of bishops. Osius then read aloud, in Greek, this formula, re-echoed since by every Christian voice: "We believe in one God, the Father Almighty, Creator of all things visible and invisible; and in one Lord Jesus Christ, only Son of God, born of the Father before all ages: God of God, light of light, true God of true God. Begotten, not made; *consubstantial* with the Father, by whom all things were made, both in Heaven and on Earth; who for us, men, and for our salvation, came down from Heaven, became incarnate, *and was made man;* suffered, rose again on the third day, and ascended into Heaven, whence he shall come again to judge the living and the dead. And in the Holy Ghost. And if any say: *There was a time when the Son was not; He was not before being begotten; He was drawn from nothing;* or if any hold that *the Son is not of the same nature and substance as the Father; He is mutable and subject to changes, like a created being;* the holy Catholic and Apostolic Church anathematizes them." All the bishops present, with the exception of seventeen Arians, signed the profession. On the following day the number of its opponents was reduced to five: Eusebius of Nicomedia, Theognis of Nice, Maris of Chalcedon, Theonas and Secundus of Libya. Eusebius of Cæsarea, one of the seventeen who had, on the eve, refused to receive the term *consubstantial*, now gave in his adhesion. The emperor, meanwhile, had threatened to banish those who persisted in opposing the Catholic doctrine. The word banishment was most effective. Eusebius of Nicomedia, Theognis of Nice, and Maris of Chalcedon, found it more convincing than the most conclusive arguments of the orthodox bishops; they accordingly added their names to the signatures of the formula. But Eusebius and Theognis made use of a fraud; in signing their names, they inserted an *iota* in the word ὁμοούσιος, and wrote ὁμοιούσιος, *similar in substance*, for *of the same substance*. This *iota* afterwards renewed the whole discussion. Eusebius also distinguished between the profession of the faith and the affixed anathema. He consented to sign the former, but obstinately refused to subscribe to the latter; "For I am convinced," said he, "that Arius is not such as the fathers believe him to be; and my relations with him have made me better acquainted with him."

Theonas and Secundus, of Libya, alone remained in favor of the heresiarch, and nothing could move them to abandon his error. The council accordingly condemned them, together with him. All the writings of Arius, and especially the Thalia, were anathematized. The emperor confirmed these decrees by his authority, and gave them the force of law in the empire.

23. The council of Nice now took into consideration two questions, of less moment than Arianism: that of the Quartodecimans, and of the Meletians. The difficulty concerning the Paschal celebration had been discussed in the times of Popes St. Anicetus and St. Polycarp, and later, under St. Victor, but had never been conclusively settled. In spite of the decisions of the two popes mentioned above, the churches of Syria and Mesopotamia still followed the Jewish custom of celebrating the feast on the fourteenth day of the first lunar month, after the vernal equinox, without considering whether it fell on a Sunday or not. They were hence called *Quartodecimans*. The council decided that the festival of Easter should always be celebrated on the Sunday immediately following the fourteenth day of the first lunar month after the vernal equinox. It was decreed that the day on which the feast was to be kept in the Eastern churches should be announced, each year, by the patriarch of Alexandria, because more attention was paid in that city than in any other to the study of astronomy. To decide more easily the first day of the lunar month, and thence

the fourteenth, the fathers agreed to use the cycle of nineteen years; because the revolution of that period always brings back the new moon to nearly the same day of the solar year. This cycle, called in Greek 'Εννέας καήτερις, had been discovered about seven hundred and fifty years before, by an Athenian named Meton. It has since been called the *Golden Number*, because it was customary, in writing the calendars, to designate the first day of the new moon by golden letters. It is believed that this computation was intrusted to Eusebius of Cæsarea; it is, at all events, known that that prelate had composed a Paschal canon of nineteen years, and explained the origin and matter of the question, in a discourse dedicated to the Emperor Constantine, who thanked him for it by letter. The decision of Nice, relative to the Paschal celebration, was put into immediate practice throughout the universal Church. A few churches in Mesopotamia alone held to the ancient custom. They were encouraged in their schism by a monk named Audius, whom Constantine was forced to banish into Scythia. After remaining some time there, he made his way into the country of the Goths, where he founded several monasteries, to which he bequeathed his obstinate perseverance in celebrating Easter in the old style, contrary to the decree of the Church. This explains the existence of the Quartodecimans or Audians amongst the Goths, and it was the work of ages to root out the schismatical doctrine planted there.

24. The Meletian schism also ended in the council of Nice, but in a manner which may, perhaps, seem strange to us, accustomed as we are to look upon the first ages of the Church as those in which she used measures of the greatest rigor. We have already noticed the deposition of Meletius, bishop of Lycopolis, by the patriarch of Alexandria, for having sacrificed to idols during the persecution. Instead of submitting, he had formed a schism, and ordained bishops, priests, and deacons of his faction. When the Arians appeared, they were joined by the Meletians, not as adherents to the same doctrine, but on the common ground of condemnation by the Church.

To put an end to this schism, offspring of apostasy and abettor of heresy, the council, whilst it pronounced Meletius strictly unworthy of pardon, still wished to use mildness; he was therefore allowed to stay in his episcopal city, Lycopolis, enjoying the title and honors of the episcopate, but deprived of the right of choosing or ordaining bishops or priests, for any church whatever. Those whom he had ordained were admitted to communion, and restored to the honor and functions of their order, but they were to yield precedence of rank and jurisdiction, in every diocese and church, to those who had been before ordained by the bishop of Alexandria. They were also forbidden to hold any election without the consent of the patriarch. This measure was necessary to remove the possibility of perpetuating the cabal. St. Alexander accordingly asked of Meletius a correct list of the bishops, priests, and deacons of his party, in Egypt and the territory of Alexandria. In handing this list to the patriarch, Meletius presented to him those who were named in it, and gave up the churches which he had seized. At his death, which occurred a short time afterwards, regardless of his solemn pledge, Meletius appointed his disciple John, of Memphis, to succeed him. This irregularity prolonged the schism, which, however, passed away, half a century later, without any further measures being taken against it.

25. The Nicene fathers, after having settled these various disputes, drew up several *canons*, or rules of discipline, which were afterwards included, together with those of the councils of Arles, Ancyra, Neocæsarea (A. D. 314), and Gangres (A. D. 324), in the collection known as the *Apostolic Canons*. We purpose giving a collective view of them, as they form a code of discipline, and comprehend the whole canonical jurisprudence of the fourth century. For the sake of order, we place the matter of the canons under six principal heads: 1. The primacy of the Roman Church; 2. Hierarchical authority of Patriarchs and Metropolitans; 3. Election and consecration of bishops; 4. Celibacy of clerics; 5. Rules for public

penance, in reconciling heretics; 6. Ecclesiastical discipline relative to marriage.

I. *Primacy of the Roman Church.* "The primacy has always resided in the Church of Rome (Canon of the Council of Nice). Let the ancient custom, then, be vigorously maintained in Egypt, Libya, and Pentapolis, so that all pay the homage of submission to the bishop of Alexandria; for so the Roman pontiff orders. Let the same be observed in respect to the bishop of Antioch; and so in all other provinces, let the various churches keep their own privileges: if any bishop is consecrated without the consent of the metropolitan, the holy council decrees that he is not to be considered a bishop." To form a correct estimate of this canon, we must remember that St. Peter himself founded the Church of Antioch, the capital of the East; the Church of Alexandria, capital of Egypt, by his disciple St. Mark; and lastly, by a residence of twenty-five years, the Church of Rome, the capital of the universe; here, by his death, he fixed the seat of his power. Thus these three great churches, Rome, Alexandria, and Antioch, were three great streams, which flowed from a common fountain-head, towards the East and the West, to fertilize the world. From this origin the fathers and councils established the pre-eminence and patriarchal dignity of the three churches. "Though there were several Apostles," says St. Gregory the Great, "yet only one of them, whose place is in three different churches, could give to these a paramount influence over all other churches. St. Peter gave the first rank to the see in which he deigned to fix his authority, and to close his mortal career. It is he who illustrated the see to which he sent his disciple, the evangelist; it is he again who established the see of Antioch, in which he sat for seven years; so that they form but one and the same see."* St. Leo adds: "The three patriarchs occupy one and the same apostolic chair, because all three have succeeded to the see of Peter and

---

* GREGOR. MAG., *Epist. ad Eulog.*, Lib. xiii., ep. 4.

to his Church, founded by Jesus Christ, in unity, and to which he gave one single head to preside over three principal sees in the three patriarchal cities, that the indissoluble union of the three sees might bind the other churches more closely to the divinely constituted head."* This apostolic constitution of the Church is what is dwelt on in the canon quoted above. A careful study of the words will show that the canon is summed up in the following statement, which includes both the decision of the council and the grounds of the decision: The Roman Church holds the primacy over all the other churches. But she has ordained that Egypt, Libya, and Pentapolis shall be subject to the bishop of Alexandria; therefore these provinces cannot be withdrawn from his jurisdiction. The same conclusion holds for the patriarch of Antioch. The canon therefore declares, that any one consecrated without the consent of the metropolitan, that is, of the patriarch, shall not be considered a bishop. The Nicene Fathers also made good certain prerogatives held by the bishop of Jerusalem, but without prejudice to the metropolitan, that is, to the patriarch of Antioch, who held jurisdiction over all the East, or to the bishop of Cæsarea, metropolitan of the province of Palestine.

26. II. *The hierarchical authority of the patriarchs* is still more clearly laid down in the thirty-ninth of the *Apostolic Canons.* It is entitled: *Of the solicitude and power of the patriarch over the bishops and archbishops of his patriarchate, and the primacy of the bishop of Rome, over all.* "The patriarch," says the canon, "shall carefully watch the conduct of the bishops and archbishops in their provinces; and if he see any thing blameworthy, he shall change and regulate it, as he may deem best; for he is the father of them all, and they are his sons. The archbishop is as an elder brother amongst the bishops; the patriarch is as the father. And as the patriarch has power over those who are subordinate to him, so also the

* Epistol. S. Leonis, 104. ad Anatol.

Roman pontiff has power over all the patriarchs. He is their prince and chief, as St. Peter himself, to whom has been given power over Christian princes and their subjects, because he is the vicar of our Lord Jesus Christ. Whoever opposes this teaching is excommunicated by the council." Such is the basis, the fundamental rule, on which all the Christian communities of the East recognize their hierarchy and their canon law, and which, from the earliest times, they have attributed to the great council of Nice.

27. III. *The ordination of bishops and priests* was made the subject of numerous canons in the councils of Arles and of Nice. It is forbidden, in the first place, to consecrate two bishops for the same see. The fourth canon of Nice runs thus: "The bishop should, if possible, be consecrated by all those of his province. But if this be not feasible, either by reason of distance or from some other legitimate hindrance, there must be at least three bishops present for the consecration, with the written suffrage and consent of the absent. In every province, the metropolitan's confirmation is required." This measure had already been taken by the council of Arles, against some bishops who assumed the right of consecrating others, on their personal authority. The fifteenth canon of Nice forbids translations from one see to another. The sixteenth extends this prohibition to all clerics. "Clerics who rashly, not having the fear of God before their eyes, and regardless of the holy canons, quit the Church to which they belong, cannot be received into any other. They shall be required to return to their own diocese, and in case of their refusal, be excommunicated." The council of Ancyra decrees, on the same subject: "If any, having received episcopal consecration, and not being received by the flock to which they were appointed, attempt to seize upon another diocese, or to excite seditions against its lawful bishop, they shall be cut off from the communion of the Church. Should they wish to take their former rank among the priests, this honor shall be granted them; but if they still foment divisions, and seek

to impugn the authority of the bishops, they shall be deprived of even the sacerdotal honor." Regarding those who are to be consecrated, the council of Nice, true to the teaching of St. Paul, formally excludes neophytes, in these terms: "It has sometimes happened, whether from scarcity of subjects, or to satisfy the importunities of certain persons, that the Church's law has been set aside, and the episcopal or priestly dignity has been conferred upon men hardly free from the errors of paganism, and baptized after a hasty preparation. The council ordains that this mode of procedure be not repeated. Time is necessary for the instruction of the catechumen, and yet more for probation, after baptism. The Apostle is explicit: 'Not a neophyte, lest pride cause him to fall into the snares of the devil.'"

The council of Nice also excludes from holy orders all who have voluntarily mutilated themselves. It fixes the canonical age for ordination at thirty years, whatever may be the merits of the candidate in other respects, because our Lord Jesus Christ only began to teach at that age. The council of Ancyra forbids *chorepiscopi* to ordain priests or deacons, and the priests of the cities to undertake any thing without the written permission of the bishop. The *chorepiscopi* were often but simple priests, to whom the bishop delegated nearly all his authority in the country districts. The council of Nice excommunicated all clerics guilty of usury.

28. IV. The observance of *clerical celibacy* was so noted at this period that Eusebius of Cæsarea wrote, in his *Evangelical Demonstration:* "The state of continence is the proper state of those who are devoted to the priesthood and engaged in the ministry of divine worship; of the doctors and the preachers of the divine word, whose care it is to raise a holy and spiritual offspring, and to train to holiness, not a particular family, but the countless multitude of the faithful." The council of Elvira (33d canon) decrees that bishops, priests, and deacons who were engaged in the married state before ordination, shall separate entirely from their wives. The

council of Neocæsarea orders that any priest who marries after ordination shall be deposed. The Nicene inveighs against an abuse, which had gained footing in many places, relative to women living under the same roof with clerics, under pretext of ministering to them; they were called, in Greek, συνδίκαστοι, in Latin, *subintroductæ*. "The œcumenical council," says the canon, "forbids all, whether bishops, priests, deacons, or other clerics, to have under the same roof any woman, save a mother, sister, aunt, or other whose relationship precludes all just ground of suspicion." "It is usual," says the learned Father Thomassin, "to allege against clerical celibacy the story of the holy bishop Paphnutius, who, according to Socrates and Sozomen, obliged the Fathers of Nice to pass no decree subjecting bishops, priests, and deacons to continence with the wife they had married before ordination, as the ancient traditions only forbade the contraction of new marriages after receiving sacred orders. But the authority of Socrates and Sozomen is by no means unquestionable. The assertion may be grounded on fact, and Socrates may have erred only in what is his own in the account. But when he says that *the ancient tradition of the Church* only forbade the contraction of marriage ties in the higher orders of the clergy, without depriving them of the use of a preceding marriage, we appeal in this matter to Eusebius, St. Epiphanius, and St. Jerome, who, besides being more ancient than Socrates, were immeasurably better acquainted with the ancient customs of the Church; his assertion, therefore, is unworthy of any credence."

29. V. The custom of *rebaptizing heretics* who came back to the bosom of the Church still held ground in Africa, in spite of the contrary decisions of the sovereign pontiffs and of several councils. The council of Arles lays down this rule: "When a heretic returns to the Church, let him be required to say the creed. If it be found that he has been baptized in the name of the Father, and of the Son, and of the Holy Ghost, he shall only undergo the imposition of hands, that he may receive the Holy Ghost. If he does not answer according to Catholic

teaching, when questioned on the mystery of the Trinity, let him be baptized." As the Donatist schism was supported by the pretext that the Catholics were over-indulgent to traditors, the council also decreed that they who would give up the sacred writings or vessels, should be deposed, provided their conviction was founded on public documents, and not on mere denunciations. The eighth canon of Nice speaks thus of the Novatian schismatics: "If they return to the Catholic Church, the œcumenical council ordains that, after receiving the imposition of hands, they may remain in the ranks of the clergy. But they shall be required to declare, in writing, that they approve and are ready to follow every decision of the Catholic Church. In all places, then, whether city or village, where there are no other clerics, let them keep the rank to which they were ordained. But if any one of them come to a place where there is a Catholic bishop or priest, it is evident that the Catholic bishop will retain his episcopal dignity, and the Novatian bishop resume the rank of priest, unless the Catholic bishop consent to yield the episcopal title and rank. Otherwise the Novatian may receive the position of chorepiscopus, that there may not be two bishops in the same city." As the East was just emerging from the Licinian persecution, the council felt called to pass several decrees concerning the reconciliation of the *lapsi*. The penances imposed are generally milder and of less duration than those decreed by the particular council of Elvira—another proof that there was no fixed rule in this respect. A great latitude is also left for the indulgence of the bishops, according to the fervor of the penitents. Fleury is fond of reiterating, on such occasions, that now the rigor of early discipline was relaxing. The truth is, as F. Morin has clearly proved by historical facts, that during the first three centuries the penitentiary system was much milder than in the following ages. There are still two canons worthy of special mention. The third of the council of Arles excommunicates soldiers who, in time of war or on the field of battle, throw down their arms and desert their standard. The twelfth of

Nice condemns such as resume the military life after having forsaken it to do public penance. This rule, forbidding a return to secular warfare after the performance of public penance, was subsequently interpreted and applied in that light by the holy Popes Siricius, Innocent, and Leo, and was again appealed to after the twelfth century.

30. VI. The Roman law had heretofore allowed *marriage between brother-in-law and sister-in-law*. The first prohibition appears in the sixty-first canon of the council of Elvira, which condemns the parties to five years of penance, after separation. The council of Neocæsarea is even more rigorous. Its second canon excommunicates till death any woman who has married her brother-in-law; still she may be reconciled, at the hour of death, if she promise to break off this connection in case of her recovery. This law of the Church was transferred to the civil codes by the Christian emperors.* The Roman laws also countenanced divorce and an ensuing marriage. The tenth canon of the council of Arles reminds husbands, who detect their wives in the commission of adultery, that they are forbidden to marry again during the lifetime of the divorced wife. In process of time this law of the Church also passed into civil jurisprudence. The council of Arles further ordains that Christian women, contracting a matrimonial alliance with pagans, shall be cut off, for a time, from the communion of the Church. The council of Neocæsarea prescribes a certain time of public penance for those who marry a second time. Hence the prohibition to priests from assisting at the rejoicings attending second weddings; though tolerated, they were deemed a weakness.

31. The council wished to close its sittings by a collective letter addressed by all the bishops to the Church and faithful of Alexandria, informing them of the anathema hurled against Arius, and of the exile to which the emperor had just condemned him. "Rejoice," wrote the fathers, "at the peace

---

* *Codex Theodosian.*, Lib. iii., t. 12.

and union restored to the Church; at the extirpation of all heresies. Receive with love and respect our pious colleague, your bishop Alexander, who has rejoiced us by his presence, and whose declining years and strength have not deterred him from meeting fatigue and toils to secure to you the sweets of peace. Pray for us, also, that the rules which we have established may remain firm and unchanged, through our Lord Jesus Christ, and that they may all tend, as we hope and desire, to the honor and greater glory of God the Father, in the Holy Ghost, to whom be all praise, world without end. Amen."

With the close of the council opened the twentieth year of Constantine's reign. The emperors were in the habit of celebrating the fifth, the tenth, and the twentieth years of their reign. It was therefore observed as a great solemnity throughout the empire, and Eusebius of Cæsarea addressed a eulogy to the emperor on the occasion. All the bishops present at the council were invited to a splendid banquet in the palace. These holy confessors, on their way to the imperial residence, received the military salutes of the same pretorian guards whose arms had so long been turned against them. The emperor received them with respectful veneration, showing especial reverence to Saint Paphnutius, whose scars he kissed with affectionate piety. Before taking final leave of them he assembled them all, and, by way of reply to some Arian bishops, who had begged him to intervene in the question decided by the council, "God," said he, " has made you His pontiffs, and empowered you to judge our subjects and ourselves; it is proper, therefore, that we submit to your decisions, and do not undertake to better them. God has constituted you as our gods; how, then, can gods be judged by men? Lay your disagreements, then, before Him who is the Judge and the God of gods—or rather let us lay aside all complaints. Let us imitate the divine goodness, by forgiving one another, and abide in the union of brotherly love, to apply, in peace and union of hearts, the truth of the faith for the sake of which we assembled here." He then concluded by recommending himself to their prayers, and finally, after having made them presents according to their respective dignities, he handed them letters to the governors of the various provinces, ordering the annual distribution of a certain quantity of wheat to the Churches, for the support of virgins, widows, and clerics; he then took final leave of them, and dismissed them to their sees.

32. The bishops who had stood by Arianism to the last, found themselves in a somewhat awkward position. Eusebius endeavored to explain his attitude, in a letter which he sent before him to his flock, and in which he mentions his submission to the decree on the word *consubstantial*. He gives all the credit of it to Constantine, more like a courtier than a bishop. Eusebius of Nicomedia and Theognis of Nice bribed the librarian of the imperial archives to give them access to the documents committed to his keeping, and erased their signatures from the profession. They then began openly to teach that the Son is not *consubstantial* with the Father. The emperor one day reproached Eusebius of Nicomedia for his heresy: "If this mantle were rent asunder," replied the Arian, "I should never say that the two pieces are of the same substance, although they were alike." They openly welcomed the Arians, treated them as victims of an unjust persecution, and received them into communion. This scandalous conduct obliged St. Alexander to call a council against them, at Alexandria. Eusebius and Theognis were deposed, and the council appointed, as their successors, Amphion for Nicomedia, and Chrestus for Nice; three months after the council of Nice, the emperor banished the two heretical bishops to Gaul, where they remained three years.

33. It is more than probable that if Constantine had not relaxed the firmness displayed on this occasion, all would have been over with Arianism. How many trials would the Church have thus been spared! But the many exalted qualities of the emperor were marred by a lamentable inconstancy of character, which always spoiled the wisest measures, and threw a doubt upon the most clearly defined questions. We

shall but too soon be called upon to record some of these sad traits. The two years immediately following the council of Nice, A. D. 326 and 327, were years of blessing and peace to the Church. Downfallen Arianism hung its head in shame.

The heathens flocked to the fold of Christ in great numbers; some from a deep and sincere conviction of the vanity of the idolatrous rites, or from the examples of virtue and holiness presented in the monastic life; many, it must be granted, from less pure and disinterested motives, and to fall in with the master's wish. Whole cities, entire districts, were seen to embrace the faith of Jesus Christ, with one accord, and overthrowing their temples and statues, build upon their ruins the sanctuaries of the true God. The inhabitants of Majuma, the ancient seaport of Gaza, in Palestine, all became Christians. To reward this act of piety, the emperor raised the town to the rank of a Roman city, and called it Constantia, after his beloved sister, and his own son Constantius. For the same reason he conferred a like honor on a Phœnician borough, to which he gave the name of Constantina; and he favored Drepanum, in Bithynia, with an exemption from taxes, in honor of the holy martyr Lucian of Antioch, whose relics were kept in that city. He changed the old name of Drepanum into that of Helenopolis, from the name of the empress Helena, his mother. But his imperial generosity was displayed in a special manner in the number of churches built at his expense, and the rich endowments he lavished upon them. The single city of Rome contained eight churches raised by him, under the direction of the Pope St. Sylvester: 1. The *Basilica of Equitius*, now known as *S. Stephano dei Monti;* 2. The *Constantinian Basilica*, or *Church of the Saviour*, in the palace of the Empress Fausta, known as the *Lateran palace*, in which the council against the Donatists had previously been held. This Basilica was furnished with a baptistery, ornamented, according to the custom of the times, with a statue of St. John the Baptist. It was from this circumstance that the Church has been commonly known as that of St John of

Lateran; it is the principal church in Rome, and the popes for many centuries made it their place of residence. 3. The *Basilica of Saint Peter*, at the Vatican, raised on the site of a temple of Apollo, to honor the place of the martyrdom and burial of the Prince of the Apostles. 4. The *Basilica of St. Paul*, on the place of his martyrdom. 5. The *Church of St. Agnes*, which was built at the request of the two Constantias, the sister and the daughter of Constantine, who were baptized in it by St. Sylvester. 6. That of *St. Lawrence, extra muros*, on the road to Tibur, over the place of the saint's martyrdom. 7. That of the *Martyrs St. Marcellinus and St. Peter*, at the place called *Inter duas lauros*, where the empress St. Helena was buried. 8. In the house of Sessorius, the *Church of the Holy Cross*, called *The Holy Cross of Jerusalem*, on account of a portion of the true cross which Constantine placed in it. To these eight churches in Rome the emperor gave an annual income of twenty-seven thousand seven hundred and twenty-nine gold ases, in houses, lands, and revenue, not only in Italy, but in Sicily, Africa, Greece, Egypt and the East.* This statement does not include the gold and silver vessels for the service and the splendor of divine worship, which of themselves make a long and curious list, drawn up by Anastasius the librarian. The most remarkable fact that we learn from the old deeds, relative to these donations, is that the emperor assigned the island of Sardinia, and two others of the Tyrrhenian Sea, with all their appurtenances and revenues, to the *Church of St. Marcellinus and St. Peter* in Rome. The other cities of the empire were not forgotten. The church built in Antioch was so rich that it was called the *Golden Church*. To endow and erect these basilicas, Constantine made use of the enormous revenues of the idolatrous temples he had destroyed, and of the profane games he abolished.

34. The pious labors of Constantine were rewarded by a discovery of inestimable price, that of the true cross, which

---

* According to the usual valuation, the as is equivalent to 20 francs and some centimes; this sum would, then, amount to 554,580 francs.

was made under the following circumstances. The empress mother, St. Helena, though more than eighty years of age, had undertaken a pilgrimage to the holy places. On reaching Jerusalem, she immediately caused the temple and statue of Venus to be destroyed; this idolatrous fane had, since the days of Adrian, desecrated the place whereon was accomplished the august mystery of our redemption. All the earth brought and heaped there was removed, and three crosses were found buried at a considerable depth. There was no mark by which to distinguish the Saviour's. The Bishop of Jerusalem, St. Macarius, after a fervent prayer to the Lord, directed that they should be taken to the house of a woman of the city, who had long been suffering from an incurable disease. The three crosses were successively applied; at the touch of the third, she was immediately and entirely healed. This miraculous discovery filled the Christian world with joy. The title fixed by the Jews to the cross, and the nails with which they had pierced the Saviour's hands and feet, were also found with the crosses, but at a little distance from them. St. Helena sent them to the emperor, with a considerable portion of the cross, leaving the remainder in Jerusalem, under the bishop's care. In the following century it was exposed to the veneration of the faithful, once a year, on Good Friday; this is doubtless the origin of the pious ceremony which has since extended to all the Catholic churches throughout the universe. Constantine wore a portion of the nails in his helmet, and attached another to the bridle of his horse, as a protection in battle. The part of the cross sent him by his mother he placed in the Basilica of the Holy Cross, at Rome, together with the title, which was fixed upon an arcade, where it was found, in A. D. 1492, inclosed in a leaden box; the inscription is written in Hebrew, Greek, and Latin, in red letters, upon a board painted white. St. Helena did not long survive her journey to Palestine; she died at Rome (A. D. 327), in the arms of her son, who solemnized her obsequies in a manner worthy of her rank. The Church honors her memory on the 17th of August

35. The progress of Christianity was not confined to the limits of the Roman empire. An embassy from Sapor, King of Persia, to Constantine (A. D. 326), brought the consoling intelligence that Persia, and the country of the Seres, or China, its tributary, already counted many churches, and that the people were flocking in thousands to the fold of Christ. The emperor's heart overflowed with joy at the news. He sent ambassadors to Sapor, loaded with presents of far greater worth than he had received from the Persian monarch. "I have embraced," writes the emperor, "the faith and worship of the Most High God. It is by His help that, setting out from the far-off ocean, I have freed the earth from the tyrants that oppressed it. My army is consecrated to Him, and bears His standard as a harbinger of victory. You may judge, then, what joy we feel to learn that the chief cities of Persia are blest with Christian churches. I recommend them to your especial favor, for they will prove a blessing to your empire. By protecting and fostering them, you will do yourself and us a priceless service." The Iberians, a barbarous people, encamped near the Black Sea, were about this time converted by the example and miracles of a captive Christian girl, and they sent to Constantine, begging for bishops to instruct them in the true faith. The Christian religion had also conquered Farther India, or Ethiopia, by means of Frumentius, a Christian boy, who had been cast upon their unfriendly shores. He afterwards became their bishop, and raised many temples to the honor of the true God.

36. But the year 327 also witnessed an event which was to change the destinies of the world. Rome had become foreign to its masters. Galerius had never seen the interior of its walls. Diocletian preferred Nicomedia. Constantine, born in ancient Mæsia, brought up at the court of Nicomedia, proclaimed emperor in Britain, had no sympathy with Rome. Julius Cæsar had once wished to rebuild Troy, the fabled cradle of the Roman race, and to make it the seat of empire. Constantine took up the idea, with a modification, however, and fixed his

throne in Byzantium. The site was unsurpassed. Seated, like Rome, on its seven hills, but under a mild and healthy sky, and in a region of natural fertility, washed by two seas, the Propontis and the Black, Byzantium commanded the shores both of Europe and of Asia. The channel of the Bosphorus, which separates the two continents, affords it a vast and safe harbor, and the ships of both worlds lay at its feet the treasures of the universe. Here the emperor laid the foundation of the new city to which he gave his name—*Constantinople*. He declared that "it was by the command of God he undertook this herculean task." The order was given him, he said, in a vision; whilst he was asleep, one day, under the walls of Byzantium, he saw a woman, bowed down by age and infirmities, suddenly changed into a young girl, beaming with health and grace, who then put on the imperial ornaments. Constantine obeyed his interpretation of the dream, as a voice from Heaven; lance in hand, he led on the workmen who were tracing out the limits of the city. It was remarked that the space already taken in was immense. Constantine replied: "I follow the invisible guide who goes before me; I shall stop only when my leader halts." The rising city was enriched with the spoils of Greece and Asia; they brought the idols of the now unworshipped gods and the statues of great men. The old metropolis also paid its tribute to the youthful rival now growing up at its side; this drew from St. Jerome the expression that Constantinople had clothed itself by the nakedness of other cities. The families of senatorial and equestrian rank were brought from the banks of the Tiber to those of the Bosphorus, here to find palaces equal to those they had forsaken. Constantine built the Church of the Apostles, which disappeared twenty years after its dedication, to make way for the Basilica of St. Sophia, dedicated by Constantius to the Eternal Wisdom, but more celebrated for its name than for its beauty. There are judgments which historians are accustomed to pronounce without reflection. It has been often said that Constantine hastened the fall of the Cæsars' power by destroying the unity of its seat; but the foundation of Constantinople was, on the contrary, the very means of preserving the Roman power so far into modern times. Rome would have been no better defended, even had it remained sole metropolis. The empire would have fallen with it, when it yielded to Alaric, had not the new capital stood as a second head to the empire, which was only cut down, more than a thousand years later, by the sword of Mahomet II. But the influences that favored the temporal power, as constituted by Constantine, were fatal to the spiritual power of the Church, which he claimed to protect. The emperors, fixed in the West, under the influence of Latin gravity and the sound sense of the German races, would not have been entrapped by the subtleties of Greek policy; fewer heresies would have distracted the world and the Church. Constantinople was born Christian, and had not, like Rome, a religion to deny; but she fouled the altar that Constantine had given her.* The emperor left no want unsupplied in the churches of his new city; he directed Eusebius of Cæsarea to engage the best copyists, and to furnish fifty copies of the Sacred Scriptures, for distribution among the churches of Constantinople; they were to be legible and of portable size, clearly and correctly written.

37. The preceding year (A. D. 326) had been marked by the death of one of the most devoted champions of the true faith. St. Alexander, patriarch of Alexandria, had closed his career in peace, with the glory and consolation of having been the principal instrument in settling the great Arian question, by the œcumenical Council of Nice. He left the patriarchal throne to St. Athanasius, who also inherited to the full the zeal, the virtue, the energy, and the activity of his holy predecessor; nor was it long before these qualities were all called into action. The Princess Constantia, sister to Constantine, had always entertained a secret attachment for Eusebius of Nicomedia and the doctrine which he professed. On her death-

---

* M. DE CHATEAUBRIAND: *Études Historiques,* p. 298.

bod she recommended to Constantine's favor an Arian priest, in whom she placed the greatest confidence. This priest succeeded in persuading the emperor that the Council of Nice had condemned the heresiarch without knowing his real sentiments. Constantine accordingly recalled Arius, who showed him a profession of faith couched in vague and ambiguous terms, in which the word *consubstantial* was omitted; and it was stated that the Word was *produced* or *created* by the Father, before all ages. The emperor was satisfied with this insidious declaration, and the exile of Arius was at an end. This lamentable inconsistency renewed all the discussions which had been settled by the Council of Nice, and opened the way to endless disputes. After recalling Arius, the emperor could hardly refuse the same favor to Eusebius of Nicomedia and Theognis of Nice, who returned in the year 328 to their churches, and expelled those who had been consecrated in their stead. The spirit of cabal necessarily came in with them. Eusebius of Nicomedia was particularly incensed by the firmness with which St. Eustathius, patriarch of Antioch, constantly battled against the Arian heresy, in his profound and eloquent writings. The heretic called a conventicle of Arian bishops at Antioch, and deposed St. Eustathius. This condemnation was based on an infamous calumny. Eusebius of Nicomedia brought the testimony of an abandoned creature, who appeared before the bishops and accused the holy patriarch of an abominable crime. The wretch held a child in her arms, which she declared to be the fruit of her connection with Eustathius. She confirmed her statement with an oath. This victim of Eusebius's wickedness, when brought to her deathbed, declared to the assembled bishops that Eusebius of Nicomedia had hired her to play her infamous part; but that her oath was not altogether false, since the child was the son of a coppersmith with whom she had lived in a state of concubinage, and who bore the same name as the holy Patriarch Eustathius. Such was the evidence on which Eustathius was deposed, and Constantine had the weakness to send him into exile. Paulinus of Tyre, an Arian, was appointed to succeed him, but he soon after died, and was followed in quick succession by Eulalius, Euphronius, and Flaccillus, in the usurped see. The Catholics, meanwhile, held their meetings apart, and refused to communicate with the hirelings who were sent to them under the false title of pastors.

38. The Arians were yet to meet the strongest opposition from the see of Alexandria. Arius had made an attempt to re-enter the city. St. Athanasius openly rejected all his advances. Eusebius of Nicomedia wrote to the holy patriarch, laying great stress on his credit with Constantine, and threatening him with the imperial indignation if he refused to receive Arius. Athanasius replied that no threats or other human considerations could ever lead him to go against the decisions of the council of Nice. The Eusebians despaired of overcoming this energetic character; they joined the Meletians in accusing Athanasius of fomenting divisions throughout Africa, by his unjust refusal of communion. The emperor then wrote to the holy patriarch, in language which it is painful to quote from the pen of Constantine: "Knowing my will on the subject," he wrote, "give free entrance to all who wish to come into the Church; for if I hear of your refusing admittance to any one, I shall give immediate orders to have you deposed and sent into exile." St. Athanasius answered, with modest firmness, that it was impossible for him to obey; that a heresy impugning the divinity of Jesus Christ could have nothing in common with the Catholic Church. The Eusebians now resorted to a calumny, which they thought must produce an irresistible effect upon the emperor's mind. They brought a juridical accusation against the patriarch of having entered into a conspiracy against the life of Constantine, and of having sent a chest of gold to *Philumenos*, the chief of the conspirators. Athanasius presented himself before Constantine, whom he early convinced of his innocence, and returned loaded with the gifts and praises of the inconstant emperor. The noise of the strife excited in Alexandria by the Arians had reached

the ears of St. Anthony in his desert solitude; this and the persecution directed against his disciple and friend, St. Athanasius, drew him down from his mountain cave to protest against the impiety of the heretics, by the authority of his presence, his words, and his miracles. His path was thronged by the faithful. Some of his disciples wished to disperse the crowd, in order to free him from their importunity: "Let them alone," said the holy hermit, "they are not more numerous than the demons we fight on the mountain." He taught the multitude that stood about him that the Word is not a creature; that He is eternal and *consubstantial* with the Father. "Do not communicate with the Arians," he continued; "you are Christians; but they say that the Son of God is a creature. They do not, therefore, differ from pagans, since they adore a creature instead of the Creator." Having fulfilled the mission to which he had been urged by his zeal for the glory of God, St. Anthony returned to his solitude, followed by the admiration of all whom he had edified by the example of his virtue.

39. But the Arians had not exhausted their charges against St. Athanasius. Those which they now brought against him surpass all that we are prepared to look for, even from men who have taken leave of the last vestige of principle. The very enormity of the calumnies which they circulated through their agents should have sufficed to excite mistrust. But the Emperor Constantine was no longer the youthful hero who had escaped the snares of Diocletian's court and the manœuvres of Galerius—whose bold and steady genius had triumphed over Maxentius and Licinius. Nothing could be more at variance with the first part of his life than the second. A hundred times he had seen the falsehood of the charges made by Eusebius of Nicomedia against St. Athanasius; yet each new insinuation of that courtier prelate found him as credulous as the one that went before it. He accordingly named a commission, to meet at Antioch, composed of the Censor Dalmatius, his uncle, of Eusebius of Nicomedia himself, Theognis of Nice, with several other Arian bishops, whom he directed to inquire

into the conduct of the holy patriarch. He wrote to St. Athanasius, summoning him to appear before this tribunal, to clear himself from the charges alleged against him. The patriarch objected to the commission, on the ground that it was wholly made up of his personal enemies. Constantine then appointed a council to be held at Cæsarea, A. D. 331. This city was the choice of the Arian bishops themselves, as they reckoned its prelate, Eusebius, among their chief abettors. St. Athanasius again refused to appear, and wrote to the emperor to state his motives, which were perfectly justified by the care of the two bishops Eusebius that no prelates but those of their own party should be admitted to the council. This refusal of the holy patriarch furnished Eusebius of Nicomedia with a plausible pretext to accuse him, to the emperor, of obstinacy, disobedience, and open revolt against the laws of the empire. His constant refusal, alleged the heretic, only proved his guilt the more. The irritated emperor changed the place of meeting, and ordered that the council should meet at Tyre, in A. D. 335, and wrote to St. Athanasius that if he again refused to appear, the imperial guards should seize his person, if necessary, even on the patriarchal throne. Solemn preparations were ordered for this assembly. Count Flavius Dionysius, late proconsul of Phœnicia, was sent with a body of troops, for the ostensible purpose of maintaining order, but with the real intention of supporting the party of Eusebius of Nicomedia, and to influence the decision of the Fathers. A great number of bishops were present from Egypt, Libya, Asia and Bithynia, from all parts of the East, from Macedonia and Pannonia. The Arians were in vast majority. The most celebrated were Eusebius of Cæsarea and Eusebius of Nicomedia, Flaccillus, intruded bishop of Antioch, Theognis of Nice, Maris of Chalcedon, Narcissus of Neronias, Theodore of Heraclea, Patrophilus of Scythopolis, Macedonius of Mopsuesta, George of Laodicea, Ursacius of Syngidon, and Valens of Mursa; the two latter cities were in Pannonia. Amongst the Catholic bishops, were St. Maximus of Jerusalem, who had lost his right eye and had one of his tendons burnt during the persecution of Maximin; Marcellus of Ancyra, Alexander of Thessalonica, Asclepas of Gaza, and the two illustrious bishops of Upper Thebais, St. Potamon and St. Paphnutius. When St. Athanasius, the illustrious and courageous patriarch of Alexandria, entered the council, he was made to stand as a criminal at the bar before his judges. This outrage moved St. Potamon to tears. Turning to Eusebius of Cæsarea, with that venerable bearing which compelled respect and gave a superhuman eloquence to his words, he exclaimed: "What, Eusebius, are you seated on the bench to judge Athanasius, who is virtue itself? Who can bear this? Answer me: were you not in prison with me, during the persecution? For my part, I lost an eye in it, but I see you are whole and sound. How did you escape without violence to your conscience?" At this unexpected and powerful appeal, Eusebius, confounded, thunderstruck, rose and left the assembly.

Posterity has yet to learn the reply and vindication of Eusebius. St. Paphnutius then turned to Maximus, bishop of Jerusalem, passed through the whole assembly, approached and took his hand, saying: "We have also suffered together for the name of Jesus Christ; you bear the marks of it as well as myself. Come, for I cannot see you seated in the assembly of the wicked." Then, taking him aside, he made him acquainted with the plot against St. Athanasius, and fully convinced him of the patriarch's innocence. The Egyptian bishops at the same time entered a protest, by which they objected to seeing their archbishop judged by those who had openly declared themselves his personal enemies; especially the two Eusebiuses, Narcissus, Flaccillus, Theognis, Maris, Theodore, Patrophilus, Macedonius, George, Uracius, and Valens. They reproached Eusebius of Cæsarea for his apostasy, and George of Laodicea that he had been juridically deposed by the Patriarch St. Alexander. No document could have rested on better legal grounds than this protestation; still, it was disregarded, and the council passed to the exam ination of those terrible accusations against Athanasius, which, for five years past, had been the talk of Arian circles. He was accused: 1. Of having been clandestinely consecrated by five or six bishops, against the wish and universal protestation of the clergy and faithful of Alexandria; 2. Of having outraged a virgin consecrated to God; 3. Of having murdered Arsenius, bishop of Hypsele, in Egypt, and of having kept his withered hand for magical operations; 4. Of having, during an episcopal visitation to a village in Mareotis, broken the chalice, overturned the altar, and trodden the sacred mysteries under foot. It is plain that weight, at least, was not wanting in the charges brought against St. Athanasius by his enemies. The first charge, respecting the pretended clandestine consecration, the Egyptian prelates easily answered by a simple statement of the facts, to which they had been eye-witnesses. At the death of St. Alexander, patriarch of Alexandria (A. D. 326), when the bishops met to give him a successor, the faithful cried out, with one voice, that they wished Athanasius to be their pastor. He was vainly sought for in the assembly, as he had fled into the desert to avoid the burden of the episcopate. He was forcibly brought back on the 27th of December, A. D. 326, and consecrated patriarch of Alexandria, with the unanimous consent of the bishops, nearly all of whom were present at the ceremony, which was performed in the sight of the whole city and province. This historical explanation defeated the first charge; the second was then taken up. A young girl was brought forward, bathed in tears, exclaiming that she was forever miserable because the Bishop Athanasius, abusing the hospitality she had given him, and regardless of her vow of virginity, had brutally ravished her. The wretched creature had never seen St. Athanasius, with whom she was utterly unacquainted. The patriarch having instructed one of his clergy, named Timothy, the latter rose, and turning to the woman, said to her: "What, you pretend that I lodged at your house, and offered violence to you!" "Yes," answered she, "you are the very person I accuse," adding at large the details of time and place. Most of those present could not forbear laughing at the discomfiture of a plot so poorly planned, and so skilfully thwarted. St. Athanasius called for the arrest of the wretched woman, that the calumny might be traced to its authors; but the Eusebians quickly drove her out of the assembly, and would not consent to prosecute a matter which it was so much in their interest to hush. They broke out into tumultuous cries that there were crimes of greater importance to examine, which could not be removed by ingenious subtleties, and that it would only be necessary to see the proofs, in order to be convinced of the guilt of Athanasius. They then produced and opened a carefully sealed box, and took from it a withered human hand. "Athanasius," they exclaimed, "here is your accuser! Behold the right hand of Arsenius, bishop of Hypsele! It is for you to tell us how and why you cut it off!" A murmur of indignation was heard in the assembly; when silence had been restored, Athanasius inquired if any of the bishops present were personally acquainted with Arsenius. Several arose and said that they had known him intimately. Then Athanasius gave a sign to one of his priests, who soon brought in a man whom the patriarch presented to the council. "Is this the Arsenius," he asked, "whom I put to death, and whose right hand I cut off?" It was indeed Arsenius, whom the Eusebians had removed to a desert place; on learning the interpretation put upon his absence, and the consequent danger of Athanasius, he had come, of his own accord, to the patriarch, who showed him to his enemies at the very moment of what they deemed their surest triumph. Arsenius stood with his cloak wrapped about him. Athanasius, throwing it partly open, uncovered first one hand, then the other; and turning to the Fathers, he said: "Here is Arsenius with two hands. God gave us no more. Let my accusers point out the place for the third, and tell you whence they took the one they have shown you." Thus triumphantly refuted, the rage of the Arians knew no bounds. They threw themselves upon Athanasius, crying out that he was a sorcerer, who charmed their eyes by his magic spells. The imperial officers were forced to interpose, in order to save the holy patriarch from being torn to pieces; and for further security, he was embarked, the same night, on a vessel of the imperial fleet. The fourth charge was thus left pending, by which he was accused of breaking the chalice of a priest who was celebrating the Holy Sacrifice, and of having trampled upon the Sacred Species. This calumny was grounded on the following facts. A certain Ischyras, residing in the province of Mareotis, who had never received any orders, had, on his own authority, arrogated to himself the priestly office, in a little hamlet in which he dwelt. In the course of his usual visitation of the province, St. Athanasius had sent a priest named Macarius who accompanied him, with orders to require Ischyras to put a stop to the scandal and to cease the sacrilegious intrusion. Macarius found Ischyras dangerously ill; he told the usurper's father of the patriarch's express command, bidding him communicate it to his son, on the latter's recovery; his duty thus peacefully discharged, he returned to the patriarch. Such was the act which the Eusebians had been able to color so highly, with their usual honesty and good faith. From the Council of Tyre, they sent a commission to examine the facts on the spot. With all the ill-will of the deputies, they could make nothing of the case, further than that Ischyras, at the time of the alleged crime, was sick in bed, and that he was, consequently, not celebrating the Holy Mysteries; that the day of Macarius's visit was not a Sunday, the only day on which the Holy Sacrifice was offered in these little hamlets; in a word, that there had been no altar overthrown, nor books burnt, nor chalice broken. On their return to Tyre, the commissioners gave in their report to the Arians, who made away with it, declared Athanasius guilty of all the crimes imputed to him, and deposed him from the episcopacy, forbidding him to reside in Alexandria, lest his stay should cause fresh troubles. All the Catholic bishops refused to sign the monstrous falsehood. The most abominable feature was the signature of Arsenius, bishop of Hypsele, amongst the subscribers to the sentence; so that Arsenius appeared alive to sign a sentence condemning Athanasius for causing his death. This reflection is made by the historian Socrates.

40. The reports which daily reached Constantine of the proceedings of the Council of Tyre were all prepared by the Arians, who omitted nothing to ruin St. Athanasius in the opinion of the emperor. The holy patriarch sailed in the public vessel on which he had embarked, to Constantinople, where he hoped, by his presence and explanations, to dissipate the false impressions made on the emperor's mind respecting him. At the moment when the emperor entered the city on horseback, St. Athanasius presented himself before him, in the midst of the imperial escort, and requested an audience. Constantine, surprised at this unexpected encounter, refused to hear him, because he regarded him as being legally condemned by a council. Athanasius exclaimed: "The Lord will judge between you and me, since you take the part of those who calumniate me." These words, pronounced with the accent of innocence, and the air of sanctity which shone in the person of the patriarch, struck Constantine. Apart from the official messages of the Arian bishops, he had received information from the Count Flavius Dionysius, that the Council of Tyre had often been the theatre of scenes of tumult and scandalous disorder. The conscience of the weak emperor hesitated in this conflict of men and things. He promised Athanasius to do him justice, and wrote to the bishops assembled at Tyre to come immediately to Constantinople and give an account of their conduct. The two Eusebiuses, Theognis, Patrophilus, Ursatius, and Valens only, obeyed this order. They relied on their ascendency, their artifice and intrigues, again to deceive the conscience of Constantine. When they were in his presence they said nothing of the clandestine ordination, nor of the outraged virgin, nor of the murdered bishop, nor of the chalice broken by Athanasius, but invented a new calumny. The preceding year the holy patriarch had purchased, during the winter, at his own expense, the wheat which he had dis-

tributed to the poor of Alexandria. Egypt was, as it is known, the granary of Rome, and, since the foundation of the new capital, its wheat was sent every year to the shores of the Bosphorus. Eusebius of Nicomedia accused St. Athanasius of hindering the convoys of wheat from reaching Constantinople. The emperor had just then condemned to death Sopater, one of his favorites, for the suspicion only of this crime. Constantine thought that he used great forbearance in sparing the life of St. Athanasius. He exiled him to Treves, then the capital of Gaul. St. Maximin, of Poitiers, who was bishop of Treves, received the illustrious proscribed with the highest honors. Constantine the younger, who commanded the legions of that province in the name of his father, treated him as a martyr to the faith, and this unjust exile only served to enhance the glory of him who suffered it, by making manifest his great merit and virtues.

41. The bishops assembled at Tyre having closed their council, as they called their factious assembly, went, by Constantine's order, to Jerusalem, to dedicate the new church which had just been erected. A vast multitude had gathered from all the provinces of the empire, to assist at this solemnity, of which Eusebius of Cæsarea has described all the ceremonies. He distinguished himself personally by an elaborate panegyric of Constantine, for which he deemed this a suitable occasion. The dedication took place September 14, A. D. 335, on the festival of the Holy Cross. Arius profited by the presence of the bishops at Jerusalem, to lay before them, in concert with the priest Euzoius, his confidant, and the most zealous of his supporters, the profession of faith which he had already submitted to Constantine. The Eusebians received this communication with favor, admitted Arius and Euzoius to the communion of the Church, and wrote a synodal letter to all the bishops of Christendom, to give them information thereof.

42. On the last day of December, A. D. 335, died Pope St. Sylvester I., after a pontificate of twenty-one years and eleven

months. He was deposited in the cemetery of St. Priscilla, in the *Salarian* way, and was removed by Paul I., in 762, to the church of St. Sylvester, in *Campo Marzo*, vulgarly called *St. Sylvester in capite*. In six ordinations, all in the month of December, the pontiff had consecrated sixty-three bishops, forty-two priests, and twenty-six deacons. Of all the popes, St. Sylvester is the only one, St. Peter excepted, in whose honor has been celebrated the feast called of Precept, for the twentieth year of a pontificate. Among other decisions, St. Sylvester decreed that in baptism the baptized should be anointed on the head with chrism. He also decided that the days of the week, except Saturday and Sunday, should be called *Ferias*, a name already in use with some ecclesiastical authors, particularly Tertullian. Monday is termed the *second Feria*, Tuesday the *third Feria*, and so on until Friday, which is termed the *sixth Feria*. Neither the *first Feria* nor the *seventh Feria* are mentioned. These two days preserve the ordinary names of *Sunday* (*Dominica Dies*) and *Saturday* (*Sabbatum*). It is not certain that it was St. Sylvester who ordained that altars should be of stone; but this became a rule of the Church from this epoch: it is still observed in the usage of the consecrated stone which is always placed in the middle of the altar, at the spot where repose the adorable body and blood of Jesus Christ. Nearly at this time, also, commenced the custom of consecrating the popes on a Sunday or other festival. There has been no exception to this rule but for the preconization of Paul III., Clement VII., and Leo X.

CHAPTER II.

§ I. PONTIFICATE OF ST. MARK (Jan. 18, A. D. 336—October 7, 336).

1. Election of St. Mark to the Sovereign Pontificate.—2. Arian Council of Constantinople; Deposition of Marcellus, Bishop of Ancyra; Restoration of Arius; His tragic Death.—3. Death of Pope St. Mark (October 7, A. D. 336).

§ II. PONTIFICATE OF POPE ST. JULIUS I. (Feb. 6, A. D. 337—April 12, 352).

4. Election of Pope Julius I.—5. Letter of St. Anthony to the Emperor Constantine. Exile of St. Paul, Patriarch of Constantinople. Death of Constantine the Great.—6. Recall of St. Athanasius to Alexandria, and of St. Paul to Constantinople. Second exile of Paul. Eusebius of Nicomedia takes possession of the Patriarchal See of Constantinople.—7. First Arian Council of Antioch.—8. St. Athanasius is a second time driven from Alexandria. Gregory of Cappadocia takes possession of his See. Council of Rome, convoked by Pope St. Julius I.—9. Recall of the Patriarch St. Paul to Constantinople. His third exile.—10. Second Arian Council of Antioch.—11. Catholic Councils of Milan and Sardica.—12. Return of St. Athanasius to Alexandria after his second exile. Return of St. Paul, Patriarch of Constantinople.—13. Death of St. Paul, the first hermit.—14. Circumcellians; Council of Carthage in regard to them.—15. Persecution of the Christians by Sapor II., King of Persia.—16. Raising of the first siege of Nisibis by Sapor II. Continuation of the Persecution in Persia.—17. Raising of the second siege of Nisibis by Sapor II. St. Ephrem, disciple of St. James of Nisibis.—18. Murder of Constans, Emperor of the West. Triple usurpation of the Empire.—19. Council of Sirmium. Fourth and last exile of St. Paul, Patriarch of Constantinople. His martyrdom.—20. Apparition of a miraculous cross at Jerusalem.—21. Death of Pope St. Julius I.

§ I. PONTIFICATE OF ST. MARK (Jan. 18, A. D. 336—Oct. 7, 336).

1. On the 18th of January, A. D. 336, St. Mark was elected to succeed St. Sylvester. Some years before, he had been appointed as one of the judges of Donatus, which sufficiently

proves that he was at that time known for his piety, wisdom and justice. It is believed that it was he who ordained the recital at Mass, after the Gospel, of that authentic and fundamental charter of faith, the Nicene Creed, *Credo in unum Deum.*

2. After the dedication of the church at Jerusalem, the bishops who had presided went to Constantinople, where the Eusebians desired to assemble a new council, ostensibly to examine the doctrine of the Bishop Marcellus of Ancyra, whom they accused of Sabellianism, because he sustained the Nicene faith. Marcellus taught, with the Catholic Church, that the distinction of persons in the Holy Trinity does not imply division of substance. "The Word," said he, "proceeds from the Father, and it is written of the Holy Spirit, sometimes that He proceeds from the Father, sometimes that He proceeds from the Word; consequently, He proceeds at the same time from both. Now it is impossible to conceive that He proceeds from both, if the Father and the Son are separated by nature. Since, then, He proceeds from the Father and the Son, they are one only God." The two often named bishops Eusebius condemned this doctrine and its author without discussion, which proves either their flagrant bad faith, or their absolute ignorance of Catholic theology. They excommunicated Marcellus of Ancyra, and deposed him from his see. They then occupied themselves with the restoration of Arius, who, since the exile of St. Athanasius to Treves, had vainly attempted to re-enter Alexandria. The people of this city, faithful to their holy patriarch and to the Catholic faith, had risen, on the approach of the heresiarch, and had driven him from their walls. The attempt having thus failed at Alexandria, the Eusebians undertook to make it succeed at Constantinople, the imperial city, and in the view of the world. Their first movement was addressed to the patriarch of Constantinople, St. Alexander. They prayed him to have compassion on a priest, so long, they said, and so unjustly persecuted. The saintly old man, then more than ninety years of age, had neither less firmness, nor less attachment to the faith, than

his namesake, St. Alexander, Patriarch of Alexandria. "The favor which I should extend to Arius," he replied, "would be a real cruelty to the Catholics. The laws of the Church do not permit me, by a false compassion, to contravene that which I have myself decreed with all the holy Council of Nice." The emperor then, of his own authority, fixed on a Sunday, when Arius should be solemnly received in the principal church of Constantinople, and admitted to communion in presence of all the people. He signified to St. Alexander to cease his opposition on pain of exile. The patriarch had recourse henceforth only to spiritual arms. By the advice of St. James, bishop of Nisibis, who was then in Constantinople, he recommended to the faithful a fast of seven days, to implore help from heaven in this pressing danger of the Church. The eve of the appointed day, the holy old man, prostrate before the altar, his face to the ground, in the effusion of his soul, and with many tears, offered this prayer: "Lord, if Arius must be received in this Church on the morrow, withdraw Thy servant from this world. But if Thou hast yet pity on Thy Church, suffer not Thy heritage to be profaned. Let Arius be stricken with the weight of Thine anger, and let not heresy be longer puffed up with its victory."

Meanwhile Arius went about the city, surrounded by a crowd of his partisans, who formed for him a sort of triumphal escort. Having reached the great public place in view of the basilica where St. Alexander prayed, he was seized with a nervous trembling, and asked leave to retire into a secret place. As he remained an unusually long time, his friends entered, and found him lying dead, bathed in his blood and his entrails gushing out. The horror of such a spectacle made even his sectaries tremble. The scene of this tragic end ceased to be frequented; no one dared approach it, and it was pointed out as a monument of divine vengeance.

3. These events occupied the whole of the short pontificate of St. Mark, who died October 7, A. D. 336, within the year of his exaltation. He was interred in the *Via Ardea-*

tina, in the cemetery of St. Balbina, and thence transported to the Church of St. Mark, which he had dedicated. This pontiff had imposed hands on twenty-five bishops, twenty-seven priests, and six deacons. After his death the holy see remained some time vacant.

§ II. PONTIFICATE OF ST. JULIUS I. (Feb. 6, A. D. 337—April 12, 352).

4. St. Julius I. was elected successor of St. Mark, after an interregnum of three months. One of the first cares of the new pontiff was to collect, in special archives, all that concerned the history of the Church in Rome—acts, donations and testaments. Cenni believes that this was the origin of the pontifical library.

5. The death of Arius had made a deep impression on the mind of Constantine. Eusebius of Nicomedia was himself in consternation. An accident so unforeseen was too evidently out of the line of ordinary facts, and disconcerted all calculations. The emperor felt it a duty, for the enlightenment of his conscience, to ask the advice of the patriarch of the desert, St. Anthony. When the officers of the palace arrived on the mountain, bearers of the imperial message, the monks could not conceal their joy at the honor conferred on their Father. "Be not surprised," said the saint, "that an emperor writes to a mortal man; be astonished, rather, that God designed to write His law for men, and to speak to them by His own Son." He replied to Constantine by counsels full of wisdom, and reminded him of the frivolity of the things of earth and the approach of eternal judgment. He pressed the emperor to revise the trial of St. Athanasius, and to put an end to his exile, which was as unjust towards an innocent man, as it was injurious to the reputation of the prince who had ordered it. At the moment of the arrival of this letter at Constantinople, the emperor had just consented to the exile of Paul, Catholic patriarch of Constantinople, and successor of St. Alexander, at the solicitations of Eusebius of Nicomedia, who wished to seat himself, by a

third intrusion, in a see which did not belong to him. Constantine, however, was approaching the term of his life, and the counsels of St. Anthony acted upon a conscience which became more clear-sighted as he approached the tomb. He formed the resolution to recall St. Athanasius, but death left him no time. He asked for baptism, which was administered by Eusebius of Nicomedia, whose obsequious familiarity pursued the dying emperor even on his bed of death. After he had received this sacrament, the emperor quitted the purple, and would wear only the white dress of the neophytes, until his death, which happened on the day of Pentecost, May 20th, 337. A hero in the first half of his life, wise in policy, and fortunate in war, the first of the emperors who had understood the influence which Christianity must exercise on civilization, and who had seconded it by merciful laws and institutions, Constantine would have been a faultless prince, if the second part of his life had not been given up to all the intrigues, all the artifices of the courtiers. Yet his name has always been dear to the Church: his memory will ever be blessed, and the good which he effected can never be effaced by the evil which he did not always prevent. None of the sons of Constantine was present to close his eyes: his body was laid in the great hall of the guards of the palace of Nicomedia, elevated on a catafalque covered with purple, and surrounded with lights which burned in golden candlesticks. He was subsequently transported to Constantinople, and interred in the Church of the Apostles, which he had chosen for his tomb. The empire was divided among his three sons: Constantine the younger had Spain, Gaul, and in general all the Roman provinces beyond the Alps; Constantius, Asia, the East, and Egypt; and Constans, Italy, Africa, Sicily, and Illyria, A. D. 338. This division was soon modified by the crime of Constans who caused his brother Constantine the younger to be assassinated, and took possession of his dominions (A. D. 340), so that the empire was resolved into two grand divisions—the East where Constantius reigned, and the West governed by Constans the fratricide.

27

'6. Constantine the younger had had time, during his ephemeral reign, to restore the orthodox bishops who had been deprived of their sees by the Arians. St. Athanasius returned to Alexandria (A. D. 338), where he was received with the acclamations of all his people, and with a pomp worthy of an emperor. Asclepas of Gaza, Marcellus of Ancyra, and Paul of Constantinople, all regained possession of their churches. These acts of justice in Constantine the younger inspire regret for his premature end. Constantius, who assumed the government of the East, agitated by the Arian dissensions, had all the faults of his father, without his good qualities. Of a character feeble and undecided, always wavering, his conduct was without unity of purpose or consistency, and full of contradictions; he reigned by his favorites. It was said of him: "It must be admitted that the emperor has much influence with Eusebius, chief of the eunuchs." This eunuch Eusebius had been at first gained over to Arianism by Eusebius of Nicomedia. The empress participated in his views, and the Arian priests whom Constantine I. had admitted to his favor on the recommendation of his sister Constantia, and to whom he had afterwards confided his last will, became all powerful at the new court of Constantius. It is not difficult to foresee the part which Eusebius of Nicomedia would take in circumstances so favorable to his views. Death was striking down those most dear to him, and had taken from his side, the same year, his namesake, Eusebius of Cæsarea, his other self, more courtier than bishop, more erudite than profound, more rhetorician than theologian, always more favorable to error than to truth. This example made no impression on Eusebius of Nicomedia; the ambitious, so long as there are honors to be won, think themselves immortal. He procured an assemblage of bishops at Constantinople; on calumnious accusations, they deposed the holy Patriarch St. Paul, who again returned to exile, and this time Eusebius saw his intrigues crowned with complete success. He seated himself finally, by his own authority, in the see of Constantinople, which for so many years had been the subject of his dreams.

7. His hatred of Athanasius only increased with the means of satisfying it. An Arian priest, named Pistus, whose life and morals were in ill repute, was consecrated bishop by Secundus of Ptolemais, who had been himself deposed by the Council of Nice. Pistus was sent, with the title of patriarch, to Alexandria, while St. Athanasius, welcomed as a father by all the Catholics, resumed the possession of his legitimate authority. Eusebius of Nicomedia at the same time sent to Rome a deputation to St. Julius I., charged with letters of accusation against St. Athanasius, and of recommendation of Pistus, the intruded patriarch. To answer these calumnies, St. Athanasius assembled at Alexandria a council of nearly a hundred bishops from Egypt, the Thebais, Libya, and the Pentapolis. They read all the accusations hitherto brought against the holy patriarch; pointed out all the calumnies, the nullities, the irregularities which marked them; and afterwards addressed a synodal letter to Pope St. Julius, and to all the churches of the world, to protest against all that the enemies of St. Athanasius had said or done against him. The deputies, bearers of this vindication, arrived at Rome at the same time with those of Eusebius of Nicomedia. It was not difficult to reduce the slanderers to silence; but the Eusebians did not consider themselves as beaten. An Arian council assembled at Antioch, where Constantius held his court, for the dedication of the Basilica of that city (A. D. 341). After the compilation and rejection of three professions of faith, they agreed on a fourth formula, where the word so formidable to Arians, *consubstantial*, was not found. They then, without waiting the sentence from Rome, proceeded to the deposition of St. Athanasius, and elected as his successor, not Pistus, whom they abandoned because of his bad reputation, but Gregory of Cappadocia, who was consecrated as patriarch of Alexandria, and sent with an escort of soldiers furnished by Constantius, to take, by arms, possession of the

see. The canons of discipline were made to conform to these iniquitous acts. "If a bishop," they decreed, "has been once condemned by a council, he can be no more judged by others: and the sentence will take effect." "If he continue to trouble the Church, he will be rebuked as seditious by the secular power." This was to appeal, against St. Athanasius, to the secular arm, which was then called Constantius, and to reject the intervention of the pope. They then deposed Marcellus of Ancyra, and Asclepas of Gaza, and the Eusebians could rejoice in their triumph.

8. Gregory of Cappadocia meantime arrived at Alexandria, supported by the authority and the military force of the apostate Philagrius, whom Constantius, at the solicitation of the Eusebians, had just named, for the second time, prefect of Egypt, with orders, at any cost, to force away St. Athanasius. The church was taken by assault, the virgins consecrated to God were infamously outraged; the religious, who continued faithful to their legitimate patriarch, were maltreated, and some were put to death: the sacred vessels were given up to pillage, and Gregory after this manner took possession of the see, to which he was elevated by the arms of Constantius, and the abused power of the Eusebians. St. Athanasius was proscribed, and a price set on his head by order of the governor: all who were devoted to him were cast into the public prisons, and he took refuge in the monasteries near Alexandria. The intruded patriarch, with an escort of soldiers, undertook a visitation of the province. Most of the bishops refused to acknowledge a metropolitan imposed by force, to whose election they had not been summoned. The only reply was made by loading them with irons. Sarapammon, bishop of Upper Thebais, was banished for his courageous resistance; the illustrious and aged St. Potamon, whose virtues the two Councils of Nice and Tyre had admired, was beaten with rods, and died of his wounds, with the glory of a double martyrdom. Against so much violence, Athanasius opposed the calmness of an unassailable right and an unyielding conscience. He addressed a

circular letter to all the bishops in the world reciting the facts, and beseeching them not to hold communion with the intruder. This duty being fulfilled, to avoid compromising the monks who had given him hospitality, by a longer sojourn, he departed for Rome, where Pope Julius I. received him as a hero of the faith. The sovereign pontiff announced his intention to bring the judgment of this affair before his own tribunal. To this effect, he appointed for the year A. D. 342, a council to be held at Rome, and he sent two Roman priests, Elpidius and Philoxenus, to the Eusebians, to require their attendance. The Eusebians detained the legates several months under different pretexts, and finished by sending them away with a letter in which they expressed, in equivocal terms, their respect for the holy see, and declared that it was not possible to be present at the Council of Rome, since the time remaining was insufficient. The council was already assembled when Elpidius and Philoxenus arrived. It was composed of fifty bishops from Italy, Africa, and Gaul, who unanimously admitted to the communion of the Church St. Athanasius, Marcellus of Ancyra, and Asclepas of Gaza, and declared null the nomination of the intruders who had robbed them of their sees. St. Julius, in concert with the Fathers of the council, wrote to the Eusebians, in reply to the letter which they had sent by Elpidius and Philoxenus. The pope declares that the faith of the Council of Nice is the Catholic faith; that whatever has been done against the decisions of that œcumenic council is null and of no effect. He justifies St. Athanasius, Marcellus of Ancyra, and Asclepas of Gaza, from all the calumnies levelled against them, formally condemns the intruders who had forced them from their churches, and opposes the irregularity of all that had been done without the approval of the see of Rome. "Know you not," he says, "that the canonical rule was to recur first to our authority, and that the decision must proceed from it? Such is the tradition that we have received from the blessed Apostle Peter, and I believe it to be so universally acknowledged, that

I should not recall it here, if these deplorable circumstances did not constrain me to proclaim it." This letter of Pope St. Julius, admirable for its majesty, gentleness, and true eloquence, is one of the most precious monuments of the wisdom and firmness of the Roman Pontiff.

9. When this letter reached Constantinople, Eusebius, the intruded bishop, the courtier-prelate, abettor of Arianism, whose intrigues had created and perpetuated so many agitations and troubles within the Church, had just expired in his usurped see (A. D. 342). The Catholics of Constantinople, freed from his tyrannical yoke, hastened to recall, before the return of Constantius, who was at Antioch, their legitimate patriarch, St. Paul, from his unjust exile. The public joy broke forth in long acclamations when the venerable old man landed on the shores of the Bosphorus; and it might have been thought for a moment, that the days of union and peace for this desolated Church had returned. But the spirit of Eusebius survived in his party. The Arian bishop Theognis of Nice, and Theodore of Heraclea, protested against the restoration of the true patriarch; to an intruder they resolved to give an intruder for successor, and consecrated as Archbishop of Constantinople, Mardonius, an unworthy priest, who afterwards added his name to the list of heresiarchs. This sacrilegious election was the signal of a civil war, and a frightful sedition at Constantinople. The Emperor Constantius, warned by the Arians, sent the prefect of his guards, Hermogenes, with orders to remove St. Paul, and to reconduct him to exile. The Catholics defended their bishop—the passions of all were excited, and knew no bounds: the multitude seized Hermogenes, burnt his palace, murdered him, and dragged his mutilated body through the city (A. D. 342). Constantius, on hearing of this, left Antioch, and in spite of the rains and snows of winter, crossed Asia Minor on horseback, and reached the gates of Constantinople, resolved to punish it with fire and sword. The people in tears, the senate as suppliants, all orders of the state in mourning, came to meet him: he

yielded to their prayers, and pardoned all the rebels on condition that St. Paul should be banished. The patriarch left his church for the third time, and it fell again into the power of the usurper.

10. St. Julius meantime had sent legates to the Emperor Constans at Treves, to present the synodal letter from the council at Rome, and to inform him of the banishment of the patriarchs of Alexandria and Constantinople. Constantius, on his side, sent to Treves four Arian bishops to explain to Constans the whole matter treated of at Antioch. St. Maximin, bishop of Treves, refused to communicate with them; he welcomed, on the contrary, the delegates of the sovereign pontiff with public marks of his veneration, and declared that he would never have any other faith than that of Rome. Constans was of the same mind. The Arian prelates returned to the East, and saw no other alternative than to call a new council at Antioch. It was held the following year (A. D. 345). The entire Arian party was convoked. They rejected absolutely the term *consubstantial*, and after stormy discussions they agreed upon a long formula of faith, composed almost entirely of words taken from Scripture, which was to be the new creed of Arianism.

11. The Orientals sent it the following year (A. D. 346) to the Council of Milan, which Pope St. Julius had just convoked. It was unanimously rejected, and the angry Arians appealed to a more numerous council, where the bishops of the East and West should be united. The pope consented to this demand. In concert with the Emperors Constans and Constantius, a council was assembled at Sardica (A. D. 347). Three hundred Catholic bishops, having at their head Osius of Cordova, responded to the call of the Sovereign Pontiff. The Arians were fewer in number, but they were accompanied by the Count Musonian, and Hesychius, general of the imperial armies, and hoped that the weight of arms might incline the decision in their favor. Osius of Cordova was designated by St. Julius as his legate, and the council proceeded to its

deliberations, admitting neither the count nor the general, and resolved to come to a decision entirely independent of political influences or court intrigues. St. Athanasius presented himself furnished with all the documents necessary to prove his innocence, and the bad faith of his enemies. The bishops who had been banished from their sees by Gregory, the intruded patriarch of Alexandria, appeared with the chains which had been put upon them, and ocular witnesses came to testify to the violence they had seen committed. Entire churches sent deputies, who called upon the Council of Sardica to restore their legitimate pastors, who had been banished, outraged, or persecuted by the Arians. They recounted the frightful treatment endured by the consecrated virgins, by venerable and holy pontiffs, by monks, and anchorets. The original of the famous report of the inquest made on the subject of the affair of Ischyras, in the province of Mareotis, was laid by St. Athanasius before the Fathers; and the innocence of the patriarch was confirmed by the testimony of his enemies themselves. The bishops of the East could not approve deliberations, where so little regard was shown to the material force at their disposal. They abruptly retired from the council, and rejected the overtures made by the Catholics for their return. Osius of Cordova went even so far as to submit to them the following proposition: "If the result of our proceedings establishes the guilt of Athanasius, you may be assured of the rigor of his condemnation. And if he succeed in proving his innocence, and you persist in refusing to receive him to your communion, I engage to take him with me to Spain." St. Athanasius subscribed to these conditions, but his enemies had so little confidence in the justice of their cause, that they refused to hear any thing, and departed immediately for their churches, under the frivolous pretence that the emperor had written to them to offer thanksgivings to God on the occasion of his recent victory over the Persians. The retreat of the Arians hindered in nothing the progress of the council. Three subjects were submitted for its examination: 1. A declaration of the Catholic faith on the question raised by Arianism; 2. The cause of the bishops driven from their sees, and accused by the Arians; 3. The complaints made against the Arians by their victims. On the first point, it was decided by an immense majority to adhere to the creed of Nice, as defining in an explicit and precise manner the Catholic faith in the divinity of the Son of God. They passed immediately to the appeal in the causes of St. Athanasius, Marcellus of Ancyra, and Asclepas of Gaza, driven from their sees by the Arians. All the accusations before submitted to the Council of Tyre were brought up, examined anew, and unanimously rejected, as infamous calumnies. Marcellus of Ancyra, and Asclepas of Gaza, were declared innocent. As a consequence, the three prelates were solemnly admitted to the communion of the Church; their legitimate authority over the sees from which they had been ejected was confirmed, and the usurpers were anathematized. It now remained to institute an inquiry into the conduct of the bishops of the East, who had never ceased, in spite of the decision of the œcumenic Council of Nice, to communicate with the Arians, to sustain them with their credit at Constantinople, and to intrude them by violence into the sees of the principal churches. The chiefs of the faction, until then tolerated, were by name deposed from the episcopate, and excommunicated. They were eight in number, viz.: Theodore of Heraclea, Narcissus of Neroniad, Stephen of Antioch, Gregory of Laodicea, Acacius of Cæsarea in Palestine, Menophantes of Ephesus, Ursatius of Singidon, and Valens of Mursa. The two last had been anathematized by the Council of Nice. The Fathers then entered upon the discussion of canons of discipline, in which they acknowledge and categorically explain the right of appeal to the pope, the jurisdiction of the See of Rome over ecclesiastical causes, and the obligation to submit to its judgment, or to that of the legates commissioned by the sovereign pontiff, to examine facts at the place where they occurred. These delegates have been since named legates *a latere.* Other canons forbid arbitrary translations from one bishopric to another, and the nomination of bishops to sees of which the titulars have appealed to the popes, in advance of the definitive judgment of the sovereign pontiff. The acts of the council were immediately sent to Pope St. Julius, and to the two emperors Constantius and Constans, at Antioch and Treves. Thus terminated the peaceful session of the Council of Sardica. It has not been placed in the rank of œcumenic councils, although bishops were assembled from all the provinces of the world. But it made no new formula of articles of faith, and it confined its action to the recognition of the creed of the Nicene Council, of which it may be regarded as a consequence and corollary.

12. The decision of the Council of Sardica was received with the applause of the Christian world. Vainly the Arian bishops attempted to fix an odious calumny upon the two bishops, Vincent of Capua, and Euphratas of Cologne, who were appointed to bear to the Emperor Constantius the synodal letter of the council. On their arrival at Antioch, Stephen, the bishop of that city, bribed a domestic of the two legates to introduce a woman of bad life by night into their apartment. The wretched creature, conscience stricken on seeing the two venerable men, fled, divulging everywhere in the city the detestable treason to which they had wished to make her an accomplice. This incident served to open the eyes of the too feeble Constantius. After a judicial inquiry, in which the Arian Stephen was convicted of having plotted this infamous machination, the emperor sent the judgment to the bishops then present at Antioch, who deposed and excommunicated him. Constantius admitted the envoys of the council to an audience, received favorably their message, and decreed the recall of the exiled prelates. He even manifested a desire to see St. Athanasius, and wrote with his own hand three letters, to pray him to visit his court. The patriarch was at this moment in Rome, with Pope St. Julius I., to whom these tidings gave great joy. Before parting with St. Athanasius, the sovereign pontiff wrote to the

clergy and faithful of Alexandria a letter of congratulation. "Finally, well-beloved brethren," he said to them, "all your desires are fulfilled. Athanasius, your bishop, is restored to you. Welcome with all honor this illustrious witness of our holy faith. You have been his consolation when among foreign nations; your fidelity has sustained him in the midst of perils and persecution. Our heart thrills with pleasure when we represent to ourselves the return of our venerable brother to your midst, the shouts of joy on his passage, the piety of the people who go to meet him, the transport of the multitude who are attracted from all quarters. What a day for you! The past will be ended. This so much desired return will henceforth unite all minds and all hearts. We ourselves participate the more in your joy, as God has given us the grace to know personally so great a man." Such were the sentiments of universal charity which animated the soul of the Roman pontiffs; such also was the veneration inspired by the virtues and genius of Athanasius the Great. St. Julius allowed him to depart, loaded with benedictions, for Antioch, where Constantius then held his court. The emperor received the saintly patriarch with a benevolence to which neither of them was accustomed. He ordered to be effaced from the public acts in the archives of the empire all that had been written against Athanasius, and swore to him solemnly never to listen to his calumniators. He ordered letters to be sent to the Egyptian churches to inform them "that to be united in communion with the venerable Athanasius would be a sufficient proof of good dispositions." Finally, he commanded the magistrates and people of Alexandria to receive the patriarch with the same honors as they would their sovereign. Preceded by these eminent testimonials of the imperial favor, St. Athanasius appeared at Alexandria (A. D. 347). All the bishops of Egypt and the two Libyas were there to receive him; the magistrates and people awaited him in their holiday garb; the city was hung with tapestries and garlands of flowers; a multitude bearing green boughs escorted the illustrious exile; no trace of former discords troubled this day of universal joy. Gregory of Cappadocia, the intruder, had perished some months before, in a popular tumult. The joy which the return of the legitimate patriarch spread throughout Alexandria was manifested in good works, and by an increase of fervor and Christian piety. The charity of the people was enkindled; they fed and clothed the poor and the orphans, and each house seemed to have become a church appropriated to prayer and the practice of virtue. They who had been until then the most bitter persecutors of St. Athanasius, hastened to ask to be restored to his communion. Ursatius and Valens addressed to Pope St. Julius a formal retractation of their conduct. "All that we have hitherto written against Athanasius," said they, "all the accusations produced against him, and sustained by us, we declare to be atrocious calumnies, and we ask pardon of your holiness and of him. And besides, we anathematize the heretic Arius and his abettors, and supplicate you to receive us into the communion of the Church." The other exiled prelates were at the same time restored to their sees: St. Paul at Constantinople, Asclepas at Gaza, Marcellus at Ancyra; and, for the moment, it seemed that Arianism was forever vanquished.

13. Great was the joy in the solitudes of Nitria and the Thebais, on the return of St. Athanasius to his patriarchal city of Alexandria. But none of the religious felt it more sensibly than St. Anthony, whose soul had participated in all the tribulations of the illustrious proscribed. The preceding year, St. Anthony, guided by the Divine Spirit, had, alone, leaning on the cane which supported his feeble age, plunged into the remote regions of the desert. A grotto, closed by a stone which the hand of man must have brought there, caught his eye. "Open," said the patriarch, knocking at this entrance; "you know who I am, whence I came, and why. I am not worthy to look upon your face, but for the love of Jesus Christ, open for me, or I shall die at your door." An aged man, whose white hair fell upon a body emaciated by age and

the austerities of penance, more like a skeleton than a man, wearing a girdle of palm-leaves, came to open the door. It was Paul, the first of the hermits, who had lived, since the year 250, unknown to all men, fed by a half loaf of bread which a raven deposited every morning before his grotto. The two saints saluted each other by name, though neither had ever heard of the other. Seated on a rock by the fountain which had given for nearly a century its limpid water to this veteran of the solitudes, Paul said to his guest, "What are men doing now? Do they still build new houses in their old cities? What master do they obey? And do they always persecute the Christians?" Anthony replied to all these questions, and leaving the hermit, returned to his monastery for the mantle which St. Athanasius had given him, in which St. Paul desired to be buried. St. Anthony made the journey with all the haste that his exhausted strength permitted; but on his return, he found only the inanimate remains of the aged saint. He buried him with respect. A lion came to dig, in the sand at his feet, a grave where the body of St. Paul was deposited, to await his blessed resurrection. These touching details, related by St. Athanasius himself, in his *Life of St. Anthony*, which he wrote for the brethren of the Thebais, went far to awaken in many souls the love of solitude, and a holy ardor for eremitic perfection. Captivated by the powerful attraction of this life, mysteriously flowing onwards in contemplation and prayer, a crowd of young men and pious virgins tore themselves away from the tumult of the world, to confide to the cloister the secret of their hopes and their destinies. Rome beheld the formation, within her limits, of monasteries which rivalled the zeal and fervor of the blooming deserts of Nitria, and the religious life was thus inaugurated in the Church, under the influence of illustrious and holy examples.

14. While the great contest of Arianism had agitated all the East, and virtue seemed to have retired to the desert, with the Pauls, the Anthonys, the Hilarions, and their disciples,

the Church of Carthage had not ceased to be rent by the schism of the Donatists. Two of the name of Donatus had succeeded to the famous Donatus *de Casis Nigris*, whose intrigues we have recounted; one had made himself the schismatic Bishop of Carthage, the other had usurped the Episcopal See of Bagaia. Their partisans, spread over the country, and around the cottages of the peasants, *circum cellas*, had taken the name of *circumcellians*, and gave to the world the spectacle of a new and strange fanaticism. They inspired the multitude with the desire of death, in order the sooner to reach heaven, and bands of desperate people claimed a self-inflicted martyrdom by casting themselves headlong into mountain chasms—into the deep waters of rapid streams—or into the flames of vast pyres lighted by their own hands. Sometimes, disdaining to take their own lives, they forced passers-by to render them this service. A young man one day encountered a troop of these frantic creatures, who offered him a naked sword, with orders to kill them all, if he did not wish to be immolated himself. The stranger feigned to lend himself with a good grace to their fancy, but declared that they must first be all bound, for fear of reprisals. The madmen consented; when all were securely fastened, the young man lashed them vigorously, and wishing them better luck, continued on his way. The circumcellians, in their ardor for martyrdom, held it right to subject others to it. They pretended it was a work of mercy to beat to death inoffensive travellers, and thus send them to heaven by the shortest road. Their disorders soon made the intervention of the imperial authority necessary. Constantius sent two considerable personages of his court, Paul and Macarius, to Carthage, with power to put an end to their excesses. The means of conciliation which the two lieutenants of the emperor attempted, were powerless against madmen resolved to die. They were obliged to resort to an armed force, which dispersed them after an obstinate resistance. Donatus, the intruded Bishop of Carthage, fled with all his clergy: his namesake of Bagaia threw himself into a well; Maculus, who had put himself at the head of the rebels, threw himself headlong from the top of a rock. The remainder of this frenzied sect hid themselves in the desert, and gradually disappeared; with them was extinguished the schism of the Donatists, who, since the year 311, had troubled the Church of Carthage. Gratus, the Catholic bishop of that city, assembled a council at the end of the year 348, to complete the measures to be taken respecting the schismatics in good faith, who in crowds entreated to be restored to the communion of their legitimate pastor. The fourteen canons which they decreed, bear the impress of the spirit of merciful charity which preserves discipline without compromising union through excess of rigor. They forbid the readministration of baptism to those who have received it from heretics or unworthy ministers, provided it has been given in the name of the Father, of the Son, and of the Holy Ghost. It is known that the contrary practice was precisely the error of the Donatists. They declare that the title and honors of martyrdom cannot be awarded to those who in the face of Heaven put themselves to death, after the manner of the circumcellians. Finally, they give rules of conduct to the clergy and faithful.

15. The peace which the Catholic Church enjoyed after the reunion of the East and West at the Council of Sardica, and the dispersion of the circumcellians, was troubled only by the persecution which Sapor II., King of Persia had waged against the Christians in his states since the year 327. The relations which this prince had at first entertained with the Emperor Constantine the Great, were soon changed into open hostilities. Sapor invented tortures for the faithful, still numerous in the churches of Persia which had escaped the ingenious cruelty of the Roman proconsuls. All the churches and altars were overturned, the monasteries burnt, and the religious hunted like wild beasts. In the city of Lubaham, two Christian brothers were seized, Jonas and Birch-Jesus, who had brought to the Christians imprisoned for the faith

the aid of their charity and devotion. Jonas was fastened to a stake, half impaled, and beaten with rods, until his bones were exposed. In this state he was plunged into a freezing pond, where he passed the night. The next day the martyr was led before the tribunal, and summoned anew to adore the sun and the fire, divinities of Persia. "Life," replied Jonas, "is a seed which the Christian spreads over the earth: if we have patience to await the time of harvest, it will produce in the next world immortal glory." The judges at these words ordered the joints of his feet and hands to be cut off, one by one, bone by bone, and spreading them over the marble floor of the pretorium, said to him: "Now thou hast only to await the harvest; thou seest how we have sown thy fingers; they will produce for thee feet and hands by the hundred." "God who created them will know how to restore them to me," said the saint. Quickly they proceeded to tear the skin from his head, and threw him into a caldron of boiling pitch; but, by the visible protection of Providence, the pitch suddenly escaped from the vessel without hurting the martyr. The judges then crushed his limbs under a wooden press. They sawed his body in pieces, threw it into a pit, and placed guards to prevent the Christians from taking away his precious relics. His brother, Birch-Jesus, suffered tortures not less horrible. They applied plates of red-hot iron under his arms: "If thou let one of these plates fall," said the judge, "we will affirm that thou hast renounced the Christian faith." "Minister of an impious king," cried the saint, "I fear not your fire; I will not move my arms, and will keep all the heated irons you may please to place in them." Upon these words, the judges ordered melted lead to be poured into his nostrils and eyes, and remanded him to prison, to pass the night suspended by one of his feet. On the day following, his tortures had in no way weakened the constancy of the saint. The tormentors began by striking him with thorns, then buried in his flesh sharp points of reeds, and when his whole body was covered, they bound him with cords and rolled him on the ground, which was dyed with his blood. After this horrible torture, they poured into his mouth boiling pitch and burning sulphur. During this last torment he expired. The remains of these illustrious brothers, redeemed by Abtusciatas, one of their friends, for six hundred drachmas, were buried with honor by the Christians.

16. These cruelties, which were practised throughout Persia, by the order of Sapor, were redoubled in consequence ot a check which the arms of this prince met with under the walls of the city of Nisibis in Mesopotamia. The death of Constantine the Great appeared to Sapor to offer a favorable occasion for an irruption into the Roman Empire. He came, therefore, in A. D. 338 to besiege Nisibis, where St. James was bishop. The army of the Persians was immense, both in cavalry and infantry. Entire regiments of elephants, carrying high towers, accompanied it, with martial engines of every description. But after sixty-three days of siege, Sapor was obliged to retire ignominiously, and to return to his dominions. His army, harassed by the Roman troops, exhausted by fatigue, decimated by disease, pestilence, and famine, nearly all perished. On his return he visited upon the Christians the shame of his defeat. Horsemen were sent into all the provinces, with orders to bring as prisoners to the capital all adorers of Jesus Christ. It was feared that the aversion to these executions would increase, by multiplying them in each locality, and therefore the persecution was to be centralized, so far as was practicable. History has preserved the names of some of the most illustrious martyrs who at this time gave their blood in testimony of their faith (A. D. 339). These were Sapor, bishop of Beth-Nictor, Isaac, bishop of Seleucia, Abraham, Mahanes, and Simeon. Mahanes was flayed alive; Simeon was buried up to the breast, and pierced with arrows; Abraham had his eyes burned out with a red-hot iron, and died two days afterwards; Isaac was stoned; the bishop Sapor was struck on the face with such violence as to break all his teeth, and he was then beaten to death. Such cruelties only aug

mented the numbers of the faithful in Persia. We have always seen persecutions produce this effect in the Church. The next year (A. D. 340) King Sapor published a general decree against the Christians, which condemned their persons to slavery, and their property to confiscation. Simeon, bishop of Seleucia, was a venerable old man, of whom Sapor himself said: "I have travelled over distant lands, yet never have I seen any thing comparable to the august majesty of his countenance." He refused to give up the sacred vessels, and other valuables of his church, and replied to the king, who urged him to do it, "It is the patrimony of the poor; I would rather die than give away this sacred deposit." On this reply they led away the holy bishop to a dungeon. Among the crowd assembled at the palace gate to see his departure, was an aged eunuch, named Guhsciatade, who had been the tutor of Sapor, and who enjoyed high consideration at court. He had once professed the Christian faith, but the fear of persecution had made him an apostate. At the sight of the holy bishop, he fell on his knees to beg his benediction. Simeon passed, turning away his eyes, to mark the horror which his apostasy inspired. Guhsciatade understood the mute eloquence of this reproach. He went immediately to lay aside the splendid garments which he wore in his office of grand chamberlain of the king, covered himself with vestments of mourning, and returned to the palace to present himself to Sapor. "Send me to execution," he said; "I merit the heaviest punishment for betraying my God, and violating the faith which I promised him." "What," cried the furious Sapor, "is that the cause of thy sorrow? Cure thyself of this madness, or I shall force thee to obey me." "Henceforth I will obey the true God alone; I will no longer adore creatures." "I, then, adore creatures, caitiff!" "Yes, and what is most deplorable, inanimate creatures." "Die, then," said Sapor, and he ordered his aged preceptor to execution. As a last favor, and in order to repair, as far as he could, the scandal of his apostasy, Guhsciatade requested the king to publish that he was put to death for his fidelity to the God of the Christians. The tidings of this martyrdom consoled the holy bishop in his prison. The next day he was again brought before Sapor, whose threats found him inflexible; the king ordered a hundred Christian prisoners to be executed in his presence, among whom were bishops, priests, and deacons. Simeon encouraged them to suffer death courageously for the name of Jesus Christ. Last of this glorious phalanx of heroes—he was himself beheaded. The two priests who accompanied him, Abdaicla and Hananias, met the same fate. While Hananias laid aside his garments to prepare for the execution, he was seized with an involuntary trembling. Phusikius, superintendent of public works of the king, who was present at the execution, remarked to the confessor: Have confidence, Hananias, close your eyes, and in a moment you will see the divine light of Christ." These few words, reported to Sapor, won for Phusikius the crown of martyrdom. Sapor resolved that his punishment should be accompanied with extraordinary cruelties. It was not easy to imagine new tortures. The tormentors pierced his neck, and through the opening tore out his tongue. He expired under this frightful operation. These different executions took place April 16th and 17th, A. D. 341. The exasperated Sapor published an edict the same day, April 17th, which condemned to death all Christians from whom the judges could not procure an explicit renunciation of the name of Jesus Christ. In a short time nothing was seen in all Persia but instruments of torture. The Christians, far from betraying their faith, hastened generously to death, and the executioners, wearied with slaughter, confessed themselves, more than once, overcome by the patience of their victims. "The cross," said St. Maruthas, bishop of Mesopotamia, witness of this atrocious butchery, "germinated in streams of blood." The names of all those martyrs, glorious before God, are for the most part unknown to men. That of the virgin Tharba, who was taken with her sister and her servant, has been preserved. The Magi caused their bodies to be sawed in two. They then cut each half into six parts, and threw them into as many baskets, which were suspended upon stakes in two lines. The queen, who was then ill, and whose ill health was attributed by the Magi to enchantments of the Christians, passed between the bloody fragments in the hope of recovering her strength by the sight of the mutilated remains of these victims, May 5th, A. D. 341. Some months afterwards, the governor of the province of Chaldea, Hormisdas, and Narses, his brother, pierced with their poniards the Bishop of Susa, St. Milles. Before he expired, the aged saint prophesied that the day following they would kill each other. The murderers laughed at the prediction. The next day, in a great hunt, the two brothers pursued from opposite directions a stag which had escaped from the hounds. They discharged their arrows at the same moment, and struck each other at the same hour as that on which they murdered St. Milles. Nearly at this time, Barsabias, abbot of a monastery in Persia, was arrested, with ten of his monks. The judge ordered the tormentors to crush their knees, to break their legs, to cut off their arms, the flesh of their ribs, and their ears. They then beat them in the eyes and face with thorny reeds. Finally, the governor ordered them to be beheaded. Barsabias was reserved for the last. During the execution, one of the Magi, accompanied by his wife, his two children, and several servants, happened to pass by the place. Touched by grace, as he saw the joy that shone on the faces of the martyrs, he exchanged clothes with one of his servants, threw himself at the feet of Barsabias, and implored to be admitted into the number of his disciples, and to obtain the glory of martyrdom. The abbot consented, and offered him to the executioner, who beheaded him without knowing who he was. Barsabias, the spiritual father of all these martyrs, was the last to be decapitated (June 3d, A. D. 342). This year St. Sadoth, successor to St. Simeon in the See of Seleucia, was put to death with a hundred and twenty-eight other Christians, in the city of Seleucia, where Sapor abode. Two years later, the priest Daniel and the virgin Verda (*Rose* in Persian) were arrested by order of the governor of the province of the Razicheans. During three months they suffered the most cruel torments. Among other tortures, their feet were pierced, and kept five days successively in freezing water. Their constancy remaining unshaken, the governor condemned them to be beheaded (Feb. 21st, A. D. 344). This same year a hundred and twenty Christians, arrested by Sapor in the province of Adiabene, met a like fate. A pious widow collected their bodies, which were interred five together, in the country near Seleucia (April 21st, A. D. 344). Barbascemin had succeeded St. Sadoth in the metropolitan See of Seleucia. Sapor ordered him to be confined in an infected prison, where the dead bodies of animals in putrefaction had been thrown. The holy martyr suffered there for eleven months the pains of hunger and thirst. He was at length beheaded with his companions, Jan. 14th, A. D. 346, at Ledan, in the province of the Husites. A fearful apostasy afflicted this desolate Church almost at the same time. A priest, named Paul, who possessed immense wealth, was denounced to the governor. He was arrested with five virgins consecrated to God—Thecla, Mary, Martha, another Mary, and Anna. The governor began by confiscating the goods of Paul for his own profit. He summoned him before his tribunal, and commanded him to renounce Christ and adore the sun. "Thus thou shalt recover the money which has been taken from thee." The wretched man, who loved his wealth more than his soul, consented to abjure. This weakness thwarted the views of the governor, who desired to retain for himself the confiscated goods. He said to the apostate: "If thou wilt prove the sincerity of thy recantation, thou must kill with thine own hand these five virgins whom thou hast instructed in thy belief, and who have been arrested with thee." The apostate consented to this infamous condition, and seizing a naked sword, advanced to the generous martyrs. "What," said they, "treacherous pastor, is it thus that you fall upon your own flock, and murder your own sheep!" Paul paid no attention to these reproaches. In the midst of a crowd, who looked on him as an execrable murderer, he accomplished his horrible work, and beheaded these five virgins (June 6th, A. D. 346). Even at this price he was unable to regain possession of his property. The governor, to secure for himself the money he had seized, had him strangled the following night.* The persecution continued with the same fury to the end of Sapor's reign, who died A. D. 380, after seventy years of barbarity and cruelty.

17. During his reign, one of the longest recorded in history, he constantly pursued the double policy of annihilating Christianity in his dominions, and of extending his limits at the expense of the neighboring provinces of the Roman Empire. In 350, Constantius, who had advanced towards Persia to defend his frontiers, was suddenly recalled by important events to the West. Sapor II. profited by this unexpected withdrawal to renew on the city of Nisibis the enterprise in which he had had such ill success in 338. He returned, therefore, the second time, with considerable force, and a multitude of elephants and warlike engines. The kings of India accompanied him with auxiliary troops. Sure of victory, he summoned the inhabitants to surrender, on pain of having their city utterly destroyed. Encouraged by St. James, their bishop, they prepared for a vigorous resistance. For seventy days Sapor put forth every effort; having filled a part of the moat, he battered the walls with his engines—then sought to undermine them, and finally turned the Mygdonius from its course, to cut off the supply of water. The courage of the citizens defeated all these expedients; the wells and springs furnished water in abundance. Sapor conceived a design scarcely credible. He stopped the river above the

* The authentic acts of the persecution by Sapor II. in Persia, were not known in Europe until the pontificate of Clement XI. (A. D. 1700–1721), who, at an enormous expense had copies made from the manuscripts preserved in the monasteries of Nitria, and which the Egyptian monks would never part with, even at their weight in gold. The importance which this great pope attached to these records is the best guarantee of their authenticity.

town by a dike between two mountains. Below the city he raised a second dike, still higher. He then opened the upper dike; the waters rushed down with fury against the walls of the besieged city, but these did not fall. Retained by the lower dike, the water soon formed a sea, in the midst of which was Nisibis, always invincible. The Persians availed themselves of this situation, which they had foreseen, and attacked the besieged from a multitude of boats. The inhabitants were not disconcerted; they captured, with boat-hooks, the boats that approached near enough to the walls, and broke or sunk others, by hurling large stones upon them. In the midst of this strange contest, the lower dike gives way, the pent-up waters are precipitated through the breach, carry with them the boats of the besiegers in spite of the rowers, and also throw down a portion of the wall. Sapor thinks himself at last master of the city. He commands his army to prepare to mount the breach the next day. The assault was furious. The Persians advance over moist and miry ground. They are allowed to approach to the border of the ditch, which was very broad, and deep with the miry deposit of the restrained waters. Then, while the Persians seek for some means of passing over it, they are assailed with a shower of stones, fire, and darts. Some are thrown down, others attempt to fly, but those who come behind force them forward; men, horses, machines, elephants, sink and perish in the mire. Sapor, forced to sound a retreat, postponed the attack for a day, to allow time for the earth to grow more firm. He returned to the charge, and was greatly surprised to find behind the breach a new wall, which the besieged had raised with incredible activity. In his fury he shot an arrow against heaven, and put to death several satraps who had promised him a magnificent triumph. This admirable defence was commanded by the father-in-law of Jovian, who will at a later period assume the imperial purple. Heaven crowned it with a miraculous success. The deacon St. Ephrem conducted the venerable bishop of Nisibis, St. James, to the ramparts, that he might, like Moses, raise his hands before the Lord, to obtain from Him the victory. In view of the countless multitude of the Persians, whose tents covered all the plain, St. James prayed God to confound their pride. Suddenly a cloud of gnats, such as are sometimes seen in the East, fell upon the army of Sapor. These insects penetrated the trunks of the elephants, the nostrils and ears of the horses and beasts of burden, which, becoming furious, threw their riders, broke the ranks of the troops, and fled, taking with them their unseizable enemy. Sapor, forced to acknowledge the power of God, raised the siege, after three months of unavailing efforts, and retired in shame. St. James died a few days afterwards, leaving the memory of a holy life and an uncounted number of miracles wrought by his intercession. St. Ephrem, his disciple and deacon, retired to a hermitage in the environs of Edessa. Descended from a pagan family, grace had prepossessed his heart; he came to throw himself at the feet of St. James of Nisibis, who received him as his son, ordained him deacon, and took him, notwithstanding his extreme youth, to the Council of Nice. The humility of St. Ephrem was so great, that, accused of a crime committed by another, he submitted a long time to public contumely without complaint, and consented to justify himself only to avoid giving occasion for scandal. In his solitude he lived in a grotto formed naturally at the foot of a rock, and passed his days and nights in meditation on the Holy Scriptures. An aged hermit, under whom he had placed himself, found him one day concluding his commentary on Genesis. Having read it, he took it, without speaking to the author, to the magistrates, professors, and priests of Edessa, whose admiration it excited. The reputation of Ephrem quickly spread over the East. The Gnostic chants of Harmonicus, son of Bardesanes, had been preserved by tradition in the memory of the people of Asia. Ephrem composed Catholic verses in Syriac, in a measure full of melody. He taught the Christian virgins to sing them in the assemblies of the faithful. The chants of the heretic were soon forgotten, and to this day the Christians of Syria repeat these pious canticles. Ephrem had a particular talent for the pulpit. Often, in the midst of his preaching, he was obliged to pause to permit the sobs of his auditory to have free indulgence. The labor of the ministry and the instructions which he composed for the monasteries occupied all his time. He left his retreat but once to see St. Basil of Cæsarea, whose reputation for eloquence and sanctity had reached even to him. Returning to his grotto, Ephrem composed a panegyric in praise of this great bishop. All his works were written in Syriac, the mother tongue of the holy deacon, who ended his peaceful and glorious career January 28, A. D. 379.

18. The unexpected event which had called the emperor Constantius from the frontiers of Persia to the West, was a triple usurpation. Constans, his brother, who reigned at Treves, had raised from slavery to the grade of captain of the guards, an officer named Magnentius. One day, in a mutiny, the soldiers, discontented with the favorite, attempted to kill him. Constans covered him with his mantle, and saved his life. Magnentius found the burden of his gratitude too heavy. On a hunting party, he murdered his benefactor, and seized his crown. Gaul, Spain, Africa, and a part of Italy, declared for the new emperor (A. D. 350); and on hearing of this murder, Nepotian, nephew of Constantine the Great, by his mother Eutropia, put himself at the head of a troop of gladiators, surprised Rome, seized it (June 3, A. D. 350), and shed torrents of blood. Proclaimed emperor, he wore the purple only twenty-three days. After this brief delay, Rome was retaken by a general of Magnentius. The latter hastened to enjoy his triumph in person, ordered the head of Nepotian, fixed on a spear, to be carried about the streets, and massacred all who were related, far or near, to the imperial family of Constantine the Great. Meantime, as early as March 1, A. D. 350, the legions of Illyria had proclaimed emperor their old general Vetranion. This new Cæsar was unable to read, but he instantly began to study the alphabet. Constantius inter-

rupted his literary ardor. Arrived in Dalmatia, he deposed him, granted him his life, and sent him to Prussa, in Bithynia, to finish his days in an opulent retreat. Vetranion lived there six years in the practice of Christian piety. He succeeded in learning to read and write, and sent word to Constantius: "You are wrong not to renounce the empire yourself, and take your share in the happiness which you procure for others." Magnentius was a more formidable rival; but two successive victories, the first at Mursa, in Pannonia (September 28, A. D. 351), where nearly fifty thousand men remained on the field of battle, the second in Gaul (August 11, A. D. 353), ended the contest in favor of Constantius. Magnentius, threatened by his soldiers, put to death all his relatives and friends, killed his own mother, and finally himself. Decentius, his brother, whom he had created Cæsar, strangled himself with his own hands; and Constantius became master of the whole empire.

19. The death of Constans was deplored by the Catholics. St. Athanasius, whom this prince had always loved, shed bitter tears at the intelligence, even in presence of the emissary of Magnentius, who brought it to him. Constantius, in restoring peace to the Church, had done it chiefly at the solicitation of his brother and colleague of the West. Free henceforth to follow his own instincts, which inclined towards Arianism, he recommenced his part as persecutor of the Orthodox Church. The eunuch Eusebius was always his counsellor and favorite. Ursacius and Valens, whose solemn recantation addressed to Pope St. Julius had only been a hypocritical dissimulation, were perpetual residents of his court. The Oriental bishops, Narcissus of Neroniad, Theodore of Heraclea, Basil of Ancyra, Eudoxius of Germanicia, Demophilus of Berea, Cecropius of Nicomedia, Sylvanus of Tarsis, Macedonius of Mopsuesta, and Mark of Arethusa, most of them Arians, followed their example, and manifested far more assiduity in the emperor's tent, or in the antechambers of the palace, than fidelity to their canonical obligation of residence. All these prelates, and others, formed themselves into a council at Sirmium, metropolis of Illyria,

whither Constantius resorted after the battle of Mursa. The ostensible object of this council was the condemnation of Photinus, bishop of Sirmium, who taught the doctrines of Sabellius and Paul of Samosata, and maintained that Christ had no existence anterior to Mary. Photinus had already been deposed by the Catholic Council of Sardica, but he had maintained himself in his see by the popular favor, which he knew how to win. The Council of Sirmium renewed against him the anathema, and this was approved by all Catholics; but the bishops present afterwards resolved to prepare a profession of faith. This was the sixth which the Arians attempted without result. The word *consubstantial* was omitted by design, and replaced by deceitful and equivocal expressions capable of being interpreted in an orthodox sense without precisely opposing the Arian error, which explains the different opinions that holy fathers have since expressed of it. St. Hilary of Poitiers, who made a thorough examination of it, finds it satisfactory. Others have regarded it as liable to strong suspicions. And in reality the deliberate omission of the word *consubstantial* employed by the Council of Nice, is of itself a legitimate subject for suspicion. The extreme care which the Arian party employed at a later period to have this formulary subscribed, will, moreover, not without reasons, make us regard it as an insidious compromise between error and truth. The Council of Sirmium thus opened a way for the future persecutions of Constantius. This prince, at the beginning of the year, A. D. 351, had secretly sent orders to Philip, prætorian prefect at Constantinople, to arrest the Patriarch Paul, and send him into exile. The virtue of the venerable archbishop gave umbrage to the courtier prelates, and the first use of the liberty to trouble the Church, which the death of his brother had left to Constantius, was against him. Philip inveigled the saintly patriarch into the governor's palace, under the pretence of an official communication, threw him into a vessel that was at anchor, and sent him away, for his fourth and last exile from his church at Constantinople. The intruder, Macedonius, entered by force of arms over the corpses of three thousand of the faithful, who had determined to resist his usurpation. Conducted to the deserts of Mount Taurus, Paul was cast into a dungeon, and left six days without any kind of food. As he still breathed, the executioners strangled him, and Constantius welcomed the news of his death with more joy than a victory over Magnentius or the Persians would have given him.

20. Heaven spared not the most solemn warnings to this unhappy prince. Almost at the same time he received from St. Cyril, bishop of Jerusalem, the following letter: "In the times of Constantine the Great, your father, of happy memory, the precious wood of the true cross was found at Jerusalem. In your days, prince, miracles come not from the earth, but from heaven. During the last festival of Pentecost, on the nones of May (7th May), towards the hour of tierce (nine o'clock in the morning), an immense luminous cross appeared in the air above Mount Golgotha, extending even to the Mount of Olives. It was not a passing phenomenon; it remained during many hours, visible to every eye, more brilliant than the sun, whose light would have effaced it if its own had not been the stronger. All the people in the city ran in crowds to the church, with sentiments of fear mingled with joy. Young and old, men and women, Christians of the country, and strangers, even pagans, all, with one voice, praised our Lord Jesus Christ, the only Son of God, who made his power to shine in such wonders." St. Cyril closes his letter by expressing his hope that the emperor may forever glorify the holy and *consubstantial* Trinity. This hope was not to be realized; and Arianism, subdued for a moment, was soon to arise more threatening and more terrible.

21. Pope St. Julius I. did not live to see the new storm which was lowering over the Church that he had so courageously defended. He died at Rome, April 2, A. D. 352, after a pontificate of fifteen years. His remains were deposited in the cemetery of *Calepodius*, in the *Via Aurelia*, and afterwards

translated to the church of *Santa Maria in Trastevere*. It has been said that Julius was the first to decree the celebration of Christmas on the 25th of December. Pagi is of this opinion; but in the great collection of councils (tome ii., p. 1255) the institution of this solemnity is placed after the time of St. Julius. In three ordinations this pope, so eminent for his piety, his resolute constancy and his truly apostolic eloquence, created nine or ten bishops, eighteen priests, and five deacons.

CHAPTER III.

SUMMARY.

§ I. PONTIFICATE OF LIBERIUS (May 22, A. D. 352—September 24, 366).

1 Election of Pope Liberius.—2. The Arians bring new charges against St. Athanasius. Fall of Vincent of Capua.—3. Pope Liberius disavows the conduct of Vincent of Capua, his Legate.—4. Council of Milan (A. D. 355). —5. St. Athanasius banished by Constantius (A. D. 355).—6. Letter of Pope Liberius to the exiled Prelates.—7. Banishment of Pope Liberius to Berea, in Thrace.—8. Fall of Osius of Cordova. Second Arian Council of Sirmium.—9. The controverted fall of Liberius.—State of the Question. —10. Semi-Arians. Anomœans. Ætians. Eunomians. Eupsychians.— 11. Arian Councils of Cæsarea, Antioch, Ancyra, and third of Sirmium.— 12. Council of Rimini (A. D. 359).—13. Council of Seleucia (A. D. 359). —14. Council of Constantinople (A. D. 360). First Council of Paris.— 15. Council of Antioch (A. D. 361).—16. Death of the Emperor Constantius.—17. First studies and intimacy of St. Gregory Nazianzen and St. Basil of Cæsarea.—18. St. Cyril of Jerusalem. His Catechetical Instructions.—19. St. Nerses, Patriarch of Armenia.—20. Doctors of the West. St. Hilary of Poitiers. St. Martin of Tours. St. Eusebius of Vercelli. St. Paulinus of Treves. Lucifer of Cagliari. Birth of St. Ambrose. Jerome and Augustine.—21. Julian the Apostate, Emperor.—22. Nature and Causes of the Persecution of Julian the Apostate.—23. Edict to recall the banished, and to deprive the Clergy of their immunities, and the Churches of their possessions.—24. Return of St. Athanasius to Alexandria, (A. D. 362).— 25. Council of Alexandria.—26. Edict of Julian the Apostate, forbidding the study of Belles Lettres to the Christians.—27. Julian's attempt to rebuild the Temple of Jerusalem. Death of Julian.—28. Macedonius. His heresy. —29. Death of Pope Liberius.

§ I. PONTIFICATE OF LIBERIUS (May 22, A. D. 352—Sept. 24, 366).

1. ON the 8th of May, A. D. 352, Liberius, a Roman deacon, ordained by St. Sylvester, was raised to the chair of Peter. He had discharged the duties of his station with a

remarkable degree of virtue and humility, and made a long resistance to the elevation thus pressed upon him. Had he a presentiment of the storms which were bearing down upon the bark of Peter, or did he obey an interior sentiment of modesty natural to his soul? History is silent on this point, but she has, with scrupulous fidelity, recorded the honorable resistance of Liberius, at a period when a pagan author Ammianus-Marcellus, thus wrote regarding the sovereign Pontificate: "When I reflect upon the splendor attached to the See of Rome, I can understand any intrigue that might be used to reach it. The bishops of that city receive the most costly gifts from the Roman matrons; they appear in public, seated in brilliant chariots, in sumptuous attire, and their table surpasses those of kings in magnificence."* Making due allowance for whatever exaggeration such a statement may contain, coming, as it does, from the malevolent pen of a pagan, it still proves the care of the fourth century to surround the sovereign Pontiff with honor, and serves to enhance the merit of the young deacon who could refuse such a dignity. Though the name of Liberius has been a subject of dispute among men, it has still this incontestable glory before God.

2. Since the exile and martyrdom of the patriarch St. Paul of Constantinople, the Arian bishops incessantly urged Constantius onward in the persecution of the Catholic faith. St. Athanasius was ever the chief object of their hatred. Ursatius and Valens began by publicly retracting their submission to the Council of Sardica, attested though it was by an instrument they had themselves written, signed, and delivered to St. Julius I. They then resumed their system of recrimination and calumny against the holy patriarch of Alexandria. They made it a crime in him to have won the favor of the Emperor Constans. They charged him with having embraced the cause of Magnentius, because, during the ephemeral reign of that usurper, he had received into his

---

* Ammian.-Marcellin. Lib. 27, No. 3.

palace at Alexandria, Maximinus, the holy bishop of Treves, from whom he had received the most generous hospitality during his exile. They succeeded, at length, in ruining him in the opinion of Constantius, by incriminating a very simple and indifferent action. A new church had been built in Alexandria, at the public expense; the archbishop had inaugurated it without the participation of the emperor. This was sufficient to blot out from the remembrance of Constantius all his former letters to the patriarch, and his solemn promise ever to turn a deaf ear to his accusers. He appealed to Pope Liberius, to beg that Athanasius might be condemned (A. D. 352). Liberius assembled a council in Rome, and laid before it the emperor's letter, together with those of the Egyptian bishops, who unanimously proclaimed the innocence of their metropolitan. The council decided that it would be contrary to all law, human and divine, to anathematize a bishop whose faith was that of the Church, and whose virtue was the admiration of the whole world. The answer of Liberius was the expression of this sentiment. Constantius gave vent to his irritation at this result, in an edict of banishment against all who would not subscribe to the condemnation of Athanasius. In the hope of appeasing the emperor's anger, Liberius sent to him Vincent of Capua, who had presided, with Osius of Cordova, in the Council of Nice, as legate of Pope Sylvester. The prelate was charged to urge the emperor's approval of a general council to be convened, during the following year, at Aquileia, and thus to determine, by an irrevocable decision, these endless disputes. Vincent met the emperor at Arles, surrounded by the Arian bishops, who followed him in all his journeys; they had met in council, and were proceeding to the condemnation of St. Athanasius. The legate, seduced by the intrigues of the courtiers, terrified by threats, forgot the character with which he was vested, and in a moment of shameful weakness, subscribed the anathema pronounced against the patriarch of Alexandria. St. Paulinus, who had lately succeeded St. Maximinus, in the see of Treves, gave a noble example of courageous resistance. He was banished to Phrygia, and died a glorious confessor, after five years of exile suffered for justice and truth.

3. The heart of Pope Liberius was filled with grief upon the fall of Vincent of Capua. He immediately wrote to Osius: " I had placed great hope in his intervention. He was personally known to the emperor, to whom he had formerly presented the acts of the Council of Sardica. Yet he has not only failed to fulfil his mission, but has even been guilty of a deplorable act of weakness. I am doubly grieved at it; and I beg of God that I may rather die than ever have a part in the triumph of injustice." The afflicted pope wrote in the same strain to Fortunatian, bishop of Aquileia, whom he held in particular esteem, on account of his great virtue, and to Eusebius of Vercelli. Eusebius had just been raised to the episcopal throne, which he adorned by his eminent piety. He was the first to show, in the West, how the monastic can be joined to the clerical life. The holy prelate and his clergy followed the exercises of the monks of the desert, dividing the time between prayer, penitential practices, reading holy books, and manual labor. Their community, thus regularly established, even took the name of monastery, and became a school which subsequently gave many illustrious bishops to the Church. In this austere life, St. Eusebius of Vercelli found the strength which afterwards enabled him to bear up under the persecution of the Arians. Liberius not only availed himself of the counsels of these holy men, but also commissioned Lucifer, bishop of Cagliari, metropolitan of Sardinia, with the priest Pancratius, and the deacon Hilary, to deliver to the emperor a letter full of respectful firmness, disavowing the conduct of Vincent of Capua, and urging anew the necessity of calling a general council, for the careful examination of the points at issue, "and to preserve," writes the pope, "in its full integrity, the belief unanimously expressed by the Catholic Church, in the presence of Constantine the Great, your father of holy and glorious memory" (A. D. 354). The emperor

readily agreed to the convocation of a council, and named Milan as the place of meeting. Never did prince with more satisfaction join in theological discussions, for which he had a real passion; or appear in the assemblies of bishops, which he believed himself able to bring to his own opinion, either by cunning or violence. The Arian bishops, who honored him with a title which they refused to the Son of God, *Your Eternity*, were careful to keep alive their master's mania, by their frequent conventions, in which his opinion was received as an oracle; and many prelates, bearing the name of Christian, did not hesitate, even in matters of faith, to follow the teaching of a crowned theologian, unbaptized, and not even a catechumen.

4. The Council of Milan, then, met in the beginning of the year 355; the Western Church was represented by more than three hundred bishops. The ranks of the Eastern hierarchy were much thinner. Three legates presided in the name of Pope Liberius; they were the same whom the pope had sent to Constantius the preceding year: Lucifer of Cagliari, the priest Pancratius, and the deacon Hilary. At the very opening of the session, Eusebius of Vercelli proposed that all the Fathers should subscribe the Nicene profession, in order that they might then proceed, in unity of faith, to the examination of the other questions. Dionysius, bishop of Milan, immediately set about signing his name; but Valens, bishop of Mursa, snatched the pen and paper from his hands, protesting that they would accomplish nothing by such means. This act of violence was followed by a scene of tumultuous confusion; the cry arose from the people assembled around the church; "The bishops have betrayed the faith!" Fearing a sedition, Constantius ordered the Fathers to adjourn to a hall in the palace. This was a death-blow to the freedom of the council. The emperor sent in an instrument written by himself, in which he supported the Arian doctrine, and made its recognition binding on all the churches in the empire. The legate, Lucifer of Cagliari, replied with noble firmness:

"Though Constantius should arm all his legions against us, he will never compel us to renounce the belief of Nice, or to assent to the blasphemies of Arius." Threats were equally fruitless to obtain the condemnation of St. Athanasius. The emperor, provoked by this unexpected resistance, summoned before him Lucifer of Cagliari, Eusebius of Vercelli, and Dionysius of Milan, the three prelates who wielded the greatest influence in the council. "I am the personal accuser of Athanasius," said Constantius; "you must believe the truth of my assertion." "This is not a question," answered the bishops, "of a temporal nature, in which the imperial authority would be decisive; but an ecclesiastical judgment, in which equal impartiality must be shown both to the accuser and the accused. Athanasius is absent, he cannot be condemned without a hearing. The rule of the Church forbids it." "But my will," replied Constantius, "must be the rule. The Syrian bishops recognize it. You have to choose between submission and exile." The prelates bowed and withdrew. It is said that Constantius was so overcome by anger as to draw his sword upon them. The morrow saw them led away, by military tribunes, to their place of banishment, through dense crowds of the faithful who thronged their path, shedding tears at the thought of losing their legitimate pastors. The deacon Hilary, whose firmness had been most offensive, was scourged in the public square before starting for his place of exile. The remaining bishops, even Fortunatian of Aquileia, had the weakness to sign the condemnation of Athanasius.

5. In all the calmness and tranquillity of a good conscience, Athanasius had been awaiting the storm at Alexandria. In the year 353, the Arians had forged a letter, written in his name, to the Emperor Constantius, in which the patriarch was supposed to beg permission to appear at court. Constantius immediately sent an officer of his guard with an answer granting the request, and affording every facility for the journey. St. Athanasius, who had solicited nothing, saw the snare, and remained with his flock. From that time the course of events

had been hurrying on; each day brought with it some new danger. The faithful of Alexandria were watching over their pastor. Immediately after the tragical close of the Council of Milan, Syrianus, commander of the troops in Alexandria, had received an imperial order to arrest the patriarch and send him into exile. Syrianus was much perplexed at receiving such an order, in a city perfectly devoted to its archbishop. He showed the imperial rescript, and pledged his oath not to put it into execution before the return of a deputation he had sent to Constantius, beseeching him to reconsider his decision. This solemn promise, followed by twenty days of the deepest quiet, soothed all anxiety and set every fear at rest. On the 7th of February, A. D. 356, towards midnight, the church of St. Theonas was crowded by the faithful, who had come together, with St. Athanasius, to keep the vigil of a solemn feast (probably that which opened the Lent of this year), when suddenly the holy temple is surrounded by a band of five thousand pagan soldiers under the command of Syrianus. The doors are broken in; the armed troops rush into the basilica; the solemn harmony of the psalms is interrupted by the loud notes of the trumpets; the darts, flying about in the vast assemblage, strike their victims at random; swords and lances, drawn against a defenceless multitude, spare neither sex, nor age, nor priestly character, not even the virgins consecrated to their Lord. The people press in confusion through every avenue of escape; the ruthless soldiery pursue and butcher still. Athanasius alone did not leave the throne he occupied. His clergy entreat him to look to his safety. "The pastor's post is in the midst of his flock," replied this great bishop. At length his priests attempt to carry him forcibly away, and to pierce the throng of soldiers and fugitives, but Athanasius, rudely jostled on all sides, stifled by the crowd, fell in a swoon, and was borne away as a corpse. By a kind of miracle, he escaped the eager pursuit of his persecutors, and a few days after he was in the desert, amid his dear religious, who received him as an angel from heaven. But he missed St. Anthony, who had gone, on the 17th of January, A. D. 356, at the age of one hundred and five years, to receive the crown he had won by his virtues. By his own order, two of his religious had buried him in a place known only to themselves. He had bequeathed his tunic of sheepskin to St. Athanasius; and the illustrious patriarch received, in exile, this legacy of the Father of the Desert. The persecution went on in Alexandria, after the departure of Athanasius. The pagans consigned to the flames, at the doors of the churches, the books and sacred vessels. Christian women and virgins were brutally outraged, and, to crown all their excesses, the Arians intruded into the see a rude, uneducated bankrupt, George, or Gregory, of Cappadocia. He was placed in possession of the see, by force of arms, during the Lent of the year 356. The faithful who lost their lives on this occasion are ranked, by the Church, among her martyrs. The persecution extended to the bishops of Egypt, most of whom had remained faithful to Athanasius. Sixteen were banished, and thirty were driven from their sees by intruders. At the solicitation of Macedonius, Arian bishop of Constantinople, the emperor issued an edict declaring all supporters of the *Consubstantial* guilty of high treason; they were to be driven from every city, and their churches destroyed. This decree was put into execution with the utmost severity; and the acts of violence to which it gave occasion conferred on many Catholics the crown of martyrdom.

6. In a circular letter to the exiled bishops, Pope Liberius expresses the most tender and devoted sentiments. "What praise can I bestow on you," he writes, "divided as I am between grief for your absence and joy for your glory? The best consolation that I can offer you is, to beg that you will believe me to be in exile with you. I could have wished, dearly beloved brothers, to be the first victim offered for you all, and to give the example of the glory you have acquired; but your merit has won for you that high prerogative. I therefore entreat you, in your charity, to imagine me present with you, and to believe that my greatest grief is the privation

of your society. Since your tribulation brings you nearer to
our Lord, offer your prayers to Him for me, that I may
patiently bear the violence with which I am daily threatened.
Entreat the divine mercy that the faith may remain inviolate;
that the Catholic Church may be preserved from division.
Send me an account of the combat you have sustained for the
faith, that your exhortations may restore my courage, and even
the wasted strength of my body, oppressed by complicated
diseases."

7. The threats of which the pope writes very soon grew
into open persecution. The Arian eunuch, Eusebius, whose
unlimited power over the weak mind of Constantius had
reduced the Church to its present sad condition, was sent to
Rome by the emperor to deceive Liberius, and force him to
sign the condemnation of Athanasius. The eunuch found
presents and threats equally ineffectual; he then procured a
rescript ordering Leontius, governor of Rome, to convey Liberius to Milan, where Constantius held his court. The interview
between the pope and the emperor, as might have been foreseen, was full of passion, recrimination, and violence on the
part of Constantius; dignified, reserved, and firm, on that of
Liberius. Two days later, the pope was seized and exiled to
Berea, in Thrace. The emperor sent him five hundred gold
pieces (about ten thousand francs), to defray his expenses.
Liberius sent them back, with these words: "Tell the emperor
to keep his money for the support of his army." A like tender
from the empress met with a like reply. When the eunuch
Eusebius had the effrontery to make a similar proffer, the indignant pontiff answered: "You have desolated the churches
throughout the world, and do you offer me an alms, as to a
criminal! Go and begin by embracing the true faith." Liberius had hardly left the soil of Italy, when the emperor caused
the Arian faction to consecrate an antipope in Rome. The
bishop of Centumcellœ was, on this occasion, the organ of
the imperial will. He caused the choice to fall upon Felix, an
archdeacon of the Roman Church. Three eunuchs represented

the assembly of the people; three bishops, one of whom was Acacius of Cæsarea, consecrated him in the palace of the emperor. The Roman people had no part in this irregular ordination; they would hold no communion with the usurper, and remained always faithful in their attachment to Liberius. Antiquity, however, does Felix the justice to testify that he always kept the belief of Nice, and that his conduct was irreproachable, save in the one particular of his relations with the Arians.

8. The war so fiercely waged against the Catholic cause was met with the most vigorous energy by the exiled prelates. From every quarter of the world to which the blind tyranny of Constantius had consigned them, they raised their unanimous voice to proclaim the dogmas of the true faith. Eusebius of Vercelli, Hilary of Poitiers, whose name and history we have still to record, and St. Athanasius, redoubled the efforts of their zeal. From the solitude of his retreat, the patriarch of Alexandria addressed to the faithful of the Church, to the bishops of Egypt and of the whole world, letters and treatises, in which he set forth the Catholic doctrine, and opposed it to the errors of Arianism. Osius of Cordova, who had now reached the venerable age of more than a hundred years, at first shared the labors of these eloquent apologists. He addressed to the Emperor Constantius an admirable letter, in which he received the whole course of the Arian intrigues, and begged the prince to put an end to the persecution against the Catholics. His courageous protest was followed by an order of the emperor to bring the bishop of Cordova to Sirmium, where the Arian prelates were a second time assembled to draw up a seventh profession of faith. In this new creed they reject not only the term *consubstantial*, but also that of *similar in substance*, and substitute other expressions which suppose in the Son a different nature from that of the Father. The author of this new formula was Potamius, bishop of Lisbon, who had found a sufficient inducement for embracing the Arian heresy in the gift of a manor-land, made him by Con-

stantius. The unworthy prelate did not limit his courtly zeal to this impious composition. He beset with his insidious toils Osius of Cordova, whom a century of years rendered venerable, and who had now been held in close confinement for a year, at Sirmium. The fall of this illustrious patriarch, which raised a cry of triumph in the Arian camp, threw a veil of mourning over the whole Church. St. Phebadius, bishop of Agen, in a treatise which he wrote, at this time, against the Arians, spoke as follows: "I am aware that our adversaries hold up to us, as an incontestable authority, the name of Osius of Cordova, the most ancient of all the bishops, and one whose faith was always so firm. But we must choose one of two alternatives: either that great man is now, or he always was, in error; in either case, what can be the weight of his authority? His sentiments, until his present advanced age, are known to the entire world; no one is ignorant of the firmness with which he defended the Catholic faith at Sardica and at Nice. If he now maintain what he before condemned, or if he condemn what he always maintained, once more, his authority, in matters of faith, is worthless. For, if he has lived in error during a period of ninety years, how can I be persuaded that what he believes when he has passed the period of ninety years is the truth? The precedent found in his authority has therefore no force, since that authority destroys itself" (A. D. 357).

9. The course of events has brought us to the point where a brief summary of the controversy touching the supposed fall of Pope Liberius is necessary. We give, word for word, the account of the historians who admit the fall as an indisputable fact, and immediately follow it up with the relation of those who treat it as a calumny invented by the Arians. Whatever opinion we adopt, in this historical collision, we deem it proper to preface the discussion with the words of Bossuet, surveying the whole dispute. "It is certain," says the illustrious Bishop of Meaux, "that Pope Liberius ended his long pontificate in communion with the holiest bishops of the Church;

with a St. Athanasius, a St. Basil, and others of equal merit and reputation. We know that he is praised by St. Epiphanius, and by St. Ambrose, who twice mentions him as Pope Liberius of holy memory; and in one of his works inserts entire, together with these expressions of praise, a sermon of this pope, which celebrates the eternity, the omnipotence, in a word, the divinity of the Son of God, and His perfect equality with His Father. But the fact is certain, that Liberius yielded only to open violence (here Bossuet sides with the historians who admit the fall of Liberius as a fact); and it is equally certain, that he returned to his duty of his own accord. These two important facts should not be overlooked, since they remove the whole difficulty. It is well known, by the constant testimony of St. Athanasius and of all cotemporary writers, that Constantius shed torrents of blood, and that those who opposed his will in the affair of Arianism had every thing to dread from his anger, so obstinate was he in support of the heresy. I do not say this to excuse Liberius; but to *call to mind, that every act extorted by open violence is null by every title, and protests against itself.*"*

Bossuet, whose words we have just quoted, evidently looks upon the fall of Liberius as an historical fact. In his *Apology for the Declaration of the Gallican Clergy*, he thus expresses himself upon the subject: "We have no intention of entering upon a discussion of the profession of faith drawn up at Sirmium. The most learned men had their doubts in this controversy, and would make no positive assertions. For our part, we incline to the opinion that Liberius signed the most innocent of all these professions. Still, it is equally certain that Liberius, who was so well acquainted with the intrigues and

---

* Œuvres complètes de Bossuet (Outhenin-Chalandre), t. XII., pp. 110 et III. All discussion on the Infallibility of the Pope seems to us utterly idle, in connection with the conduct of Liberius, even admitting the fact of his fall. If it be universally granted that Liberius yielded only to open violence, and that *every act extorted by open violence is null by every title*, it cannot reasonably be maintained that the pope, in the *free exercise* of his authority, and teaching *ex cathedrâ*, has erred; and this is the only ground on which a serious controversy on the subject could be based.

errors of the Arians, did very wrong in signing a profession of faith which dissembled the doctrine that Christ is *consubstantial* with the Father, and of the same substance with Him."* Fleury, in his Ecclesiastical History, adopts the same opinion, and says: "Pope Liberius had suffered two years of an exile which daily increased in severity, until it had taken from him his deacon Urbicus. Fortunatian, bishop of Aquileia, was the first who urged him to submit to the will of the emperor, and he gave him no peace until he had subscribed. Demophilus, bishop of Berea, when Liberius was in exile, laid before him the profession of Sirmium, that is, according to the most probable opinion, the first one composed against Photinus, in the council of the year 351, at which Demophilus had assisted; in this the terms *consubstantial* and *similar in substance* were pliantly omitted, but it was still capable of being defended, as it has been, by St. Hilary. Liberius approved and signed it as Catholic, renounced the communion of St. Athanasius, and embraced that of the Orientals, or in other words, of the Arians.†

Rohrbacher, in his *Universal History of the Catholic Church*, thus presents the facts relating to the return of Liberius to Rome, and refutes the arguments of those who admit the fall of the pope: "The Emperor Constantius saw Rome for the first time, as he entered it towards the end of April, A. D. 357, in triumph for his victory won six years before over Magnen-

---

* We quote, *verbatim*, the note here inserted in the *Œuvres complètes de Bossuet*, from which we have taken this passage (Defens. Cler. Gall., Lib. IX., Cap. 33—Edit. Outheuin-Chalandre, t. XVI., p. 475): "Eruditissimi inter Catholicos hodie stant pro omnimoda innocentia Liberii, et quidem argumentis haudquaquam contemnendis. (Vide *Dissert. Critique et historique sur le Pape Libère, dans laquelle on fait voir qu'il n'est jamais tombé*; par l'Abbé Corgne. Paris, 1726;—et multo fusius, *Commentar. critico-histor. de sancto Liberio Papa*, a P. Stiltingo, inter *Acta Sanctorum Septembris*, ad diem XXIII., t. VI., p. 573.) Illud interea constat, multa hic adferri adjuncta, aut plane incerta, aut omnino supposita; et plura taceri, quæ minime omitti debuissent. Certe vix intelligo quomodo ea cohærsant cum iis quæ Ipse illustrissimus auctor dixit (2ª Instruction sur les promesses de l'Eglise, Nos. 105 et 106). Cetorum ex diario D. Ledieu (Bossuet's Secretary), colligitur voluisse Bossuetium ea delere quæ hic scripsit de Liberio, tanquam ad suum scopum non satis pertinentia. (Vide *Hist. de Bossuet*; Pièces justificatives du liv. VI., p. 396. Edit. Versail.)

† L'Abbé Fleury, Hist. Ecclés., liv. XIII., t. III.; Edit. in-12, p. 468.

tius. Liberius had now lingered out two years of exile; the Roman matrons urged their husbands to petition the emperor for his restoration. They answered, that they feared the anger of the emperor, who would not, perhaps, pardon the request if made by men, and that the matrons themselves would be more favorably received; that, though their prayer should be denied, still no harm could accrue to them from it. The ladies, therefore, presented their supplication to the emperor, entreating him to pity so great a city deprived of its pastor. Constantius replied, that Rome possessed a pastor capable of governing it, without assistance from another; he meant Felix. The Roman ladies rejoined, that nobody entered the Church whilst Felix was there; for though he kept the Nicene faith, he still held communion with those who corrupted it. The emperor doubtless promised to attend to their request; for, some time after, he wrote to Rome, announcing that Liberius was to be recalled, and to govern the Church in conjunction with Felix. But when the letter was read in the circus, the people ironically exclaimed: *'That is just, indeed! As there are two factions in the circus, distinguished by their colors, each one will have its bishop!'* Having thus expressed their contempt for the imperial letter, they cried out with one voice: *'One God, one Christ, one Bishop!'* Matters were carried to yet greater extremes. Seditions were excited in Rome, and its streets were even stained with blood. It was on this account, according to the historian Socrates, that the emperor reluctantly consented to the return of Liberius to his pontifical throne." "The admirable Liberius then," says Theodoret, "returned to his beloved city." Other ancient authors inform us that he entered Rome in triumph; that the whole city, full of joy, went out to meet him, and expelled Felix.

"It may cause some surprise that we make no mention of the fall of Pope Liberius, the famous fall which Bossuet has endeavored at great length to prove. We are aware that, in his *Apology for the Declaration of the Gallican Clergy*, Bossuet spares no efforts to prove that Liberius fell by subscribing the

Arian profession of faith; but we also know, from his secretary, that in a later revision of the work, Bossuet erased the whole passage concerning *Pope Liberius, as not proving conclusively enough what he wished at the moment to establish.**

"What Bossuet thought it his duty to erase from his *Treatise on the Ecclesiastical Power*, we deem it proper to erase from the *History of the Church*; what twenty years of meditation and research have not enabled Bossuet to prove to his own satisfaction, we deem simply indemonstrable. The reasons of this are given in detail, in the dissertation of a doctor of Paris, published a few years after the death of Bossuet; in a more recent treatise of the learned Zaccaria, in the profound Gallaud, of Venice, in the fifth volume of *Library of the Ancient Fathers*; and especially in the *Critical History of the Holy Pope Liberius*, inserted in the *Acta Sanctorum*, on the 23d of September.† We shall only remark here, from what we have just seen, that the Roman people could not endure Felix, because, whilst he professed the belief of Nice, he still communicated with the Arians; that Pope Liberius entered Rome like a conqueror; that the people gave him a triumphal reception, and drove out Felix. In the face of this conduct of the Roman people, how can it be supposed that this same Pope Liberius had just disgraced himself before the Church, by condemning St. Athanasius, by subscribing to Arianism, and by sending to the principal Arians letters of communion, as pitiful in style as they were abject in sentiment? We have seen the scandal to which the fall of Osius gave rise, the advantage taken of it by the Arians, and the striking reply of St. Phebadius of Agen. Now, if Liberius had likewise fallen, the scandal would have been much more horrible, the Arians would have proclaimed a greater triumph, St. Phebadius would have found a much more urgent call for a reply.

---

* Histoire de Bossuet, liv. VI., Pièces justific., p. 396. Edit. de Lebel.
† *Dissert. sur le Pape Libère*, par l'Abbé Corgne. Paris, 1726; in-12. Tr. Ant. Zacharia, *Dissert. de commentitio Liberii lapsu*, in Thes. theol., Venet., 1762; in-4°, t. II. p. 589. Gallaud, Biblioth. Veter. P. P. t. v.—Acta Sanctor., t. VI, Septemb.

This utter silence, on all hands, conclusively proves the nullity of the fact.

"It may be objected that St. Athanasius refers to the fall of Liberius, both in his *Apology against the Arians*, and in his *History of the Arians*, which latter work was addressed to the hermits; but it is universally granted that the *Apology against the Arians* was written at the very latest in A. D. 350, two years before Liberius became pope. The passage which speaks of his fall is, then, evidently a subsequent addition, made by a strange and unskilful hand; for far, from giving any force to the *Apology*, it only makes it pointless and ridiculous. The *History of the Arians* was also written at a period prior to that of the supposed fall of Pope Liberius. This unfavorable passage is, then, another interpolation, equally unconnected with what precedes and what follows. But by whom could these interpolations have been made? We know that even during the lifetime of St. Athanasius the Arians forged a letter, in his name, to Constantius. What they could do whilst he was still alive, was certainly easier of accomplishment after his death. Did not the Donatists invent a similar account of a fall on the part of Pope St. Marcellinus, which was long received, but which all critics now acknowledge as false? Besides, the Arians were not the only enemies of Liberius; the Luciferian schismatics were quite as eager to defame him. In the words of Rufinus, written about fifty years after this period, we perhaps see the first dark spots on the horizon, foreboding the storm of calumny which was soon to break upon the head of Liberius. He says: "Liberius, bishop of Rome, had returned whilst Constantius was still alive; but I cannot positively state whether it was that he had consented to subscribe, or that the emperor would please the Roman people, who, at his departure, had begged this favor." Rufinus was a priest of Aquileia; in his youth he may have known Liberius; he had certainly known Fortunatian, bishop of Aquileia, to whom the fall of Liberius is imputed. And yet Rufinus knows nothing of it, undoubtedly because the calumny was only beginning to spread abroad; for if Liberius had actually signed an Arian formula, had he actually penned the pitiful letters of defection ascribed to him, the Arians, who were all-powerful, would have left no one in ignorance of the fact. It would have been impossible for Rufinus to retain any doubt upon the subject.* The *Greek Menology* relates the facts as we have given them. It speaks as follows: "The Blessed Liberius, defender of the faith, was Bishop of Rome, under the empire of Constantius. Burning with zeal for the orthodox faith, he protected the great Athanasius, persecuted by the heretics for his bold defence of the truth, and driven from Alexandria. Whilst Constantine and Constans lived, the Catholic faith was supported; but when Constantius was left sole master, as he was an Arian, the heretics prevailed. Liberius, for his vigor in censuring their impiety, was banished to Berea, in Thrace. But the Romans, who always remained true to him, went to the emperor and besought his recall. He was therefore, on this account, sent back to Rome, and there ended his life, after a holy administration of his pastoral charge."†

With this statement before us, giving the facts and substantiating arguments of both parties with equal impartiality, it cannot be hard to form a conscientious opinion. We have no wish either to solicit or to bias. It will suffice to end this discussion with the solemn words of Bossuet, whose name we quote the more readily, as its authority has been so often invoked against the prerogatives of the holy see. "Though one or two sovereign pontiffs," says the illustrious prelate, "contrary to the custom of their predecessors, should, either from violence or surprise, have failed in maintaining the faith with sufficient constancy, or in explaining its doctrines with perfect clearness, still, personal errors could make no impression on the chair of Peter. Not more traceless are the waters which a ship has cleaved in its passage."‡

* M. l'Abbé ROHRBACHER: *Hist. Universelle de l'Église Catholique*, 2e Edit., t. XI., pp. 430, 431, 432.
† ROHRBACHER: *Hist. Universelle de l'Église Catholique*, tom. xi, p. 374.
‡ BOSSUET: *Sermon on the Unity of the Church*.

10. The constant excitement caused by the Arian wrangling on questions of dogma soon split the public mind into different hostile factions. Heresy cannot free itself from the consequence of its fundamental law; it must, by its very nature, undergo continual change. Arianism, even thus early, presented this spectacle of rapid transformation. It was already divided into the *Semi-Arian* and the *Anomœan* sects (ἀνόμοιος, dissimilar). The *Semi-Arians*, who were in the majority, denied the consubstantiality of the Word, and rejected the expression *consubstantial*, contained in the Nicene profession. Still, they attributed to the Son of God a resemblance, in all things, to the Father. The great majority of the Eastern bishops had embraced this opinion; and we can easily understand how captious and amphibological their professions of faith could be, since, like the first of Sirmium, they might appear perfectly orthodox, with the single exception of the omitted term *consubstantial*. The *Anomœans*, on the other hand, not only denied the consubstantiality of the Word, but even taught that God the Son is dissimilar (ἀνόμοιος) to His Father, in essence and in all other points. These sectaries owned the leadership of Ætius and Eunomius: hence their names also of *Ætians* or *Eunómians*. Ætius was a Syrian adventurer, who had left his native city, Antioch, to follow the fortunes of travelling merchants, and later, of strolling actors (A. D. 347). Tired of this wandering life, he returned to his home, and became remarkable for the ardor with which he embraced the Arian tenets. His intimacy with Leontius, afterwards Arian bishop of Antioch, and with Eusebius, Arian bishop of Sebaste, inspired him with an ardent desire to perfect himself in dialectics, that he might be enabled more successfully to defend his error. With this intention, he went to Alexandria, where he soon acquired the pitiful facility of the Sophists, in reducing every thing to an argument or a syllogism. At his return, he began to discuss the nature of God with so much boldness, that the terrified people gave him the title of Atheist, which did not, however, hinder Leontius from

ordaining him deacon, nor deter the pure Arians from acknowledging him as their chief. Eunomius had been a disciple of Ætius, until he was consecrated bishop of Cyzicus, in A. D. 360. when, by the addition of some new tenets to those learned from his master, he formed a new sect, of which he became the leader. He maintained that he knew God as well as God knows Himself; that the Son of God was not truly God, and had only been united to humanity by His virtue and operations; that faith alone is sufficient for salvation, in spite of the greatest crimes, and even of impenitence. He denied that Jesus had any knowledge of the day or the hour appointed for the last judgment. He rebaptized all who had received the baptism of the Church in the name of the Holy Trinity. He rejected the triple immersion, then used in baptism, and the honors given to martyrs and to the relics of the saints. His followers, calling themselves *Eunomians*, soon formed a subdivision, under the name of *Eunomio-Eupsychians*; they taught that the Saviour knew the day and the hour of the last judgment, which truth the Eunomians refused to admit. The master of this new school was named Eupsychias; hence the name *Eunomio-Eupsychians*, under which the sect appeared.

11. In the midst of this general conflagration of minds, whilst most of the legitimate bishops were lingering out a life of exile, and intruded heretics held their sees; when, to use the energetic expression of St. Jerome, *the whole world seemed to have waked up Arian*, Constantius gave his whole attention to the multiplication of formulas of faith, to the assembling of councils; and spent his time in constructing Arian theology in the midst of his courtier bishops. God alone could now save His Church from the peril into which it had been precipitated by the emperor and the Greek bishops, who seemed to look to the court of Constantinople for their dogmatic definitions. This deliverance could not be long deferred; still, the hour was not yet. In the year 357, a council assembled at Cæsarea, the metropolitan see of Palestine, by Acacius the Arian bishop, had, in opposition to all canon-law, deposed St. Cyril, bishop

of Jerusalem; the saint set out for Tarsus, where he was honorably received by the bishop, in spite of the repeated threats of Acacius. In A. D. 358 another council, convoked by Eudoxius, Arian bishop of Antioch, was making every effort to exonerate Ætius from the charges so justly brought against him. But the people who were true to the faith, whilst so many bishops were betraying it, stoutly opposed the heresiarch, and resisted his admission to the Catholic communion. The council, therefore, failed in its object; but the bishops who were present condemned the terms *consubstantial* and *similar in substance,* and sent letters of congratulation to Ursatius and Valens, praising their zeal for the propagation of Arianism. Meanwhile, the *Semi-Arians* were assembling in council at Ancyra, under the presidency of Basil, bishop of that city. They anathematized Ætius and the *Anomœans*, who denied that the Son is similar to the Father, and sent their profession of faith to all the churches; this formula would have been irreproachable but for the studied omission of the term *consubstantial*. Basil of Ancyra, Eustathius of Sebaste, and Eleusius of Cyzicus, were deputed to present this new profession of faith to the emperor, who was then at Sirmium. On their arrival, they held another council at Sirmium, in which Basil of Ancyra procured the adoption of his profession, and the condemnation of the second profession of Sirmium, which had been signed by Osius of Cordova. Valens and Ursatius, the authors of the anathematized formula, were the first to desert it, because such was the desire of Constantius, who presided at all these petty councils. Ætius and Eunomius were banished to Phrygia, with seventy of their followers. The emperor's mania for councils only increased with his years. He called a general council, for the following year, at Nicomedia. But the total destruction of that city, by an earthquake, on the 24th of August, A. D. 358, obliged him to think of another place of meeting. This afforded matter for long and serious deliberations in what might be called the permanent council, which held its sittings in the court of the emperor, at Sirmium. On the 22d of May, A. D. 359, a tenth profession of faith was signed here, "*set forth*," as the bishops announced, "*in presence of our lord, the very pious and victorious Emperor Constantius, august, eternal, venerable; in the consulship of Flavius Eusebius and Hypatius, at Sirmium, the 11th of the Kalends of June.*" The new creed, which rejected the word *substance* as unknown to the people, and affording an occasion of scandal, was signed by all the bishops present at Sirmium, and made binding for the two approaching councils. In the versatile mind of Constantius, the original idea of a general council to be assembled in order to give additional effect to the condemnation of the Anomœans, had been suddenly metamorphosed into that of two simultaneous councils, for the East and the West; the one to be held at Rimini, in Italy, for the West, the other at Seleucia, in Isauria, for the East.

12. The Council of Rimini accordingly met, in the month of June, A. D. 359, without any further convocation than that of the emperor; Pope Liberius was neither consulted, nor even invited—a somewhat remarkable circumstance; for in the hypothesis of a recent fall, it does not readily appear how the emperor could have helped availing himself of this occasion to show to the world the spectacle of a Roman pontiff in full communion with Arianism. However this may be, Liberius afterwards protested against the irregular convocation of the Council of Rimini, in these words: "The impious and sacrilegious Arians have succeeded in assembling the bishops of the West at Rimini, with a view to deceive them by false discourses, and to force them, by means of the imperial authority, either to strike out or openly to condemn a term very wisely inserted in the profession of faith. But the artifice has failed." Four hundred bishops met at Rimini, from Illyria, Italy, Africa, Spain, Gaul, and Great Britain, but only eighty of the whole number were Arians. The Catholic prelates held their sessions in the principal church in the city; the Arians refused to pray with them, and met in a small oratory in the neighborhood. Ursacius and Valens at first appeared before the Catho-

lic bishops, and read the last profession of faith adopted by the emperor, at Sirmium. But all the Fathers indignantly rejected it. "We have not come together," said they, "to learn what we are to believe; we hold our faith from our fathers, the confessors and martyrs, whose successors we are; from the many saints assembled at Nice, some of whom are still with us. What means your profession of yesterday? Were there no Christians before that date? And shall we believe that so many saints who, before that day, fell asleep in the Lord, or gave their blood for the faith, knew not what they should profess?" The council then went into an examination of the other professions of faith, drawn up by the Arians, during the past twenty-five years, and amounting to the number of about fifty. They were all, in turn, rejected. The Nicene Creed was then read, and adopted as the legitimate, full, and complete expression of the Catholic faith. A decree to this effect was drawn up, and signed by all the orthodox bishops, without a single exception. Valens, Ursacius, Caius, Germinius, and the other Arians were condemned and deposed from their sees, by an act which is still extant. Thus far the bearing of the Council of Rimini is irreproachable: this is due to the fact that its deliberations had not been trammelled by violence, and the true spirit of the Church was free to display itself. Still, Constantius had at the outset sent Taurus, prefect of the pretorium, to Rimini, to watch the workings of the council. But the imperial lieutenant lacked the nerve for the execution of vigorous measures, in presence of so imposing an array of Catholic bishops. This state of affairs did not last long. Ten Catholic deputies had set out from Rimini, to lay before Constantius the decision of the council. The Arians had also sent ten of their faction, who, by dint of expedition, reached the court at Adrianopolis before the Catholics. They had no difficulty in prepossessing the mind of the emperor in favor of their cause, and when the Catholic envoys appeared, they were received with the utmost coldness and disdain. They soon found themselves surrounded by the intrigues of the Arian bishops; and after many negotiations, in which promises and threats were successively brought into action, they had the weakness to sign the Arian profession of faith drawn up at Sirmium, on the 22d of May, A. D. 359. Constantius at once instructed Taurus, his imperial lieutenant, to oblige all the bishops of Rimini to sign the same profession, and in order to intimidate the rest by a show of great severity, to send fifteen of the most obstinate into exile. The necessity of such a measure was unhappily obviated: discouraged by a long residence in a strange land, terrified by the threats of the emperor, the greater number yielded, and subscribed to whatever was proposed. Only twenty still held out, amongst whom were St. Phebadius, bishop of Agen, and St. Servasius, bishop of Mæstricht. Ursacius and Valens then protested that the profession of Sirmium explicitly condemned the Arian heresy; that the term *consubstantial* was omitted only to put an end to such incessant disputes; but that in other respects it was substantially a profession of the Nicene doctrine. They repeated these assertions before a general assembly of the clergy and faithful, and publicly read the following anathemas:

"If any one saith that Jesus Christ is not God, Son of God, begotten of the Father before all ages, let him be anathema!

"If any one saith that the Son of God is not co-eternal with the Father, let him be anathema.

"If any one saith there was a time when the Son of God was not, let him be anathema.

"If any one saith that the Son of God is a creature, like to other creatures, let him be anathema."

All applauded this last proposition, unheeding the hidden venom it contained; for the Catholics understood by it, that the Son of God is not a creature, in any sense of the term, whilst Valens meant that He is indeed a creature, but more perfect than other creatures. This whole triumph of Arianism thus rests upon a pitiful equivocation, not observed at the moment; but they had gained every thing by the signing of a profession in which the term *consubstantial* was not contained; Pope Liberius therefore felt bound to annul the acts of the Council of Rimini, and history must ever record, as a standing reproach, the weakness of the bishops who could depart, however slightly, although perhaps in good faith, from the Nicene Creed. The prelates now set out for their respective sees, without molestation, whilst Ursacius and Valens hastened to the imperial court, to reap the reward of their successful intrigues.

13. On their arrival at the court, they found the envoys of the Council of Seleucia, which had been sitting since the month of September, A. D. 359. It was composed of about one hundred and sixty Eastern bishops, divided in creed as follows: nineteen *Anomœans*, or pure Arians; one hundred and five *Semi-Arians*, admitting the *similar in substance;* the rest, all from Egypt, were zealous Catholics, supporting the term *consubstantial*, and the faith of Nice. We give this estimate on the authority of an eye-witness, St. Hilary of Poitiers, who assisted at the council, during his exile in Phrygia. Two commissioners of the emperor were present, with a body of troops at their disposal. It was not an easy matter to present a profession of faith equally acceptable to the three parties composing the council. Acacius, bishop of Cæsarea, and leader of the *Anomœans*, proposed one which was rejected. The Semi-Arians obtained the adoption of the formula composed in the Council of Antioch held in A. D. 341, and which sanctioned their doctrine. They restored St. Cyril, who had been unjustly banished from Jerusalem, two years previously, and formally deposed, as heretics, Acacius of Cæsarea, George of Alexandria, Eudoxius of Antioch, Patrophilus of Scythopolis, and other leading members of the *Anomœan* faction. The acts of the council, and the profession of faith which it had approved, were laid before Constantius, together with those of Rimini. The emperor, on his own authority, decided that the profession of Rimini should alone be binding; exacted subscription to it from all the deputies, and

banished Ætius to Phrygia. With these proceedings closed the year 359.

14. In this factious age, one council had seldom closed before several others began to assemble. In the beginning of the year 360, Constantius celebrated, with extraordinary splendor, the dedication of the basilica of St. Sophia, which had just been completed. He availed himself of the presence of the Eastern bishops, whom he had summoned to the dedication, to hold a council, in which he wished to secure the adoption of the profession of faith signed at Rimini, with which he was now quite infatuated. He of course obtained what he wished. Ætius was anathematized as the author of the scandals and divisions then rending the Church, and this by bishops who believed precisely what he had taught. St. Cyril of Jerusalem was again deposed; Eudoxius transferred himself from Antioch to Constantinople, after causing the deposition of its intruded bishop, Macedonius; and this afflicted church was freed from the rule of the first usurper, only to fall under the power of a second. As soon as the Council of Constantinople had issued its decrees to the satisfaction of the emperor, he sent instant orders to all parts of the empire, demanding the immediate assent of all prelates to the formula of Rimini, with the alternative of exile for all who would refuse. Fear drove many of the Eastern bishops into heresy. Pope Liberius and Vincent of Capua met every solicitation and threat with equal firmness: their courageous attitude consoled the Catholics, and supported them in their attachment to the true faith. The bishops of Gaul held a council, called the First Council of Paris, in which they annulled all that had been wrongly done, with intention or through ignorance, concerning the omission of the term *substance*. Many of the Eastern bishops who had subscribed to the Arian formulas, held to the sense of the term *consubstantial*, as the expression of Catholic faith, only yielding the term itself. Several among them hastened to atone for their error, publicly declaring their belief in the doctrine of the consubstantiality, asserting, at the

same time, that they had always retained this belief in their hearts. Notwithstanding, therefore, the favor given to Arianism by their signature, their perseverance in teaching the Catholic dogma shows them to have been, in reality, with the faithful defenders of the truth, and that the Arian majority was only apparent. The Church of Spain did not yield to that of Gaul in sincere attachment to the faith. The fall of Osius of Cordova was a source of deep grief, but led to no second defection. Gregory, bishop of Elvira, in particular, gave an example of invincible firmness, and remained ever unshaken by the repeated solicitations of the Arian faction.

15. The year 361 opened with another council; but this one was the last that Constantius was to assemble. The war against the Persians had brought him to the East. Whilst here he called together a considerable number of bishops, through whom he wished to condemn both the Catholic doctrine of the *consubstantial*, and that of the Anomœans, or pure Arians, in favor of the Semi-Arians, whose cause he had made his own. The council gave its whole attention to the choice of a bishop for Antioch, to fill the vacancy left by Eudoxius, who had, on his own responsibility, transferred himself, the year before, to the imperial see of Constantinople. Catholics, Arians, Semi-Arians, all contended for the election; each party aimed at directing it to one of its own members. The good cause triumphed, by the direction of Providence. The unanimous vote fell upon St. Meletius, bishop of Sebaste. The new patriarch had been remarkable from early youth for the regularity of his life, his mild disposition and austere morals. He was just, sincere, simple, and feared God. The Arians looked upon him as one of themselves, and the chief movers of his promotion to the see of Antioch were Acacius of Cæsarea, and George of Laodicea, the foremost leaders of the Anomœan faction. The decree of election, signed by all the bishops present, was placed in the hands of Eusebius of Samosata. The arrival of the patriarch at Antioch caused the liveliest sensation. His inaugural address was awaited

with an almost feverish impatience, as it would rank St. Meletius as an adherent of one of the three parties contending for the honor of possessing him. Constantius had ordered his stenographers to note each word of the address as it fell from the prelate's lips; he had moreover required that the patriarch should take for his text the celebrated passage from the Proverbs, upon which the Arians chiefly rested their denial of the eternity of the Word: *Dominus possedit me in initio viarum suarum.** The Greeks gave to these words the meaning that *the Lord had created the Word in the beginning* of his ways.† Perfectly unconcerned with all the intrigues by which he was beset, St. Meletius began his discourse, in the presence of Constantius, of the bishops, of all the dignitaries of the empire, and of an immense concourse of people who had come to hear him. We are indebted to St. Epiphanius for the text of this discourse, enriched throughout by the very words of Holy Writ. The patriarch clearly affirms that the Word is the Son of God, God of God, One of One, similar to the Father, and His living image. He explains the words of the *Proverbs*, in the Catholic sense, by other analogous texts of Scripture, and ends by denouncing the rash curiosity of heretics, who would sound the depths of the divine nature, and reject the simplicity of faith. So unexpected a train of reasoning threw Constantius into a violent rage. But few days were allowed to pass, ere the patriarch was thrown into one of the governor's chariots, and led away to exile. But in those few days the people of Antioch had learned to love their holy bishop; in their indignation they would have massacred the governor, who was seated in the car beside his prisoner. He owed his life to St. Meletius himself, who covered him with his cloak. The emperor, and the Arians whose tool he was, now repented of having intrusted the certificate of the election of Meletius to Eusebius of Samosata. Constantius sent an officer of his

* Lib. Proverb. cap. viii. 22.
† According to their interpretation, it followed, from this text, that the Word was but a creature.

palace to demand the document, with an order to cut off the bishop's right hand in case of refusal. The intrepid bishop, having read the imperial letter, held out both hands towards the officer, and said: "Cut off both, for I shall never give up the decree, which so clearly proves the duplicity of the Arians." This noble answer disarmed the emperor, who neither insisted any longer, nor could refuse the tribute of his admiration to such greatness of soul. To come to some final arrangement, however, for the occupation of the see of Antioch, he sent for Euzoius, one of the first disciples of Arius, who had been deposed from the deaconship, at Alexandria, by the holy bishop Alexander. In defiance of every law of the Church, this deposed deacon, who had never been restored to his office, was consecrated by the Arians, and proclaimed patriarch of Antioch.

16. Whilst Constantius was engaged in holding councils, in changing professions of faith, and receiving from his courtiers the title of *Eternal*, his end had come. The Cæsar Julian, his nephew, to whom he had committed the government of Gaul, had just caused himself to be proclaimed emperor, at Lutetia (Paris). According to Libanius, Constantius had neither the heart of a prince nor the head of a captain. The news of this event found him without courage or foresight. After yielding, at first, to a fit of fruitless rage, and then to cowardly despair, he at last found resolution to lead his troops against the rebel: but death met him on the way. He died at Mopsucrene, in Cilicia, after having received baptism at the hands of the same Euzoius whom he had just intruded into a patriarchal see. The death of Constantius was the salvation of the Church. She was, indeed, about to suffer the contemptuous and ironical persecution of an apostate; but the faith had nothing to fear, with paganism for its adversary; it had every thing to lose, when given up to the caprices of a court of eunuchs and of a crowned theologian.

17. Before entering upon the details of the new struggles into which the Church was plunged under an apostate emper-

or, during a season of pagan *renaissance*, we must retrace our steps, to study the great historical figures that arose both in the East and in the West, during the theological campaigns of Constantius. Whilst borne along by the tide of Arian discussions, already too complicated of themselves, we could not pause to insert the personal biographies which we now present. The two names which first meet us, in the order of time, are those of two holy doctors and illustrious friends—Gregory Nazianzen and Basil of Cæsarea. Drawn together by proximity of birth-place, their hearts were more closely knit by community of studies and of pious practices. Gregory was born in A. D. 316, at Nazianzum; his mother was St. Nonna; his brother and sister rank in the Church's calendar as St. Cesarius and St. Gorgona. At the time of his birth, his father, after whom he was called, was still a pagan, professing the doctrines of the Hypsistarians (adorers of the Most High God, Ὕψιστος). But the head of a family of saints could not long remain in darkness. From the period of his conversion, he showed so much fervor, and made such rapid progress in every Christian virtue, that four years later, at the age of fifty-five years, he was elected Bishop of Nazianzum, and in the discharge of a holy and laborious pontificate reached a happy old age, having lived nearly a hundred years, when he went to his reward. Gregory, his son, was prevented, in tender infancy, by heavenly graces and benedictions. At that period of life when the germs of virtue or of vice begin to unfold in the human heart, he was favored with a marvellous vision: he saw by his side two virgins in white apparel, of more than mortal majesty, with a look of angelic modesty, who leaned towards him to kiss his forehead. Gregory asked their names. They replied that they were Chastity and Temperance; that they ministered before the throne of God, and took particular delight in chaste souls. Then they urged him to give his heart into their keeping, that they might one day present him in the train of virgins that follow the Lamb. This vision left the heart of the youthful Gregory inflamed with a pure love for virtue. With a clean heart, he had received also a noble and vast intellect. He advanced with equal pace in piety and science. He had soon exhausted the course of studies furnished to the youth of his day, and was then sent to Cæsarea in Palestine, where he availed himself of the advantages afforded in the school founded by Origen, and of the famous library collected by his disciple, the martyr St. Pamphilus, and increased by the learned Eusebius. St. Cæsarius, his brother, had repaired to Alexandria, to learn wisdom and science at the feet of the blind sage, Didymus, who had inherited both the chair and the learning of Origen. Didymus had lost his sight at the age of five years. He had the letters of the alphabet engraved on wood, and succeeded by force of ingenuity in learning to read: he was thus enabled to enjoy the teaching of the best masters, and at the age of forty-five years his knowledge equalled that of the greatest doctors of the age. The renown of his eloquence and exalted science placed him at the head of the Alexandrian school. But neither his glory, nor even his great virtue, was able fully to compensate for the loss of sight. One day he candidly admitted this fact to St. Anthony, who had come to visit him: "I am surprised," said the holy patriarch, "to find a wise man lamenting the loss of what we have in common with flies and gnats, instead of rejoicing in the possession of what has been left us by the saints and apostles. Far more precious is the vision of the intelligence than that of the body, since a single glance of the corporal eye may cause the eternal loss of the soul." Gregory Nazianzen joined his brother Cæsarius in Alexandria, and for some time profited, with him, by the teaching of the illustrious sufferer. They soon parted, however; Cæsarius returned home, and Gregory set out for Athens, which was always looked upon as the metropolis of science and literature. Here he met a youth whom the hand of God was also leading to great things: it was St. Basil. He was born at Cæsarea, in Cappadocia, at the same time with St. Gregory, towards the year 317. Holiness seemed to be an heir-loom in his family also. His father Basil, his mother Emily, with Macrina his sister, Gregory bishop of Nyssa, and Peter bishop of Sebaste, his brothers, have all been honored by the Church with a place in the ranks of her saints. Young Basil was first sent to the public school of Cæsarea, in Palestine, and then to Constantinople, always far outstripping his fellows in rapid progress, quick intelligence, and especially in the solid piety which gave life to his brilliant talents. In the last-named city he studied elocution under the celebrated Libanius, who was then at the full height of his reputation. Though himself a heathen, Libanius could not refuse the tribute of his unbounded admiration to the extraordinary talents of his youthful disciple, which received additional lustre from the surpassing modesty and virtue that accompanied them. He says in his *Epistles*, that to hear Basil speak in public always transported him quite out of himself. He ever afterwards kept up a continual correspondence with him, and always took occasion to show the high esteem and deep veneration he had conceived for his distinguished merit. Basil at length left Constantinople for Athens, whither he had been preceded by Gregory. These two noble souls, so worthy of one another, were soon bound together by the ties of an undying friendship. Each opened to the other the inmost recesses of his heart; they mutually communicated their aspirations after Christian perfection. They dwelt together in studious retreat, shared the same table, and divided their hours between common labor and prayer. "We had both the same end in view," writes St. Gregory himself: "we were both in search of the same treasure, virtue; we sought to make our union unending, by preparing ourselves for eternal happiness; we were our own masters and guardians, mutually exhorting one another to piety; we held no communication with those among our companions whose morals were at all relaxed, and only sought the society of those whose modesty, reserve, and wisdom could urge us forward in the practice of virtue. We knew but two streets in Athens: the one led to the Church, the other to the

public schools; those which led to the places of worldly
amusement, to plays, and public assemblies, were altogether
unknown to us." Foremost in the way of wisdom, the two
friends held the same rank in the paths of science and literature. Besides his proficiency in rhetoric, poetry, philosophy,
and dialectics, Basil possessed a knowledge of geometry and
astronomy, which placed him on a level with the ablest men
of the day. In the maladies resulting from his austere and
mortified life, he found an occasion for adding to his other
acquirements a knowledge of medicine, at least of what is
most philosophical in that science. So much learning and virtue
caused a corresponding degree of admiration, and wherever
mention was made of Athens and its great masters, the names
of the marvellous pair, Gregory and Basil, were always heard.
Amid the student-throng that then frequented the Athenian
schools, was a youth of some twenty years, of medium height,
with thick-set neck, quick, ever-restless, wandering eyes, un-
combed beard and broad shoulders, which were always in a
state of uneasy, restless agitation: such was the Cæsar Julian,
nephew of the Emperor Constantius, and the only member
spared by the emperor, in the general massacre of his own
family. Julian sought to share in the intimate relations which
existed between Basil and Gregory; but God had given to the
holy pair, even at that early age, the too uncommon gift of a
keen perception of human character. They rejected Julian's
advances, and Gregory, perceiving his affectation of austerity
and his deceitful piety, could not forbear exclaiming: "What
a viper does the Roman empire cherish in its bosom; but God
grant I prove a false prophet!" These sad forebodings were
but too correct; the youthful hypocrite at Athens was the
apostate emperor of later years. But the two friends had now
fully completed their course of studies. Basil and Gregory
must leave Athens, and separate. The whole city was affected
by the prospect of such a loss; professors and students press
around them and beg them to remain. But Basil at last tears
himself away from so much regret. Gregory was forced to

accept a chair of elocution; but he soon succeeded in escaping secretly from his disciples, and went to share his friend's seclusion in Cappadocia. Here, in the quiet of a pious and profitable retreat, they await the hour of Providence, and prepare themselves for the great work God has in store for them.

18. Another father of the Greek Church was meanwhile gaining honor for his native city, Jerusalem. St. Cyril, whilst but a simple priest, was commissioned by Maximus, bishop of Jerusalem, to preach every Sunday in the assembly of the faithful, and at the same time to instruct the catechumens. Of his *Catecheticals*, or familiar oral instructions, twenty-three have reached us, of which the first eighteen are devoted to the explanation of the Creed, and the remaining five to the sacraments of baptism, confirmation, and the Eucharist, which the neophytes received on the same day. This is a monument of inestimable worth, on account of the clearness and order with which the Christian doctrine is explained and defended against the attacks of heathens and heretics. These catechetical instructions, which generally lasted about an hour, were given under the porticos of the churches, and not within the sacred precincts, to which the unbaptized hearers were not, as yet, admitted. St. Cyril here gives the name of faithful to all who believe in heart, and profess by word, whatever the Church believes and teaches, even though they have not yet received the sacrament of regeneration. The talent and eloquence displayed in this series of instructions naturally pointed out Cyril as the fit object of the votes of both clergy and people, when the death of Maximus left the patriarchal throne of Jerusalem vacant. The illustrious priest, therefore, was hailed with universal applause as bishop of his native city. The apparition of the miraculous cross, in A. D. 351, splendidly confirmed the many marks of divine favor which God was pleased to bestow upon the labor of the holy prelate. His attachment to the Nicene faith soon drew upon him the persecution of the Arians. Acacius of Cæsarea brought about his deposition, in A. D. 357, on the false pretence that St. Cyril

had squandered the treasures of the Church. It is true that whilst the country about Jerusalem was suffering from famine, the starving flock applied to its bishop for food. As Cyril had exhausted his funds, he sold some golden vases and precious stuffs to feed the suffering members of Jesus Christ. On such charges as this did the Council of Cæsarea condemn a Catholic bishop! St. Cyril was restored in A. D. 359, by the Council of Seleucia, only to be again deposed by that of Constantinople (A. D. 360), and he was only enabled to return to Jerusalem by the death of Constantius, which gave back to their homes so many suffering exiles. But new struggles awaited him here.

19. In the far East, Armenia lavished its admiration upon a new apostle, the patriarch Nerses I., surnamed the Great. He was of the royal race of the Arsacidæ, and had received his early training at Cæsarea, in Cappadocia, and afterwards in Constantinople, where he had studied Greek literature. Here he had contracted an alliance with the daughter of a distinguished personage. Three years later he was left a widower, returned to his native country, and embraced a military life. Having passed through several grades in the service, he was honored with the dignity of chamberlain to King Arsaces. In all the freshness and vigor of youth, his brilliant virtue and distinguished valor had won him general esteem, whilst he inspired respect by his imposing figure and majestic bearing. In the year 340 the patriarchal throne of Armenia became vacant. Since the time of St. Gregory the Illuminator, there had been some scandalous patriarchs; religion had suffered much in consequence; two of their successors, though, indeed, possessed of virtue, yet wanted energy equal to the deeply rooted evil; the work called for a second Gregory the Illuminator. This necessity had given occasion to a great assembly, which was now in session. Many voices begin to speak of a holy patriarch who had arisen, worthy heir to the virtues of a great ancestor. The name of Nerses is uttered; the vote is unanimous, and, with one concert of praise, the patriarchal sceptre is awarded to him. From every quarter the cry is raised: "He alone shall be our pastor!

No other shall sit upon the episcopal throne." Unconscious of this wonderful movement, taken by surprise, Nerses strives to escape the honor thus forced upon him. He attempts to fly; but the king himself stops him, and ungirding the sword he wore as a badge of his rank, orders him to be instantly vested in the pontifical attire. The Armenian Catholics had no reason to regret their choice. Under the culture of the new patriarch the faith soon flourished again in Armenia; the ruined churches and altars were restored; new temples, dedicated to the true God, arose over the ruins of idolatrous shrines; hospitals and monasteries were founded; public morals began to assume a new tone; and the blessings of education were placed within the reach of all. Towards the year 355, whilst the persecution of Constantius against the Catholic bishops was at its height, the king of Armenia sent him an embassy, headed by the patriarch Nerses. The emperor undertook to win him to Arianism. Failing in the attempt, he became so enraged as to violate, in the saint's person, the sacred rights of an ambassador, by banishing him to a desert island.

20. Whilst the Eastern Church was rejoicing in this rich harvest of great men, the West also numbered illustrious defenders of the faith. The name of Hilary of Poitiers was the brightest ornament of the Church of Gaul. Sprung from one of the noblest families of the land, Hilary had been brought up a pagan. He cultivated the profane sciences with distinguished success, and gave particular care to the study of eloquence. Every gift had been lavished upon this chosen intellect. The grace of God sought him out in the midst of his literary engagements, and of his predilection for Quintilian, whom he had chosen as master and model. He thus records the particulars of his conversion: "I deemed the most desirable state, in a natural point of view, to be repose in the midst of plenty; but I saw that we possess this happiness in common with irrational animals. I understood, then, that the happiness of man must be of a higher order. As the present life is but a tissue of miseries and troubles, it seemed to me that it

has been given us only to afford the occasion of practising the virtues of patience, moderation, meekness, and that the God of mercy could not have given it to make us more miserable by taking it from us. I then felt in my soul an enthusiastic desire to know this God, the author of all good; I plainly saw the absurdity of the heathen doctrine touching the Divinity—dividing it amongst many persons of both sexes, attributing it to animals, plants, statues, and insensible objects. I saw that there could be but one God, eternal, all-powerful, immutable. Full of such sentiments, I read, with admiration, these words, in the books of Moses: 'I am Who am.' And in Isaiah: 'Heaven is My throne, and the earth My footstool. He weighs the heavens with His palm; He hath poised with three fingers the bulk of the earth.' And in the Psalms: 'Whither shall I go from Thy Spirit? or whither shall I flee from Thy face?' These words taught me that all things are subject to God; that He is beyond all, in all, and everywhere present; that He is the source of all beauty—infinite beauty. In a word, I understood that I must believe Him incomprehensible. My desires reached even beyond this, and I felt the need of an immortality, as the reward of a life devoted to good works; but the weakness of my understanding threw me into a strange perplexity, when the writings of the Apostles and Evangelists opened a new world to my wondering mind. In reading the opening passages of the Gospel of St. John, I learned that God had a Son coeternal and consubstantial with His Father; that the Son, the Word of God, had been made flesh, that man might, in turn, become the Son of God." From that moment, his conversion was complete. His wife followed his example, and embraced the true faith, and their daughter, St. Apra, consecrated her virginity to the God who had thus revealed himself to her family. The new convert became the model of the faithful of Poitiers, and when death removed their bishop, Maxentius, brother to St. Maximus of Treves, Hilary was unanimously elected to fill the vacancy (A. D. 353). He was a pastor ever ready to defend the faith, even at the cost of his life

Towards the year 356, in the name of all the bishops of Gaul, he addressed to the emperor, Constantius, a bold remonstrance against the violence of the Arians. His conclusions were expressed with an independence of style and language worthy of an apostle: "Let the Catholic churches," he writes, "no longer suffer such intolerable persecution from their brothers; let secular magistrates no longer undertake to judge in ecclesiastical matters, nor continue to show open favor to the partisans of heresy; give to the faithful the right to receive the teaching of their legitimate pastors, instead of being compelled to hear the corrupters of holy doctrines; recall the exiled bishops to their flocks; amongst others, Eusebius of Vercelli, Dionysius of Milan, and Athanasius of Alexandria, in whose case every form of justice has been grossly violated. The fruitful cause of all this evil is clearly traceable to this new plague, the Arian imposture, lately brought amongst the faithful by the two Eusebiuses, Narcissus of Neronia, Theodore of Heraclea, Stephen of Antioch, Acacius of Cæsarea, Menophantes of Ephesus, and two presumptuous youths, Ursacius and Valens, whose ignorance is only equalled by their malice." Such firmness on the part of Hilary drew upon him all the hatred of the Arians. Saturninus, bishop of Arles, their partisan, together with Ursacius and Valens, who had been so deeply branded in the remonstrance to the emperor, opened a council at Beziers, in A.D. 356, where Hilary succeeded in thwarting all their intrigues. They revenged themselves by causing his banishment to Phrygia; but his flock at Poitiers were always true to him, and from his far-off exile in Asia, Hilary still governed his church. Banishment could not damp the ardor of the confessor. It was at this time that he wrote his twelve books on the *Trinity*. As he was the first to develop this doctrine in the West, where the terms were consequently not yet well fixed, we find in his treatise some inexact expressions, which must be explained by the collation of his general teaching and doctrine. He often deplores the poverty and insufficiency of human language to hold converse with

God. After recalling the incoherent and doubtful character of human philosophy, he shows the invariable and harmonious method of Christian teaching in both Testaments. In the Old, God defines Himself: "I am Who am;" this more than human expression Hilary exhibits in its full force. In the New, a Galilean fisherman, rising above and far beyond all created things, seems to dive into the very bosom of the Divinity. St. Hilary then comments on the opening words of the Gospel of St. John, and displays their full depth and sublimity. The chief object of this work is to prove, by means of the Old and New Testaments, the Trinity and the *Consubstantiality* of the Divine Persons, but especially the divinity of Jesus Christ, and to refute the objections of Sabellius and Arius. In this work we can perceive an emanation from the fountain of living waters that flow unto eternal life. We are impressed throughout, by the unbounded fulness of faith and vigor, which of itself proves that the Catholic Church, though under such bitter persecution, was by no means near to destruction. St. Hilary lays down, as an undeniable truth, that whenever, in the Old Testament, God appeared in human form to the patriarchs and prophets, it was the Word, thus showing Himself, in order that man might become, so to speak, accustomed beforehand to the real Incarnation. This is but a reproduction of the doctrine taught by the first fathers, St. Justin, St. Irenæus, Origen, Theophilus of Antioch, Clement of Alexandria, Tertullian, and St. Cyprian. Even the Arians admitted this; Eusebius teaches it, in his *Demonstration of the Gospel;* and the Council of Sirmium, against Photinus, pronounces an anathema against all who hold the opposite doctrine. This tradition, handed down through St. Ambrose, St. Augustine, St. Leo the Great, and all the most illustrious doctors, has been worthily taken up and renewed, at a more modern date, by Bossuet. This view gives the deepest and clearest insight into the harmony and surpassing beauty of the two covenants.

We have seen that Providence led St. Hilary to the Eastern council convened at Seleucia (A. D. 360). At the close of this council, the Bishop of Poitiers set out for Constantinople, and presented a petition to the emperor, begging a twofold favor: 1st, the privilege of being confronted with Saturninus of Arles, Ursacius, and Valens, to give a public refutation to their errors; 2d, that of being admitted to the imperial presence, in order to treat the question of faith in the Catholic sense. "Your majesty seeks the truth," said he; "learn it, then, not from new formulas of yesterday, but from the books of God. Remember that it is not a question of philosophical demonstration, but the teaching of the Gospel." Constantius gave no heed to this private communication; he continued to push his doctrinal despotism to the last excess. St. Hilary now published a new appeal, addressed, not to the emperor, but to the Catholic faithful. He opens with all the vehemence of an apostle: "Let us await Christ, since Antichrist now rules. Let the shepherds speak, because the hirelings have fled. Let us lay down our lives for the flock, for the wolves have broken into the fold, and the raging lion seeks to devour the sheep. Let us hasten to martyrdom, for the angel of Satan has transformed himself into an angel of light. Impious prince, you receive bishops with a kiss like that by which Judas betrayed Christ; whilst you bow your head to receive their blessing, your foot is raised to trample on their faith!" The Eastern bishops, terrified by the holy audacity of his language, urged Constantius to rid himself of Hilary, by sending him back to Gaul. His return to Poitiers was a general triumph. He soon became the centre, so to speak, of the bishops of Gaul, who rallied about him as to the living rule of the faith. We have seen St. Phebadius of Agen, with like intrepidity, take his stand in the breach, to beat back the Arian heresy. A second champion, worthy of St. Hilary, was the illustrious disciple who one day came to him from a company of imperial veterans, levied in the far-off region of Pannonia (the present Hungary). Martin, son of a military tribune, a Christian in spite of his parents, a soldier of Jesus Christ before enlisting under the standard of the empire, so alive to the call of charity as to cut his cloak in two to share it with a half-naked beggar at the gates of Amiens, sought his discharge on the day following a battle in which he had displayed the most heroic courage, and hastened to throw himself at the feet of the Bishop of Poitiers, to learn from him the virtues which were one day to shine so brightly in the great St. Martin, bishop of Tours. Meanwhile, Eusebius of Vercelli, and St. Paulinus of Treves, by their courageous efforts and eloquent writings, nobly labored in defence of the faith. From his remote exile, Lucifer of Cagliari sent forth a series of works addressed to Constantius. These works are remarkable for purity of faith, and for the energy with which Lucifer reproaches Constantius for his attachment to Arianism. They comprise the *Defence of St. Athanasius*, the book of *The Apostate Kings*, the two treatises, *That we must not spare those who resist God; That we must die for the Son of God.* Thus the West was nobly represented in the great intellectual movement which animated the Catholic Church in the fourth century. The line of its great doctors by no means closes here; for at this time St. Ambrose, the future Bishop of Milan, was beginning his course of studies in Rome; St. Jerome first saw the light in Dalmatia (A. D. 351), and St. Augustin at Tagaste (A. D. 354). What splendor were these three names destined to reflect upon the Latin Church!

21. Constantius had ruined the imperial treasury by the hire of public conveyances to bring the bishops to his councils. Julian, his successor, completed the work of draining it, in rebuilding the idolatrous temples destroyed by Constantine, and in the purchase of the oxen needed for his hecatombs; such was his extravagance in this particular, that he actually received a satirical note, in these terms: "The white oxen salute the Cæsar Julian. It is all over with us, if you triumph." The youth who sought the friendship and intimacy of St. Gregory and St. Basil, in Athens; who had gone so far in his fervor, as to become *lector* in the Church of Nicomedia, and whose youthful piety had been pushed even to supersti-

tion, once clothed in the imperial purple, thus shows himself in the proclamations published throughout the world: "We serve the gods openly, and the multitude of troops at our command is pious. We sacrifice oxen to the tutelary divinities of the empire, and we have already offered them several hecatombs, in thanksgiving for our victory (A. D. 361)." The piety of the troops, of which Julian boasts, was nothing else than the very natural eagerness on the part of the Gallic and German soldiers to secure their share of meat and wine, in these imperial slaughters. Their devotion, in this respect, was so fervent, that as Ammianus-Marcellinus testifies, "the passersby were often obliged to carry them to their quarters." An edict forthwith appeared, for the restoration of idolatry, with the dignities of sacrificers, aruspices and augurs, in all the cities throughout the empire. All the temples destroyed by Constantine were to be raised from their ruins, and endowed with their original revenues; the Christians were bound to restore, at their own expense, those which they had destroyed, and to give up to them all the endowments bestowed by Constantine upon the churches. So unexpected a revolution in the titles of property set the whole empire in a blaze. In the course of the few preceding years, Mark, bishop of Arethusa, at the head of his flock, had destroyed an idolatrous temple. Too poor to make restitution to the full value of the property destroyed, the prelate was seized, by virtue of the Roman law which gave up to the creditor the person of the debtor. After undergoing a cruel scourging, his beard was plucked out, and his body rubbed with honey; and in this condition, the holy old man was suspended naked in a net, and exposed, under a burning sun, to the stings of flies and other insects. It was Mark who had rescued the infant Julian from the rage of Constantius, and the general massacre of his family: this was the apostate's return! In this case, which had every claim upon his generosity, Julian was cruel by exception, for it formed no part of his plan to crush the *Galileans*, as he called them, under the blows of a bloody persecution. He was too well versed in the history of the religion he was persecuting, to renew the attempt in which the emperors, from Nero to Diocletian, had met with such signal failure. Ridicule, public contempt, derision and satire, were the weapons he deemed powerful against a Church which torrents of blood could not overwhelm. The sword of sarcasm was shivered in the hands of Julian, and the philosophers of the eighteenth century, who so eagerly gathered up the scattered fragments, have met with the same success as the apostate. They fondly imagined themselves the inventors of a new system, and their invention is reduced to a plagiarism from a persecutor of the Lower Empire. Julian's apostasy was not wanting in the natural accompaniment of hypocrisy. The Gallic soldiers who had followed him from Lutetia, where he was proclaimed emperor, to Rome, where the Senate recognized his accession, had sworn, upon their swords, to die for him. Yet many of them were Christians; but Julian had deceived them. A short time before quitting Gaul, on the feast of the Epiphany, he had gone into the Church, at Vienne, where he spent some time in prayer. Ammianus-Marcellinus asserts that, at that very moment, he secretly professed paganism; this double dealing of the deceitful Cæsar surely justified the indignation it excited. As he was once offering sacrifice in the Temple of Fortune, Maris, bishop of Chalcedon, sharply upbraided him with his apostasy. Julian said to him: "Old man, the *Galilean* will not restore you your sight." Maris was blind. "For that I thank Him," answered the bishop, "since it spares me the pain of looking upon such an apostate." "The first publication of Julian's edict for the restoration of idolatry," says St. Chrysostom,* "brought together, from every quarter of the world, numbers of magicians, sorcerers, soothsayers, augurs, and all, in fact, who dealt in professional imposture and delusion: and now the imperial palace was filled with vagabonds and worthless characters. Many of them had long lived in

* Tillemont's translation.

the last extreme of misery; some had just come forth from the dismal confinement of the prison or the mines, to which their magic and evil-doings had condemned them; others, again, dragged out a miserable existence, in the most vile and disgraceful employments; and these impostors now suddenly found themselves invested with the pontifical dignity, and raised to the highest distinction. The emperor, disregarding his generals and magistrates, disdaining to grant them even the favor of a word, went about through the city surrounded by his court of dissolute youths ruined by debauchery, and of courtesans who had just left their infamous dens. The emperor's horse and attendants followed him at a considerable distance, whilst this vile multitude surrounded his person, appearing in the public places, with every mark of rank and honor, indulging in the words and actions that might be expected from such characters."

22. Apostasy led Julian to fanaticism; from fanaticism he passed on to persecution: when a man has committed a fault which he deems irreparable, pride leads him to seek a defence in the very fault itself. Julian tried two very difficult experiments: to rekindle the zeal of the idolaters for an extinct worship; to provoke defections amongst the Christians. He offered gold and honors as the price of apostasy: he failed with the fervent faith of the disciples of Jesus Christ, and with the dead faith of the pagans. He complained, himself, that he found so few persons disposed to offer sacrifice; he upbraids the inhabitants of Alexandria with having forsaken the gods of Alexander, for a Word, which neither they nor their fathers had ever seen.* If now it be asked what intrinsic or extrinsic causes could excite in Julian so deep an antipathy for a religion which he had himself professed with all the zeal of a neophyte, it seems to us that they can be summed up in the following view of his nature and disposition: Julian's was one of those lively imaginations better fitted for poetry than for

---

* Hunc vero quem neque vos, neque patres vestri vidire, Jesum Doum esse Verbum creditis oportere. (Julian., Epist. li.)

the realities of the governmental and positive world. His soul, fascinated by the fables of Greece, was allured by the beauty of the pagan ceremonial. The gods of Homer were, to him, the fairest creations of genius, and his unbounded admiration of their poet led him to the conviction that he was called to restore their worship. But deeper than this literary enthusiasm was the bitter hatred he bore Constantius, the murderer of his father, who had handed over his brother to the executioner, and had long threatened his own life. He thought to revenge his murdered kindred by proscribing the religion of the prince who had been their executioner. Extrinsic influences also gave new force to his personal motives. Heathenism, peremptorily outlawed by Constantine, had long been awaiting the period of reaction. The Greek and Latin sophists, the rhetoricians and philosophers of Athens, Alexandria, and Rome, who had persistingly opposed the light of the Gospel, were offering up all their vows for the restoration of the gods of Homer and Virgil, of Aristotle and Plato. Moreover, the manners, habits, and worship of a whole people are not changed by a stroke of the pen; all the interests, passions, and self-love which had been wounded in the triumph of the cross, clustered around Julian, at the period of his accession, crying out: "Without Julian Augustus, all power is lost, for the provinces, the army, and the republic."* It must be allowed that the state of society, at the death of Constantius, was such as to justify the most sanguine hopes of the pagans. The heresy of Arius had produced divisions and subdivisions without number: there was but one unceasing cross-fire of anathemas; legitimate bishops were driven from their sees, by force of arms, to make way for usurpers; schism came to add its portion to the disorders already produced by heresy. These strifes, which resounded in every city, village, and hamlet, weakened the empire without, paralyzed its interior strength, and made its administration difficult and perilous. The sedi-

---

* Ammianus-Marcellinus. Lib. xx. Cap. II.

tions excited by the Arians occupied all the attention of the judges and governors. Julian might then have believed that he would at once repress every evil, by making all the sects yield to the ancient worship;* to effect this object, he applied the ironical levity of a sophist, the fanaticism of an idolater, the cold calculation of a sceptic; and his fruitless attempt only added another evidence of the divine immortality of the Christian religion, "that anvil," said a celebrated orator, "on which all hammers have been shattered."†

23. As early as the year 362, Julian published an edict granting to every one the free exercise of religion, and recalling all who had been banished for a religious cause. He sought to foment the divisions between Catholics and Arians, to weaken them by means of one another, and then to crush both under the weight of public contempt. The religious liberty which he ostensibly granted to the Christians was but a hard slavery: he did not, indeed, condemn them to death, by a public edict, but he still took the surest means to overwhelm them. Every favor was lavished upon the heathens; the Christians received from him but disdain, vexation, and disgrace. In order to lower the clergy, he abolished the privileges of ecclesiastics; he cut off the pension allowed for the support of clerics and virgins consecrated to God. "Their admirable law," he said, "enjoins upon them to renounce the goods of this world, in order to reach the kingdom of heaven; with the gracious desire to make their journey the easier, we order that they be relieved of the weight of all their goods." When the Christians dared to complain, he said: "Is it not the vocation of a Christian to suffer?" The bishops addressed to him an apology for Christianity, through Diodorus of Tarsus; he sent it back to them with these three Greek words: Ἀνεγνων, εγνων, κατεγνων (I have read, I have understood, I have condemned). All the churches were stripped, and their costly ornaments transferred to the idolatrous temples, which

---

* *Etudes Historiques* de M. de Chateaubriand (passim). † M. l'Abbé Combalot.

he was repairing at the expense of the *Galileans*. Those who were weak in the faith he tried to win over by promises. The firmness of those who resisted his solicitations was made a State offence; but those who weakly yielded, and sacrificed their conscience to a fortune, were loaded with honors and favors. Apostasy was the avenue to every preferment; it supplied the want of talent and merit; it threw a veil over every past crime, and purchased an unlimited right to the commission of fresh ones.

24. By a glorious exception, Julian had especially excluded St. Athanasius from the privilege of returning to his episcopal see, which was granted to all other exiles. "It would be dangerous," said the apostate, in a letter to the inhabitants of Alexandria, "to leave an intriguer at the head of the people; not a man, but a worthless little abortion, who esteems himself the greater, in proportion to the dangers he invokes upon his own head. Never, therefore, receive that wretch, Athanasius. He has dared, in my reign, to confer baptism upon some Greek women of illustrious rank." But the course of events determined matters otherwise. The Arian bishop, George, who had held the See of Alexandria since the banishment of St. Athanasius, had incurred the odium of all parties: of the Catholics, by the persecution he had brought upon them, under Constantius; of the Arians, by obliging them to subscribe the condemnation of Ætius, one of their leaders; of the pagans, by pillaging their temples, and by the vexations he indiscriminately inflicted upon all classes of people. The pagan reaction availed itself of existing circumstances to throw George into prison. He hardly had been consigned to custody, when the people assembled in crowds, seized and dragged him through the city, trampling him under foot, with every kind of indignity. George expired in the midst of fearful agonies. His body was placed upon a camel, and conveyed, amid the shouts of a maddened people, to the sea-shore, where it was burned, and the ashes scattered upon the waters, lest the Christians should honor them as those of a martyr; this had lately happened in

the case of Artemius, governor of Egypt, hom Julian had put to death on a charge of embezzlement, but in truth, to punish the zeal he had shown in the destruction of idolatrous temples. No like demonstration need have been feared in the case of the intruded bishop. It was too notorious a fact, that religion had no share in causing his death, and that his crimes had rendered him odious to all. When Julian heard of the sedition, he appeared displeased only with the form of the execution. Indeed, it could not but be pleasing to him to see religious resentments embittered, and to witness the mutual destruction of sects so hateful to him. He contented himself with writing to the Alexandrians in these terms: "George deserved the treatment he received. I will even add that he deserved a yet more severe chastisement, but it did not belong to you to inflict it. Even though you show no regard for Alexander, your founder, or rather for the great god Serapis, how could you forget the common duty you owe to humanity, and what is due to me—to me, whom the gods, and especially the great god Serapis, have invested with the empire of the universe?" By such addresses did this literary Cæsar hope to appease popular tumults. Under the circumstances, St. Athanasius seeing no obstacle to his return, notwithstanding Julian's antipathy to him, determined to go back to Alexandria, after an exile of seven years. His entrance was a triumph worthy of a disciple of Jesus Christ. The Saviour of the world entered Jerusalem seated, in the words of the Holy Text, "upon the foal of an ass." It was in just the same manner that Athanasius appeared amid his beloved Alexandrians, surrounded by a countless multitude who had gone forward, two days' journey, to meet him. All Egypt seemed to have met around the illustrious patriarch. Every height was crowded by multitudes eager to look upon him; they thronged around him to catch the least tone of that revered voice; the mere passing of his shadow seemed a pledge of blessing and sanctification. If it may be said that no man ever suffered such a life-long persecution as did Athanasius the Great, it must with equal truth be admitted, that never did a people show themselves more devoted, more enthusiastic, more true to their legitimate pastor, than did the faithful of Alexandria. The triumphant procession passed through an atmosphere fragrant with burning perfumes, a path strewn with flowers; the whole city was illuminated; joyful feasts were held in every square. Never did father meet a gladder welcome on his return to the domestic circle; never did a beloved monarch receive more general proofs of a people's love. St. Athanasius treated his most bitter persecutors with so much mildness, that they had no cause to regret his return. He made himself the visible providence of all the needy, the unfortunate, and the oppressed, without distinction of party; all minds, all hearts were irresistibly drawn to him by the charm of his gentleness and of his virtue.

25. In his return from Thebais, whither he had been exiled by Constantius, St. Eusebius of Vercelli tarried at Alexandria to confer with St. Athanasius. The two prelates conjointly called a Council, small in numbers, but composed almost wholly of confessors of the faith—men such as St. Asterius, bishop of Petra in Arabia, Caius, Ammonius, Dracontius, Adelphius, Paphnutius. It was necessary to decide upon the line of conduct to be adopted in regard to the bishops who had been so weak as to sign the heretical professions of faith. The majority of those who had allowed themselves to be ensnared at Rimini, had since given manifest proofs of their repentance. The Council of Alexandria decided that they should not be excluded from the ecclesiastical communion. It was also decreed that the leaders of the Arian faction who would renounce their errors should obtain pardon for the past, but not their former rank among the clergy. Those who had yielded only to violence, and were received back to the communion of the Church, after due retractation, were not to lose their place in the hierarchy. The question of dogma was then settled by the condemnation of the new doctrine taught by Macedonius, intruded Bishop of Constantinople; this doctrine, which was beginning to gain ground, attacked the divinity of the Holy

Ghost. The council fixed the catholic sense of the term *hypostasis*, which had been used with different acceptations in the course of the controversy. Some, understanding this term as synonymous with *substance*, admitted but one *hypostasis*, in God. Others, giving it the signification *person*, recognized three. Having decided upon these points of theological language, they proceeded to the solemn condemnation of Arius, Sabellius, Paul of Samosata, Basilides, and Manes. The closing sessions were devoted to the examination of a disputed point in the doctrine of the Incarnation. It was recognized that the Redeemer had not assumed a body without soul or thought, in opposition to certain Greeks who believed that the soul of the incarnate Word was the Divinity itself. St. Athanasius had hardly closed the labors of the council, when the pagans, irritated by the numerous conversions due to the zeal of the holy patriarch, complained to Julian that there would soon not be left a single worshipper of the gods in their city. The apostate immediately wrote them: "That bishop, banished by the repeated orders of several emperors, should at least have waited for a new one, to return. I did, indeed, grant to the Galileans proscribed by Constantius, of happy memory, the privilege of returning to their country, but not to their churches. By what right, then, does this bold Athanasius, with his wonted impudence, presume to hold what they call the episcopal see? I hereby order him to leave the city, upon receipt of this letter, under pain of the most severe punishments if he dare to disobey. I swear by the great Serapis, that if the impious intruder be not driven from the city, or, rather, from the soil of all Egypt, before the Kalends of December, I shall exact from the company of Egyptian officers a fine of a hundred pounds in gold." It may easily be supposed that an order backed by such threats was executed with the last degree of severity. The principal church in Alexandria was once more invaded by the soldiery, and defiled by profanation and murder. Intending to seek again the secure solitude of Thebais, Athanasius hastily fled in a boat which was sailing up the Nile; but the rowers of the Governor of Alexandria, in the eagerness of the pursuit, gained upon him. Suddenly the patriarch directs the prow to be turned towards Alexandria; he meets his pursuers, and passes through the midst of them without being recognized; the rowers ask if Athanasius is far in advance. "Press on; he is very near," answered the bishop. A few hours later, under cover of the darkness, the illustrious fugitive was re-entering his episcopal city, where he remained hidden until the death of Julian (A. D. 362).

26. The apostate emperor persisted in his blind and hypocritical persecution with a truly satanical stubbornness. By a new decree, made binding in all the provinces of the empire, Christian professors were forbidden to teach, and Christian children to learn, the Greek and Latin literature. "Either cease to explain the profane authors," said the emperor, "if you condemn their doctrine; or, if you will explain them, approve their sentiments. You believe that Homer, Hesiod, and the others of the same school, are wrong; go and explain Matthew and Luke in the churches of the Galileans." This decree was carried out to the letter. The Christian teachers, thus deprived of the chairs of eloquence and literature, resorted to an ingenious device to escape the circle in which Julian sought to confine them. They composed hymns, idyls, elegies, odes, and tragedies, on moral or theological themes, or on subjects drawn from sacred history. St. Gregory Nazianzen alone wrote more than thirty thousand lines. His poems are remarkable for their sublime sentiments and beauty of expression. Julian was unwilling to assume the odious character of persecutor, but he freely allowed the pagans to harass the faithful without stint. His reign, therefore, furnished several martyrs to the calendar of the Church. At Dorostorum, in Thrace, Emilianus was cast into the fire, for overturning the heathen altars; at Myra, in Phrygia, Macedonius, Theodulus, and Tatian, for breaking the idols in a pagan temple, were roasted by a slow fire; at Ancyra, in Galatia, the priest, Basil, was torn with iron hooks, and died under his torments. The inhabitants of Cæs-

area, in Cappadocia, had remained true to the Catholic faith; Julian punished them by depriving their city of the name given to it by Constantine, and restoring the former one of Mazacca. At Hierapolis, in Phœnicia, humanity was appalled at a punishment unknown even to the torturers of Diocletian. Virgins consecrated to God, after being exposed, naked, to the gaze and outrages of the mob, were cut open and stuffed with barley, and then given up to be devoured by swine. These horrors were renewed at Gaza, in Palestine, in the case of priests and virgins. The Christian soldiers fared no better. Bonosus and Maximilian were beheaded for refusing to remove the cross from the *Labarum*. Such cruel outrages, such torrents of blood, add another stigma to the memory of the apostate emperor.

27. Julian was at this time planning two undertakings, which were equally to turn to his confusion. With a view to falsify the prophecy of our Lord Jesus Christ, who had foretold of the Temple of Jerusalem, that a stone should not be left upon a stone, Julian gave orders to raise the temple from its ruins. But balls of fire, bursting from the bowels of the earth, scattered the workmen. Every new effort was met by the same miraculous resistance. The formal testimony of the pagan historian, Ammianus-Marcellinus, removes all possibility of doubt from this historical fact. Julian's second dream was a war against the Persians, which would rank his name next to that of Alexander. In the spring of the year 363, an immense army, in three divisions, followed by a fleet which sailed up the Tigris, entered Persia, under the command of Julian the Apostate. The success of a preliminary engagement seemed to presage the conquest of the whole of Asia. In his assurance of success he burned his fleet, which retarded his progress. On the next day he found himself in a country laid waste by the enemy; he now saw the extent of his error, and tried to retreat, but it was too late. On the 26th of June, his rear-guard is suddenly attacked by Sapor. Julian flies to the scene of action, without taking time to put on his breast-plate. Whilst

he traverses the field of battle, issuing his orders, a javelin, thrown by an unknown hand, enters his side and pierces the liver. Theodoret says that at that moment, Julian, filling his hand with the blood that flowed from his wound, cast it towards heaven, with the exclamation: "Thou hast conquered, Galilean!" His death, which soon followed this action, ended the struggle of heathenism against the Church of Jesus Christ.

28. The Roman army, half vanquished, entangled in the mountainous regions of Persia, hemmed in on all sides, made all haste to choose a leader capable of drawing it out of its perilous position. Jovian was invested with the purple (A. D. 363). He was a Christian, and had suffered at the hands of Julian, on account of his faith. He concluded a treaty with Sapor, by which he was enabled to bring back the remains of the army to Antioch. His first care was to reopen the churches, and to restore the privileges and property of which Julian had deprived the clergy. Athanasius accordingly appeared openly in the midst of his flock of Alexandria. Jovian wished to receive instructions from the holy patriarch in the truths of the faith: he brought him to Antioch, and gave him his full confidence, in spite of the remonstrances of the Arians, who still pursued Athanasius with the most grievous accusations. A council was held at Antioch, in the hope of reuniting the various Arian factions to the orthodox faith. But the profession submitted was unanimously rejected by the Catholics, as the term *consubstantial* had been omitted; and besides, it did not establish with sufficient clearness the dogma of the divinity of the Holy Ghost. A new heresy was now in the field against this point of faith. During the whole period of Julian's reign, the heresiarch, Macedonius, intruded Bishop of Constantinople, had been constantly dogmatizing in that direction. He held that the Holy Ghost is not a divine person, but only a creature, more perfect than others; against the divinity of the Holy Ghost, he revived the Arian arguments against that of the Word. His followers were found in Thrace, in the province of the Hellespont, and in Bithynia, under the names of *Mace-*

donians, *Pneumatomachists*, and *Marathonians*; this last appellation derived from Marathonius, bishop of Nicomedia, one of the best known members of the sect. We shall now find the Catholic doctors, headed by Athanasius, engaged for the moment with these heretics. At about the same time, as though each year of the fourth century was to be dedicated to some separate heresy, the unreasonable severity of Lucifer of Cagliari refused to admit to his communion the bishops who had fallen during the Arian persecutions, notwithstanding the indulgence shown, in their regard, by the Church of Rome. Such was the origin of the Luciferian schism. Meanwhile Constantinople impatiently awaited its new emperor. Jovian hurried on to take possession of his new capital; he bore with him the good wishes and prayers of the Catholics, who centred their hopes in his person; but death overtook him on the 17th of February, A. D. 364. He was succeeded by Valentinian in the West, and Valens in the East; Milan became the capital of the former, Constantinople of the latter. Valentinian was gifted with sterling qualities, which he unfortunately tarnished by several acts of weakness and atrocious cruelty. At the very outset, he formally announced his intention of abstaining from the discussion of the doctrinal questions which were, at that time, so fruitful of bitter dissensions: "It does not become me, a mere layman," he said to Hypatian, bishop of Heraclea, "to interfere in these matters. Let the bishops judge, since theirs is the mission and authority." It happened to him, notwithstanding, to swerve from the rule he had laid down for himself, in the case of Auxentius, Arian bishop of Milan, whom he supported against St. Hilary of Poitiers, and Eusebius of Vercelli; but in this circumstance he acted in good faith, and for the maintenance of peace. Yet this intervention of the civil authority in religious matters was eloquently deprecated by St. Hilary. "Did the Apostles," said he, "ever call in the aid of some civil official to assist them in preaching the Gospel?" This was the last combat of the great Bishop of Poitiers, whom St. Jerome styles the *Rhone of Latin eloquence*. He died, in the midst of his beloved flock, in the year 367, the same which witnessed the death of his friend, St. Eusebius of Vercelli. These two illustrious champions of the Catholic faith, hand in hand, as they had fought the good fight here, went to receive the reward of their virtue and their combats. Valentinian showed his enlightened consideration by a succession of edicts favorable to religion. He began by revoking Julian's decree, forbidding Christian professors to teach Greek and Latin literature. He restored the observance of Sunday, as established by Constantine the Great. To honor the miracle of the Resurrection in a peculiar manner, he ordered that on the festival of Easter all prisoners should be released, whose crimes were not of a nature to endanger the public safety. He exempted the Christians from the fine imposed upon all the citizens to defray the expenses of the gladiatorial combats. It was decreed that comedians who might, during an illness, have received the sacraments, should not be bound by any previous engagement to reappear upon the stage. The immunity from every personal charge was extended to all ecclesiastics; and, without being exempted from the ordinary taxes, the Church property was freed from all extraordinary contributions. Fourteen physicians were appointed for the different sections of the city of Rome, with the title of physicians of the poor, and a sufficient sum assigned for their subsistence. Whilst Valentinian, who had first reached the imperial throne, was thinking of naming a colleague, he consulted one of his captains on the choice he should make. "Sire," answered the officer, "if you love your family, you have a brother; if you love the State, seek the most able man." Valentinian was not offended by the frankness of the reply, but he unfortunately failed to appreciate the advice it contained. He named Valens. Constantius seemed to have reascended the throne. Valens was a man of weak, wavering, frivolous character, full of the same theological pretensions, the same inanity as Constantius. In the year 365, a council assembled at Lampsacus proclaimed the Catholic faith touching the divinity of the Word, with the omission, however, of the term *consubstantial*, to save animosities, but replacing it by the term *similar in substance*.

The Fathers of Lampsacus decreed that the bishops who had been deposed for their defence of this doctrine should be restored to their sees, and announced to Eudoxius of Constantinople, leader of the *Anomœans*, or *pure Arians*, that they were prepared to receive him back to the communion of the Church, on condition of his renouncing his errors. The Anomœans appealed to Valens, who publicly proclaimed himself their protector and the abettor of Arianism. He began his part as persecutor, by banishing the Fathers of Lampsacus, and placing the Eudoxians in their vacant sees. In his zeal for proselytism, he sent for Eleusius, orthodox bishop of Cyzicus, and urged him to sign an Arian profession; the resistance of the prelate was at last overcome by the threats of the emperor, and he had the weakness to subscribe. On his return to Cyzicus, Eleusius deplored his fall, before his clergy and people; declared himself unworthy of the episcopal dignity, and wished to retire into solitude. But the tears of the faithful moved him to retain the government of his church. The orthodox bishops of the East, now persecuted by Valens, instinctively turned to Rome, the centre of unity, the guardian of the faith. Their envoys, accordingly, arrived in Italy (A. D. 366), bearing letters to Pope Liberius, in which they begged to be admitted to communion with him. Liberius, overjoyed at the return of the East to the Catholic faith, required them to sign the Nicene profession. They declared that the term *consubstantial*, contained in the formula, fully expressed the faith of the Church against the Arian heresy; they especially condemned the heresiarch Arius, and his adherents; they anathematized the errors of the Sabellians, the Patropassians, the Marcionites, of Paul of Samosata; in a word, all the heresies contrary to the faith of Nice. The original copy of this declaration, signed by them, in the name of all the Eastern bishops, was kept in Rome. The envoys returned to their sees, with a letter of communion from Pope

Liberius to the bishops who had sent them; the letter was expressive of the most sincere joy and the most ardent charity. On their arrival, they read it in the Council of Tyana (A. D. 367). It was joyfully welcomed by all the fathers, and the faith of Nice was solemnly received as the faith of the universal Church.

29. In the midst of this triumph of truth over Arianism, which he had followed up during the whole course of his pontificate, Liberius had passed away on the 24th of September, A. D. 366. In life, he had confirmed his brethren in the true faith, and pacified the Church in the East and in the West. When death had removed him from the scene of action, St. Basil, St. Epiphanius, St. Ambrose, speak of him as a pontiff of blessed, of holy, of venerable memory; the ancient Latin, Greek, and Coptic Martyrologies honored him as a saint. Still the Roman Church, with wonted prudence, has not ranked his name amongst the blessed whose feasts she celebrates. If we may trust the most probable historical testimony, Liberius did not fall; but the single slight suspicion left, suffices to suspend the Church's judgment. Liberius had worn the tiara fourteen years and some months. Of the many monuments of Rome, he founded and dedicated the basilica of *St. Mary Major*, sometimes called the *Liberian Basilica*.

CHAPTER IV.

§ I. Pontificate of St. Damasus (Sept. 24, A. D. 366—Dec. 11, 384).

1. Ursinus Antipope.—2. Arianism in the East, under the Emperor Valens.—3. Basil of Cæsarea and the Prefect Modestus. Death of St. Athanasius at Alexandria.—4. St. Martin, Bishop of Tours. Election of St. Ambrose to the Episcopacy.—5. St. Optatus, Bishop of Milevum. St. Jerome.—6. Gratian calls Theodosius the Great to the Government of the East. Death of St. Basil the Great.—7. St. Gregory Nazianzen is appointed to the See of Constantinople. Schism of Maximus at Constantinople.—8. Council of Constantinople. Death of St. Meletius. Troubles arising from it. Retirement of St. Gregory Nazianzen. Rights of the various Patriarchates.—9. Priscillian. His Heresy condemned in the Council of Saragossa. Death of St. Damasus.

§ II. Pontificate of St. Siricius (Jan. 1, A. D. 385—Nov. 25, 398).

10. Decretal of St. Siricius to Himerius, Bishop of Tarragona.—11. St. Ambrose persecuted at Milan, by the Empress Justina. Mission of St. Ambrose to the Usurper Maximus.—12. Revolt of Antioch. St. Flavian. St. John Chrysostom. Clemency of Theodosius.—13. Massacre at Thessalonica. Penance of Theodosius. Massalians. Death of Theodosius the Great. Death of St. Ambrose.—14. Conversion of St. Augustine.—15. St. Jerome retires to Bethlehem. St. Martin of Tours. St. Paulinus of Nola. St. Delphin and St. Amandus of Bordeaux. St. Victrix at Rouen. St. Sulpitius Severus.—16. St. John Chrysostom elected to the See of Constantinople. Synesius. Death of St. Siricius.

§ III. Pontificate of St. Anastasius I. (Nov. 26, A. D. 398—April 27, 402).

17. Dismissory Letters. First Council of Toledo.—18. Disgrace of Eutropius. Discussion between St. Jerome and the Priest Rufinus.—19. Death of St. Martin, Bishop of Tours. Death of St. Anastasius I.

§ I. Pontificate of St. Damasus I. (Sept. 24, A. D. 366—December 11, 384).

1. Saint Damasus I., who succeeded Liberius (Sept. 24, A. D. 366), was born at Guimaraens, in Portugal, but had been

brought up and resided in Rome from his early childhood. The talents and virtue which he showed in the discharge of the successive inferior grades of the hierarchy attracted universal attention. These eminent qualities were brought into greater prominence by his promotion to the pontificate. As he was himself deeply skilled in the knowledge of the Scriptures, and the author of some excellent works, he was enabled to give a powerful impulse to the study of the sacred science. The confidence he bestowed upon St. Jerome is precious to the Church, by the translation of the sacred writings known as the *Vulgate*. Notwithstanding the attention he gave to encouraging the labors of the doctors, he never slighted the least of his great pontifical duties. He was the support, the prop, the centre of unity, for the East, so lamentably divided, in the reign of Valens. God had reserved for St. Damasus the consolation of seeing the long triumphant heresy of Arius sink under the power of the great Theodosius. The holy pontiff met with his share of struggles. He had hardly taken his seat upon the chair of Peter, when an antipope, Ursinus, a deacon of the Roman Church, elected by some few intriguers, tried to contest the sovereign power with him. The people took part in this schism. The quarrel became so warm that Ursinus wished to have recourse to arms, to uphold an ordination held against every law of the Church. But Damasus was backed by an overwhelming majority, and the usurper soon found himself alone. Though protected, at the outset, by Valens, he was banished, by Theodosius, to Cologne; yet he still held out in his schism during the life-time of St. Damasus I.; this powerless opposition, however, made not the smallest change in the unanimity with which the Catholic world recognized the sovereign power vested in the rightful pontiff.

2. The East, with one accord, turned its eyes towards the supreme head of Catholicity. Valens had just received baptism from Eudoxius, of Constantinople, leader of the Arians (A. D. 367) Vetranion, bishop of Tomi, capital of Roman Scythia, and situated at the mouth of the Danube, for refusing to deny the

true faith, had been banished. St. Evagrius, a Catholic bishop, elected, A. D. 370, to succeed Eudoxius, had shared the same fate. Eighty ecclesiastics, sent by the Catholic bishops of the East to complain of these acts of violence, were drowned in the Gulf of Nicomedia, by Modestus, Prefect of Constantinople, acting by the order of Valens. In the year 367, the Prefect of Alexandria, with the design of seizing the patriarch, had forcibly entered the principal church, in which St. Athanasius generally resided. But the bishop had foreseen the coming storm, and took refuge in his father's tomb, the only shelter now left for his persecuted virtue. Here he remained concealed four months, till the people of Alexandria called so earnestly for their pastor, that Valens, to hinder even greater disorder, at last allowed Athanasius to return to Alexandria. This prince had evidently inherited all the hatred of Constantius for Catholicity. But the spirit of the East was no longer the same. Arianism, now confined to a small circle of obstinate followers, had lost its power over public opinion. The majority of the Eastern bishops were eager for the unity in faith, which brought such peaceful repose to the West, under the rule of the Bishop of Rome. This tendency towards the orthodox faith soon showed itself with new energy, when it found an organ in an eloquent, skilful, persuasive leader, whose holiness was universally respected. This leader was St. Basil, whom the bishops and the faithful had just made Metropolitan of Cæsarea (A. D. 370). He no sooner found himself installed, than he addressed a letter, in the name of all the Eastern bishops, to Pope Damasus and the bishops of the West, begging their intervention to bring back peace to the Church. "What lamentation," said he, "can equal our misery! What fountains of tears can correspond to such great evils! Hasten, then; hasten you, our true brothers, whilst there is still left a trace of what once was; and before the churches become a complete wreck, hasten to help us. Stretch out a helping hand to those whom you see kneeling before you!" The solicitude of St. Damasus did not need these earnest entreaties to rouse it to action. During the preceding year (369), he had called a council in Rome, which, after condemning the Antipope Ursinus, had given its earnest attention to the state of the Eastern churches. The leaders of the Arian faction were anathematized. The term *hypostasis* was adopted to express the Persons in the Trinity. Then passing over to a particular question, the pope examined a notorious subject of dispute existing in the Church of Antioch, on which all minds were then held in suspense. The government of that metropolitan see was held by three bishops, the Arian Euzoius, and two Catholics, Paulinus and St. Meletius. Since the Arian had long been excluded from the Catholic communion, his claim was not to be considered; but it was harder to settle the matter of the two orthodox bishops, both elected under extraordinary circumstances, in the midst of persecution, and each exercising authority, in perfectly good faith, over portions of the population, equally devoted to their respective pastors. St. Basil and St. Athanasius seemed to lean towards St. Meletius; whilst Pope Damasus did not think the ordination of Paulinus unlawful. Seeing the utter impossibility of choosing between two bishops equally worthy, without exposing a part of the population of Antioch to the danger of a schism, St. Damasus decided that Paulinus and Meletius should together govern the Church of Antioch, with this express condition, that on the death of either one of the two, the other should remain sole bishop. This decision was applauded throughout the East. Another discussion had arisen, touching the orthodoxy of Marcellus of Ancyra. This prelate was charged with impugning the eternity of the Son of God, teaching that He did not exist before coming forth from the Father, and that He ceased to be, after having returned to Him. St. Basil had written to St. Athanasius on the subject, in order to be made better acquainted, by him, with the real sentiments of Marcellus. The accused bishop, on the other hand, sent a deputation to the Patriarch of Alexandria, to represent his attachment to the Nicene faith, in terms which leave no doubt as to the orthodoxy of Marcellus, who died in the course of the same year (370.)

3. As soon as the pope's directions reached the East, St. Basil had them adopted in several particular councils, where the Nicene Creed was proclaimed to be the faith of the Church. But Valens, maddened by this marked return to the teachings of Rome, came in person to Cæsarea, and ordered Modestus, his prætorian præfect, to bring about the apostasy of St. Basil, at any cost. Modestus ordered the holy bishop to appear before him, and threatened to use the sternest measures against him— the confiscation of his property, exile, torments, and even death— if he dared to resist the imperial order. "The confiscation of my property!" answered St. Basil: "I own nothing but these poor clothes, and a few books, which are my whole life. You cannot make me an exile; the whole world is the country of the children of God. You may torment my body, it is my greatest enemy. I do not fear death, it will only send me the sooner to enjoy my God." Astounded at this reply, Modestus exclaimed: "Never have I heard such language before!" "Perhaps," answered St. Basil, "you have never yet had to deal with a bishop." Even Valens was struck by this bold reply, and withheld, for a season, his projects of revenge. He even expressed a wish to assist publicly at the Holy Mysteries, celebrated by Basil, on the feast of the Epiphany (A. D. 372). But the Arians succeeded in removing from the emperor's mind these favorable impressions in regard to St. Basil, and brought an order of banishment against the holy bishop, for his signature. The reed, which was then used to write on the tablets, three times broke in the hand of Valens, who then refused to have any share in so unjust an action. The hatred of the Arians was not satisfied. On some false charge, they had Basil dragged to the tribunal of Eusebius, governor of the province, uncle of the Empress Domnina, and, like her, an Arian. Eusebius ordered the saint to be struck, and to be torn with iron hooks. St. Basil only replied: "If you would but tear out my liver, you would be doing me a great favor; you see how much it troubles me." (The saint suffered greatly from it.) Meanwhile the people of Cæsarea, hearing that their bishop had been arrested, hastened to the

rescue; a raging multitude were seeking the governor to tear him to pieces; St. Basil threw his cloak about the intended victim, and insured his safe-conduct to the palace. Valens still persecuted the orthodox bishops. St. Meletius, one of the two Catholic bishops of Antioch, was exiled to Armenia. The same punishment was inflicted upon St. Eusebius of Samosata, and St. Barses, bishop of Edessa. The utmost disorder and confusion reigned in the churches thus desolated and bereaved of their pastors. The religious were forced to tear themselves from their peaceful retreats, to go and evangelize the orphaned flocks. Valens, meeting the anchoret St. Aphraates at Antioch, reproached him with having left his retirement for the commerce of the world. "My lord," answered the intrepid old man, "were I a virgin, confined to my father's house, and should I see it set on fire, what would it be my duty to do? You have set fire to the house of God, and we are hurrying out to extinguish the flames." St. Sabas, a celebrated hermit of Osrhoene, had followed the same course, and was confirming the faithful of Antioch, in their devotion to the doctrine of Nice, not less by his miracles and the example of his virtue, than by his earnest exhortations. But the most illustrious champion of the faith, the dauntless athlete who had struggled through forty-five years of episcopacy, ever persecuted, never conquered, who had fought so many battles in its behalf, and supported it by his pen, his example, and all the influence of his virtue, St. Athanasius, dying in the midst of his faithful flock, at Alexandria, found at last the peace which the world had been unable to give him (A. D. 373). His works, written under the ever uplifted sword of persecution, in exile, in the desert, in inaccessible retreats, and even in his father's tomb, form one of the most precious monuments of the Greek Church. At the earnest request of the Alexandrians, he had pointed out his successor, in the person of Peter, one of his priests. The new patriarch was hardly consecrated by the bishops of his province, when an order from Valens consigned him to exile (A. D. 373). St. Basil alone was left to console the widowed Church of the East. But his energy was equal to the call. His letters went everywhere to renew the waning fervor of the weak, to encourage the confessors, and everywhere to keep alive the sacred fire. He took care that bishops should be ordained for vacant sees; settled all difficulties; multiplied himself to meet every necessity; silenced the heretics; and, in spite of the calumnies heaped upon him by the Arians, compelled the admiration and respect of Valens himself. Yet the weight of so extensive an administration forced him to seek another self, who might divide with him the vast responsibility. He accordingly consecrated his friend, St. Gregory, Bishop of Sasima, a small town in the province of Cæsarea. St. Gregory made a long resistance, but at last, in his own beautiful expression, *bowed his head rather than his heart*, and offered his sacrifice on the altar of friendship, giving up a peaceful, studious seclusion, in exchange for the heavy burden of the episcopacy. Now the two friends together share the charge of the Eastern Church. Basil, with unflinching firmness, holds his position against the Arians. Gregory undertakes to keep a watchful eye upon the *Pneumatomachists* or Macedonians, and, when necessary, to meet their attacks. Providence sent them an illustrious assistant, in the person of St. Epiphanius, who had been made, in A. D. 367, Archbishop of Salamis, the metropolis of the island of Cyprus. This new doctor of the Greek Church was born in Palestine, about the year 310, and now entered the lists, after a youth of hard study and the austere practices of a monastic life. He had been educated by St. Hilarion, a disciple of St. Anthony, and was thoroughly acquainted with the Hebrew, Egyptian, Syriac, Greek, and Latin languages. His first work was a complete refutation of Arianism, which appeared under the name of *The Anchorage*, because it was intended as a saving anchor, to fix the minds unsettled by the subtlety, the doubts, and the objections raised, during the past century, against the true faith. He soon followed it up with his great *Treatise against all the Heresies;* he counts eighty up to his own time, and meets them all with the unchangeableness and apostolic tradition of the faith.

4. The Latin Church vied with the Eastern in fruitfulness,

and gave a rich harvest of great men. The episcopal throne of Tours was filled by St. Martin, the disciple of Hilary of Poitiers (A. D. 372). The life of this great Gallic bishop was but a constant succession of miracles. His holiness won for him the admiration of the people, and the respect of the emperors themselves. He used every means in his power to blot out the last traces of paganism from Gaul. The prodigy of the sacred pine, cut by his orders, is well known. The pagans had tied the saint to the lower side of the leaning tree; by a wonderful prodigy, at the moment of the fall, the tree threw itself back in the opposite direction, nearly crushing the pagans, who thought themselves in the safest position. In the midst of the labors which filled his ever-active life, he built himself a monastery at the foot of a rock, on the bank of the Loire, at some distance from his episcopal city; here he gathered about him eighty disciples, with whom he practised all the exercises of an ascetic life. This was the origin of the Abbey of Marmontiers, so celebrated throughout all Gaul. At this time (A. D. 374), Ambrose, governor of Milan, a simple catechumen, was elected bishop of that city, in spite of his earnest opposition. The Fathers of the Church, far from seeking the episcopal dignity, sometimes even calumniated themselves to escape it: this was sometimes carried to such a degree, that the Council of Valencia, in Gaul, which was held in the course of the same year, thought it necessary to draw up a special canon against those who falsely accused themselves to escape ordination. When Valentinian heard of the election of St. Ambrose, he said to those who had informed him of it: "It affords me unspeakable satisfaction to find that I have appointed a judge who is worthy to be sought as a bishop." The name of Ambrose, his virtue, charity, disinterestedness and eloquence, were soon known throughout the East as well as the West. It was commonly said of him, that in his infancy a swarm of bees had deposited its honey upon his lips, such was the sweet and resistless eloquence which flowed from them. The governor, once become a bishop, gave all his property to the poor, devoted himself to the study of the Sacred Writings, and of the Fathers of the Church, and entered into intimate relations with St. Basil, for whom he expressed the most genuine admiration. He made especial efforts to banish from his church all traces of Arianism, left by his predecessor, Auxentius, whose orthodoxy, justly suspected by St. Damasus, had led to his condemnation by a council held in Rome (A. D. 371). Valentinian placed unbounded confidence in St. Ambrose. The holy bishop was one day asking redress for some grievance committed by the magistrates, against the interests of the Church of Milan. The emperor replied: "I always knew your freedom of speech, yet this did not deter me from approving your ordination. Go on, then, fearlessly applying to our sins the remedies appointed by the divine law." Italy was, at the same time, illustrated by two other great bishops, St. Valerian of Aquileia, and St. Philastrius of Brescia. Spain also gave her doctor, St. Pacian, bishop of Barcelona, whose eloquent writings prove him a stanch defender of Catholic faith and unity. The unity of the Church was ably and boldly maintained in Africa by St. Optatus, bishop of Milevum, who attacked the errors of the Donatists. This Father thus lays down the marks of the true Church: to be one, to be catholic, and to hold by unbroken tradition the primacy of the Roman See, as a warrant of the integrity of the faith, and purity of discipline. Finally, in the midst of this galaxy of great names, that of St. Jerome shines with peculiar brightness. He was born about the year 331, of a noble and wealthy family of Stridonium, in Dalmatia. Endowed with an ardent, passionate disposition, capable of the greatest actions, thirsting for knowledge, Jerome spent a part of his youth in travelling through Gaul and Asia. At Rome he made himself familiar with Aristotle and Plato; but his mind was particularly captivated by the teachings of the Scriptures, which he had never studied. He was baptized; and from that moment, showing the same zeal in the study of religion that he had devoted to the pursuit of worldly knowledge, he visited Syria, Palestine, and Thebais, to form himself to the religious life, by the example of the monks and saintly hermits whom he there met.

Above all these doctors of the Latin Church, seated upon the chair of St. Peter, towered the great St. Damasus, who controlled them with all the authority of his apostolic power. The *Donatists* of Africa, and the Luciferians of Sardinia, vainly struggled with united efforts to oppose their Antipope Ursinus, to the legitimate successor of the prince of the Apostles. It is Damasus who gives hospitality to the exiled successor of St. Athanasius, Peter of Alexandria; it is to Damasus alone that all the contending factions of the East send their deputies; it is from him that St. Jerome, from the solitude of his Syrian desert, would learn whether to follow in the communion of St. Meletius or of Paulinus, in Antioch. It is to him that St. Basil makes the most earnest appeal to restore peace to the churches of the East. It is St. Damasus, who, in a council held in Rome, in A. D. 377, solemnly condemns the error of Apollinaris, bishop of Laodicea. This heresiarch maintained that Jesus Christ had no human understanding, but only a body and a sensitive soul, in which the added divinity supplied the want of human understanding. He also taught that the body of Jesus Christ had come down from heaven, and ceased to subsist after the ascension. His disciples, calling themselves *Antidicomarianites* (adversaries of Mary), denied the virginity of the mother of God. An opposite sect, known as the *Collyridians*, from the Greek word Κολλυριδες (sacred cakes), exaggerated the honor due to Mary, worshipped her as a divinity, and as such, made offerings to her. St. Damasus established the Catholic teaching against these opposite heresies, and showed himself the living rule of the Church's faith.

5. Valentinian had just died, leaving the West equally divided between his two sons: Valentinian the Younger ruled over Italy, Illyria, and Africa; Gratian governed Gaul, Spain, and Britain (A. D. 375). In this change Valens saw only a means of satisfying more fully his hatred against Catholicity. Seeing that the monks formed one of its strongest bulwarks, he passed a law, obliging them to bear arms (A. D. 376). Tribunes were sent into the Egyptian deserts, and numbers of hermits perished by

the violence of the brutal soldiery. Like scenes of blood were enacted in the other provinces of the empire, especially in Syria. The persecutors attacked the cells of the hermits, burned their crops, and drove the solitaries themselves from their desert home. St. Basil opened wide his doors to the persecuted monks, and wrote them affectionate and tender letters to console them in their sufferings. But now the time was come when the excesses of Valens were to meet with their final check. Divine Providence chose, as its instrument for this end, the barbarians who had long been hanging upon the frontiers of the Roman Empire, ready to pounce upon it and divide it as their prey. In A. D. 377, a deputation from the Goths appeared before Valens, begging the privilege of settling, as allies, upon the imperial territory. The embassy was headed by the Bishop Ulphilas, author of the celebrated Gothic version of the Bible, so highly praised by St. Jerome himself, for its scrupulous fidelity. Valens granted all that they asked; but when the Goths, trusting to his plighted faith, unarmed and unprovided, set foot upon the Roman territory, they met generals who took their wives and daughters from them, and refused to furnish the promised subsistence. Such a wrong could not go unpunished, and in the following year, A. D. 378, the people, whose friendship had been rejected, appeared in considerable force, and pushed their inroads to the very walls of Constantinople. A general consternation reigned in all the cities. One universal cry of malediction arose against Valens. The emperor, terrified at the approach of so fearful an array of enemies, thought to win the favor of Heaven by recalling all his decrees of proscription, and restoring Peter of Alexandria, with the other exiled bishops. But this too long delayed atonement was of no avail. As he was marching out of Constantinople, at the head of his army, the hermit Isaac, who was universally revered as a saint, called out to him: "Prince, whither are you going? It is God who has sent the barbarians against you. Cease your warfare against Him, or you will not return alive from this expedition!" Valens, in a rage, ordered the prophet of evil to be thrown into a dungeon, saying to him, as he went off: "At my return you shall lose your head." But he never returned. On the 9th of August, A. D. 375, the armies met under the walls of Adrianople. Never, since the battle of Cannæ, under Hannibal, had the Roman arms met a more disastrous defeat. Two-thirds of the imperial army, with thirty-five generals, were left upon the field. The emperor himself, wounded and unable to keep his saddle, was lying in a neighboring hovel whilst his wound was dressed. The Goths set fire to the hut, and Valens, with all his attendants, perished in the flames. The prophecy of the hermit Isaac was more than fulfilled.

6. The rout at Adrianople might have seemed, for a time, to forebode the fall of the empire. "The Roman Empire is falling to pieces," wrote St. Jerome, at this period. The borders of the Tigris and the Euphrates were threatened by the Persians, the Iberians, and the Armenians. Illyria and Thrace had been invaded by the Goths; Fritigern, their leader, who had just won so brilliant a victory over Valens, had it in his power to strike off, at a single blow, both heads of the empire—Constantinople and Rome. The Taiphalæ, the Huns, and Alani, nations unknown to the first Cæsars, were sweeping down from the great plain of Tartary, driving the Goths before them: the country bordering on the Rhine and the Danube was attacked by the German tribes, the Alemanni, the Franks, and the Suevi. Where should Rome find a hero able to cope with so many enemies at once! The champion appeared at the appointed hour, and his promotion was due to a prince of nineteen years. Gratian, who had ascended the throne of the West, at the age of fifteen, on the death of his father, Valentinian I., had incurred the deep guilt of unjustly beheading, at Carthage, Count Theodosius, a skilful general, whose high endowments moved the envy of the courtiers. This victim of imperial injustice left a son called after himself, Theodosius, who was living in the retirement of a studious solitude. It was this son, in whose person he wished to repair the injustice done to the father, that Gratian suddenly appointed to the throne of the East. The whole world applauded

this signal satisfaction, as well as the judgment of the prince, hardly yet past the period of boyhood, who had sought out, from the extremity of the world, the hero destined to raise the empire from its ruins. Gratian had already enacted a law recalling all the bishops banished by Valens, and restoring their churches to all who would embrace the communion of Damasus. These banished prelates now gave a beautiful example of disinterestedness. Some of them, after the example of Eulalius, bishop of Amasea, in Pontus, finding their sees filled by Arians, offered to leave them in the full enjoyment of the episcopal power if they would profess the faith of Rome. St. Damasus I., wishing to make some return to Gratian for the favors he had granted religion, called a numerous council at Rome (A. D. 378), in which, by united suffrages, the bishops expressed their thanks to the two emperors of the West, Gratian and Valentinian the Younger. Gratian did not stop here; he used severe measures to crush the intrigues of the Antipope Ursinus, and ordered that all the bishops condemned as heretics by St. Damasus should be brought to Rome, to make their submission at the feet of the pontiff, and should only be entitled to jurisdiction when rehabilitated by him. Thus the supremacy of the Church of Rome became a law of the empire. Prostrate Arianism no longer dared to raise its head. Only one layer from the parent tree remained, which had struck root in the soil of the North. The poison of this heresy passed from the Goths to the Gepidæ, their neighbors, who in turn spread the infection amongst the Vandals. From the Vandals it was communicated to the Burgundi (Burgundians), where we shall find it, for some centuries, resisting all the efforts of the papacy. The accession of Theodosius the Great (January 19, A. D. 379), confirmed all the hopes of the Catholics. The universal rejoicing which reigned throughout the Church was suddenly checked by the death of St. Basil (January 1, A. D. 379.) He was mourned by the world as the doctor of the truth and the bond of peace in the East. Amongst the numerous works of this Father of the Greek Church, the best known are, his *Ascetics*, comprising a rule of life for hermits; his

Treatise on Studies; the *Hexaëmeron,* or exposition of the work of the six days of creation; the *Book of the Holy Ghost,* against the *Pneumatomachists;* and his *Letters,* which are a true model of epistolary style. St. Basil's style is so pure that, Erasmus did not hesitate to compare it to that of the old Greek orators— even to Demosthenes himself. There was but one thing wanting to this great bishop—the joy of seeing the East restored to the peace and unity for which he had worked and prayed so long. The law *Cunctos populos,* published by Theodosius immediately upon his accession, was, in substance, an order that all the subjects of the Roman emperors should hold the faith of the Roman pontiff. Those alone who were in communion with the pope were entitled to the name of Catholics; all others were looked upon as heretics. The legislation of Theodosius breathes throughout the true spirit of Christianity, whose discipline he had embraced in ascending the throne. St. Ascholus, bishop of Thessalonica, had administered to him the sacrament of baptism (A. D. 380); and every exercise of his newly acquired power showed an obedient and devoted son of the Church. He confirmed the decree of Valentinian I., for the release of criminals on Easter-day, and, whilst signing it, he uttered the sublime sentiment: "Would to God it were in my power to raise the dead!" During the season of Lent he suspended all criminal cases in the courts of law: "It does not become the judges to punish criminals," said he, "at a time when they themselves look to the Divine goodness for the forgiveness of their own crimes." The seed of the Gospel had evidently borne fruit abundantly in the heart of Theodosius. The same spirit reigns in his civil laws. He prescribes the severest punishments against informers; he orders that the prison registers be examined every three months by an inspector, in order to shorten the time of detention before trial. He took measures to systematize the assessment of taxes, to put a stop to embezzlement and peculation, to check the needless extravagance of provincial governors, who ruined their subjects by costly and useless structures. The care he bestowed upon the internal wants of the empire did not hinder his securing an honorable peace with its external enemies. The barbarous tribes, held in awe by the weight of his name and of his arms, settled as allies in the provinces he assigned them. The Visigoths found a home in Thrace, the Ostrogoths in Phrygia and Lydia. The court of Theodosius was a refuge for the oppressed of all nations. Athanaric, king of the Visigoths, driven from his kingdom by Fritigern (A. D. 381), sought an asylum there, and was received with all the honor due to a great man in misfortune.

7. The Church of Constantinople had long been given up to Arian bishops, and was accordingly the most desolated of the East. The death of Valens and the accession of Theodosius gave the Catholics a promise of brighter days. They called upon St. Gregory Nazianzen to take upon him the government of their church. It was now some years since he had retired from the See of Sasima, and had been enjoying his loved solitude. His body was prematurely bent; his bald head, his face dried up by tears and austerities, even his language, which had retained something rough and foreign, at first excited the ridicule of the Arians. But his resistless eloquence, his virtues, his miraculous life of abstinence and privations, soon drew such throngs of listeners, that they broke through the railing of the sanctuary where he was preaching. The private dwelling in which he preached was no longer capable of holding the ever-swelling crowd; it was converted into a church, called the *Anastasia*, because St. Gregory had there, in some sort, raised to life the Catholic faith, so long dead in the city (A. D. 379). Such was the reputation enjoyed by the holy patriarch, that St. Jerome undertook the journey to Constantinople for the sole purpose of hearing him. The Latin doctor one day asked him the meaning of an obscure expression of the Gospel; St. Gregory answered, laughing: "I will tell you to-night, in the church, where everybody applauds me. You must needs seem, at least, to understand me there; for if you alone do not applaud you will be taken for a barbarian." We see here what St. Gregory thought of popular applause, " which shows most admiration for

what it least understands," says St. Jerome. But Demophilus, Arian bishop of Constantinople, left nothing untried to destroy the influence of Gregory. Theodosius, failing in all his efforts to bring him to the true faith, determined to banish him (A. D. 380). This measure seemed to promise a return of quiet. But an Egyptian, named Maximus, who had hitherto professed the cynic philosophy of the Epicureans, came to Constantinople, succeeded in gathering a party about him, and had himself consecrated bishop of the city (A. D. 380). This outrage filled the Catholics with grief. St. Gregory, unwilling to be even the innocent cause of a division, made known his intention of quitting a see which he had only entered with so much violence to every personal inclination. He was, however, led by the entreaties of the faithful to stay with them until a council, which was soon to meet in Constantinople, could choose a Catholic bishop. The question was brought for decision to Pope Damasus, who protested against the irregular election of Maximus. He wrote to St. Ascholus to avail himself of the approaching council to choose a bishop of Constantinople. St. Gregory still continued to beg the permission to retire into his solitude. As he was urging his claim upon Theodosius, the emperor replied: "God makes use of me to keep you in this church. The city is in such a state of excitement on this subject, that it even seems ready to force me to its wishes; but it is well known that very little violence is needed to win my consent."

8. The Council of Constantinople met in the month of May, A. D. 381. St. Damasus had been notified of its convocation, and approved it. He had given his directions to St. Ascholus regarding the chief question to be treated—the election of a successor to St. Gregory. The questions of dogma had already been settled by him in his letters to the Asiatic bishops. The profession of faith which he sent them had been signed by more than a hundred and fifty of their number. All the orthodox bishops had received the additions made to the Nicene Creed, and confirmed by the Fathers of Constantinople, concerning the divinity of the Holy Ghost, the

marks of the Church, the unity of baptism, the resurrection of the body, and the life of the world to come. We call attention to these particulars, because the Council of Constantinople, which was the second ecumenical or general council, was not presided over by papal legates; which fact has been urged to prove that a council could have ecumenical authority without the sanction of the sovereign pontiff. The Council of Constantinople was, in fact, ecumenical only through the sanction of the popes, who confirmed all its acts, approved of its letter and spirit, and pronounced its doctrine to be that of the Universal Church. The bishops present at the council at first assembled under the presidency of St. Meletius, bishop of Antioch. The first subject of discussion was the election of Maximus the Cynic, which was unamiously pronounced irregular. The fathers of the council declared that he could not be considered a bishop; that those whom he had ordained, of whatsoever clerical rank, were not to be admitted to the discharge of its duties, and that all his episcopal acts were null and illegal. Having driven the usurper from the See of Constantinople, it remained to find a worthy incumbent. Theodosius, who was an ardent admirer of the eloquence and virtue of Gregory Nazianzen, found none more worthy to fill so important a station; he made known his conviction to the whole council. St. Gregory resisted even to tears; but he was at length overcome, and St. Meletius, president of the council, solemnly installed him. This was the last act of the holy Bishop of Antioch. Meletius went to his reward, and St. Gregory was unanimously called to preside. Troubles soon arose in the council, occasioned even by the death of St. Meletius. According to the agreement made between the parties, with the consent of St. Damasus, Paulinus was alone entitled, as the surviving bishop, to govern the Church of Antioch. Still a faction of the bishops proposed to appoint a successor to Meletius, and actually consecrated the priest Flavian as such. This was a means of perpetuating the division in the Church. Gregory had done all in his power to oppose this measure. The failure of his efforts, his declining health, and the infirmities of old age, at last brought him to the determination of throwing off the burden of the episcopacy. His farewell address to the assembly, which is still extant, is a model of eloquence, of self-denial, and of charity. "Farewell," said the eloquent archbishop, "our Anastasia,* name once so promising, and due to our pious confidence; farewell, memorial of our triumph, new Siloë, where we first set down the holy ark, disturbed and wandering for forty years, in the desert; farewell, too, great and illustrious temple, our new conquest, which owes your present greatness to the Word of God; town of Jebus, of which we have made a Jerusalem; farewell, all ye sacred abodes of the faith, second in dignity, which embrace the different sections of the city, and form a bond of union among them; farewell, holy apostles, heavenly colony, who have been my model in all my struggles; farewell, pontifical throne, coveted and perilous honor, council of pontiffs, adorned by the virtue and the years of priests; you, ministers of the Lord at the holy table, who are so near to God, when He comes down to us; farewell, choir of Nazarenes, harmony of the psalms, holy vigils, sanctity of virgins, modesty of women, assemblies of orphans and widows, looks of the poor, turned towards God and to me; farewell, hospitable dwellings, friends of Christ, and strength of my weakness; farewell, you who loved my discourses; eager throng in which I saw the rapid pencils that stole away my words; farewell, rails of the sacred enclosure, which so often yielded to the throngs who pressed forward to hear my voice. Farewell, O princes of the earth, palaces of kings, servants and courtiers, faithful, it may be, to your master, but certainly, for the most part, unfaithful to your God. Applaud your new orator, raise him to the skies! The voice which displeased you shall now soon be hushed. Farewell, sovereign city, friend of Christ (for I bear this testimony of it, though its zeal be not always

---

* Resurrection.

according to science, but the moment of separation softens my words); come to the truth, amend at least now, though it be but late. Farewell, guardian angels of this Church, who watched over my presence here, who will still protect my exile. And Thou, Holy Trinity, my constant thought and my glory, may they keep Thy faith, and do Thou save them all—save my people!"*

Nectarius was chosen to succeed him, and St. Damasus ratified the election. The questions of dogma were next taken up. Thirty-six bishops, headed by Eleuzius of Cyzicus, refused to subscribe to the term *consubstantial*, and were solemnly pronounced heretics. The profession of Nice, with the traditional additions mentioned above, and in the form in which it is now sung in the Mass, was declared to express the belief of the Church. The seven canons of discipline, then drawn up by the council, regulate the jurisdiction of bishops, confining it to the limits of their diocese, always saving the supremacy of the Roman See over the other Churches; translation of bishops from one see to another; the form of juridical accusation against bishops; the manner in which heretics are to be received, when they return to the orthodox communion. The *Arians, Macedonians, Novatians, Quartodecimani,* and Apollinarists are to be admitted, on delivering a written abjuration of their errors. The heretics who had changed the form of the sacrament of baptism, as the *Eunomians*, the *Montanists*, and the *Sabellians*, who baptized with a single immersion, or without the Catholic invocation of the three persons of the Blessed Trinity, could only be reconciled to the Church, having received Catholic baptism. The most celebrated of all these canons is the third, which ascribed to the Patriarch of Constantinople the precedence, after the Roman pontiff, for the reason that Constantinople was the new Rome. It was on this ground that the patriarchs of Constantinople subsequently based their claim of jurisdiction over all the

---

* *Tableau de l'Eloquence chrétienne au IVe siècle.* Translation of M. Villemain.

churches of Asia, and took to themselves the pompous title of œcumenical patriarchs of the East. This canon of the General Council of Constantinople never received the approbation of the See of Rome. Pope St. Leo the Great (A. D. 451), in his letter to the Council of Chalcedon, declares that, by this want of sanction, it had been, from the first, utterly nullified; and he sums up the apostolic tradition touching the rank of the patriarchs in this invariable rule: "The See of Alexandria shall lose nothing of the dignity it derives from St. Mark, the disciple of St. Peter; the Church of Antioch, birth-place of the name of Christian, by the preaching of the same apostle, shall keep the rank assigned it by the regulation of our fathers; let it never lose its place as third in order." The second ecumenical council closed with a great solemnity, attending the translation of the relics of St. Paul, patriarch of Constantinople, who had died for the faith, under Constantius. The acts of the council were sent to the pope; and Photius, who states the fact, positively asserts that *blessed Damasus, by his authority, confirmed the second council.*

9. Whilst the integrity of the faith was thus maintained in the East, the Council of Saragossa (A. D. 380) had condemned the *Priscillianists*, who had already infected the greater part of Spain with their error. Priscillian, from whom the sect borrowed its name, had been the disciple of an Egyptian Manichee, named Mark. His doctrine was but a tissue of the errors of Manes, with a mingling of Gnostic visions and astrological absurdities: a few bishops, amongst whom were Instantius and Salvian, had fallen into this heresy, which was condemned with its authors. At the close of the year A. D. 381, St. Ambrose was presiding, at Aquileia, in a provincial council of Italy, for the condemnation of Palladius and Secundianus, two Illyrian bishops, and the only prelates in all the West who still held the Arian doctrines. The ravages of Manicheism in Egypt, in the north of Africa, and in the provinces of Syria, determined Theodosius the Great to establish against these heretics a law enjoining upon the prætorian præfect of the East the establishment of an

inquisition, to seek out and pursue them (A. D. 382). This is the first appearance of the name *inquisitor* against the heretics, in the history of the Church. In the course of the same year, the pope assembled a numerous council in Rome; amongst the attending bishops were St. Epiphanius of Cyprus, St. Paulinus of Antioch, St. Ambrose of Milan, and St. Ascholus of Thessalonica. The council annulled the election of Flavian, which was a preparation of schism in the Church of Antioch. The condemnation of the heretic Apollinaris, and his disciple Timothy, was confirmed. St. Damasus, writing on this subject to the Eastern bishops, commended their submission to the Holy See. "When your charity, dearly beloved sons," wrote the pontiff, "pays to the Apostolic See the respect due to it, the greatest advantage comes back to yourselves." This was the last solemn act of the pontificate of this truly great pope. The East and the West, bound together in a common faith, acknowledged the legitimate authority of the successor of St. Peter. To preserve for future times, and irrevocably to fix the text of the Sacred Scriptures, the pope had just caused St. Jerome to furnish, under his personal supervision, an exact translation from the original Hebrew. This is the version which the Council of Trent afterward declared *authentic*. In the course of this immense labor, besides the encouragement of the pope, St. Jerome received also that of the most illustrious Roman ladies, who made the sacred text their only study. Sts. Melania, Marcella, and her sister Asella, Paula and her daughter Paulina, Lea and Fabiola, and the virgin Eustochium, members of the most illustrious houses of the time, became the disciples of the austere anchoret of Palestine, who has made their names and their virtues immortal in his eloquent works. The pope lavished upon St. Jerome the honors due to his talents, but painful to his modesty. He made him his private secretary, and intrusted him with the charge of his extensive correspondence. It was in the midst of such engagements that death came to end the glorious works of St. Damasus I. (December 11th, A. D. 384). Time had still been left him to recommend to Theodosius the deacon Arse nius, as governor to his son, Arcadius Cæsar; and by this choice, even at his last hour, he rendered a most important service to the world, as he would have been instrumental in giving it a master trained in the school of virtue, had Arcadius answered to the care of Arsenius.

§ II. PONTIFICATE OF ST. SERICIUS (January 1st, A. D. 385—Nov. 25th, A. D. 398).

10. St. Sericius, a Roman priest, was elected pope on the 1st of January, A. D. 385. He inaugurated his pontificate by an answer to a consultation on various points of discipline, addressed by Himerius, metropolitan of Tarragona, in Spain, to St. Damasus, who had died in the interval. This is the first *decretal* which has come down to us. Decisions of this nature are so called, because they have the force of laws. This decretal furnishes rules for the reconciliation of heretics; for the period of conferring solemn baptism, which custom then placed between Easter and Pentecost; for the infliction of public penance, the age of candidates for ordination, and the intervals to be observed between the reception of the different orders. The pope required thirty years for sub-deacons and acolytes. Five years of deaconship were necessary to entitle the candidate to receive priestly orders, and ten years of priesthood to make him eligible to the episcopacy. Another important particular, treated by St. Sericius, is the celibacy of clerics, which he lays down as an apostolic tradition. Another decretal was soon after addressed to Anysius, disciple of St. Ascholus, and his successor in the See of Thessalonica. The pope urges him to look to the episcopal ordinations in Illyria, and not to allow, in his capacity as metropolitan, any bishop to be consecrated without his consent. In the event of his inability to preside personally at the election and consecration, he is to delegate the prerogative to some bishop whose fitness he approves.

11. The bright and cheering promise of Gratian's youth was suddenly blasted by his assassination at Treves (A. D.

383]. The murderer, Maximus, an officer of his army, had clothed himself with the imperial purple, and usurped his victim's throne. He was soon to turn his attention to Gratian's brother, Valentinian the Younger, who reigned at Milan. The Empress Justina, mother of the youthful prince, was too entirely given up to the Arians, to think of taking any precautions against such an attack. Her attention was wholly devoted to the persecution of St. Ambrose, who refused to yield one of the Milanese churches to the Arians (A. D. 385). In the following year, the influence of Justina obtained the publication of an edict, which enabled these heretics to assemble, and publicly profess the doctrine of Rimini (A. D. 386). Benevolus, chancellor of the empire, who was a zealous Catholic, refused to sign the decree. He threw down his insignia of office at the empress's feet, and was exiled to Brescia. The repeated solicitations of Justina drew from St. Ambrose but one reply: "Naboth would not give up the heritage of his fathers, and shall I give up the heritage of Christ?" He was several days kept in a state of siege, in the basilica, surrounded by a troop of soldiers; the people, meanwhile, were watchful of their bishop's safety. In these delicate circumstances, obliged to make a daily exhortation to the multitude that shared his imprisonment, St. Ambrose was able to avoid the least expression that could have tended to arouse or imbitter the passions of his audience. He availed himself of this turn of affairs, to awaken feelings of piety and faith in every heart. The wonderful discovery of the relics of Sts. Gervasius and Protasius, and the miracles attending their translation, completed the work begun by the eloquence of the holy bishop. The Arians and the Empress Justina at length made an end of their persecution. This unlooked-for change was not a little due to a fear of Maximus. The report was circulated, with great show of probability, that Maximus was marching upon Italy, to dispossess Valentinian III. In the hour of peril, the empress instinctively turned to the holy bishop, whom she had so lately treated as an enemy. The reputation of Ambrose was immense, throughout all Gaul. Some Franks once asked Arbogastes, general of the imperial armies, if he knew the Bishop of Milan: "I know him," replied Arbogastes, "and he honors me with his friendship." "It is not strange, then," returned the Franks, "that you win so many victories, since you are the friend of a man whose only word would stop the sun in its course." Justina accordingly had recourse to Ambrose, to check the hostile designs of Maximus. He was begged to go as an ambassador to the usurper, with the ostensible object of claiming possession of the remains of Gratian. The holy bishop, forgetting all the outrages he had received, immediately set out for Treves. Maximus met all his requests by evasive answers (A. D. 387). The court was crowded with Spanish bishops, urging the most extreme measures against the Priscillianists. Ambrose represented to them that God wills not the death of the sinner, but his conversion, and he sought to recall them to the true spirit of the Church, the spirit of sweetness and charity. As these obstinate hearts remained hardened, he refused to communicate with them in the holy mysteries. Maximus finding his instincts of cruelty seconded by these bishops, openly proclaimed himself their protector; he ordered that all Priscillianists should be put to death, and required St. Ambrose to communicate with the Spanish bishops. The Bishop of Milan refused to comply. His example was followed by St. Martin of Tours, who was also then at Treves. The enraged usurper hereupon sent an order to St. Ambrose to return to Milan. The fruitless issue of this embassy furnished a pretext to the enemies of St. Ambrose for renewing their intrigues against him. They complained of his rigid inflexibility. A diplomatist was sent to Maximus, who received him with every mark of good-will. St. Ambrose warned the empress to be on her guard against an enemy who cloaked his hostile designs with a hypocritical show of friendship. He was not believed: but the last favorable report had hardly reached Milan, when Maximus marched a formidable army over the Italian frontier. Valentinian and his mother had hardly time to embark for Thessalonica, where they put themselves under the protection of Theodosius. This protection did not fail them in their necessity. The great prince hurries on to Pannonia, defeats, in two pitched battles, the forces of Maximus, twice as numerous as his own, pursues the usurper, whom he overtakes at Aquileia, where the murderer of his sovereign meets a disgraceful death—just punishment of his crime (July 28th, A. D. 388). This victory left Theodosius master of all the West. Valentinian III. had never held sway beyond Italy, Illyria, and Africa; Theodosius returned these countries to him, and added all the jurisdiction of Gratian—that is, Spain, Gaul, and Great Britain—only admonishing the young emperor to honor the God from whom all power derives, and no longer persecute the Catholics, who were his most faithful subjects.

12. This act of moderation increased the glory of Theodosius throughout the world. In the course of the preceding year (A. D. 387), this emperor had given to all time a shining example of clemency. An extraordinary subsidy had excited a sedition in Antioch. The city had been, for a season, given up to the last excesses of popular madness; the statues of Theodosius, torn down from their pedestals, were dragged through the mire, and then left to the insults of the children, who carried the fragments through the streets, amid jeers and execrations. When the hour of frenzy had passed, a dull stupor fell upon every guilty heart. The city awaited, in consternation, the moment of retribution. The inhabitants, in hurried flight, escaped across the fields, and Antioch soon resembled a vast tomb. Every thing gave occasion to forebode a terrible chastisement. At the first tidings of the outbreak, Theodosius, doubly angered because of his constant kindness to Antioch, gave instant and most severe orders. His couriers come upon this desolate people; all hope seems lost; but there still remains for the salvation of Antioch the self-devotion of its Bishop Flavian, and the eloquence of St. Chrysostom. The magistrates were persuaded to delay the execution of the imperial decrees until the return of the holy bishop, who, careless of the wintry severity of the weather, re-

gardless of his age and infirmities, set out, at once, nor rested day or night until he had entered the gates of Constantinople. Meanwhile John Chrysostom, to whom he had left the care of consoling the flock in his absence, from the eminence of the Christian pulpit, whence his winning and tender accents went forth to draw and fix every heart, shortened these days of uncertainty and cruel agony. This priest, whose name has become immortal, as the type of a superhuman eloquence, was only thirty years of age. He had renounced the prospects of a brilliant youth, had torn himself from the tearful pleadings of a mother's fondness, to hide himself in solitude. Flavian had dispensed, on justifiable motives, with the usual discipline, and had ordained him priest before the canonical age. John more than realized the most sanguine hopes entertained in his regard. In the present sad crisis, he was able to dry the tears of the people and to calm their worst terrors. The city so hopeless in its consternation, owed to him the return of quiet. During this time of trial, he delivered twenty discourses, which are still extant, and are fully equal to the most brilliant specimens of eloquence ever produced by Rome or Athens. They show a most marvellous skill. In his uncertainty as to the course Theodosius will pursue, he combines the hope of forgiveness with a contempt for death, thus preparing his hearers to receive with submission and resignation the orders of Providence. He always affectionately shares the feelings of his fellow-citizens, but he cheers and strengthens them at the same time. Never dwelling too long on the thought of their evils, he soon bears them up from earth to heaven. To free them from their present fear, he inspires them with one more lively, bringing before them the remembrance of their vices, encouraging them to amend, and then shows them the arm of God, infinitely more powerful than that of earthly king, uplifted to strike them for their sins. But Flavian had reached the court of Theodosius, and stood before the emperor a weeping suppliant. The address of the holy bishop, which is supposed to have come from the pen of St. John Chrysostom, is an unapproachable model. When he ceased speaking, the emperor could hardly contain his emotion. At length, giving free course to his sobs, he replied: "What marvel if a man forgive men, his brothers, when Jesus Christ, the Lord and Master of the universe, crucified by the Jews, asks his Heavenly Father to forgive his executioners? Go, my father, return to the bosom of your flock; restore peace to the city of Antioch; after so fierce a storm, it can feel sure only when it once more sees its pilot." Flavian hurried back on his way; but lest he should withhold from his people even a few moments of happiness, he sent couriers before him, who brought the emperor's letter to Antioch, with incredible speed. It was read in the public square, amid the deepest silence, but when the words were uttered by which Theodosius recalled the orders previously given for the punishment of the city and its inhabitants, one universal cry of joy rent the air. In an instant every street is decked with festoons and wreaths; banquets are spread in the public places; the following night is bright as the clearest day; the whole city is illuminated; and a few days later Flavian enters the city in triumph.

13. It is to be regretted that Theodosius was not himself on a similar occasion. The city of Thessalonica, the capital of Illyria, had revolted on account of the arrest of a rider in the circus, for whom the people showed a most enthusiastic admiration (A. D. 389). The city magistrates were butchered, and the governor, Botheric, who had signed the order of imprisonment, was stoned by the mob. This revolt was doubly blamable, for simple justice exacted the arrest of the criminal, who had led a notoriously infamous life. When informed of the sedition, Theodosius, in the first impulse of his anger, spoke of annihilating the guilty city, thereby to impress all minds by a terrible example, and to prevent the recurrence of a like disorder. St. Ambrose succeeded in allaying this first outbreak of passion, and the emperor promised to follow the rules of justice. The case was brought before the imperial council, where it was determined to punish Thessalonica by a general massacre. The order was kept secret, not to arouse the solicitude of St. Ambrose. The whole population of the devoted city was gathered together in the cir-

eus, for the supposed purpose of witnessing a chariot-race; but instead of the expected signal for the opening of the games, another was given to the troops who surrounded the circus, to begin the massacre. The carnage lasted three hours; citizen and stranger, the feebleness of infancy and the decrepitude of age, the virgin and matron as well as the strong in manhood, crime and innocence, in one indiscriminate slaughter, lay a bloody sacrifice to imperial wrath; seven thousand persons perished in this massacre. The grief of St. Ambrose was unbounded. Theodosius himself, appalled at his own deed, a prey to bitter and continual remorse, dared not approach the church for a period of full eight months. St. Ambrose forbade him entrance; and when Theodosius urged the example of David, whose crime God had forgiven, the bishop replied: "You have followed him in guilt, follow him also in penance." At length, on the feast of Christmas, Theodosius came to St. Ambrose, who caused him first to sign a decree, that a sentence of death or of confiscation should only take effect thirty days after being pronounced, that reason might have time to regulate the first impulse of anger; then he gave him absolution. Theodosius entered the basilica of Milan, and there, before the assembled multitude, putting aside his imperial decorations, he prostrated himself upon the pavement, which he bathed with his tears, repeating the words of David: *Adhæsit pavimento anima mea: vivifica me secundum verbum tuum.* The remembrance of the massacre of Thessalonica haunted Theodosius till the hour of his death. The desire of atoning for this crime redoubled his zeal against paganism; the idols and temples were destroyed by his order, at Alexandria, and throughout the whole of Egypt. The statue and temple of Serapis were overturned; then were brought to light the mysteries of iniquity so long practised by the pagan priests, and the deceits they had used to mislead their votaries (A. D. 391). In his watchful zeal to put down all abuses, Theodosius made a law against the vagrancy of the *Massalians*, a body of heretical monks already condemned by St. Flavian of Antioch (A. D. 390). They maintained that prayer alone is necessary for salvation, to the exclusion even of the sacraments. On this principle of loose morality they led an idle life, wandering through the provinces of Syria, and given up to every disorder. Matters of a more serious character however soon called for the intervention of Theodosius. Count Arbogastes had caused Valentinian III. to be strangled (May 15th, A. D. 392). Since the death of his mother, the Empress Justina, the influence of St. Ambrose was gradually bringing out the good qualities of this youthful emperor. The murderer then placed on the imperial throne a scholar named Eugenius, a mere shadow of a monarch, through whom he himself hoped to reign. St. Ambrose, true to the memory of Valentinian, would hold no communion with the murderer, but fled from Milan, at his approach. Eugenius and Arbogastes swore, in their rage, that they would revenge themselves by turning the basilica of Ambrose into a stable, and by obliging the Milanese clergy to bear arms. Theodosius left them no time to put their threats into execution. He hurried forward, and met them in Italy; and with the battle of Aquileia ended the ephemeral reign and the life of Eugenius and Arbogastes (September 6th, A. D. 394). Theodosius immediately sent tidings of his victory to St. Ambrose, asking him to return thanks to heaven for this signal favor. The holy bishop made use of his influence with the emperor, to obtain the pardon of all who had shared in the revolt of Arbogastes, which was readily granted. The emperor, who now began to feel the effects of shattered health, made the necessary dispositions to secure a quiet succession, in the event of his approaching death. He divided his states between his two sons. Arcadius, the elder, received the East; Honorius, the West. Neither of these two princes made an effort to dispel the world's regret at the loss of Theodosius the Great, who died at Milan, on the 17th of January, A. D. 395; the name of St. Ambrose was the last word that passed his lips. Theodosius was the model of a Christian ruler. The spirit of the Gospel seemed to inspire his administration, his laws and the great actions of his reign. The massacre of Thessalonica gives us a truer view of his greatness, in all the humiliation of penance, than the hour of his most glorious triumph. The funeral oration pronounced by St. Ambrose over this great emperor, moved the assembled multitude, and even the soldiers, to tears. "I loved the hero," said the saint, "who wept over the sin into which the intrigues of others had drawn him; and wept for it during the remainder of his life! He had but lately returned victorious from the most just of wars, and yet he forebore, for a time, to approach the sacred mysteries, that he might not make an offering at the holy table with blood-stained hands. I loved the merciful and clement hero; therefore from my heart do I weep for him. I loved him; and my prayers and tears shall incessantly plead before the Lord, that he may be admitted to the holy mountain of God, in the true land of the living." The whole Church shared the sorrow of St. Ambrose, and she still holds the memory of Theodosius in veneration. The holy bishop did not long survive the prince he had loved so well. He had just received an embassy from Fretigil, a queen of the Marcomanni, asking to be instructed in the truths of the faith. His answer, which was written in the form of a catechetical instruction, is a master-piece. The queen, induced by the reputation of the virtue of St. Ambrose, came to Milan, to receive baptism at his hands. But she arrived only in time to learn that the saint had gone to receive the reward of his labors, on the 4th of April, A. D. 397, in the fifty-seventh year of his age. The numerous works of St. Ambrose, on the Sacred Scripture, and against heresies, his books on morals and his letters, all abound in a wonderful unction and sweetness of style. In his writings we find the first mention of the word *mass*, in relation to the Holy Sacrifice of the altar. The Church still sings several hymns of his composition. They had become so celebrated that they were long called by the general name, *Ambrosianum*, because St. Ambrose had first brought their use into the Latin Church. Tradition attributes to St. Ambrose the *Te Deum*, the solemn anthem of thanksgiving adopted by the whole Church. The chanting of psalms, by alternate choirs in public worship, is also said to have been introduced by him, when the faithful of Milan, imprisoned in the basilica, guarded their holy bishop against the persecution of the Empress Justina. But this can only refer to the Western Church, for the custom had long prevailed in the East.

14. The most glorious, the undying praise of St. Ambrose, is to have been the father of St. Augustine in the life of grace. Augustine was born in the year 354, in the little city of Tagaste, near Madaura and Hippo, in Numidia (the present Algeria). His mother, St. Monica, brought him up in the fear of God; but the ardent disposition of the youth led him into the path of pleasures which he joined to an unquenchable thirst for knowledge. At the age of twenty-eight years, Augustine had mastered the whole circle of human science then taught, and gained the unbounded applause of all his masters. He was then a celebrated professor of rhetoric at Carthage. His morals were those of the wealthy youths of his time. When an occasional ray of the light of grace found its way into his heart, and gave him the passing desire of a life more worthy of a man and of a Christian;—when he was thus moved by a wish to quit the ways of vice, he begged of God to give him a pure heart; but quickly starting back affrighted at the apparent austerity of virtue, he checked himself and added: "Not yet! not yet!" Still St. Monica wished to bring forth anew this well-beloved son, by opening to him the gates of heaven, as she had ushered him into this terrestrial world. Augustine showed no inclination to correspond to this mother's care, and as if to shut out every remaining hope of conversion, he had lately taken up the heresy of the Manichees. St. Monica told her grief to a pious bishop, and begged him to labor for the salvation of this dear soul. "Go," said the holy bishop, "it is impossible that the child of such tears should be lost." The prediction was to be soon accomplished. Augustine went to Italy, and obtained the chair of rhetoric in the city of Milan. It was at this time that the whole world was resounding with the praises of St. Ambrose, as an orator. Augustine must hear him. The mind of the youthful professor was powerfully affected by the sweetness of his gentle

and impressive language, by the elegance, the majestic flow and gracefulness of his discourses, which gave to the language of Virgil all the attic purity of that of Plato. His whole attention, in the beginning, was fixed on the delivery; little by little, however, his mind was led insensibly along, by the train of thought, and the matter outweighed the form. Without, however, giving up the passions that were wearing away his life, he gave himself to the serious study of St. Paul, whose sublimity pleased his eager intellect. In the midst of his dissolute friends, whose conduct often put him to the blush, though he still kept up an illicit connection in which he prided himself on a certain degree of fidelity, he was ever unwittingly followed by divine grace. It pursued him by means of the stings of remorse, of momentary returns to self-knowledge, in which he felt his weakness, and asked of God, with many sighs, the strength necessary to overcome himself. In one of these moments of extraordinary feeling, arising from an account which he had just heard of the life and austerities of St. Anthony, he suddenly arose and left the room, saying to his friend Alypius: "What! the ignorant take heaven by violence; and we senseless wretches! with all our miserable science, rise not above flesh and blood!" With these words, he buried himself in the solitude of a deserted walk in the garden, there to calm the storm that troubled his heart. Now was the season of grace. Yielding to a hitherto unknown emotion, he threw himself upon his knees, exclaiming: "How long, O Lord! shall I always say: to-morrow! to-morrow! Why not to-day? Why not now, at this very moment!" As he uttered these words he heard an interior voice saying to him: "Take, and read." A volume of St. Paul lay at his feet; he opened it at random and read this passage: "*Sicut in die honeste ambulemus; non in comessationibus, et ebrietatibus; non in cubilibus et impudicitiis, non in contentione et æmulatione, sed induimini Dominum Jesum Christum, et carnis curam ne feceritis in desideriis.*" * All his past life, with

---

* Rom. xii. 13, 14.

its many disorders, passions and ambitious aims, lay unfolded before his mind, in all its hideous deformity. His understanding was bathed in a supernatural and irresistible light, whilst his heart had yielded to the charms of virtue. Augustine was converted. The power of passion was at an end; the empire of grace began. He quitted his chair of rhetoric, gave up the hope of a wealthy alliance, and all the bright promise which the world held out to his talents. He retired, with his mother, his son Adeodatus, and a few friends, to a solitude in the neighborhood of Milan. His treatises, against the *Academicians*, on *Happiness*, on *Order*, the *Soliloquies*, and the work on *Music*, were the fruits of these hours of retreat, out of which he only came forth on Easter-day, in A. D. 387, to receive baptism from the hands of St. Ambrose. Monica, the happy mother, witnessed this ceremony, for which she had so long and so fervently prayed. She died in peace, at Ostia, towards the end of the same year, admonishing her son to remember her at the altar of the Lord. The first duty to which St. Augustine devoted himself, after his baptism, was the conversion of the Manichees, whose errors he had just cast off. To this end he wrote two books, called: *The morality of the Catholic Church*, and *The morality of the Manichees*. These he followed up with a yet more important work, entitled: *On Free-will*, where he most thoroughly tests the question of the origin of evil, and answers the most specious objections against the goodness and providence of God, by which it is embarrassed. In A. D. 388, he left Italy, and returned to Africa, where he continued his life of solitude and study, near Tagaste. At this very period, Valerius, bishop of Hippo, was beginning to sink under the weight of years and infirmities. The holy old man, finding himself unable longer to fulfil the duty of preaching to his people, felt the want of a learned and able priest to whom he could intrust that important ministry. Regardless, therefore, of the convert's repugnance for all public employments, Valerius ordained him priest. So successfully did Augustine discharge his sacred duties, that the bishop was encouraged to

ask a favor almost without precedent at the time, that of
having Augustine consecrated as his coadjutor. The Church
was opposed to this usage, as it might cause such schisms as
that of Antioch, which had so long kept the public mind in a
state of division. But the united suffrages of the bishops of
the province, who had met at Hippo, approved the choice, and
St. Augustine was consecrated (A. D. 395). Humility, love of
retirement, passion for study, regular and frugal habits, all
clung to Augustine even amid the honors of the episcopacy.
His priests lived with him, and together they led the regular,
uniform life of cloistered monks.

15. Whilst Augustine was thus ascending the scale of ecclesiastical dignities, and was destined soon to take the lead in the
great religious movement of his time, another of the brightest
lights of the Latin Church sought to hide its lustre in the solitude of
a contemplative life, to escape the employments and the renown
by which it was encircled; this was St. Jerome. Since the
death of St. Damasus I., his friend and protector, St. Jerome
had felt the attacks of a thousand secret jealousies, a thousand
rivalries, which had been concealed during the season of favor.
The power of his words, his apostolic freedom in pointing out
and branding abuses, had created enemies. His great soul was
above these petty strifes, and he resolved to win peace by yielding to envy; he left Rome, returned to Palestine, and made his
abode in Bethlehem. St. Paula and her daughter, St. Eustochium, followed him and placed themselves under his direction.
The last days of St. Jerome's life were devoted to the study of
Holy Writ, the guidance of souls, and the exercise of hospitality
towards strangers, and from the midst of these saintly labors, he
passed away to receive the reward of his long life of holy toil.
Gaul was not debarred from a share in the great movement
which made the fourth century the richest in great names, of
the Church's History. By the side of St. Martin of Tours, in
the veneration and grateful remembrance of posterity, a place
has been given to St. Paulinus, who was born at Bordeaux (A.
D 353), of a senatorial family; he was ordained priest at Barce

lona, and went to end his days at Nola, by the tomb of St. Felix, whose glory he has immortalized in his charming and elegant Latin poems. Among the other illustrious names of this period, are found those of St. Delphin, bishop, and St. Amandus, a priest of Bordeaux; St. Aper, bishop of Toul; St. Victricius, bishop of Rouen, apostle of the regions inhabited by the Marini and Nervii, now comprised in the provinces of Picardy, Hainault and Flanders; and St. Sulpitius Severus, who was of a noble and wealthy family of Aquitaine. He had so perfectly mastered the style of the authors of the Augustan age, that he might almost be classed amongst them. He became a disciple of St. Martin of Tours, and wrote his life. He also compiled a *Sacred History*, or Ecclesiastical History, from the beginning of the world to the year 400 of the Christian era. This work is a master-piece of precision and elegance.

16. The East was not backward in sending its laborers into the Lord's vineyard. Whilst the weak emperors Arcadius and Honorius let fall the sceptre from their nerveless grasp, Stilicho and Rufinus, their ministers, were making profit of the employments and offices which they sold to barbarians; and now the Church of God was stretching out her empire, and was clothed with greater splendor and power than ever. In the year 398, St. Gregory Nazianzen had ended his long career of saint, doctor, bishop and hermit. He died in the retreat of Arianzus, solacing his last moments by the pious flights of Christian poetry. His poems treat the loftiest themes of Christian spirituality. He wrote on the *Principle of Beings*, on the *Trinity*, on *Providence*, the *Angels*, the *Soul*, the *Harmony of the two Testaments*, the *Incarnation of the Word*, the *Miracles of Christ*, *Virginity*, and the *Monastic Life*. At the same period, death also removed St. Gregory of Nyssa, brother of St. Basil, one whose holy life, precision of thought, powerful reasoning, and pure style in his numerous writings, made worthy of such a relationship. His writings were chiefly directed against the errors taught in his time, by the *Arians*, *Sabellians*, and *Pneumatomachists*. But all these great names were followed by one whose renown was given

back by every echo in the Greek Church. John of Antioch, who was made patriarch of Constantinople in A. D. 398, and surnamed Chrysostom, or the *Golden Mouth*, achieved a reputation which deservedly ranks amid the most illustrious and best merited of antiquity. To avoid a popular sedition, it had been found necessary to remove him secretly from Antioch. Thus torn from the enthusiastic attachment of that Church, he was thrown like a prisoner into a carriage, and carried, without a halt, to Constantinople. There he was consecrated by a council called for the purpose by the eunuch Eutropius, who had supplanted Rufinus as the favorite of Arcadius. John of Antioch ascended the episcopal throne, weeping over his lost repose and former independence; but he did not allow himself to be overcome by useless regrets. His first care was the reformation of his clergy and the entire extirpation of heresy. His charity, motherly in its solicitude, reached every want, founded and endowed hospitals, houses of refuge for virgins, and directed all the efforts of his eloquence to induce the rich of the world to make consecrated temples of their abodes, by receiving in them Jesus Christ, in the persons of His poor. The first year of St. John Chrysostom's episcopate was marked by the arrival at Constantinople of the Christian Pindar, Synesius, whom his native province Cyrenaïca had delegated to Arcadius, to beg for help against the inroads of the barbarians. Synesius, both philosopher and poet, traced back his lineage to the ancient kings of Sparta. He was gifted with a most brilliant imagination, and with so flexible a mind, that he could imitate, at will, all the authors he read, however different in style and varied in the turn of their ideas. He had been formed by the most celebrated masters; in Alexandria he had frequented the school of Hypatia, daughter of the astronomer Theon, a prodigy of learning, who gave public lectures on mathematics and on the philosophy of Plato. Athens had opened to him its schools, in which studious youth was urged on by so many noble memories and great examples. He turned at last towards the land of his birth, richly laden with treasures of imagination and intellect, gathered together in his many wanderings, and which he devoted, in the highest order of poetry, to erect a monument to the faith. His hymns are so many poetic aspirations, bearing him by degrees above every order of created being, until he rests in the very bosom of God; but the swelling tide of his sentiments finds no expression in human language capable of conveying it; he often complains of this poverty, which obliges him to multiply figures, some of which may thus be wanting in exactness; for this he humbly asks pardon. This poetical feature of Christianity, which had now attracted such minds as St. Paulinus of Nola, St. Gregory Nazianzen, and Synesius, shows a new tendency. The struggle with paganism, and the theological contests against the Arians, had given way to the poetical development of Christian intellect. Eloquence, literature, the fine arts, legislation, all became subservient to the triumphal progress of religion. But this flight was not long: it soon shared the fate of all the old world, in the barbarian invasion.

17. St. Sericius had seen his pontificate successively illumined by all these splendors of the church. His watchful care reached every part of the world, and his authority was everywhere acknowledged and blessed. He had repeatedly condemned the excessive zeal of the Spanish Ithacians, who urged on the magistrates and tribunals to extreme measures against the Priscillianists. The whole church approved his decision, which was founded on the law of charity. The particular provincial councils sought his concurrence. Those held at Carthage (A. D. 393–398) consult him respecting baptism conferred by the Donatists, and ask if it is allowed to ordain those who have received it. A council of Gallic bishops, assembled at Turin, refers to Pope Sericius the validity of the election of Felix, bishop of Treves, who had been ordained by the Ithacians (A. D. 397). He was also consulted by the bishops of Gaul, who wished to know, on the authority of the Apostolic See, what the canon laws required in regard to the continence of clerics, ordinations, and monasteries for virgins. Sericius answered by a decretal, in which he repeats the in-

structions sent, some time before, to Himerius, bishop of Tarragona. In the most unaffected modesty and humility, the pope lays down, with apostolic firmness and vigor, the teaching of the ancient discipline. If the dignity of his tone and bearing show him to be the ruler of the Church, the *Vicegerent of God;* the Father of Christendom, the Pastor of pastors also speaks in the meekness, gentleness and charity which eminently characterize his every word. St. Sericius died on the 25th of November, A. D. 398, after a pontificate of nearly fourteen years. Tradition attributes to him the introduction, into the prayers of the mass, of the *Communicantes,* and the exclusive application to the Sovereign Pontiff of the title of pope. The name had been common to all priests. It expressed the spiritual paternity of the pastor over his flock. It was subsequently limited to bishops. St. Sericius introduced the now universal tradition of confining its application to the Roman Pontiff alone.

§ III. PONTIFICATE OF ST. ANASTASIUS I. (Nov. 26th, A. D. 398—April 27th, 402).

18. St. Anastasius I. was raised to the pontifical throne on the 26th of November, A. D. 398. St. Jerome styles the new pontiff "*a man of most rich poverty, and endowed with apostolic zeal.*" Tradition ascribes to this pope, a decree, by which the entrance to holy orders is closed against those who are affected with any bodily blemish. This measure was based on the necessity of securing respect for the priestly ministry, and to save it from even the most unjust occasion of ridicule. S. Ambrose, whose merciful charity yielded only to a stern sense of duty or justice, strictly withheld holy orders from a young cleric, who had one shoulder more prominent than the other. The Catholic priesthood may not be treated less honorably than that of the Old Law, which multiplied the precautions to be observed in the choice of its ministers. Another regulation aimed at the reform of an abuse which was creeping into the

Churches. Foreign clerics or monks were ordained priests in the Church where they happened to be at the time, without the consent of their bishop. St. Anastasius forbade any such ordination, unless authorized by a letter bearing the signature of the bishop to whom the candidate was subject, and who alone had authority over him. This is the real origin of the *dimissorial* letters. St. Anastasius also decreed that, during the reading of the gospel, the priests should stand, that their attitude might express the respect due to the good tidings which brought salvation to the world. This custom has also become general in the Church.

The short pontificate of St. Anastasius carried on the work begun by St. Sericius, of establishing a regular and uniform discipline throughout all the Churches of the world. The fifth Council of Carthage (A. D. 400) had just succeeded in quieting the African Church, and was engaged with the error of the Manicheans and of the Donatists, which still survived in that country. The first Council of Toledo (A. D. 400) brought together the bishops of all the Spanish provinces, who solemnly recognized and professed the faith of Nice. It also made all the necessary regulations for the clerical life, and for the dispositions relative to marriage, which it emphatically declared to be one and indissoluble, which characters were unknown to the Roman law. In virtue of the principle laid down by St. Sericius, the Council of Toledo gives to the bishop of Rome the name of *pope*, as a distinctive title. This is the first monument of ecclesiastical history that furnishes this peculiarity.

19. The attention of the East was now fixed upon two facts of a far different character. One belongs to the domain of politics, and would claim no mention in ecclesiastical history but for the part taken in it by St. John Chrysostom, patriarch of Constantinople; we refer to the disgrace of Eutropius. The other is the famous dispute between two friends of twenty years' standing, both renowned for their holiness, their labors, and their ecclesiastical knowledge—St. Jerome and the priest

Rufinus. We propose to analyze these two events, which alone fill up the pontificate of St. Anastasius I. The eunuch Eutropius, in the pride of his power and of the favor lavished upon him by Arcadius, ruined whole provinces, sold positions of trust, and squandered the public revenue, to supply the demands of his luxurious prodigality. He had statues raised in his own honor, under the pompous titles of *Father of his country*, of *Third founder of Constantinople*, of *Invincible Warrior*. His boldness went so far as openly to resist an order of the empress Eudoxia. It was his last excess, and filled the measure of his outrages. The emperor Arcadius was weary of this tyranny of an inferior, and ordered the arrest of Eutropius. The minister who but yesterday held the whole world at his beck, now finds not a single door that will open to shelter his disgrace. Dismayed, terrified, distracted by a blow equally sudden and crushing, he seeks refuge in the church, and places himself under the protection of St. John Chrysostom. But the imperial troops, who had long groaned under the hateful and humiliating tyranny of the insolent eunuch, were eager to wreak a pitiless revenge upon his person. They surround the church and call for their victim. The holy patriarch resists their violence; he is himself seized and carried as a rebel to the palace. St. John Chrysostom appears before the emperor and obtains the pardon of Eutropius. But neither the people nor the soldiery seem disposed to ratify this act of mercy; the emperor's voice is unheeded, and the night is disturbed by the cries and imprecations of the bloodthirsty multitude. On the next day, St. John Chrysostom, placing all his confidence in the power of Christian eloquence, whose triumphs he had so often witnessed, appeared in the pulpit, surrounded by a dense mass of the excited people. All eyes were fixed upon Eutropius, the imperious minister, but lately the idol of the court and the terror of the empire, now forsaken, pale, trembling, cowering in the shadow of a pillar, finding an asylum in the church which he had despised in the hour of prosperity. This striking contrast was eloquently brought out by the sacred orator; the storm of popular passion was lulled by the influence of those merciful accents, and angry hatred found vent in tears of pity; Eutropius was saved (A. D. 399). Whilst Constantinople witnessed this display of human vicissitude, all Palestine was engaged with the dispute between St. Jerome and Rufinus. Rufinus was a native of Friuli, but had first embraced the monastic life at Aquileia, where he was subsequently ordained priest; he then came to Bethlehem, accompanied by St. Melania, who lived there under his direction. He was bound to St. Jerome by the closest ties of friendship, and shared his labors, studies, and ascetic life. For twenty years the world was held in admiration of this union, so fruitful in beneficial labors. Still it was not proof against a trifling circumstance which cast the seed of a lamentable division into the souls of the two friends. A charge of teaching the errors of Origen was brought against St. Jerome and Rufinus, by some *Anthropomorphites*, a heretical sect, who ascribed to God a human shape. Rufinus deigned them no reply; St. Jerome, on the contrary, felt bound to justify himself. This different line of conduct opened the dispute. It was embittered by a translation of the Περι άρχων, Origen's work on *Principles*, undertaken by Rufinus. St. Jerome wrote against his old friend with a certain degree of sharpness; Rufinus replied in the same strain. The debate was carried to Rome (A. D. 400). The translation of Origen's work was condemned by St. Anastasius I., yet saving the translator's intentions, which might be free from reproach. St. Epiphanius of Salamis, who had lately come to Palestine, also took part with St. Jerome, against Rufinus, and publicly preached against Origenism. St. Augustine, who had learned of the dispute, from the pen of St. Jerome himself, replied. "How sad to see two souls, once so closely united, whose friendship was the admiration of nearly all the Churches of the world, now fallen into a state of discord! What hearts shall hereafter dare to hold interchange of confidence? Where shall we find the friend into whose bosom we may, with safety, pour our most secret thoughts and feelings, without a fear that he may one day become an enemy, since we see and deplore this misfortune in Jerome and Rufinus?" Was the heart of St. Jerome moved by these touching words? It may be easily believed. From that moment, he ceased to write against Rufinus; and the mediation of St. Melania soon publicly reconciled the two old friends. Rufinus continued his labors; a *Translation of the Ecclesiastical History of Eusebius*, an *Explanation of the Creed*, a great number of *Lives of the Fathers*, engaged his attention until his death, in the year 410.

20. St. Martin of Tours had died in the second year of the pontificate of St. Anastasius (A. D. 399), at the age of more than eighty years. Moved by the tears of his disciples, who stood around his death-bed, he exclaimed: "Lord, if I can still be useful to Thy people, I refuse not to labor; but Thy will be done." A few moments later, he added: "My brethren, let me look to heaven rather than to earth, that my soul may wing its flight to God." He had himself stretched out upon a sackcloth covered with ashes, to end a life of austerity and self-denial by an act of humility and mortification. His countenance, after death, was lighted up by a look of heavenly joy. The body of the holy bishop was buried in his episcopal city, in the spot afterwards crowned by the church and monastery of St. Martin of Tours. This sanctuary became a place of frequent pilgrimage in the early days of the French monarchy. He was succeeded by St. Brice, one of his disciples.

At about the same period, St. Anastasius received a deputation from the African bishops, asking leave to keep the converted Donatists in the ranks of the clergy. This measure had been approved by a council held at Carthage, on the 16th of June, A. D. 401, both on account of the scarcity of clerics, and to open to the Donatists an easy return to the Catholic faith. The request met with a favorable reception from the pope. The apostolic solicitude of St. Anastasius was about to be called into action, on behalf of the Church of Constantinople, and of its holy patriarch; against whom the empress Eudoxia was just opening a persecution; but death came to the relief of the holy pontiff, in the midst of his good works (April 27th, A. D. 402). His pontificate had lasted but three years, and in that brief space he won the tribute paid him by Innocent I.: "Anastasius," said he, "governed the Church in the purity of an exemplary life, the fulness of an unimpeachable doctrine, and the just firmness of ecclesiastical authority."

CHAPTER V.

SUMMARY.

§ I. PONTIFICATE OF ST. INNOCENT I. (April, A. D. 402—March, 417).

1. Letters of St. Innocent I., to various bishops of France, Spain and Africa.—2. First exile of St. John Chrysostom.—3. Second exile and death of St. John Chrysostom.—4. Invasion of Rome by Alaric.—5. *City of God*, by St. Augustine. Pelagianism.—6. Death of St. Innocent I.

§ II. PONTIFICATE OF ST. ZOSIMUS (August, A. D. 417—December, 418).

7. Labors and death of St. Zosimus.

§ III. PONTIFICATE OF ST. BONIFACE I. (Dec. 30, A. D. 418—Oct. 25, 422).

8. Election of St. Boniface I. Antipope Eulalius. Question of the right of appeal to the Holy See agitated by the Bishops of Africa.—9. Pretensions of Atticus, Bishop of Constantinople, to jurisdiction over all the Asiatic Churches.—10. Death of St. Jerome and of St. Boniface I.

§ IV. PONTIFICATE OF ST. CELESTIN I. (Nov. 3, A. D. 422—April 0, 432).

11. Semi-Pelagianism.—12. Cassian. St. Simeon Stylites. Invasion of Africa by Genseric. Death of St. Augustine.—13. The Franks in Gaul. St. Lupus of Troyes, St. Eucherius of Lyons, St. Germanus of Auxerre, &c.—14. Nestorius. Third General Council, at Ephesus. Death of St. Celestin I.

§ V. PONTIFICATE OF ST. SIXTUS III. (April 26, A. D. 432—March 28, 439).

15. Election of St. Sixtus III.—16. Prudentius. Sedulius. Predestinarianism. St. Prosper.—17. Theodosian Code. Barbarian invasion of the different Provinces of the Empire. Death of St. Sixtus III.

§ I. PONTIFICATE OF ST. INNOCENT I. (April, A. D. 402—March, 417).

1. The fifth century opens with the pontificate of St. Innocent I., who ascended the chair of St. Peter in A. D. 402

The decline of the Roman Empire, in the West, dates from this period. In the inscrutable designs of Providence, always watchful over the Church's destinies, all things were so disposed that in the downfall of the old world, the power of the pope and of the bishops should alone remain standing amid the universal wreck. The barbarians, breaking in upon the Roman Empire, at every point, everywhere meet, in the religion of Jesus Christ, a moral power far higher, more imposing, more commanding than that of arms. The authority of the Roman Pontiff rises simultaneously with the fall of the Cæsars; victor and vanquished together kneel before the conquering cross, and under the hand of the vicar of God on earth. Innocent I., who was to witness the first invasion of Rome, by the Goths, ascended the pontifical chair, to find the Roman Empire in the hands of two princes, equally incapable of ruling it, or of freeing themselves from the sway of their own ministers. Honorius, in the West, had placed all his power in the hands of his favorite, Stilicho, a Vandal, whose daughter he had married. In the East, Arcadius was the tool of his eunuchs, and of the caprices of his empress, Eudoxia. The political condition of the empire was most lamentable; but the Church seemed to gain in strength, union and harmony, what the empire lost in greatness. The rule of Innocent I. was marked by a singular prudence; his enlightened views, correct judgment, and deep penetration, drew from St. Augustine expressions of the highest praise. The new pope retained all the members of the preceding administration: "New-comers," said he, "only embarrass matters, before they understand them." His decretals went to all parts of the world, to confirm the established discipline. In one of these letters, addressed to St. Victricius, bishop of Rouen (A. D. 404), the pope recalls the canons relating to the ordination of bishops and priests, and to the exclusive cognizance of spiritual matters by the ecclesiastical tribunals. Another (A. D. 405) decides several particular cases referred to the Holy See, by St. Exuperius, bishop of Toulouse. The law of clerical celibacy, the indissolubility of the marriage tie, and the rules of penance, are there laid down in accordance with the constant and invariable tradition of the Church. Africa, still ravaged by the violence of the Donatists, earnestly begged the help of the Roman Pontiff. Three councils had met at Carthage, to consider the means of obtaining peace (A. D. 402, 403, 404). In every city, the Catholic prelates had proposed to the Donatists to hold public conferences. The proposals had been everywhere rejected. The council at length resolved to send a deputation of bishops to the emperor, urging him to enforce against the Donatists the laws of Theodosius the Great, relative to heretics. The embassy bore a letter of recommendation to the pope, St. Innocent I. The emperor granted their request. In his answer to the fathers of the council, St. Innocent calls their attention to the canonical obligation of bishops to residence, and admonishes them to guard against the absence of prelates from their dioceses, unless for most weighty reasons. At this period, the watchful energy of St. Innocent I. stifled, at its birth, a schism about to come to light in Spain. The council of Toledo had consented to communicate with Symphosius, Dictinus, and several other bishops of Galicia, who had abjured the heresy of the Priscillianists. These prelates were allowed to retain their rank and authority. This decision seemed too indulgent in the eyes of the bishops of Bœtica and of the province of Carthagena, and they refused communion with those who received it. The matter was referred to the pope, who approved the decision of the council of Toledo, and commanded the Spanish bishops to communicate with all whom the council had restored.

2. But the holy pontiff's care was now chiefly called to the religious state of the Eastern Church. Its most eloquent and zealous bishop, St. John Chrysostom, found himself accused, condemned, persecuted, exiled by his brethren in the episcopacy, and saw but one hand outstretched to save, and not to strike, that of the successor of St. Peter. The holy patriarch of Constantinople had made himself many enemies, by his zeal

for the reformation of his clergy, and the suppression of every abuse. In a council called by him, at Ephesus, he caused the deposition of six simoniacal bishops, convicted of having bought their ordination from their metropolitan (A. D. 403). He also deposed the bishop of Nicomedia, Gerontius, for procuring his ordination by Helladius of Cæsarea, at the price of an important office at court, obtained for a relative of Helladius. He was entangled in new difficulties, by a matter of a yet more important nature, in which he acted with his usual uprightness. Theophilus, patriarch of Alexandria, was exceedingly irritated against the hermits of Scete, for receiving a priest he had driven from his church. He accordingly called a council, in which he had them convicted of Origenism, though they had not been granted a hearing. Acting under an inconceivable excess of rage, he even headed a troop of soldiers who attacked the monasteries, committing to the flames the sacred writings and the holy mysteries, and putting pious and harmless solitaries to the sword (A. D. 401). The monks thus ruthlessly driven from their holy retreats, first sought shelter in Jerusalem, whence the influence of Theophilus succeeded in banishing them. At every point, enemies were raised up against them by the anger of the patriarch. St. Epiphanius was deceived by his false account, and convened a council at Salamis, where the condemnation of Origenism was renewed. St. Epiphanius did not doubt that the monks of Egypt were ardent partisans of the heresy. He followed them to Constantinople, whither they had gone to seek the protection of St. John Chrysostom, and refused to communicate with the holy bishop whom he looked upon as an abettor of heretics. St. John sent to offer him the hospitality of his palace; Epiphanius refused to accept it, and even ordained a deacon, without asking the consent of the metropolitan. Meanwhile the Egyptian monks, who had indeed found a protector in St. Chrysostom, presented themselves to St. Epiphanius, and said to him : "We are the Egyptian monks you persecute: we would ask whether you ever saw our disciples and our writings." St. Epiphanius answered that he had never had the opportunity. "How then," they replied, "can you condemn without knowing us?" The saint was moved by this consideration, and received them kindly. The interview doubtless hastened his departure. He left Constantinople, without, however, coming to a reconciliation with St. Chrysostom. He died during the passage (A. D. 403), and the Island of Cyprus, which revered him as a father, received his mortal remains as precious relics. The dispute between him and the illustrious patriarch of Constantinople, was maintained with perfect good faith on both sides, and has not hindered the popes from placing the name of St. Epiphanius in the calendar of saints. The Greek Church ranks him among her doctors. He won this twofold title of honor, by the purity of his life, the ardor of his zeal, and the learned works he composed in defence of the truth. Theophilus of Alexandria soon came himself to Constantinople, to carry out his system of destruction against the monks. He gathered a powerful party, composed of all the saint's enemies. A sermon of the patriarch's, against the luxury and licentiousness of women, was represented to the empress Eudoxia as aimed at herself and the ladies of the court. Wounded vanity never forgives. The empress, seconding the efforts of Theophilus, urged the emperor to the most unjust measures. A cabal, which met in the village of the Oak, near Chalcedon, deposed St. Chrysostom (A. D. 403). The only canonical objection that could be brought against him, was that he made the faithful drink a little water after communion, lest they should run the risk of throwing out with the saliva the least particle of the sacred species. But his accusers gave more prominence to a comparison attributed to St. John, in which the courtiers discovered the guilt of high treason. St. Chrysostom had drawn a parallel between the empress and Queen Jezabel. The condemnation of the patriarch, by the false Council of the Oak, was immediately followed by an order for his banishment. On that very night, St. John Chrysostom was taken on board a vessel, and carried to the coast of Asia, near

Prœneste, in Bithynia. This exile lasted but a day. As soon as the people had learned the banishment of their holy bishop, they filled the churches and public places with their clamors. On the following night the city and vicinity felt the shock of an earthquake. To the terrified empress, this was a mark of the divine wrath. The earliest dawn revealed the Bosphorus covered with boats searching the coast for the retreat of St. Chrysostom, which was yet unknown. He was found at last; an officer of the empress handed him a letter from that princess: "I assure your holiness," she wrote, "that all this was done without my knowledge. I am innocent of this act of injustice. The plot is the work of perverse and wicked men. God sees the tears I offer in sacrifice. I cannot forget that my children received baptism from your hand." St. John reached his episcopal city at night; on his approach he found himself surrounded by his flock, who had come out to meet him, carrying lighted torches in sign of rejoicing. Attended by more than thirty bishops, he proceeded to the church of the Apostles, amid the enthusiastic shouts of the multitude, and there ascended the pulpit. But for once his very eloquence was prejudicial to the orator, for the assembled throng broke out into such energetic and prolonged applause, that he was unable to end his discourse (A. D. 403). All the holy patriarch's enemies were reduced to silence, and disappeared before this splendid display of the Catholic sentiment. Even Theophilus of Alexandria ceased to persecute the monks of Thebais. His war against the doctrines of Origen had gradually given rise in him to a wish to read his works. This study made him a most sincere admirer of the great doctor; and when asked how he had thus suddenly been changed from a persecutor into an admirer, he replied: "His works are like an enamelled field: I pluck the flowers without touching the thorns."

3. The quiet so unexpectedly restored to Constantinople, lasted but two months. The still smouldering hate of Eudoxia was again blown into a flame. A silver statue had been erected to the empress, in the square before the church of St

Sophia. The dances and shows to which the inauguration of the statue gave occasion, disturbed the solemnity of the sacred mysteries. The patriarch, with apostolic freedom of speech, complained of the abuse. This was the signal for a new persecution. Eudoxia took offence, and revived her former intrigues with the enemies of the orator. "Herodias has become furious," exclaimed St. Chrysostom one day, "she is again dancing, and asking for the head of John." This time she obtained it. A cabal composed of the personal enemies of the saint, deposed him without a hearing. Arcadius sent him an order to quit his church. "I received it from God," answered the patriarch, "I shall leave it only when your soldiers take me from it." The basilica was soon surrounded by Thracian troops. It was the holy Paschal time (A. D. 404), and according to the custom of the period, St. John Chrysostom was just conferring solemn baptism. Men and women were driven out at the point of the sword, the faithful clerics and priests cast into prison, the body and blood of Christ profaned. The patriarch withdrew into the episcopal residence, now surrounded and defended by the whole people, who had armed themselves for the purpose. The emperor dared not attack him. At length, on the 10th of June, A. D. 404, he sent Patricius, his intendant, to warn the patriarch that if he would not consent to leave the city of his own accord, the troops would engage the armed multitude. St. Chrysostom turned to the bishops who accompanied him, and said: "Come, let us pray together, and then take leave of the angel of this Church." After a fervent prayer, he gave the kiss of peace to his bishops, with abundant tears. Then tearing himself from his loved flock, he left the church by a private door, and entered a boat which carried him to Nice. This was the first stage of his exile. By an imperial order, received on the 5th of July, A. D. 404, he was removed to Cucusus, a lonely town among the ridges of Mount Taurus. The health of the patriarch was completely shattered by so many shocks, to which was added the long and painful journey performed at a season of parching heat, in the burnings of a fever which lasted more than thirty days. All the care and attention of Sabiniana, a deaconess of Constantinople, whose devotion kept her near the holy bishop, were fruitless to restore him to perfect health. Still Eudoxia was not satisfied. She vented her hatred upon the clergy who stood firm in the communion of their lawful pastor. One of them, named Eutropius, died under the hands of his executioners, whilst they tore his face and body with iron hooks. Arsacius, an intruded bishop, was placed upon the throne of the rightful prelate. The Church of Constantinople, in its desolation, appealed to the sovereign pontiff for help. St. Innocent I. wrote a letter of consolation to St. Chrysostom, who received it in his remote mountain exile of Armenia. The pope also wrote to the clergy and faithful of Constantinople : " We are not so far removed from you," writes the pontiff, " that we cannot share your grief. Who can bear with such unjust and criminal conduct on the part of those whose only care should be to establish peace and quiet in the bosom of the Church ? By a strange subversion of the most sacred laws, guiltless bishops are dispossessed of the government of their sees. Such is the unjust treatment inflicted upon your bishop, John, who is bound to us by the closest ties. By an audacious violation of all canonical law, a successor has been appointed to his throne; but such an election is a sacrilegious intrusion." The pope did not limit his zeal to this show of sympathy for the afflicted Church, but urged Honorius to write to his brother Arcadius, in behalf of St. John. Several bishops were sent to bear the dispatch of Honorius to Constantinople; but they were stopped on the way by order of Eudoxia, and only allowed to return home after undergoing the last degree of outrage and the sufferings of a long and painful imprisonment. St. Chrysostom, in his exile, heard of the efforts made by the pope in his behalf, and sent him several letters of thanks. " Upon you," says the holy bishop, " rests the burden of the whole world; for to you it belongs to do battle in the cause of widowed churches, of scattered flocks, of persecuted priests, of exiled bishops, and for the prescriptions of our fathers, now so wantonly trampled under foot" (A. D. 406). The exiled patriarch was even yet too near to allow his enemies to feel at rest. They drew from Arcadius an order to have him removed to Pityus, a deserted spot in the country of the Tzanians, on the coast of the Euxine Sea. The journey lasted three months, during which the illustrious exile was not allowed the least repose, notwithstanding the desperate state of his health. He never reached the place of banishment destined for him. At Comano he became so ill that the soldiers dared not move him further. They laid him in a church dedicated to St. Basiliscus. He had himself clothed in white, in token of deliverance, distributed the little that he had to those about him, received the Holy Eucharist, and breathed his last whilst pronouncing these words of thanksgiving: "Glory be to God for all things!" (A. D. 407). Thus, in a strange land, far from his beloved people, that splendid light of the Eastern Church was extinguished; the eloquent voice, which had won him the title of *Golden-mouth*, was hushed forever. Several popes have styled him the *Augustine of the Greek Church*. Literary men, struck by his splendid eloquence, rich at once in the fire of Demosthenes and the flowing elegance of Cicero, have said of him that he was the *Homer of Christian orators*. We have from this father several dogmatic treatises, commentaries on various parts of the Bible, some letters, and a number of discourses, homilies, and panegyrics of the saints. His most valued works are the *Treatises on the Priesthood*, on *Providence*, and on *Virginity*. The pope was careful of his memory after death, and refused to communicate with the Eastern bishops until they had made solemn reparation and recalled all who had been banished on his account. The persecutor did not long survive his victim. In the following year (A. D. 408), the death of Arcadius, that weak emperor who had nothing of the sovereign but the name, left the throne of the East to his son, Theodosius the Younger, then but a child. His mother, the Empress Eudoxia, had been dead two years.

This loss, which to most other children would prove an irretrievable misfortune, was a special blessing of Providence in the case of the infant emperor. His first years were passed under the tender care of Pulcheria. Anthemius, præfect of the prætorium, held the regency. At any other period, Theodosius, with his gentle, humane, and sympathetic disposition, would have made an accomplished prince; but now that hordes of armed barbarians surrounded the empire, the strong arm of a warrior was needed to meet them. The Huns and Scirri profited by the weakness of the court at Constantinople, to invade Thrace.

4. These partial inroads in the East hardly deserve mention by the side of the deluge of barbarians that now poured over the boundaries of the Western Empire. As early as the year 405, a detachment of the great nation of the Goths, to the number of two hundred thousand men, had crossed the Alps, under Radagasius. Stilicho, the minister of Honorius, aided by an army of Huns, crushed this formidable invasion, in the mountains of Northern Italy; this time, Rome owed her safety to the barbarians themselves. The torrent of invasion had but surged back for a moment to return with redoubled fury. In A. D. 407, Gaul was overrun by a swarm of Vandals, Suevi, Alani, Alemanni, and Burgundians. Mentz was taken and sacked; several thousands of Christians, with their bishop, Aureus, were murdered; Worms, Spires and Strasburg were burned. Tournay, Terouanne, Arras, St. Quentin, were powerless to stem the torrent. The barbarians, half Arians, half pagans, added many names to the martyrology of Gaul. St. Nicasius, bishop of Rheims, and St. Didier, bishop of Langres, were beheaded; Besançon witnessed the massacre of its bishop, Antidius. Marseilles was destroyed. Toulouse, vainly besieged by the invaders, owed its safety to the prayers of its holy prelate, Exuperius. For three years did these ravages deluge the country with blood, without calling from Stilicho a single effort to check them. Though father-in-law of the emperor, he was accused of a design to dispossess his son-in-law, with

a view to bestowing the crown on his own son, Eucherius. He was at this time in constant communication with Alaric, king of the Visigoths. Alaric was one of those destroyers of nations called by Providence to parcel out the ruins of the Roman world. From his home on the banks of the Danube, an unknown power urged him irresistibly on in his path of destruction. "A voice," said he, "ever cries within me, 'Go, and destroy Rome!'" Two victories won by Stilicho over Alaric's Visigoths (A. D. 402–403), checked the invader's progress. In A. D. 408, Alaric once more stood on the frontier of Italy. Was it for the safety of Rome, or to further his own ambitious views, that Stilicho now opened negotiations with him? History gives no answer; but Honorius leaned to the latter opinion. An imperial decree declared the general an enemy to his country, and Stilicho met his death upon the scaffold (A. D. 408). Alaric, whom nothing could now withstand, sat down before the very gates of Rome; he had turned the course of the Tiber and cut off all communications, and the city soon became a prey to all the horrors of famine and pestilence. An enormous ransom bought the withdrawal of the Visigoths. Honorius, shut up in Ravenna and unable to fulfil the conditions of the treaty, saw his title to the empire disposed of by Alaric, in favor of Attalus, prefect of Rome (A. D. 409). The following year (410) was marked as the period for the destruction of the Eternal City. On the 24th of August, Alaric, with his Visigoths, entered the city of the Cæsars. The troops were licensed to pillage; but the very barbarians stood in awe before the majesty of the Christian religion. The churches of St. Peter and St. Paul were named by the conqueror as places of refuge. All the sacred vessels brought to Alaric from the church of St. Peter were sent back by him to the priests, as holy articles, and the soldiers themselves were seen guiding consecrated virgins to the appointed asylums, to save them from outrage. The pope, St. Innocent I., did not quit Rome in the hour of peril; nor was his presence unrecognized in the marks of respect paid by Alaric to Christianity

The pope had already been honorably received and treated by him, when he came as bearer of the propositions of Honorius (A. D. 408). Men were becoming accustomed to see the majesty of the Sovereign Pontiff rise superior to the din of arms, and the Church came forth triumphant from this first invasion, which was to last from Alaric to Odoacer.

5. But the colossal fabric of the Roman Empire could not crumble into ruins without awakening an echo that shook the world. The heathens attributed these unequalled disasters to the anger of the gods, and held the religion of Jesus Christ answerable for the humiliation of the Capitol. The Christian doctors undertook to answer these bitter complaints. Whilst St. Jerome, like another Jeremias, wept over the Roman ruins, and showed by his writings that the decline of the empire was due to the corrupt state of pagan morality, and to the degrading influence produced upon character and courage by centuries of unbridled licentiousness and luxury, Paul Orosius, a Spanish priest of Tarragona, in his *Epitome of Universal History*, undertaken at the request of St. Augustine, was establishing the same conclusion, by a statement of facts. St. Augustine himself was writing his immortal work, the *City of God*; here, in a parallel embracing the whole field of history, he shows the kingdom of truth rising upon the ruin of empires, and displays the plan of Providence in the institution of the Church, and in its development throughout all time. This great work, which would have taken up an ordinary lifetime, was but an incident in that of St. Augustine. The Donatist controversy found the indefatigable champion ever in the gap. At Carthage, he held, with the leading spirits of the faction, a public conference, over which Honorius had directed the tribune, Marcellinus, to preside (A. D. 411). St. Augustine spoke for the Catholic bishops. The conference lasted three days. The eloquent orator conclusively proved that there can be no just cause for leaving the Church; that the true Church could not have been confined till now to a single spot in Africa, and that the Donatists, by their very name, by the very fact of

their breaking with the rest of the Catholic world, were already condemned. The discourse made a deep impression; but the words of the holy doctor were confirmed by an unparalleled example of disinterestedness, more powerful than all human eloquence. At his desire, the two hundred and eighty-six Catholic bishops present offered to give up their sees to the Donatists, if they would agree to return to the communion of the Church. This splendid self-denial, enhanced by the evident obstinacy of the Donatist prelates, brought back a number of heretics to the faith. From this time, the inveterate schism which had desolated Africa since the days of Cecilian, was consigned to oblivion by public contempt. The few remaining members of the lost faction made an effort to appeal from the decision of Marcellinus to Honorius. The emperor's only answer was an order to the Governor of Carthage to treat the refractory Donatists as open rebels. This schism had hardly been crushed, when a new heresy was planted in the soil of Africa, by two natives of Great Britain, Pelagius and Celestius. The subject of dispute was the fundamental dogma of *grace*, the basis of man's spiritual regeneration. This equally arduous and important question had in Pelagius a formidable antagonist, and in St. Augustine an intrepid champion. Now that Jansenism has in our own time once more called attention to this question, we can understand the difficulty of treating it with theological precision, rigor, and completeness. In the year 405, Pelagius, who gave his name to the new heresy, left the monastery of Bangor, in Wales, and went to Rome. His subtle, captivating mind, skilled in the art of dissimulation and deceit, had long been fostering the germs of his system of the omnipotence of the human will. He began openly to unfold it in a journey to Carthage with his disciple and friend, Constantius. In his book of *Confessions*, begun in A. D. 397, St. Augustine had said: "*Domine, da nobis quod jubes, et jube quod vis ;*" Pelagius attacked this proposition, in an assembly of bishops. The Bishop of Hippo took up the gauntlet thus thrown, and never again laid it down. The more he owed to grace, the more he felt bound to restore to it. Twenty years he followed up Pelagianism; and was able to console his last hour with the assurance that the heresy pierced by so many darts could not long survive him. The errors of Pelagius are summed up under three principal heads: original sin, free-will, the necessity and gratuitousness of grace. I. The fundamental error of Pelagius was the denial that the sin of Adam and Eve has been transmitted to their posterity. In his system, the sin of our first parents could hurt no one but themselves, and if it had been prejudicial to their descendants, it was not as an hereditary fault, but, at most, as a bad example; baptism is therefore given to children not to wash away an original stain, but to stamp them with the character, the seal of adoption. II. On the subject of free-will, Pelagius taught: 1, that it is as entire, as strong in us, as it was in Adam, before the fall; 2, that the power of free-will is sufficient, in man, to enable him, without any supernatural help, to fulfil all the divine precepts, to overcome every temptation, to rise to the highest degree of perfection, and to win everlasting life; 3, in such a system grace was, in fact, destroyed. But since it would have been impossible to do away with its name, Pelagius placed this gratuitous gift in the very free-will which God, without owing it, gives us. St. Augustine objected that Jesus Christ has brought us a more plentiful grace, without any apparent increase of the amount of free-will in the New Law over the Old. Pelagius replied that this grace of the New Testament consists in the good example of the Redeemer. St. Augustine retorted: "Why, then, does this good example act so efficaciously upon some, and leave others in indifference?" Thus driven back to his last intrenchments, Pelagius agreed to admit an interior illuminative grace in the understanding, which facilitates the operation of the will. This useful grace is not, however, indispensable; nor is it preventive or gratuitous, and God is not free to refuse it to whoever deserves it by a good use of his natural powers.

These preliminary remarks will suffice to give a view of the nature and bearing of Pelagianism. The first condemnation of this new heresy was pronounced by a council held in Carthage (A. D. 412), at which Augustine was unable to be present. The anathema was directed against Celestius, as Pelagius was no longer in Africa; he had gone to visit the cities of the Syrian coast. The errors of Celestius had been reduced to seven leading propositions: 1. Adam was created subject to death; 2. His sin was a personal offence, and was not communicated to his posterity; 3. Children are, at the moment of their birth, in the same state of innocence as that of Adam before his fall; 4. The sin of Adam is not the cause of death to the whole human race; the resurrection of Jesus Christ is not the cause of the resurrection of man; 5. The law of Moses leads to heaven as well as the law of Jesus Christ; 6. Before the coming of Jesus Christ, there were impeccable men; 7. Children who die without baptism have a right to eternal happiness. After his condemnation, Celestius appealed to the Sovereign Pontiff, but without waiting to urge the appeal, left for Asia, where he continued to dogmatize. Pelagius had in the mean time been denounced by the Gallic bishops, and especially by Heros of Arles and Lazarus of Aix, as a heretic; he was now striving to clear himself in the eyes of the bishops of Palestine, by a public conference held at Jerusalem, and in a council of fourteen bishops, held at Diospolis. His chief opponents were Orosius of Spain and St. Jerome. The fathers of Diospolis, misled by the false representations of Pelagius, cleared him from the charge of heresy, without awaiting the reply of Innocent I., to whom the matter had been referred after the conference at Jerusalem (A. D. 415). St. Augustine was at the same time bringing out a series of works against the principal errors of Pelagianism: the *Treatise on Nature and Grace; Merit and the Remission of Sins; The Grace of the New Testament; the Perfection of Righteousness; Free-will.* St. Jerome followed in his footsteps, and published his *Dialogue between a Catholic and a Pelagian.* The intricacies of the question were mostly removed by the light which these two great writers threw upon it. The Councils of Carthage and Milevum decided, conformably to the Catholic belief, that the sin of Adam has been transmitted to his descendants, and that, without an interior grace inspiring good-will, we can do no supernatural good, nor any thing useful for salvation. The Fathers of these councils wrote to Pope St. Innocent I., begging him to confirm the decision by the authority of the apostolic see. To the synodal letters of the African bishops, the Sovereign Pontiff replied: "You have followed, as becomes the episcopate, the institutions of our fathers, who indeed held by divine tradition, that nothing can be regulated in the most distant countries without the cognizance of the Holy See. From this fountain-head the pure and running waters of truth flow out, to water and fertilize all the regions of the universe." The pope then ratifies the decisions of the two councils, and solemnly condemns Pelagius, Celestius, and their followers: he declares them to be cut off from the communion of the Church, unless they forsake their errors. After this decree of the pope, St. Augustine exclaimed: "Rome has spoken, the cause is finished. God grant the error be so too!"

6. Filled with grief at the sad state to which the barbarian inroads had reduced Gaul, Spain, and Italy, Innocent I. enlarged his charity to take in the full extent of his children's desolation: he made collections to relieve the suffering and want which such a revolution had multiplied to a fearful extent. Alaric had survived the sack of Rome but two years; but the Visigoths had given his place to his brother-in-law, Adolphus. The pope kept his laborers in the vineyard, and these barbarians were gradually taught to bend under the yoke of the Gospel. His zeal was urged on to renewed activity by the earnest wish to see unity of discipline established in the bosom of the Church. We have still a precious monument of it, in a decretal addressed to Decentius, bishop of Eugubio, in Umbria, who had consulted him on several points of liturgy and discipline. "If the bishops of the Lord,"

said the pope, "would but follow, in their full extent, the ecclesiastical institutes as they have been left us by the blessed Apostles, there would be neither diversity nor variety in what regards consecrations and the celebration of the sacred mysteries." Like decisions are found in other letters of St. Innocent, to bishops in Italy and Macedonia. The death of the holy pontiff took place in A. D. 417. St. Innocent I. is the first pope who absented himself from Rome, to serve the general interests of the Church. In the year 400 he had gone to Ravenna, to urge Honorius to greater punctuality in fulfilling his contract with Alaric. Had the advice of the pope been taken, the Eternal City would have been spared the horrors of the invasion of A. D. 410.

§ II. PONTIFICATE OF ST. ZOSIMUS (August, A. D 417—Dec. 26, 418).

7. St. Zosimus was called to succeed St. Innocent I. on the 19th of August, A. D. 417. His pontificate, which lasted but a year, was almost entirely taken up with the question of Pelagianism, which, under the mask of a hypocritical submission to the authority of the Church, had been steadily spreading its poison. Celestius came to Rome (A. D. 417), protested the purity of his intentions, solemnly declared that he *condemned all that St. Innocent I. had condemned*, and was received by St. Zosimus into communion with the Church. Pelagius wrote to the pope in the same strain, and the merciful pontiff absolved him also from the censures pronounced against him. Still the two sectaries continued to preach their errors, and more boldly than ever, as they now declared themselves in communion with the See of Rome. The bishops of Africa assembled to the number of two hundred and fourteen, in a council at Carthage, and represented to the pope that notwithstanding their seeming submission, Pelagius and Celestius still continued to dogmatize. The Sovereign Pontiff called the case once more before his tribunal, and after mature delibera-

tion, ratified the sentence of the African bishops, renewed the sentence pronounced by his predecessor, and declared that if the two heresiarchs would abjure their error, they should be received to public penance, otherwise they were to remain excommunicated. The doctrinal letter of the pope was sent to the bishops of Egypt and of the East, and to the patriarchs of the great sees, Antioch, Alexandria, Jerusalem, and Constantinople. This ecclesiastical judgment was followed by an imperial rescript of Honorius, condemning the two heresiarchs and their followers to exile (A. D. 418). At the same time St. Augustine had the Catholic doctrine acknowledged by a new council held at Carthage (May 1st, A. D. 418). The decision of the Holy See was received by all the churches throughout the world. Only one bishop, Julian of Eclanum in Campania, refused to subscribe. In conjunction with several Pelagian bishops, he drew up an heretical profession of faith, and appealed from the decision of the pope to a general council. St. Zosimus expressly condemned Julian and his accomplices. They were deposed, and their sees given to Catholic bishops. In the midst of the cares attending the examination of these important questions, St. Zosimus had found time to settle a dispute concerning the metropolitan jurisdiction of the second Narbonese, claimed, at once, by the churches of Vienna and Marseilles, to the detriment of Arles, which had always enjoyed it. The pope confirmed the claim of the latter church, "founded upon the apostolate of St. Trophimus," and condemned any thing opposed to this decision. He wrote to the clergy and faithful of Marseilles, that if their bishop persisted in usurping the canonical prerogative of his metropolitan of Arles, he should feel bound to depose him, and to place in his stead a pastor more worthy to govern them (March, A. D. 418). The holy pontiff showed the same apostolic vigor in every thing else relating to ecclesiastical discipline. He also addressed a decretal to Hesychius, bishop of Salona, the metropolitan See of Dalmatia, in which he inveighs against the ambition of laymen and monks, who seek to reach, at one

step, the highest degree of the priesthood, without regard to
the intermediate grades established by the canons. This vigilant and zealous pastor was snatched from the Church by a
premature death (December, A. D. 418).

§ III. Pontificate of St. Boniface I. (Dec. 30, A. D. 418— Oct. 25, 422).

8. The election of St. Boniface I. presents the first instance
in the Church's history of a secular power interfering in the
choice of a Roman pontiff. The clergy and people of Rome
had met to proceed to a canonical election, when the Deacon
Eulalius forcibly seized upon the Lateran Basilica and obliged
the Bishop of Ostia to consecrate him. On the next day, the
regular assembly hailed the legitimate pastor in the person of
Boniface I., a Roman priest. Symmachus, prefect of Rome
had in the mean time sent to the Emperor Honorius a statement favorable to the antipope. The emperor called the
case before his own tribunal, summoned Boniface and Eulalius
to appear at Ravenna, where he was then holding his court,
and caused them to sign an agreement not to return to Rome
until he had pronounced sentence. In spite of this solemn
promise, Eulalius returned to Rome with the intention of celebrating the Easter solemnity (A. D. 419). But the people, true
to their lawful pastor, expelled the usurper, and, two days
later, Boniface was received in triumph and recognized by the
emperor, the senate, and the whole city. Hardly had the authority of the sovereign pontificate been secured in his person,
when St. Boniface was called to defend it against the sixth Council of Carthage (May 25, A. D. 419), which sought to abolish
appeals to the pope. The discussion originated in the case of
Apiarius, a priest of Sicca, in Mauritania, who had been excommunicated by his bishop, Urban, and appealed to the See
of Rome. St. Boniface sent three legates to Carthage, to
examine the matter; they were Faustinus, bishop of Potentina, in Italy, with Philip and Asellus, priests of the Roman

Church. When, in the heat of the discussion, the right of the Sovereign Pontiff was questioned to judge the cases brought to him by appeal, the legates quoted the canons of the Council of Sardica, to which the pope referred in the written instructions given them. But, strange to say! the Council of Sardica held in A. D. 347, though Carthage was represented there by its bishop, Gratus, was altogether unknown to the African bishops of the year 419. The fathers of the Council of Carthage then asked for time to examine the original acts of the Council of Sardica. The difficulty was thus held in permanence, and was only finally settled in the pontificate of Celestin I., in A. D. 427. Apiarius, the first cause of the whole discussion, made his peace with his bishop, and was received into the communion of the Church.

9. The solicitude of St. Boniface I. extended equally to all the churches in the world. On the 13th of June, A. D. 419, he referred to the judgment of the Gallic bishops the case of Maximus, bishop of Valence, who was charged with Manicheism, and the commission of abominable crimes. The pontiff directed the bishops of Gaul to meet in council on the 1st of November, in order to look into the matter, on condition that their judgment should be subject to the revision of the pope. St. Boniface at the same time authorized the translation of Perigenes, bishop of Patras in Achaia, to the metropolitan See of Corinth (A. D. 419). Atticus, patriarch of Constantinople, protested against this decision of the Roman court. He asserted that no bishop could be ordained in the Hellespont and other provinces of Asia without the consent of the Patriarch of Constantinople. He enjoyed sufficient credit at court to obtain from Theodosius the Younger the passage of a law to this effect (A. D. 421), and assembled a council at Corinth to discuss the translation of Perigenes, in spite of its solemn confirmation by the authority of the Holy See. By this constitution the emperor also claimed to take from the bishops of Thessalonica their canonical jurisdiction over Illyria, and to bestow it on the bishops of Constantinople, "who enjoy," he

said, "*the prerogatives of ancient Rome.*" In a juncture when the primacy of the chair of St. Peter was called in question, St. Boniface I. showed himself worthy to guard and defend it.[a] He sent deputies to the Emperor Honorius, begging him to use his influence with Theodosius the Younger to obtain the revocation of the decree. He had in the mean time written to Rufus, bishop of Thessalonica, a most energetic letter. "The attempts recently made," he writes, "to lessen your authority neither can nor will succeed. Strong in your undeniable right, arm yourself as a soldier of God. Fear not these new storms; the blessed Apostle St. Peter will be with you, and will not allow the rights of his see to be touched." Other pontifical letters to the bishops of Thessaly were equally explicit. "It is certain," says the pope, "that the Church of Rome is, to all the churches throughout the universe, what the head is to the other members of the body. Whoever, then, withdraws from it, becomes an alien from the Christian religion, since he is no longer in unity. The same principles are laid down with equal energy in a circular letter to all the bishops of Macedonia, Achaia, Epirus, and Dacia (March 11, A. D. 422). The pope cited facts of history clearly sustaining the rights of the Roman See. "The great Athanasius, Flavian of Antioch, and Chrysostom of Constantinople, always sought counsel from the successor of St. Peter, and their example fully proves the tradition in the great Churches of the East." The zeal of St. Boniface was crowned with success; Theodosius the Younger withdrew the offensive decree, and Perigenes governed the Church of Corinth until his death.

10. Whilst the attention of the East was taken up by this discussion, a great light of the Church had gone out in Palestine; St. Jerome had died on the 30th of September, A. D. 420, at the age of eighty years. St. Jerome brought to the service of the truth more learning than any other Father of the Latin Church. His immense labors on the Scriptures are equalled only by his incredible mortification, his love of retreat and poverty, and his burning charity, which moved the great St. Augustine to compare him to St. Paul. His style is energetic,

rich in figures and in lofty and concise thoughts, sometimes reaching the highest standard of pure Latinity. The reproach made to him in a vision is well known. Our Lord Jesus Christ asked him if he was a Christian. "Yes, Lord," answered the saint. "No, you are still a Ciceronian." His predilection for profane authors from that moment gave place to an unbounded love for the Sacred Writings, which led him, at the age of sixty years, to undertake and to pursue with distinguished success the study of Hebrew. His solitary life did not keep him out of the lists, when heresy was to be met; this is clearly shown in the Pelagian difficulty. He was at the same time engaged in a no less arduous contest with Vigilantius, an heretical priest of Comminges, in Gaul. The heretic, whose errors are known to us only through the writings of St. Jerome himself, condemned the veneration of saints and of relics, as well as clerical celibacy. A few clerics of lax morality had adopted a doctrine which favored their disorders, and formed the nucleus of a party. St. Jerome pursued the new sectaries with his usual energy; and there is every reason to believe that Vigilantius yielded to the influence of grace and subsequently retracted, for he died at Barcelona, in the communion of the Church.

In the hour of his triumph over the proud pretensions of the Patriarch of Constantinople, St. Boniface had been called away to enjoy a more lasting triumph in heaven (Oct. 25th, A. D. 422). He had renewed St. Fabian's ordinance, fixing the canonical age for the priesthood at thirty years. He also abolished the *vigils* of saints, that is, the assemblages held at a saint's tomb, on the night before his feast. These meetings were by degrees falling away from primitive gravity and decency; but he still held to the precept for the liturgy and fast of vigils

§ IV. PONTIFICATE OF ST. CELESTIN I. (Nov. 3, A. D. 422— April 6, 432).

11. St. Boniface was succeeded by the deacon St. Celestin, a very near relative of the Emperor Valentinian. The new

pope ascended the throne on the 3d of November, A. D. 422, and opened his pontificate by the condemnation of a heresy sprung from the errors of Pelagius. Pelagianism, crushed by the decisions of Rome and the eloquence of St. Augustine, was gradually dying out; but from its ashes arose another sect, which smoothed over all the most revolting features of its archetype, and held a middle course between the doctrine of Pelagius and the orthodox faith. This mitigated form of Pelagianism was started by some priests at Marseilles, who were called *Semi-Pelagians*. They attributed to free-will the beginning of faith, and the first steps of the human will towards good. According to their teaching, God, in consequence of man's first efforts, gives increase of faith and the grace of good works. Thus the Semi-Pelagians agreed with the Catholics in admitting the existence of original sin and the necessity of an interior grace to do good; but they held that man may deserve this grace by a beginning of faith, by a first impulse of virtue, of which, however, God is not the author. St. Augustine brought all his energies to bear upon this baneful error. The case was summoned before the tribunal of St. Celestin. The pontiff condemned the priests of Marseilles, and defined, against them, that God so operates in the human heart, that every holy thought, pious intention, and, in a word, every right impulse of the will to the end of salvation comes from Him, and that if we can do any good work, it is by Him, without Whom we can do nothing. This sentence was received with respect throughout the Christian world, and disunion was at an end.

12. The attention of St. Celestin was next called to the case of Apiarius, begun in A. D. 419, under the pontificate of his predecessor. The African bishops still refused to admit the validity of appeals to the Holy See. Apiarius, though readmitted to the communion of the Church, again drew upon himself the censure of his bishop, and appealed to the pope. St Celestin sent Faustinus, the same legate already employed by St. Boniface, to examine on the spot the charges brought

against this priest. They were found to be well grounded. Apiarius himself showed a deep repentance, confessed all his crimes, and was removed from the sacred ministry. The African bishops seized this occasion to beg the pope that he would show less readiness in granting his protection to the foreign clerics who might apply for it. Whatever importance may be attached to this document, it cannot, in the least degree, impair the so often admitted rights exercised by the popes long before this controversy, and still maintained at every period, in spite of these protestations (A. D. 426).

Whilst the Church was suffering from this internal agitation; whilst the world was distracted by political revolutions, in the midst of which Castinus, commander of the militia, placed upon the throne, at the death of Honorius (A. D. 423), a mere shadow of an emperor, who perished miserably within two years, leaving the purple to Valentinian III. (A. D. 425), the religious life was spreading with renewed fervor in Gaul. St. Romanus founded the monastery of Condate in Franche-Comté (now the episcopal See of St. Claude); the celebrated abbey of St. Victor was established at Marseilles (A. D. 427), by John Cassian, a Scythian by birth, known as the author of the *Monastic Institutions*, and of the *Conferences*, and by the journeys he made into Egypt to visit the solitaries of Thebais. The same period witnessed the erection by Honoratus of the famous monastery at Lerins, an island in the Mediterranean, on the coast of Provence. Syria, meanwhile, held the living miracle of anchorites, in the person of St. Simeon Stylites,[*] who spent thirty years on the top of a lofty pillar, whither he had retired, to give himself more uninterruptedly to meditation and prayer. But now the world was thrown into a state of consternation, by the report of a Vandal invasion into Africa, headed by King Genseric. The whole province, which was looked upon as the granary of the universe, on account of its wealth, fertility, and numerous cities, was wasted by

---

[*] From the Greek word στύλος, a column.

fire, the sword and famine. The invaders were mostly Arians, and turned their rage principally against the Catholics. All the churches were destroyed. Bishops, priests, monks, virgins consecrated to God, were led into captivity or ruthlessly murdered by their conquerors (A. D. 430). The Church, hitherto so flourishing, was thus extinguished in the blood of her children, only to revive at some period far in the future, known and marked out by Divine Providence. As if to add to the calamity, the same year closed the career of the great St. Augustine; he died as the flames kindled by the barbarians devoured his episcopal city of Hippo (28th of August, A. D. 430). With him died Christian and civilized Africa. He has left ever-enduring monuments of his zeal and learning in his works, which Possidius, a contemporary author, computes at one thousand and thirty, including sermons and letters. St. Augustine has sometimes been charged with a want of exactness in his theological discussions on grace. We have already had occasion to answer this objection, in speaking of the works of other doctors. We must remember that the language of theology was not till afterwards, by the decisions of the councils, brought to its present state of perfection. These slight blemishes are more than redeemed by a lively faith and fervid eloquence, rich in figures,—and they have not been deemed sufficient to rob him of the title of *Doctor of Grace*. The most glorious monument has been raised to his memory by the Roman Church: the statue of St. Augustine, with those of Sts. Ambrose, Athanasius, and Chrysostom, support the chair of St. Peter, in the Vatican. A wonderful coincidence gave to the same century the glory of producing the two most illustrious Fathers both of the Greek and of the Latin Churches.

13. The religious life, lately extinguished in Africa, was advancing with marvellous fruitfulness in Gaul; it seems to be the destiny of the Church never to lose a jewel from her crown without seeing it replaced by a brighter one. The provinces of Gaul had till this period been divided between the different tribes of barbarians who had settled there after the

former invasion: the Goths held Aquitaine; the Burgundians had founded an empire, to which they gave their name, Burgundy; the Alani had received from the Roman general Ætius the territory of Valence, on the Rhone; whilst the Romans held very little more of their original possessions than the two Narboneses and Provence. During the period between the years 430 and 438, the northern part of Gaul began to be visited by the nation that was to conquer and settle it permanently, and to found, under the name of France, a kingdom which still endures. The Franks had for some centuries lived along the banks of the Rhine, in the country which has kept the name of Franconia; under their chief, Clodion, they made themselves masters of the cities of Cambray, of Tournay, and of Amiens. At the time when this yet pagan people first set foot upon Gallic soil, the episcopal sees of the province were filled by a generation of illustrious and holy bishops. St. Germanus had just succeeded St. Amator in the government of the Church of Auxerre. His friend, St. Lupus, illustrated the See of Troyes by his virtue, his eloquence, and his miracles. St. Hilary, a school-fellow of these two great men, had torn himself from the holy solitude of Lerins, to fill the metropolitan See of Arles. At Lyons, the virtue, piety, and learning of St. Irenæus were revived in the person of St. Eucherius. In St. Oriens, bishop of Auch, the most eminent degree of virtue was allied to the gift of a soft and flowing style. But these were not the only lights that shone in Gaul; St. Prosper was engaged in his *Chronicles*, and his *Poem against the enemies of Grace*. Salvian, called the *Jeremias of the fifth century*, was composing his work *On Providence*, and his *Treatise on the Church;* and St. Vincent of Lerins was preparing to publish his admirable *Memorial*. This exuberance of holiness and faith, overflowing the limits of the Church of Gaul, reached the shores of Great Britain, then infected by the Pelagian heresy. St. Germanus of Auxerre and St. Lupus of Troyes landed on this island in A. D. 429, where the influence of their preaching, their miracles, and the holiness of their lives.

restored the first fervor of the faith. It was in this journey that the two saints, on their way through Nanterre, consecrated to God the holy virgin St. Genevieve, whose name and memory have become so wide-spread in later times. The pope, St. Celestin, had just ordained St. Patrick bishop of Ireland; the saint became the apostle of the island, till then steeped in idolatry. Crowds of pagans were won by his words. He founded the monastery of Sabhal, near Down, and made his disciple, St. Dunnius, its abbot; he also established the metropolitan See of Armagh (A. D. 431).

14. The East seemed to be marked out as the common birthplace of the great heresiarchs of the fourth and fifth centuries; its great see, Constantinople, was now filled by a bishop soon to give his name to a new error against the Catholic faith. This was Nestorius, who had been made patriarch in A. D. 427. The heresiarch was proud, superficial, with great pretensions to depth, and bombastic rather than eloquent. He divided Jesus Christ into two persons: one, the person of the man, Jesus Christ; the other, the person of God, the Word. Whence it followed that Jesus was not God, but a man united to God in a more special and intimate manner than any other. Then, by logical consequence, the Blessed Virgin was not the mother of God, but only the mother of a man called the Christ, to whom the Word had united Himself. This doctrine thus destroyed the mystery of the Incarnation, the divinity of Jesus Christ, and the divine maternity of the Blessed Virgin. The heresy made its first appearance in a sermon preached on Christmas-day (A. D. 428), in which Nestorius said, "that to call the Virgin the *mother of God*, Θεοτόκος, would justify the pagan folly of giving mothers to their gods." These blasphemies shocked the Catholic mind of Constantinople; but the patriarch gave no heed to the public feeling, and encouraged his priests to spread the doctrine. Dorotheus, bishop of Marcianopolis, who had taken up his error, preaching one day before Nestorius, in the church of St. Sophia, pushed his blasphemous impiety so far as to utter the words: "If any one

saith that Mary is the mother of God, let him be anathema!"
At these words the people, with a loud cry of indignation,
rushed from the church. All the East was moved at the
report of this scandal. When it came to the ears of St.
Cyril, patriarch of Alexandria, he at once wrote to the
solitaries a letter, which forms a complete treatise against
Nestorianism. The matter was brought before St. Celestin
by St. Cyril, and even by Nestorius himself. The Sovereign
Pontiff was alarmed at the spread of the impious doctrine, and called upon Cassian to meet it; the acquittance of
the charge was the *Treatise on the Incarnation*, in which the Catholic faith is nobly vindicated. Still, Nestorius never ceased to
preach his error under the favor and protection of the court
of Constantinople. St. Cyril of Alexandria, worthy successor
of the great St. Athanasius, redoubled his zeal and energy in
defence of the truth. He wrote to the emperor and his sisters
in the most eloquent strain, showing the doctrine of the
Church on the Incarnation, and upholding it by Scripture and
tradition; he meanwhile sent to the pope a general view of
the state of the question. St. Celestin at once called a council at Rome, in which Nestorius was anathematized. The pope
communicated this decision to St. Cyril, and directed him to
excommunicate the heresiarch if he refused to submit. The
words of the pontiff on this occasion are worthy of note: "By
the authority of the Holy See, and acting in our stead with the
power granted to us, you will execute the sentence with exemplary severity." (In obedience to the pope's instructions) St.
Cyril called a council of the Egyptian bishops, and drew up
twelve anathemas against each point of Nestorius's errors;
these he sent to the heresiarch, with the injunction, according to
St. Celestin's letter, to sign them (A.D. 430). Nestorius refused,
and proposed to change the word Θεοτόκος (mother of God)
to Χριστοτόκος (mother of Christ). The discussion grew in bitterness. Andrew of Samosata and Theodoret of Cyrrhus wrote a
tract against the twelve anathemas, whilst Marius Mercator defended them in a very spirited and learned work. Meanwhile, St.

Cyril himself was not idle; he successively published his *Reply to Andrew of Samosata*, the *Apology against Theodoret*, and a *Refutation of the Sermons of Nestorius*. Nestorius adopted the artifice common to heretics of all times—he appealed (from the pope) to an ecumenical council. His patron, Theodosius the Younger, wished to grant him this satisfaction. The third general council was therefore appointed for the month of June, A. D. 431, to meet at Ephesus. St. Cyril presided as Papal Legate. The session was opened with great solemnity. Two hundred bishops were present in the great church of Ephesus; on a golden throne in their midst they had placed the book of the Gospels, to represent the assistance of Jesus Christ, Who has promised to be with the pastors gathered together in His name. Nestorius had come to Ephesus escorted by an armed troop; but he refused to appear in the council. The Fathers thrice summoned him to attend the meetings; their messengers were always turned away by the guard about the house in which the heresiarch kept himself shut up. The council was thus forced to proceed, in the absence of the Patriarch of Constantinople, to the examination of his writings. They had no sooner been read than the assembled bishops with one voice exclaimed: "Anathema to such impious teaching! anathema to whoever holds such opinions! they are contrary to Sacred Scripture and to the tradition of the Fathers!" Pope St. Celestin's letter was then read, and inserted in full in the acts of the council. Finally, solemn sentence was pronounced in these words: "Nestorius having refused to answer our summons and to receive the bishops sent to him, we have been obliged to enter upon an examination of his impieties. He is convicted, on the evidence of his letters, his writings and his discourses, of holding and spreading scandalous and heretical opinions. Bound by the holy canons, and by the letter of our Holy Father Celestin, bishop of Rome, we are reduced, not without tears of heart-felt sorrow, to the cruel necessity of pronouncing this sentence against him: Our Lord Jesus Christ, whom he has blasphemed, decides, through this most holy council, that he is deprived of the episcopal dignity, and cut off from every ecclesiastical body." This sentence, one of the most solemn ever uttered by the Church, gives Bossuet occasion to note that *the Fathers recognize, in the pope's letter, the force of a juridical sentence, to which they feel bound to subscribe.* The people of Ephesus had besieged the church doors during the whole day, in anxious expectation of the decision. As soon as it was publicly announced, the multitude broke out into enthusiastic transports of joy. The bishops were escorted to their dwellings with lighted torches; they were covered with flowers, carried in triumph; the whole city was illuminated; and the smoke of precious incense going up from before the statues of Mary, filled the atmosphere with a rich fragrance.

The popular indignation had been particularly aroused by the injury done to the honor of the Blessed Virgin in the Nestorian doctrine. In a discourse delivered at the second session of the council, St. Cyril expresses this sentiment with a rare happiness of eloquence and faith. "Hail, O Mother of God!" he exclaims: "O Mary! rich treasure of the universe, everburning lamp, light of the Church, crown of virginity, sceptre of orthodoxy, imperishable temple, Mother and Virgin, through whom He is, that cometh Blessed in the name of the Lord! We hail thee who didst, in thy virginal womb, contain Him Who is immense, incomprehensible! Thee, through whom the Holy Trinity is adored and glorified, the cross honored and venerated throughout the universe; in whom heaven triumphs, the angels and archangels rejoice, the demons are put to flight; thee, through whom the fallen creature is raised up to heaven; thee, through whom the whole world, when crushed under the yoke of idolatry, was brought to the light of truth; through thee, holy baptism and the unction of spiritual joy are imparted to the faithful; through thee, all the churches of the world were founded, and nations brought to penance. Through thee, in fine, the only Son of God, *the Orient from on high hath visited us, to enlighten them that sit in darkness, and in the shadow of death:* by thee the Prophets foretold, and the Apostles preached salvation to the nations; through thee the dead rise again, and kings reign in the name of the Blessed Trinity!" This apostrophe of the holy Patriarch of Alexandria, given back by every popular echo, drowned the discordant voices of a few bishops, met in a cabal, to uphold the errors of Nestorius. Truth prevailed, and its light reached Theodosius himself, in spite of the efforts of Count Candidian, who commanded the soldiery, and was devoted to the cause of the heretics. The prelates had written to make the emperor acquainted with their decision, as soon as it was pronounced; but Candidian intercepted their letters, and joined Nestorius in prejudicing the emperor against them by a false account. The emperor was carefully guarded against the letters and the envoys of the council. Vessels and highways were watched; every approach was closed to them, and truth must have fallen, had not God given it strength to overcome all obstacles and to thwart all intrigues. At last an envoy of the council, disguised as a beggar, gained access to the palace, bearing the true account in a hollow staff. When the emperor was informed of what had really taken place in the Council of Ephesus, he banished Nestorius to a monastery at Antioch; but as the heresiarch continued to preach his errors, he was exiled to Oasis, in Upper Egypt, where he shortly after perished miserably. He was succeeded in the See of Constantinople by Maximian. The pope wrote to the Eastern bishops, approving the promotion, and congratulating them upon their choice.

This letter, and that which he wrote at the same time to the bishops of Gaul in defence of St. Augustine's teaching, then assailed by the Semi-Pelagians in that province, were the last public acts of St. Celestin's pontificate. He died on the 6th of April, A. D. 432. Tradition attributes to this pontiff, the addition made by the Church to the Angelical Salutation: "*Sancta Maria, Mater Dei, ora pro nobis,*" which he composed on receiving, at Rome, the decree of the Council of Ephesus.

§ V. PONTIFICATE OF ST. SIXTUS III. (April 26, A. D. 432—March 28, 439).

15. St. Sixtus III. was a priest of the Roman Church, long distinguished by the depth and purity of his faith. St. Augustine addressed to him a celebrated letter on the dogma of grace. He was elected pope, by a unanimous vote, on the 26th of April, A. D. 432. The first care of the newly-elected pontiff was to write to the Eastern bishops, confirming by his apostolic authority all that had been done at the Council of Ephesus. Up to this period the Patriarch John of Antioch had held to Nestorius and refused communion with St. Cyril; but this schism was at length ended by the care of the pope and the good offices of Paul, bishop of Emesa. John of Antioch now acceded to the condemnation of Nestorius and his adherents (A. D. 433). He was followed by Theodoret of Cyrrhus, who anathematized the heresy, but withheld judgment on the person of the heresiarch. The paternal heart of the holy pontiff gave vent to its joy at this pacification, in the affectionate letters he wrote to the patriarchs of Antioch and Alexandria on the occasion. The threatening growth of the Nestorian heresy was thus checked by the energy with which it was met at the very start; but it still maintained its position as a sect, and yet counts a few adherents in some parts of the East.

16. The West had not been disturbed by this controversy. Its doctors brought, as before, the inspirations of faith, eloquence, and poetry to the service of the truth. Whilst St. Vincent of Lerins, illustrious brother of Lupus of Troyes, was engaged in his *Admonitory against Heretics* (A. D. 434), Prudentius, a Christian poet of Saragossa, had ended his days by a holy death, leaving the most elegant compositions as a monument of his faith. He made a rich display of spirit and elegance in his work entitled Περὶ στεφανῶν, or, *The Crowns*, in which he scatters the flowers of poetry upon the tombs of the martyrs. Amongst the other productions of this gifted writer, we have a work *On the Deity*, against the errors of the Jews and Pagans; one on *The*

Origin of Sin, in which he opposes the Marcionites; *On the Combat of the Soul against Vice;* two *Treatises against Symmachus*, refuting his discourse in the Roman Senate, for the reconstruction of the altar to victory; the *Cathemerinon*, or book of hymns for every day, and every hour of the day; and the *Enchiridion*, or *Manual*, an abridgment of Sacred History, in verse.

The Priest Sedulius was at the same time bringing out his *Paschal Poem*, and the *Life of Christ*, in verse, from which the Church borrows the hymns appointed for the festivals of Christmas and the Epiphany. A false rendering of St. Augustine's writings had, in the beginning of the fifth century, given rise to the error of the *Predestinarians*, who taught that God sincerely wishes to save only the predestined, and that Jesus died only for them. By the efficacious graces granted them, they are necessitated to do good and to persevere in it, since man never resists interior grace. The reprobate are, by a parallel train of reasoning, placed in the impossibility of doing good, as they are either positively determined to evil, by the will of God, or deprived of the grace necessary to abstain from it. This system of fatalism, which utterly destroys human liberty, was destined to be revived in the ninth century by a monk named Gotescalc; in the twelfth, by the Albigenses; in the fourteenth and fifteenth, by the Wickliffites and Hussites; in the sixteenth, by Luther and Calvin; and in the seventeenth, by Jansenius. The Predestinarians were refuted at their very first appearance in the world, by Gennadius, a priest of Marseilles; by the younger Arnobius, in his *Commentaries on the Psalms*, and in the *Prædestinatus*, an anonymous work attributed to him; by St. Prosper, in his *Abridged Chronicle of Ecclesiastical History;* and especially by the unknown author of the celebrated work called *Vocation of all Nations*, attributed by some critics to St. Prosper. Whilst the doctors of the West learnedly discussed the question of grace, its prodigies in the hearts of the humble and lowly held the East in admiration, in the very midst of its Nestorian troubles. St. Mary of Egypt became an inhabitant of the desert-solitude for forty-seven years of unremitting penance, to expiate her youthful irregularities; St. Maro spent his days under a tent, in continual contemplation of the mysteries of religion; his disciple, St. James the Syrian, lived exposed to the inclemency of the weather; parched in summer by the heat of the sun, buried beneath the winter's snows; always loaded with iron chains, and living on undressed herbs. St. Baradat remained for several years a self-imprisoned captive of the Lord, enclosed in a kind of wooden cage, so low and so ill-fastened, that he was completely cramped in it, and exposed to rain and heat.

17. Constantinople was at length freed from Nestorianism. Maximian had died in the odor of sanctity, leaving the see to Proclus. Since their condemnation by the Council of Ephesus, the Nestorians had been vainly trying to restore their error, by connecting it to the writings of certain ancient authors, and especially of Theodore of Mopsuesta. But this new manœuvre proved as fruitless as the preceding ones. Theodore, who had now been dead several years, had used some rather inexact terms, in trying to explain the separation of the two natures in Jesus Christ. As his real attachment to the orthodox faith had not been deeply shaken by this, and as he had moreover died in the communion of the Church, the attempt to restore the Nestorian doctrine on the foundation of his writings proved a complete failure. The internal union of the Church of Constantinople was completed by a solemnity demanded by the voice of the whole people; it was the translation of the relics of St. John Chrysostom, which were brought by order of the Emperor Theodosius, at the request of Proclus, from the scene of his holy death at Comana. The faithful met the relics with the same marks of loving enthusiasm they would have shown the eloquent patriarch had he come back to them alive. The venerated remains were taken to the Church of the Apostles, on the 27th of January, A. D. 438, on which day the Latin Church celebrates the saint's festival. The Emperor Theodosius reverently kissed the

shrine in which the relics were contained, and in the name
of his father and mother begged the saint to forgive their
unjust sentence against him. This prince, though he shared
the weakness common to those who successively occupied the
throne in that degenerate age, seems to have possessed some
sterling qualities. In the course of the year 438, he published
the *Theodosian Code*, a systematic collection, in sixteen books,
of the imperial laws and ordinances made since the time of
Constantine, for civil, military, and ecclesiastical administration. Such a work was a public benefit. Since legislation
had followed the emperors into the sphere of Christianity,
and numerous laws made under the influence of paganism had
never been revoked, there was a loose and contradictory
medley of decrees, widely different in spirit and origin. The
Theodosian Code, inspired by the spirit of Christianity, brought
back legislation to the unity which constitutes its power, consecrated the fundamental principles of all society by proclaiming the holiness and indissolubility of the marriage-tie, protecting the innocence of childhood and the honor of woman, and,
in some sort, restoring to humanity its lost dignity. The code
was intended for the East, where it did not survive eighty
years. Justinian abrogated it to make way for a new one;
but in the West it outlived the fall of the empire, and forms
the basis of modern public law. The West especially suffered
from the repeated inroads of the barbarians. Africa, which
was now in the hands of Genseric, on the 19th of October,
A. D. 439, saw Carthage forever blotted out from the list of cities.
The Vandals plundered it, and banished its chief inhabitants.
Spain and Gaul were invaded by the Suevi, the Goths, Alani,
Burgundians, and Franks. But the most destructive of all
these scourges came down from the interior of Tartary, sending terror before him, and leaving general devastation and
ruin behind. Attila, with his hordes of savage Huns, having
wasted Illyria, Pannonia, and Thrace with fire and sword, and
pushed his victorious arms to the very walls of Constantinople,
suddenly turned back upon the provinces of the West (A. D.

439). St. Sixtus III. was spared the miseries of this formidable invasion; he died on the 28th of March, A. D. 439, having held the pontifical power eight years. The last days of his reign were also devoted to the support of the ecclesiastical jurisdiction against the attempted encroachments of the Patriarch of Constantinople. He wrote to Proclus, in A. D. 437, admonishing him not to infringe upon the rights of the Metropolitan of Thessalonica, and to admit no Illyrian bishop to the communion of the Church without a letter in form from the See of Thessalonica. He gave the same instructions to Perigenes of Corinth, and reminded him that he also depended upon the same metropolitan. Thus the watchful care of the Roman pontiffs ever kept up a uniformity of government in the Church. They exercised their power only to protect the rights of all, to check usurpation, to crush schisms, to destroy growing errors, to extend the truth, and subject the world to the yoke of Jesus Christ.

CHAPTER VI.

§ I. Pontificate of St. Leo I. the Great (September 1, A. D. 439—April 11, 461).

1. Works of St. Leo the Great against different Heresies.—2. Eutyches. *Latrocinale of Ephesus.*—3. Marcian, Emperor of the East.—4. Council of Chalcedon, the Fourth of the General Councils.—5. Attila. He invades Gaul and Italy. Retires before the Majesty of St. Leo the Great.—6. New Troubles raised in the East by Eutychianism.—7. Invasion of Rome by Genseric.—8. Timothy Ælurus at Alexandria. Death of St. Leo the Great.

§ II. Pontificate of St. Hilary (Nov. 12, A. D. 461—Sept. 10, 467).

9. Election of St. Hilary.—10. Efforts of St. Hilary to uphold the Laws of the Ecclesiastical Hierarchy.—11. Councils of Arles, of Tours, and of Vannes, in Gaul.—12. Earthquake at Antioch. Burning of Constantinople. Death of St. Simeon Stylites.

§ III. Pontificate of St. Simplicius (Sept. 27, A. D. 467—To the fall of the Western Empire, August 23, A. D. 476).

13. Election of St. Simplicius.—14. St. Epiphanius of Pavia. St. Patiens of Lyons. St. Sidonius Apollinaris.—15. Odoacer, King of the Heruli, overthrows the Western Empire.

§ I. Pontificate of St. Leo I., the Great (Sept. 1, A. D. 439—April 11, 461).

1. The Church, and indeed the world at large, called for a Sovereign Pontiff endowed with an energy of character, with a moral power and dignity equal to the importance of coming events. Divine Providence, ever watchful of the welfare of His Church, had prepared for the appointed hour the man of His own choice. Leo, a Roman archdeacon, was then absent in Gaul, whither he had been sent on a mission to the General

Ætius. The esteem in which he was generally held is sufficiently clear from the fact that, though absent, the vote in his favor was unanimous. A deputation was sent to lay at his feet the homage of the whole city of Rome; and when the newly-elected pastor appeared in the midst of his flock, he was received in triumph by the people to whom he was about to devote his life. Every quality of the great man was united in St. Leo, with the deep humility and eminent virtues which adorn the saints. His flowing eloquence charmed the people; we have still the homilies and sermons delivered by him on the different solemnities. When the great pontiff, from the commanding height of his apostolic throne, cast a glance over the world, he found matter enough to awaken all his care and zeal. The Arian Vandals were pillaging the churches of Africa and Sicily; the Manichean fugitives from Carthage were pouring into Italy, and threatening to infect Rome; the Priscillianists were arousing themselves in Spain, the Pelagians in Venetia; the provinces of Gaul were shaken by internal commotions; whilst Nestorianism was still alive in the East. St. Leo proved equal to his task. He restored the churches ravaged by the Vandals, and consoled the flocks; he severely punished the abominations committed by the Manichees in their mysterious meetings (A. D. 443). An authentic account of this investigation was drawn up; and it were impossible to peruse, without a thrill of horror, the record of the fearful crimes committed by this sect of darkness. The pope wrote to all the Italian bishops, to warn them against the heretics, and to guard them against their errors (A. D. 444). St. Turribius, bishop of Astorga, sent him the report of his inquisition against the Priscillianists in Spain. St. Leo replied (A. D. 447) by a long letter, in which he meets all the errors of Priscillian, bringing them into conjunction with Manicheism, and includes them all in one condemnation. Septimius, bishop of Altinum, in Venetia, made known to the pontiff that, in his province, priests, deacons and clerics of other orders had been admitted to the communion of the Church, from the Pelagian ranks, without being previously required to make a full abjuration. The pope immediately directed the Bishop of Aquileia, metropolitan of the province, to call a council, in which all persons suspected of Pelagianism should be required to give in an open and written abjuration of the heresy. In the Gallic provinces St. Hilary of Arles was the life of the councils, and led the religious movement now manifested in that country. In A. D. 439 he presided over a council at Reez, in Provence, to put an end to a schism in the Church of Embrun, by giving it a lawful bishop. In A. D. 441 he held the first Council of Orange, celebrated by a series of thirty canons, the most noteworthy of which forbids, for the future, the ordination of deaconesses. During the same year he directed the Council of Vaison, where provision was made for the care of children abandoned in the public streets; for this barbarous custom had been retained, notwithstanding the imperial edicts which, since the days of Constantine, had continually opposed the unnatural crime. Another council, held at Besançon, drew St. Hilary into more serious difficulties. Chelidonius, bishop of Besançon, was accused of having been ordained in opposition to the canons, and of having been twice married before his promotion to the episcopacy. St. Hilary deposed him, whereupon he appealed to the pope, and set out for Rome in person. St. Hilary followed. The case was brought before a council assembled in Rome, by St. Leo (A. D. 445). Chelidonius cleared himself of every charge brought against him, and was restored to his see. The settlement of this question brought the Bishop of Arles into disfavor; and the Sovereign Pontiff deprived him of his metropolitan jurisdiction over the province of Vienne. This last decision was strengthened by a rescript of Valentinian III. (8th of July, A. D. 445), by which it was forbidden to undertake any thing in ecclesiastical government without the authority of the Apostolic See Such was the public law of the fifth century: the supremacy of the Roman Pontiff was universally recognized as a fundamental principle of religious society. St. Hilary of Arles was the first to give an example of the most respectful submission; he left no means untried to effect a reconciliation with St. Leo the Great, who was not slow to appreciate the zeal, virtue, and humility of the Bishop of Arles. The death of St. Hilary soon after threw a gloom over the whole Gallic province, and, indeed, over all the Catholic world (A. D. 447). At the moment when this holy pastor was just quitting the field of his struggles and labors, St. Germanus of Auxerre, accompanied by St. Severus, bishop of Treves, was setting out on a second mission to Great Britain. The preaching and miracles of the two holy missionaries proved too powerful for Pelagianism, which they had come to combat. They were granted the consolation of seeing the whole nation folded in the true Church before their departure from the island. St. Germanus had not had time to rest from the fatigue of the voyage, when his zealous charity urged him on to Ravenna to obtain from Valentinian III. the pardon of the rebellious Armoricans. All Italy was in wondering admiration of the prodigies which marked his journey; but death awaited him at Ravenna, the term of his pilgrimage. On the last day of July, in the year 448, he closed a holy and laborious episcopate of thirty years.

2. Four years earlier the East had been called upon to weep the loss of the Athanasius of Nestorianism. St. Cyril of Alexandria left to posterity a monument of his piety and learning, in a series of works comprising no less than seven folio volumes. He was succeeded by a bishop unworthy of the name. Dioscorus, by his slavish compliance with the imperial will, and by his bearing in regard to Eutychianism, seemed determined to blot out the noble precedents of his antecessors, St. Athanasius the Great and St. Cyril. In A. D. 448, Eutyches, the superior of a monastery near Constantinople, in combating the error of Nestorius, which divides the persons in Jesus Christ, fell into an error no less repugnant to the doctrine of the Incarnation. He asserted that there was but one nature in Jesus Christ—the divinity—which had absorbed the humanity in the process of uniting with it. The obstinacy shown by Eutyches in upholding his error, in spite of the

admonitions of his friend Eusebius of Dorylæum, and the wise counsels of Flavian, who had recently been promoted to the See of Constantinople, clearly showed his ignorance and bad faith. The true explanation of his conduct was, that he had long coveted the metropolitan dignity, which he hoped to reach by the influence of the eunuch Chrysaphius, a favorite of Theodosius, who, in his early days, had been his pupil. A disappointed ambition thus acted as the motive power of that covetous heart: how often has the Church been torn by heresies springing from the same source! Eusebius of Dorylæum made to the cause of truth the sacrifice of a life-long friendship, and became the accuser of him who had been the companion of his childhood. He arraigned him before a council assembled by Flavian at Constantinople, in A. D. 448. Eutyches at first refused to appear, but finally presented himself in the last session (November 28th); as he persisted in his error, he was condemned, deposed from the priesthood and from the government of his monastery, and excommunicated. The sentence was signed by all the bishops of the council, and by twenty-three abbots who were present.

Eutyches, after the manner of all heresiarchs, refused to submit; for the character of heresy is, after all, not so much the error of the human mind, which is but too prone to fail, as perseverance and obstinacy in clinging to the wrong opinion. Flavian sent to the pope the acts of the Council of Constantinople. Eutyches also wrote to complain of injustice in his condemnation. St. Leo foresaw at a glance all the damage that such a doctrine was calculated to inflict, if thrown into the East at a moment when all minds were turned, by the Nestorian controversy, to an inquiry into the dogma of the Incarnation. His answer to Flavian was a confirmation of every act of the council, and an encouragement to follow up the new sectary. Eutyches had also written to St. Peter Chrysologus, bishop of Ravenna, to win him over to his cause, but received, in reply, only the following eloquent appeal to forsake his error: "When Jesus Christ uttered his infant wail in the manger, the heavenly host was chanting *Glory to God in the highest!* and now, when at the name of Jesus every knee is bent in heaven, on earth and in hell, a question is raised concerning His origin! We exhort you above all things, beloved brother, to submit to what has been written by the holy Roman Pontiff; for St. Peter lives and presides in his See, and gives the truth of faith to all who sincerely seek it." Even the words of Chrysologus were powerless to move his obstinate heart. By means of Chrysaphius, Eutyches found a protector in Dioscorus of Alexandria. Through the joint influence of these two friends he obtained from the weak Theodosius the convocation of a council, which was to be ecumenical, and where the question should be once more debated. St. Leo was consulted on this subject by the court of Constantinople. He sent, as legates, Julius, bishop of Pozzuoli, in Campania; René, priest of the title of St. Clement, who died on the journey; the deacon Hilary, and Dulcitius, a notary. They bore written instructions, in which the pope establishes, beyond contradiction, the Catholic dogma concerning the two natures in Jesus Christ. One hundred and thirty bishops were assembled from the provinces of Egypt, of Asia, Pontus and Thrace; but this assembly was now to form a mere cabal, branded by history with the name of the *Latrocinale of Ephesus* (August 8th, A. D. 449). The eunuch assumed the authority of appointing the presiding officer, who was Dioscorus. The Papal Legates were given the second place, contrary to all precedent and canonical law. Some authors even assert that Dioscorus shut them out from all share in the deliberations of the council. Two counts, sent by Theodosius, with an armed escort, undertook to dictate the sentence and to carry out the orders of their master. Moreover, from the very opening of the first session, Dioscorus refused to read the instructions given by St. Leo to his Legate; but he caused the letters of convocation sent to him by the emperor to be publicly read. The council insisted upon being made acquainted with the rescript of the Roman Pontiff.

Seven times Dioscorus made the promise, but as often did he find means to put off the reading of the much-dreaded letters. He then summoned Eutyches to appear before the council. The Fathers, with St. Flavian at their head, demanded that Eusebius of Dorylæum should likewise be summoned as his accuser. The merest notion of justice would have made this a law; but Count Elpidius, the emperor's agent, objected, on the ground that Eusebius of Dorylæum, in his character of accuser, had forfeited his right to a place among the judges. Eutyches thus enjoyed the privilege of speaking alone, and without opponents. He was merely made to sign the Nicene profession, without any mention of the capital point of his error. Dioscorus pronounced him solemnly absolved from all censure previously uttered against him, and restored to the communion of the Church, to the dignity of the priesthood, and to the government of his monastery. The head of this false council then read an act of deposition against Eusebius of Dorylæum and St. Flavian of Constantinople, *who had publicly* in the words of Dioscorus, *calumniated the faith of Eutyches.* A unanimous cry of indignation broke from the assembly. The bishops who, through weakness, had signed the absolution of Eutyches, were staggered by such arbitrary despotism. To terrify them into submission, Dioscorus called upon the commissioners, who surrounded the church with armed troops. The majority of the bishops yielded to violence; but the Papal Legates openly resisted, and their protestation had to be inserted in the acts. From all sides arose the cry: "Tear in pieces all who divide the natures! Drive them out! Kill them!" From threats the soldiers came to blows and wounds. The bishops were confined amid this tumult till a late hour of the night; not even those who were oppressed by the suffocating atmosphere were allowed to go out and breathe the fresh air. At this price did Dioscorus buy one hundred and thirty signatures. To crown such a triumph, he caused a sentence of deposition to be passed against Theodoret, bishop of Cyrrhus, Ibas of Edessa, Sabinian of Perrha, and Domnus of Antioch, all remarkable for holiness and a strong attachment to the Catholic faith. He even dared to pronounce sentence of excommunication against St. Leo himself. With this excess of madness closed the *Latrocinale of Ephesus.* Eusebius of Dorylæum was thrown into prison. St. Flavian of Constantinople died in exile of the wounds he had received on this occasion. Dioscorus ordained, to fill his see, Anatolius, a deacon of his church of Alexandria, and thought to have thus planted heresy in the imperial city.

3. Theodosius immediately issued a decree, confirming, by the imperial authority, all that had been done at the Latrocinale of Ephesus. Meanwhile, St. Leo, informed by his Legates of the deplorable issue of affairs there, had called a council at Rome, where all the acts of the false council were rejected, all those unjustly condemned by it were restored, and all its sentences declared null. This circumstance showed the tireless activity of the pontiff. He simultaneously wrote letters full of burning zeal and apostolic energy to the Emperor Theodosius, to the Empress Pulcheria, to the clergy and people of Constantinople, to the superiors of the monasteries in that city, to Anastasius of Thessalonica, and to St. Flavian, whose death had not yet been communicated to him. His letter to Theodosius is full of a calm majesty which the storm cannot disturb, of feeling charity for the fallen, and of the most delicate consideration for a weak and deluded prince: "Let the bishops," says the pontiff, "enjoy the liberty of defending the true faith, which no human power can ever destroy. In supporting the cause of the Church, we uphold the cause of your empire and your own welfare. Protect the constitutions of the Church against heretics, that Christ may also protect your empire." The remedy which suggested itself to the mind of the Sovereign Pontiff in the existing crisis, was the convocation of a truly œcumenical council; and to this end he directed all his energies. To effect his object, he made use of the influence of the court of Ravenna with the Emperor Theodosius (A. D. 450). Valentinian III., and his mother, Placidia, wrote to Constantinople, to

urge the request. But Providence had reserved to itself the task of removing the obstacle presented by the weakness of Theodosius, and that in quite an unlooked-for manner. On the 28th of July, A. D. 450, the emperor died, at the age of fifty years, by a fall from his horse; the Empress Pulcheria gave the succession to Marcian, an officer whose talents and virtue called forth the admiration of the world, and made him an emperor truly worthy of the name (August 24th, A. D. 456). The new Cæsar gave his first thoughts to the pacification of the Church. When the Papal Legates reached Constantinople, with their letters for Theodosius, they found a council assembled under the auspices of Marcian, and presided over by Anatolius, St. Flavian's successor. Dioscorus's deacon, once in the patriarchal chair, showed himself, to his patron's great astonishment, a true follower of Catholic doctrine. In presence of the Papal Legates, at the head of his council, he solemnly anathematized Eutyches, his doctrine and his followers. The remains of St. Flavian were brought to Constantinople, and placed near the relics of St. John Chrysostom. All the bishops banished by the *Latrocinale of Ephesus,* for their devotion to the faith, were recalled: those who had been so weak as to subscribe the measures imposed by Dioscorus were left at the head of their dioceses, but not admitted to the communion of the Catholic Church, until an ecumenical council should have pronounced upon their case. St. Leo approved all these acts, and sent letters of communion to Anatolius, which he had hitherto refained from doing, to give himself time to learn the true sentiments of a prelate whose election, by the favor of Dioscorus, made him an object of justifiable suspicion (A. D. 450).

4. The Pope St. Leo I., and the Emperor Marcian, were equally desirous to see peace restored to the Church, by the meeting of a general council. Nice was first named as the place of meeting, but a threatened inroad of the Huns made Illyria too unsafe. The city of Chalcedon, situated on the coast of Asia Minor, near Constantinople, was then chosen. Five hundred bishops, from all the provinces of the East, met on the 8th

of October, A.D. 451, under the presidency of the Papal Legates, Pascasinus, bishop of Lilybæum, in Sicily; Lucentius, bishop of Ascoli; Basil and Boniface, priests of the Roman Church. The first session of the fourth ecumenical council was taken up by an inquisition into the acts of the *Latrocinale of Ephesus;* Dioscorus now appeared as the accused party. All the irregularities of the false council were brought forward;—the inferior rank assigned to the Papal Legates;—the refusal to read the pope's letters;—the protest of St. Flavian, and of Eusebius of Dorylæum, set at naught;—the violent measures adopted to force the bishops to sign an unjust sentence. At this particular point the Eastern bishops cried out: "We were struck; the soldiers loaded us with insults and blows. We have all erred, we beg pardon and mercy." In the second session, the doctrinal letters sent with the legates by St. Leo were publicly read. The pontiff, with an authority becoming the successor of St. Peter, here lays down the Catholic doctrine in opposition to the error of Eutyches. So exact and so pure was the statement of the doctrine, that the bishops, with one voice, exclaimed: "It is the faith of our fathers! it is the faith of the apostles! Peter has spoken by the mouth of Leo! This is the faith we all hold!" The dogmatic difficulty being thus settled, the council, in its third session, proceeded to the explicit condemnation of Dioscorus, who was unanimously anathematized. The sentence condemning him as guilty of heresy, of crime, and violation of the ecclesiastical canons, was announced to him and to the faithful of Alexandria by deputies from the council. Anatolius, Patriarch of Constantinople, signed it with the other Fathers. The Emperor Marcian banished Dioscorus to Gangres, in Paphlagonia, where he died in the year 454. The fourth session was spent in considering the various petitions sent in by Egyptian monks, whom Dioscorus had led to beg from the Fathers a recall of the sentence of deposition. But it was maintained in all its rigor. "Dioscorus has been juridically deposed!" said the Fathers. "It is God Himself Who has condemned Dioscorus!" Finally, in the fifth session, a profession of faith was drawn up in opposition to Eutychianism: "We unanimously declare," said the bishops, "that all must confess one and the same Jesus Christ, our Lord; perfect in divinity and perfect in humanity, true God and true man; possessing a reasonable soul and a body; consubstantial with the Father in divinity, and consubstantial with us in humanity; like to us in every thing save sin; begotten of the Father before all ages, as to His divinity; in these last times born of the Virgin Mary, as to His humanity, for us and for our salvation; one and the same Jesus Christ, only Son, Lord, in two natures, without confusion, without change, without division, without separation; in whom this union hinders not the difference of natures: on the contrary, preserved to each what is its own, they meet in one single person, in one hypostasis; so that Jesus Christ is not divided into two persons, but is one and the same Lord, the Word, the only Son of God." This clear, explicit, categorical expression of the dogma of the Incarnation, was received with acclamations by all the Fathers, and unanimously subscribed. To add solemnity to the reading of the profession of faith, the Emperor Marcian was present in person at the sixth session, where it was published. He announced that after the example of Constantine, he had come into the holy assemblage only to lend the imperial authority to the decisions of the council, and not to interfere with the freedom of suffrage. This noble expression of sentiment drew from all the bishops the exclamation: "Long live the new Constantine! Long live the pious and orthodox emperor and empress! A long and happy reign to Marcian!" The emperor called for the reading of the profession of faith, and asked if all agreed upon what they had just heard. They all replied: "We have but one faith and one doctrine. This is the belief of the holy doctors; it is that of the Apostles. This faith has saved the world!" Marcian published a decree confirmatory of the profession of faith drawn up by the council, and condemning Eutyches, who soon afterwards died, at the age of seventy-five years. In the remaining sessions, the Fathers gave their attention to some matters of discipline: forbidding the erection of a monastery without the consent of the bishop and of the owners of the place; the submission of monks to diocesan authority; forbidding clerics and religious to take upon themselves any tutorage or administration, and to pass from one Church to another, without permission of the Ordinary. So far all the acts of the council had been perfectly regular. The only dissonance which affected the harmony existing between the Papal Legates and the Fathers of the Council of Chalcedon, arose from an attempt of Anatolius. The besetting ambition of the patriarchs of Constantinople had ever been to raise their see to the second place in the Church, and to make it first after that of Rome. Anatolius thought this a favorable moment to renew the attempt; the service he had done the Catholic cause, the zeal displayed by him against the Eutychian heresy, the letters of communion, so lately received from the Sovereign Pontiff, all inspired the most sanguine hope of success. The twenty-eighth canon of the Council of Chalcedon was then drawn up to that effect; but the legates loudly protested against the innovation. "The holy and Apostolic Pontiff," said they, "gave us these amongst his other instructions: Should any prelate, looking too much to the splendor of his city, wish to arrogate to himself any prerogative whatever, oppose the attempt with all becoming firmness." The legates supported this noble sentiment, by reading the sixth canon of the Nicene Council, where the question had, as we have seen, already been decided. The close of the council was not delayed by the debate thus left pending. The bishops separated (November, A. D. 451), with the hope that their harmony and pious efforts had secured long years of peace to the Church. They had sent the acts of the council, with a synodal letter, to the pope. They begged him especially to confirm, "by his Apostolic authority," the privilege they had deemed it right to grant to the See of Constantinople. Anatolius urged the same petition in private letters. St. Leo stood out firmly against this claim. His reply to Anatolius, and his letters to the Emperor Marcian and the Empress Pulcheria (A. D. 452), show a pontiff most watchful to guard the prescriptions of the hierarchical canons, even at the risk of displeasing the powers of earth. The pope's refusal to confirm the twenty-eighth canon, relative to the pre-eminence of the See of Constantinople over the apostolic patriarchates, gave occasion to the partisans of Eutyches to assert that St. Leo had not ratified the acts of the Council of Chalcedon. The Sovereign Pontiff accordingly found it necessary to make a public statement of what he had already written to the emperor and to Anatolius. He confirmed all that had been decided in questions of dogma; but still protested against the ambitious attempt of the Patriarch of Constantinople.

5. Whilst this great pontiff thus brought back peace and unity of faith to the Church in the East, he had in the West checked the onward course of the fierce king of the Huns, who was pushing on his victorious hordes over the ruins of the Roman world. Attila, the most formidable *mower of men* who had yet led on the barbarian invaders, seemed born for the terror of the world. He had come originally from the forests of Tartary, and his destiny appeared to be attended by something inexplicably terrific, which made a fearful impression upon the generality of men. His gait and carriage were full of pride and haughtiness; the movements of his body and the rolling of his eyes spoke his conscious power. His short stature, broad chest, and still larger head, thin beard, and swarthy features, plainly told his origin. His capital was a camp in the fields by the Danube. The kings he had conquered kept guard by turns at the door of his tent. His own table was set with wooden platters and coarse food, whilst his soldiers sported with gold and silver vases. Enthroned upon a low stool, the Tartar chief received the ambassadors of Valentinian III. and Theodosius the Younger, whose credulity he deceived in a manner that would have done credit to the most practised courtier of Constantinople or of Rome. He said of himself, with savage energy: "The star falls, the earth trembles; I am the hammer

of the universe. The grass never grows again where Attila's horse has once trod." He claimed the official title of *Scourge of God*. The two emperors of Ravenna and of Constantinople thought to stop the barbarian at their gates, by allowing him the title of *General of the Empire*, and allowing him a tribute which they regarded as his pay. The Hun remarked on this subject: "The generals of emperors are servants; Attila's servants are emperors." He one day sent two Goths, one to Theodosius II., the other to Valentinian III., with this message: "Attila, my master and yours, orders you to prepare him a palace." This meant an invasion.* Dragging along with him a train of tributary princes and five hundred thousand barbarians, he crossed the Rhine and pushed on through the provinces of Gaul (A. D. 451). This was the precise period at which the fourth general council was to have met at Nice, in Illyria; the terror inspired by the arms of Attila had caused it to be transferred to Chalcedon. Maestricht, Rheims, Arras, Cambray, Besançon, Langres, and Auxerre were given up to pillage and to the violence of an unbridled soldiery. Metz had provoked a redder vengeance by a longer resistance, and saw its streets flowing with the blood of the greater part of its inhabitants. The survivors, with their bishop, were led away captives, and the city, given up to the flames, was soon but a heap of ashes. Troyes was threatened with the same fate. Its holy bishop, Lupus, importuned the mercy of God by his ceaseless prayers, tears, fasts, and good works. At length, inspired with a supernatural confidence, he goes forth in full pontifical attire, to meet the barbarian, and asks him: "Who art thou that dost overcome so many kings and nations, ruin so many cities, and subdue the world?" Attila replied: "*I am King of the Huns, the Scourge of God!*" "If thou art the scourge of my God," returned the bishop, "remember to do only what is allowed thee by the hand that moves and governs thee." Attila, astonished at the boldness of this address, and awed by

---

* M. DE CHATEAUBRIAND: *Etudes Historiques.*

the majesty of the holy prelate, promised to spare the city, and passed through it without doing it any harm. In Paris, such was the dismay that the inhabitants were preparing to leave the city, with their wives and children, to seek the protection of some more strongly fortified place. St. Genevieve, the humble virgin of Nanterre, consecrated to God by Sts. Germanus and Lupus, became the patroness and mother of the city. She restored the failing courage, provided for every want, procured means of subsistence for the affrighted multitude, and promised, in the name of Heaven, that Attila should not approach the walls of Paris. In effect, Attila, suddenly changing the direction of his march, fell, with his savage hordes, upon the city of Orleans. This city, which seemed marked out for miraculous deliverances, was then governed by the holy Bishop St. Aignan, to whom it owed its safety. He had been able to go to Arles and solicit help from Ætius, the Roman general. Just as Orleans was on the point of opening its gates to the besiegers, the combined armies of Ætius and Theodoric, king of the Visigoths, came within sight of its walls. Attila, foaming with rage, raised the siege, and in the plain of Chalons sought a field in which he could display his forces and meet his opponents. The confederates counted a body of Franks commanded by their Prince Meroveus. The two armies, now encamped face to face, numbered about a million warriors. They met; and then ensued one of the bloodiest battles that crimson the pages of history. Three hundred thousand slain encumbered the field; a little neighboring stream was swelled like a torrent by the quantity of blood that flowed into its channel. Theodoric fell, but his valor had won the victory for the allies. Attila was utterly defeated, and recrossed the Rhine in hasty flight. In the following year (A. D. 452) he reappeared, more formidable than ever, on the borders of Italy, leaving Pannonia and Noricum wasted by fire and sword. Valentinian III. made a precipitate retreat from Ravenna, and hastened to seek shelter within the walls of Rome. Attila besieged and destoyed the cities of Aquileia, Padua, Vicenza, Verona, Brescia, and Bergamo; Milan and Pavia were given up to pillage. The Hun pushed on amid the smoking ruins of the conquered cities, and halted near Mantua, on the banks of the Mincio; the terrified inhabitants fled at his approach, and sought, in the marshes where Venice now stands, a refuge from the violence of the victorious barbarians. The last hour of the Roman Empire seemed at hand; St. Leo succeeded in warding off the threatened ruin. He appeared before Attila as the ambassador of Heaven, as a herald of peace. The two great sovereignties of the Word and the Sword stood face to face; and the Sword bowed before the majesty of the Gospel. Attila was awed by the bearing of the great pontiff whose fame had reached the remote borders of Tartary, and he lent a favorable ear to his propositions; quitting the soil of Italy, he withdrew across the Danube, where death suddenly snatched him from the midst of his plans of destruction (A. D. 453). On his return from the successful embassy, the pope was received in triumph, and the enthusiastic people bestowed upon him the title of Great.

6. The bright halo of genius shed around the person of the holy pontiff, wonderfully enhanced the splendor and majesty of the Apostolic See. His letters were received in all the Churches of the world with marks of the deepest veneration and filial submission. The bishops of Gaul wrote to him to express the universal admiration they excited among them. "It is just," wrote the bishops, "that the primacy of St. Peter's See should be established there, where the tradition of the oracles of the Apostolic spirit is maintained." They met in council, to receive the condemnation of Eutyches, and thanked the holy pontiff for his care in warding off the errors which had not yet taken root among them. The same peace and harmony did not, however, reign in the Eastern Churches. The deposition of Dioscorus, by the Fathers of Chalcedon, gave rise to serious disorders in Alexandria. The inhabitants were divided between Proterius, snewly elected, and Dioscorus, in exile. The partisans of Dioscorus insulted the magistrates and stoned the soldiers sent to put down the sedition. The

troops took refuge in the Temple of Serapis, where they were besieged by the enraged mob. This furious populace, maddened by resistance, set fire to the temple, and burned the prisoners alive. The Emperor Marcian took severe measures to repress the outbreak. Proterius, the new patriarch, had, meanwhile, written to Pope St. Leo, to have his election confirmed by the authority of the Apostolic See; having given satisfactory evidence of the purity of his faith, he received letters of communion from the pope (A. D. 454). Palestine was at this time in the hands of a Eutychian faction, who refused to submit to the Council of Chalcedon. Theodosius, an intruded bishop, had seized upon the patriarchal throne of Jerusalem, and was supported by the intrigues of some monks attached to Eutychianism, and especially by the favor of Eudoxia, widow of Theodosius II., who was now residing in Palestine. St. Leo, anxious to withdraw this princess from the path of error, wrote her an admirable letter, which forms a complete treatise on the dogma of the Incarnation. The controversy between the two parties had taken the form of a grammatical logomachy, and turned upon the difference between the particles *of* and *in*. The schismatics held that Jesus Christ, God and man, is *of* two natures; the Catholics maintained that Christ, being true God and true man, is not only *of* two natures, but also *in* two natures. To make the latter expression more clear, it must be understood that Eutyches and Dioscorus, by the expression, *of* two natures, implied *before the Incarnation;* teaching that they had afterwards been blended in a single nature in the Man-God. Hence the earnestness with which the Catholics insisted upon the expression: *in two natures*. To the monks who had fomented these divisions the pope wrote the most eloquent letters: "To what would you have been brought by bloody persecution, iron hooks, tortures and executioners, when the weak efforts of wretched heretics have sufficed to rob you of the purity of your faith! You think yourselves arrayed in defence of the truth, whilst you dare to wage war against the truth! You take up arms in the name of the Church, but in reality you rend the bosom of the

Church! Is this what you have learned from the Prophets, the Evangelists and Apostles?" These exhortations, seconded by the watchful energy of the Emperor Marcian, produced their effect. The intruded bishop was driven from his usurped throne, and the lawful patriarch, Juvenal, restored to the full enjoyment of his rights (A. D. 454). Not one of the many questions then troubling the harmony of the Eastern Churches was excluded from the solicitude of Leo the Great. On learning the restoration of Juvenal to the See of Jerusalem, he immediately wrote to the Patriarch of Antioch, encouraging him to a steady defence of his rights as metropolitan, which the bishops of Jerusalem had attempted to dispute. "No individual ambition," wrote the pontiff, "shall ever lessen the privileges of the Church of Antioch; I hold the Nicene canons in too great esteem ever to allow their infringement by any innovation." With a view to establish unity of government on a firmer basis, he constituted Theodoret, bishop of Cyrrhus, his legate for the provinces of the Euphrates and Armenia. Julian of Cos held the same powers at Constantinople; he acquainted St. Leo with the suspicious conduct of Anatolius, patriarch of the city, in regard to the few remaining Eutychians who still kept up their cabals. Ætius, a Catholic archdeacon, had been unjustly deprived of his position which was given to a Eutychian. The pope required the patriarch to restore Ætius to his dignity. Marcian also used his influence to the same end, and Anatolius complied. He still, however, claimed the privileges granted him by the surreptitious canon of the Council of Chalcedon. The pope reproved him severely for this, and the patriarch, without urging the matter again, replied by acknowledging the necessity of the pontifical sanction in the case. "As to the decision in favor of the See of Constantinople," says the patriarch, "rest assured that I have had no part in it. Besides, it has been left to the authority of your Holiness to confirm every thing that was done in the council." These exterior occupations did not suffice to absorb the tireless energy of St. Leo; he now set about regulating the time of the Paschal celebration. By his direction Victorius of Aquitaine undertook to draw up a Paschal canon, more exact, extensive, and scientific than any yet adopted. In this work the learned Gaul traced up the whole succession of lunations and days to the beginning of the world, according to the chronology of Eusebius. He carried out his system to the year 559 of the Christian Era. The cycle of Victorius, published in A. D. 457, became the standard of the Latin Church, and served as a basis for all future undertakings of a like nature.

7. Political events of fearful import were thickening in the West. Valentinian III., wholly given up to pleasure and to his eunuchs, was unable to govern himself. Ætius, who had won imperishable glory on the field of Chalons, soon became hateful to the weak emperor. One day Valentinian III. summoned him to the palace, and in the heat of the discussion ran him through with his sword. Among the courtiers there was one Roman worthy of the name, who had the courage to say to the emperor: "You have just cut off your right hand with your left." But a few days later Valentinian himself fell under the daggers of assassins paid by the Senator Maximus, who aspired to the throne (A. D. 455). The murderer immediately assumed the purple, purchased at the price of crime, and obliged the Empress Eudoxia, widow of his victim, to receive his hand, still red with her husband's blood. Eudoxia thought to avenge her honor and her husband's death, by sacrificing to resentment her country's sacred interests. She invited Genseric, king of the Vandals, to Rome, promising her help to put him in possession of the city. The barbarian king sailed from Africa with a formidable fleet. The tidings of his approach went before him, and spread terror throughout the whole of Italy; the crowned assassin, Maximus, was preparing to fly from Rome, and showed a dastardliness which excited the contempt of his own courtiers. Some of his attendants murdered him, cut him in pieces, and threw the mangled members into the Tiber (June 12th, A. D. 455). Genseric was now three days' march from Rome. But one power remained unshaken in the threatened capital; one man alone, in the general consternation, had kept all his

courage, all his energy. This power was the papacy; this man was St. Leo the Great. Once before he had saved Rome from the invasion of Attila; now again he shielded it from the fury of Genseric. The pontiff went forth to meet the Vandal king, without the walls of the city, and exacted from him a promise to respect the lives and honor of the unfortunate Romans, and to spare the public monuments. More than this could not be expected from a royal barbarian, leading on his savage hordes to the sack of Rome, as to a long-looked-for reward. The pillage lasted fourteen days. Amongst the richest treasures seized by the barbarians were the sacred vessels brought from Jerusalem by Titus. The Vandals led away several thousand captives; the Empress Eudoxia, who had brought on the invasion, was forced, with her two daughters, to follow in captivity; bitter mockery of a pitiless barbarian! The band of wretched exiles found, upon the shores of a strange land, a consoler and father, in the holy Bishop of Carthage, called *Deogratias*. To redeem the captives, he sold all the gold and silver vessels used in the service of the altar. He provided a shelter for them by making hospitals of two large churches in Carthage, which he furnished with beds and straw, and here he spent whole nights, with his own hands attending those whom fatigue and grief had prostrated. When death snatched away the pious pontiff from the midst of these charitable cares, the Roman captives felt as though they had again fallen into slavery. Their sad condition was aggravated by the cruelty of Genseric towards the Catholics. The Vandal closed the Church of Carthage, and scattered its priests and ministers in different directions to the shores of Spain and Italy, to Sardinia, Sicily, Greece, Epirus and Dalmatia, and even into Venetia. As he was sailing out of the port of Carthage, on one of his errands of rapine, his pilot asked him to what country he should shape his course: "To that one on which God's anger rests!" answered Genseric. The Roman Empire thus became in some sort the domain of the barbarians. Emperors succeeded each other at the will of Count Ricimer, who, with the title of general of the empire, really wielded the sovereign power through these ephemeral monarchs. From the year 456 to 461, Avitus, Majorian, Severus, successively sat upon the imperial throne, displaying different qualities, but all equally powerless to shake off the rule of Ricimer. Whilst the West was thus beginning to feel the throes of its last agony, the Eastern Empire mourned an accomplished prince, its Emperor Marcian (A. D. 457). Burning with all the zeal of Constantine for religion, he was free from that emperor's deplorable inconsistency, which overthrew heresy at the outset, only to restore it to a life of many centuries. He possessed all the good and generous qualities of Theodosius the Great, without his violent fits of anger. Though of an obscure origin, he raised the fallen majesty of the empire; and when Attila imperiously claimed his payment of an annual tribute, he answered with true Roman dignity: "I have gold for my friends, but steel for my enemies." Pope St. Leo, his friend and admirer, pronounced his memory holy and venerable; the Greek Church honors him together with his empress, St. Pulcheria, on the 17th of February. The Eastern sceptre passed into the hands of Leo the Thracian, governor of Selymbria, who was raised to the imperial throne by the influence of a barbarian, the patrician Aspar. Aspar hoped to find in him a pliant tool; but his hopes were cruelly disappointed. When the patrician required the new emperor to confer the title of Cæsar upon one of his sons, according to a previous understanding, with the remark that "it does not become one who wears the purple to break his word,"—"Does it become him better," answered Leo, "to be treated as a slave?"

8. Still, Leo the Thracian, with all his instincts of sovereignty, was far from being a great prince, and though he professed Catholicity, he yet by no means showed the same zeal as Marcian in its support. In the beginning of his reign the Eutychian party revived in Egypt. Timothy Ælurus,* a

---

* Ælurus, from the Greek word αἴλουρος (cat); which name he obtained by running during the night to the cells of the monks, calling them by name, and speaking to them through a hollow reed. He told them he was an angel sent from heaven, to warn them

monk interdicted on account of his attachment to heresy, gathered, by means of bribery, a band of seditious characters in the neighborhood of Alexandria. With these followers he entered the city, and proceeded to the church, and even there murdered the holy patriarch, Proterius, whose body was dragged through the streets, amid the jeers of the mob. Timothy then publicly assumed episcopal jurisdiction in Alexandria. He pronounced an anathema against the Council of Chalcedon and all who received it, including, of course, St. Leo, Anatolius of Constantinople, and Basil of Antioch. All the Catholic bishops of the province were driven from their sees, and creatures of the intruded metropolitan substituted in their place. Julian of Cos, the pope's Legate at Constantinople, informed St. Leo of the lamentable state of the Church of Alexandria. Timothy Ælurus and his partisans had petitioned the emperor, Leo the Thracian, to call a council for the purpose of revising that of Chalcedon. The pope strenuously opposed the measure, which was likewise rejected by all the Eastern metropolitans. "The troubles of the Church would never cease," wrote the pope to the emperor, "if discussions were renewed at the will of the heretics" (A.D. 457). To give his views more weight at the Court of Constantinople, St. Leo sent two legates, Domitian and Geminian (A.D. 458), bearing ample instructions for the emperor. At their request, Leo the Thracian determined to send positive orders to Styla, imperial governor of Alexandria, for the expulsion of Timothy Ælurus. The usurper was sent in exile to Chersonesus, under a strong guard, and replaced at Alexandria by a lawfully elected patriarch, Timothy *Solofaciolus*, who immediately begged the confirmation of his election by the Sovereign Pontiff. The decisions of the great pope were sought for by all the bishops of the world, at a time when the torrent of invasion, pouring over every point of the Roman frontier, added daily increasing difficulties to the administration. St. Leo's correspondence is an immense collection of solutions of every sort—of

to fly the communion of Proterius, and to elect in his stead Timothy, that is to say, himself.

theological discussions; of cases of conscience cleared up by the canonical rules. In the hundred and seventy-three letters which we have of him, pastors will ever find a finished model of spiritual government. Death at last relieved him from so much care and labor (April 11, A. D. 461). He has left us an imperishable monument of his apostolic eloquence in sixty-nine discourses, in which he exposes, with admirable clearness, the highest mysteries of Christian philosophy. Though the writings of St. Leo the Great are not entirely free from some slight blemishes, due to the bad taste of the age in which he lived, they are yet very remarkable for loftiness and elegance of style, precision and clearness of thought, powerful reasoning, and the moving bursts of a brilliant eloquence, which captivates the mind and pierces the heart. To these labors of the closet we must join the great deeds of his glorious pontificate: the ignominy attached to the Catholic faith by the *Latrocinale of Ephesus*, redeemed by the Fourth General Council of Chalcedon; Rome saved, once from the invasion of Attila, and again from murder and flames threatened by Genseric; the East rescued from the pollution of Eutychianism, placing itself under the shadow of Peter's Chair, to walk hand in hand with the West, under the guidance of the great Roman unity; and then we shall understand how time has but confirmed the title of Great given by a loving people to a pontiff who worked so many wonders amid the din of ceaseless revolutions and crumbling thrones, of murdered emperors and a ruined world. St. Leo is supposed to be the first pope who accredited apostolic nuncios to foreign courts. We have seen that Julian of Cos resided in that capacity at the Court of Constantinople, under the Emperor Marcian. That nuncio's credentials are worthy of note. "I beg," writes St. Leo to Marcian, "that you will receive with affection and kindness our venerable brother, the Bishop Julian; in his respect and attention you will find a living image of my presence. I trust in the sincerity of his faith, and have delegated to him all my powers against the heretics of our time; I have moreover required him, for the better maintenance of

throughout the Eastern Churches, to remain close to your person." Such is the first trace we find in ecclesiastical history of apostolic nunciatures, now established in every Christian court, to represent the authority of the Holy See, and to guard the great interests of religion, with sovereigns and nationalities. Shortly before his death St. Leo had abolished the custom then creeping into some churches, of reading aloud the sins of those who were subjected to canonical penance. The pope decreed that they should not pass beyond private confession, made to an approved priest, which was all that was needed.

§ 2. PONTIFICATE OF ST. HILARY (Sept. 10, A. D. 461—Nov. 17, 467).

9. St. Leo the Great was succeeded by the Archdeacon Hilary, one of the legates of the Holy See to the *Latrocinale of Ephesus*, where he had shown equal nobleness of soul and courage (Sept. 10, A. D. 461). The first act of St. Hilary, in his new dignity, was to write a decretal to all the Eastern Churches, confirming the Councils of Nice, of Ephesus, and of Chalcedon; he also renewed the condemnation of Nestorius and Eutyches, with their adherents, and recalled the great principle of authority and of the primacy of the Apostolic See, as the centre and basis of the government of the Church. He at the same time addressed a circular to the Western bishops, to inform them of his election to the Sovereign Pontificate. "As the Roman Church is the mother of all the others," wrote Leontius of Arles, in reply, "we are rejoiced to learn that in the midst of the general consternation, in this great infirmity of the age, you have been promoted to judge the people, to direct the nations in their way upon earth."

10. The trouble of the times to which Leontius alludes was complicated by political events, and by the daily increasing imminence of a barbarian invasion. The din of arms resounded through the whole empire, and directions were no longer received from the emperors of the West, who succeeded each

other on the throne according to the caprice of the Goth,
Ricimer. But in the midst of this general decline, St. Hilary
held the reins of ecclesiastical power with a firm hand. The
acts of his short pontificate all tend to draw closer the hierarchical bond, to keep in the episcopal sees zealous and able
prelates, and to check the ravages of heresy. In A. D. 460,
Rusticus, Bishop of Narbonne, had begged St. Leo's consent
to retire from his see and lead a life of solitude and quiet.
The holy pontiff had refused his permission, at the same time
urging the pious bishop to place the general good of the Church
before his personal inclination. Rusticus submitted. In A. D.
451 he consecrated his archdeacon, Hermes, Bishop of Beziers.
The inhabitants of Beziers refused to receive Hermes: pending the difficulty Rusticus died, and Hermes procured his own
election to the See of Narbonne. This translation was denounced to the pope as contrary to canonical rule. Two
bishops, Faustus of Reez, and Auxianus of Aix, appointed to
examine into the matter, came to Rome and assisted at a
council which was then sitting there (November 19, A. D. 462).
The case of Hermes was discussed, and the pope communicated the result of the council to the bishops of the provinces
of Vienne, Lyons, Narbonne, and the Alps. It was determined
that, for the sake of peace and to be indulgent towards Hermes,
he should remain in the See of Narbonne. But lest this case
should be urged as a precedent, it was further decided that
Hermes should not be empowered to ordain the bishops of
his province; this power was transferred to the Bishop of
Uzes, the most ancient in the province. At the death of
Hermes, the right of ordaining was to revert to the Bishop of
Narbonne, as metropolitan. The maintenance of hierarchical
subordination between bishops was all-important at a period
when multiplied revolutions worked continual changes in the
temporal rulers of the provinces. The popes, therefore, kept
an ever-watchful eye to this matter; St. Hilary showed this
in the case of Mammertus, Bishop of Vienne, whose name now
appears in the catalogue of saints, and who had just instituted

the feast of the *Rogations*, or annual processions to invoke the blessing of God upon the fruits of the earth. In his quality of metropolitan, Mammertus claimed jurisdiction over the Church of Dia,* where he consecrated a bishop against the wish of the people. Leontius of Arles, to whom this prerogative rightfully belonged, appealed to the pope, who censured the conduct of St. Mammertus, and directed that the election of the Bishop of Dia, to be valid, should be confirmed by Leontius of Arles.

11. The same principle was established at the same time against Sylvanus, Bishop of Calahorra, in Castile. He had also consecrated a bishop without the consent of his metropolitan of Tarragona. The case was examined by a council assembled in Rome, and a decision rendered similar to that against St. Mammertus; and the new bishop was sent to his metropolitan to receive the confirmation of his authority. The attention of the Council of Rome was called to another violation of the canons, in the Church of Barcelona. The Bishop Nundinarius, had, on his death-bed, expressed a desire to leave the see to Irenæus, already bishop of another city; in accordance with the wish of the deceased prelate, the translation took place. Some examples of similar proceedings gave a color of regularity to the translation. To guard against any such abuses for the future, the pope declared the translation of Irenæus null, and ordered the see to be filled by the regular process of election. He earnestly inveighed against the tendency to make the episcopacy hereditary, thus lowering to the level of a bequest, a dignity which can be conferred only by the grace of Jesus Christ. With a view to enforce the canonical rules and the observance of these decrees in Spain, the pope sent the sub-deacon Trajan to that court, as his Legate. He recommended the holding of provincial councils, as one of the best means for keeping up a true spirit of discipline in the various churches.

* Dia, *Dea Vocontiorum*. This city was until the thirteenth century the see of a suffragan of Valence. It is now included in the department of the Drôme.

It is a remarkable fact in the history of the Church, that the regular development of its institutes, discipline, and liturgy is always in exact proportion to the freedom enjoyed by the bishops to meet in council and discuss matters of general interest. As the interference of the temporal power in the councils held under such princes as Constantius and Valens was productive of the most afflicting evils, so the councils freely assembled, and unrestrained by exterior influence, bore the happiest fruits of prosperity to the Church, of uniform direction in government, and of spiritual good in the hearts of the faithful. The Gallic bishops entered fully into the views of St. Hilary. The Councils of Arles, Tours, and Vannes were held at this time, and gave proof of their zeal in carrying on the work begun by the Holy See, as well as of the apostolic vigor with which they had determined to maintain the rules of canonical discipline. The Council of Arles was called upon to settle a question of episcopal jurisdiction over monasteries, in the case of the famous Abbey of Lerins. It was decided that the Bishop of Arles should alone be entitled to ordain clerics to the different orders; but all the lay-religious were to remain subject to the abbot, whose election and administration were to be free from episcopal jurisdiction. The Council of Tours renewed the ordinances relating to the continence of clerics, and ordained that they should not quit their diocese without the bishop's cognizance: the degrees of the hierarchy and the rights of the various jurisdictions were also established by the same council. The Fathers of Vannes confirmed most of the ordinances passed at Tours, and extended to monks the prohibition to travel without letters of recommendation from their bishop. A particular ordinance was passed by the council concerning divination, or *the lot of the saints*, and the most severe punishments were decreed against it. It is not unworthy of remark, that this superstitious practice began to prevail in the West at a time when actual occurrences full of trouble and suffering naturally led the mind to peer into the mysterious darkness of the future. And besides, the total disorder into which the barbarian inroads had thrown the political world, necessarily produced its counterpart in the moral and intellectual world, which thus sunk to a somewhat lower level.

12. During the short pontificate of St. Hilary the East presents the unwonted sight of an interval of peace, in which the heretical spirit of discord seems for a season to slumber. The barbarians, in the magnitude of their preparations for the great Roman invasion, seemed to disregard the Greek Empire. This period of religious quiet is marred by only two disastrous events: the almost total ruin of the wealthy and prosperous city of Antioch by a violent earthquake, which destroyed most of its monuments; and a conflagration which lasted seven days, and laid in ashes eight of the twelve districts composing the opulent city of Constantinople. These two terrible disasters gave occasion to a proportionable marvel of charity. St. Simeon Stylites lived near Antioch. After the destruction of the city, a countless multitude of the inhabitants came to the miraculous pillar of Stylites to seek protection from the wrath of Heaven. "I do not think," says an eye-witness, "that the desert ever saw such a multitude within the memory of living man. God seemed to have drawn all the nations of the world from their homes, to gather them together under the care of His servant." St. Simeon directed his disciples to satisfy the wants of the immense throng, whilst he restored their courage by his words, his fervent prayers, and boundless charity in their behalf. The concourse of people lasted fifty days, when he again addressed the crowd, exhorting them to keep the commandments of God and the practices of a Christian life; then he added: "Return now to your homes; go without fear to your various duties; God will have mercy upon you." One month later St. Simeon Stylites received the final summons; he turned his eyes towards the four quarters of the world, gave them his blessing for the last time, and leaning his head upon the shoulder of one of his disciples, expired. Constantinople saw an imitator of this virtue, and of the same extraordinary manner of life, in Daniel the Stylite. When the flames had destroyed two-thirds of the

city of Constantine, the inhabitants also hastened to place themselves under the protection of the Stylite, who seemed placed between heaven and earth to offer up the prayers and tears of men in atonement to divine justice. The Emperor Leo the Thracian came himself, with the empress, to beg his intercession on behalf of his people; the prayer of the holy hermit became a sort of buckler to the empire (A. D. 465).

Ricimer had, in the mean time, seated upon the Roman throne another shadow of an emperor; Anthemius, a son-in-law of Marcian, had come from Constantinople to assume his short-lived honors. He was accompanied by a Macedonian heretic called Philotheus, who sought by means of his position at court to introduce his errors at Rome. St. Hilary met the attempt with his wonted energy. As the emperor was present one day at a solemnity in the basilica of St. Peter, the pope addressed him publicly, and made him promise to oppose the efforts of the Macedonians. With this act of apostolic energy the career of the holy pontiff fitly ends; he died on the 10th of September, A. D. 467. St. Hilary had ordered the establishment of two libraries in the Lateran basilica. Thus papal vigilance opened a repository for the treasures of intellect, during a period when their existence was threatened for centuries by barbarian invasions.

§ III. PONTIFICATE OF ST. SIMPLICIUS, *First Part* (Sept. 27, A. D. 467, to the extinction of the Western Empire, Aug. 23, A. D. 476).

13. When St. Simplicius ascended the chair of St. Peter (Sept. 27, A. D. 467), the Roman Empire was already tottering to decay. The internal revolutions by which it was torn awaked no echo amongst the indifferent people. They saw Anthemius murdered by Ricimer and succeeded by Olybrius, who was soon in turn displaced by Glycerius, commander of the imperial guard. The vital power of this society, with its barbarian element, accustomed to political strife, careless of its ceaseless

change of masters, was wholly centred in the Catholic Church, the only government which presented the spectacle of an intellectual and moral unity. Following the tradition of his predecessors, and with a view to draw the various nations closer to the Holy See, St. Simplicius named a Vicar-Apostolic to Spain. It is probable that the same custom was then established in regard to all the other kingdoms. We have already seen it carried out in Constantinople, as also in Illyria and Armenia.

14. The lowered standard of moral character, that unfailing forerunner of the fall of empires, was strikingly visible in the political world. But the Church escaped the universal degeneracy. Miracles of holiness illustrated the principal Western Sees. Pavia was in a transport of love and admiration for its bishop, St. Epiphanius, then only thirty years of age. No character, however passionate or fierce, had yet been found to resist the heavenly influence of the young and pious prelate. His contemporaries said of him: "Epiphanius would persuade the most savage beast. When he comes to ask a favor, it is offered before it is known. His countenance is like the very radiance of life." St. Epiphanius sometimes interposed in the strifes occasioned by Ricimer's ambition, between himself and his sceptred victims, and always with the success that attended his every act. He was especially triumphant in an embassy on which he was sent by the haughty minister to the Emperor Anthemius. War appeared unavoidable, and Italy seemed fated to see the crowning of her miseries by an intestine strife, in which her children should meet to shed each other's blood. The universal voice of the people called for St. Epiphanius as the only possible mediator. The Ligurian nobles came to Milan, and throwing themselves at the feet of Ricimer, with tears in their eyes, begged him to put an end to such fatal dissensions by choosing the holy Bishop of Pavia for his ambassador. Epiphanius was accordingly sent to Rome, with propositions of peace to Anthemius. Shouts of enthusiasm met him in all parts of the city; he received public marks of veneration; and when he appeared before the emperor, it was in the midst of a proces-

sion of Romaus, who bore him on in triumph. His eloquent and persuasive words softened the harsh and resentful feelings awakened in the emperor's breast by the conduct of Ricimer. "Through your mediation," said the emperor, "I now first tender the favor which I had determined to refuse an arrogant minister. If he has deceived you, he will but injure himself. For myself, I place my person and the empire in your keeping." This splendid homage had been won by the eminent virtue of St. Epiphanius—his patience, mortification, burning charity, zeal for study and love for the sacred writings, recalled the life and the labors of the most illustrious doctors. Whilst this light shone in Italy, Gaul was not without its holy bishops, to guide the flocks in safety through the ruin and desolation that filled the land. St. Patiens, metropolitan of Lyons, had made himself the living providence of all his suffragan churches. A general famine, a relic of the barbarian inroads, ravaged the southern portion of Gaul. St. Patiens multiplied the resources of his charity to meet so many wants. Great cargoes of wheat, shipped by his care on the Saône and Rhone, carried plenty and life to Arles, Riom, Avignon, Orange, Viviers, and Valence. "Thus," says Sidonius Apollinaris, to whom we owe these details, "when the storm of barbarian invasion has ruined the harvests, a bishop supplies the wants of a whole people; the universal misery finds relief in him alone." The bishops now began to be viewed by the people in a light which explains the political attitude they were soon, by force of circumstances, obliged to assume before the world. It has not been carefully enough remarked that the movement which led the Church to take the direction of temporal matters, and which shows its ever-increasing activity in great political events, was a spontaneous and natural impulse of the people, who gathered of necessity about the only centre of power and life. The Papacy and the Episcopate were no usurping powers; the very instinct of preservation brought the conquered to seek their protection; a recognized moral superiority compelled the homage of the conquering tribes: thus every force which sunk the empire of

Pagan Rome, only gave a new elevation to the power of Christian Rome. St. Sidonius Apollinaris, the poet, historian, and polished writer, whose works give us the best account of this period of transition, was Bishop of Clermont. Nephew of the Emperor Avitus, whom the fleeting favor of the Goth, Ricimer, had raised to an hour of imperial dignity, Sidonius made his first public appearance in the conduct of political affairs, and discharged his high and important duties, with all the qualities of a great man. He possessed every gift that could have made him an ornament in worldly circles—wit, learning, goodness, prudence, and a winning and fervid eloquence; but his piety was above them all, and led his mind into the channel of a higher and holier vocation. In A. D. 472, Eparcus, bishop of Clermont, his native city, died, and Sidonius, though a layman, was elected his successor. This promotion was hailed with joy by all the Gallic churches, whose most illustrious bishops were already on friendly terms with Sidonius. St. Lupus of Troyes wrote to him in these terms: "Your noble connections have placed you on the dizzy steeps of imperial eminence; you have won honor and applause in the discharge of the highest offices of state, and reached the point to which the anxious flight of human desire tends, as the most glorious gift the world can offer. But now the order is changed; you have reached the highest dignity in the house of the Lord. If I loved you when you trod the barren paths of worldly honor, what can you think of my feelings towards you now that you follow the fertile ways that lead to Heaven?

The same period was illustrated by St. Euphronius of Autun, St. Valerius of Antibes, St. Gratian of Toulon, St. Demetrius of Nice, and St. Leontius of Frejus. Most of these holy prelates became glorious martyrs in the invasion of the Visigoths; their virtue, however, was equalled by a holy Pannonian monk named Severinus. His birth and country were unknown. When questioned on this point, he only answered: "If you believe that I sincerely seek my heavenly country, what need to know my home on earth?" He practised the austerities of the hermits of Thebais, eating only after sunset, and but once a week in Lent. At night he slept, with a sackcloth about him, on the hard ground of his oratory. The territory of Pannonia* and Noricum—now comprised within the limits of Bavaria and Austria—had become for the barbarians the great highway to Italy. The Roman military posts, once stretched along the banks of the Danube, were never garrisoned in the decline of the empire, and the way was left open by their gradual disappearance for the advance of the barbarians. The Rugi, who then inhabited the soil, considered themselves the allies of the Romans; but they were themselves attacked by new tribes, the Heruli, Turci, and Allemani. A universal war was now raging, to which no end could be foreseen; cities were taken and ruined, the population of whole districts led away into bondage. Severinus was their only refuge in these disastrous times. His presence put the barbarians to flight, and saved Comagena. Vienna, in the horrors of a general famine, found relief from his prudent charity and care. The kings of the Rugi, Flacciteus and his successor, Fava, entered upon no undertaking without first consulting the man of God. Severinus used his influence with them to redeem the numerous captives reduced by the continual war to a state of slavery. He became the central point of all the active charity of the times, and established the tithe for the poor and captives, which was spontaneously contributed by the neighboring people. Thus it was that the religious element, under all its various aspects, rose above barbarism, and became the conservative principle amid the revolutions of the age. Severinus had retired one day to his solitary cell, a few leagues from Vienna, when his quiet was interrupted by a passing body of barbarians, on their way to Italy; they stopped to ask his blessing. Among them was a youth so tall that he could not stand erect in the hermit's cave. He was poorly clad; his low extraction gave him no ground for ambitious hopes. The holy hermit looked upon him as he stood thus bent before him, and said: "Enter, my son, upon this soil of Italy, now open before you. You are now covered with the spoil of beasts; soon you shall divide among your comrades the spoils of the world." The young barbarian was Odoacer.

15. Three years later, Odoacer had passed through many changes and adventures, and found himself invested with an important charge in the Italian Guards. Julius Nepos, who had removed Glycerius from the imperial throne to the See of Salona, was, in turn, disposessed by Orestes, who placed the imperial purple upon the person of his son, Romulus Augustulus. Odoacer, backed by the Alani, the Scirri, the Rugi, the Heruli, and the Turci, demanded of the emperor that a third part of the lands of Italy should be divided among them. Orestes, who governed under his son, thought himself strong enough to resist. Odoacer besieged him in Pavia, stormed the city, took and murdered him. On the 23d of August A. D. 476, this Goth, an Arian in creed, was proclaimed by his soldiers *King of Italy*. Romulus Augustulus, surprised in Ravenna, was degraded from the purple. Odoacer fixed the annual allowance of the last Roman emperor at six thousand pieces of gold, and assigned the ancient villa of Lucullus for the place of his exile or retirement. The empire of the West was fallen. The Church, against which it had struggled for three centuries, now stood erect amid the ruins, to console the conquered and to civilize the conquerors.

CHAPTER VII.

SUMMARY.

§ Review of the Second Period of the History of the Church (A. D. 312—476).

1. Advance of the Gospel in the East.—2. Advance of the Church in the West.—3. Pagan Polemics. Apologists of the Second Period.—4. Heresies, Doctors, and Councils.—5. Growth of Monastic Institutions.—6. Government, Discipline, and Worship.

1. The second period witnessed the spread of the Church's conquests beyond the limits of the Roman world. In the East, Armenia had received the light of the Gospel from St. Gregory the Illuminator, a lineal descendant of the royal race of the Arsacidæ (A. D. 386). The Iberians, who inhabited what is now Georgia, lying to the north of Armenia, separated from the Caspian Sea by the Albani and from the Black Sea by Colchis, also received the faith, about the year 326. A Christian captive became the apostle of that nation, which was converted through the miracles worked by God at her intercession. Persia at this period also counted many churches, whose martyrology was swelled by the bloody persecution of Sapor. The province of Adiabene, from its contact with Armenia and Osrhoene, was already nearly Christianized. The new faith found the best soil in the western provinces, which enjoyed a closer intercourse with the Syrians; thus we find the long list of Persian bishops almost entirely made up of Syrian names. Nestorianism subsequently found an entrance among this Christian people, and committed disastrous ravages. Fostered by the favor of the reigning monarchs, error took root in this soil, and was perpetuated until the invasion of Mahometanism. Abyssinia had

been brought to the faith, about the year 326, by two young Syrians, Frumentius and Edesius; and successfully resisted the attempts of the Emperor Constantius to plant the Arian heresy in its soil. The Abyssinians remained strongly attached to the Catholic faith. The Patriarchs of Alexandria have kept the prerogative of appointing and consecrating the metropolitan of that country, with the title of *Bishop of Ethiopia*, in memory of Frumentius, consecrated by St. Athanasius the Great. Christianity was also making rapid progress in Arabia: this is evidenced by the efforts of Constantius to introduce Arianism into the country. Even India, according to Philostorgius, did not resist the mighty influence which was drawing on the world towards the truth of the Gospel. It possessed, in the fourth century, a church already ancient.

2. The progress of Christianity was not less rapid and steady in the West. The German tribes were bent to the yoke of the faith, without much resistance, excepting the Saxons, who persisted in the worship of idols and in hostility to the Christian religion, with an obstinacy which tried even the genius of Charlemagne two hundred years later. But those tribes which emigrated to the western provinces of the empire, with the exception of the Franks and Anglo-Saxons, received a mutilated form of Christianity, disfigured by the errors of Arius. This is the true cause of the momentary preponderance won by Arianism in the fourth century, under Constantius and Valens. The obstinacy with which all these nations, except the Visigoths and a portion of the Lombards, supported this heresy, even in the midst of Catholic communities, seems to find its explanation in the natural connection between Polytheism and Arianism. Having been originally converted by Arians, they never rose to the thought of one Church, the same for all nations; they had been accustomed, from the beginning, to regard the different religions as expressions of nationality, and they looked upon Arianism as the genius of their race. The Goths were the first Germans baptized. Setting out from their home in remote Scandinavia, beyond the North Sea, they had made

their appearance, in the year 215, on the left bank of the Danube. Once settled on the banks of that river and on the northern and western shores of the Black Sea, they proved themselves formidable enemies to the empire. They formed two great tribes under two dynasties: the Ostrogoths stretched from the Dniester to the Don; the Visigoths, from the Dniester to the Theiss. The Gospel found entrance amongst them towards the middle of the third century, by means of some captives whom they had brought back from their expeditions into Greece and Asia Minor. There was even a Gothic bishop, Theophilus, present in the Council of Nice. The Catholic faith prevailed amongst them until the reign of the Emperor Valens, who made use of their bishop, Ulphilas, to infect them with the Arian heresy. It is a known fact that this prelate, won by the promises of the imperial court, in the course of an embassy with which he was charged by King Athanaric, agreed to betray the faith and to spread the Arian heresy among the Visigoths. This treacherous work was much facilitated by the influence he had acquired in his country, by giving it an alphabet modelled on that of the Greeks, and a translation of the sacred writings, from which, however, according to Philostorgius, he curtailed the book of Kings, lest that reading should encourage the taste of the Goths for warlike undertakings. Though Arianism predominated among the Christian Goths since the time of Ulphilas, there were still some who retained the faith, and indeed their number was sufficient to induce St. John Chrysostom to build a special church in Constantinople, for the use of the Gothic soldiers who served in the Roman armies; the divine service was here conducted in their own language by priests of their nation. The respect shown by the Goths to churches and those who took refuge in them, in the sack of Rome by Alaric, their king, in A. D. 410, was probably due to their regard for the Christian religion. St. Jerome tells us that these fair-haired barbarians had portable churches among their tents, where they assembled to pray. From the Visigoths, Christianity, with its mixture of Arian error, passed to their allies, the Ostrogoths, the Gepidæ, and thence to the Vandals, the Alani and Suevi. The Vandals already numbered many Christians in their ranks when they crossed the Rhine and invaded Gaul; and if Idacius's account be true, that their king, Genseric, who began to reign in A. D. 428, passed from Catholicity to the Arian heresy, it is certain that they did not receive their first religious instructions from the Goths alone.

The Burgundians came from the northeastern part of Germany, settled the country as far as Helvetia and Savoy, and overcame the Gauls on both sides of the Rhone and of the Saône. They treated the natives in their territory not as conquered enemies, but as brothers in religion; such is the testimony of Orosius towards the year 417, at which time that people were already converted. Another and a less important branch of the same nation received baptism, according to the testimony of Socrates, as late as A. D. 430. The Burgundians persevered in the faith under their kings, Gondikar, Gondioch, and Chilperic, who fixed his capital at Geneva; but after the year 430, under King Gundebald, who put to death his brother, Chilperic, with all his family, they became Arians at the monarch's instigation. Catholicity was re-established on the death of Gundebald, in A. D. 517, by his son and successor, Sigismund. The Vandals, the Alani and King Hermeric, with his Suevi, crossed the Pyrenees in A. D. 409, and divided among them the Spanish peninsula. Galicia and the western portion of Spain fell to the lot of the Suevi and Vandals; but the latter people, in the year 420, passed over into Africa, and the Suevi were left at liberty to overspread the country more freely, and, under the leadership of Rechila, subdued the whole northwestern portion of the peninsula. The Visigoths, led by Alaric, in A. D. 410, to the conquest of Rome and of Italy, and those whom Adolphus had, two years later, brought into Gaul, were pushed by the Romans, in A. D. 414, into the Spanish peninsula. Here they seized upon the greater part of the country, leaving but a small share of Galicia and Lusitania to the Suevi; and under their kings, Wallia, Theod oric, and Euric, they gradually gained footing in the southern provinces of Gaul, as far as the Loire. Toulouse then became the capital of the great empire of the Visigoths. The pagan king of the Suevi, Rechila, was succeeded by a Catholic; but Remismund, who had married the daughter of the Visigoth Theodoric, introduced Arianism among his people, in the year 469, by means of a Galatian priest named Ajax, who had, like himself, gone over to the heresy. It was not till ninety years later, about the year 560, that Galicia returned to the true faith under King Theodomir. In the southern provinces of France, under the Arian rule of Visigoth princes, Catholicity was subjected to many vicissitudes. Driven by motives of political distrust and by an incredible Arian fury, the Visigoth King Euric carried on so bloody a persecution against the Catholics, that, to use the expression of Sidonius Apollinaris, "It was doubtful whether he was as solicitous for the extension of his own power as for the extirpation of Catholicity." He ordered the doorways of the churches to be filled with packs of briers, and then set fire to the buildings; he imprisoned the priests, of whom some were banished, others put to death. The bishops were the particular objects of his hatred, and he insisted upon their sees remaining vacant. Thus Bordeaux, Périgueux, Rhodez, Limoges, Gévaudan, Cause, Bazas, Comminges, and Auch were long deprived of pastors. The final triumph of Catholicity, in the struggle, was only secured ninety years later, when the throne of Toulouse was held by Clovis. We have already had occasion to speak of the persecution suffered by the Catholics from the Arian Vandals in Africa. This desolate Church was not destined to rise again from its ruins. The oppression of the Vandals was followed by that of the Mahometan Moors, and the long lethargy of the Catholic worship in that country was to be interrupted only in our own day, when the arms of the most Christian king have given Africa, as a crowning trophy of victory, to France and to religion. But the progress of the Gospel in the British Isles presents a consoling offset to the gloomy picture we have just traced. The labors of St. Patrick had, in the beginning of the fifth century, brought about the conversion of the Scoti in Ireland.* Patrick was born in A. D. 387, as he tells us himself, at *Bonaven Tuberniæ*,† that is, at Boulogne, in Picardy, on the coast which was then called Armorica. At the age of sixteen years he was seized by a sea-rover from Ireland, who was cruising along the Gallic shore, and in his captivity was set to keep his master's flocks. The youth then felt a rising wish for piety and a holy life. After a thraldom of six years he at length found means to escape, and on reaching Gaul repaired to the monastery of Tours, where St. Martin had founded a celebrated school, in which he spent four years in the study of the sciences and of Christian morality. After his return to his parents, he felt himself called in a vision by night to the conversion of Ireland. Either mistrusting this first call, or to make preparation for obeying it, he attached himself, in A. D. 418, to St. Germanus, bishop of Auxerre, who sent him to Lerins, to finish his course of studies. These completed, he returned to St. Germanus, and then went to Rome, where Pope Celestin charged him with the task of preaching the Gospel in Ireland. He was consecrated bishop at Eboria (probably Evreux), and took with him several companions, amongst whom are mentioned Auxillius and Isserninus, with whom he landed among the Scoti, in the year 432.‡ He found the pagans here given up to the worship of the stars and of springs.§

The usual places for religious rites were the hills and mountains. Patrick preached the Gospel in the presence of the king and an assembly of the principal chiefs.‖ His word was fruitful, and in a short time three bishoprics were established in Ireland. A church which he built in the district of Macha

---

* See Note (1), p. 629.

† *Bonaven* is nothing more than the Latin *Bononia* (Boulogne), and *Taberniæ*, or *Tarverniæ*, designates the country of *Tarrabanna*, or *Tarvenna* (Térouanne), in which Boulogne is situated.

‡ It was eighty or ninety years from this date before the name *Scoti* became common to all the Irish, and then their island began to be as well known by the name of *Scotia* as by that of *Hibernia*. The Scotland of to-day only received its name of *Scotia* in the eleventh century.

§ See Note (2), p. 629. ‖ See Note (3), p. 629.

became the centre of a city, which grew, by degrees, under the name of Ardmacha or Armagh; here the apostle fixed his see, which afterwards became the metropolis of the Irish Church. Together with Auxillius and Isserninus, he held a synod, in which he published a series of canons constituting the new Church of Ireland.* He died in his retreat at Sabhal, in the year 465, leaving the whole island as a rich legacy to the true faith, which it has ever preserved, in the midst of political storms, with such unshaken constancy and devoted love. The north of Britain, now Scotland, was then held by the Picts or Caledonians, a people who had immigrated hither from Scandinavia. The Southern Picts, who held the country between the Forth and the Grampian Hills, were converted about the year 412, by Ninyas, first Bishop of Witherne, in Galway. One hundred and fifty years elapsed before the Northern Picts received the faith, from their apostle, St. Columban.

3. The barbarian inroads into all parts of the Roman Empire brought the Church face to face with new nations, who were successively to yield to her resistless influence. Christianity had, at the very outset, found itself opposed to an entire and regularly constituted heathen community, and it conquered. But it cannot escape the notice of the historian that civilization was a greater stumbling-block than barbarism to the advance of the Church. Roman paganism, subdued by Constantine, who strove to remove its least traces from the laws and manners, from institutions, education and literature, produced a powerful reaction under Julian. The sophists who beset the imperial apostate might well have exulted for a moment in the prospect of the downfall of Christianity, under the accumulation of measures contrived with such system against it. The philosopher Maximus, and the rhetorician Libanius, endeavored to restore the worship and the poetry of the Homeric gods. Julian himself, laying aside the sceptre and sacrificial knife, found time, amid his imperial duties, to write polemical works, which

---

* See Note (4), p. 630.

assumed to prove that Theognis, Orpheus, Phocilides, and Isocrates were far superior, as politicians, legislators, and moralists, to Moses and Solomon. St. Cyril of Alexandria undertook to refute these imperial lucubrations; and performed his task with a spirit, a logical precision and force of eloquence that left no room for reply. Arnobius had already taken his place among the apologists of this period. His works have been mentioned in their place. Lactantius, his polished disciple, also consecrated the seven books of his *Divine Institutions* to the refutation of the pagan objections against Christianity. Eusebius of Cæsarea was in the mean time writing his fifteen books of *Evangelical Preparation*. In A. D. 345, Firmicus Maternus presented to the Emperors Constantius and Constans his book on the *Falsehood of Profane Religions*, a spirited work, in which the author aims at exhibiting the most shameful and immoral features of the pagan superstition. St. Athanasius also published two treatises or discourses: *Against the Pagans*, and *On the Incarnation of the Word*. The plan is equally correct, noble, and simple. Athanasius proves the first fall to have been the principle of heathenism and estrangement from the true God; and then proceeds, gradually refuting the pagan objections, to establish the possibility, the necessity, and the reality of the incarnation of Jesus Christ. But the noblest and most perfect apology for the Church are the twenty-two books of the *City of God*, opposed, by St. Augustine, to the City of the World—to paganism. The first ten books are devoted to an analysis of the three classes of polytheistic mythology mentioned by Varro and by the Pontiff Scævola—the poetical, the political, and the natural or philosophical. The illustrious author particularly attacks the neo-Platonist school, of which he seems to make Porphyry the chief representative; he upbraids this school with its bold idolatry, its apotheosis of demons, the absurdity of its liturgy, and of its doctrine of the transmigration of souls. Then laying down, as a foundation, the principle that the knowledge of God is possible only in and through Jesus Christ, he builds, so to speak, in the last twelve books, the *City of God*, beginning with the creation and the fall of the angels, and following up the progress of this divine kingdom through the old dispensation until the last judgment, to the eternal felicity of the just. The most popular pagan objection against the Christians was drawn from the rapid decline and daily-increasing weakness of the empire. The heathens compared its present situation with its early glory, with the boundless grandeur and magnificence it once enjoyed under the protection of the gods. Then Rome was strong and powerful within, ever victorious, ever invincible without, spreading far and wide over nations and tribes the terror of its name. Now that the gods were despised, the sacrifices abolished, and that the honor due to them was given to the God of the Christians, misery, disunion, impotence were hurrying on the empire to destruction. "Now," bitterly exclaimed Libanius, "in place of the immortal gods, they are honored who bring all these evils upon us." The Christians answered that their present misery and disgrace was but the necessary fruit of the seed sown by polytheism in past ages; that a Christian posterity was atoning for the faults of its heathen ancestors; and that the approaching fall and dissolution of the empire were already visible whilst the worship of the gods still prevailed. "And after all," exclaims St. Augustine, "what do they regret, they who wish to make us Christians answerable for the crumbling empire? They can regret but external splendor, wealth, impunity for their enjoyments, the freedom with which the wealthy and powerful could satisfy every passion. They would bring back a state of things in which license, disorder, and corruption ruled without stint. They then regret precisely what has caused the internal ruin and decay of the Roman Empire, and what has, in consequence, brought about its outward decline." In spite of the recriminations of the people and of the rhetoricians, in spite of the boundless credit enjoyed by the sophists at Athens and Alexandria in the fourth century, notwithstanding the restoration attempted by Julian the Apostate, paganism ran its downward course until its last vestige had disappeared, with the rest of ruined social order, under the blows of the barbarians.

4. From the conversion of Constantine, the Christian religion showed itself fearlessly, and gained by publicity; the sublime promises it held out, the weight and beauty of its laws, its pure morality, magnificent ceremonial and high festivals, soon won all hearts. Men were astonished and confounded to see how wide they had wandered in following superstition, and hastened to pay atoning homage to the true Church, by pouring into its fold in throngs; whole cities joined in destroying their temples, and raising churches on their ruins. This universal current, which carried the whole world into the bosom of Christianity, doubtless caught up a considerable number of weak and timid souls, drawn into the Church rather by the influence of general example, the official protection given to Christianity, or whatever other extrinsic motive, than by a solid conviction or the working of grace. St. Augustine, St. Jerome, and Salvian mention in their writings the relaxation introduced, in the beginning of the fifth century, by this accession of so many neophytes, still wearing their heathen habits and morals; so that in its very triumph the faith met a new source of danger. The Church seems gifted with the faculty of drawing new power from the very storms let loose against her. Although the fourth and fifth centuries brought no general persecution, still they were not wanting in those trials which temper courage, quicken faith, and give new prominence to great minds. In the West, the Donatist schism, the Pelagian and Semi-Pelagian heresies, the local persecutions of the Vandals in Africa, and those of the Visigoths in the south of Gaul; in the East, the Arian, Macedonian, Nestorian, and Eutychian heresies, gave more trouble to the Church, and made almost as many victims, as the most cruel persecution could have done. But what a consoling offset to this growing generation of errors is presented by the array of Catholic doctors raised up by Providence to meet them! In these two centuries genius would seem to have become an heir-loom, to be perpetuated in

the bosom of the Church, in the illustrious names of Ambrose, Augustine, Jerome, Athanasius, Basil, Gregory Nazianzen, and Chrysostom. This bright array of great names, any one of which would have sufficed to fill a period of history, were not the only adornments of the fertile field of the fourth and fifth centuries. We mentioned those of Sts. Ephrem, Epiphanius of Salamis, Epiphanius of Pavia, Cyril, Gregory of Nyssa, Hilary, Optatus, Lupus, Sidonius Appollinaris, and a host of other doctors, both in the East and the West, who were ever ready, ever armed to defend the Catholic faith and unity. Such a galaxy of great lights gave a peculiar splendor and glory to the general councils assembled at this period. The conversion of Constantine had opened to the Christian bishops the way to every portion of the empire. If Arius, Macedonius, Nestorius, or Eutyches dare to attack a fundamental dogma of the faith, the great Councils of Nice, of Constantinople, Ephesus and Chalcedon, presided over by legates of the pope, inspired by the Holy Ghost, blast the heresy and schism. Some particular events of the fourth and fifth centuries are alleged, as facts, to support its cause, by a school of theology ever busy for the benefit of local opinions, in turning over the pages of history to seek arguments weakening the authority of the Holy See. The question *whether the pope is superior to the general council, or the general council to the pope*, is agitated with a vehemence bordering on passion. The very statement of the question presents an inadmissible hypothesis. To discuss the question on an acceptable ground, it would be necessary to find a general council acting without the pope, or a pope standing apart from the general council. But the two ideas are impossible.* No council can be ecumenical without the pope; no argument can, therefore, be founded on the hostile attitude of the two powers, when, by the very fact of their separation, one must cease to exist. We have also considered the debate—arising from the disputed fall of Pope

---

* *Vide* M. DE MAISTRE: *On the Pope.*

Liberius—concerning *the infallibility of the pope in matters of faith*. One expression uttered by our Lord Jesus Christ settles the whole question: *Ego rogavi pro te, ut non deficiat fides tua; et tu aliquando conversus, confirma fratres tuos.*

5. The general advance of the Church at this period was followed by the development of monastic institutions. Monks were at first divided into three classes: the *Cenobites*, who lived in communities under a superior; the *Anchorets*, who lived alone in the desert solitudes; the *Sabaraites*, who lived, two or three together, in cells; the latter class had but little duration. Cassian has drawn a graphic picture of the edifying life led by the solitaries of his day. They were wholly occupied in prayer and manual labor; their daily food was bread and water, their bed a rush mat, their pillow a handful of leaves. Egypt was the birth-place of the monastic life; from thence it passed into Syria, Pontus, Asia Minor, and the West. Then the Gauls had also their celebrated monasteries, and we have had occasion to mention the foundation of those of Tours and of Lerins. The name of St. Augustine is also associated with a code of monastic rules destined to lead generations of religious to the height of sanctity. Most of the monks were laymen, and Cassian tells us that those of St. Pacomius's monastery depended upon the priests of the neighboring villages for the celebration of the Holy Mysteries. The monastic life debarred them from the priestly state. The manual labor to which they assiduously devoted themselves furnished them not only the means of procuring their coarse and slender fare, but even of giving plentiful alms. The Alexandrian poor were relieved by boat-loads of wheat which had been raised from the burning sands of the desert by the patient toil of the monks of Arsinoe. St. Augustine notices the same practical charity in the monks of Northern Africa. Yet some of these solitaries were occasionally torn from their desert-homes to be incorporated among the clergy of the neighboring episcopal city; but they then became seculars, as was the case with those who were raised to the episcopate. In his

letter to Dracontius, written about the year 353, St. Athanasius reckons seven monks who had already been made bishops. Such was the increase of solitaries at the end of this century, that the single city of Oxyrinchus, in Lower Thebais, numbered ten thousand monks and twenty thousand virgins.

6. The government of the Church developed itself without restraint upon the basis already established at the end of the first century. To the authority of the Holy See were referred all the important questions raised in every quarter of the Christian world. The central power of Rome radiated to every European court through the Apostolic Legates sent to all the Christian princes. Ambitious pretensions were checked by the decisions of the Nicene Council concerning the patriarchal jurisdiction. We have seen how the efforts of the Bishops of Constantinople to raise their see above all the Churches of the East, though backed by the favor of the Greek emperors, yet failed before the firm and steady resistance of the Sovereign Pontiffs. Canonical discipline was also upheld by a wise and prudent rigor. The great example of Theodosius, humbly bowed upon the pavement of the Cathedral of Milan, at the feet of St. Ambrose, was a living picture of public penance. Although the customs of the various churches were regulated in the essential prescriptions, a certain variation is still perceptible in particular observances. Thus St. Augustine informs us that the fast of Saturday, which was observed in some places, was not of universal obligation. In some churches the Holy Sacrifice was offered up daily, in others only on Saturday and Sunday; the faithful received the Holy Eucharist every day or only once a week. St. Augustine says that the faithful are free to follow either practice, and that the best rule in such cases is to conform to the tradition of the Church in which they find themselves at the time. It is plain that these differences only reach particular and optional cases of discipline or ritual. The great law of unity, in more weighty points, stood firm and unshaken. At a period when the political world, undermined by barbarian inroads, presented

a spectacle of universal license, despotism and disorder, unity of government, even were it not the fundamental and divine law of the Church, became an imperious necessity; and we shall again have occasion to record the steadiness with which it preserved, in the midst of an agitated world, that principle of authority which outlives the wildest storms, profits by all revolutions, and repairs every ruin.

NOTES.

(1.) EVEN before the mission of Palladius, who preceded St. Patrick, to Ireland (A. D. 431), it is probable that Christian communities had been founded on the island; for between Ireland and Gaul there existed a considerable commerce, and we know, from Tacitus, that the ports of Ireland were better known and more frequented by merchants than those of Britain. We may suppose, also, that the Irish may have become acquainted with the doctrines of the Christian religion by means of the many captives whom, in their expeditions of plunder, they bore away from the British and Gallic shores. Cœlestius, the companion of the heretic Pelagius, was, as we learn from St. Jerome, an Irishman (Scotus). This beginning of Christianity in Ireland attracted the attention of Pope Celestine, who consecrated the Roman deacon, Palladius, and sent him from Rome, in 431, as first bishop of the Irish.—(*Prosperi Chron. ad annum* 431.) So great was the success of the new bishop, that Prosper could venture to say that, by the care of Celestine, Ireland had become a Christian country.—(*Prosper, de Gratia Christi, Ch.* 41.) Intimidated, however, by the threats of the infidels, Palladius left the island, and died in Britain. The entire conversion of Ireland was reserved for St. Patrick, for, according to the ancient Irish proverb: "Not to Palladius, but to Patrick, did God give the Irish."—(DÖLLINGER, *Hist. of the Church.* London edition, vol. ii. p. 19.)

(2). As they honored water as a beneficent deity, they considered fire as a principle of evil. The use of idols of their gods was not general; they are, indeed, sometimes mentioned, but they were no more than rude figures of stone. The chiefs of the religion, who, in the history of St. Patrick, are called Magi, appear to have practised magic and soothsaying. They were as distinct from the Druids as the religion of Ireland was different from the religion of Britain and of Gaul. The people formed two separate classes—the ancient aborigines, who, according to the traditions of the country, were Milesians that had come from Galicia, and the more recently arrived Scots.—(*Ibid.*, p. 22.)

(3.) St. Patrick preached before the chief king of the island, Leogaire, an the princes who were assembled around him. The first-fruit of his preachin was the conversion of a famed poet, named Dubtach. The most powerfi princes of the land soon listened to his words, and Corrall, a brother of th chief king, was amongst the earliest of his disciples. Many sons of chieftain whose good-will he had won by presents, followed him, and shared in his apostolical labors; virgins, whom he had converted, embraced an ascetic state of life, and the number of these nuns seemed to increase in proportion as they were persecuted by their parents.

But the most celebrated and the most numerous conversion was in Connaught, where St. Patrick arrived when the seven sons of a king, and a large body of people, had met there in assembly. He baptized the young princes and one hundred and twenty thousand of the people in the fountain of Euardhac.—(*Ibid.*, p. 23. *Usher's Antiq.*, Dublin edition, p. 865.)

(4.) The only one of the letters of St. Patrick which has been preserved appears to have been written in the earlier part of his labors; it is a circular epistle against Coroticus, a British chief, and his followers, who had made a predatory descent upon the Irish coast, and had violently borne away, as captives, many of the natives whom St. Patrick had baptized. In this letter he pronounces excommunication against the chief and his companions, and requests the faithful into whose hands the letter may fall, to read it in the presence of the people, and even of Coroticus himself. He remarks that the Roman and Gallic Christians sent large sums of money to redeem Christian captives from the power of the Franks, whilst he, Coroticus, carried on a detestable commerce with the members of Christ, that he might sell them to the heathens.

By the prudent ordinances of St. Patrick, ecclesiastical schools and seminaries, which were named cloisters, and were under the guidance of the bishops, were established in Ireland. Some of these were founded during his life, and many more after his death. One of these institutions was the school of the Bishop Fiech of Sletty; others were formed by Bishop Ailbe, by Ibar of Beg-Erin, and by Olcan at Dorcan. St. Patrick had previously erected one at Armagh. Abodes of piety were provided by St. Bridget, who, towards the close of the fifth century, introduced into Ireland rules for nuns, and established several nunneries in different parts of the island. Of these, the largest and most celebrated was that founded A. D. 490, at Kildare. At the instance of St. Bridget, an episcopal see was also erected at the same place.

END OF VOL. I.

www.ingramcontent.com/pod-product-compliance
Lightning Source LLC
Chambersburg PA
CBHW021219300426
44111CB00007B/358